P9-CDO-571

Old and New in Southern Shona Independent Churches

CHANGE AND CONTINUITY IN AFRICA

MONOGRAPHS UNDER THE AUSPICES OF

THE AFRIKA-STUDIECENTRUM · LEIDEN

MOUTON · THE HAGUE · PARIS

M.L. DANEEL

Old and New in Southern Shona Independent Churches

Volume I: Background and Rise of the Major Movements

MOUTON · THE HAGUE · PARIS

Library of Congress Catalog Card Number: 79-171101

Printed in the Netherlands

To the

Zionist Bishops: Samuel Mutendi, David Masuka (Jr.)
and Andreas Shoko;
Apostolic Priests: Abero and Makebo Maranke;
Topia Bishop: Nheya Gavure;
Chibarirwe President: Mheke Zvekare Sengwayo, and
African Reformed Church President: Kumani Sibambo,

whose reassuring trust, goodwill and
unfailing aid largely contributed to this study.

Foreword

The increase of studies of African Independent Churches seems to be keeping pace, almost, with the phenomenal rise of such religious movements in various parts of the continent. There are also forthcoming the more or less authoritative sweeping generalizations supposedly applying to the Continent as a whole, or to specific regions.

The need for thorough local observation and research is felt all the more. It is, in the last resort, only on the basis of such patient field work that real progress in this area can now be made. Dr. Daneel's study is therefore especially welcome.

For his work he has had unique opportunities and he has obviously used these to the full. Born in Rhodesia and well acquainted with the local Shona language from his childhood he had an enviable head-start for this enquiry. His discriminating and charming book on 'The God of the Matopo Hills' proves his intimate knowledge of the African religion in this area. The Afrika Studie Centrum, Leiden, Holland, has with characteristic generosity and far sightedness provided him with the means and the tools for his research, and – what is perhaps even more important – with sustained encouragement, guidance and inspiration for his task.

The study is conceived on a generous scale. This book is only the first in a series of, possibly, four volumes devoted to the study of the structure and life of Southern Shona Independent Churches. As the study evolves, it will prove, I am convinced, that its real strength lies in the concentrated attention which the author has given to the local scene, 'Anything, to be real, must be local'.

Magnificent photos enhance the value of the book and of its highly interesting material.

Independent African churches are a response to a complicated, sometimes harsh social situation. They provide a great challenge to Mission-oriented churches in Africa. Dr. Daneel's book is to be welcomed for bringing this to our notice, as it deals with a controversial situation of great interest.

Uppsala, Sweden, July 1971.
Bengt Sundkler

Acknowledgements

I wish to thank the representatives of the Free University, Amsterdam, for granting me paid leave to engage in a prolonged period of fieldwork (March 1965-June 1967) in Rhodesia and for supporting me financially while writing up the results in the Netherlands; the Netherlands Foundation for the Advancement of Tropical Research (WOTRO) for covering the major costs of the field project, and the Afrika Studiecentrum, Leiden, under whose auspices I worked, for contributing substantially towards field expenses and statistical data-processing as well as the preparation and printing of the manuscript. Without the generous grants of these institutions I would never have been able to undertake such an extensive study nor to spend a lengthy period working out the acquired material.

Much of the inspiration for this study derives from the far-reaching influence of two remarkable missionary leaders to whom I remain deeply grateful: the late Rev. A. A. Louw, founder of the Dutch Reformed Mission in Rhodesia, who, through his ability to communicate effectively with the members of a different race, awakened my interest in the elusive art of 'patiently listening to the other party'; and my former tutor in Missiology at the Free University, the late Prof. J. H. Bavinck, whose mastery of this particular art impressed me. Prof. Bavinck's keen interest in Javanese mysticism and his penetration of the thought-world of its exponents – while he was serving as a missionary in Indonesia – were based on the conviction that one could only effectively communicate the Gospel message cross-culturally, if sympathetic consideration was given to the traditional religious life and beliefs of the people concerned. Having drawn my attention to the missiological significance of traditional concepts of God, not least by assigning to me the task of writing a pre-doctoral script on the subject of 'Missionary Instruction and the Tribal African Beliefs in God', he wholeheartedly supported my plan of undertaking a field study and finally wished me an inspiring 'fruitful stay in Africa' a few days before his death in 1964.

Persons to whom I am indebted for their assistance during the preparatory stages of the project are: Prof. J. F. Holleman, who, as director of the Afrika

Studiecentrum, deliberated with the Free University authorities about the possibilities of a joint research project; Prof. L. Onvlee, who acted as the representative of the Free University in the Advisory Board of the Afrika Studiecentrum and enthusiastically supported the project (in which he has shown a keen interest ever since); Bishop B. G. M. Sundkler of the University of Uppsala, Dr. H. von Sicard, former Swedish Lutheran missionary in Rhodesia, Prof. Daryll Forde and Dr. M. Douglas of the University College of London, Sr. Mary Aquina, then at the University of Manchester; and several others, for orientating discussions before I left for Rhodesia. From these persons I received many useful suggestions about possible research methods.

In the course of my investigations in Rhodesia I was ably assisted by several African and European friends. A special word of thanks is due to:

my regular assistants, Janis Mutumburanzouh, who helped me to settle down at Zion City during the first months of research; J. S. Bvumburai, a former theological student at Morgenster Mission, who intelligently and patiently helped me to trace the strains of traditional religion and philosophy in Shona Christianity; Herbert Mukapa, Raymond Munzararikwa, and Taripa Munyai, who rendered valuable assistance in tape-recording interviews and writing up the information acquired; Howard Muremba, Samson Dzikati and Virimai Muzondo, who became so closely associated with the entire project that they assisted me for a much longer period than was initially planned and thus formed the core of my regular staff; they took the strain of regular camp-shifting with grace, shared the joys of exciting new findings as well as the frustrations of an incomplete survey in the Mucheke township at Fort Victoria, and were always ready to discuss complicated aspects in the acquired information which needed unravelling;

the 'camp-superintendent', Daveson Njarava, a former DRC evangelist, who was my trusted friend and counsellor throughout the entire project; his wise counsel and moral support during long spells of isolation from fellow-Europeans enabled me to cope with the strain of adapting to the living conditions in tribal areas and to avoid unnecessary mistakes in my contact with tribal dignitaries;

the following African teachers and students, who formed the team which assisted me in conducting the random sample survey in the Chingombe chiefdom:

I. M. Bofu	S. Dzikati	P. J. Maisiri	Z. J. Nkomo
S. Chingombe	S. Hamutyi	E. K. Makamure	J. K. Nyemba
M. Choga	W. Hove	J. Maronga	T. Shuro
P. J. Dondo	T. A. Hungwiri	V. Z. Muzondo	F. Tavatya;

their interest in the project and their willingness to work long and hard furthered the completion of the sample survey in the planned time;

the principal leaders of the Independent Churches, to whom this study is dedicated, their subordinate officials and followers, as well as the Shona people generally, who accepted me with friendship and hospitality, allowed me to attend their meetings, festivals and rituals, and always proved willing to discuss religious and other topics;

the personnel at Alheit Mission, Rev. Shiri, Headmaster Chindanya and School Manager Gopoza; as well as at Mutero Mission, Fathers Haag, Kaufmann and Augustin Urayai, including teachers Mutero and Paradza, all of whom contributed towards a fruitful stay at these mission stations;

Rev. A. Brand and Mr. C. Jackson (Pamushana Mission), Rev. E. Esterhuizen (Morgenster Mission), Dr. Oskar Niederberger and Fr. Joseph Kumbirai (Chikwingwiza Seminary) who kindly provided me, through interviews and correspondence, with their views on subjects relevant to my investigation;

the District Commissioners of the Gutu and Bikita districts: Messrs. Ploughden, De Bruyn, Menzies and Dodds, and the members of their staff, who not only gave me their assistance and advice, but also offered me their kind hospitality; and

the staff-members of the Department of Sociology at the University College, Salisbury: Prof. Clyde Mitchell, Dr. Kingsley Garbett and Dr. J. van Velsen, whose valuable comments on two of my seminar papers opened up new perspectives to me in my field of enquiry.

Back in the Netherlands I became indebted to a number of people for their assistance during the process of sifting field notes and preparing the manuscript. I wish to thank in this connection:

Mr. J. M. Bidima of the Institut des Recherches du Cameroun, who drew the maps of this study with meticulous care;

Mrs. Elisabeth Wessels-Eybers, and Drs. V. February of the Afrika Studiecentrum, who revised my manuscript and whose interest went beyond the purely linguistic aspects of this study;

Mrs. P. E. M. Lijphart-Hemans, the computer analyst, who treated the statistical data with precision and patience;

Mrs. M. M. Smit-Huisinga, Mrs. Selma Wolfaardt and Mrs. A. M. Benink-Catier, who ably typed and re-typed various drafts of my manuscript;

Mr. D. G. van der Heij, Mrs. H. M. Jansen van Veuren and Mrs. M. B. Isaacs, who read the proofs; and

the administrative staff and other members of the Afrika Studiecentrum, Leiden, for giving me every facility and moral support to carry out a time-consuming task.

It is with a deep sense of gratitude that I mention the names of Prof. J. F. Holleman of the University of Leiden, Prof. J. Blauw and Prof. D. C. Mulder, both of the Free University, Amsterdam, under whose supervision I was privileged to write this study. Prof. Holleman gave me the scientific support I needed in the field. After years of experience as a fieldworker in Mashonaland he could render advice and guidance directly relevant to the situations I encountered. His unceasing interest in the project and personal encouragement during two visits to Rhodesia while I was in the field challenged me to subject my research methods to a constant critical re-appraisal. Moreover, his willingness to examine and discuss each draft chapter in great detail, his insistence on the clearest possible presentation of material, penetrative analysis and appropriate style greatly contributed towards an improved final draft. Prof. Blauw, who acted as my co-promotor, spent several weeks with me in 1966 and accompanied me to the headquarters of some of the largest Independent Churches to attend the annual festivities. In addition to the privilege of sharing his companionship, I benefitted from his penetrative observations of and comments on some of the more elusive aspects of religious life. His quick and thorough scrutiny of draft chapters, followed up by constructive comments, were always stimulating and encouraging. Prof. Mulder, who, as representative of the theological faculty, acted as my main promotor, was always willing to assist me with his patient and understanding supervision. His exhaustive scholarship, critical mind and tactful indications of errors in the draft chapters helped to improve the quality of this study. To him and the other two supervisors I wish to extend my sincere appreciation. I benefitted immensely from their enriching insights, valuable suggestions and sustained interest in this study.

I am also indebted to Prof. W. J. van der Merwe and Drs. N. Smith of the Dutch Reformed Theological Seminary, University of Stellenbosch; Prof. H. W. Turner, formerly of the University of Leicester and now at the Candler School of Theology, Emory University, Atlanta; Dr. David Barrett of the University of Nairobi and Prof. Marshall Murphree of the University College of Rhodesia – for discussions during and/or after the period of fieldwork, as well as for reading through and commenting on my manuscript. They have provided me with valuable suggestions which contributed towards the improvement of this study. I greatly appreciate the interest they have shown in my work and their willingness to provide me with their views and advice whenever I needed it.

To my parents and my wife I owe a deeper gratitude than can be expressed in words. With them I have shared the excitement and joys as well as the strains and frustrations of my work. Under all circumstances could I rely on the loyalty and understanding of a father and a mother, whom I admire and respect for their wise counsel and for their challenging example of Christian living, set during a lifetime of selfless missionary service in Mashonaland. I considered it a special privilege to subject my use of the vernacular in the manuscript to the able revision of my mother, who has been a teacher in Chikaranga for many years. My wife, Beulah, joined me in the field during the last and in many ways the most difficult phase of research work. Adapting herself to the changing and sometimes uncomfortable living conditions with admirable ease, she created a pleasant home for us, from which base I could operate with renewed interest and confidence. She introduced a new and most meaningful dimension into my relationship with African friends and informants. Her devotion and patient companionship has been a source of inspiration which enabled me to complete the working out of a substantial part of the information acquired. Finally, I owe everything to Him, our Master, whose ways with man fills one with awe and wonder.

Afrika Studiecentrum,
Leiden,
January, 1971.

the hope and understanding of a father and a mother whom I admire and respect for their wise counsel and for their challenging example of Christian [illegible] during a lifetime of selfless missionary service in Madagascar. [illegible] a special privilege to [illegible] the [illegible] in the [illegible] the able revision of my manuscript, who has been a teacher of Cantonese for many years. My wife, [illegible] during the last and in many ways the most difficult years of research work. A special [illegible] for the [illegible] and [illegible] the [illegible] [illegible] a [illegible] which [illegible] interest and [illegible] a new [illegible] with African friends and [illegible] partnership has [illegible] to complete the working out of a [illegible] Finally, I owe [illegible] to Him [illegible] whose [illegible] with [illegible]

[illegible]
L[illegible]
[illegible] 19[illegible]

Table of contents

APPENDIXES

List of plates and maps

LIST OF PLATES *opposite or between pages*

LIST OF MAPS

Introduction

The aims of this study

The study of Independent Churches in Africa has become of vital importance for an understanding of the rich variety of forms in which Christianity manifests itself on this continent. Since the end of the last century there has been a rapid growth in the membership of the Independent Churches. According to Barrett, there are at present more than 6,000 of these Churches with a total membership approximating 7 million, to be found in more than 275 African tribes.[1] He estimates that the entire movement is growing at a rate of approximately 3-400,000 adherents per year. The spectacular increase during the past few decades has given rise to the publication of a number of studies dealing with this phenomenon, such as the pioneering work of Sundkler in South Africa,[2] Andersson's valuable description of the Messianic movements in the Congo,[3] Turner's penetrative account of the Church of the Lord (Aladura) in West Africa[4] and Barrett's recent study in breadth[5] (which provides an illuminating perspective of the entire phenomenon), to mention but a few. It has also convinced some missionaries, as well as African leaders of the Mission Churches – who found themselves directly confronted with this mushrooming movement in the field – that intensive thought should be given to the phenomenon in order to determine their future attitude to and possible forms of co-operation with representatives of Independent Churches. Various forms of religious expression, for example, are provided by these Churches which seem

1. Barrett, 1968, Chapter 1.

2. B. G. M Sundkler, *Bantu Prophets in South Africa,* 1948 (second revised edition, London, 1961). See also B. A. Pauw, *Religion in a Tswana Chiefdom,* London, 1960.

3. E. Andersson, *Messianic Popular Movements in the Lower Congo,* Studia Ethnographica Upsaliensis XIV, London, 1958.

4. H. W. Turner, *African Independent Church,* Vol. 1: *The Church of the Lord (Aladura)*; Vol. 2: *The Life and Faith of the Church of the Lord (Aladura),* Oxford, 1967.

5. D. B. Barrett, *Schism and Renewal in Africa,* Oxford University Press, 1968.

to fulfil the needs of numerous Africans more adequately than some of the Western-orientated Mission Churches appear to have done. This fact in itself poses a challenge to the Mission Churches to engage in a thorough self-examination, since it at hints at limitations and failures in the Western type of presentation of the Gospel to the African, due to a lack of understanding.

The motivation for a study of a few of these African Independent Churches was not a purely academic one. It derives partly from the conviction that any planning of the future strategy of Missions in Africa should take this phenomenon into consideration, since the growth of the entire movement is conditioned to a considerable extent by the reaction of Africans to Western forms of worship. In addition, the Young Mission Churches which came into being as a result of missionary work, can greatly benefit from comprehensive studies of Independent Churches in their own struggle to become indigenous in character and working method.

But the motivation for a study in depth in this field involves more than the benefits it may yield to the established Missionary agencies and Young Mission Churches. While I was in the field it became increasingly clear to me that the Independent Church leaders, whose movements I was studying, feel the need for official recognition and co-operation with Mission Churches. They themselves are generally aware of the Christian imperative of Church unity, which, to their way of thinking, necessitates the building of bridges of understanding and reconciliation. In the effort to do so Independent Church officials find themselves confronted with the wide divergence between the ideal of Christian unity and the bewildering reality of a multiformity of fissiparous Church groups to which they belong and to which they contribute in their own way. They have difficulty in their continual struggle to 'place' their own movement in its historical context, in its relation to the Western and ultimately the primal Christian community. I was therefore much inspired by the idea that the study of a few Independent Churches, however limited its scope, might contribute towards clarifying some problems of the Independent Church leaders themselves. Several Shona Church officials expressed the wish that their own 'Church History' should be written. Their wish to understand and interpret their own movement in the wider context of Christianity greatly stimulated the presentation of the accumulated material in its present form.

The main objective of this study is to provide a descriptive account of a few selected Independent Churches, representative of the Spirit-type (the prophet-healing groups, known as the Zionist Churches in South Africa and the Aladura Churches in West Africa) and Ethiopian-type (non-prophetic) movements among the Southern Shona. This includes an historical survey, based on interview and archival material, an analysis of the community structure of these Churches by means of socio-anthropological methods, a description of these movements as religious phenomena, and subsequently a theological evaluation of the practices and beliefs described. Working on the assumption that the new religion introduced by European missionaries is accepted as the point of departure in these circles, an effort was made throughout the study to analyze both *old* and *new*, since it is obvious that, in contrast to Mission Churches, a completely different and diversified pattern of attitudes towards traditional religion and custom was emerging in these Churches. By relating the leadership structure to kinship and hereditary law, the organization and life of the Church community to village and town activities, and Church ritual and belief to traditional practices, an idea was obtained of the process of *adaptation*, where old and new are merged into a syncretic whole, as well as the process of *rejection*, where the choice of Christianity involves a break with the system of the past.

From the missiological point of view the material thus presented leads to such subjects as the dialogue between Christianity and the non-Christian religions, Church indigenization and syncretism. Without depth studies of this kind, a sound theological evaluation of the Independent Churches, of how *they* relate the Christian message to the thought-world conditioned by traditional religion, of the question whether they are to be regarded as sects or Churches, of their forms of prophecy, exorcism, faith-healing and their interpretation of the Holy Spirit, etc., cannot be achieved.

A number of studies dealing with African Independent Churches have been written primarily from the historical or sociological point of view. A few observers have interpreted this phenomenon rather one-sidedly in terms of political or social protest. Some contributions appear to be products of field-workers who incidentally came across these religious groupings while engaged on other projects, or by missionaries who had taken an interest in the activities of one or other group with which they came into contact in the course of ministering to their own congregations. On the whole such studies, some of which contain brilliant accounts of the personalities and groups concerned, are highly informative and valuable. Yet the limitations of many of these accounts, caused by the lack of a comprehensive approach and by the lack of close identification of the observer over a long period of time with the groups studied, are only too obvious.

It was therefore felt that, in order to be really meaningful, a study of the Southern Shona Independent Churches should be conducted from the level of *participational observation* during a two and a half year research period of sustained and direct contact with leaders and members of the selected groups in the field. An enquiry had to be held as far as possible *from within* these

Church groups. The task which I had set myself was that of finding the answers to the following basic questions:

Who join the Independent Churches? *Why* and *under what circumstances* do people join these Churches? *How* do they interpret and practise Christianity in their own (rural and urban) environments?

The use of an interdisciplinary methodology – the combination of an historical, socio-anthropological and theological approach – seemed the most appropriate way of dealing with this subject. It is hoped that such a combination will provide at least part of the comprehensive perspective needed for an appreciation and understanding of the rich variety of factors involved in the origination and life of these Churches. It should be stated, however, that the inclusion of an historical account of the Churches studied and the use of anthropological methods in the search for information in the field does not imply any pretence of expertise, since my studies in theology did not include any academic training in history or anthropology. In the effort to cope with this handicap I availed myself of the advice of experts in various disciplines during the different stages of enquiry and writing up of the material.

This is also a *comparative study* in that the Mission and Independent Churches within the surveyed area are compared with each other as regards their major attractions, doctrines, beliefs, religious expressions and especially their attitudes towards traditional customs and ritual. No effort was made to cover the extensive literature on the subject or to relate each facet of this study to those of similar movements elsewhere on the continent. Reference to the Independent Churches in South Africa is only made in the historical context so as to clarify the influence of these movements on the initial development of religious 'Independency' in Rhodesia, and also at other points in the study where such comparisons seemed relevant.

Choice of environment and research design

The choice of environment for the study was conditioned mainly by two considerations. *First*, it coincided with my interest in the Southern Shona of the Victoria Province where I was born. Knowledge of the Karanga language, derived from my early contacts with boyhood friends, enabled me to conduct interviews in the vernacular from the outset without the assistance of an interpreter. Thus most notes could be extracted from interviews in Chikaranga and, when necessary, translated into English at a later stage. By making notes in the vernacular my assistants, who were otherwise reasonably well versed in

English, could avoid confusion of concepts in this intricate field of religious expression. *Secondly*, very little has thus far been published on the Independent Church movements amongst the Southern Shona. Aquina has written some interesting articles on a few of the larger movements in the area with which I was concerned, and these deserve attention.[6] But an extensive study of these groups, comparable to Sundkler's treatment of the 'Separatists' in South Africa, has not yet been undertaken and it is towards the bridging of this gap that my research program was directed.

For the purpose of studying four Independent Churches on a comparative basis it was desirable to confine the study to a culturally and linguistically homogeneous area. This was not always possible since the research design was based on three different levels of enquiry, namely of Church life (1) at *Church headquarters*, (2) in *local congregations* (Tribal Trust and Native Purchase Areas) and (3) in *urban congregations*, which necessitated the extension of the project over a fairly wide geographical area. Nevertheless, the main focus of the study was restricted to one chiefdom in the Gutu district, where practically all the Churches concerned were represented by local congregations. Only in the case of two Church centres, the Ethiopian-type Church in Ndau territory and the major Apostolic Church in Manyika territory (see map 3), was it necessary to go beyond the boundaries of the Karanga-steaking tribes.[7] Fortunately this particular extension of the study did not unduly complicate the total comparative picture, because the traditional religious background of the Ndau and the Manyika tribes, with the exception of minor variations, largely corresponds with that of the Karanga.

Once the initial survey of the Churches in the Southern Shona territory had been made in March, 1965, a choice of two Spirit-type and two Ethiopian-type Churches was made. The Spirit-type Churches are: the *African Apostolic Church of Johane Maranke* (AACJM), and the Zionist movement which consists of two distinct groups, Rev. Samuel Mutendi's *Zion Christian Church* (ZCC) and the *Ndaza* ('holy cord') or robed Zionists. Of the latter group Bishop David Masuka's *Zion Apostolic Church of South Africa* (ZAC of SA) and Bishop Andreas Shoko's *Zionist Apostolic Faith Mission* (ZAFM) are the

6. Sr. Mary Aquina OP, *Christianity in a Rhodesian Tribal Trust Land,* in African Social Research, No. 1, June 1966; *The People of the Spirit: An Independent Church in Rhodesia,* in Africa, Vol. XXXVII, No. 2, April 1967; and *Zionists in Rhodesia,* in Africa, Vol. XXXIX, No. 2, April 1969. Dr. Marshall Murphree's study (*Christianity and the Shona,* London, 1969) includes a thorough description of one Independent Church – the *Vapostori* of Johane Maranke, also to be dealt with n this treatise – amongst one of the Northern Shona tribes, the Budgja.

7. For the geographic distribution of the Shona tribes, see map 1.

main bodies from which numerous Zionist secessionist Churches have sprung. The Ethiopian-type category includes the *African Congregational Church* (ACC) of President Zvekare Sengwayo and the *First Ethiopian Church* (FEC) of Bishop Nheya Gavure.[8]

Each of these Churches had to be studied on the threefold level as indicated above, which implied visits varying from several days to two or more months at the headquarters of each Church. The first four months were spent among the Zion City community of Rev. Mutendi in the Bikita district, before a shift of camp took place to the Chingombe chiefdom in the Gutu district. In Chingombe I built my quarters in the vicinity of congregational centres and Church sites of several Independent Churches. A neutral site was chosen because too close an identification with any particular group could complicate the study of rival groups. From July 1965 to the end of 1966 the research comprised regular interviews with Independent Church officials and ordinary members, the participational attendance (where possible) and observation of a variety of traditional religious, Mission and Independent Church activities, with spells of absence from Chingombe in order to visit some distant Church headquarters. During these periods of absence one or two members of a team of trained assistants remained in Chingombe in order to maintain continuity of work in this area. They interviewed people according to my instructions with the aid of tape-recorders, which enabled me to cross-check on dubious aspects or follow up important information at a later stage. During these periods they also kept in touch with local people whose involvement in any particular part of the religious field, over a set period of time, was of specific importance for my study.

At Church headquarters, where identification with the central community of adherents was as close as the circumstances and inclination of the people permitted, much time was spent in the company of principal Church leaders, all of whom I personally interviewed. Living in these communities enabled me to obtain a fair idea of Church organization, the hierarchic pattern of leadership in relation to the kinship structure and the program of religious life in the immediate vicinity of the main leaders themselves. Those assistants who accompanied me on such trips usually concentrated on the Church members of the central congregation who lived in the villages close to the Church headquarters. In this way information was obtained, not only from the nuclear group of Church officials, but also from closely or loosely affiliated members and outsiders in the immediate environment, which shed some light on inter-

8. For the use of the terms 'Spirit-type' and Ethiopian-type' Churches, see pp. 285, 350.

group attitudes. Sessions of Church council, Passover ceremonies, baptismal rites and all possible types of Church activities were regularly attended. The repeated and generous invitations by *all* the Church leaders whom I met, to conduct sermons or to attend Church dances, enabled me to participate in religious activities in a way which made close identification possible without the risk of being excluded from other communities. When I was allowed to accompany Zionist officials during some of their country-wide missionary campaigns towards the end of my stay at Zion City, I regarded it as a sign of their acceptance of my presence as a *munyori weHistory* ('writer of history') although they were fully aware of my own affiliation to a Mission Church.

Towards the end of 1966 a mass of material had been collected on the basis of *casual sampling*. The quantitative material supplied by my assistants could be added to the qualitative information gathered through sustained, direct and personal contact. Up to this stage sampling was used primarily for interviews with regular and casual informants apart from, or in connection with, observations in the field. The accumulation of basic data on tribal affiliation, age, educational standard and occupation of Church members was mostly followed up by questions concerning religious history, contact with Missions, reasons for joining Independent Churches, attitudes towards other Church groups, etc. In addition to obtaining answers to prescribed questions regarding the life histories of individuals, the assistants were allowed considerable freedom in eliciting information on a number of topics relevant to our subject.

Since the material was only representative of those Churches with which we are concerned, a general frame of reference was needed in which the results of our findings could be assessed within the total structure of the Chingombe community. Thus a *random sample survey* was conducted in December 1966 and January 1967, with the aid of sixteen Shona schoolteachers, most of whom resided in Chingombe. The teachers were briefed on the questionnaire and had to conduct a few trial interviews, the results of which were jointly discussed and criticized, before they commenced work. Of the 110 villages in Chingombe, 21 were selected by taking every 5th kraalhead from the order in which their names appeared on the tax register. This meant a 20% sample of the total number of villages in the Chingombe tribal area, and the selected villages proved to be fairly evenly distributed within the boundaries of the whole area (see map 4). A smaller sample, based on this type of selection, could hardly be used in view of the uneven distribution of Churches. I was satisfied with the geographical spread of the 21 villages since most of the sectors where Independent and Mission Church influence is felt were included.

The enumerators were subdivided into three teams, each with its own leader, whose task it was to check the information obtained by his team after a day's work, to hand in the answer sheets at Alheit Mission station where I was staying at the time, to keep the team supplied with writing material and to see to it that time was not unduly lost at homesteads where beer parties coincided with interview appointments. Through a regular perusal of the work done by the enumerators, mistakes and gaps could be detected and corrected the next day. Only in the initial stages of the survey was it required of an enumerator to repeat one or two whole interviews, after it had become apparent that some of the questions had been misinterpreted. Each of the teams operated in its own demarcated territory in North, Central and South Chingombe, where team members could lodge with relatives or at the nearest schools. Loss of time through travelling was avoided in this way.

The questionnaire was an abbreviated version of the one we had used for the casual sampling. Next to the basic data on education, age, kinship ties in relation to head of homestead, marital state and religious affiliation, brief questions about the nature of Church affiliation, reasons for joining a Church, or for moving from one Church to another, and about a number of theological subjects (e.g. conversion, salvation, heaven, hell, etc.) were asked. Descriptive accounts were avoided in the sections dealing with beliefs in the spirit world. Instead of requiring, for example, a description of the spirits and their various forms of manifestation, short questions, based on previously obtained information, were put. This method often implied a positive or negative reply to questions that implicitly posed some traditional attribute ascribed to the spirits, such as: Can the *midzimu* (ancestral spirits) kill? Can they protect their descendants? Can they mediate between us and God? Does the alien *shavi* spirit provide the *nganga* (diviner-herbalist) with curative powers? Does the *ngozi* (vengeful) spirit kill? Superficial though these questions may seem, the quantified answers nevertheless provided a means of determining, on a representative basis, the persistence of traditional beliefs in non-Church and Church circles.

Accurate data on economic conditions were the most difficult to obtain. I had avoided a detailed enquiry into this field during the first few months of my stay in Chingombe, because it was evident that questions concerning livestock roused the suspicion among some village elders that the project might lead to destocking measures by Government officials. According to them, an agricultural survey in the past had resulted in strict destocking measures. Although much of the suspicion had been overcome by the time the random sample survey (RSS) was conducted, the figures on the ownership of livestock cannot be regarded as fully reliable. Neither are the figures given by subsistence farmers on the number of bags of maize, finger millet, groundnuts, etc. completely accurate, since many people do not normally estimate the total crop yields of their lands in these terms. Consequently, economic estimates were primarily used as an indication of the general pattern of rural production and stock ownership, or as a means of distinguishing between the lower, middle and upper economic classes, which could in turn be correlated with Church affiliation. They should not be taken as a comprehensive and complete assessment of the economic situation.

Once the RSS had been completed, the research shifted to a Dutch Reformed and a Roman Catholic Mission station, the former in Chingombe and the latter situated in Nyamande, the chiefdom adjacent to that of Chingombe. Special attention was given to organization, social relations and the approach to traditional religion. Apart from discussions with Church leaders also ordinary Church members on the Mission station, in its immediate vicinity and further afield, were interviewed along lines similar to those followed among Independent Church members. It should be stated, however, that the study of Mission Churches was of a limited nature, and that reference to their policies is made in this study only in so far as these have a direct bearing on the Independent Churches.

The last months of my fieldwork, from April to June 1967, were spent in Fort Victoria. A representative study of the town community could not be made during such a brief stay. I personally contacted the leaders of Mission and Independent Churches in an effort to assess the numerical strength of each Church and to discuss religious matters with them. This was followed by a schedule of regular interviews with adult members of all the officially recognized Churches, conducted by myself and three of my trained assistants who had also participated in the Chingombe survey. Much of the work had to be done at night. The township manager permitted me to move about at night. Thus I could meet Church people, attend some of their nightly prayer-meetings and spend hours watching town *nganga* (diviner-herbalists) at work.

Not all the information collected in Fort Victoria was used for quantification. Small samples of adult members of the most influential Mission and Independent Churches, as well as 35 traditionalists, were selected to get a general idea of some of the most important religious factors in an urban area. Care was taken with the selection of Church members to include people of the widest possible range of occupations in town. Yet it should be noted that a sample of 10 Independent Church adults sometimes comprised either the entire leadership nucleus or the total adult community of a Church, since the Independent Church groups are represented in town by relatively small numbers.

For the purpose of this study the quantifiable material can therefore be labelled according to its source of information: the *random sample survey*

(RSS) which is representative of the Chingombe chiefdom, a territorially defined rural community; a *casual sample* containing information on adult members of four Independent and two Mission Church communities in the Chingombe area and at the Churches' headquarters (referred to as CSR – Casual Sample, Reserve); and a *casual town sample* (CST). In this form the information can be presented as pertaining to either *rural* or *urban* communities, which presents, where necessary, a further distinction between headquarters (Mission Church or central Independent Church community) and local congregational levels in rural areas. Sometimes the information of all three samples is grouped together when certain aspects, beliefs or attitudes of any one Church group in contrast to another, are described.

Presentation of the material acquired

During the process of working through life histories, recorded sermons, field notes and statistical data, I came to the conclusion that the best method would be to present this study in a series of companion volumes. The advantage of this is that one can concentrate on a limited number of aspects in each volume, the publication of which is not dependent on or delayed by the working out of all the acquired information. In this way a drastic condensation of case material – which would have been necessary if the entire range of the enquiry had to be covered in a single volume – could be avoided. It was felt that, in the effort to probe as deeply as possible into the motivation of individuals for joining the Independent Churches and to understand their interpretation of Christianity, *their* responses to questions, *their* narratives of religious and other experiences and the contents of *their* sermons should be given full space in this study. Thus the reader is presented, not only with the author's impressions and deductions, but also with numerous verbatim accounts by Africans as they were tape-recorded in the field. This combination of 'raw' interview material with scientific analysis in some respects disturbs the balance of the analytical framework. Yet it is hoped that through this method the reader will gain a deeper insight into the rich and sometimes subtle variation of factors and experiences involved in these movements.

Broadly speaking, the entire study is planned to comprise four main themes, possibly to be presented in as many volumes:

In the first place a sketch of the *socio-economic* and *religious background* of the Southern Shona serves as an introduction to an account of the *rise of the Independent Churches*, as well as to the entire study. This, in short, is the scope of our first Volume.

Secondly, attention is given to the *patterns of affiliation* of Independent Church members and the *patterns of recruitment*, in order to determine the *major attractions* of these movements. Using as a guide-line the answers of adherents to the question *why* they had joined their particular Church groups, the practices and circumstances most frequently referred to are subjected to close scrutiny. Subjects dealt with in some detail, are: adaptation to the traditional High-God and ancestral cults, the vital role of dreams in some groups as a decision-making factor, the substitution of traditional divinatory and healing practices with prophetic faith-healing and exorcism, as well as the 'Christianized' version of witch-finding.

Thirdly, the *structure, organization and leadership* of Independent Churches are considered. An idea is given of how the local congregations, regional circuits and headquarters of each Church are structured, how they function as a whole and what annual programs are followed. In addition to their inner structure, Church groups are also viewed in relation to their environment, which includes their attitude towards other religious groupings, their participation in or abstention from village, tribal and national political activities, etc. Leadership hierarchies, types of leaders, the appointment, duties, powers and succession of Church officials all form part of the composite picture.

In the fourth place, *ritual and belief* are dealt with. Baptismal, holy communion, marriage and burial rites are described in detail. On the basis of interview material, sermons and some written sources, e.g. sacred books and hymns, a number of beliefs concerning the triune God, conversion, sanctity, salvation, damnation, etc., are analyzed. In conclusion, a brief theological evaluation of the Christian character of the Independent Churches will be attempted. This is done in the effort to contribute towards the theological reorientation which both Mission and Independent Churches, in their dealings with each other, will have to undertake sooner or later.

It should be noted that this fourfold classification is still subject to revision and change. Since the presentation of findings in several volumes involves a long-term program, with much of the material still to be worked out or recast, this can only be a tentative outline of the proposed working scheme.

As far as this first volume is concerned, the first three chapters all deal with the background of our subject of study. Chapter 1 concerns the socio-economic conditions of the rural and urban Shona people. Attention is paid to the social structure within a typical chiefdom, ward and village; to kinship patterns and distribution of authority; to subsistence farming, land allocation and labour migration, all of which have a direct or indirect bearing on the origination and character of the Independent Churches.

Chapter 2 deals with traditional religious practices and beliefs: the High-God and ancestral cults, the alien and avenging spirit ceremonies, magic and wizardry. An attempt has been made not only to give an account of the main procedures and objectives of traditional rituals, but also to assess their present-day significance.

Chapter 3 contains an account of the two major Mission Churches – Dutch Reformed and Roman Catholic – operating in the area of our enquiry. Their respective theories and practices relating to Church expansion, auxiliary services (education and medical aid) and especially traditional religion and customs are discussed, to indicate the different ways in which the new religion was introduced into Southern Shona society. Chapters 2 and 3, lengthy as they are, form the pivot of the entire study. They provide the essential background for an analysis of the way in which the *old* religion continues to condition – whether in camouflaged or modified form – Independent Church life; and the influence of the *new* religion, the essence of which was largely accepted while many of its outward forms were rejected by the Independent Churches.

In the first volume, Chapters 1 to 3 (i.e. Part I) contain more detail account than the following three chapters (Part II), which deal with the rise of the Independent Churches. This lengthy background study should, however, be viewed in the context of the whole survey, because much of what is presented here is directly relevant to the descriptions and analyses appearing in the following volumes. For instance, a discussion of the land problem and economic conditions, introduced in Chapter 1, receives fuller treatment in Volume 2, and the extent to which Church leadership is conditioned by the kinship patterns, also mentioned in Chapter 1, is dealt with more fully in Volume 3.

Chapters 4 and 5 trace the development of the Spirit- and Ethiopian-type Independent Churches, from their inception up to modern times. The focus is mainly on the experiences of the principal leaders, their contact with Mission Churches in Rhodesia and with 'Separatist' Church leaders in South Africa, their first campaigning activities amongst fellow tribesmen and the extension of activities further afield. For each major group or subdivision the geographic distribution, approximate numerical strength and the schisms which had occurred up to 1965, are given. Chapter 6 is called 'Conflict and recognition', for it deals with the attitudes of the Rhodesia Administration, tribal authorities and Mission Churches towards the budding Independent Churches during the past few decades. The struggle of the IC leaders for official recognition and the problems of control confronting local District Commissioners and tribal chiefs are reflected in archival documents and historical accounts in the 'canonical' books of some of the most outstanding Church leaders.

The statistical analysis employed in this study varies in accuracy according to the subject concerned. Quantified data on tribal affiliation, approximate age and educational qualifications of individuals, are more reliable and accurate than those on such topics as stock ownership and crop production, or on religious ideas. The problem of interpretation and reduction, in order to distill the essentials from the lengthy responses of interviewed persons to open-ended questions, arose frequently. In some cases the detailed narratives of informants obscured the actual point they were driving at, which rendered accurate interpretation and classification nearly impossible. Nevertheless, the statistical data, even on abstract subjects, retain their validity, if not for accurate scientific demonstration at least as indications of emerging patterns of thought or of differentiated emphases within the various religious groupings.

Subjectivity and bias inevitably enter into a study of this kind. I have nevertheless tried to be as objective and fair as possible in my approach to this intricate field. The term 'Independent Churches' has been chosen since these movements are 'independent' from the Western Mission Churches in finance, organization and forms of worship. 'Separatist' is an often used but misleading term. It is usually based on the assumption that Independent Church leaders draw most of their followers from the flocks of the established Mission Churches. This is not the case with the four Church movements I studied, since the majority of their members had either never attained full membership of a Mission Church, or, for all practical purposes, had left the Mission Churches long before joining an Independent Church. Only a minority of members had defected directly from Mission to Independent Churches. Furthermore, the term 'Church' is used, not in the first place on the grounds of theological evaluation, but because it seems fair and appropriate that these movements, for descriptive purposes at least, should be characterized in terms corresponding to their own interpretation.

Part 1

Socio-religious background

History and socio-economic background

African Independent Churches have been described as protest movements in relation to oppressive colonial governments, as reactionary groups that resent the paternalistic approach of missionaries, or as deliberate attempts to adapt Christian belief and worship to their specific ethno-religious backgrounds. Presumably the factors of 'situation coloniale',[1] missionary strategy and ethnic background all feature prominently in the origination of many of the Independent Churches, but any *one* of these has never yet by itself proved a sufficient basis for a comprehensive interpretation of the phenomenon of African Church Independency in its totality. Theories concerning the origin of this movement[2] have often obscured the complexity of the originating factors involved. In order to achieve a balanced evaluation of these Churches in any particular area special attention should therefore be given to the historical and social context within which they originate. In the case of the Southern Shona we shall concern ourselves with a cursory glance at the historical past, with the most relevant aspects of the urban and rural social structure, with the all-important kinship structure and with the implementation of land legislation, which was bound to lead to reaction and protest from the side of the Africans.

1. EARLY HISTORY

According to African tradition one of the first Shona tribes to settle south of the Zambesi was the Mbire (totem: *Shoko*). Chief NeMbire is supposed to have migrated from the vicinity of Lake Tanganyika with his own and several subordinate Karanga elans early in the 14th century.[3] Linguistic and

1. Balandier, 1963, pp. 41-65.
2. For a summary of the principal theories forwarded by recognized investigators during the past few decades, see Barrett, 1968, pp. 62-68.
3. Abraham in Stokes and Brown, 1966, p. 33.

material evidence confirms early contact with Central and West African tribes.

When the European settlers arrived in the country towards the end of the 19th century, the Shona-speaking people made the impression of being completely cowed by the warriors of the Ndebele monarch, Lobengula, Mzilikazi's successor, and of being organized in small chiefdoms throughout the whole country without any form of centralized control. As a result the settlers tended to underrate the Shona people. To them the scattered *amaSvina* (people of dirt) – also called the 'dogs of the Ndebele' – represented the underdog whom they had come to liberate from the tyranny of the well-organized Ndebele power. In spite of temporary suppression by the Ndebele, the Shona carried with them the heritage of a rich past. Their culture had evidently reached a higher peak than most of the surrounding Southern and Central African tribes. They were technically more advanced, of which fact their pottery and gold mining activities bear proof. The stone constructions at Kami and Dhlo-Dhlo, as well as the magnificent Zimbabwe ruins, are directly associated with them. These buildings of shaped rocks are the remnants of state headquarters reminding us of the remarkable past era of centralized government.

Apparently there were two Shona dynasties, known as the 'Monomotapa' and the Rozvi empires. In the 15th century the Tavara people, living to the south and in the immediate vicinity of the Zambesi, were conquered by a group of Southern Shona, today known as the Northern Kore-Kore, under the leadership of Mutota. The latter was given the name of '*Mwene Mutapa*' – i.e. the master of the ravaged land – a title which became a hereditary praise name, and in the course of time was generally referred to as Monomotapa. Portuguese traders came into contact and kept up trade relations with the powerful rulers of this empire as far back as the 16th and 17th centuries.[4] At that stage the tribes paying allegiance to the Monomotapa rulers covered the vast areas of what is today known as Zambia, Rhodesia and much of contemporary Portuguese East Africa. In a recent account of the Monomotapas, Gann tells us that 'the Monomotapas in time managed to build a great tribal confederacy. Hoe cultivation and small-scale industries like weaving, gold mining, pottery and the production of ironware built up a surplus; trade in luxury goods enhanced the country's wealth . . . The king himself used great nobles in his household which formed the nucleus of a rudimentary state organization. He also received assistance from a body of tribal intellectuals, part royal spirit mediums and part official historians, who were supposed to voice the will of ancestral kings, and maintain the tradi-

4. Kuper, 1955, p. 16.

tions of their race.'[5] The Monomotapa ruler's influence therefore covered both political and spiritual affairs. With the aid of officially recognized spirit mediums, whose task it was, amongst other things, to name the successors of deceased tributary chiefs or of the Mutapa himself, it became possible for the rulers to achieve a ritually sanctioned hegemony.

Internal strife between the vassal states, aggravated by the increasing trade demands of the Portuguese, led to the disintegration of the Monomotapa kingdom. The rulers, Ranger asserts, were 'caught between Portuguese demands and the resistance of these by their vassals; if they accommodated themselves to the Portuguese they faced rebellion; if they accommodated themselves to the demands of most of their subjects and attempted to exclude Portuguese influence they faced the military strength of this early colonial power.'[6] Thus the centralized state started to disintegrate, so that the only remnant left of it in the 19th century was the continuation of the traditional religious role played by the influential *vasvikiro* (spirit mediums) in the succession of chiefs amongst the Kore-Kore.

The Rozvi empire to the south, with its capital first at Zimbabwe ('houses of stone') and later in the Matopo country, near present-day Bulawayo, has its roots in the 15th century. For a long time it coexisted with the Monomotapa dynasty, but it differed from the northern state in two important aspects. In the first place the Rozvi *Mambos* (Kings) managed to steer clear of the Portuguese influence by keeping the traders coming into their territory under control, and in the second place, by making use of the centralized Mwari High-God cult to achieve an even stronger religious tie with their vassals than had the northern state. Unlike the military power on which the highly centralized states of the Zulu and Ndebele were based, the Rozvi confederacy consisted of loosely affiliated vassal states, stretched over a vast territory, with the Rozvi claim to leadership based not exclusively on military superiority but on the widespread belief that Mwari, the Shona High-God himself, had called the Rozvi monarchy into being.

As the Israelites depended on the Levites for their priestly function, so members of the Mbire Shoko tribe became the acknowledged guardians of the Mwari shrines and ritual office-bearers of those Shona tribes that belonged to the Rozvi empire. Tradition has it that Dyembewu, the first Rozvi *Mambo*, was the son of Chief NeMbire's granddaughter, whom some believed to have been impregnated by Mwari himself.[7] Thus the Mbire chief and

5. Gann, 1965, p. 9.
6. Ranger, 1967, p. 8.
7. Abraham in Stokes and Brown, 1966, p. 33. The information was obtained from the present spirit medium of Chaminuka.

priests became closely associated with the royal Rozvi tribe. The central Mwari shrine was conveniently situated at the Zimbabwe state headquarters, where the priests conducted cult ceremonies on behalf of the whole empire.[8] Because of this close identification with the Rozvi power the cult's influence naturally spread, together with the expanding boundaries of the Rozvi confederacy.

Blake Thompson and Summers aptly described the royal dwellings of the Rozvi as follows: 'Zimbabwe was a religious centre. All the miscellany of buildings on the hill and the valley were attracted here because of the special sanctity of the site. Some were undoubtedly royal dwellings, other administrative buildings or even trading places, but they crowded round the sacred areas as King, Parliament, Government trade and commerce all crowd round the royal church at Westminster Abbey.'[9] It is not fully clear whether the transfer of the Mwari shrine to Matonjeni (Matopo mountains) coincided with the shift of the Rozvi administrative headquarters after they had conquered the Matopo country in the 17th century. The close link between Rozvi rulers and Mbire priests nevertheless continued to exist and to play an important role in the minds of the Southern Shona people after the Rozvi power had been broken by the Nguni invaders. It is of great importance to take note of the widespread prestige of the Rozvi tribe at this early period, since it was partly the appeal of the traditional religious authorities to the glories of this dynasty that enabled them to rally the rebellious Shona against the European settlers in 1896. It was this same prestige which enabled Zionist Bishop Mutendi, one of the most influential of the present Independent Church leaders, to draw several Southern Shona chiefs into his Church from the 1930's until this day, and it was this pre-Ndebele past that African Nationalist leaders invoked with the rise of African Nationalism after 1950.

The Rozvi reign did not necessarily imply peace within the empire. There is ample evidence of intertribal disputes. Invasions of certain territories by chiefs who wished to expand the boundaries of their own chiefdoms within the empire was often followed by the subdivision of tribes and the fragmentation of clans through the movement and resettlement of people. As Chingombe, a chiefdom in the Gutu district, is the area of our particular concern we must now briefly turn to its pre-Ndebele past, which will throw some light on the presence of a considerable number of tribal segments in this territory to this day.

8. In 1871 Karl Mauch obtained an account of how the ritual ceremonies were conducted. See Summers in NADA, 1952, and Van der Merwe, 1957, pp. 24-25.

9. Blake Thompson and Summers, in NADA, 1956.

Prior to the arrival of the Rufura tribe, members of several other Shona tribes had settled in different parts of what is known today as Gutu district. The Hera (*mutupo*: Shava; *chidao*: Museamwa),[10] who lived in the east under the leadership of Chief Nyashanu, started moving across the Nyazvidzi river (see map 2) which now forms the eastern border of Gutu. At approximately the same time members of the Chamutsa tribe (*mutupo*: Moyo; *chidao*: Mugonderwa) – later to be called the Chagonda or Rasa people – moved in from the south-east. They followed Kariwara Marumbi, a reputed rainmaker who had to flee from the wrath of her brothers after she had obtained the rainmaking powers from her father, who was a blood relative of Shoshangane, the powerful Gaza ruler north of the Sabi river. Marumbi became the wife of Chief Nyashanu who fathered her only son, Chinamashabwa. The descendants of Chinamashabwa are today called the Munyaradze people and they have their own sub-chiefdom in approximately the centre of the Gutu Tribal Trust land. Marumbi was to play an important role as a rainmaker, activities which brought her in contact with the Mwari cult priests at Matonjeni. After she was forced into, and had won a rainmaking competition with another reputed rainmaker at Matonjeni during a period of critical drought, she finally settled down at Mt. Rasa, near the Chingombe border, where the descendants of her younger brother, Neusaka, continued to play an important role as rainmakers in the old traditional way.

Segments of the Duma tribe (*mutupo*: Moyo; *chidao*: Chirandu or Gonyohori) had migrated from the present Bikita district where their great chief, Fupajena, reigned. They settled to the south-west of the Devure river. Wandering Rozvi clans, who were known as iron-smelters, occupied patches of land between the Hera and Duma that had not yet been claimed by others. When the Rufura tribe (*mutupo*: Gumbo; *chidao*: Madyirapazhe) arrived in the country from Musana near Salisbury in the north, they found a dwelling place amongst the occupants of the territory. These were the four Rufura brothers with their followers: the two elder brothers, Nemashakwe and Munyikwa, settled at the junction of the Devure and Nyazvidzi rivers in the east; NeNdanga moved to the south into what is now called the Ndanga reserve, and Mabwazhe went and lived in the western regions with his Hera *sekuru* (maternal uncle), Chasura.

It was Chasura who taught his *muzukuru* (sister's son) how to use powerful medicine against his enemies. Mabwazhe eventually turned the medicine against his instructor and drove Chasura and his people from the district. This was only the beginning of several invasions. The surrounding chiefs,

10. *Mutupo* = clan name; *chidao* = sub-clan name.

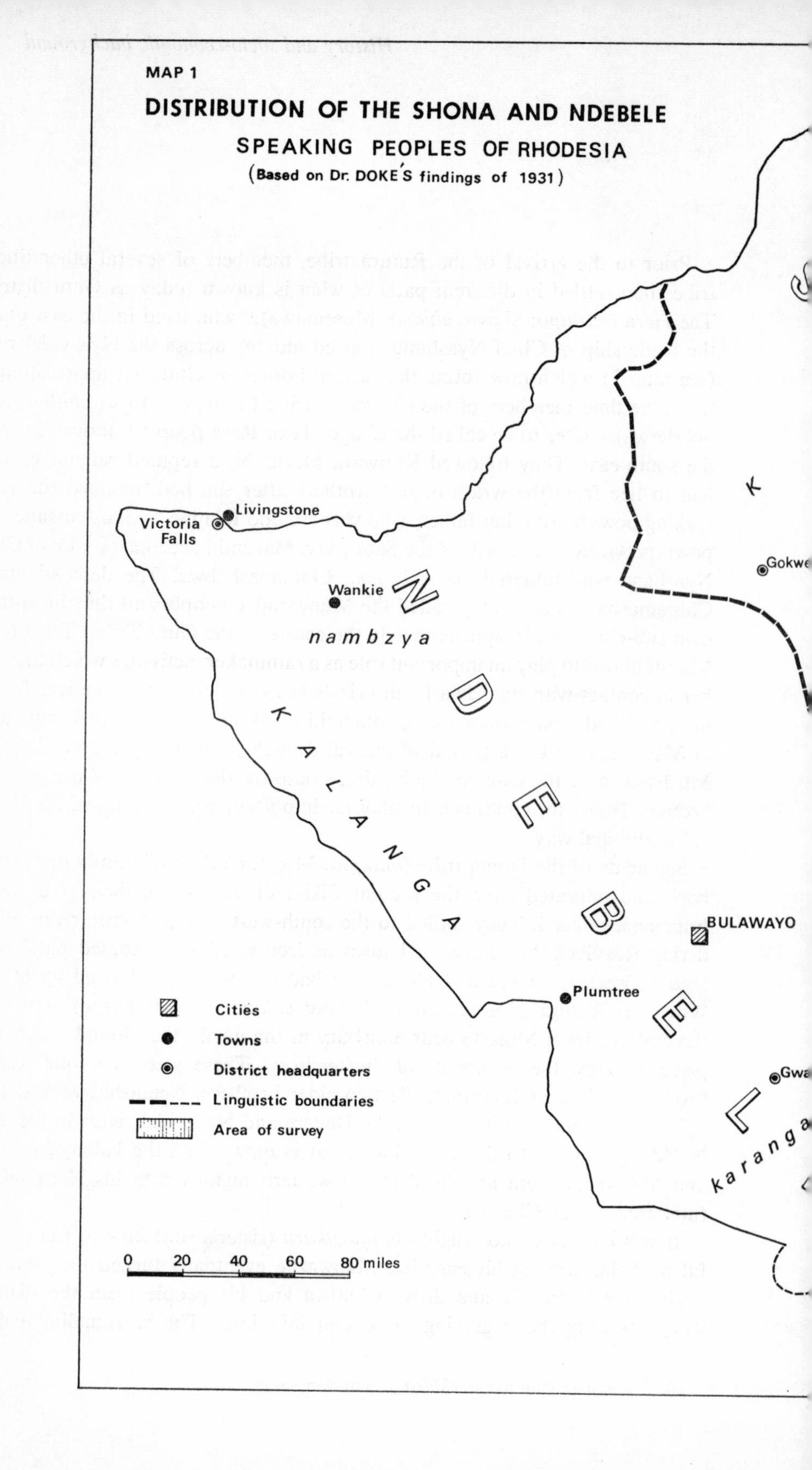
MAP 1
DISTRIBUTION OF THE SHONA AND NDEBELE
SPEAKING PEOPLES OF RHODESIA
(Based on Dr. DOKE'S findings of 1931)
Livingstone
Victoria Falls
Wankie
Gokwe
NDEBELE
nambzya
KALANGA
BULAWAYO
Plumtree
karanga
Cities
Towns
District headquarters
Linguistic boundaries
Area of survey
0 20 40 60 80 miles

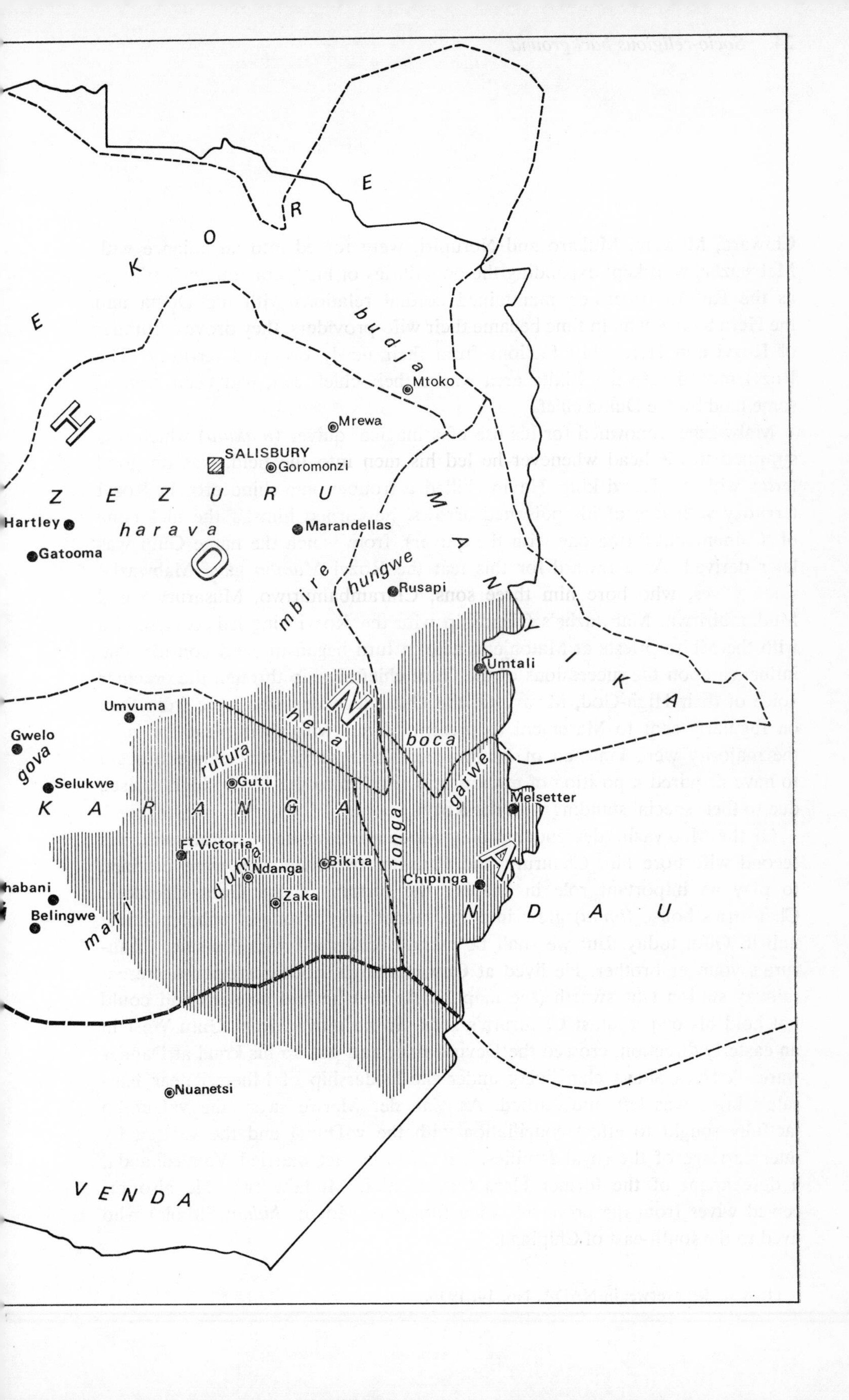

K O R E
E
budja
Mtoko
Mrewa
H
SALISBURY
Goromonzi
Z E Z U R U
Hartley
harava
Marandellas
Gatooma
M A N Y I K A
O
mbire
hungwe
Rusapi
Umtali
N
Umvuma
hera
Gwelo
boca
gova
rufura
Selukwe
Gutu
garwe
K A R A N G A
Melsetter
tonga
Ft Victoria
A
duma
Ndanga
Bikita
Chipinga
habani
Zaka
Belingwe
mari
N D A U
Nuanetsi
V E N D A

Chiwara, Mawere, Mukaro and Norupiri, were forced into an alliance with Mabwazhe, who kept expanding the boundaries of his 'paramountcy'. Whereas the Rufura tribesmen maintained cordial relations with the Duma and the Hera Shava, who in time became their wife-providers, they drove a number of Rozvi and Hera Shiri factions from their newly occupied territory. The Rozvi moved into the Bikita area where their chief, Jiri, had been granted some land by the Duma chief.

Mabwazhe, renowned for his use of a magical quiver (*mukutu*) which was strapped to his head whenever he led his men into the field, was on good terms with the Rozvi king. Having killed a troublesome rhinoceros in Rozvi territory with one of his poisoned arrows, he earned himself the nickname of 'Chinamakutu' (the one with the quiver), from which the name Gutu was later derived. As a reward for this feat the Rozvi *Mambo* gave Mabwazhe some wives, who bore him three sons, Chirambamuriwo, Musarurwa and Mudambirirwa. Mabwazhe's friendship with the Rozvi king led to close ties with the Mbire priests at Matonjeni, who in turn began to exert considerable influence upon the successions of the Gutu chieftainship through the oracular voice of their High-God, Mwari. Of the Gutu degelates who were from then on regularly sent to Matonjeni to present Mwari with their pleas for rain, the majority were kinsmen of Mabwazhe. These *vanyai* (messengers) seem to have acquired a position of authority in relation to the Mwari high priests, due to their special standing with the Rozvi.

Of the Mabwazhe descendants only Mudambirirwa had several sons. His second wife bore him Chaurura and Rutsate, two men who were destined to play an important role in shaping the history of the Gutu chiefdom. Chaurura's house (*imba*) grew into the numerically strongest tribal political unit in Gutu today. But we shall be mainly concerned with Rutsate, Chaurura's younger brother. He lived at Guwamatanga, not far from the present railway station Chatsworth (see map 2). At first he had no sons and could not hold his own against Chaurura's sons. So he moved from Gutu West in an easterly direction, crossed the Devure river and put up his kraal at Dandaware. A Hera Shava clan living under the leadership of Mheresi near Rutsate's kraal was left undisturbed. As Van der Merwe says: 'the vaGumbo tactfully sought to effect conciliation with the vaDuma and the vaHera by intermarriage of the royal families.'[11] Rutsate in fact married Vamazikanda, a descendant of the former Hera Shava chief, Mudakurewa. He also received wives from the powerful Ndau (*mutupo*: Moyo; *chidao*: Sithole) who lived to the south-east of Chipinga.

11. Van der Merwe, in NADA, No. 14, 1936.

With the aid of his Ndau *vatezvara* (wife-providing in-laws), who were reputed for their bravery as warriors, Rutsate waged war against the sons of Chaurura. These small-scale civil wars undoubtedly caused considerable unrest and a shifting of the minor groups in the Gutu district. Chaurura complained about the fighting. Yet he was forced to recognize the independence of Rutsate east of the Devure river since his younger brother had acquired sufficient power to subject and politically organize the splintered tribal groups within his own sphere of influence. Since Rutsate became known as a warrior who could defend himself, Chaurura somewhat depreciatingly gave him the nickname of Chingombe (little ox); a name which inferred that Rutsate was 'just an animal'. Thus the Chingombe chiefdom gradually came into being, eventually comprising the two wards of Mheresi's Hera Shava and Rutsate's vaGumbo descendants.[12]

It was only when the Nguni invasions confronted the Gutu inhabitants with a common enemy that the fissiparous segments of the Karanga-speaking tribes were welded into a unified people. Zwangendaba invaded the weakening Rozvi empire in 1830. His army consisted mainly of Swazi and Zulu refugees who had fled from Shaka's kingdom. The invaders penetrated the country from the south-east, leaving destroyed and looted villages behind them as they went along. Mabaiwemazha, the reigning Rozvi *Mambo*, was 'skinned alive'[13] and his forces scattered all over the country. But the Zwangendaba invaders soon moved northwards to establish themselves as various independent communities in contemporary Malawi and Zambia. In their wake followed the Ndebele under their king, Mzilikazi. They came from a southwesterly direction after they had clashed with the Boer 'Voortrekkers' at Mosega, where they had lived for some years following their expulsion from Shaka's domain.

Having finally overpowered the Rozvi rulers, Mzilikazi established himself near the Matopos, where Bulawayo is situated today. This became the royal headquarters of the Ndebele military state. The Shona tribes in the immediate vicinity were subjected and their youths incorporated in the Ndebele *impis* (armies). Tribes further afield were regularly raided by the Ndebele, and the scattered Shona chiefs could offer no unified resistance. The Rufura tribesmen were constantly harassed by Shoshangane's armies from the east and Mzilikazi's warriors from the west. They managed at first to ward off

12. Information concerning the historical background of the tribes in the Gutu district was obtained from the African Extension Officer, Mr. Vandira, the High-God cult messenger, *Munyai* Vondo Mukozho and others.

13. Gann, 1965, p. 30.

small raiding parties, but once they had become demoralized by the fighting power of the Ndebele, the chiefs sought refuge in the granite strongholds whenever an attack occurred. Mt. Rasa, near Chingombe's western border (see map 4), a mountain with steep granite flanks, proved an ideal stronghold for the Chingombe and Nyamande people. 'On one occasion' writes Van der Merwe, 'the Matabele laid siege to Rasa for a whole month. Famine also raged fearfully. Then the powers of nature came to the aid of the starving Vakaranga. A flash of lightning from the clear sky struck the camp of the enemy. A considerable number of benumbed warriors were left as an easy prey to the assegais of the Vakaranga pouring down the mountain sides. The Matabele were profoundly impressed by what seemed so ostensible an intervention of Supernatural Powers on behalf of the Vakaranga.'[14] The Gutu inhabitants state that after this episode the Ndebele never returned in great numbers to their territory. As a result of the raids, the Karanga-speaking tribes under Rufura leadership achieved a greater sense of unity; but nevertheless the picture of tribal complexity was increased through the displacement of Ndau, Tonga and other groups, some of whom remained in Gutu after the Ndebele threat had passed.

European traders and hunters started crossing the borders of Mzilikazi's kingdom after Livingstone's discovery of the Victoria falls in 1855. The Inyati mission station was founded by the London Missionary Society near Mzilikazi's capital as early as 1859, but it was only after the discovery of gold, and when Mzilikazi's successor, Lobengula, had 'signed away' the mineral rights in his territory in the much disputed Rudd Concession, that the Europeans arrived in numbers large enough to ensure a permanent European settlement. Lobengula was defeated in the Matabele war of 1893 and the Shona-Ndebele resistance broken with the repressions of the Rebellions of 1896-7.

Instead of allowing the installation of another Ndebele king, the BSA Company Administration, which was the ruling power in the new colony until 1923, recognized a number of separate Shona and Ndebele chieftaincies whose boundaries were clearly defined in the course of time. In this way Shona and Ndebele chiefs were placed on an even footing, and permitted a limited (civil) jurisdiction over their followers under the local control of European officials called Native Commissioners. Guramatanga, the senior son of Chaurura, who was acting as chief at the time of the risings, had urged his followers not to take part in the fight against the Europeans. This fact, as well as his regular contact with the European administrators, led to

14. Van der Merwe, in NADA, 1936.

his recognition as paramount chief of the whole Gutu tribal area. All the chiefs in the district acknowledged Gutu's leadership, although the Munyikwa descendants were senior to the numerically stronger group of Mabwazhe kinsmen. Each of them attained the position of sub-chief or headman, but in practice the forms of allegiance varied considerably, due to the variegated historical past. Chingombe, for example, had always proved to be somewhat of a rebel. Consequently he retained a relationship of semi-independence with regard to the Gutu paramount, a status which was about to be officially raised to that of an independent chieftainship when I left the district in 1967.

2. POPULATION AND TRIBAL DISTRIBUTION

According to the final report of the April/May Census of 1962 in Rhodesia, the Europeans numbered 223,000 in contrast to the total African population of 3,618,000.[15] Approximately 48 million acres of land belonged to the Europeans and the Crown, whereas 42 million acres had by then been allocated to the Africans. The African areas mainly comprise three categories of land:

a) Native Reserves (now called Tribal Trust Land) – set aside in terms of the Constitution, covering about 21 million acres;
b) Special Native Areas (set aside by act of Parliament) – approximately 13 million acres;
c) Native Purchase Areas – approximately 8 million acres.[16]

Of the total African population 51.1% lived in the Tribal Trust Land in 1962, a figure which rises to about 65.5% if the labour migrants who come and go between rural and urban areas are included in this category. Of the indigenous African population 19.2% lived in the European farming areas and only 15.3% in urban areas. In the Gutu district the total African population was distributed in the different sectors as follows:

TTL (Reserves)	–	100,130
N.P.A.	–	10,410
European farms	–	13,350
'Urban area'		
Gutu township and Chatsworth	–	1,200
Total:		125,090[17]

15. The 1969 preliminary report of census results (mimeographed report from the Central Statistical Office, Salisbury) indicates a population of 228,590 Europeans, and 5,070,400 Africans.

16. Rogers and Frantz, 1962, p. 189.

17. Final Report of the April/May 1962 Census of Africans in Southern Rhodesia,

The vast majority of Africans are therefore still living in the rural areas, especially in the Reserves, with considerable numbers on the European and African (NPA) farms. Compared to most of the other Reserves in Rhodesia, Gutu has a large number of inhabitants, even though the ratio of 45 persons per square mile compares favourably with the 69 per square mile in the densely populated Goromonzi reserve. The approximate average of the whole of Southern Rhodesia, including the main town and cities, amounts to 24 persons per square mile.

Of the African indigenous population of Rhodesia more than 70% belong to the Shona-speaking peoples. They live throughout the country in varying degrees of density. The initial division of the country into the two administrative divisions of Mashonaland and Matabeleland therefore does not correspond to the linguistic and ethnic distribution (see map 1). The borderline demarcating Mashonaland stretches roughly from the Kariba gorge in the North, to Gwelo, and from there in a south-easterly direction to include the districts of Ndanga, Bikita and Melsetter. In Mashonaland proper the main linguistic distribution (according to the classification of Doke)[18] comprises the Karanga or Southern Shona, the Zezuru or Central Shona, the Kore-Kore or Northern Shona, the Manyika in the Eastern Umtali and Inyanga districts, and the Ndau in the Chipinga and Melsetter districts. The majority of the Ndau and considerable numbers of the Manyika-speaking people today live in the adjacent Portuguese territories. Of the Western Shona, the Kalanga in Plumtree district and the Nambzya at Wankie represent the main groups.[19]

Fortune estimated the Shona in the 1950's at 1,712,280 out of a total indigenous population of 2,221,000. His figures for the people speaking the main dialects are as follows:

Kalanga	–	50,000
Ndau	–	60,000
Zezuru	–	429,000
Karanga	–	615,000
Manyika	–	212,000
Kore Kore	–	336,880 [20]

Salisbury, 1964, p. 57.

18. Kuper, 1955, pp. 12-13.

19. Prof. Murphree points out that the people referred to as Nambzya, prefer the designation Nambiya. The former term, which dates back to the period of Ndebele occupation, has derogatory connotations (personal communication – 1970).

20. Fortune, 1959, p. 6.

While at present all given areas carry more people than the given figures indicate it is clear that the Karanga represent proportionately the most compact and largest of all the Shona groups. The Karanga sub-dialects coincide only partly with the ethnic distribution. These dialects are mainly spoken by the Duma speakers of Victoria, Ndanga and Bikita; Jena of Victoria; Mari of Chibi; Rufura (or Govera) of Gutu, Chilimanzi and Victoria; Gova of Selukwe; and Nyubi of Mzingwane, Matopo and Gwanda. It is difficult to determine the correlation between the ethnographic and linguistic factors on the basis of written sources. Holleman doubts whether the linguistic classification is ethnologically valid, as no detailed comparative study of the tribes has been attempted. Furthermore, from the African point of view, the affiliation of the tribes usually classified under one of these headings, e.g. Zezuru, is meaningless, as it is not supported by ties of a political or other nature.[21] Broadly speaking some religious traits coinciding with the main linguistic divisions can be distinguished, such as the prominent role played by the *svikiro* (spirit medium) of the *mhondoro* (tribal) spirits in important tribal matters of the Northern Kore-Kore in contrast with the well-developed High-God cult with its Mwari messengers found in the majority of chiefdoms of the Southern Karanga. On the other hand, numerous variations often characterize the cultures of relatively small political units situated in one linguistic area. This is due to the integration of a great number of tribes, as we have seen in the case of the Gutu district. The VaRemba, for example, now living in one of the Gutu sub-chiefdoms, still adhere to a code of life, including such ceremonies as circumcision and the ritual killing of all livestock used for personal consumption, which is foreign to Rufura custom.

The total population of the Chingombe chiefdom was about 8,000-9,000 in 1966-7. In the 21 villages of the chiefdom which were covered by the random sample survey there were 97 Rufura and 31 Hera Shava adult males, representing respectively 35% and 11% of the adult male population (table 1). These small bodies of agnatic kinsmen form the nucleus around which tribal unity is built[22] and they trace their descent through Rutsate back to Mabwazhe or through Mheresi back to Nyashanu, the recognized senior ancestors at the apex of the Rufura and Hera lineage hierarchies. The Rufura

21. Holleman in Colson and Gluckman, 1951, p. 354. Murphree, on the other hand, points out that a term like Zezuru within certain contexts – especially as an out-group designation – does have significance (personal communication – 1970).

22. Holleman, 1952, p. 15.

kinsmen are called the *vachinda* to distinguish them as members of the chief's lineage from the Hera and other males who, as *vatorwa* (foreigners), designate groupings of different origins. In the two Chingombe wards (see map 4) we find, apart from the Rufura and Hera kinsmen, small groups of Duma (11%), Ndau (7%), Rozvi (5%), Manyika (4%), Mbire (1%), Gargwe (3%), Hungwe (3%) and others, who together constitute the adult male community. Thus the historical past is still clearly reflected in the composite tribal structure of the Chingombe community. The fact that 79% of all the adult males were born in Chingombe and 14% (table 2) had migrated from other Gutu sub-chiefdoms shows that the small segments from different tribal backgrounds represent stable groups of which the majority have become permanent residents with a 'local history' of at least one or more generations. In the two tribal wards the majority of males stood in an affinal or cognatic relationship to the Rufura and Hera kinsmen, and the Hera were regarded as the main 'wife-providers' of the Rufura.

Judging from the figures relating to adult women, besides the Hera women (11%), the Duma (9%), Ndau (7%), Rozvi (7%), Manyika (7%), Mbire (8%) and Gargwe (6%), had become the most important wife-providing groups (lineages in the wide sense of the word) of the Rufura and other males (table 2). Since Shona marriages are exogamous it is understandable that only 52% of all the adult females had been born in the Chingombe chiefdom itself. Apart from women from the adjacent and other Gutu chiefdoms, the wives come from the Bikita, Victoria and Buhera districts, which explains the comparatively large numbers of Duma, Mbire Shoko and Rozvi women (table 2).

Although the nucleus of Rufura kinsmen forms a minority group in relation to the bulk of the population, it is significant that not a single other agnatic unit constitutes a numerically stronger group. In addition to this core of the dominant clan group, the political unity of the tribe finds its expression within the borders of the demarcated tribal territory. The rights to a specific area are ritually sanctioned by the respected spirits of the founding ancestors of the tribe. If the total African community in the Gutu paramountcy is therefore referred to as the Rufura tribe, it should be kept in mind that the term 'Rufura' strictly applies to the minority group of a politically dominant lineage, but in normal usage comprises a multitude of interrelated Karanga-speaking 'tribes'. For the purpose of this study the term *rudzi* (tribe, lineage, kind) will therefore be used either with a territorial connotation, to indicate a politically integrated community within defined boundaries, e.g. the Rufura of Gutu; or to distinguish members of lineages belonging to geographically scattered clans (and by implication, tribes) of a different origin, e.g. the Rufura, Mbire, Duma and Rozvi.

In comparison with the African communities of the rural areas, those of the urban areas present a completely different picture. According to the 1962 Census, 4,640 Africans were living in Mucheke, the Municipal African township at Fort Victoria. The township manager estimates, however, that more than 2,000 Africans live within the township without being registered. If the 3,260 Africans living in the European residential and commercial areas are added to the approximate 7,000 of Mucheke township, the total African population at Fort Victoria must amount to more than 10,000.[23] The majority of people come from the surrounding administrative districts. Of the 157 interviewed adults (35 Traditionalists and 122 members of the Mission and Independent Churches) included in the casual urban sample, 22% were from Gutu, 21% from the Victoria reserve and the rest from Bikita, Ndanga, Buhera, Chipinga, Chibi, Umtali and other Shona areas (table 3). Only a small number of people came from beyond the Rhodesian borders, and they were nearly all Malawians.

The large representation in town of people from the Victoria and Gutu rural communities accounts for the presence of proportionately numerous Hera (15% of sample) and Duma (13% of sample), as indicated in table 4. Of the adult males the largest group are vaDuma but only a few of them are related to each other within the span of two to three generations. They nevertheless acknowledge a common descent. From the tribal point of view, the absence in the town community of a politically dominant kin-group, the lack of a defined territory in the immediate vicinity to which a related group of founding ancestors claim a common right, and a constantly changing society, characterize the urban community as a multi-tribal group of temporary residence which lacks cohesion. In contrast to the total Chingombe adult population of which 63% (table 2) were born in the chiefdom, only one person of the casual urban sample had been born in town (table 3), 28% of the townsmen had lived in the Mucheke township for more than 10 years while 52% of them had been there for less than 5 years (table 5). These figures are indicative of the fact that a stable core of townsmen, who regard the urban area as 'home', had hardly begun to take shape in Fort Victoria; this may not be representative of other urban communities such as Salisbury and Bulawayo, but it does reflect the high incidence of labour migrancy.

23. According to the 1962 Census, Salisbury counts more than 215,000 and Bulawayo more than 154,000 African inhabitants.

3. SOCIO-POLITICAL ORGANIZATION

a) *Tribal area*

In the tribal areas the local organization is based on a hierarchy of three interrelated units.[24] The smallest unit of administrative importance is not the elementary family unit but the village (*musha*) which falls under the direct jurisdiction of its headman (*sabuku*). Several villages of varying sizes constitute a ward (*dunhu*) under a ward headman (*sadunhu*: lit. 'owner of the ward'), whilst the widest grouping, incorporating a number of wards, is called a *nyika* (lit. 'country'), i.e. a chiefdom, with the chief (*ishe*) at the apex of the tribal political structure. Strictly speaking the Gutu tribal area constitutes a *nyika* in which Chingombe counts as one of the numerous wards, but, with intertribal political ties in a state of transition during the period of study, one could hardly call Chingombe with its 110 villages and 8,000-9,000 inhabitants a *dunhu*. Neither was it recognized by the Administration as an independent chiefdom. It still had only one tribal court of justice (*dare*), which was subject to chief Gutu's tribunal and had little more jurisdiction than the ordinary ward court. The boundary-line subdividing the Hera and vaGumbo territories into two distinct wards had also not yet been officially recognized. Nevertheless, for the purpose of this study, we will refer to Chingombe as a chiefdom with two wards (*matunhu*).

Each of the types of local unit has to be considered separately:

i) *The village*

The average Chingombe village consists of more than 10 homesteads, and seldom exceeds 25 households. Familial groupings at the different homesteads are composed of elementary families, i.e. a man, his wife and unmarried children, or of complex and extended families. Judging from table 6 the former pattern predominates in this patrilineal and patrilocal society. The mother, brother, sister or grandchildren of the head of a homestead occasionally reside with the latter, but his affinal relations seldom do.

Each village is composed of a nuclear group of male family heads agnatically related to the *sabuku*. The rest of the males are either his other cognatic kin, affines or *vatorwa* ('foreigners'). For the surveyed Chingombe villages

24. See Holleman (1952, pp. 3-22) for a general analysis of the Shona political structure.

the proportion of the male homestead heads, related to their kraalheads, is as follows:

Agnatic kin: 45% – the majority of these male homestead heads were sons or younger brothers (*vanunguna*, pl. for *mununguna*) of the kraalhead;
Other cognates: 20% – i.e. the kraalhead was either *sekuru* (maternal uncle) or *muzukuru* (sister's son) to the heads of homestead;
Affines: 14% – the kraalhead was in these cases *tezvara* (father- or brother-in-law) of the homestead head;
Vatorwa: 21% – no relationship between *sabuku* and homestead head (table 7).

This distribution indicates that the composition of the village community tends to support the *sabuku*'s authority. The *vatorwa* sometimes form separate village sections, but they remain under the control of the headman.

Segmentation of villages is a common feature in Shona society. It usually occurs after the death of a kraalhead, when some of the younger married sons prefer to start a new village of their own, instead of living under the control of their eldest brother who succeeds to the position of the deceased father. Should a married male with an exceptionally large household, or with sufficient followers, wish to establish a new village, he has to obtain the permission of the ward headman and the kraalhead. In earlier years the allocation of a site for a new village became official once the *sadunhu*, as Holleman describes, had 'driven a peg (*kudzikira bango*) into the ground on the spot where the hut of the principal wife (*vahosi*) of the new village headman is to be built.' Nowadays the possession of a separate tax-register (*buku*: book; from which the term *sabuku*: 'owner of the book' derives) marks the independence of the new village.[25] The new village is usually situated in close proximity of the parental village. Such is the case, for instance, with several of the Hera villages in Chingombe which in the past two to three generations have hived off from and still pay allegiance to the parental villages of Shumba and a few other closely related, senior descendants of Mheresi, the local clan ancestor. They are all situated in the northern part of Chingombe. This 'kraalsplitting' practice is of great importance to the study of Shona Independent Churches because it has a direct bearing on the fissiparous tendencies in Church life.

The main functions of a *sabuku* are to allocate land to the family heads and other adults under his jurisdiction, to settle domestic or other minor dis-

25. Holleman, 1952, p. 6.

putes and to see to it that the traditional ritual obligations, such as the keeping of *chisi*, the day of rest in honour of the senior tribal ancestors, or the provision of *rukweza* (finger millet) for the beer-brewing preparations of the annual rain rituals (*mikwerere*), are fulfilled. The *sabuku* is assisted in his task by village elders whom he calls together for village court (*dare*) meetings whenever disputes must be settled. Such proceedings have an informal character. The *sabuku* acts, as Holleman says, as an 'arbitrator, trying to settle a dispute (*kuenzanisa nyaya*) in an informal manner, rather than (as) a judge formally deciding a case (*kutonga mhosva*).'[26] Serious offences are referred to the ward headman.

Land allocation by the *sabuku* does not imply individualized land ownership. The land is communally 'owned' by the members of the village, whose rights to cultivate an allocated patch of land derive from membership of the village unit. The system of land allocation will be briefly dealt with below. Yet in this context the implementation of the 'village-line' system, as part of the Government's agrarian reform measures, should be mentioned because it directly influenced the whole structure of rural communities. Whereas villages originally consisted of clusters of homesteads, a few of which, according to traditional standards, had reached outsize proportions before the Rebellions, the villages now had to be built along a surveyed 'line' which divided arable and grazing territory. As a result village buildings were strung out along plotted 'lines' with clusters of dwellings and granaries situated from a few hundred yards up to more than a mile apart. In hilly country different 'village lines' sometimes cross each other with the result that adjacent homesteads do not necessarily belong to the same village. The visual impression of a rural community is that of a conglomeration of small farmholdings, with mud-and-pole or brick huts stretched along the foot of kopjes or mountains. Grazing areas are mostly in the hills and the arable fields in the plains (*mapani*; sing. *bani*). Sometimes the establishment of popular Independent Church communities has led to larger clusters of homesteads than usual, with temporary or permanent transformations of geographic village patterns as a result.[27]

The collective 'ownership' of arable lands does not exclude the individual rights of any cultivator to the crops produced on his or her patch of land, but usually does involve collective agricultural activities such as sowing, ploughing, weeding and reaping. Members of the family work on the lands allocated to their family head, but whenever extensive labour is required a

26. *Ibid.*, p. 8.

27. This feature will be dealt with in one of the following Volumes.

nhimbe party is organized. Much beer (*doro*) is brewed for the occasion, because beer is a tangible form of 'compensation' (not as payment in the strict sense of the word, but in recognition of the principle of reciprocity) given to the village members who offer their services on the appointed day. Beer brewing for a *nhimbe* party is heralded well in advance. As such it is an integral part of Shona social life but with distinctly economic implications. *Doro* itself became the symbol of the economic and social interdependence of cultivators who rely greatly on subsistence farming. To those families whose members did not form a labour force large enough to cultivate their own fields, repeated beer brewing during one season was a sure way of obtaining the necessary assistance. Holleman states in this connection that 'participation in the *nhimbe* system both as host and as working guest is a matter of social urgency, because anyone, who for some reason or other keeps himself and his family apart from these activities cuts himself off from the communal life.'[28]

The *nhimbe* system provides villagers with a loosely organized but controllable labour force, since it actually prompts relatives and neighbours from other villages to participate in the farming and social activities which rotate in a specified area from one field to another. Even for those who have sufficient means to become economically independent, the *nhimbe* parties remain of great social importance. It is an occasion when people, otherwise scattered, meet in large numbers. When the heat becomes unbearable towards midday, several hours will be spent in joint discussions and drinking in the shade of trees. It is therefore understandable that membership of a Christian Church that strictly prohibits any form of beer drinking would, if taken seriously by a villager, have far-reaching social and economic implications for him.[29]

ii) *The ward* (*dunhu*)

The number of villages in a ward and its territorial size vary considerably. Some wards in sparsely populated areas like the Southern Sabi reserve may comprise only 8 to 20 'villages' with a total population of less than 200 inhabitants,[30] but others may have well up to 100 villages with a few thousand inhabitants. Unlike the traditional village boundaries, which were flexible and often changed due to shifting cultivation, the ward boundaries, following

28. Holleman, 1952, p. 11.

29. Stringent application of restraining Church laws was bound to create an atmosphere of resentment, especially in the conservative rural communities, which in turn provided fertile soil for dissent among Church members. See below, pp. 259-262.

30. Holleman, 1952, p. 11.

rivers, hill-tops and streams, are fixed and well known. The recognition of set boundaries distinguishes the ward as a distinct unit within the greater tribal context. The unity of a *dunhu* is based on territorial and genealogical factors, but the former are undoubtedly of greater importance, since the *dunhu* is in the first place a land unit.

'Home' for the African is not the village but the ward. Ward membership, whether one is related to the ward headman or not, is the qualifying factor for the right to cultivate land within its boundaries. *It is the ward which forms the basis of social security for its members.* Small enough for people to know each other well, the ward forms the background to the strongest inter-personal ties between the rural folk.[31]

The *sadunhu*, who is ward head by hereditary right, often represents one of the senior houses of the chief's lineage, but he may also be a *mutorwa* (pl. *va-*) who has been granted land and therefore pays allegiance to the chief. Should the *sadunhu* belong to the chief's lineage he is called a *jinda*.[32] Chingombe, for example, is regarded as *ishe* (chief) by his subordinates, but as a descendant of Mabwazhe, he is also considered to be *jinda*. That there is a substantial number of Chingombe's agnates in his ward is due to the fact that, like the kinship pattern of villages, the *dunhu* community usually includes a nuclear body of the ward head's kinsmen. Apart from the Rufura village headmen in Chingombe, who are mainly descendants of Chingombe's numerous sons, such as Mudyanadzo, Chivasa and Makonese, or of the Hera headmen, all of whom trace their descent back to Mheresi through the houses of Mushosho, Shumba, Mafudza and others, there are also a few villages whose headmen are foreigners. These men were granted permission by the *sadunhu* to settle in the territory. Although political control in the Chingombe area therefore

31. 'A village was not a home – it stayed for only a short while on the same spot. The tribal territory was not a home – it was too wide and vague for a man to grasp. But the *dunhu* (or ward) was home. It was big enough for a man's children and his children's children to settle in; it was small enough to know everyone who lived in it. Within the *dunhu* boundaries a man could make use of the land for the purposes of his family unit . . . within a *dunhu* the people felt they belonged so closely together that they would help each other to cultivate their fields or build their villages as a matter of course. They thought of themselves as one big, old family . . . The *dunhu*, the land and its people, and the invisible spiritual bonds with the ancestors who lived and died there for generations, all these together made the intimacy of home. And even a man who leaves this place to settle elsewhere will leave it in such a manner that the door . . . is never closed to him. For he knows that there will come a day when he wants to come back to it, if only to die there and be buried in the soil that contains his ancestors.'
See Mangwende Report, p. 18.

32. Kuper, 1955, p. 28.

lies primarily with the Rufura and Hera notables in their southern and northern Chingombe wards respectively, it should be remembered that the Rufura people actually 'invaded' the territory, that the Hera *dunhu* for many years never had a ward council of its own – being represented only by *Sabuku* Shumba, one of the principal councillors in Chief Chingombe's court – and that the boundary between the two *matunhu* (see map 4) does not wholly separate the Rufura from the Hera villages, as there are kraalheads of both tribal groups on both sides of the *dunhu* boundary. In spite of the Rufura dominance in the political field, the chief nevertheless acknowledges the Hera *sadunhu's* own jurisdiction. For instance, a Rufura kraalhead has to obtain the Hera *sadunhu's* permission if he wants to settle in or shift his village in the latter's ward. Rufura headmen in the Hera ward also rely on Hera ritual officers if they want to conduct rain ceremonies on behalf of their village members. Thus the Rufura people acknowledge that land rights in the Hera ward are partly vested in the Hera ancestors who were there first.

In addition to his responsibilities concerning land allocation, protection of the community against land misuse and the settlement of land disputes between villages, the *sadunhu* also has jurisdiction in other fields of conflict. He presides over the *dunhu* court which functions along somewhat more formal lines than the village 'court'. It is a court of appeal midway between the village and chief's *dare*. Limited court fees are levied. Although serious offences should all be referred to the chief's court, it does sometimes happen that a *sadunhu* in practice handles important cases related to witchcraft or stock-theft. Judgement, on the other hand, is reserved on most cases, even petty ones falling directly under the jurisdiction of the *sadunhu*, if it becomes apparent that a satisfactory decision for both parties is not to be achieved at the *dunhu* court. This midway position of the *dunhu* court at times impairs its effectiveness because people realize that there is always a higher tribal court of appeal.

Traditionally the *sadunhu's* authority regarding land matters was naturally extended into the ritual field. He had to take the initiative in rain and thanksgiving ceremonies (called *mukwerere* by the vaDuma and *mutoro* by the vaRozvi). As ritual officiant he was responsible for addressing his lineage ancestors on behalf of the ward community during the big annual ceremonies especially arranged for such occasions. All the ward adults were supposed to attend and dance and feast in honour of the ancestral spirits. With the gradual curb on the *sadunhu's* land-distributing powers through the various forms of land legislation, the ritual function of the *sadunhu* lost some of its relevance. Consequently *mukwerere* rituals are now mostly conducted on the decentralized village level, although in some of the Gutu wards, e.g. Nyamande, ward rituals still take place.

iii) *The chiefdom* (*nyika*)
The *nyika* is the widest territorial and political tribal unit. As in Gutu, the chief himself is usually the senior member of the dominant patrilineage within the chiefdom. His own lineage members form the skeleton of the tribal political hierarchy. They are often widely dispersed throughout the entire chiefdom, living in wards controlled by minor houses of their own lineage, or even in those wards in which political leadership is vested in a *mutorwa* lineage. As we have already indicated, the chiefdom is composed of several wards with the inhabitants of a great variety of tribes and clans grouped together under the different ward headmen. Upheavals in the past have greatly contributed to tribal and clan fragmentation. Even today the process of foreigners settling in territory other than that of their own *rudzi* continues, though more restrictedly, as the cognatic and affinal relatives of those already living in the tribal area settle near their kin. The population of the chiefdom can therefore be broadly classified in two main categories: *vachinda*, the people belonging to the chief's patrilineage, which provides the basis for tribal unity, and *vatorwa* (foreigners). This distinction does not necessarily imply social discrimination. 'No *muchinda*, unless he occupies a position of authority in the tribal organization, ranks higher than a "mutorwa".'[33]

Tribal unity is in some respects an extension of ward unity on a broader level, in the sense that, just as kraalheads recognize the political superiority of the *sadunhu's* lineage, the ward heads formally acknowledge their subordination to the chief's house (Chaurura in Gutu). This political unity can only be of significance within the demarcated tribal territory, since the unity of tribe and land, as Holleman tells us, 'is a natural conception. It is based economically on the fact that the tribe depends exclusively on its own territory for its subsistence; it is legally supported by the occupation of successive generations of tribesmen; and religiously and magically this conception is strengthened by the belief that the tribal ancestors who founded the tribe established the communal right on the land for the benefit of the future generations of their own kin (and of those incorporated in the tribal unity), and that their spirits are still closely interested in, and connected with, the land.'[34]

Shona chiefdoms are generally small and a Shona chief's power is relatively limited in comparison to the military-structured Ndebele kingdom of the past. Shona chiefs as a rule did not have large regiments through which they could exert military control, although the Rozvi kings seem to have expanded

33. Holleman, 1952, p. 15.
34. *Ibid.*, p. 17.

the boundaries of their empire through peaceful as well as military means. But even then Rozvi military power was never as centralized as that of the Zulu or Ndebele kings.

Succession to chieftainship under Shona law follows the collateral principle.[35] The chieftaincy descends in principle from older to junior brothers in the dominant patrilineage until the generation of brothers is exhausted. Then the chieftaincy passes from the last brother to the oldest agnatic male descendant in the next generation and from there to the grandsons according to their order of birth. The rightful heir may be bypassed in cases of physical disability, absence from the tribal territory or previous insubordination. It seldom happens that a candidate's claim to seniority is unanimously accepted by the tribal notables. There are usually quite a number of potential candidates. Rival claims can remain unsettled for years before a final agreement is reached. In Gutu it happened that an *interregnum* lasted nearly 4 years – during which period (1963-7) Munyonga, a close relative of the deceased chief, was in office as acting chief – before a new Chief Gutu was officially installed. During the prolonged struggle between the senior representatives of the Chaurura sub-houses, the advice of both the oracular deity at Matonjeni, whose political influence has not completely disappeared after the fall of the Rozvi empire,[36] and of the local *svikiro* (spirit medium) of Makuwaza, son of Chaurura, was sought.

The functions of the chief resemble those of the *sadunhu*, differing mainly in his greater authority. Originally the chief's court was the final judicial body that handled all cases on appeal from the *dunhu* courts. Its special concern were those offences that posed a threat to the tribal community as a whole, such as homicide and witchcraft. Since the advent of the European Government, the chief's judicial powers have been severely curtailed. Under the provisions of the Native Law and Courts Act, he retained civil, but not criminal, jurisdiction. At the local level magisterial powers were vested in the position of the District Commissioner. In practice it did happen that the chief was left some scope to treat cases between Africans, involving minor criminal aspects. But it is only in recent years and under pressure of political circumstances that the Government, in the effort to consolidate and strengthen both its own position and that of the tribal authorities, made a move to restore some of the chief's former powers.[37]

35. For a more detailed exposition, see Holleman, 1952, pp.

36. For an analysis of the role played by the Matonjeni cultists in the succession to the Gutu chieftainship, see Daneel, 1970, pp. 71f.

37. For a penetrative analysis of the position of the Shona chief in a fermenting polit-

Court organization and procedure is of singular importance for a study of the Independent Churches, since the procedure followed at *matare* (pl. for *dare*) of these religious institutions is often very similar to that of the traditional court. We must therefore briefly look at some of the main features of the chief's court. The chief is assisted by two categories of tribal officials.[38] These are the hereditary ward headmen who are occasionally summoned to the chief's village to act as councillors, in which capacity they are called *makota*; and a number of close relatives of the chief, who live at or near to the chief's village. This second group of people act as the chief's close advisers in all circumstances. During court sessions they act as intermediaries, messengers, spokesmen and assessors. Some of them are always present in case they are needed by the chief. They are usually chosen by the chief from the ranks of his subordinate relatives. Consequently the most common pattern is that the chief's younger brother, senior son or sister's husband take these positions. But there is also the chief's *muzukuru* (usually sister's son) who stands in a cordial relationship of relative equality to his *sekuru* (maternal uncle). He is the person whose relationship to the chief, in spite of his being a 'junior', is least dominated by the principle of subordination, which places him in a unique position to advise the chief and, if necessary, censure him. It stands to reason that the *muzukuru* who is appointed as a councillor at the chief's *dare* is in a position to effect a considerable influence on tribal affairs. In their official capacity this body of relatives are called *makurukota* (councillors). Because of their close ties with the chief they often play a more important role in tribal affairs than the ward headmen.

While the procedure of a chief's court is generally more formal, it also resembles that of a ward court. Once the necessary respect has been shown through hand clapping, during the first phase of a *dare*-session, each party concerned, whether claimant or defendant, is given ample time to give his or her version of the dispute concerned. The time spent at the chief's court sharply contrasts with the brisk approach usually adopted at the District Commissioner's office. Lengthy discussions, during which the case is viewed and reviewed from all possible angles, often carry on for hours or days. During these sessions the chief usually does little more than listen attentively to what is being said. By the time his judgment is required the majority

---

ical situation, see Holleman, 1969, p. 339 ff. Under the heading 'The Rediscovery of the Chiefs', Holleman discusses statutory changes implemented after 1960 and directly affecting the chief's powers.

38. Holleman, 1952, p. 20.

opinion has often emerged clearly and to this he gives expression. Shona philosophy, which favours a compromise solution rather than a radical 'either-or' decision, is often reflected in the chief's judgment. Both parties must receive full attention, and the chief may conclude his verdict with a fatherly admonition directed at the guilty party or at both parties.

The ritual functions of the chief are restricted to the propitiation of his clan ancestors. In this connection he may sacrifice a bull to the spirit of his deceased *tateguru* (grandfather and more remote lineage ascendants). Because of the dominant position of his own lineage within the tribal territory this ritual function would automatically place the chief at the apex of the tribe's ritual hierarchy. He nevertheless has a limited authority in this field and never acts as ritual officiant on behalf of the whole tribe. Big annual ceremonies at tribal level, such as the Ndebele 'first-fruit feasts', are unknown to the Shona. *Mukwerere* or thanksgiving rituals were never conducted at this level, the *dunhu* ritual having had the widest corporate context for mass rituals. The roles played by the *svikiro* (medium) of the tribal spirit and the *munyai* (messenger to the Mwari shrine at Matonjeni) tended to overshadow the chief's ritual powers. He retained, however, formal responsibility for rain in his territory, which involved at least close collaboration with the *munyai* and *svikiro*. The former must annually collect gifts throughout the *nyika* and the latter must testify to the ancestral approval of the gifts, before they are taken to the oracular caves at Matonjeni with a plea for rain. These ritual activities cannot take place without the chief's official consent. He must actually be present when the gifts are 'shown' to the ancestral spirits.

Nowadays, at the apex of the tribal political hierarchy in the Tribal Trust Lands, we find, in addition to the chief, an African local Council and the District Commissioner. The latter are both foreign elements in the traditional political pattern.[39] As highest local authority the DC is surrounded and supported by Government officials such as the District Officer, Land Extension, Agricultural and Community Development officers, all of whom form part of the European staff stationed at local District headquarters.

39. In his outstanding study, *Chief, Council, Commissioner* (1969), Holleman describes the unenviable position of the Rhodesian chief who, through the system in which he operates (be it in relation to his fellow tribesmen, at Council level or in direct personal contact with the District Commissioner) is nearly always subject to a division of loyalties between the tribesmen whose interests he represents and the Administration which keeps him in office. The introduction of African Councils in some areas met with opposition from chiefs who considered their own authority jeopardized. Holleman indicates that the friction between chief and commissioner, which in the Mangwende reserve had far-reaching repercussions, originated within the context of the local council (p. 123).

b) *Urban environment*

Ever since the turn of the century increasing numbers of Africans started to converge on towns, mines and European farms in search of employment. At first the conservative tribesmen were reluctant to stay for long periods and they usually returned to their homes in the reserves after short spells in the urban and other areas. This form of migrant labour initially met with much criticism from the employers, who found it difficult to maintain any form of continuity in their labour force, but the system was soon regarded as an inevitable and permanent institution in Rhodesia and other states of Central Africa. By the time Africans were seeking a permanent residence in urban areas, the migrant labour system had become part and parcel of the territorial pattern of social segregation and the structure of Rhodesian economic life. Towns were regarded as white areas, with the general consensus amongst Europeans that the African's home was in the reserves. The Land Apportionment Act of 1930 prevented Africans from obtaining permanent rights in European areas. Consequently the African was permitted to visit town 'only under stringent control, and his temporary residence was made conditional of his being in full-time employment.'[40]

In spite of the desire to keep the towns white, the interdependence of Europeans and Africans in agriculture, trade and industry inevitably led to an increasing African urbanization. Housing became a major problem. Employers were made responsible for the accommodation of their employees under the African (Urban Areas) Accommodation and Registration Act (Chapter 110). Employees could be housed upon the employer's property at the employer's expense. In Fort Victoria, approximately one third of the African population is housed within the European residential and commercial area. The rest of them live in the Mucheke township, where the (European) Municipal Council is responsible for the housing facilities.

Amendments to the Land Apportionment Act in 1960 provided for the creation of African Township Areas near towns and cities and permitted Africans to own land in municipal townships. Such townships, like Mucheke, are usually situated well away from the European residential areas, but the fact that Africans are now permitted to own land and build houses according to their own designs in these locations indicates the realization – albeit reluctantly – that a permanent African urban community is inevitably coming into being. The system of home-ownership is comparatively well advanced in the Mucheke township. The Victoria Council was second only to Bulawayo

40. Gray, 1960, p. 107.

to start implementing the scheme. Sizeable sites were directly bought by some distinguished African businessmen. Furthermore, houses were built by the Council and sold to Africans on a non-profit basis. This home-ownership scheme enables Africans to purchase their houses with a monthly payment over a period of 20 years, after which it becomes freehold property.

The presence in the fluctuating Mucheke township community of about 2,000 unregistered people reflects the shortage of accommodation. It also reflects the lenient attitude of the local authorities towards Africans who have their lawful wives staying with them in single quarters while they are awaiting married accommodation. An oft-repeated method of obtaining married quarters is for a husband to stay with his wife in single quarters, which places him in a favourable position to be considered for a three or four-roomed house. Shortly after procuring this accommodation the legal wife is sent back to the reserve to tend to the lands in the home village since land-rights may terminate through continual absence of the landholder. The husband then takes in friends and often enters into a temporary alliance with a 'town wife', who earns her living by offering her domestic and other services to the 'temporary husband'. These women are called *vakadzi vamapoto* (women of the cooking pots) to indicate the way in which they earn a livelihood. They mostly lead a shifting kind of existence because few lawful marriages result from temporary alliances of this nature. Difficulties in obtaining accommodation, together with the absence of tribal authorities with sufficient powers to uphold traditional law and customs, and the resultant breakdown of the rural norms of society in the urban areas, have greatly contributed to the acceptance by the townsmen of this expedient form of 'matrimony'.

Indicative of an essentially different set of values operative in urban, in contrast to rural areas, is the election of young businessmen and teachers on the township's Advisory Board.[41] The seniority and hereditary principle, important for tribal leadership in the reserves, had to make place for qualities of efficiency and competence in the business or educational fields. This does not mean that the tribal authorities have completely lost their influence over townsmen. Civil matters are often taken by the latter to the tribal tribunal in the home-reserves. To meet with the need of a judicial authority in town that could handle civil cases at a less advanced level, and in order to alleviate

41. African Advisory Boards became a necessity in every urban residential area when the Natives (Urban Areas) Accommodation and Registration Act was passed in 1964. These Boards have the responsibility of reporting on by-laws or any matter affecting the interest of Africans in the local Authority area. In Fort Victoria the Local Advisory Board, consisting of seven regularly elected African members, forms an Advisory Committee of the Municipal Council.

the task of the local DC, a Chief's Court was introduced in the Mucheke township. Provision was made for a monthly visit of at least two chiefs from the tribal areas within the Victoria Province. These chiefs are accompanied by their own councillors when they come into town on such occasions. During a few days' stay at the chief's quarters and chief's Hall, civil cases that are brought forward voluntarily by the townsmen are dealt with. Townsmen still generally prefer to go directly to the DC as they have done in the past, but it is envisaged that in time the chiefs will appoint local councillors in the location, instead of relying on rural councillors. This will serve to make the Chief's Court more effective in civil matters arising in the urban environment.

Social life in town differs greatly from that of the reserve village. Numerous organizations, such as the YMCA, YWCA, Women's Institute, Handicraft Club and Helping Hand Association, provide townsmen with a wide choice of activities after working hours. A library and regular night classes enable them to participate in part-time studies and to improve their educational standard, which in turn enhances their chances of getting a better job.

Favourite leisure-time activities are the attendance of dances and cinema shows, but the most popular social centre is the beerhall in the centre of the township. When off-duty, Africans have a chance of meeting friends and relatives or members of the same tribe at the beerhall. The young men are thus presented with an opportunity of demonstrating their respect for the tribal elders in town by buying them some beer. The beerhall is a place where the toils of the day can be forgotten, where serious discussions and instructions in traditional custom take place; it is also the place where young men have the opportunity of meeting girls or 'women of the pots'. Due to the less constructive social aspects associated with the beerhall, it becomes the target of regular attacks during sermons in the Spirit-type of Independent Churches. The local municipal authorities take a different view. They regard the drinking of beer as a customary and therefore unavoidable practice. The provision of liquor in large quantities is justified with reference to the fact that 'the profit goes entirely to African Welfare where it is put to good use'.

Whatever the moral implications of beerhall connections for townsmen, for many of them this social centre has become one of the brightest aspects of town life.

4. KINSHIP ORGANIZATION

The importance of the Shona lineage within the tribal political structure has already been referred to. Chief, ward headman and kraalhead, each attains his politically important position through his seniority in the dominant lineage of the tribe, ward or village concerned. Social relations are furthermore defined in terms of kinship within the ranks of a single lineage, or in terms of lineages, related to one another as corporate entities. The kinship system as a basis for an organized society meets, in the words of Holleman, two essential requirements:

'a) It provides a definite pattern of social order in which any two persons or classes of persons of the same sex, closely or remotely related by blood or by marriage, are placed in a position of relative superiority or subordination;

b) it regulates the reproduction of unilineal and exogamous kingroups with due respects to Native concepts of incest, and the existing social order referred to above.'[42]

We are here mainly concerned with those basic aspects of kinship terminology and organization that are of direct relevance for an understanding of the congregational structure of the Independent Churches and the distribution of power in the leadership hierarchy. Knoob has postulated that the ideal conception of the extended family is projected onto the Independent Church congregation, as it was extended to clan and tribe in the past.[43] For an analysis of this idea in the coming chapters, we therefore need to reflect briefly on the socially defined position of people within their own lineage ranks, and in relation to members of other lineages.

In Shona society there are several distinct but overlapping groupings. The widest grouping is that of the patri-clan (*rudzi*), whose members are scattered over a vast territory, surpassing chieftain boundaries. The clan as such does not function as a corporate unit, although dominant lineages (also *rudzi*) of a particular clan within a specified territory, as has been indicated for the Rufura, form the nucleus of tribal unity within that area. The importance of this *rudzi* is that it has a common *mutupo* (clan name) and one or more *zvidao* (pl. of *chidao*: sub-clan name) which enables all members to claim a common descent, through the acknowledged patrilineage, even if all the ancestral iinks cannot always be traced. Agnatic kinship is therefore presupposed between all people with the same *mutupo* and *chidao*, with the exogamous marriage laws automatically pertaining to the group as a whole, whatever their territorial distribution.

42. Holleman, 1952, p. 30. For a description of Shona kinship I have drawn on Holleman's material. His account of kinship terms and obligations generally applies to the central, southern and eastern Shona.

43. Knoob, 1961, p. 122.

A group that does function as a corporate unit is the *chizvarwa*, a lineage segment which usually comprises the first, second and third generation agnatic descendants of one man, i.e. his sons, daughters and son's children or grandchildren. A certain amount of local unity is maintained by the male members of this group, but the females are scattered through marriage. On special occasions, such as the propitiation of a recently deceased elder of the *chizvarwa*, succession to the name of the common grandfather or the inheritance of property, *all* the members of this group are called together. Rituals undertaken on behalf of group members call for a manifestation of group unity. Distant members are usually informed well in advance of such ceremonies to ensure a full ritual representation, which is a precondition for the favourable disposition of the ancestor concerned.

The *imba* ('house') is an agnatic unit founded upon a common male or female ancestor. As a sub-division of his patrilineage (*rudzi*), a man's house may be identified with a distinct political unity.[44] The house of Mabwazhe, for example, today comprises most of the politically significant Rufura houses in the Gutu district. But in a more limited family context, and often when inheritance of 'house' property is at stake, the concepts of *imba* is narrowed down to the agnatic offspring of a particular wife.[45]

The political significance of component houses within the lineage may change in the course of generations. In Gutu the junior house of Chaurura, Mabwazhe's grandson, managed to establish a political supremacy, so that the chieftaincy became associated solely with his house. The houses of Chitsa and Chingombe, the senior and junior brothers of Chaurura, though excluded from succession to the paramountcy, do, however, form the nuclei for ward unity in their respective areas within the wider political framework of Gutu's chiefdom. In Chingombe the majority of Rufura kraalheads belong to the houses of the 2nd and 3rd generation descendants of Rutsate's numerous sons.

Apart from the *imba*, another distinction is made at the village level to denote a group of kindred. This group is called *mhuri* ('family' or 'kindred') and includes almost any combination of relatives, such as a man, his wife, or wives, and children, together with maternal, uterine and affinal kin who live in the same or neighbouring villages. This is essentially a non-political unit, fused on grounds of near kinship and residence; a group that shares the experiences of birth, marriage, illness, etc. of each of its members.

Holleman has provided a thorough analysis of the Shona kinship system.[46]

44. Holleman, 1952, p. 26.
45. *Ibid.*, pp. 28-29.
46. *Ibid.*, pp. 23-71.

The following brief description of some behaviouristic patterns within the inter-lineage framework, which are relevant to our study, is based to a large extent on his findings.

Within the patrilineage each member's status is determined by two factors, sex and seniority, the latter being expressed by terms either denoting, in the same generation, relative age; or inter-generation differences. The reciprocal term between brother and sister (also in classificatory sense) is *hanzvadzi*. *Mukoma* means either a man's elder brother or a woman's elder sister; *mununguna* his younger brother or her younger sister. Male members of the first and second ascending generations are 'fathers' (*madzibaba*), addressed like one's own father, and referred to as *babamukuru* or *babamunini* if they are respectively older or younger than one's father. 'Grandfathers' are all *tateguru* (sometimes: *sekuru*). The first descending generation is called *mwana* (pl. *vana*), but a descriptive distinction is made between *mwanakomana* (boy child) and *mwanasikana* (girl child). The second descending generation are all 'grandchild', *muzukuru* (pl. *va-*) regardless of sex. There is, therefore, no equality in rank, only relative seniority or juniority, with concommitant positions of relative superordination or subordination among brothers as among sisters, and (more prominently) between agnates of different generations within the lineage hierarchy.

Emotionally the relation between grandchild and grandfather or grandmother (*mbuya*) is one of the closest and most intimate in the Shona family, while that of father to child is strictly authoritarian. Children are spiritually and economically dependent on the family head. 'During the life-time of his father a son never attains full independence, unless he breaks away from his family . . . a married son gradually attains greater freedom of action as he grows older and carries his weight as the head of his own domestic unit, but in all matters of importance he remains the child of his father and is treated accordingly.'[47] Consequently a greater 'social distance' usually exists between father and son than between grandfather and grandson. If a father dies while at loggerheads with his son, his vengeful spirit becomes a menace to the well-being of his son's family, which requires special propitiatory rites before appeasement is achieved.

The *vatete* (father's sister) holds an authoritative position in relation to her brother's children, because of the assumption that her marriage cattle enabled her brother to marry – whether she is the actual *chipanda* (his linked sister, whose marriage cattle are used for his *roora* arrangements) or not. This position manifests itself perhaps even more clearly in her relation to

47. *Ibid.*, p. 61.

her brother's wife. As *samukadzi* or *vamwene* she is the recognized 'owner' of her brother's wife. She is the arbitrator in family feuds, and one of the leading ritual officiants in the religious ceremonies following her brother's death. In this latter capacity she has the right to *ngombe yovutete* (ox or cow of the aunt) which the senior son of her deceased brother owes her, as well as the power to supervise the distribution of property and estate of the deceased. Her mystical power is believed to be considerable, and akin to that of a mother-in-law. Should the *ngombe yovutete* be still outstanding when the *vatete* dies, her dissatisfied spirit is believed to have the power to 'grip the wombs' of her brother's daughters or brother's son's daughters, causing barrenness until the necessary obligations are fulfilled by her '*vana*' ('children', i.e. nephews).

The relation of *vana* (children) and *mai* (mother) is intimate. She is not, except when they are very young, in a commanding position because she does not belong to the lineage of her husband. Children experience their organic unity with their mother much more vividly than with their father. Consequently the ties between 'children of the same womb' (*dumbu rimwe*) are usually closer than that between children of the same father but different mothers. The importance of the matrilineal descent in this predominantly patrilineal society is illustrated by the mother's right to receive a cow (*ngombe youmai*) and a goat (*mbudzi yeimbwazukuru*: goat of the grandchildren) in addition to and separate from the bride-price (*roora*) from her daughter's husband. Of these animals the former is used for the propitiation of the mother (*mai*) and the latter for the propitiation of the mother's mother (*mbuya*) These female spirits of the matriline are directly associated with the procreative powers of their female descendants. If they are not remembered and honoured in the proper way, or if the daughter's husband unduly delays the payment of *ngombe youmai* and *mbudzi yeimbwazukuru* these female spirits avenge themselves by 'stealing the granddaughter's menstrual blood', thus causing temporary or permanent barrenness.

The *mukoma's* position of relative superiority in relation to his or her *mununguna* (younger brother or sister) is more evident among males than among females, because the latter do not have hereditary representative positions within their lineage. After the death of his father, the eldest son receives the deceased's name, becomes ritual officiant of the family, and is placed in charge of family matters such as the provision of his younger brother with *roora* cattle. When the younger brother wants to marry or when he turns to the new head of the family for propitiatory directives in times of affliction, his dependence on his older brother becomes manifest. In everyday life, however, the senior son does not carry as much authority as his father did. Those *vanunguna* (younger brothers) who have hived off with their families and started a new village are practically independent of their *mukoma* apart from the occasional ceremonial gathering when they are expected to obey their 'father'. As was indicated above, the structural relationship between a brother and his sister (*hanzvadzi*) is determined by her cattle-providing potential. Should she become the recognized *svikiro* (spirit medium) of one of the deceased lineage males, however, her status and power, as interpreter of the ancestral demands, reaches far beyond that of the ordinary woman within her family.

Marriage places all the members of a husband's and wife's lineage in a relation of wife-receivers and wife-providers. Being exogamous, a lineage-group must seek its wives in another group. Once a marriage is officially recognized, all the affinal male relatives of the wife-receiving lineage become *vakuwasha* (sons-in-law) to the males of the wife-providing lineage, who become their *vatezvara* (father-in-law). The *mukuwasha's* lineage is placed in a position of relative subordination to that of the *tezvara*, because all the *tezvara* males, regardless of their generation level, are placed as a unit on the level of the first ascending generation, i.e. they are all 'fathers'. In practice, however, there is no question of complete subordination. The *mukuwasha*, as 'child' of the *tezvara*, must respect him, he must help him in his fields, with the building of a house, with food in times of scarcity and with the slaughtering of any animals killed for ritual purposes. On the other hand the *tezvara* owes certain obligations to his *mukuwasha*. He must be well fed during visits and should be allowed a reasonable amount of freedom with his potential 'wives', the younger sisters or daughters of his *tezvara*. A *tezvara* usually regards his *vakuwasha* as well suited for the positions of spokesmen, councillors or messengers since they are *vatorwa* (members of a foreign lineage) and can therefore never aspire to *sadunhu*- or chieftainship within the *tezvara's* tribal territory. Their obedience and loyalty, necessitated by the link between the two lineages, can furthermore be taken for granted by the *tezvara*.[48]

The women of the wife-providing lineage, in turn, are all placed by imputation in the same generation as their relative, married off to the wife-receiving lineage. As such they are called *varamu* by the receiving husband and his male relatives. The term itself connotes potential connubium. To the wife all the males of her husband's lineage who are of the same generation are her *varume* (husbands) and the males of his senior generations are her *vatezvara*. Whereas her own male relatives are in a commanding position in re-

48. *Ibid.*, p. 69.

lation to her husband, the wife's position is reversed in the house of her husband. She falls directly under the authority of her husband's sister, who is her *vamwene* (owner) and who calls her *muroora* (sister-in-law).

A different pattern of mutual obligations and privileges concerns the relation of children and their maternal kin. In contrast to the social superiority of the *tezvara* over his *mukuwasha*, the relation to his *muzukuru* (sister's son) is one of greater cordiality and freedom of action. The child addresses all the females of the same generation as his mother as *mai* (mother) and the females of his paternal grandmother's generation as his *mbuya* (pl. *vadzimbuya*. The men of both his mother's and paternal grandmother's generations and lineages are called *sekuru* ('grandfather'). Of all the kinship ties, that between *sekuru* (maternal uncle) and *muzukuru* (sister's son) is possibly the most intimate and equal. It is referred to by the Shona as a 'playing relationship' (*ukama okutamba*),[49] which is usually marked by the absence of the strife and competition that characterize agnatic ties. This relationship is based on the direct link of the son with his mother's lineage. He is of the same blood as his maternal kin, which makes him *mwana mukati* – a 'child inside' his mother's lineage. To his *sekuru* he owes obedience and respect, but simultaneously he shares some of the authority his mother can exercise in respect of his uncle's family affairs and estate on account of her position as provider of marriage cattle to her brother. In this free relationship of give and take, of mutual respect and obedience, the *muzukuru* can make use of his *sekuru's* property and be free and easy with his *sekuru's* wife as long as he remains within the limits of proper conduct.

Death of a married partner need not terminate the marriage relationship completely, because the tie concerns many more people than the partners concerned. If a woman dies without having borne any children, either a divorce is effected, or one of the *varamu* takes her place. The wife-providing lineage is exempted from any further obligations if the deceased woman has already produced a satisfactory number of children. If the husband dies, his wife is inherited by a younger brother or another male relative within the same lineage, depending on the woman's consent. Should she be past child-bearing age, she will still be taken care of by the inheritor, or she may return to her home village. Should the husband die before his wife had produced a male name-bearing child, the younger brother may act as genitor to raise a name-bearer for his elder brother. Normally, however, the successor is paterfamilias of the children he begets himself. In the light of these patterns all Shona marriages are potentially polygamous. Kinship obligations, together with the inher-

49. *Ibid.*, p. 67.

ently African vision of the child as the consummation of marriage, often provide the motivation for taking a second wife if the first one is barren, or for the inheritance of a deceased brother's wife, quite apart from another traditionally important factor, namely the association of wives and children with wealth and prestige.

The Shona kinship structure has indeed been influenced by the Western culture, Christianity and the process of urbanization. Especially in the towns, the unity of the larger kingroups is breaking down and the emphasis is increasingly on the elementary family of parents and children. This does not mean that town-life completely eliminates the obligations to more distant relatives. It is often the assistance of a distant relative that provides a person with the kind of social backing and stability that is needed for a successful adaptation to the urban environment. The system of labour migration normally causes persons to be only temporarily isolated from their relatives in the rural areas where traditional kinship ties are as yet far from breaking down. It is, in fact, kinship obligations that often drive the rural farmer to the urban area where sufficient money can be earned to meet the basic needs of his relatives at home.

5. ECONOMIC FACTORS

a) *Land*

In South Africa the resentment of Africans against the distribution of land has a direct bearing on the rise of the Independent Church Movement. Sundkler tells us that 'the increase of the numbers of Bantu Independent Churches could be shown on a diagram as a parallel to the tightening squeeze of the Natives through land legislation. Some of the African land-buying syndicates before 1913 were composed of Ethiopian leaders, and even today one of the highest ambitions of a successful church leader is to find land for the founding of a church colony of his own.'[50] The Africans felt that the Native Lands Act of 1913, which restricted African purchase of land to reserved areas, was especially discriminating. The alienation or reservation of land for Europeans in South Africa has of course assumed proportions unparalleled in any of the other African states South of the Sahara. According to Yudelman's estimate approximately 89.0% of the land in South Africa had been reserved for the Europeans by 1959, the Europeans numbering 19.4% of the

50. Sundkler, 1961, p. 33.

total population.[51] It stands to reason that the restriction of land rights on such a massive scale would provoke a strong protest from people who traditionally are used to a rural economy and that they would see the limitation of their rights to land as a threat to their livelihood and security. It also seems likely that the correlation between resentment about land-alienation and flocking to the Independent Churches should be higher in this territory than in countries where the land problem was less pressing.

For a critical evaluation of the element of protest against land legislation within the Shona Independent Churches, an introductory assessment of the Rhodesian situation is needed. First a distinction between the Ndebele and Shona territories should be kept in mind. Whereas the allocation of land in Mashonaland largely coincided with the Shona homelands which they were occupying when the Pioneer settlers arrived, the Ndebele were deprived of large portions of what they considered to be their homelands after the overthrow of the Ndebele monarchy in 1893. During the land rush that followed this conquest, land was granted to Europeans at random. The preference of speculators and settlers for the black and red loamy soils surrounding Bulawayo led within a year to the alienation of the most fertile regions in Matabeleland.[52]

Although the direct causes of the Rebellions in 1896-7[53] can be attributed

51. Yudelman, 1964, p. 19.

52. That the Ndebele were more adversely affected than the Shona by the allocation of land is clearly reflected in the letter of the Superintendent of Natives, Bulawayo, to the Chief Native Commissioner in 1920. He wrote: 'The formerly dominant tribe of this territory, through whom the first titles of the Territory were secured by whites, are of all tribes now in the worst position in respect of land... Their [the Ndebele] misfortune was in the first place their national predilection for the red and black loams... within a few months of the European occupation practically the whole of their most valued region ceased to be their patrimony and passed into the private estate of individuals and the commercial property of the companies. The whole of what the term "*nga pakati kwe lizwe*" (the midst of the land) conveyed became metamorphosed, although they did not early realize it, into alien soil, and passed out of the direct control even of the Government. (Not so the tribes of Mashonaland who were for the most part left in possession of the granite soil preferred by them to all others.) In the native concept Government and Ownership of land are indivisible. That land on which people live, and have lived for generations, can be purchased for money is hard to understand. White men of varied origin and race become in a day their landlords, their overlords, with power to dispossess and drive forth.' Superintendent of Natives, Bulawayo, to Chief Native Commissioner, 1st June 1920. National Archives 3/16/9. Quoted from Ranger, 1967, pp. 102-103. See also Ranger, 1966, pp. 178-179.

53. The rising tension in the new colony was brought to a climax by the unpredictable forces of nature – rinderpest, drought and locusts – and the rebellions which broke out, eventually cost the settler community a 10 % loss of lives. See Gann, 1965, p. 137.

to the general dissatisfaction caused, among other things, by the mismanagement of some of the newly appointed 'Native Commissioners', the land problem already played an important role at this early stage. The Ndebele were dissatisfied with the lands allotted to them beyond the territory originally inhabited by them. The majority of them had refused to move into the newly created reserves, and as a result found themselves on the private property of European farmers, who could subject them to rental charges or eviction. Many land grants were held by Europeans *in absentia.* Yet the Ndebele soon noticed that the Europeans had taken charge of what they (the Ndebele) regarded as their home-land. One of the senior Ndebele *indunas,* Gambo, stated at the peace talks held towards the end of the rebellions, that 'one cause of dissatisfaction and unrest is, that after we had lived many years at a spot we are told that a white man has purchased it, and we have to go.'[54]

As for the Shona, an important reason for their opposition to the Chartered Company derives from the fallacy of the European authorities that Lobengula's authority was established and accepted throughout the whole of Mashonaland. The British Government had accepted Lobengula's concessions as being applicable to the whole region and the Company acted accordingly. Mineral rights were therefore issued to miners within the Shona chiefdoms without the local tribal authorities having any say in the matter. Several Shona chiefs, however, had in fact maintained their independence during the Ndebele rule, so that Company action was regarded by them as an unlawful breach of their land-rights.

During the years following the Rebellions, after Mashonaland and Matabeleland had been joined in 1898, the 'Cape Clause' was introduced into the Colony. This clause theoretically enabled any African to hold or dispose of land under the same conditions as anybody else. But in practice Africans were not encouraged to buy land. To the majority of them the purchase of land was a foreign conception, apart from the fact that few of them had the means to obtain sizeable farms. As a result only 45,000 acres were privately owned by Africans compared to the 31,000,000 acres in the possession of Europeans towards 1925, when the settlers started pressing for the Cape Clause to be repealed. In the meantime Native Commissioners were requested to make recommendations on lands to be allocated to Africans. They did so, without the application of uniform principles. Their recommendations generally referred to the land not yet alienated by Europeans. Thus

54. Ranger, 1967, p. 105, with reference to the Bulawayo Chronicle, 26th June 1897.

the reserve system came into being, which, for the Shona, in the majority of cases actually implied the recognition as tribal territories of areas already occupied by them.

During the two decades preceding Responsible Government, in 1923, the Ndebele aristocracy tried to create a 'National Home' for their dispossessed tribesmen, and to revive the Kingship. At this early stage the Ndebele leaders were already assisted by some of the prominent members of the 'Ethiopian' Independent Church Movement in South Africa. Rev. Ncayaya, for instance, in his capacity as leader of the 'Ethiopan Church of South Africa' became the spokesman of Nyamanda, the oldest son of Lobengula, who was organizing the resistance of Ndebele malcontents. The petition which he handed to the king of England on behalf of the Ndebele, during his visit in 1919, amongst other things urged the king to 'hand back the so-called unalienated land to the family of the late king Lobengula in trust for the tribe according to Bantu custom and the right of the chieftainship therein to be restored and acknowledged.'[55]

That the Ndebele efforts eventually failed is of little importance at this juncture. The essential point is that the Ndebele were offering organized resistance of a sophisticated nature before Responsible Government in 1923, while the Shona people were still largely relying on the traditional religious authorities, especially the oracular deity at Matonjeni, to voice their protests. Ethiopianism had spread to Matabeleland at an early stage. Independent Church leaders identified themselves with the Ndebele struggle for land, which involved their active participation in the political field. The Southern Shona, on the other hand, only started responding to the campaigns of returning labour migrants who had been converted to the Independent Churches in South Africa during the early 1920's. A spread of this movement in significant numbers amongst the Southern Shona started only after 1930. Even then the link between the Shona Independent Churches and forms of political protest against land allocation was much less evident, or possibly more subtly organized, than was the case with the Ndebele. Discontent about land gradually grew after the Rebellions, with only sporadic local outbursts to signify its existence. Consequently the Shona Independent Church Movement in its initial stages was much less of a land-protest movement – with a leader 'leading his followers to Canaan' – than many of the South African and Ndebele Churches, an argument which will be elaborated on in Vol. 2.

Several Land Commissions were appointed in the course of time to inves-

55. *Ibid.*, pp. 178-193.

tigate and report on the important issue of land distribution. Of these the Morris Carter Commission, which was appointed in 1925, had a significant influence on land legislation. The members of this Commission brought out a report in favour of territorial segregation which they thought would aid the prevention of racial friction.[56] The Commissioners also stressed that special 'purchase areas' should be reserved for Africans, where they could buy individual land holdings free from European competition.

The outstanding legislative measures which directly or indirectly caused discontent and provoked protest from the African community concerns the Land Apportionment Act and the Native Land Husbandry Act. With these we will briefly concern ourselves:

i) *The Land Apportionment Act.*
Acting on the recommendations of the Morris Carter Commission, the Government passed the first Land Apportionment Act in 1931. More than 28 million acres of land were then classified as Native Areas. In 1941 a revised Land Apportionment Act was passed in which the final allocations amounted to 48 million acres for Europeans, 42 million acres for Africans, 3,000 acres Forest Land and 57,000 acres unreserved land. The latter division left Africans with approximately 35 acres per person, which compared favourably with the 5.8 acres, in the Union of South Africa.[57] In several important aspects Rhodesian territorial segregation differed from that of South Africa. Rhodesia dealt with the problem while there was still land to divide and it could allot more to the Africans than in South Africa. The Rhodesian approach to segregation was less dogmatic and had fewer religious overtones. It was then generally regarded as a temporary solution, with the result that this policy was initially much less rigidly applied. Instead of decreasing, the number of Africans on Crown and private European lands actually increased in the years following the approval of the Land Apportionment Act. Serious attempts to move these Africans on a large scale to the areas especially allocated to them only took place after the 2nd World War, when the opening

56. The view was taken that 'however desirable it may be that members of the two races should live together side by side with equal rights as regards the holding of land, we are convinced that in practice, probably for generations to come, such a policy is not practicable, nor in the best interests of the two races, and that until the native has advanced much further on the path of civilization, it is better that points of contact between the two races should be reduced.' See *Report of the Land Commission*, 1925; quoted from Yudelman, 1964, p. 69.

57. Gray, 1960, p. 55.

up of new farms for returning white servicemen directly highlighted the so-called squatter problem.

Distinct disadvantages of the Land Apportionment Act can be pointed out. Although Africans had received some fertile lands, the Europeans generally had the best of the deal.[58] With the exception of a few reserves, tribal areas mostly fall in the zones with a low annual rainfall. The railway lines were only indirectly accessible from tribal reserves, which complicated the marketing of produce. Perhaps the most outstanding feature of the Act was the philosophy on which it was based. The point of departure was the provision of enough land for each African family to sustain itself at subsistence level. One of the weaknesses of this approach was that the urbanization of the Africans was not clearly foreseen or provided for at an early stage. This in itself is an understandable error, if one considers that, at the time when the Morris Carter Commission drew up its report, only about 3% of the total African population were to be found in urban areas, and that of these the majority were labour migrants. The Act of 1931 actually confirmed the already existing pattern of labour migration in which Africans were regarded as temporary 'visitors' in European areas, and township planning was left to the initiative of the municipalities. In turn the Land Apportionment Act became the tool which perpetuated the labour migration pattern. It divided the country's labour force into two sections comprising non-competing racial groups.

Since the implementation of the Act was delayed for a considerable time, its effect on the African community remained obscure for some years. Other factors, however, caused a wave of discontent in the early 1930's. During the years of depression, Africans in particular experienced difficulties with maize marketing. Most of them were too far from the railway lines to profit from the newly introduced legislation which guaranteed stricter control of maize marketing through the Maize Control Board. They were dependent on individual traders who paid low prices for African maize, because of the ready assumption that native-grown maize was of an inferior quality, and also because of the great distances that had to be covered to reach the African producers.

Another cause of African resentment was the destocking measures applied by the Administration since the late 1930's. Africans had been used to the traditional system of shifting cultivation, but once their movements were restricted to certain areas, the movement of villages could take place less regularly, or not at all. Soil was therefore being used continuously without

58. Gann, 1965, p. 280.

the necessary intervals of regeneration, and stock increased disproportionately to the grazing capacity of the land. This latter aspect added to the dangers of soil erosion, and compulsory destocking measures became inevitable. Such measures were at first applied by 'administrative persuasion', but were soon legalized under the Natural Resources Act of 1944. The discontent caused by these measures can only be understood in the light of the traditional Bantu evaluation of cattle, which still largely persists in the rural areas of this day. Cattle have always been a symbol of wealth and prestige; used for *roora* purposes, cattle were directly associated with the African marriage institution, representing as such the 'wife-acquiring' and therefore reproductive potential of family and lineage. Animals dedicated to family ancestors obviously attained the kind of sacral significance which prohibited their use for other than propitiatory purposes. Destocking measures amongst a people whose social fabric and self-respect were so intricately linked with the cattle they possessed was bound to have grave consequences. A chief could be persuaded of the necessity to limit the stock in his chiefdom once he was convinced of the dire effects of overstocking on his lands. Yet it became increasingly difficult to convince him that the remedy was fewer cattle and not more land.[59]

ii) *The Native Land Husbandry Act*

In 1951 the Native Land Husbandry Act was passed to counter numerous land problems, such as the fragmentation of landholdings, soil erosion and declining crop yields. Revolutionary in its conception, the Act was directed at a gradual abolition of the customary landholding system. In the place of the traditional method of land allocation by the ward headman the act proposed a new system of individual landholding together with communal grazing rights. Farming rights had to be registered with the Native Commissioner. Once obtained, farming rights could be sold, but holdings could no longer be fragmented at will, and succession to land rights could only take place with the approval of the NC. The sizes of landholdings were determined by such factors as local rainfall, soil fertility and the availability of land. Tracts of land were to have fixed boundaries to counteract land fragmentation. As in the past grazing was to remain communal, but the methods of destocking were radically changed. Instead of applying destocking measures *after* overgrazing had taken place, each communal grazing area had to be rated according to pre-assessed carrying capacity. In order to prevent soil erosion and ensure good farming methods a set of new regulations were introduced. Any landholder convicted more than three times for non-compliance with these rules

59. Gray, 1960, p. 67.

could be forced to sell his holding. Thus a means was devised which aimed at eliminating the necessity to combine periodical labour migration and soil cultivation in the tribal areas. A cultivator could be required to maintain his presence on his holding in order to retain his land rights. Although labour migration is not specifically mentioned in the Act, the authorities hoped that the implementation of the Act would bring about a division between good agriculturalists and permanent wage-labourers. If landholdings could be consolidated so that families could reasonably subsist on it, the supplementary income derived from labour migration would become unnecessary.

When the Act was passed in 1951, it was a novelty in the Central and East African colonies.[60] But for all its ingenious planning and far-sighted consideration of soil conservation, the implementation met with difficulties and resistance from the side of the Africans. Uneven distribution of the cultivators in the different territories caused great variations in the size of holdings. In southern Mashonaland there were 79,000 cultivators, but only land enough for 32,000 full-sized holdings. Eastern Mashonaland had land to spare next to full-sized holdings for all its cultivators. In some of the more densely populated reserves less than 30% of the families could be allotted full-sized holdings.[61]

More important, however, was the threat of a serious disruption of the African's social fabric, due to the application of measures essentially alien in character. Convinced of the necessity to force the pace, in order to check the deterioration of land in the reserves, the Administration did not favour long-term experimentation. Thus the impact of the new measures on African society was not always sufficiently considered. Instead of enhancing agricultural security, the new land legislation was felt by many Africans as a threat to the kind of security which land had provided in the past. To them ward membership and tribal affiliation implied the inalienable right to a part of the communally held land. The tribal land to which one belonged represented a real link with the past and safeguarded the hereditary right to

60. Nyasaland at that stage was still experimenting with a centralization system that had been introduced in Rhodesia in the 1940's. 'In East Africa it was revolutionary that the Royal Commission of 1956 should put individual land tenure in the forefront of their disposals.' Gray, 1960, p. 69.

61. Holleman (1969, p. 57) points out that by the time the Land Husbandry Act was implemented 'the over-all man-acre ratio dropped from 1 : 28 in 1913 to 1 : 14 in 1953, while the over-all ratio of cattle shrank from 53 acres per head to 17 acres.' The population pressure on the land had therefore more than doubled since the beginning of the century.

exist in one's preferred milieu.[62] Excluding tribesmen from what they regarded as their indisputable right to land – irrespective of periods spent away from their home reserves – could not but have a serious effect on the internal fabric of ward life.

In addition to the introduction of a foreign, individualized principle of land-rights which stood diametrically opposed to the traditional system of land tenure, there were also other factors which caused the Land Husbandry Act to become extremely unpopular among Africans. Like the Land Apportionment Act it implies restrictive measures, the implementation of which once more emphasized the manipulative powers of the European Administration. When the allocation of landholdings took place insufficient consideration was given to the wishes of ruralists who were temporarily engaged in wage labour in the urban areas. Consequently large numbers of males returning from town with the intention of settling down in the tribal areas found themselves 'landless' because they were not present on the 'prescribed date'. Furthermore an economic recession instead of the expected industrial boom during the crucial period of implementing the unpopular Act, only served to aggravate matters and to intensify, especially in the cases of jobless individuals, the feeling of insecurity.[63] But, as Holleman suggests, the main reasons for the failure of this Act should perhaps be sought in 'the lack of understanding of the human factors involved in the complex of social, economic and mental adjustment during rapid transition, and the over-confidence of the architects and executors of the Act in the remedial power of the legislative and administrative action imposed from above.'[64]

iii) *Rural and urban landholders*

For an assessment of the possible correlation between land legislation and the growth of the Independent Churches, the actual situation in the Chingombe and Fort Victoria communities, as far as landholding is concerned, should be considered.

A standard land allocation pattern was introduced under the Land Husbandry Act.[65] It was stipulated that a minimum of 6 acres of unirrigated land would be necessary to sustain a household, consisting of a man, his wife and children. In densely populated areas, with little land for allocation,

62. Yudelman, 1964, p. 111.
63. Holleman, 1969, p. 61.
64. *Ibid.*, p. 66.
65. Government Publication: *What the Land Husbandry Act means to the Rural African . . .* 1955.

a special formula could come into operation which permitted the registration of allocations previously made by tribal authorities, even if the holdings concerned fell below the minimum requirements.[66] In those areas where enough land was available a polygamist could claim one-third of a standard holding for each additional wife, provided that his total holding did not exceed the standard holding more than three times. These additional arrangements, together with factors of soil fertility and rainfall, account for the deviant figures on the acreage of arable land per household in every tribal area.

In Chingombe with its relatively low rainfall a full-sized holding for households, averaging some 6 to 7 members, amounts to about 12-13 acres. The results of the random sample (table 8) indicate that 44% of the adult male cultivators (and by implication also of the chiefdom's households, since practically all adult males – above 18 yrs. of age – included in the sample, represent a household or consumption unit of varying size) have access to an arable acreage (10-15 acres) approximating the standard allocation. With only a few exceptions of large households cultivating more than the average amount of acres, an additional 25% of the households have to sustain themselves on 6-9 acres, while 31% fall below the above-mentioned minimum acreage as stipulated in the Land Husbandry Act.

Included in the category of households (14%) which have no registered land rights at all, are a few comparatively small units (e.g. households consisting of recently married couples) which are still economically dependent on the parental consumption unit. The family heads of these units are not necessarily landless because they normally have access to and cultivate land registered in the names of their fathers. Other family heads who claimed to be landless belong to a group of dissatisfied males who were away from the chiefdom when allocations, under the provisions of the Land Husbandry Act, were made. They have no registered landholdings and supplement their food resources with products from the fields of their relatives.

Despite these additional distinctions it remains a fact that the members of approximately 31% of the households in the chiefdom have to sustain themselves on an acreage below or well below the minimum requirements of 6 acres. Such conditions inevitably stimulate increasing numbers of tribesmen periodically to engage in wage labour beyond the chiefdom's borders. Here we have a potent source of discontent and resentment.

At present nearly all the available arable land in Gutu-East has been allocated to registered holders under the provisions of the Land Husbandry Act. Precise figures are therefore available on the number of cultivators per

66. Garbett, 1963, p. 192.

land unit. Yet these figures bear little relation to the actual situation in the tribal areas where the majority of people still cultivate land that had been 'traditionally' allocated to them by their tribal leaders.[67] The full impact of the new legislation has therefore not yet been felt by all cultivators in tribal areas. Thus the actual change of landholding from the traditional to the individualized system can be expected to become a prolonged process, which might well have a marked effect on religious life in the future.

Indicative of the premium on land rights even for labour migrants who spend proportionally few years in the tribal areas, is the fact that the majority of townsmen in Fort Victoria still hold land in their home reserves (table 8). Some of them (28%) have full-sized landholdings of 10 acres and more, with a few exceptions claiming to be owners of farms in the Purchase Areas. Retention of land rights is especially important as a security factor to labourers whose positions are not secure in the competitive urban labour market. To the majority of townsmen landholdings remain a scurce of subsistence to their families, which enables them to save up some capital in town, be it for bride-price, farm improvement or educational purposes. In the event of good crop returns the worker in town himself is regularly provided with foodstuffs from home.

In view of the continuing reliance of urbanites on landholdings in the tribal areas, it seems significant that a considerable proportion of urban households (29%)[68] are represented by adult males who have lost all land rights. If there had been a direct correlation between the discontent caused by restricted land rights and the increase of Independent Church adherence, one would have expected the urban environment with its 'landless' males to be the ideal setting for intensified recruitment of Independent Church membership. That this has not been the case derives from the fact that the Southern Shona Independent Churches still represent a predominantly rural phenomenon. This does not mean that land legislation has no bearing on the surveyed Independent Churches. For although the statistical data still to be presented do not support the postulation of discriminatory land legislation as a conclu-

67. Hughes (1965, p. 35), an Extension Officer who conducted an experimental socio-economic survey in the Gutu East Tribal Trust Land (including Chingombe) in 1963, indicates that in a sample of 85 homesteads, a total number of 86 Land Husbandry Act allocations have been made, compared to a total number of 245 'traditional allocations'.

68. Although the urban and town samples are not strictly comparable, due to differences of circumstances and of households, the higher percentage of 'landless' households in town probably reflects the increasing concentration of people without registered holdings in this environment; people who have become or are in the process of becoming fully dependent on cash earnings for a livelihood.

sive explanatory theory for religious separatism, the importance of these measures as a background factor, contributing generally to a psychological climate conducive to the formation of 'separated' Church groups, cannot be discarded.

b) *Livestock and agricultural production*

Although the agricultural production in Chingombe, as in other unirrigated areas, is generally low, there are significant differences between the various farmers of this area. Those who have received a training on experimental farms or who proved themselves capable of farming well under the supervision of Land Extension Officers or Agricultural Demonstrators, are given certificates as 'master farmers'. Then there are plot-holders and 'co-operators' who, under supervision, apply such farming methods as crop rotation or the use of fertilizers. Ordinary farmers make no use of supervisory aids. The latter category still forms the largest group in tribal areas. In 1960 it was estimated that about 70% of the African producers had not yet made use of improved agricultural techniques, a factor which contributes towards the low crop yields per acre. There were then approximately 9,000 'master farmers' in the country.[69] In 1967 only 4% of the adult male cultivators were 'master farmers' in Chingombe (table 9), but considerable numbers of cultivators were making use of the services provided by the Government. Due to frequent periods of absence (64% of all the small farmers were also occasional labour migrants – table 9) African cultivators had not yet been able fully to exploit the supervisory aid at their disposal.

In spite of the process of converting traditional farmers into 'co-operators' or 'master farmers' being retarded through labour migration and other factors, the impact of new agricultural techniques on the Chingombe community is noticeable. As can be deduced from the tables below, some of the farmers harvested considerable crops on a limited acreage in 1966. Especially the 'master farmers' and some of the more progressive 'co-operators', together with the teachers and the successful businessmen at Basera township, are at present emerging as an economic upper class. As the agricultural elite of the chiefdom, 'master farmers' frequently wear their badges on social occasions, a sign of their being proudly aware of their status. They are the people who come into consideration for farms in the Purchase Areas, depending on the

69. *Report of the Secretary for Native Affairs*, Salisbury, 1960, p. 78.

recommendations of extension officers once it is evident that they have become financially strong enough for such a venture.

The combination of a rural semi-subsistence economy with cash income derived from periodic wage labour complicates a comparative assessment of the economic strength of rural households. As far as income is concerned there are three major components:

a) crops harvested;
b) increase of livestock;
c) wages earned during migrant labour sorties.

Cash income is mainly derived from wages and the sale of crops and stock. In Chingombe migrant wage earnings appear to amount to about half of the total cash income.[70] Most crops, however, are not sold but consumed, and also the number of livestock sold probably accounts for less than its actual increase. This means that wage earnings represent considerably less than half the *total* income of rural households, and that crop yields and (increase of) stock holdings are probably better indicators of the relative strength of such households. Moreover, it proved to be difficult to obtain accurate information about periodic wage earnings, individual stock sales and increases. Our main purpose being to get some idea of a possible correlation between economic status and Church affiliation, the random sample survey in the Chingombe area therefore merely aimed at a simple assessment of the number of livestock per household at the time of survey and of the total crop yields and major sales of agricultural produce during the preceding season. The data thus obtained should provide a limited yet fairly reliable basis for a distribution of households into three (admittedly arbitrarily defined) economic classes: 'lower', 'middle' and 'upper'. Here we briefly sketch the general picture:

As far as livestock is concerned Chingombe ruralists still highly prize the ownership of cattle. The customary practice of judging a man's wealth in terms of the cattle he owns still features strongly in this society. Consequently farmers set great store by at least a small herd of cattle. Quantity is more important than quality, with the result that, despite veterinary services, the condition of cattle is generally on the poor side. Only 23% of the households have no cattle compared to the 36% without any (or supplementary herds of) goats, and 80% without sheep (table 10).[71] The average ratio of livestock units (one unit amounting to one head of cattle or four head of small

70. Hughes (1965, p. 31) has estimated that 56.3% of the total cash earnings of homestead groups in Gutu-East derived from migrant labour, 11.5% from crop sales and 22.3% from stock sales.

stock: goats and/or sheep) per household, amounts to 21% with no livestock units; 33% with 1 to 5 units; 35% with 6 to 15 units and only 11% above 16 units (table 11). In terms of livestock ownership this classification would imply that about 54% of the chiefdom's households – with no, or only small herds of livestock – belong to the lower economic stratum popularly referred to as the *varombo* (the 'poor') with only a small number of households clearly distinguished from the 'middle class' owners of sizeable herds (6 to 15 units), as the really prosperous livestock owners, the *vafumi* (rich people) with herds exceeding 16 livestock units.

An analysis of crop production in Chingombe, in 1966, reveals that this is a predominantly millet- and groundnut-growing area, as in fact most of the low rainfall areas in Rhodesia are.[72] Whereas 83% of the household produced bulrush millet (*mhunga*), 58% finger millet (*rukweza*), and 73% groundnuts (*nzungu*), only 47% produced maize (table 12). Finger millet is widely produced, but only in small quantities, as is clear from the figures of the households which have produced more than 5 bags. On the other hand bulrush millet and groundnuts are produced in large quantities and used as saleable crops. Groundnuts especially form the major cash crop. Not only did the largest number of crop-selling household sell groundnuts in 1966 (52% of all households), but the largest quantities of crops sold consisted of groundnuts. Compared to the few exceptional households selling more than 5 bags of maize or millet in 1966, approximately 25% of the households sold more than this amount of groundnuts; some even sold more than 20 bags. A mere 6% of the households sold maize.

Despite the low rate of maize production, this type of grain forms the staple diet of the ruralists in Chingombe. Millet and millet products – especially beer –, groundnuts and other secondary crops, such as pumpkins, potatoes and beans, serve to supplement the staple diet. Cash earnings, derived from crops sold, invariably provide the means with which to buy maize products for consumption. Thus a large number of the chiefdom's farmers sell *mhunga* and *nzungu* at the business centres of the Basera and Chingombe townships and buy maize meal (*upfu*) in return. During periods of drought or bad maize harvests the economically weak homesteads may temporarily switch to a staple diet of millet porridge. Considering the 41% of non-maize-producing households in 1966, and the relatively low percentage

71. Whereas a high percentage of households (58 %) owned less than twelve head of cattle, the number of households with large herds of goats (in excess of 20 head) was slightly higher than those with equally large herds of cattle.

72. Johnson, 1964, p. 181.

of households (39%) storing maize in that period – some of which had to supplement the harvested supplies with maize products they bought – then an estimated 60% or more of the households had to buy maize or switch to another diet in order to sustain themselves. If the major grain crops and the groundnut crops harvested by each household in 1966 are added up, at least 47% of the households had harvested no, or less than 20, bags (table 13). The majority of these households (at an average of 6 to 7 inhabitants per household) can reasonably be said to have had a shortage of harvest yields in this year. As regards crop production they can therefore be classified as belonging to the chiefdom's economically lower stratum (the *varombo*). The 38% of households with total yields of 21 to 40 bags represent the 'middle class' units producing sufficient grain and nuts to sustain themselves, whereas the 15% with total yields above 40 bags represent the economically more virile category of 'upper class' *vafumi* with the chiefdom's surplus potential.

In Volume 2 figures on livestock ownership and crop production will be related to the religious categories of Traditionalist, Mission Church and Independent Church 'households' to determine whether the Independent Churches are particularly identified with any of the rural economic strata. A similar threefold classification based on the urban economy of average cash incomes per month (see below) will be applied to the sample of wage-labourers in Fort Victoria to determine the economic status of Church-affiliated townsmen. The limitations of such a classification are obvious. Earnings deriving from migrant labour have not been included for the rural households, while rural production has not been added to the wages of townsmen who are still supported from back 'home'. Nevertheless such categorization retains some comparative validity, since the various households in each sample were subjected to essentially the same criterion.

c) *Labour migration*

As elsewhere in Rhodesia, labour migration in the Southern Shona districts was not really curbed by the provisions of the Land Husbandry Act but seems to have remained a well established practice. Perhaps it is too soon to judge the effect of legislation on the present-day trends, since it is only in recent years that legislation has made it possible for Africans to settle permanently in urban areas. The increase of the number of people participating in the wage labour economy, together with the new schemes of home-ownership in townships, may in time create a stable urban community. There are already signs pointing in this direction. The sample of adults resident in the Mucheke township at Fort Victoria (table 5) shows that 28% of them have been living in town for more than 10 years, 9% for more than 20 years, while 30% have been in town for less than 2 years. These figures point at an increase of the stability of the town community, if compared with those of a survey conducted in 1953, when among 3,600 Africans only 5.9% had remained in town for more than 10 years, 5.7% between 5 to 10 years and nearly 60% for less than 10 months.[73]

Labour migration causes an uneven sex ratio in rural and urban areas. There is a surplus of males in the urban, and females in the rural areas. A U.C.R.N. Sample Survey of 132 African labourers in Salisbury in 1958 showed that 53.8% had no families with them. Of the 96 adult males interviewed in the Mucheke township (table 14) 44% had their families and children staying in the reserves, 41% had their families with them, although some only for brief periods each year, especially after the harvests; and 16% of the males were single. As has been mentioned, husbands often reside with their wives in town until they obtain married quarters, and then send them back to the reserves,[74] so as not to forfeit their land rights. The wife's continued presence on the allocated patch of land, supported by relatives who do not own but cultivate the fields, as well as by regular visits of the labour migrant himself, has made it more or less impossible for the Administration to alienate such land rights. At the same time, however, cultivation often deteriorates on the fields of labour migrants, with a subsequent decrease of production. As yet the increase of yields of those cultivators co-operating with the extension staff has not been achieved on a large enough scale radically to alter the over-all economic position in the reserves. What has in fact happened is that regular contact with the Western culture has increased the needs of rural Africans. Especially the cost of education, the importance of which is now fully appreciated by the Africans, in addition to traditional family obligations (the rural family still forms a socio-economic unit) continues to force many men to periodical participation in the wage labour market. Thus a vicious circle seems to perpetuate itself. Low agricultural returns, in relation to increasing demands, stimulate labour migration and perpetuate absentee landholding. Simultaneously the lack of sufficient social security in urban areas, such as unemployment funds or old-age pensions, tends to strengthen the traditional outlook which associates land with social

73. Garbett (1963, p. 193) calculated it from the Demographic Survey 1953-5.

74. This practice often has a negative bearing on family life. The prolonged periods of a wife's absence in town enhances the chances of her husband entering into a temporary alliance with a 'woman of the pots' (*Supra*, p. 43) which in turn may lead to domestic conflicts or even to the complete breakup of family life.

security. Spells of employment are therefore followed up by a return to the tribal lands, where again the kinship obligations are so demanding that the benefits of individual landholdings cannot be fully exploited. Even without the further fragmentation of land, so many relatives become dependent on the available holding which was planned to provide subsistence for a man, his wife and their children only, that the returning labour migrant soon finds it necessary to leave his little farm once more.

This movement between reserve and town varies considerably in different parts of Rhodesia. By 1956, 63.8% of males between 15-49 years of age were employed outside the reserves.[75] Garbett found that in a Zezuru-speaking district 49.6% of the married males and 83.4% of single males between 15-20 years were absent from their homesteads in 1958.[76] Chingombe, which is further removed from a big urban centre, has fewer adult men absent at any particular time. The adult community present in 1967 showed a ratio of 41.2% males to 58.8% females. Only 47 women reported that their husbands were absent due to labour migration, which means an absentee rate of approximately 17% of the married male population (table 15). It follows that, in spite of the great majority (about 80%) of all male adults having entered the wage-labour market at some time or other, it is only a minority of Chingombe males who are absent at any one time.

Of the adult males in Chingombe, only 20% had *never* entered the wage-labour market; 15% had been employed outside Rhodesia, 62% inside Rhodesia, and 12% of the adult male residents were employed or self-employed in or near the chiefdom, in addition to carrying on with their cultivation activities (table 16). The majority of this latter group were landholders working as salesmen, carpenters, builders, tailors or butchers in the Basera township, the chiefdom's largest business centre. A few of them were employed as farmhands in the Devure African Purchase Area.

As to the locality of employment of the Chingombe wage-labourers, 74% of them had been employed in urban and peri-urban areas, and the rest in rural areas which include townships, farms, railway stations and district headquarters. The two cities, Salisbury and Bulawayo, and large towns like Umtali, Gwelo and Fort Victoria, with large industrial concentrations, draw the majority of labourers (56%). Of those employed in rural areas, the great majority sought jobs within easy reach of the chiefdom, i.e. within a 100-mile radius of their home villages (table 17). 41% of the wage-labourers have in the past engaged in more than one job, some of them having been employed

75. Garbett, 1963, p. 193.
76. Garbett, 1960, p. 43; quoted by Crawford, 1967, p. 13.

more than six times (table 18). These figures reflect the mobility of African labour and suggest that quite a number of males have spent more than one wage-earning period away from home.

The spells of absence seldom exceed more than 5 years at a time. Of the Chingombe labour migrants only 7% had been away from the chiefdom for periods exceeding 5 years, 52% for 2 to 5 years and 42% for periods of less than 2 years (table 19). Preference is therefore given to relatively short spells of absence. During such spells most of the men occasionally return home for weekends if they are near enough, or for brief vacations.

Average cash incomes of Africans are still very low, compared to those of the Europeans. In recent years, however, there has been a noticeable increase. I have not calculated the wage rates earned by Chingombe labour migrants in the past few decades in table 20, but if it is considered that some 60% of them were earning an average wage of less than £9 per month and an estimated 40% were earning £4 and less, during periods of employment preceding the 1960's, then the wages of the Fort Victoria townsmen in 1967 show a marked increase in cash income. Few townsmen earned £4 or less per month; some 28% were earning £5 to £9; 58% earned £10 to £19 and 13% were receiving upwards of £20 per month (table 20).

It is within the framework of this economic setting that we will view the Southern Shona Independent Churches. Against this background too, we shall later on return to the questions of whether the religious bodies studied in essence represent protest movements as a reaction particularly to restrictive land legislation, and/or to the colonial situation with its white supremacy, generally. In anticipation of the case material yet to be presented it should be stated at this juncture that the element of protest in the economic and political fields is much less evident than may have been expected. Some of the Church groups deliberately avoid nationalistic political involvement and derive their powers of attraction in the first place by meeting the religious needs of Africans with adapted and indigenized ritual practices. Others have vested interests in Government projects aimed at the improvement of economic conditions. They co-operate in land development schemes, serve in the police force and other branches of Government Service and in some cases even publicly oppose radical nationalistic activities aimed at revolutionary changes in the existing order. On the other hand, some elements of antagonism and protest against white supremacy and its restrictive legislation cannot be denied even if these tendencies in some groups are in embryonic form or obscured or as yet only indirectly expressed.

TABLES 1-20

TABLE 1. *RSS – Tribal affiliation in Chingombe*

Rudzi (Tribe)	*Mutupo* (Clan name)	*Chidao* (Sub clan name)	Adult males* n	%	Adult females n	%	Total n	%
Rufura	Gumbo	Madyirapazhe	97	35	79	20	176	26
Hera	Shava	Museamwa/Mukahuru	31	11	43	11	74	11
Duma	Moyo	Chirandu/Gonyohori	29	11	36	9	65	10
Ndau	Moyo	Sithole	19	7	26	7	45	7
Rozvi	Moyo	Mondizo	14	5	27	7	41	6
Manyika	Duwe	Tembo/Mutasa	10	4	27	7	37	6
Mbire	Shoko	Vudzijena	4	1	30	8	34	5
Gargwe	Shumba	Sibanda/Muwawarirwa	7	3	23	6	30	5
Hungwe	Shiri	Chasura/Maokomawi	7	3	17	4	24	4
Ngara	Mambo	Zimuto	10	4	10	3	20	3
Gwai	Chuma	Mutingwende	12	4	4	1	16	2
Chamutsa	Moyo	Mugonderwa/Biriviri	7	3	9	2	16	2
Mlambo	Dziva	Dondo/Save	8	3	8	2	16	2
Others**			21	8	55	14	76	11
Total:			276	102	394	101	670	100
(Sample percentage)				(41.2)		(58.8)		

* Adult = 18 yrs. and above.

** Others: Shangaan, Ndebele, Remba, Tonga, Njanja, etc. – small groups of two to four persons per tribal unit.

TABLE 2. *RSS – Districts from which Chingombe inhabitants originated*

Districts (mostly reserves)	Adult males		Adult females		Total	
	n	%	n	%	n	%
Born in Chingombe	218	79	205	52	423	63
Other Gutu areas	38	14	99	25	137	20
Chipinga	2	1	5	1	7	1
Bikita	8	3	34	9	42	7
Ndanga	–	–	6	2	6	1
Victoria	3	1	11	3	14	2
Buhera	–	–	11	3	11	2
Umtali	2	1	4	1	6	1
Outside Rhodesia	1	0	7	2	8	1
Other territories*	4	2	12	3	16	2
Total	276	101	394	101	670	100
(Sample percentage)		(41.2)		(58.8)		

* Other territories: One to three persons from each of the following districts: Matabeleland, Chibi, Chilimanzi, Que-Que, Belingwe and Nuanetsi.

TABLE 3. *CST – Districts which Fort Victoria townsmen come from*

Districts (mostly reserves)	Adult males		Adult females		Total	
	n	%	n	%	n	%
Born in Fort Victoria	–	–	1	2	1	1
Chibi	5	5	4	7	9	6
Victoria	19	20	14	23	33	21
Ndanga	9	9	4	7	13	9
Bikita	10	10	5	8	15	10
Chipinga	5	5	4	7	9	6
Gutu	23	24	12	20	35	22
Buhera	8	8	4	7	12	8
Umtali	2	2	3	5	5	3
Outside Rhodesia	4	4	2	3	6	4
Other Shona territory	11	11	8	13	19	12
Total	96	98	61	102	157	101
(Sample percentage)		(61.1)		(38.9)		

TABLE 4. *CST – Tribal affiliation of Fort Victoria townsmen*

Tribal affiliation	Adult male		Adult female		Total	
	n	%	n	%	n	%
Hera	14	15	10	16	24	15
Duma	16	17	5	8	21	13
Mbire	8	8	8	16	16	10
Gargwe	11	12	4	7	15	10
Rufura	9	9	3	5	12	8
Rozvi	5	5	5	8	10	6
Ndau	6	6	3	5	9	6
Ngara	3	3	4	7	7	5
Manyika	4	4	3	5	7	5
Other tribes*	20	21	16	25	36	23
Total	96	100	61	102	157	101
(Sample percentage)		(61.1)		(38.9)		

* Other tribes: Two to three persons per tribal grouping: Ndebele, Hungwe, Remba, Tonga, Njanja, Mlambo etc.

TABLE 5. *CST – Period of residence of townsmen in Fort Victoria*

Period in town/number of years	Adult males		Adult females		Total	
	n	%	n	%	n	%
20 +	10	10	4	7	14	9
10 – 20	20	21	9	15	29	19
6 – 10	20	21	13	21	33	21
2 – 5	20	21	14	23	34	22
0 – 2	26	27	21	34	47	30
Total	96	100	61	100	157	101
(Sample percentage)		(61.1)		(38.9)		

TABLE 6. *RSS – Chingombe chiefdom: Kinship patterns within homesteads*

Relation to head of homestead	Number of persons	Percentage of sample population
Heads of homestead	247*	15
Wife	311	17
Son	585	32
Daughter	588	32
Mother	25	1
Brother	11	1
Sister	10	0
Daughter's daughter	13	1
Daughter's son	11	1
Brother's daughter	4	0
Brother's son	2	0
Sister's son	3	0
Sister's daughter	1	0
Mother-in-law	5	0
Paternal aunt	1	0
Other (foreigners)	3	0
Total	1,820	100

* There were more households in the random sample villages than the number (247) of heads of homesteads in this table indicates. Married and unmarried males representing 'households' that are still in a transitional stage – i.e. households that are not yet fully economically independent from the parental family unit – were classified in this table as belonging to the original household.

TABLE 7. *RSS – Chingombe chiefdom: Village kinship structure*

Relation of adult males to their village headmen	Number of adult males (18yrs and above)	Percentage
Agnatic kin	124	45
Cognatic kin	55	20
Affines (in-laws)	39	14
Vatorwa ('foreigners')	58	21
Total adult males	276	100

TABLE 8. *RSS and CST – Acreage per household*

Number of acres allotted	Chingombe households (all adult males)		Households of townsmen (married males only)	
	n	%	n	%
None	38*	14	20	29
2 acres	7	3	1	2
3 to 5 acres	38	14	5	7
6 to 7 acres	32	12	11	16
8 to 9 acres	37	13	12	18
10 to 12 acres	24	9	9	13
13 to 15 acres	96	35	8	12
15 to 20 acres	4	1	–	–
20 + (farm in Purchase Area)	–	–	2	3
Total	276	101	68	100

* Unmarried or recently married males some of whom are still reliant on the fields of their fathers, and whose 'households' as a result have not yet become agriculturally independent.

TABLE 9. *RSS – Agricultural position of ruralist males in Chingombe*

Agricultural position	Adult male cultivators	Percentage
Master farmer and occasional labour migrant	8	3
Master farmer only	3	1
Small farmer and periodical labour migrant	175	64
Small farmer only	43	16
Owns no acres	20	8
Small farmer in conjunction with father	18	6
Small farmer with employment in immediate surroundings	9	3
Total	276	101

TABLE 10. *RSS – Number of livestock per household in Chingombe*

Number (head) of livestock	Cattle		Sheep		Goats	
	Number of households	%	Number of households	%	Number of households	%
None	60	23	206	80	93	36
1–2	21	8	9	3	25	10
3–5	60	23	17	7	46	18
6–8	41	16	12	5	29	11
9–11	37	14	7	3	16	6
12–14	19	7	2	1	10	4
15–17	11	4	1	0	13	5
18–20	4	2	2	1	4	2
20+	6	2	3	1	23	9
Total	259	99	259	101	259	101
Herds of 1–11 head	159	61	45	19	116	45
Herds of 12–20 head	34	13	5	2	27	11
Herds of 20+ head	6	2	3	1	23	9

TABLE 11. *RSS – Ratio of livestock units* per household in Chingombe*

Number of animal units owned		No. of households	Percentage	
Lower stratum	None	58	21	54
	1	28	10	
	2	7	3	
	3	2	1	
	4	26	9	
	5	28	10	
Middle stratum	6–10	50	18	35
	11–15	47	17	
Upper stratum	16–20	17	6	11
	20–30	13	5	
Total		276	100	

* One livestock unit = 1 head of cattle or 4 head of small stock (goats or/and sheep)

TABLE 12. *RSS – Food and cash crops per household in Chingombe in 1966*

Number of bags		Harvested (1966)		Sold (1966)		Stored (1966)	
		Household	%	Household	%	Household	%
MAIZE: (*mabarwe*)	None	112	41	223	81	137	50
	1 to 5	66	24	17	6	75	27
	6 to 9	28	10	–	–	18	7
	10 to 20	30	11	1	0	7	3
	20+	6	2	1	0	5	2
	Others*	34	12	34	12	34	12
	Total	276	100	276	99	276	101
BULRUSH MILLET (*mhunga*)	None	15	5	204	74	23	9
	1 to 5	51	19	37	13	96	35
	6 to 9	58	21	–	–	46	17
	10 to 20	87	32	1	0	62	23
	20+	31	11	–	–	15	5
	Others*	34	12	34	12	34	12
	Total	276	100	276	99	276	101
FINGER MILLET (*rukweza*)	None	82	30	211	76	98	36
	1 to 5	107	39	30	11	109	40
	6 to 9	29	11	–	–	22	8
	10 to 20	20	7	1	0	10	4
	20+	4	1	–	–	3	1
	Others*	34	12	34	12	34	12
	Total	276	100	276	99	276	101
GROUND-NUTS (*nzungu*)	None	41	15	98	36	95	34
	1 to 5	53	23	75	27	114	41
	6 to 9	50	18	28	10	16	6
	10 to 20	52	19	25	9	16	6
	20+	36	13	16	6	1	0
	Others*	34	12	34	12	34	12
	Total	276**	100	276	100	276	99

Households *producing* maize = 47%; bulrush millet = 83%; *rukweza* = 58%; *nzungu* = 73%.
Households *selling* maize = 6%; bulrush millet = 13%; *rukweza* = 11%; *nzungu* = 52%.
Households *storing* maize = 39%; bulrush millet = 80%; *rukweza* = 53%; *nzungu* = 53%.

* Others: Several unmarried or recently married males representing 'transitional households' which are still in the process of evolving from their parental units. A few households from which only inconclusive information could be obtained, are also included in this category.

** The number of households (276) approximates that of the adult males (above 18 yrs of age) included in the random sample. Of the 36 unmarried males (see table 8), practically all represent consumption units – counting a few members – which have attained various degrees of economical independence from the main households. For this reason they are included as 'households' in this sample.

TABLE 13. *RSS – Bags of grain and groundnuts harvested per household in Chingombe in 1966*

Grain (maize, bulrush millet, finger millet) and groundnuts *(nzungu)*. Total number of bags harvested.		Number of households	Percentage	
Lower stratum	None	41	15	47
	1 to 5	10	4	
	6 to 10	23	8	
	11 to 20	56	20	
Middle stratum	21 to 30	57	21	38
	31 to 40	46	17	
Upper stratum	40+	41	15	
Total		276	100	

TABLE 14. *CST – Absence or presence of spouse in Fort Victoria*

Position of adult	Male		Female		Total	
	n	%	n	%	n	%
Husband absent (stays in reserve)			3	5	3	2
Wife absent (stays in reserve)	42	44			42	27
Husband present			49	80	49	31
Wife present	39	41			39	25
Person is single	15	16	9	15	24	15
Total	96	101	61	100	157	100
(Sample percentage)		(61.1)		(38.9)		

TABLE 15. *RSS – Chingombe chiefdom: absence of spouse from residence*

Spouses present and absent	Male		Female		Total	
	n	%	n	%	n	%
Husband is absent (labour migrant)			47	12	47	7
Husband absent (illness)			1	0	1	0
Wife absent (illness)	8	3			8	1
Spouse absent (travel, vacation, divorce)	2	1	8	2	10	2
Husband present			253	64	253	39
Wife present	228	83			228	33
Unmarried adults in chiefdom	36	13	85	22	121	18
Unknown	2	1			2	0
Total	276	101	394	100	670	100
(Sample percentage)		(41.2)		(58.8)		

TABLE 16. *RSS – Labour history/Employment of Chingombe adult males*

Employment	Number of adult males	Percentage
Has never been a wage-labourer	54	20
Was employed outside Rhodesia	14	5
Was employed outside and inside Rhodesia	28	10
Was employed in Rhodesia only	143	52
Is employed in Rhodesia at present*	30	11
Self employed at present	2	1
Unknown	5	2
Total	276	101

* The majority, in or near Chingombe

TABLE 17. *RSS – Locality of employment of labour migrants*

Place of last or present employment of Chingombe labour migrants			Labour migrant	Percentage
Urban & peri-urban areas	Large industrial centres	Salisbury	38	19
		Bulawayo	21	11
		Umtali	14	7
		Fort Victoria	16	8
		Gwelo	22	11
	Small towns	Other urban centres eg. Shabani, Selukwe.	37	19
Rural areas	In Chingombe and within 100-mile radius		46	23
	In areas beyond 100-mile radius of of Chingombe		6	3
Total			200	101

TABLE 18. *RSS – Number of jobs done by Chingombe wage-labourers*

Number of jobs done	Wage-labourers	Percentage
1	130	59
2	51	23
3	25	11
4	7	3
5	3	1
6+	4	2
Total	220	99

TABLE 19. *RSS – Average duration of absence of labour migrants outside Chingombe*

Average duration of period(s) of absence*	Number of adult males	Percentage of adult males	Percentage of lab.migrants
Less than 6 months	7	3	4
6 – 12 months	27	10	15
1 – 2 years	40	15	23
2 – 3 years	41	15	23
3 – 4 years	39	14	22
4 – 5 years	12	4	7
5 – 10 years	9	3	5
10 + years	3	1	2
No period of absence	78	28	
Unknown	20	7	
Total	276	100	101

* The period of absence for each individual is based on the only period or the average of all the periods of employment spent beyond the chiefdom's borders, since 1910.

TABLE 20. *CST – Cash income of wage-labourers in Fort Victoria*

Average cash income per month	Number of wage-labourers (present job)	Percentage
£1 to £4	2	2
£5 to £9	24	28
£10 to £14	40	47
£15 to £19	9	11
£20 to £24	6	7
£25 to £29	3	4
£30 +	2	2
Total wage-labourers	86	101

2

Traditional beliefs and ritual

For descriptive purposes Shona beliefs and religious practices can be classified into four distinct but interrelated categories associated with 1) the High-God, 2) the spirit world, 3) the diviner-herbalist, and 4) the wizard (sorcerer or witch). The first category recognizes the general belief in a Supreme Being, the second covers a wide range of activities related to ancestral and alien spirits, while the third category concerns the divinatory and magical practices of the most versatile specialist in Shona religion, the *nganga* (diviner-herbalist). The fourth category also deals with magical practices, although in this case the purpose of the manipulation of dynamistic forces, unlike that of the healing *nganga*, is predominantly destructive or negative.

Efforts to systematize the different aspects of religion have often obscured the meaning of component parts within a composite picture. An effort will therefore be made to indicate the relevancy and frequency of the various traditional religious facets and practices to the individual in every-day life. It is only in its totality and in its relevance to the actual behaviour of individuals in their specific social context that the significance of traditional religion can be appreciated.

Looking at the historical past of the Shona from the religious point of view, it appears that it was precisely their loyalty to their own characteristic conception of the divine, manifested in a common adherence to traditional practices, which rendered them 'immune' to the early Catholic missionary endeavours of the 16th and 17th century. Of this failure of the Portuguese missionaries, a Jesuit priest writes as follows: 'What was the result of these hundred years of devoted effort? Almost nothing. It is one of the most complete failures in missionary history. During these years when the missionaries were struggling to Christianize the Zambesi valley and the north east of Mashonaland, Xavier's work on the Fishery Coast on the southern tip of India was being continued, and Christianity remains vigorous to this day . . . Japan, too, had its converts during these years, some of whom remained faithful through one of the worst persecutions of history . . . None of these regions bear comparison with this part of Africa, where, though there were no notable external trials, the Christian faith which had been taught so long and so devotedly, perished so completely and so soon.'[1]

This passive resistance to foreign influence was shaken when, during the 1896-7 Rebellions, the traditional religious authorities failed, at the command of the High-God, Mwari, to rally all the Shona and Ndebele powers in an effort to dispel the European settlers from the country. From then onwards there was a marked change of attitude towards Missions, and the growth of Christianity, which had been inhibited for many years, started in real earnest. The numerical strength of Mission and Independent Church membership at present may easily lead one to assume that traditional religion is losing ground in the process of acculturation. But nominal affiliation to Christian Churches proves to be a highly deceptive criterion for measuring the virility of traditional religion, because much of what was practised in the past continues to exist in disguise, in syncretized or adapted forms, within the different Churches; moreover, many Christians alternately participate in either the Christian Church or in the traditional religious realms, or in both, as the occasion demands. After the rebellions, the High-God cult was temporarily driven 'underground'. Yet the cult officials continued to play an important role, inconspicuous though it may have seemed, in the politico-religious field. The efforts of African nationalists, in recent years, to channel the aspirations of their people into organized political parties stimulated and partly resulted from the revival of this cult.

A study of the Independent Churches, in which Africans could decide for themselves what elements of the traditional religion to eliminate or adopt, reveals much about their own approach and what *they* regard as important or idolatrous in the traditional religion. For such an analysis it is important that first the main aspects of the traditional system are briefly discussed:

1. THE HIGH-GOD

a) *Concept of God*

The Shona concept of the Supreme Being has never been polytheistic. The great number of names designating the Supreme Being reveal a variety of functions and the association of the divine with different phenomena of nature rather than suggesting the existence of a number of deities. For centuries the Shona have believed in Mwari as the final authority above and

1. As quoted by Ranger, 1967, p. 25.

behind their ancestors, a High-God who seemed perhaps less directly involved in their individual lives than their ancestors were, but one who could be consulted on matters of national importance. Far from being a *deus otiosus* or *deus remotus*, this Mwari was believed to control the fertility of Shona-occupied country, to give rain in times of drought and to advise on the course of action to be taken during times of national crises. Especially at times when invasions and occupation by foreign powers threatened the national identity of the Shona, Mwari's presence was felt to be very near and His demands particularly compelling.

The name *Mwari* is the one most commonly used. Its origin, according to Shona tradition, dates back to the time when the Mbire tribe migrated from the Tanzanian lake regions.[2] The name 'Muali' is still used in the vicinity of Mt. Kilimanjaro and designates God as the 'Sower' and therefore the God of fertility. It seems that the tradition of the Mbire past lends support to Von Sicard's view that there is a definite relationship between the Kilimanjaro Muali and the Shona Mwari. The similarity between the two concepts strengthens this assumption, since Mwari too, is primarily concerned with the fertility of crops and women. His interests in tribal and national politics derives from the time when the Rozvi had started exploiting the cult as a centralizing agency in an effort to consolidate their political control over their widely scattered vassals,[3] and also from the period when the oracular element was more fully developed in the Matopo hills near the present-day city of Bulawayo. As the God of the fertility of crops, Mwari is first and foremost regarded as the rain-giver. Political issues may sporadically, under the stress of circumstances, become the major topic of 'discussions' when delegations from many parts of the country visit the oracular shrines at Matonjeni, but to this day the messengers (*vanyai*) who move between their home districts and Matonjeni still regard the petition for rain as their main assignment. When they approach the caves of the oracle, they all use Mwari's most popular praise-name: *Dzivaguru*! (the Great Pool) which is directly associated with the idea of rain. As *Dzivaguru* or *Chidziva chopo* (the little pool that is always there) Mwari can be relied upon to provide the people with rain.[4] When this deity reveals His presence in the loud thunder-clap after a period of drought the Shona rejoice at the prospect of rain with the exclamation: *Dziva*! *Dzivaguru*!

2. Van der Merwe, 1957, pp. 2-5.
3. *Ibid*., p. 3.
4. The ritual centre at Matonjeni is especially known as *Mabweadziva* (rocks of the pool) which illustrates how closely Mwari's dwelling place is associated with a pool of water. In this case the *dziva* has the connotation of an everlasting supply of water.

The terms *Dziva*, *Mbuya* (grandmother) and *Zendere* (the name of the young woman who is regarded as Mwari's emanation) represent the feminine attributes of this deity, who is both male and female. As a male, He is *Sororezhou* (head of the elephant; and as such: father),[5] *Nyadenga* (Possessor of the sky) and *Wokumusoro* (the One above). The female is probably best represented in the symbolic identification with the pool, and rain-sustained fertility. In this form Mwari is the 'God from below'. But as the owner of the skies Mwari is also the male God of light, the Father of creation who manifests himself in lightning or in the shooting star from above.

As *Musiki* (from *kusika*: to create), *Musikavanhu* (Creator of mankind) and *Muvumbapasi* (Founder of the earth), all commonly used terms, the Supreme Being is indicated as the Creator.[6] Mwari as Creator is furthermore qualified in relation to His creation by some other interesting appellations: *Matangakugara* (You, who settled first) and *Mawanikwa* (You, who were found to exist), which makes Him the eternal and original Being, who existed before anything else. Generally the act of creation is only vaguely described, presumably because the Shona are not greatly interested in the original source of creation. What Tanner says of the Sukuma is also true of the Shona: 'Their speculation is confined to the causes of their present-day troubles and, in the absence of any need to consider creation in order to understand these immediate causes, they do not speculate about it.'[7] Contemporary Shona traditionalists would rather refer to the impressive rock formations in the country or to the Zimbabwe ruins as special manifestations of God's creation than elaborate on the 'how?' of God's initial activities.

The interpretative concept that emerges from the above-mentioned names is that of an ambivalent deity, both immanent and transcendent. Ever present in His creation He stands in direct relation to the life-giving water. His association with all things created evokes an almost pantheistic conception because a clear distinction between Him and His creation is not conceived. As Taylor puts it, 'no distinction can be made between sacred and secular, between natural and supernatural, for Nature, Man and the Unseen are inseparably involved in one another in a total community.'[8] The popular Shona saying: 'God is Spirit (Mweya); He is everywhere (*pose-pose*), even in the

5. Von Sicard, 1944, p. 150.

6. Van der Merwe, 1957, p. 8. The verb *kusika* basically means to make fire by rubbing two pieces of wood together. Van der Merwe therefore suggests that the Shona idea of creation seems to be that of producing something new by using something that had existed before.

7. Tanner, 1968, p. 7.

8. Taylor, 1963, p. 72.

wind that rustles the leaves', testifies to His involvement in the total community of things and living beings. It should be stressed, however, that this concept of an immanent deity coincides with the Shona's intuitive awareness of His presence rather than with a rational projection of the nature of His being. Mwari, in the final analysis, is not an 'abstract power' void of anthropomorphic attributes. His close association with the apex of the hierarchically structured world of human ancestors contributes towards His anthropomorphic character and makes of Him the transcendent but personal God, the One above. Had it not been for the oracular shrines He might have become as remote as some of the African High-Gods of whom Taylor writes, 'beginning in this world as part of the "human" hierarchy of the living and the ancestors, they the gods are eventually, as we might say, pushed through the skylight and lost sight of.'[9]

Mwari was not totally lost sight of but, in the composite picture of Shona traditional religion, He did become the Personal Being beyond and above the ancestral hierarchies and therefore could only be approached indirectly through the mediation of senior lineage ancestors (*mhondoro* or *varudzi*), or through the messengers who went to distant shrines to hear what Mwari had to say about the community as a whole. To the individual, who in private life had to depend on the family ancestors for his well-being, this God of fertility 'spoke' far off at Matonjeni; as *Wokumusoro* (the One above) He occasionally manifested Himself in lightning, clouds or the shooting star. Although this God was the recognized Power on which the whole of creation ultimately depended, and although He could retaliate strongly by striking with lightning or drought if people failed to keep His holy days (*chisi*), the belief in Him was rather the necessary prerequisite for the ancestral rituals conducted in the tribal communities than the inspiration for regular prayer by individuals. The average Shona person is content to accept the final authority of Mwari as the ultimate controller of the *midzimu* (ancestral spirits), to contribute to the prescribed annual fees which are forwarded to the cult shrines in order to procure from Mwari much needed rain; and to act on the advice of this God in times of national crises. But this suffices because the ancestors are felt to be much closer and can therefore be spiritually approached more effectively. Private petitions are therefore addressed to the family ancestors (*midzimu yapamusha*), who either transmit the pleas through the senior lineage ancestors to Mwari, or act upon them directly. Apart from the activities of the officially appointed Mwari messenger (*munyai*), whose task of collecting the gifts (*zvipo*) for Mwari inevitably

9. *Ibid.*, p. 85.

focuses the attention of the commoners on the High-God, Mwari comes into the daily life of the tribal community mostly upon the uttering of a special oath or invocation.[10] During traditional rituals in the family circle His name is hardly ever mentioned. Only during the annual rain rituals (*mikwerere*) will there be references to Mwari waMatonjeni, when the senior tribal spirit is asked to further the plea for rain, through 'those [ancestors] whose names have been forgotten', to the *great Mambo*[11] behind them. The use of the latter name, which was the prerogative of the Rozvi kings, hints at the close link believed to exist between Mwari and the royal ancestors. It is possible that some of Mwari's anthropomorphic attributes derive from those of the divine rulers of the Rozvi empire. This does not imply, however, that Mwari is a deified ancestor[12] but it does substantiate Cullen Young's assertion, that 'no approach to any appreciation of indigenous ideas regarding God can take any path but through the thought-area occupied by the ancestors.'[13]

What confronted the Christian missionaries of this century was a highly syncretized traditional concept of God. Early contact with the tribes of West Africa, of whom the Dogon, Ambo and Ashanti are known for their well developed High-God cults, may have contributed to the development among the Shona of a clearer concept of the Supreme Being than most of the Southern and Central African Bantu tribes have. Semitic, Islamic and early Catholic influences making themselves felt through trade relations with the East Coast as well as the 16th century missionary efforts, may also have had an influence on the concept of this High-God. Even so, there is very little evidence that extraneous ideas did in fact radically alter the indigenous conception.

Internal migratory and political factors rather than external and foreign influences served to mould the concept of this High-God. The Mbire God of fertility had attained additional female and sexual connotations through the influence of Tonga tribes in the Zambesi basin. Rozvi influence greatly stimulated the personification of this deity who became less remote through His interest in the political cohesion of His people. As the tribal spirits could be approached through their spirit mediums so this oracular God could eventually be consulted at His shrines. European presence in the country at first

10. Abraham in Stokes and Brown, 1966, p. 37.

11. In everyday life it is only a chief of high standing or a highly respected person who will be addressed as *Mambo*.

12. Bullock (1927, p. 38) correctly states that 'Mwari is not the deified spirit of some human progenitor – some remote ancestor.'

13. Young in Smith, 1950, p. 38.

turned Him into a militant God,[14] after which He attained, in addition to His rainmaking activities, His present role as the Protagonist of traditional law and culture.[15] As a conservative force He has become the final bulwark against foreign influence and His messages form the source of inspiration for the passive resistance to innovation which still characterizes the 'Shona way of life' in this modern era of acculturation.

The influence of Christianity upon the traditionalists and the continuation of traditional notions within the Shona Churches will be discussed later in more detail. At this stage it will suffice to consider that the missionaries' use of the term *Mwari* for the Biblical God has inevitably led to the transfer of a number of pre-Christian attributes to the Biblical God in the minds of many nominal and active Christians. On the other hand the idea of a personal God directly involved in everyday life has penetrated the community of non-Christians. It may reasonably be assumed that the recent revival of the High-God cult, and its central significance in the lives of those living in remote tribal areas, has indirectly been influenced by Christianity. Christ Himself is acknowledged by many traditionalists; yet, as Mediator, He is suitably fitted by some into the traditional pattern. This means that He is placed at the spiritual apex of a European ancestral hierarchy, in much the same way as Chaminuka, or one of the other popular tribal spirits at the top of a Shona hierarchy, represents numerous descendants in their relation to God. That the Christian concept, in addition to being fitted into the traditional pattern, also exerts its influence upon that pattern is best illustrated in the now common description of Mwari, by traditionalists, as *Mweya mutsvene*, the Holy Spirit. In this way the Shona concept of God has gained essentially new dimensions.

14. Ranger (in Stokes and Brown, 1966, p. 96) gives us an excellent account of the important role played by the Mwari cult officers as co-ordinators in the organization of the 1896-7 rebellions. He rightly asserts that they did not provoke the rebellions, but 'embodied and set the seal of ritual approval on the decision of the community as a whole. Their general involvement in the risings was in itself an indication of the total commitment of most of the traditional society to them.' The nature of the messages 'transmitted' by the High-God during the rebellions, comes out in the following command that He is reported to have given: 'They (the Europeans) killed your fathers, sent the locusts, caused this disease among the cattle and bewitched the clouds so that they have no rain. Now you will go and kill these white people and drive them out of our father's land and I (Mwari) will take away the cattle disease and the locusts and send you rain.' (Ranger, 1967, p. 148; with reference to Flemming: *Siege of Peking*, 1959, p. 35.)

15. For the nature of His present-day oracular messages concerning chieftain succession issues, and His emphasis on strict adherence to customary law, see Daneel, 1970, pp. 71-87

b) *Ritual and organization*

A number of permanently appointed cult officers, who live in the priest colonies near the main shrines at Matonjeni, are responsible for conducting regular ceremonies each year. Of these offices the hereditary high-priestly functions of the male and female *vapinzi vebasa* (lit: those who control the work) are the most important. These functions are performed by a brother and sister belonging to one of the main Mbire-Shoko lineages. They are assisted by a *muchengeti* (keeper or guardian of the shrines), a *mbonga-svikiro* (female 'child of God' dedicated to Him and acting within the cave as His 'Voice' during rituals) and a host of junior priests. The latter are the *mbonga* (females from all over the country who have been dedicated by their parents as 'wives' to Mwari) and *vaHosana*, the male 'children of God'.

The top functions belong to the members of the three interrelated clans, namely the Mbire priests, the Venda keepers and the Rozvi female *mbonga*. The relation between the priests and keepers is that of relative equality, the latter having become the priests' *vazukuru* (sister's children) through intermarriage. Subordinated to the priests are the Rozvi *mbonga* women who are often married to them.[16] Traces of the close ties between the Mbire and Rozvi tribes in the past are therefore still to be found at the cult's centre. At the priest colony itself the Rozvi women fall under the strict control of the Mbire priestesses. As imputed *vamwene* (wife-owners) of their brothers' wives, these women exert their authority over their *varoora* (sisters-in-law); a position which enables the senior priestess to influence the interpretation of the message spoken by Mwari in the cave, since the 'Voice' is preferably the wife of her eldest brother, the high priest. This ritual authority of the Mbire priests and priestesses is, however, not absolute. They greatly respect the 'Voice' who represents the age-old link between their own and the royal Rozvi tribe. Thus the Rozvi dominance of the past is not completely lost, because the majority of the more than 60 *mbonga* still living at Matonjeni are vaRozvi. As wives of the priests and keepers, these women on the one hand guarantee Rozvi continuity in the important office of *mbonga-svikiro*

16. Van der Merwe states that he had not come across any MuShona who supports Bullock's statement that the *mbonga* dedicated to Mwari waMatonjeni really become the wives of the officiating priests at the cult caves. (See Van der Merwe, 1957, p. 33; Bullock, 1927, p. 122.) Many of these women do in fact leave the cult centre when they are married, as Van der Merwe suggests, but at the Wirirani cult centre a number of *mbonga* no doubt become the recognized wives of priests and keepers. During my stay at Matonjeni in 1967, the acting 'Voice' of Mwari was a certain MaMoyo, a MuRozvi and *mbonga*-wife of the deceased high priest, Chokoto.

at the shrines, and on the other perpetuate the ancient and customary kinship pattern of mutual obligation and privilege between the priestly Mbire and the royal Rozvi, being representatives respectively of the wife-receiving and the wife-providing lineages of the ancient past.

Observed by an uninitiated observer in a tribal area like Gutu, some 250 miles away from the shrine, the influence of the cult seems to be limited to the sporadic visits of the local messenger (*munyai*) who reports back to the chief and headmen what Mwari has said at the caves. But an analysis of the messenger's present functions sheds some light on his obscure yet far-reaching influence. Most of the Mwari messengers belong to the chiefly lineages of their home districts; their appointment is determined by hereditary principles, a special calling from Mwari himself or the preference of the local chief. Vondo Mukozho, the present influential messenger of the Gutu district (see plate 1), traces his descent via Makuwaza and Chaurura to Mabwazhe, the recognized founding ancestor of the Rufura tribe.[17] As a kinsman of the local rulers, Vondo is regarded as a true representative of his district. Once officially installed, he became part of a seemingly disintegrated but in reality well-organized cult system, whose influence stretches over a very wide area. Simon Chokoto, the present-day high priest at Matonjeni, estimates that well over 40 messengers still annually visit the Wirirani shrine, which is only part of the Matonjeni complex of shrines. The majority come from the Southern Shona districts: Belingwe, Shabani, Chibi, Victoria, Gutu, Chilimanzi, Ndanga, Bikita (all of these districts falling in what one can culturally define as the Karanga-speaking block of Shona tribes); and also from further east, namely Melsetter and Chipinga in Ndau territory. Others come from districts north of Bulawayo, from the west as far as Plumtree, from Gwanda and further south from the Venda-inhabited territories, on both sides of the Limpopo river.

The task of a cult messenger includes the collection of gifts for Mwari throughout the entire district under his care. This is done in various ways. Sometimes the chief will call a meeting of *vachinda* (sub-chiefs and ward headmen) and order them to collect money from their kraalheads, or else, as in recent years, circular letters will be sent out to the different wards to inform sub-chiefs that the messenger will shortly visit them. Each kraalhead is supposed to collect a few pennies from the head of every homestead under his jurisdiction. The total sum per village is consequently quite low and often does not exceed 2/6, but Vondo assures me that the sum of money taken to Matonjeni on behalf of the whole district normally amounts to about

17. *Supra*, pp. 21-22.

£30. More important than the amount of money, which is primarily the evidence of a general recognition of Mwari as the 'owner of the land', is the regular contact between the messengers and the local ward headmen over such a wide area. On his rounds the messenger sometimes stays for several days in one ward, where he will visit traditionalist kraalheads, attend tribal court sessions and instruct people in the procedure of rain rituals. The latest messages from Matonjeni are thus conveyed to the widely dispersed population of a district through direct and personal contact which in African usage has always been the most effective form of communication. The messenger thus becomes one of the most important agents (next to the traditional *nganga* – diviner-herbalist) of keeping the traditional rituals operative and of giving the traditionalists a sense of unity beyond the tribal boundaries where they live.

Under normal circumstances the *munyai* undertakes two visits to Matonjeni per year: before the rainy season commences and after harvest time. Having visited the wards of his district, Vondo meets the chief and principal district *svikiro* (spirit medium) in September or October before the heavy rains start falling. Reference has already been made to this occasion[18] when the tribal ancestors must be 'shown' the presents collected by their descendants for Mwari. The messenger never leaves for Matonjeni before the spirit medium has assured him of the official approval and guidance of the tribal spirits. It is believed that the tribal spirits have already informed Mwari about the local state of affairs by the time the messenger arrives at Matonjeni. They are the main informants in the mystic background who keep Mwari abreast of the shortcomings of their living descendants. In turn Mwari tells the messenger at the shrine in what way the inhabitants of His district have 'sinned' and why He has retaliated by damaging personal property through lightning or by causing a prolonged drought. From the remote district a spiritual link with Mwari waMatonjeni is therefore established by the principal *svikiro* through his contact with one of the senior tribal spirits before the messenger's departure. But Mwari does not 'reply' through the tribal spirit. His reaction is heard only at the cult shrine.

Although the September-October visit of the *munyai* is not necessarily planned to coincide with the big annual rain ceremony at Matonjeni, it often does. In such a case the usual two days' stay in the priests' colony may be extended to allow the messenger to participate in the dancing and other festivities. On such occasions all the senior priests, *mbonga*, *vasvikiro*, *va-Hosana*, several *vanyai* and delegations from the Nganga Association, or

18. *Supra*, p. 41.

individual diviners and herbalists are present at the cult centre. Much *rukweza* (finger millet) beer, preferred by the tribal spirits, is brewed by *mbonga* who are past the child-bearing stage. Of the participants a great number are the official mediums of senior and junior tribal spirits (*mhondoro*), or *shavi* (alien) spirits. They need to 'feed the spirits' with *rukweza* beer, before these spirits 'come out' (*buda*) through the possession of their hosts during the dancing ceremonies. One or more black cows will be ritually slaughtered in honour of Mwari.[19] The climax of the proceedings lies in the approach to the Supreme Being when the delegations, representing the people from different parts of the country, are led by the ritual officiants to the cult caves to commune with Mwari.

The approach of the High-God on this occasion follows the same procedure as on any other, when a solitary cult messenger, diviner-herbalist or barren woman arrives at the cult centre requesting rain, curative powers or fertility. Requests are now presented on a massive scale, but they basically involve these three issues, which are regarded as Mwari's direct concern.[20] The delegates are taken to the shrines after sundown or just before sunrise. They take off their shoes before they approach the sacred cave (plate 2), clap their hands, ululate and intermittently call out Mwari's praise-names: '*Dziva*! *Mbedzi*! *Shoko*!' Once they have been officially welcomed by the Voice of the 'Unseen One', they sit down with their backs to the cave, facing eastwards.[21] The high priest, high priestess and keeper sit nearest to the mouth of the cave. All three act as interpreters but the initiative is taken by the high priestess who is best acquainted with the trance-like and high-pitched voice speaking in the ancient chiRozvi dialect from the cave. Having presented their gifts, which are placed at the mouth of the cave, delegates often enter into lengthy 'discussions' with the Voice through the interpreters. Some may procure a promise of good rains and successful harvests from Mwari, but it frequently happens that others are rebuked because their people neglected customary laws and traditional obligations. The High-God often complains about the educated young Africans (*vana vamabuku*: children of the books) who 'discard the customs of their fathers' (*rasha tsika dzamadzi-*

19. Black is the colour normally preferred by the ancestors. In this context a black cow may symbolize the black rain clouds which are sought from Mwari.

20. Mwari's concern with curative powers characterizes Him as the source of all dynamistic forces. His interest in the tribal political affairs of His people is still very real. He is well informed on the political development in distant districts and exerts a certain amount of influence on chieftain successions through the *vanyai*.

21. Informants tell me that this is done because Mwari originally arrived from the east (*mabvazuva*: where the sun comes from).

baba awo), and He blames European influence (*chirungu*) for this. He will send the visitors away with the final summons: 'Go and give the ancestors their cattle! Don't work on the third day of the week [His holy day in most districts]. Arrange the chieftainship according to seniority!'[22] In this way the conservative God sends His messengers and 'children' back to advise their people in the outlying home districts. As the preserver of tradition He expects them to fulfil their customary obligations to His subordinate but demanding spirits further afield.

During the whole ceremony at the cave the high priestess is regarded as being nearest to Mwari. In her ritual capacity she is called *mbuya venyika* ('grandmother of the country') and the mother of all people because, for a brief spell, she is then the 'wife' of Mwari. As such she temporarily assumes command over her brother, the high priest, to whom she is usually subordinate. Another outstanding feature of the oracular session is the complete identification of the medium (the 'Voice') in the cave with Mwari himself. Hers is a secretive office and the priests take care to impress upon the people that it is God Himself (*ndiye Mwari*!) speaking from the cave. Even if one should press them with questions regarding the role of the *mbonga-svikiro*, who should not be seen entering the cave during the ritual, it becomes evident that for the duration of the ceremony, God and medium assume a single and indivisible identity. A common characteristic in the pattern of Shona symbolic representation is that, at certain stages of the ritual process, the representative symbol (human being, animal or inanimate object) becomes the personification of the spirit-being or the power so represented, and is addressed and treated as if the latter were a living reality.

Mwari waMatonjeni has remained the God of many rural, that is tribal, people. To those living at an essentially subsistence level, dependent on a rain-giving God for their crops, and those involved in the intrigues of tribal politics, the God of Matonjeni is still a power that counts. In Chingombe and the other Gutu chiefdoms the gifts for Mwari waMatonjeni are still regularly collected by the kraalheads. The messenger, Vondo, goes about his duties with conviction and personal zeal. His devotion to his task, combined with his persuasive personality, in all probability contributed to a resurgence of the cult's influence in the Gutu area in recent years. That Mwari's instructions were obeyed without protest throughout the whole district in 1966 – He wanted a change of *chisi* ('holy' day) from Thursday to Wednesday,[23] and He

22. In Shona: '*Endai mundopa midzimu ngombe yavo*! *Musabata nezuva reChitatu*! *Fambisai ushe noukuru*!'

23. These 'holy' days are kept in honour of the tutelary spirits of the different tribes.

gave advice in the latest dispute about the succession to the Gutu chieftainship[24] – proves that He is still regarded by many rural people as a major power.

In the bustle of town life the need for this God is felt less and although townsmen generally know about this deity they often remark: 'Mwari waMatonjeni is the God of the *vakuru* [old people] in the tribal lands'. It now seldom happens that a woman travels from the Mucheke township at Fort Victoria to Matonjeni in search of *chibereko* (lit. 'fruit', i.e. child-bearing power), something which, townsmen recollect, used to be common in the past. An organized system of 'messengers' does not exist in this urban community. Yet it should be noted that the rising popularity of the 'Nganga Association' (Herbalist Association of Africa) has led to the sending of *nganga* delegations from nearly all the Rhodesian towns to the annual meetings at Bulawayo, close to the Matopos and its Mwari shrines. In Fort Victoria alone there are at least six acknowledged members of this Association who are in contact with their senior officials at Bulawayo. Judging from a recent newspaper report individual journeys of *nganga* to Matonjeni are now being replaced by delegations of the Association sent to ask Mwari for the powers of healing. Of the ritual ceremonies at Matonjeni in 1967 it is stated that 'members of the Nyanga Association had played an important part throughout the ceremony... They had reported their work which was welcomed, and were promised healing powers. The Nganga delegation was led by the Association's president, Mr. M. C. Chakari.'[25] In this way a new and indirect kind of presentation of Mwari's powers for townspeople is possibly taking shape. The influence of the urban *nganga* as 'revivalists' of the traditional religion is considerable. To them the God of Matonjeni is in the first place the 'owner' of curative power and it is mainly in this role that they present Him to urban dwellers.

2. THE SPIRIT WORLD

In the Shona spirit world one can distinguish three main categories. These are the *midzimu* (sing. *mu-*), ancestral spirits; the *shavi*, alien spirits that do

Acceptance of Mwari's orders to change *chisi* from Thursday to Wednesday points at the general recognition of His overriding powers and authority in the spirit world. It also reflects the assumption that Mwari has already arranged matters with those tribal ancestors near to Him.

24. Mwari's involvement in the chieftain succession issue is discussed in Daneel, 1970, pp. 71f.

25. *The Chronicle*, 23rd October, 1967.

not belong to the same clan, tribe or ethnic group as their hosts; and the *ngozi* or avenging spirits. These different types of spirits often co-operate, and in certain situations may be interdependent for the fulfilment of their tasks. Each of these categories will have to be considered separately:

a) *The ancestral spirits* (*midzimu*)

i) *Their nature and powers*

When a Shona is asked, 'Which of your *midzimu* is responsible for your well-being?', he will invariably reply: '*Ndinochengetwa navabereki vangu chete-chete*', i.e. 'I am looked after only by those who have borne me.' The parents referred to are the *midzimu yapamusha* (home ancestors), and include a person's deceased father (*baba*), mother (*maï*), and paternal grandparents (*tateguru* and *mbuya*). These four ancestors are directly concerned with the welfare of all the members of one's household. The spirit of a woman's mother or of her maternal grandmother is believed to have a direct influence upon her procreative powers; the *vatete* (paternal aunt), again, can interfere with the child-bearing capacity of her brother's daughters. The spirits of both the matri- and patrilines are therefore involved in the most vital affairs of the family unit. As far as the guardianship of the family is concerned, the spirit of the paternal grandfather (*sekuru*, or commonly referred to as *tateguru*), and of the deceased father, play the most important roles. 'Above' these 'home ancestors' in the ancestral hierarchy, a senior ancestor, mostly a male, fulfils the function of guardian in the wider sense of the word. This male ancestor guards over the members of a number of houses (*dzimba*). To the Rufura and Hera kinsmen in Chingombe, the senior guardian spirits are undoubtedly Rutsate and Mheresi. Since these spirits are usually two to three generations removed from the living, their deceased sons and grandsons in the course of time take over their protective function. Members of the families who rely on these guardian spirits often call them *sekuru*, without further differentiation. It is customary for this spirit to be represented amongst his living descendants by a male or female medium.

Strictly speaking both of the above-mentioned types of spirit fall under the 'home ancestor' category, because of their presupposed preoccupation with the different units of their living descendants; but the senior lineage ancestors stand in a more direct relationship to the tribal ancestors (the *mhondoro* or *marudzi*). This alliance is brought about by the gradual change in function of the *sekuru* guardian as his descendants increase and, through the segmentation principle, are divided into an increasing number of 'houses'. When the junior spirits have completely taken over his function, the guardian spirit himself moves up in the hierarchy of known ancestors and may in time become a *mhondoro*[26] (tribal spirit) himself. The less prominent tribal spirits are closely associated with the progenitor (*musikarudzi*) of the dominant lineage which constitutes political unity in the territory concerned.[27] In contrast to the family ancestors the tribal ancestors are concerned with the welfare of the tribal community as a whole. Their main task is to act as mediators between the tribal community and Mwari, usually when rain is needed. The most senior of the tribal *mhondoro* are the *mhondoro vematenga* (*mhondoro* of the skies). Kumbirai, a Shona Catholic priest and specialist on Shona traditional religion, suggests that the '*mhondoro* of the skies' get their orders directly from Mwari and that each of them has the boundaries of the area under his care fixed by Mwari. Within these boundaries, which may comprise several chiefdoms and administrative districts, the sky-*mhondoro* acts as a rain spirit. To this category belong the well-known spirits as Nehanda, Chaminuka, Nyakasikana and Kaguwe.[28] The exact identity of these *mhondoro* is often not known and, because of their multi-tribal significance, some of the Shona people refer to them as the '*midzimu mikuru isina mutupo*' (the senior ancestors without a totem or clan name). Should such a spirit 'come out' (*buda*) in a local medium, it often refuses to reveal its real identity to the participants of a ritual ceremony, with the suggestion that they would not know him in any case. Since the territorial scope of the sky-*mhondoro* is much bigger than that of the ordinary tribal spirits, he is not represented by a spirit medium in all his districts, with the result that the inhabitants of some districts such as Gutu, are mainly concerned with their own tribal spirits. It should also be noted that the tribal spirits can remain 'silent' for many years after their officially recognized mediums have died. Periods may therefore occur in a chiefdom during which not a single *mhondoro* is officially represented. On the other hand it can happen that several *mhondoro* spirits are operative through their hosts in one chiefdom during the same period.

26. This term is used both in the singular and the plural.

27. The Hera *mhondoro* are directly associated with Nyashanu and the Rufura *mhondoro* (or *marudzi*) with Mabwazhe. In Chingombe both the terms *mhondoro* and *marudzi* are rarely used. Tribal spirits are commonly referred to as *midzimu mikuru yorudzi* (senior ancestors of the tribe).

28. Kumbirai, Unpublished Manuscript on Shona Religion. These spirits, especially Chaminuka, have in the course of time attained a position of multi-tribal significance. Chaminuka has had *masvikiro* acting as his hosts in various parts of the country. His spirit's claim to the ownership of large areas in Mashonaland fits the ideology of African nationalist politicians. They urged the ruralists to appeal to Chaminuka in their struggle for more land, a trend which may become more manifest as the political strife intensifies.

Thus we find a well differentiated spiritual hierarchy. It is the extension of the Shona lineage (*rudzi*) which, as a continuing entity, embraces the dead, the living and the yet unborn members. Hence the structure of the (ancestor) spirit world is the same as that of the living, with the principles of super and subordination, mutual interaction and obligations, already mentioned in connection with kinship organization, also applying to this realm. At the base of the structured, ancestral hierarchy are the agnatic and other cognatic 'home ancestors' whose close ties with their living relatives are expressed in the terms '*vari pedo nesu* – they are near to us'. Above these spirits the deceased paternal lineage members, whose names are remembered by their descendants, form a unity of several generations deep. The guardian spirits of the families are to be found amongst the seniors of the remembered ancestors. Although such spirits are further removed in time than the recently deceased persons of the family concerned, they are also in a 'relationship of nearness' (*ukama uri pedo*) to their living members. The distant ancestors whose relationship to the family is described as *kure* (far-off) belong to other houses of the same lineage or to the category of apical tribal ancestors. Far or near in the spiritual hierarchy therefore suggests genealogical rather than physical distance. A distant relationship (*ukama uri kure*) may indicate cognatic ties with ancestors who are not directly involved, and are therefore not mentioned by name during family rituals. During family rituals concerning the agnatic ancestors, the names of all the male *midzimu* of the first three ascending generations up to the guardian *sekuru* may be mentioned, with a final request that the specific plea be passed on to the known and unknown ancestors 'behind' them. It is only during the rain rituals that all the prominent ancestors are mentioned. On this occasion Mwari waMatonjeni may also be mentioned as the One to whom the request for rain should ultimately be directed.

As has been mentioned, Mwari, as the owner of the whole creation, is the source of the power wielded by the ancestors. The tribal spirits are nearest to Him and therefore communicate directly with Him on matters of a communal nature. Private affairs may be submitted to Mwari by the 'home ancestors' who pass the petition through the whole hierarchy of spirits. As such the ancestors fulfil the essential function of mediation. On the whole, however, the *midzimu* have *simba guru* (great power) and, when properly propitiated, they themselves meet the needs of their living descendants: the agnatic spirits acting specifically as protectors of the family and the maternal spirits safeguarding the procreative powers of its female members. The obligation of the living relatives of their nearest family ancestors is to remember and honour them according to kinship norms. They even have to perform a special rite to assist the spirit of the deceased relative to attain full ancestorhood. In return they expect to be protected by their father and mother-group of ancestors against the evils and misfortunes of life. This protective task is the most outstanding of all the family *mudzimu's* benevolent functions. Nearly all the Shona believe that the home ancestors protect the family (*midzimu yapamusha inorinda mhuri*). In fulfilling this essential task the ancestors are believed to assist a person in the enterprises of everyday life, such as obtaining a good job, getting married, having children, etc. But all these benefits derive from the basic protection offered by the ancestors 'at the doors' of the houses of their descendants. At night, when evil spirits and witches operate, the protecting ancestors are believed to stand at the door (*mira pamukova*), where they ward off these forces.

Once the anger of the *midzimu* is aroused by the neglect of their living descendants, they are capable of unleashing destructive powers on one or several members of the family concerned. The Shona say that their ancestors can kill (*uraya*), hurt (*rwadza*) and be troublesome (*kunetsa* or *kutambudza*). These are the key terms used to indicate the manifestations of the ancestors' anger. Kumbirai suggests that it is the maternal spirits that are regarded as the most dangerous. He says: 'If the mother's *mudzimu* wants to kill somebody, nobody can stop her . . . If an ancestral spirit has caused death in the family, it is always that of the *mai* . . .' The patrilineal ancestors afflict but they do not kill. They say: 'We do not kill our own children, but our wives kill because they do not belong to our family.'[29] On the other hand, Gelfand states of a Southern Shona tribe that 'sickness may be caused by spirits on the maternal side although it is not as common as on the paternal side.'[30] In Chingombe the general consensus is that both the matrilineal and patrilineal ancestors can cause death, but this is hardly ever thought of as a direct act of the *midzimu* themselves. It is a matter of deliberately withdrawing their protective powers, to expose the members of their forgetful families to the evil powers of the *vavengi* (enemies), rather than of just killing their living descendants. The most frequent reply about the cause of illness, death or other misfortunes is that the 'ancestral spirit was offended and consequently opened the door (*mudzimu washatirwa nokuzarura mukova*)'. To forfeit the protective powers of the *midzimu* means facing the inevitable destruction of the family, or at least the death of several of its members. So there is a strong incentive to maintain or regain the goodwill of the ancestral spirits.

Basically the *midzimu* have the power to protect (*kurinda*) and to kill (*uraya*). The resilience of the belief in these powers, in spite of the far-reaching

29. Kumbirai, Manuscript and personal communication, 1967.
30. Gelfand, 1966, p. 60.

impact of Christianity, can be gauged from the answers of Africans in both the rural and urban areas. In Chingombe 77%, and in Fort Victoria 71% of the interviewed adults stated that they believed the ancestors to have protective powers over their living descendants. The belief in their ability to kill is just as strong (82% of the Chingombe ruralists and 78% of the townsmen – tables 21 and 22). That there is hardly any difference between the rural and urban area on this point is not so surprising in the light of the constant flow of labour migrants between the two areas. Christian beliefs about the concern of a personal God in the lives of individuals may have started to supplant the ingrained belief in the protective powers of the ancestors but it is clear from the above-mentioned figures that the belief in the destructive powers of the ancestors is still a dominant reality in the lives of most of the Shona people. The persistence of these beliefs seems all the more remarkable if it is considered that more than 80% of the total adult community in Chingombe claim to be nominally if not actively affiliated to one of the Mission or Independent Churches. As long as these basic beliefs remain, propitiatory rites will continue to take place, even though the incidence of such ceremonies may be reduced to intermittent family crises.

There are various ways in which a person becomes a *mudzimu*. During this life every person already has a spirit, but it is often regarded as being only latent because his grandfather's spirit is operating in him. His own spirit only achieves a separate and independent identity after death. As Holleman says of the North Eastern Shona, the personal soul is potentially there as long as a person is alive, but it cannot 'come out' (*buda*) and reveal itself. 'Until a man dies it is therefore the spirit of his *sekuru* (and not his own) that may be active . . . When death occurs the personal spirit gets its own identity, separate from the *sekuru's* spirit.'[31] If this is generally true for the Shona, it follows that for them the *mudzimu* of a living person is only a potential entity which cannot be identified with his own individuality or his own conscious ego.[32]

31. Holleman, 1953, pp. 27-28.

32. Murphree (1969, p. 33) disagrees with Holleman's analysis which regards the *mudzimu* as incarnate within a person during his lifetime and as 'coming out' (*kubuda*) of the body after death. The *mudzimu*, he argues, does in fact come into existence at the time of a person's birth, yet 'it is not incarnate within him, but as it were, a separate "shadow" existence beside him.' Instead of having spatial connotations, as Holleman seems to infer, the term *kubuda* (to come out) according to Murphree rather has revelational connotations which means that a man's spirit 'comes out' in the sense of revealing itself as an independent entity and not by way of dislodgement from the deceased's body. This line of argumentation seems perfectly logical if Murphree's basic assertion that the *mudzimu* exists as a separate shadow next to the individual during life is accepted. Yet, as he himself admits, the *locus* of the *mudzimu* is not the object of precise

A person's spirit only obtains its full identity and independent existence within the ancestral hierarchy when the necessary rituals have taken place after death. On the other hand the notion that every living human being has a small white shadow (*bvute* or *mvuri*) and a large black shadow that represent his person (*munhu*) and physical stature (*muviri*) respectively, is widespread amongst the majority of Shona tribes. The small white shadow can be regarded as identical with the embryonic '*mudzimu*' during life, because it is this being which actually becomes the *mudzimu* after death. Sometimes this distinction is not made and people will merely refer to a person's 'shadow', without any further qualification. When death occurs the white shadow immediately departs from the body and hovers as a spirit (*mweya*) – but not yet as *mudzimu* proper – near the grave. Although the *mweya* has not yet attained full spiritual ancestorhood at this stage it is the continuation of the deceased's spiritual force, which had become mysteriously powerful the moment it dislodged itself from the body. It remains near the grave for some time to satisfy itself that the relatives are taking the necessary precautions against witchcraft. During this period it may also appear to relatives in dreams to inform them about the cause of death, or to instruct them in connection with some outstanding obligations that must still be fulfilled. Then a period ensues during which the spirit just wanders around desolately in the bush (*dondo*). People say: 'The spirit simply stays and wanders around in the bush (*mweya unongogara uchifamba mudondo*)' – which is a way of stating that the spirit has not yet achieved its full status through inauguration into the spiritual hierarchy of its lineage.

In the meantime the deceased's *mweya* might reveal him or herself in the form of an animal in the vicinity of the home village or grave. Kumbirai suggests that the spirit of the deceased must of necessity grow into some living animal and he traces the origin of the *mutupo* (clan name) back to the progenitors of the tribes, whose spirits were believed to have grown into the animals which in time became the totem of the clan and therefore taboo to their descendants. The black shadow is supposed to come out of the dead person's head in the form of a little worm (*chikonye*). It is breathed upon by the

---

definition on the part of the Budjga. On the basis of the information acquired from the Southern Shona, it seems to me that one cannot qualify the latently existent *mudzimu* as being 'inside' or 'next to' the living person's body. It is only after death when the induction rite (*kugadzira*) is performed, that the deceased's *mweya* (spirit) achieves full ancestorhood and thereby becomes *mudzimu*. The term *kubuda* in this context has in fact both spatial and revelational connotations: at death the deceased's spirit 'comes out' of his body or simply leaves it, and afterwards – both before and after its transformation into a real *mudzimu* – it is capable of 'coming out' (in the sense of appearing from its new domain) in order to reveal the deceased's wishes to his or her living descendants.

white shadow, and then grows into a spotted lion (also called *mhondoro*), leopard, battaleur eagle (*chapungu*) or some other animal. The black and white colours of these '*mudzimu*-animals' symbolically represent the black and white shadows, in other words the complete psycho-somatic essence of the deceased. At present, however, this belief is no longer very common. In Chingombe it is primarily the spirits of distinguished persons, e.g. a reputed rainmaker or a distinguished diviner-herbalist who are still believed to reveal themselves occasionally in the form of animals or birds.

Having roamed about in the *dondo* (bush) for about six to twelve months or longer, the *mweya* (spirit) is officially 'brought back home' by its living descendants.[33] The ritual activities of this occasion signifies the formal introduction of the wandering spirit into the ranks of the family ancestors. Full ancestorhood thus being attained, the *mudzimu* is now endowed with its full powers to protect or harm. Propitiatory rites cannot be effective before the 'home-bringing' ceremony has taken place. The latter remains the key ritual and prerequisite to all subsequent forms of 'ancestor worship'. The roles played by kinsmen and others during such 'home-bringing' rituals will be discussed below.

Since social maturity in everyday life depends on marriage, full ancestorhood can only be achieved by a deceased who has been married. 'Home-bringing' ceremonies are not conducted for the spirits of the unmarried dead. They are relatively unimportant unless they *pfuka* (turn against someone) and return as avenging spirits to demand retribution from those who had unduly wronged or harmed them in life. In such cases propitiatory rites, resembling *ngozi* rituals (see below) are performed.

Ideas about the habitat of the ancestors vary considerably. Many people think of them simply as 'being with God – *paMwari*'. Traditionally *paMwari* would probably have indicated the state of the deceased as being 'closer to' God than to the living, but Christian influence seems to have strengthened the notion of being specifically 'with God'. At the same time the ancestors, as guardians of their families, are near the homesteads of their kith and kin. During the daytime they will occasionally reveal their presence in the tree leaves rustling in the wind, but they normally dwell in the 'wards [i.e. places] without water' (*matunhu asina mvura*) until the sun sets and they draw nearer home to protect their relatives. That is why spirit-possession or the ritual communication with the ancestors mostly takes place late in the afternoon, at night or early in the morning. When a *mudzimu* 'comes out' in a spirit medium, it receives water for drinking and washing, because of its journey from the

33. See the *Kugadzira* ritual below, pp. 104f.

'dry places'. If delayed through ritual until the late morning, it will complain to the participant relatives that its fellow-*midzimu* are already on their way to their distant abode. In addition, the ancestors can also be conceived of as being inside a person, for male and female *vazukuru* (grandchildren) can all 'have' the spirit of their *sekuru* or *sekuru's* sister respectively. A spirit can therefore be with God, in a dry ward (or place), at home or within several grandchildren, depending on time and circumstances.

The dead communicate with the living through dreams, or by causing illness and misfortune. In the case of dreams the interpretation of the *nganga* need not necessarily be sought because the ancestor's wish may be clear enough; but when serious illness befalls a person or when inexplicable misfortunes come his way, he is likely to consult a *nganga*. Should a *sekuru* or *baba* ancestor visit a person in a dream, it is experienced as a real encounter between the dream-soul of the sleeper and the spirit. Guidance about general conduct, medical advice and instructions for a new venture may be given. Complaints about the reluctance of the sleeper to meet the needs of the ancestor for a *jira* (blanket), a *ngombe* (ox), *gono* (bull) or beer, may also be vented. Thus, on the one hand, service is offered by the ancestor while, on the other, demands are made; demands that are legally valid between kinsmen.

Whenever a *nganga* diagnoses the cause of illness or misfortune he or she usually works according to a more or less standardized pattern of possibilities. The major objective is to find out which spirits may have caused the affliction and to prescribe the ritual measures that should appease the angered spirit. If, for example, barrenness is divined to be caused by one of the maternal spirits 'gripping the womb' (*kubata pamimba*) of the unfortunate woman, the prescription invariably includes the suggestion that her husband supply the in-laws as soon as possible with a *ngombe youmai* or *imbwazukuru* for propitiatory purposes.[34] Or if a man is repeatedly sacked from his job the *nganga* may say: 'The spirit of your deceased father is angry because his home-bringing ceremony is long overdue. He says that he will cause his son to be in the bush [be without a job] just as he himself is wandering in the bush without a home. You will have to go and *gadzira* [accommodate] your father!' Any kind of misfortune can also be caused by the *tateguru* (paternal grandfather) who wants a bull to be dedicated to him, or an already dedicated bull to be slaughtered in his honour. All these, and other possibilities, are well known but commoners need the authoritative interpretation and diagnosis of a diviner before rites of an extensive nature are undertaken. Thus the *nganga* becomes one of the most important activating forces behind the practice of traditional religion.

34. *Supra*, p. 48.

Another way of communicating with the living is for the ancestor to select a medium (*svikiro*) amongst the living descendants. A male *mudzimu* selects either a male or a female, but a female hardly ever selects a male medium. Female mediums are far more numerous than males, partly because of the effort of women to rise above their normally subordinate social positions. Once a woman becomes a recognized medium of one of the distinguished spirits of her own lineage she is entitled to certain privileges otherwise beyond her reach. When she is in a state of possession her husband has to address her as 'father-in-law'. As medium of his *tezvara*, she is identified as such. In everyday life she has a privileged position and need not perform certain feminine duties; she is entitled, for instance, to refuse her husband's sexual advances if she prefers to do so, and she is hardly ever beaten by him, lest the spirit she represents retaliate with punitive action.

A long-drawn-out illness is often a sign that an ancestor wants to 'come out' in the person whom he or she has selected as future medium. A *nganga* diagnoses the cause, and advises the family members to arrange for an initial installation ceremony, with sufficient finger millet (*rukweza*) beer. On this occasion beer is 'offered' (*kupira* or *kusuma*) to the ancestor concerned, once it has made known its presence through the shaking of the body and grunting noises of the new medium. In a state of possession, the medium's personality is temporarily suspended and he or she 'is' the *sekuru*, or whichever spirit is being represented. The *mudzimu* is now questioned by his or her relatives, and in this manner the dead advise their descendants on family matters and future rituals. If the possessing ancestor has a particular animal in which it manifests itself, it may warn the family members in the house to keep the children inside, since its *mhuka* (wild animal) is waiting nearby in the bush.

After the first ceremony, several others follow, such as the 'beer of acceptance' (*doro rokubvuma*) party, when the new medium's husband officially welcomes the spirit into his household, or the killing of the first sacrificial beast for the visiting spirit. On this latter occasion the *svikiro* must drink the raw blood of the beast or eat the raw liver as the sign of his/her authority. A true medium will perform this feat without vomiting, because he or she *is* the *mudzimu* or the '*mudzimu*-animal' itself, that drinks the blood or eats the liver. Kumbirai gives a realistic explanation of this act. He says that the '*mudzimu*-animal', as soon as it has consumed the blood or liver, is believed to return to the bush where it shares the 'food' with the lesser *midzimu* who do not participate in social life. 'It vomits the blood in the bush and the little *midzimu* dash for it.'[35] Some mediums repeat this act whenever a sacrificial beast is slaughtered for the particular ancestor. Once the medium is officially recognized, he or she retains this function for life and the family is provided with a direct 'channel of communication'. If the medium is frequently consulted, the association between her/him and the ancestral spirit becomes so real that she/he is identified with the *mudzimu* represented whether in a state of possession or not. Frequent consultations lead to a limitation of the ritual activity preceding the 'coming out' of the spirit. In contrast to the initial prolonged spells of dancing, drumming and feasting, the mere donning of the *mudzimu's* apparel or the shaking of the rattle causes the spirit to put in an appearance.

The reason why the Shona, like Africans elsewhere in Africa, literally live with their ancestors, is that the ancestral cult somehow meets the need for survival that lies deep down in human nature. The community of the unborn, the living and the deceased, has to be perpetuated, and in order to achieve this objective the inner unity between the ranks of the living and the deceased must be maintained. The ancestors are regarded as the guardians of this inner unity. They take action as soon as this unity is disrupted, and in this way they provide the supporting sanction behind the code for proper conduct woven into the kinship system. In the case of a family conflict the *sekuru* guardian spirit will protest against backbiting or any other sinful act indulged in by the members of the opposing parties within the family. He may reveal an internal family quarrel as the reason why he causes illness among the members of the family. Thus the ancestors uphold a set of moral imperatives, the observance of which is important for an ordered society. Their authority is binding. Due to their mystical powers they should not be opposed by the living, and there is little else one can do to safeguard his future existence than to follow the directions of the ancestors. Because of the reciprocity of the relationship between the living and the dead the effectiveness of the ancestors' protective powers is conditioned by the loyalty of their living descendants. Consequently the unpardonable sins which provoke the anger (*kutsamwisa*) of the ancestors are *neglect* and *forgetfulness*. Their wrath can turn them into dangerous tormentors, which adds to the relationship of dependence, the element of fear.

ii) *Propitiatory rites*

The kugadzira ritual. The *kugadzira* is the most important and the most elaborately organized of all the Shona post mortem rituals. Derived from the term *gadza* (settle or repair), *kugadzira* in this context means to 'settle the spirit of the deceased' or 'to put the deceased's spirit to rest'. Amongst the

35. Kumbirai, Unpublished Manuscript.

North-Eastern Shona this ritual is called *bona* (from *kupona*: to give or sustain life), which implies that the ritual action 'gives birth to a new spiritual being' in that it acquires full ancestorhood. A parallel ceremony in Central Mashonaland is called *kurova guva*, which literally means 'to hit the grave'.

The purpose of the ritual is to accommodate the wandering spirit of the deceased (which up to this moment remains an uninitiated 'outsider') into the spiritual hierarchy of his or her lineage. His formal induction into the family ranks, which implies the elevation of the spirit to full ancestorhood, should be ceremoniously accompanied by the spirit's living relatives and other ritual participants. If this ritual is not performed, the spirit remains 'outside' (*panze*) without officially recognized status; an incomplete spiritual being whose name is not mentioned during family rituals. The incentive to conduct the ritual is strong because of the common belief that a spiritual being, left out in the veld (*dondo*) too long, will turn his or her destructive powers against the kinsmen responsible for the ceremony or against some other close relatives. In this state it is a potential and unpredictable danger to its close relatives. Practical family considerations also necessitate this ritual because on this occasion the senior son, if the deceased was a married male, officially succeeds to the position of head of the family, while the position of the surviving wife (or wives) is decided upon and the possessions of the deceased are distributed.

Originally the *kugadzira* was conducted 6 to 12 months after a person's death, but people nowadays often delay the ritual until the misfortune or illness of one of the family members is diagnosed by a *nganga* to be an indication of the deceased's wish to 'come home'. It seems as if this has become a popular diagnosis of *nganga* in town. Quite a number of *kugadzira* rituals held in Chingombe in 1966-1967 were requested by adults who had failed to adapt themselves to the urban environment, who had lost their jobs or become ill, and who were subsequently told by diviners that they had to return home to *gadzira* a deceased father or mother who had caused the unfortunate events. Serious conflicts amongst members of a family without an officially (i.e. ritually) instated family head, or indirect affliction by other ancestors such as can happen when a mother's *mudzimu* starts 'hurting' her own daughter, if, for instance, her deceased son had not repaid the cattle he owed her before his death, also call for the *kugadzira* ritual. The afflicted daughter, in the latter case, then requests her own relatives to prepare the *kugadzira* ritual, because she can only claim the outstanding cattle on behalf of her mother's *mudzimu* when the senior son of her deceased brother is instated as head of the family and in that capacity is obliged to settle the matter.

During ritual procedure a wide range of relatives of the deceased are obliged

1. *Munyai* Vondo Mukozho of the Gutu district discusses his trip to the Matonjeni cult caves with his father.

2. Cave entrance at the Wirirani shrine – Matonjeni.

3. *Kugadzira*. Final address of the home-coming spirit by the officiating *muzukuru*, who stands with beer pot in hand on the grave.

4. *Kugadzira*. Imitated sexual action on grave, which symbolizes the life-force of the deceased male.

5. *Kugadzira*. Jubilant dance of woman who 'accompanies' the spirit of her deceased relative back home, after the grave ceremony.

6. *Kugadzira*. Name-giving ceremony; seated on a reed mat the deceased's name-bearer (senior son) accepts the tokens of recognition from members of the family, while the senior *muzukuru* (with hat) closely observes the proceedings.

7. Lament of *Vatete* Marinzepi while she dedicates the finger millet (*rukweza*) to the Hera tribal ancestors in preparation of a *mukwerere* ritual

to attend and participate in the ceremonial activities. They are the agnates, members of the deceased's paternal kin; the *vazukuru*, especially uterine cousins or nephews (i.e. the children of daughters, sisters or father's sisters); the *vakuwasha* (sons-in-law), the husbands of daughters, sisters or father's sisters, and the *varoora*, i.e. daughters-in-law, including the wives of the *vazukuru*.

The preparations for the ritual are undertaken by the agnates, who provide their *varoora* (daughters-in-law) with the necessary finger millet to prepare the sacrificial beer (*doro rokugadzira*). When all the relatives and visitors have arrived at the village of the deceased, the proceedings are opened with the slaughtering of a goat and the 'showing' of the brewed beer to the ritual officiant. The closest senior relatives of the deceased all congregate in the hut where the beer is kept, and the *vatete* (the deceased male's elder sister who acts as ritual officiant and in the ritual context is generally addressed as '*vatete*' by the deceased's kinsmen), or the deceased's father, brother, or brother's son, if the deceased is a female, briefly tells the spirit that the ritual is about to start: 'Today, So-and-so, we are bringing you back to your home where the others are. This is your beer . . . Come back and look after your children!' Meanwhile the *vakuwasha*, directed by the senior amongst them, kill a sacrificial beast, usually an ox, of which part of the breast and intestines is set apart as a special offering to the spirit. Normally the master of ceremonies is the senior *muzukuru* (deceased's sister's oldest son), to whom special respect is shown, due to the cordial relation that existed between him and the deceased. He tells the dead man's *vakuwasha* when to distribute the meat and beer to the participants and remains generally in charge of the procedures.

Once the three-day ritual has started the sequence of events may follow different patterns, but there are at least five discernable stages that form an integral part of the *kugadzira* ritual. These are: (i) a visit to the *nganga* to find out if the offerings are favourably received; (ii) the 'bringing home' of the spirit from the grave; (iii) the succession to the deceased's name; (iv) the central *kupira* ('worship') ceremony in the hut of the deceased, and (v) disposal of his inheritable wives and property (*kugova nhaka*). We will briefly consider each stage.

The illustrations given below to indicate the nature of procedure generally, or to clarify some of the significant differences between ceremonies concerning deceased males and females, respectively, are based on two rituals which I have observed in Chingombe, in 1966. One of these concerned the 'bringing home' of *Mai* P.'s (mother of P.'s) spirit at her husband's village, P. being a labour migrant who had returned from Salisbury to help 'put his mother's spirit to rest'. Her restless spirit was believed to be the cause of P.'s fruitless efforts to find a proper job in the urban environment, the protracted illness of his children and the strife between other members of the family. The second ritual concerned the dissatisfied spirit of R., a deceased male who, through afflicting his children and grandchildren, made known his wish to be *gadzwa'd*.

i) One or more delegations, consisting of the closest kin of the deceased, are sent out to distant *nganga*. Nowadays a popular practice is to send such delegates to traditional diviners as well as prophets of the Spirit-type Independent Churches and then to compare the information. It is essential that the spirit of the deceased should make known its acceptance of the offerings that were shown to him or her during the opening ceremony. Special wishes of the spirit are revealed to the spirit's relatives through divination and the causation of death may be dealt with in full, especially if it had not been done properly shortly after death. Such an errand may take a full day. When the delegates return they are given the *shope-shope* (derived from *kushopera*: to divine) pot of beer to quench their thirst. Then they report on the outcome of their mission to the agnates who meet in one of the huts while the visitors carry on with the feasting outside. The reports are followed by intermittent discussions between the close relatives during the following days. The cause of death according to the latest divination, ensuing family troubles, outstanding debts of the deceased and the distribution of property are reviewed and debated in full. The nature of the deliberations depends on the value of the estate concerned and on the message brought from the *nganga*.

ii) The 'home-bringing' ceremony usually takes place on the second day of the proceedings, during the early morning or afternoon. If the grave is near to the homestead the *vakuwasha* first 'clear the road' to the grave while the ritual officiant goes into the beer hut to fetch the *musumo* or *murevo* pot (pot of calling) of beer. It is reverently handled and will occasionally be addressed with the clapping of hands as if it were the deceased him or herself. Beer is also distributed from the other pots to the 'bearers of beer' (*vasengi vedoro*) who must carry the *murevo* pot to the grave. If the deceased is a female, the wives of her own male agnates are entitled to a special pot of beer. While the beer drinking goes on the young people dance and sing.[36] Eventually the relatives of the deceased will leave for the grave, with their

36. For a description of the *dembe, ciwere* and *ngororombe* plays (dances and singing), see Holleman, 1953, p. 5.

varoora (sisters- or daughters-in-law) carrying the spirit's pot of beer. When the procession approaches the grave, the women are allowed to go on ahead. They dance, ululate and greet the deceased by shouting out his or her *mutupo*, *chidao* and other names. The grave is quickly cleared of all grass and shrub with hoes.

If the ceremony concerns a female whose husband is absent or dead, as was the case with *Mai* P.'s ritual, the *vamwene* (husband's sister acting as his representative) gives orders at the grave. When all were seated round the grave on this particular occasion the ritual officiant dipped a *mukombe* (calabash) into the *murevo* pot and poured beer on the grave with the following address: 'Today, *Mai* P., we have come to fetch you so that we can go home over there where the children are. If therefore we leave this place we go there where the children are. You must go and guard your home properly. We want to live peacefully at that village and we don't want to be troubled [hear many things]. You must love your children as you know they love you today by bringing you home.'[37]

The calabash was then re-filled and passed from the senior to the junior relatives of the deceased, each of whom shortly addressed the spirit before drinking:

Muroora (sister-in-law to deceased): '*Vamwene*, you have come today!'

Mwana (deceased's brother's daughter): '*Vatete*, your son P. refuses to give me *nhaka*!'

Vamwene (husband's sister): '*Mai* P., I am your "husband". Here is your snuff which I *durura* [pour out] for you."

P. (eldest son, who requested ritual): 'Mother, I have come from Salisbury. If I have killed you, you will come to me; if I have not done so, you will know who has killed you. I have nothing against you [*Handina chitema nemi*]. I have come to fetch you so that you can see your children.'

The addresses were followed by dancing on and next to the grave. Ululations and the clapping of hands marked the merry mood of the relatives who rejoiced at the prospect of welcoming their deceased relative home. On the way home the procession moved at a quicker pace than when approaching the grave, because the woman's spirit was in a hurry to see her children. The younger males ran ahead, shouting, whistling and calling on the elderly women supposed to be 'carrying' the spirit: '*Hendei*! *Hendei*! Let's go, let's

37. In Shona: '*Mai P. nhasi tauya kuzomutorai kuti tiende kumusha uko kuvana. Saka kana tabva pano totodzira kuvana uko, muchindorinda musha wenyu zvakanaka! Tinoda kuti tigare zvakanaka pamusha apa; hatidi kundonzwa zvinhu zvakawanda! Munofanira kuda vana venyu sezvamunoziva vanokudai nhasi, kuti muve pamusha!*'

go home where the others are!' The idea was to impress on the spirit that it was no longer left alone. Songs of rejoicing, such as '*Chikwara-kwara ndotamba mbuya*, Chikwara-kwara, I play, grandmother', were sung to welcome the spirit home. When the procession approached the deceased's hut, her *varoora* (sisters-in-law) were urged by the other participants to dance as well as they could, as a sign of their welcoming their 'owner' (*vamwene*).[38] In this manner they were reminded of and were expected to demonstrate their imputed subordination to the returning sister of their husbands. As a sign of humility they furthermore 'told' the *mudzimu*: 'We are here, your beggars (*tiri pano varombo venyu*).' Then the deceased's father and brothers-in-law entered the deceased's hut to welcome back their relative.

In the case of a deceased male the ritual procedure deviates from that of a female in so far as the deceased's sister (*hanzvadzi*) and preferably his *chipanda*,[39] who acts as officiating *vatete*, is responsible for the main address at the grave and for directing the dancing. Sometimes the deceased's senior *muzukuru* acts as leading officiant at the grave (e.g. plate 3). The address of R., which also included words of welcome and a request to 'return home', was followed up by mimicked actions of sexual intercourse (plate 4). This was vividly enacted by some women next to R.'s tombstone as a symbolic manifestation of the returning male's vitality and procreative powers. Unlike the female spirit who hastens back home the male spirit is expected to approach his abode in a dignified manner. The procession accompanying R. stopped several times in the shade of trees to rest his spirit. Back home it was primarily his agnates who assembled in his hut to greet their family head and brother.

iii) Succession to the deceased's name (*kubata zita*: lit. to 'hold' the name) in the case of a female spirit is often postponed until at a later date one of the female relatives falls ill. It is sometimes even omitted altogether. Through divination the female spirit, generally referred to as *mbuya* ('grandmother') because of her elevated status, reveals which of her granddaughters must receive her name. Beer is then brewed for the occasion. In Chingombe the 'name-giving' ceremony may take place on the last day of the *kugadzira* proceedings, in which case the deceased's 'owner' (husband's sister) – in other words the paternal aunt of P.'s daughter, who, in the above-mentioned ritual became the name-bearer – takes the initiative as ritual officiant. Gelfand states of the NaJena tribe in the Victoria district that only a granddaughter can succeed to the *mbuya's* name.[40] In Chingombe this is also the general

38. *Supra*, p. 48.
39. The sister to whom a man is 'linked' for the provision of his marriage cattle.

rule, although daughters of the deceased are not necessarily excluded as name-bearers.

Should the *kugadzira* concern a male, it is important to install the senior son as soon as possible. Thus the 'name-giving' ceremony (plate 6) takes place immediately after the people return from the grave or early the next morning. The senior *muzukuru* (deceased's sister's son) and the officiating *vatete* (deceased's sister or her representative, who acts as executrix of the deceased's estate) play the main roles at this juncture. They request the dead man's senior son (*dangwe*) to be seated on a special reed mat (*rupasa*) and the *vatete* then present him with a calabash of beer. Addressing the senior son at this stage implies official recognition of the new family head. R.'s son, for instance, was addressed by his *vatete* in customary fashion, as follows:

'R. [name of the deceased] you have come being you! [R., *mauya uriwe*!] Take good care of your family! You have been in the *dondo*, but today we have brought you back to be in our midst.'

One after another the various groups of agnatic, uterine and affinal relatives stood up to welkome the deceased. Each of them threw a 3 or 6-penny piece in a plate in front of the senior son as a sign of recognition of his legitimate succession to his father's position. They addressed him by the name of his father as if he was the deceased in person:

'R., you are with us today. You must learn to give to others as your forebears have done. You are my *babamunini* [uncle]; I give you 6-pence and hope you will '*semende*' [cement] the family ties.'

'R., I am your daughter, N. You must prepare a place for me in heaven. I have arranged for the pot of beer you told me about in the dream.'

'R., I am your brother. Before death you used to beat me, but if you do so now, it will be wrong.'

'R., you have come. You must not scold me. I have many problems. Now that you have come, you will help me solve them. I am your *mununguna* [younger brother]. You will know what to do with this '*mukono*' [little bull; which in fact was a 3d piece] of mine.'

After each address the spectators clapped their hands and ululated. Some of the personal belongings of the deceased such as a walking stick, an axe, bag of medicine, etc., which had been carefully stored for the occasion in a sealed *dura* (granary), were placed in front of the heir. The acceptance of these articles, the money of the relatives and especially the name of his father signified the successor's instalment as head of the family. What was conferred on him was the authority of his father, which implied both rights and duties.

40. Gelfand, 1966, p. 89.

In the above-mentioned addresses the general acceptance of the senior son's identification with the departed father and the responsibilities concerned are clearly reflected. Thus one of the most important objectives of the ritual is achieved. What Meyer Fortes states paradigmatically about ancestor worship, applies specifically to the *kugadzira* ritual: 'Ancestor worship' he says, 'puts the final source of jural authority and right, or to use the more inclusive term, jurisdiction, on a pedestal, so to speak, where it is inviolable and unchallenge-able, and thus able to mobilize the consent of all who must comply with it.'[41] Apart from the duty of settling family disputes and to settle *roora* arrangements for his younger brothers, the particularly important duty of officiating during traditional religious rites on behalf of the members of his house is conferred on the new namebearer for life. 'He can refuse them [the ritual duties] only at the dire peril of disaster inflicted by the ancestors; he cannot be deprived of them except at the dire peril of those who try to do so.'[42]

This particular aspect of *kugadzira* has a direct bearing on the patterns of leadership succession in the Independent Churches, as will still be indicated. It also complicates the position of the ritually and officially installed name-bearer should he consider joining a Church. Conversion for such a person inevitably leads to compromise or conflict, because of his mystically sanc-tioned, traditional office.

iv) When the meat of the sacrificial beast is distributed – during the accom-modation of a male spirit[43] – one front leg (*bandauko*) usually goes to the deceased's senior *muzukuru*, the other front leg goes to the *vakuwasha* or the *tezvara's* wives, the oldest agnate receives a hind leg and the remaining meat is dished out to the visitors. The meat set aside for the *kupira*-ceremony (pieces cut from the front of the chest, pieces of liver and especially the 'thin intes-tines'–*ura dete*) is called 'the meat that pacifies' (*nyama yokudzora*). It is prepared by the officiating paternal aunt (*vatete*) who roasts it without salt. Special thick porridge is also prepared. All the family members of the deceased congregate in his hut towards the evening of the second or third day. The sacrificial meat and porridge are distributed among the participants by the *vatete*. She passes the senior son's portion to him in a pot or container of

41. Meyer Fortes in Fortes and Dieterlen, 1965, p. 137.
42. *Ibid.*, p. 134.
43. For a description of this part of the ritual we concentrate on the procedure as observed at R's village. The differences in procedure where a female spirit is concerned exists in minor variations of roles, such as the *vamwene* of the deceased female acting as ritual officiant instead of the '*vatete*' as described above, and a slightly different pattern of meat distribution.

traditional style because, as representative of the deceased, he must eat his food in the customary way of the fathers. Before the people start eating, the *vatete* first of all kneels or stoops in front of the pot-shelf (*rukuva*) to address the spirit once more. While speaking she may face a pot of beer in front of the pot-shelf, or she may direct her words at the new name-bearer himself as if he were the deceased. Having welcomed the spirit and having stated once more that the responsibilities for the family now rest on the senior son, the *vatete* will conclude with the plea: 'Don't afflict us any longer! Protect us here, so that evil [lit. wind] does not enter and destroy us!'[44]

In this way the spirit is reminded of his protective function at the doors of his descendants' houses. This *kupira* ceremony differs from the other addresses of the spirit in so far as it is conducted in the private presence of close relatives, with a more elaborate offering than the beer which is otherwise given to the spirit. Africans nevertheless regard this meal with the *mudzimu* as the essential act of veneration. They say: '*Ndiko kupira chaizvo*! That is real "worship"!'

v) On the last day of the ritual the *gova nhaka* (distribution of the inheritable property) ceremony takes place.[45] A deceased woman's personal belongings are distributed (*kuparadza nhumbi*: lit. 'divide her belongings') in a slightly different way than those of a male. At the request of her husband, the deceased woman's father takes care of her possessions. If she had owned any cattle the *tezvara* may select an ox, which is slaughtered on the same day, but he will seldom lay claim to all his daughter's property. He is expected to hand most of it back to his *vazukuru*, the deceased's children. If his daughter had died without bearing his son-in-law any, or only a few, children, he may at a later date 'replace' the daughter who had died with another daughter. This practice is called *kumutsamapfiwa* (to provide a substitute for a prematurely deceased wife).

In the case of a deceased male who has left one or more wives behind, a special test must determine whether the women have committed adultery after their husband's death. They must all 'step across the bow' (*kudarika uta*), which is placed by the senior *muzukuru* as a kind of 'sin-detector' on a reed mat. A guilty woman will refuse to step across the bow because the mystical power of her husband, represented in the bow, will strike her down. Refusal

44. In Shona: '*Mutiregerere! Mutichengete pano kuti mhepo irege kupinda kuzotiparadza-paradza!*'

45. For a detailed account of succession laws concerning the matri- and patri-estate, see Holleman, 1952, Chapter 8.

in such a case is regarded as an admission of guilt, for which the woman's father must pay a fine. She herself is sent back to her home village. Having passed the test the wife or co-wives decide for themselves whose wives they want to become. A gourd of water is presented by each woman to the man of her choice. It is preferably one of the deceased's younger brothers (*vaningina*), but it can also be an older brother, or a son of the deceased, begotten by another woman. Should a wife refuse to be *garwa nhaka* (become an inherited wife) by one of the deceased's agnates, she simply remains seated and will not be forced against her will. Women past the child-bearing stage usually prefer to live at the homestead of one of their older sons.

After the wives have been officially handed over to their new 'husbands', the livestock and movable property, such as hoes and ploughs, are distributed by the *muzukuru* amongst the sons of the dead man. The new family head receives most of his deceased father's possessions, but not all of it belongs to him personally, since each of his younger brothers will lay claim to the beasts that are paid as *roora* for their 'linked' (*chipanda*) sisters,[46] when they themselves want to get married. On this occasion it will also be decided which sister will 'belong' to which brother, as far as *roora* cattle is concerned, and who is entitled to the outstanding *roora* cattle still to be paid for those sisters who have already been given out in marriage prior to the death of their father. The senior *muzukuru* is entitled to an ox due to his mother's position as *samukadzi* to her deceased brother. Outstanding debts (*zvikwereti*) of the deceased are once more brought to the notice of the senior son, who announces that he assumes full responsibility for repayment. With the completion of the *gova nhaka* procedure, the *kugadzira* ritual comes to an end. After the last meal a pot of beer is given to the people *kuseredza manhindi* – to make the consumed meat settle down. It is also called the *chiparadza* (dispersal) pot of beer.

Diagram 1 illustrates the roles played by the different relatives during the ritual proceedings. Suppose the *kugadzira* is conducted to accommodate the deceased A2's spirit. C1 receives his father's name on the reed mat (*rupasa*). A1, the *chipanda* sister of A2 (*vatete* to A2's descendants), is preferably the ritual officiant by virtue of her special relationship to A2, who acquired his wife with his sister's *roora* cattle. B is the senior *muzukuru* who acts as master of ceremonies. He is assisted by E1, the other *muzukuru*. The *vakuwasha* (husbands of A1 and C2) are responsible for the slaughtering of the ritual beast, while the *varoora* (wives of C1 and C3) must brew and carry the beer to the grave.

If the *kugadzira* is conducted on behalf of the spirit of A2's wife, the in-

46. See foot-note 39.

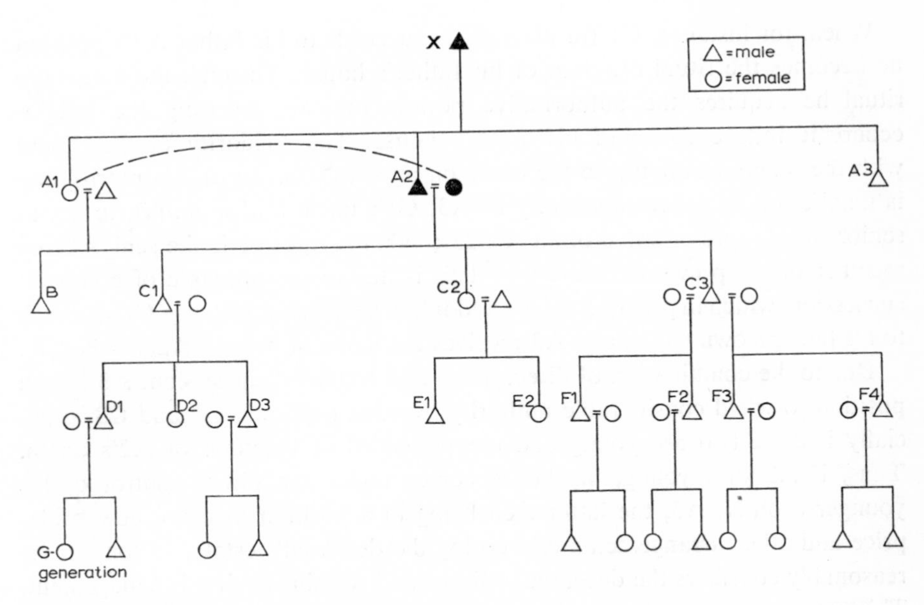

Diagram 1

laws are called in to participate in the ritual. As mentioned before, the deceased woman's 'owner' (*vamwene*) – in this case A1 as representative of A2 – acts as ritual officiant at the grave while the deceased's father or another representative of the woman's agnatic kin-group is responsible for the distribution of the inheritable property. The successor to the deceased's name in this case will be either C2 or E2, depending on the spirit's choice.

The segmentation of the Shona lineage which finds its ritual expression in the *kugadzira* ritual should also be briefly considered. Holleman's detailed analysis of segmentation is related specifically to the customary laws of succession.[47] As the general principles described in his treatise also apply to the ritual field they need not be dealt with extensively at this juncture. Important, however, for an understanding of the ritual offices within the segmented family units is the inherent conflict between the two basic tendencies: of 'a natural cohesion between the various estate [house] units based upon the solidarity of the different houses of a common patri-group' on the one hand, and the tendency of individual houses to establish their independence in relation to the other houses belonging to the common patri-group, on the other.[48]

47. Holleman, 1952, p. 324.
48. *Ibid.*, p. 325.

When, for instance, C1 (in diagram 1) succeeds to his father A2's position he becomes the ritual officiant of his father's house. Through the *kugadzira* ritual he acquires the authoritative powers to start asserting the religio-economic independence of his father's house. The solidarity of this house with the others belonging to the common ancestor (*tateguru*) X's patri-group is manifested in the responsibility of A3, C1's uncle (*babamunini*), to act as senior ritual representative of all X's descendants, since he is the senior living member of the previous generation. This is due to the principle of collateral succession, which in practice means a 'double' succession because C1 succeeds to his father's own name, and A3 receives the name of his and A2's father, X.

Due to the combination of direct lineal and collateral succession, A3 is in a position to wield considerable authority over his nephews, C1 and C3, especially if these two are young and inexperienced at the time of A2's death. Thus, if A2 dies young, his house comes under the direct control of his younger brother, A3, the latter then being in a position to make new bride-price and other arrangements concerning the deceased's estate, as long as he reasonably considers the deceased's wishes and refrains from mismanagement. This pattern of succession is often the cause of conflict between the deceased's firstborn son (*dangwe*) and his *babamunini*.

After the death of A3, C1 officiates on behalf of his own house and that of C3. His sister, C2, of course belongs to his lineage, while her children are ritually represented by the officiant of her husband's lineage. Should E1 or E2 be afflicted by the ancestral spirits of the mother's lineage, C1 may be required to propitiate his agnatic forebears on their behalf. After C1's death his first-born son, D1, officially succeeds to his position during the *kugadzira*, and he in turn can only exert full ritual power after C3's death. Then D1 officiates on behalf of the members of his own and D3's houses while F1 becomes ritually responsible for his own house and those of F2. Since each wife and her children in the case of a plural family constitute a distinct house, and because the link between the children of co-wives sometimes disappears after the death of their father, F3 may become ritual officiant of his own and F4's houses, independently of F1. With the recognition of D1, F1 and F3 as the officiating representatives of their own houses, the solidarity of X's lineage, which during the two previous generations was still strong, starts weakening. As Holleman says: 'The sense of solidarity in the patri-group is the strongest amongst near-agnates; it weakens as the ties of kinship are protracted and the various family units outgrow the tutelage of the common parent group, gaining their own independence.'[49] A sign of this weakening solidarity and of

49. *Ibid.*, p. 325.

the segmentation of X's lineage having become an established fact, is the substitution of X with A2 as the common tutelary or guardian spirit of the different houses of the G-generation, or at least of houses of the following generation. How the segmentation of lineages influences the patterns of propitiatory family rites following the *kugadzira*, will be discussed below.

Because a great number of people congregate at the homestead of the deceased during the two- to three-day proceedings, the *kugadzira* rituals can be detected by the observer with greater ease than the small-scale rituals where the domestic units congregate in the privacy of their homes. The semi-secret nature of family rituals of people who have become Church members, and who are urged by missionaries to discard all forms of the ancestral cult, makes it extremely difficult to achieve an accurate assessment of the present-day continuation of such activities. In Chingombe the *kugadzira* undoubtedly takes place frequently, for the majority of male and female married adults are *gadzwa'd*, whether they have been affiliated to a Church or not. As long as some of the family elders remain non-Christian or are only nominally affiliated to a Church, they see to it that this ritual is performed for their kinsmen and they often induce active Christians to participate in it.

These rituals are always performed in the rural areas and hardly ever in town. Since the grave itself features prominently in the *kugadzira* ceremony, one would think that the absence of the grave of a relative who was buried in town would complicate the ritual or render it impossible. Yet this is not the case. If the grave is beyond reach of the relatives, the ceremony is adapted to meet the needs of the circumstances and the spirit is 'brought back home' in any case. The *kugadzira* in its present form is often modified or changed by those who want to retain such aspects of the ritual as concerns the transfer of jural rights and obligations, but with the exclusion of the specific traditional religious connotations. Even in the traditionalist circles the ritual is sometimes pruned to the mere essentials. Nevertheless, the basic aspects and the different discernable phases of procedure, as described above, remain the same.

The gono guru (big bull) and other family rituals. The traditional conception of a kin-group, consisting of both the living and the dead, finds its ritual expression in the dedication of bulls (*makono*, sing. *gono*) to the founders of the different houses (*dzimba*, sing. *imba*) or segmented family units by their descendants. This is a sign of recognition of the continued authority wielded by the deceased over his living descendants.

A distinction is made between the 'big bull' (*gono guru*), also referred to as the *gono romusha* (bull of the homestead) dedicated to the paternal grandfather (*tateguru*) of a particular house, and that which is dedicated to the senior lineage ancestor of several generations ago, who acts as the guardian spirit of several family units. Paradigmatically it is therefore possible that the segmented family units of the G-generation (diagram 1) have bulls in their kraals respectively dedicated to their grandfathers C1 and C3, but that one of these units has a bull dedicated to the common guardian '*sekuru*'[50] spirit, A2 or X (the generation depth of a common guardian spirit, officially recognized by related lineage units, varies in the lineages of commoners and chiefs), on behalf of the whole lineage.[51] A propitiatory ceremony where this bull is sacrificed, calls for the presence of agnatic representatives of each of the segmented family units or houses, whereas the ritual killing of a bull named after C1 on behalf of D1's children requires, strictly speaking, the presence only of C1's descendants, their *vazukuru* and *vakuwasha*.

The dedication of *gono guru* to a newly instated ancestral spirit often follows quite a while after the *kugadzira* ritual. As long as members of the family enjoy good health and are relatively prosperous the home ancestors are considered to be content. Illness or an unexpected mishap causes the seniors of the family to visit a *nganga*, who diagnoses that one of the home ancestors has caused the unfortunate event as a sign of his or her wish that a *ngombe* be dedicated to him or her. It is usually the spirit of the latest *gadzwa'd* family member who seeks to assert his or her authority and who 'refuses to be forgotten' by the living. A common pattern of affliction is that of a grandparent afflicting a grandchild. Thus in the case of A2's spirit requesting a *gono guru*, after he has been *gadzwa'd* and his son C1 ritually instated as family head, the tendency is not to afflict C1, but one of C1, C2 or C3's children. Likewise the 'returned' spirit of A2's wife, as *mbuya*, tends to afflict the daughters of her own children if the latter fail to dedicate the 'mother's cow' to their deceased parent.

The dedication of a bull to the grandfather's or a cow to the grandmother's spirit follows basically the same pattern in that the senior male or female representative (in the latter case it will be the senior daughter or granddaughter of the *mbuya*) of the family performs this ritual. This person takes a calabash (*mukombe*) filled with beer sediment (*masese*) or water, and approaches the bull-calf or cow in the kraal, while the rest of the family stand by as spectators. The contents of the calabash is thrown over the animal's

50. *Supra*, p. 92.

51. It should be noted that in practice not all adult male and female spirits have *ngombe* dedicated to them. Normally a total of two to three dedicated bulls will be found in the cattle kraals of all the families of the G-generation, as presented in diagram 1.

head or back with a formal address to the *mudzimu*: 'Here, So-and-so, is your *ngombe*. We have today complied to your request!' At times the ancestor will be requested, immediately after the dedication of the animal, to allow the afflicted family member to become well again. If the animal moves its head or bellows during this ceremony it is interpreted as a favourable sign coming from the *mudzimu* itself. The dedicated beast is usually treated with greater care than the other animals. In passing, it may be called by its spiritual name. Undue lowing or bellowing will be interpreted either as a sign of the ancestor's pleasure or displeasure in accordance with the general state of family affairs at that stage. Important events in the family (especially marriages, with cattle coming and going) are often reported to the *midzimu* by addressing the dedicated animal, but otherwise little attention may be paid to it until the ritual killing takes place.

There is no specific time for the ritual killing of the 'big bull'. Family circumstances determine whether this sacrifice is made a few months or many years after the dedication ceremony. Once the *mudzimu* has made known its wish through a diviner or spirit medium that its beast should be slaughtered, the beer-brewing preparations and notification of relatives will take place.[52] The basic pattern of activities is similar to that discussed under the *kugadzira* ritual. Once again the *vakuwasha* (sons-in-law) and *varoora* (daughters-in-law) play an important role in the beer-brewing and slaughtering activities, as becomes their subordinate position in the kinship structure. Once again the *vazukuru* (uterine cousins or nephews) have honoured positions in the ritual, with one of them playing the important role of master of ceremonies. Distribution of meat varies according to the number of each group of relatives present, but the parts reserved for sacrificial purposes remain essentially the same. Pieces of meat cut from the front part of the chest and *ura dete* (thin intestines) can invariably be found in the *mudzimu's* pot.

There are certain variations as to where the ancestor should be 'fed' and 'worshipped'. In some areas a special *rushanga* (pole enclosure)[53] is built round the trunk of a *muchakata* tree (cork-tree) where part of the ceremony will be conducted, but in Chingombe this practice applies to the rain ritual (*mukwerere*) only. As is the case with the *kugadzira* the main address of the

52. For full details of such rituals, see Gelfand, 1959, Chapter 7, and Gelfand, 1966, Chapter 6.

53. A *rushanga* is a temporary pole enclosure or shrine for the purposes of the ritual. The poles are used for other purposes after the ritual, so that a new *rushanga* will have to be built for the next ritual. The same applies for the *musumo* or *murevo* pots of beer. The symbolic representation of the ancestral spirits lasts only for the duration of the ritual.

ancestor takes place inside one of the huts, when the saltless meat, thick porridge and beer is 'given' to the spirit. During this ritual the officiant will be the senior son of the deceased family head and not the *vatete* (paternal aunt). The 'prayer' itself consists of the formal presentation of the *mudzimu* with his 'food' (*zvokudya*) and an explicit request that he should protect the family. Unless a medium is present there will be no elaborate discussions with the spirit, apart from the brief address directed at the *musumo* (or *murevo*) pot of beer in front of the pot-shelf. Family members who feel that the ancestors have failed them in the past give vent to their feelings through intermittent exclamations of accusations during the main address. They also jest with the spirit. If the ritual offering concerns the beast of the *mbuya*, fewer relatives attend, but the procedure is essentially the same, with the *mbuya's* name-bearer taking care of the main 'prayer'.

Families constantly harrassed by illness and death of its members, or families too poor to afford cattle, dedicate goats to the ancestors instead. The spirits as a rule accept such substitute offerings without complaint.

One need only observe the reciprocal aid between families during and after marriage arrangements to appreciate how closely the constant obligations of the living to the dead are associated with animals, and how essential the joint participation of both families in the ritual slaughtering of such dedicated animals is to strengthen their ties. The payment of the bride-price is never complete without the *gono rabata* – a bull which the bride's father is supposed to dedicate to one of his family ancestors. If the father-in-law already has a *gono guru* in his kraal this animal may be passed on to another lineage as *roora* payment for one of his sons. In any event the link between the dedicated bull in the *tezvara's* kraal and the donor's family remains, and when it is sacrificed, the son-in-law himself or one of his representatives is responsible for killing it. In this way the goodwill of the wife's paternal ancestors is maintained, and the interfamily ties are strengthened.

In addition to *gono rababa* there are at least three other types of livestock with ritual significance that should be paid by the son-in-law's family to his *vatezvara*. These are the *masungiro* goats, the *ngombe youmai* (cow or heifer for the bride's mother) and the *imbwazukuru* goats for the maternal and paternal grandmothers. None of these animals belongs to the bride-price in the strict sense of the word. No legal action can be taken against the son-in-law to supply them, but the fear of his wife's matrilineal ancestors interfering with her procreative capacity or with the well-being of her children is sanction enough to enforce the *mukuwasha's* compliance in the majority of cases.[54]

54. *Vakuwasha* often postpone the payment of these animals until family troubles are

Holleman correctly states that these animals are provided 'in recognition of the organic bonds existing between a woman and her ascendants, especially female. They reveal a certain indebtedness or dependence of the husband's family upon the woman's ancestry, based upon a vague and mystical conception that the reproductive capacity of the woman is rooted in that of her ascendants as part of what may be termed a supra-individual procreative organism which is vitally interested in its offspring. To this organism, represented primarily by the woman's parents and parents' mothers, the husband has to pay homage in order to ensure its beneficient influence, realizing that his failure to do so might provoke mystical sanctions (e.g. barrenness of his wife, illness or death among his children).'[55]

The *masungiro* consists of a male goat given to the wife's father and a female goat given to her mother. As soon as the wife's first pregnancy is established, a 'messenger' (*munyai*) should take the two goats to the village of the father-in-law because in her pregnant state the mother-in-law's daughter forms a mystical threat to her parents. Arrangements are made for the *masungiro* ritual at the *tezvara's* homestead, where the male goat is offered to his ancestors and part of its meat eaten by the *tezvara*, *vambuya* ('mothers-in-law'), their son-in-law and his pregnant wife. This ritual eliminates the mystical threat to the parents of the pregnant woman. The female goat is not killed directly. It belongs to the *ámbuya* who dedicated it to her mother to secure her protective powers for her female grandchild and great-grandchildren. In this way the mother-in-law builds up her own herd of animals (*danga ramai*) which enables her to propitiate her maternal spirits on behalf of her children if necessary. The most important animal in the *danga ramai* is the *ngombe youmai* or *bakuro* (motherhood cow) which may be forwarded by the *mukuwasha* with the initial *roora* payment but, as usually happens, after his wife has given birth to several children. We have already referred to the importance of this animal, and mentioned that the mother's spirit causes barrenness if the *mukuwasha* fails, especially after her death, to produce this beast. If she receives this cow while alive, she first of all 'shows it to her matrilineal spirits' and then keeps it for future propitiatory purposes. Offspring of the *ngombe youmai* (motherhood cow), if any, serves to assist the woman's blood-brothers or sons with *roora* payment.[56] When the mother-in-law decides to sacrifice the *ngombe youmai*, her eldest brother who officially acts as ritual officiant of

diagnosed by the *nganga* to be caused by the angered spirits of their wives' lineages.

55. Holleman, 1952, pp. 176-177.

56. This *roora*-assistance provided by their mother places the sons, who have profitted from it, in a special obligatory position towards her *mudzimu* after her death.

the family unit to which she belongs, should be present, as well as the *mukuwasha* concerned and members of her elementary family group. The cow is killed and skinned by the sons-in-law and the sacrificial meat given to their mother-in-law, who informs her brother that the meat is ready to be sacrificed. He then addresses their mother's *mudzimu* in the hut at the pot-shelf as follows: 'This is your cow which we have killed, and this is the first roasted meat which we are giving you from the cow provided by our *mukuwasha*.'[57] Several more addresses may be made before the meat is consumed. If no beer has been brewed for the ritual, the *mbuya's* spirit will be informed that the beer, to which she is entitled, will be brewed for her soon. Should a mother-in-law's spirit cause affliction in her *mukuwasha's* family because the *ngombe youmai* has not yet been forwarded, the beast will be collected by a close relative, a brother or a sister, who will at least 'show' the beast to the aggrieved spirit as soon as possible, in order to avert possible tragedy.

The third kind of gift to be given to the in-laws concerns the *imbwazukuru*[58] to which the paternal or maternal grandmother, usually the one who cared for the bride when she was still an infant, is entitled. It seldom happens that the former grandmother receives this gift, but the latter is regarded as more directly involved in her granddaughter's child-bearing capacities, and should therefore receive her due to safeguard successful child-birth. In cases of miscarriage or complicated birth the *nganga* will advise the propitiation of the wife's maternal grandmother's spirit, if this has not yet been done. Husbands often postpone the fulfilment of this obligation until their pregnant wives show symptoms of possible complications. The mother-in-law is then given the *imbwazukuru* goat, which she dedicates to her mother's spirit without delay in front of the pot-shelf in her hut. Having poured water over the goat from a calabash and holding it by its front leg she addresses her mother's spirit as follows: 'See, mother, here is the goat you have requested from your granddaughter's husband. He has done his duty. Take good care of his *mhuri* [family]!' This goat, nearly always presented under stress of circumstance, is slaughtered immediately after its dedication to the spirit, and all the relatives present can partake of its meat.

57. Gelfand, 1959, p. 90.

58. The derivation of the term, which literally means 'dog of the grandchild', is somewhat obscure, but Holleman (1952, p. 184) considers it possible that it stands in relation to the custom of mixing a newly-born baby's with porridge and feeding it to a dog of the same sex. His informants also suggested that the grandmother's activities in cleaning the baby are comparable to those of a dog which sometimes cleans up the baby's mess by eating its dirt. 'The implications of the terms', Holleman contends, 'are that the grandmothers of the wife have taken care of her when she was an infant, and in the husband's tribute to them such services are acknowledged.'

8. A *muchembere* soaks the finger millet in a *guvi* in preparation of the beer brewing for a *mukwerere* ritual.

9. *Mukwerere*. Two Hera kinsmen greet their tribal ancestors with the clapping of hands on behalf of Rufura people who are approaching the grave in the background.

10. *Mukwerere*. With the snuff of the tribal spirits in their hands, ritual participants dance on the grave of one of their forebears.

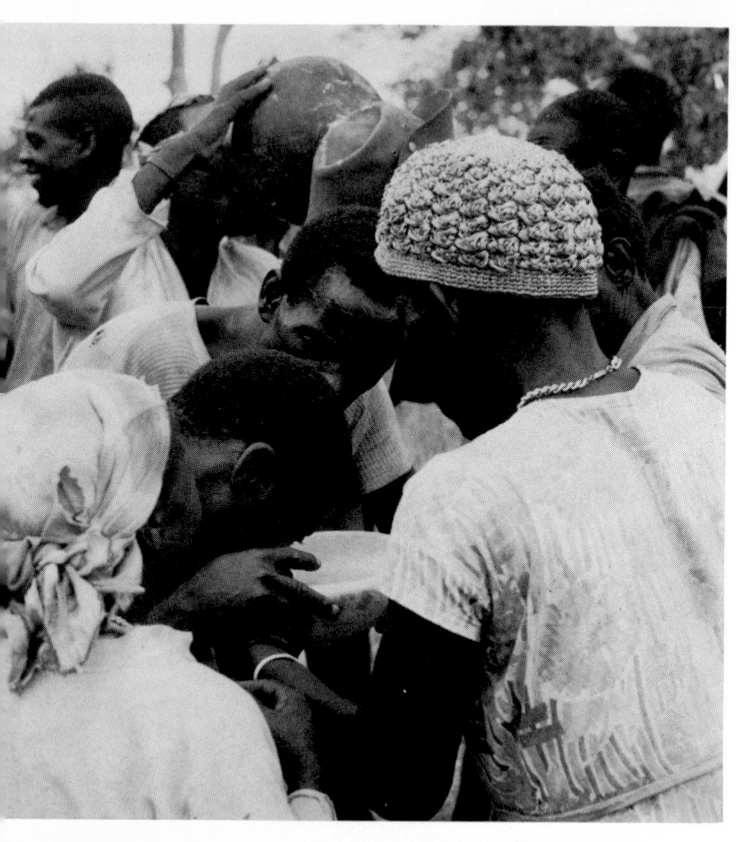

11. *Mukwerere*. Beer drinking in honour of the ancestors.

12. *Mukwerere*. An old war dance in honour of the tribal spirits.

Apart from the propitiatory rites which include the sacrifice of animals, numerous other offerings can be made to the *midzimu*. In cases of family troubles or a new venture being planned by one of its members, the 'home ancestors' frequently request either beer or a *jira* (blanket or piece of cloth). Such *kupira* ceremonies involve fewer participants than the rituals mentioned above. The family head and a few members of the elementary family may be the only attendants. The *murevo* pot is the means of communicating with the spirit in any ritual where sacrificial beer is involved. In addition to beer and meat, snuff may be left in front of the pot-shelf for the spirit to use. Spirits that are represented by a medium always ask for a blanket or a piece of cloth which is given to and used by the *svikiro*. But the spirit sometimes orders certain members of the family to be in possession of a '*mudzimu*-blanket' or piece of cloth. They are expected to keep it with them wherever they go, after it has been dedicated to the *mudzimu*. These articles, symbols of the protective power of the guardian ancestors, can be addressed by the name of the particular spirit. Thus a muShona, before applying for a new job, may take the dedicated blanket from a trunk where it is carefully kept, and demand of it: 'You, So-and-so, I am about to go and see manager X about a new job. Be with me and help me to be successful!' It is in this form that remnants of ancestor 'worship' are still found in urban areas. The larger ceremonies that include the sacrifice of animals are reserved for the home village and special or weekend arrangements are made by townsmen when the time has come for them to return home for ritual purposes. But some symbols of the ancestor's presence are taken to town, and numerous inconspicuous actions of townsmen, such as the deliberate spilling of a little beer, or the setting aside of portions of food, are tangible signs of a sence of dependence on and respect for the ancestors.

Whenever a *mudzimu* selects a *svikiro* (medium) through whom he periodically reveals his wishes to the family, much of the ordinary ritual procedure is channelled through the *svikiro*. Spells of spirit possession do not necessarily supplant other facets of a ritual, but the presence of a recognized medium tends to focus the attention of the ritual participants on this one spirit, whose 'physical' and verbalized presence is somehow more convincing than other forms of spiritual communication. The roles played by the different relatives during rituals remain essentially the same, with the one crucial difference that communication with the spirit is now more direct. One can 'discuss' family matters with the possessed *svikiro* instead of a 'prayer' being directed at a symbolic but select a medium, but in practice it is rather the exception than the rule.[59] A

59. Among the Southern Shona the *svikiro* system is politically less relevant than

silent pot of beer. Any spirit that attains full ancestorhood can theoretically male spirit usually selects one of his grandsons, granddaughters or a daughter-in-law (*muroora*), while female spirits prefer outsiders. In Chingombe the mediums of female family spirits are few while the female mediums of male family spirits are more common.

One of the main reasons why a male spirit prefers to select a second generation descendant as a medium is the relative lack of strife between the alternate generations in contrast to the conflicts often arising from the direct assertion of authority in the father-son relationship. This is also in accordance with the general conception of a close link between the grandfather's spirit and his grandchild's psyche.

The urgency with which a male spirit 'takes hold of' (*kubata*) a living descendant is often determined by the state of family affairs. Should, for instance, the spirit of A2, in diagram 1, object to the mismanagement of his estate by his younger brother A3, he may select one of C1, C2 or C3's daughters to act as the medium and voice his protest. If the *kugadzira* has not yet been performed, the new medium, say E2, will voice A2's request to be 'brought back home' from the bush in order to settle family affairs. The first efforts of A2's spirit to 'come out' in E2 become evident in her dream-life which she narrates to some of the other members of the family. She may even pass through a phase of mental disorder (*kupenga*) or illness which provides all the more motivation for a *kugadzira*. Although messages from A2 are already indirectly 'transmitted' at this stage, his spirit is still regarded as being out in the bush and only after the *kugadzira* ritual will E2 become the officially recognized medium through a series of *kusvikirwa* (to be possessed) sessions. This is of course only one of a variety of circumstances which can lead to the *kugadzira* ritual and the lifelong office of spirit medium. As a rule an ancestral spirit's selection of a spirit medium takes place *after* he or she has achieved full ancestorhood, or else the uninitiated spirit's manifest choice is only officially recognized after the 'home-bringing' rite.

The distant lineage guardian, who presumably rises to the status of *mhondoro* in the course of time, seems to be in greater need of a medium (*svikiro*) than the more recently deceased 'home ancestors'. In Chingombe several of the mediums represent this category of senior lineage spirits. The most popular

---

among the northern Kore-Kore. According to Garbett (1964, p. 44) 'the traditional political system (of the Kore-Kore) has two major components: one is the political organization of the chiefdoms, the other the politico-religious system associated with the spirit medium cult.' Although the Southern Shona medium is also consulted when a new chief is installed, his influence is generally less far reaching and direct than that of the Kore-Kore medium.

of these is *Mai* Benny who claims to be possessed by the spirit of Rutsate himself, and who acts on behalf of seven composite houses (*dzimba*) under the leadership of kraalhead Murambasvina.[60] A few Chingombe mediums are the acknowledged mediums of tribal spirits near to Mabwazhe, the founder ancestor at the apex of the Gutu spirit hierarchy. In the ward community the status of a *svikiro* is determined by the position of the spirit he or she represents in the spiritual hierarchy and by the nature of involvement of the spirit's descendants in tribal politics.

Rain rituals (*mutoro or mukwerere*). Annual rain rituals take place between September and January according to the urgency of the need for rain. A great number of minor ritual centres exist in each ward, of which at least a few will be operative during good rainy seasons and the majority of them during droughts. Such a centre is the grave of one of the senior lineage ancestors, mostly situated on, or at the foot of a granite kopje, or it may be a sacred cork-tree (*muchakata*) near the homestead of a kraalhead, around which a *rushanga* (also called *mutoro,* as indicative of a sacred pole enclosure) is built during the preparatory stages of each ritual. Originally a distinction was made in the Gutu district between the *mukwerere* ritual, which was conducted at the commencement of the rain, and the *mutoro* ritual which took place as soon as the crops started ripening. In contrast to the first supplication for rain, the latter ceremony was a thanksgiving for the *zhezha* (edible tuber),[61] of which nobody was allowed to eat before this ritual was conducted. Nowadays the Gutu people have only one ritual per year, primarily concerned with petitions for rain, and they alternately use both words, *mutoro* and *mukwerere*, for it.[62]

The *mukwerere* usually involves members of a wider range of lineages than those rituals concerning elementary or extended family units. Ward heads (*vasadunhu*) still conduct ceremonies[63] on behalf of their wards. On such occasions the most senior houses of the politically dominant lineage will all be represented. Yet the limitation of the ward head's authority and his subsequent loss of political power has reduced his representative religious activities. Nowadays it is mainly the kraalheads (*masabuku*) who are responsible for *mukwerere* rituals. Consequently the participants at the numerous rain-

60. This faction forms an opposition group to the present Chief Chingombe. They claim to have the sanction of the senior ancestral spirits behind them.

61. In this context the term *zhezha* refers to all ripening crops.

62. The vaRozvi of Bikita make exclusive use of the term *mutoro*.

63. Towards the end of 1965 I attended two *dunhu*-rituals in Chitsa and Nyamande. On each occasion several hundreds of people were present and practically all the senior houses of each ward were represented.

centres comprise one of the senior kraalheads, representing a senior house of the dominant lineage, bearing the hereditary name of one of the more ancient ancestors, together with several junior kraalheads (3 to 5) and their followers. These junior kraalheads are the ones who have hived off from the parental village at one stage or another. In some cases one or more *vatorwa* (foreigner) kraalheads are included. In Chingombe the senior kraalheads who take the initiative for their ritual centres are nearly all Rufura or Hera kinsmen.

As soon as the newly-sown seed starts germinating and the heavens show signs of withholding its rain (*denga rakweva kure*: lit. the heaven has drawn far away), the leading kraalhead tells the other kraalheads of his ritual unit that the time has come to 'fix the heavens' (*gadzira matenga*). Finger millet is then collected from the family heads of each village, irrespective of the religious convictions of its members.[64] When sufficient millet has been collected it is dedicated to the apical ancestors by their oldest living descendant; the leading kraalhead himself, one of his older *vadzibaba* ('fathers') or his paternal aunt. There are various ways of doing this, but the most common practice is to place some *rukweza* (finger millet) on a clay platter and to address the spirits while mixing it with water, or to allow the grain to trickle through the fingers into a basket while addressing the spirits. 'Prayers' vary from short pleas to lengthy, lamentatious speeches. *Sabuku* Kono, for example, in 1965 dedicated the *rukweza* to his ancestors with the single phrase: 'Here our fathers, we brew beer for you and ask you *mate emvura* [spittle of rain]'; but Marinzepi,[65] the paternal aunt of the Hera *sabuku*, Muza, had much more to say to the spirits:

'Muza, forward our plea to Mavurume, Mavurume to Mazodza, Mazodza to Tabvingwira and then to you, Mheresi, Makomora and Nyashanu. You, the fathers of my people, we are dying without water. Do you want us to die and be buried in dry soil? Soften it with rain, so that we may be buried in wet soil! Gather the people [*midzimu*] for the *mutoro*! I want all of you to be here, because I am the oldest living descendant. Give us rain, my *midzimu*, all of you! Don't put me to shame, my fathers! I thank you already, Chinezema, because as firstborn you are going to give us rain. Your children are not

64. Tactful kraalheads may skip the houses of staunch Christians. In practice few collections of millet take place by force (*kumanikidza*), but Christians usually state that they comply with the *sabuku's* order because it is *tsika yenyika* (the law of the land) which cannot be disobeyed without prejudicing one's land rights.

65. Marinzepi belongs to the ritual unit adjacent to that of Kono. She could be more outspoken is her address to the spirits (see plate 7) because she is the 'daughter' of Mheresi, while Kono as a muRufura was actually dedicating grain to the spirits of his *vasekuru*, the vaHera, who are the 'owners of the soil' in the *dunhu* where his village is situated.

lazy. They work, but they starve because there is no rain. I want the rain clouds to be here this afternoon. I, as the daughter of Mheresi and Norwira, believe that rain will fall today. I am not joking. *Look*! *Here is the grain* [*zviyo*] *we are giving you so that you can let the rain fall*!

You want your *vazukuru* to die of hunger? Who will remain on this *nyika* if all the babies die at once? Take pity on them and let them die peacefully, but not of hunger!

Nyashanu, what have we done to you? You Mundangande, Chaminuka, Mufudza, Shumba, Maruma and Mheresi, help us! *You, Mwari, help us*! *You are the owner of all things*!'

First of all the major ancestors in the direct line of descent, from the deceased Muza (Marinzepi's brother) to the founder ancestor of the Hera tribe (Nyashanu) are mentioned. Then at a later stage the names of the senior local *midzimu*, mostly the sons of Mheresi, whose descendants represent the senior Hera houses in Chingombe, and therefore also the main rain-ritual centres, are mentioned. Lastly there is reference to Mwari, without whose aid the ritual would be futile. Rain is expected by Marinzepi on the same day, because in earlier years it was customary to pour the grain in a rock cavity (*guvi*) and wait for the spirits to wet it with their 'spittle' before continuing with beer-brewing activities. At present people seldom wait for the ancestors to soak the millet. A *mhandara* (unmarried young girl) fetches water for the old women past child-bearing (*vachembere*), who soak the grain in the *guvi* (plate 8).[66] The germinating grain will be dried and ground a few days later, before the actual brewing commences. Towards the end of the fermentation stage the *vachembere* are sent out to sweep the graves of the senior ancestors. The men will construct a pole enclosure around the trunk of the ancestor's *muchakata* tree,[67] if they have no accessible graves in the immediate vicinity to go to, or else the *rushanga* is used for further communication with the spirits shortly after the main ritual has taken place at the graves. The performance of these duties may also take place on the day of the main ritual, but whatever the sequence of events, these preparatory activities always include conversation with the spirits. 'Look, father, we have come to fix your "house",' a person will say while removing shrubs from the grave or while whittling down the

66. Women in their child-bearing phase of life are regarded as ritually unclean and they are therefore not allowed to handle the sacred beer of the *vakuru* (spirit and living elders).

67. One of the reasons why the *muchakata* is regarded as the holy tree of the *midzimu* is probably that it has a dense foilage which provides ideal shade during the heat of the day; another is its ample fruit of which the Shona are fond. As such the tree symbolizes the cardinal function of the ancestors: protection.

bark from the *rushanga* poles. Pots of dedicated beer and snuff may be left at the graves or *rushanga* for the spirits to use during the night preceding the main ritual. The next day, during the early hours of the morning, the adults of the ritual unit assemble at the senior kraalhead's homestead.[68] The *vachembere* carrying the sacrificial beer lead the procession, often up a granite kopje, to the graves. Singing, ululations of the women, the clapping of hands and the occasional blast of the *hwamanda* (kudu horn) tell the ancestors of the arrival of their 'children'. Special care will be taken to put the finishing touches to the graves, a task reserved by the Hera for the *vachembere* and *vazukuru* (sister's son's descendants) of the deceased. The main address at the grave is usually delivered by the *sabuku* himself or by one of his *vazukuru* (sister's sons).

By way of illustration we will now trace the proceeding of the rituals that followed the two above-mentioned introductory addresses. In the case of the Hera *sabuku*, Muza, his sister's son washed an old pot, and then, whilst pouring the beer of the ancestors into it, he said: '*Imi vaMuza, tinokumbira hore yemvura. Muudze vaMaruma, naMheresi kuti vatireverere wo kuna madzitete-guru awo* [*vatakangangwa*]. *Madziteteguru atireverere kuna Mwari wavo paMabweadziwa.*' – 'You Muza, we ask for clouds of rain. Tell Maruma and Mheresi to intercede for us with those ancestors [meaning: those we have forgotten] so that they, the senior ancestors [*madziteteguru*], can intercede for us with their Mwari at the "Rocks of the Pool" [i.e. the Matonjeni shrine].' The participants rejoiced with loud shouts of Museamwa! Mhukahuru! – which are the two main *zvidao* (sub-clan names) of the Hera ancestors. Songs such as '*Unofa ukasiya mumwe*' – 'you will die if you leave someone' and '*Tiri pano pamuchakata wenyu*' – 'we are here at your muchakata tree' were sung in honour of the lineage ancestors.[69] Towards the end of the ceremony the *vachembere* claimed a special pot of beer reserved for them, and having 'driven the others away' they proceeded to the foot of the Marashasimba hill, where their forebears used to conduct rain ceremonies. Here they drank the beer and sent repeated requests to the spirits.

In the case of *Sabuku* Kono and his Rufura kinsmen, a senior representative of the Hera clan, Chaminuka, was asked to conduct the ritual proceedings.

68. The vaRozvi on this occasion slaughter a goat and spill the contents of its intestines at the doorstep of the first wife's hut. They then inform the *midzimu* that they themselves will not remove the dung and that they expect it to be washed away by rain in due course.

69. Other popular *mukwerere* songs, sung in Gutu and Bikita are: *Baya mabaya* (an old war song – see plate 12); *Tinoda kurima* (we want to plough), *Mbavarira inoda vane ngombe* (perseverance prefers those with cattle).

As a reflection of the Shona attitude to land, this fact is of great significance because it illustrates the common recognition of the land rights of the first historically-known inhabitants, and the dependence of the invaders, whatever the extent of their political power, on the mystical powers of these 'owner-spirits.' To ensure good crops the favour of the 'land-owning spirits' of the subjected tribes should be sought and continually fostered. Thus the Hera kraalhead, who represented the land unit in which Kono's village was situated, was invited to come and call down the 'spittle' of his forebears, on behalf of his *vazukuru*.[70] He led the Rufura procession to a cork tree where a pole enclosure (*rushanga*) was constructed under his supervision. A pot of ancestral beer was placed by Kono's *muchembere* sister at the entrance of the *rushanga*, after which she retreated a few steps to sit down amongst the elderly females. Chaminuka stepped forward, dipped a calabash (*mukombe*) into the pot of beer, and spoke to his ancestors while pouring beer onto the trunk of the cork tree. Some beer was also deliberately spilt down the sides of the pot, next to its *muromo* ('mouth') as if to feed the spirits. Meanwhile the Rufura men squatted reverently a few yards away and at the mention of each Hera *mudzimu* name they clapped hands as one would do when approaching a chief and they muttered the spirit's *chidao*: Museamwa! The supplication ran as follows:

Sekuru Chaminuka: 'My fathers, we ask your spittle [*mate*] for your *vazukuru*, these Madyira people. Here are my words, *madziwanyika* [great ones of the land], pass them to Mupangi, Mupangi to Mazodza and Mazodza to Mheresi!'

Other Hera kinsmen in unison: 'We speak to you, Museamwa [meaning Mheresi]; you, the biggest leader to come from Nyashanu's country!'

Rufura notables: 'Museamwa! Mhukahuru!'[71] With the clapping of hands.

Sekuru Chaminuka: 'I am your son, my fathers. This is the snuff I give you to share among yourselves. *Madzivanyika*, these Madyira people [Rufura] are your *vazukuru*, the children of your sister, who cry for rain. They say that they are suffering from the heat and want to be cooled [*kutonhodzwa*] by your "spittle". *Madzivanyika*, you must also tell your mountains [*makomo*] Zimbizi, Kutsvanga, Marashasimba and Mheresi.'[72]

Kraalhead Kono to the Hera spirits in general: 'You, our great maternal

70. Due to the vaHera forming primarily the wife-providing group to the Rufura kinsmen, they are now generally called *vasekuru* by their sister's sons, the Rufura nephews.

71. *Mhukahuru* literally means 'great antelope'. As praise-name of the Hera tribal spirits, it probably refers to the important personages of the Hera clan with *Mhofu* (eland) as their *chidao*.

uncles [*vadzisekuru*], you must do the work [i.e. get rain from Mheresi] as you used to do!'

Rufura notables in unison: 'We thank you, Museamwa, that you send all our cries for rain to Mwari waMatonjeni.'

As Chaminuka poured the last drops of beer on the tree trunk there was a soft clapping of hands as a request for gentle rain (*risipambvi*). It is a way of asking the *midzimu* not to send *chipondamabwe* (lit. 'pounding of the rocks', i.e. thunderstorms or hail). The rain song: '*Muturura, mvura yauya*' (Muturura, the rain has some) was then sung and a few people joined in *jukwa* dancing,[73] before they moved off to the kraalhead's homestead to spend the rest of the day in drinking and feasting (e.g. plate 11).

If one of the senior lineage ancestors is represented by a medium, he will 'come out' during the period of *mukwerere* preparations and ritual to give his living descendants advice on ritual procedure. In December 1965 the female *svikiro* of Chirambagomo,[74] a well-known Matonjeni messenger (*munyai*) of the Nyamande people in earlier years, revealed her *mudzimu's* wish to have a delegation sent on his behalf to the Matopos to consult Mwari. This had to be done before the *mukwerere* was held. The spirit also ordered the shallow well (*tsime*) at the foot of the kopje, where his house had been situated during his lifetime, to be reopened. Confirmation was received from Matonjeni that Chirambagomo's orders were to be followed up. On the day of the ritual itself a few hundred people arrived at the newly dug well to listen, amongst other things, to the ancestral *mitemo* ('laws') which were to be made known by the possessed medium. The essence of Chirambagomo's laws was as follows:

1. No European objects such as billy-cans, drums, jugs or soap should be brought near the well or Chirambagomo's hill, as this would anger his spirit and prevent rain from falling. The water could only be used for drinking purposes and was to be drawn from the well with a calabash only.
2. No human faeces were to be allowed on or near the hill.

72. These mountains are the ones on which the most important Hera ancestors are buried. 'Tell your mountains!' could therefore mean: 'Tell those whose graves are there!' Possibly we have here yet another symbolic identification of the *midzimu* with something which is closely associated with them.

73. The *jukwa* spirits belong to the *shavi* category of alien spirits, but their dwelling place is at Matonjeni. Because of their nearness to Mwari they can also mediate for rain and if they are honoured with *jukwa* dances the chances of rain are believed to be greatly enhanced.

74. *Chirambagomo* (to refuse the mountain) is a nickname which was presumably given to the *munyai* during his life. It is said that as long as he guarded the mountain the *tsime* (well) at its foot never dried up.

3. No sticks or stones were to be thrown into fruit trees[75] on or near the hill, lest the ancestors be angered. People could only use the ripe fruit that had fallen to the ground.

In this particular case we notice the reaction against European influence (*chirungu*). The prohibition of the use of European objects at the *tsime* reflects the inclination of the conservative Africans to blame the Europeans, the *varungu* (whites), for droughts, because they cause the *vatema* (the blacks: popular term used by the Africans themselves) to stray from the customs of their ancestors. During a drought the community as a whole is reminded by the ritual officers of its neglect of the ancestors, and reconciliation is sought. Due to the pragmatic nature of this type of ritual, the ancestral laws are often only partially obeyed, or even temporarily forgotten once the drought has passed, until a bad season once more necessitates a communal demonstration of goodwill through stricter adherence to the prescribed rules.

The major points of divergence between family and *mukwerere* rituals are the following: In the latter ritual corporate lineage unity is stressed, which involves great numbers of people, even if some of them participate only partly by contributing grain. The whole spiritual hierarchy, and especially the tribal progenitor, is addressed on this occasion, in contrast to the family ritual where not even mentioned. Furthermore, the link with Mwari and the people's the most senior lineage ancestors are less directly involved and, in many cases, dependence on Him as the ultimate 'owner of the country' is perceived with greater clarity during the *mukwerere*. He may be addressed directly – as Marinzepi did – or the apical ancestor is requested to forward the request to Him. Due to the spiritual superiority of the tribal spirits the attitudes of ritual participants seem more reverent than during a family ritual when, for example, the daughters-in-law are allowed to jest with their *tezvara* spirits, or the ritual officiant is heard to rebuke his *midzimu yapamusha*. Marinzepi's lament bore the character of intense pleading with Mheresi and Nyashanu, rather than of a straightforward admonition. To the western observer *mukwerere* procedure therefore seems to conform more closely to what is understood by 'worship' (religiously paying homage to), and the supplications to the tribal spirits sound more like genuine prayers than does the straightforward approach of the family ancestors. Another feature distinguishing *mukwerere* from family rituals is the focus on mountains. The temporary personification of *makomo* (mountains), closely associated with the senior ancestors, possibly serves to enhance the idea of spiritual elevation and power – the distinct attributes of these old an-

75. *Muchakata* (cork), *musvaza* (sour plum) and *mutamba* (klapper apple) trees.

cestors. *Kukwira makomo* (to climb the mountains) has become almost synonymous with *kukumbira mvura* (to ask for rain) to the Southern Shona. In this respect there is a marked similarity between the places for worshipping tribal spirits and the God of Matonjeni whose dwelling place and shrines are also closely associated with mountains.

To the Shona ruralists the *mukwerere* still functions generally as an existentially meaningful and relevant ritual. At least thirty of these rituals took place in Chingombe or its immediate vicinity during the 1965-1966 rainy season, several of which were attended either by me or by one of the assistants. This high incidence of rain rituals during a period of relatively mild drought and the involvement of several kraalheads in each ritual, seem to suggest that the majority of kraalheads, regardless of their religious affiliation, still participate in such rituals.

b) *Alien spirits (mashavi)*

The *shavi* spirits have in common that they never belong to the *rudzi* (tribe or lineage) of their hosts. They are spirits that come from afar, from under the ground, from the deep pool or merely from distant places. Their names sometimes indicate their origin, such as the *Dzviti* (Matabele), *Changani* (Shangaan), *ChiRozvi* (Rozvi) and *Murungu* (European) *shavi*, or else, as in the case of the *Muvimi* (hunting) *shavi*, the name of the spirit indicates the special kind of skill it confers on its host. The following are the *mashavi* commonly found amongst the Southern Shona, and particularly the Chingombe people: *Jukwa* and *Dzviti*, closely associated with Matonjeni; *Changani*, thought of as coming from Ndau or Portuguese territory; *ChiRozvi* and *Murungu*, originating from different places all over Rhodesia; *Njuzu* (the water spirit), *Zenda* (the hunter) *Danda, Chipuna, Bvene* (baboon) and *Zvingweme*.

Each of these names stands for a distinct category of *shavi* spirits, with clearly specified skills ascribed to it. A Shona who acts as host to one of these spirits, may refer to the spirit as generally belonging to one of the abovementioned categories without any further distinction, but in the majority of cases a *shavi* also has its own personal name (e.g. Manyahana, Djaravai or Gadzemoyo) and its own personal history, which the host can recount at length when in a state of possession.

Nearly all the *shavi* spirits are concerned with the art of healing or divination. One spirit may be particularly good at detecting the causes of illness or death, while another specializes in medicine for particular ailments. Women doctors often divine with the aid of *Zvipuna* and *Dzviti mashavi*, but the

Njuzu type of spirit is by far the most popular agent among them, when it comes to the procurement of medicines for epilepsy (*zvipusha*), scabies (*mhezi*) and especially barrenness amongst women (*ngomwa*). *Njuzu* is regarded as a water spirit living in or underneath a pool or river. At one stage or another the *Njuzu* possesses its host (hardly ever a male) and leads her to the 'city of the *Njuzu* spirits' (*Guta reNjuzu*) under the nearest dam or river, where she stays for several days.

There are numerous variations in the descriptions of the *Njuzu's* dwelling places, but the following outstanding features can be determined: No deaths occur, since the surrounding streams of boiling water prevent all witches from reaching this place. *Njuzu*land is therefore thought of as a place freed of all evil influence. All the 'people' in *Njuzu* territory are in a state of well-being, even if some of them are so old that they cannot feed themselves. Due to all the positive features of the *Njuzu* abode, the medicines prescribed by these spirits can be used for constructive purposes only. The spirits supply their mediums with medicative reeds, water plants, white clay, etc. (all medicines associated with water), which are the only things to be taken back on the return journey.

One should always refrain from accepting the mash made from pumpkins (*nhopi*) offered by the *Njuzu* spirits, because once this happens one is doomed to stay underneath the pool for ever. Only mud should be consumed to safeguard one against such temptations. It is only in a possessed state that a person is believed capable of staying submerged under water for such a long period. Once she returns with *Njuzu* medicine from the pool, a special welcoming ceremony is arranged by the villagers. This ceremony demonstrates the formal recognition of the now elevated status of the *Njuzu* host, the degree of elevation being determined by the duration of her stay amongst the *Njuzu* spirits.

The hosts of *Njuzu* spirits, like all *shavi* mediums, can only practise their occupation when their spirits take hold of them. Whenever they treat patients, a spell of ritual purification, which includes the washing of hands and face, or of the whole body, is needed to induce the spirit to put in an appearance. Thus the *Njuzu* spirit's close association with water and purity becomes evident during each healing session.

Jukwa spirits also give medical advice, but their main function is to act as rain emissaries in the spiritual realm. They come from Matonjeni and their nearness to Mwari enables them to mediate directly with God on behalf of the inhabitants in those districts where their hosts reside. Hence the importance of *kutambe maJukwa* (dance in honour of the *Jukwa* spirits) during the *mukwerere* rituals.[76]

76. In the spiritual realm several channels of communication therefore exist between

Zenda and *Muvimi* spirits are mainly preoccupied with the skills of hunting. The spirit's apparel is worn by its host on important hunts. Should he hit his quarry with a particularly good shot, the other hunters would exclaim: '*Zenda rabuda*!' (Zenda has come out!) In such an event the *shavi* is deemed to be present in its host without necessarily causing a trance-like state of possession. The same holds true for professions such as iron-smelting. The ability and skill to practise the profession is directly related to the particular type of spirit, which becomes so closely associated with its host that there is no need for regular spirit manifestations as signs of its presence. Active manifestations of *shavi* possession of these hosts only take place during the occasional *shavi* dance (*kutamba mashavi*) ceremonies.

The powers of *shavi* spirits are always subordinate to those of the ancestors. It is possible that through the influence of Christianity the *shavi*-God relationship has become closer in recent years. Several *shavi* hosts in Chingombe were practising Christians for some time before they became *shavi* mediums. These people often mention the co-operation between God and *shavi* spirits. 'They [the *mashavi*] first sit down with Mwari and receive His permission before they can do anything', is a commonly heard remark. Also, before selecting its host, the *shavi* must get permission from the family ancestors, who 'open the door' to the alien spirit to enter a prospective host's homestead. Should the spirit of a deceased *nganga*, who had practised his profession with the aid of a *shavi*, wish to possess one of his descendants, his *mudzimu* is always accompanied by the *shavi*, in which case the inheriting *nganga* will generally attribute his healing powers to both his *mudzimu* and the deceased's *shavi*, or differentiate between the divinatory powers bestowed upon him by his *mudzimu* and the curative insight he derived from the ancestor's *shavi*, or vice versa. The *mashavis'* powers never excel that of the ancestors. They hardly ever kill although they can cause grievous illness as a sign of their having selected a particular host and as a reminder of their rights to official recognition by the living.

There are several ways in which a *shavi* can reveal that he is calling a particular host. The person concerned may be caused to tread on a particular object,[77] e.g. a piece of cloth associated with the *shavi*, and when he or she picks it up the *shavi* will say: '*Ndaona nzvimbo yokugara*' – I have found a

---

the rain-giving God of Matonjeni and the rural population: 1. through the pyramidal structure of ancestral spirits; 2. through the continued activities of the deceased *vanyai* (called *vanyusa* in the state of death); and 3. through the *Jukwa* spirits.

77. This way of 'obtaining' a *shavi* spirit is referred to as *kutsika shavi* (to tread on the *shavi*).

place to stay (i.e. a host to settle in). The future host may at first not realize what has happened, until a *nganga* is consulted and the meaning of the occurrence explained. *Shavi* spirits that are affiliated with the family ancestors through generations of co-operation reveal their wishes to the chosen lineage members of each generation through dreams. But the most common procedure is to cause prolonged illness in the prospective host, until the relatives consult a *nganga* who reveals the *shavi's* wish. It is important that the *nganga* should indicate what kind of *shavi* causes the illness and what kind of outfit the spirit requires the prospective medium to wear. A *Jukwa* spirit usually demands at least a few yards of blue material or python skin, rattles (*hosho*) to be worn on the legs during dances, and perhaps a *muswe* (tail of an ox or of an *nkonkoni*, i.e. a gnu) all of which should be worn by its host during *shavi* ceremonies.[78]

While the beer-brewing preparations are under way, relatives of the afflicted person will buy the necessary cloth, beads and a few more of the articles prescribed by the *shavi*. At some future time the *shavi's* medium will personally supplement the outfit. The hosts of similar *shavi* spirits in the vicinity will be invited to this opening ceremony, which is conducted with the aim of assuring the *shavi* of its acceptance by the host-to-be and his or her relatives. After the *rukweza* beer has been dedicated to the *shavi* by one of the afflicted person's parents or spouse, the ceremony can start in all earnest. On this occasion the novice usually remains a spectator, but all the invited *shavi* mediums become possessed after a spell of preliminary dancing to the rhythmic beat of drums. Each of them wears his or her own *shavi* paraphernalia. The state of possession, which can last for many hours, starts with the noises and bodily movements peculiar to each kind of spirit. Shortly after the afflicted person has recovered another ceremony is arranged for the spirit to 'come out' in its host. As soon as the spirit puts in an appearance by responding to the special music of the occasion, it is presented with the required belongings, after which the new medium, having temporarily lost his or her own identity, sits down as the *shavi* itself and recounts its own history. It often happens that the *shavi* is cross-questioned by participants who try to detect inconsistencies in the facts presented by the spirit. The history of a family

78. Gelfand provides us with elaborate descriptions of the kind of paraphernalia associated with the different categories of *shavi* spirits. For the Kore-Kore, see Gelfand, 1959, Chapter 9, and Gelfand, 1962, Chapter 10. In Chingombe the head-gear and garments of the different types of *shavi* were not sufficiently differentiated for such a detailed classification as that of Gelfand. With the exception of a few outstanding articles particularly associated with one or another category of spirit, there is a considerable amount of overlapping in this respect.

shavi are of course well known, and the host of such a *shavi* knows that the facts should be correctly recited as a sign of authenticity. At this juncture jesting is also allowed.

A whole series of introductory ceremonies is sometimes performed before the *shavi* 'comes out' properly in its host and before the medium can fully profit from the skill imparted by the spirit. *Nganga* often work with more than one *shavi*. They frequently state that one of their *mashavi* has not yet 'come out' properly (*shavi rigere kubuda zvakanaka*), in spite of their having acquired all its necessary *nhumbi* (belongings). But once a medium has accepted a *shavi*, regular ceremonies should be held at least once a year in honour of the spirit. The number of relatives and other *shavi* mediums attending such ceremonies depends on the medium's standing and popularity. Some of the reputed *nganga* in the Gutu district invite other *shavi* diviners and herbalists from far and wide for their annual *kutamba mashavi* ceremonies. As a result the majority of *shavi* mediums annually attend at least a few large-scale *shavi* feasts in addition to the more modest ceremonies (e.g. plate 13) conducted on behalf of one kind of *shavi*. The basic principle behind the regular ceremonies, whether on a large or small scale, nevertheless remains the same. It amounts to a concrete demonstration of belief in (*kutenda*) and remembrance of (*kurangarira*) the *shavi*. Without this regular re-enactment of an attitude of gratitude and dependence, the danger of retaliation or complete loss of the spirit's beneficient powers arises. These feasts also indicate the mutual interdependence of spirit and medium. A town-*nganga* summed it up as follows: 'Through the *shavi* dances we strengthen [*simbisa*] our *shavi* spirits, so that they can be more effective in their work. If we forget them, they leave us and we stay behind as fools [*mapenzi*].'

No *shavi* dance is complete without beer. Female relatives of the medium brew the *shavi's* finger millet beer and see to it that the spirit's *murevo* pot is set aside for propitiatory purposes. Goats are often slaughtered to provide the guests with meat, but not for any sacrificial purposes. Drums, rattles and *hwamanda* (kudu horns) are the most frequently used musical instruments during *shavi* dances. Since each spirit responds only to its own rhythm or tune, subtle variations are constantly being introduced by the musicians, especially the drummers, so as to give each spirit a chance of possessing its dancing medium. The *Bvene* (baboon) spirits cause their hosts to jump around or climb trees; water spirits cause their hosts to fall down and move around on the ground like reptiles; *Zenda* and *Muvimi* spirits manifest themselves in the stalking and shooting manoeuvres of their hosts. Some of the spirits are only to be distinguished from others in minor variations of dance steps. *Shavi* dances break the monotony of village life. Because of their entertainment value and the chance of a beer drink, great numbers of guests are usually attracted to the larger *shavi* dances, which may last a full day or a whole weekend.

As can be deduced from table 23 the belief in the existence of *shavi* (and *ngozi*) spirits, both in tribal areas and in town, is still strong. No less than 95% of the rural adults in Chingombe and 90% of the townsmen considered *shavi* spirits definitely to exist, a result of the survey which clearly reflects the resilience of some traditional beliefs. Due to the impact of Western medical service, the relevancy of *shavi* spirits in the lives of individuals is being changed. They no longer need to depend solely on the curative insights and powers imparted by *shavi* spirits to the *nganga*. But this change does not necessarily eradicate the belief in the *shavi's* curative capabilities. In so far as it does, the process is slower than one might anticipate, because only 16% of the interviewed ruralists and 15% of the urbanites were willing to state that the *shavi* spirits have no healing powers (table 24). We must therefore conclude that, to a greater or lesser degree, the *shavi* spirits are still regarded as real forces, with a direct influence on the lives of people, by the majority of Africans in our field of study.

c) *Avenging spirits* (*ngozi*)

Of all Shona spirits, the *ngozi* is the most formidable, dangerous, and therefore also the most feared. It is the avenging spirit of an aggrieved person that comes back after his death to demand justice and retribution for the unrepaired wrongs that were done to him during life. Most people refer to the *ngozi* as 'very bad' (*kushata chose*), but this does not imply moral wickedness, since the spirit that 'arises to haunt someone' (*kupfuka*) as *ngozi* has a just cause and is somehow allowed by Mwari to claim its dues from the living. It is bad in the sense that it causes destruction without mercy amongst the relatives of the guilty person.

Gelfand distinguishes between four kinds of *ngozi* amongst the Zezuru: 1) the spirit of a murdered person; 2) the spirit of a person from whom something was borrowed during his life without being returned; 3) the spirit of a deceased spouse who returns to his or her surviving partner because of desertion or bad care during a period of critical illness; and 4) the parental spirit that returns to its own children to punish them for maltreatment.[79] He asserts that the *ngozi* is also known amongst the NaJena (Karanga) people, but that it

79. Gelfand, 1959, p. 153.

differs to some extent from the concept amongst the Zezuru. The additional type of circumstance, according to Gelfand, which can give rise to the emergence of an *ngozi* spirit 'are the occasions when a man goes off with another man's wife; when a loan is not repaid; or if the bride-wealth is not paid to the bride's parents.'[80] According to these motivations a spirit can turn *ngozi* in response to a wide range of injustices, which leads us towards a broad concept of the avenging spirit.

The information supplied by a great number of Southern Shona informants suggests, however, that the *ngozi* concept can be narrowed down considerably. In the first place, the *ngozi* proper is a killer who causes havoc in the family of the guilty person. In this capacity the avenging spirit is never a member of the afflicted person's patrilineage. It is always a *mutorwa*, a 'foreigner' in the sense of belonging to another (including the matri-)lineage. A person's own patrilineal spirits can never become *ngozi* to him in the full sense of the word. This distinction limits the above-mentioned point 4 of Gelfand. A father's or grandfather's spirit afflicting its descendants, for instance when it requests them to prepare the *kugadzira* ritual or rebukes them for misconduct, also appears as an avenging spirit. As a result family members may say 'the spirit has become a *ngozi*' (*mweya wava ngozi*). Yet if one inquires into the matter, it becomes evident that they do not regard such a dissatisfied agnatic spirit as *ngozi* proper, but as *ngozi* by analogy. Similarly, other spirits that are haunting (*kupfuka*) people may also be casually referred to as '*ngozi*', without the actual vengeful spirit being implied.[81]

In the second place a *mutorwa* (foreigner) spirit only turns *ngozi* as a result of fatal injury such as outright murder, or actions leading to the death or suicide of the aggrieved person, such as ill-treatment of a severe nature, refusal to feed a person, desertion during critical illness, improper care of a sick or disabled person, or the casting out of a person from the homestead where he used to be fed, which leads to eventual death. In the third place the *ngozi* always claims compensation of a retributory nature. Death can only be substituted by life, which in this context involves the transfer cattle and/or an unmarried girl (*mhandara*) from the culprit's family to the deceased's relatives, where the latter bears children as 'wife of the *ngozi*' to replace the damage done to his lineage.[82]

80. Gelfand, 1966, p. 70.

81. A motor-car that can 'kill' is sometimes called a *ngozi*, or people will say of a difficult situation '*ingozi*!' (it is a *ngozi*). Due to this wide use of the term confusion can arise as to the true nature of the avenging spirit.

82. In this respect the *ngozi* represents the interests of his lineage group as well as his own. The vengeful act therefore has more than a purely subjective motivation behind it.

According to these three basic aspects Gelfand's second and fourth categories of vengeful spirits do not necessarily belong to the Southern Shona concept of the *ngozi* proper. This does not mean that these spirits do not claim retribution, for they do, but their punitive measures are less drastic than those of the *ngozi*.

The *ngozi* does not always attack the wrongdoer, but it can cause havoc in the families of any of the latter's blood relatives. It often happens that the avenging spirit delays its disastrous actions for one or more generations before it strikes at the descendants of the culprit. This means that practically any series of inexplicable deaths in one family can be attributed to the actions of *ngozi* that had been wronged in the remote past. The *nganga* may pinpoint as the reason for such deaths the misdeeds of the 'forefathers of long ago' (*madziteteguru ekare*) of which the descendants may have been totally unaware. Thus the common guilt of the forefathers – and any lineage of course has its known or unknown 'murderers' – has fatal consequences for their descendants, because '*ngozi inongoramba inchitevera ropa romuurayi* (the *ngozi* persists in following the blood[-relatives] of the murdered)'. A whole family can therefore become so obsessed with the idea of a harassing *ngozi* that any serious trouble met by any of its members is interpreted in terms of this spirit. If the descendants of the *ngozi* spirit are known, the compensation claimed by the spirit is given to them, and they are then responsible for the ritual appeasement of their *mudzimu*.[83] Should the *ngozi's* relatives be unknown or beyond the reach of the afflicted family, the *nganga* will either try to exorcise the spirit, through action aimed at deflecting the spirit's attacks, or the family will try to pacify it by 'adopting it' more or less as one of the family ancestors, mentioning its name during family rituals.

In the former case the *nganga* will dedicate a fowl to the *ngozi* spirit and after a ceremony of ritual killing he will bury it in a remote ant-bear hole or cave with the words: 'You, so-and-so, we have today prepared this dwelling place for you. Stay here and do not return to X's (the afflicted) family.' Another way of diverting the *ngozi* is to dedicate a black cow to it and then leave the animal somewhere in the bush for the *ngozi* to follow.[84] In the latter case the head of the afflicted family dedicates one of his daughters – at the request of the *ngozi* which by this time has found a medium to voice its wishes – to

83. The lineage members of the afflicting spirit qualify it in their own family circles as *mudzimu unonetsa* (the troublesome family spirit). If they call it *ngozi*, the implication is always that it is in the first place an avenging spirit to the members of the guilty person's lineage and not to themselves.

84. If another person finds the beast and claims it, the *ngozi* may direct his attacks against this man's family. For this reason Africans seldom claim stray animals.

the spirit as compensation. Since the *ngozi's* relatives are not there to collect the compensation, the *ngozi's* 'wife' may be given in marriage to any ordinary suitor, but the collected *roora* beasts will be used from time to time as offerings to the vengeful spirit. In Chingombe the *ngozi* spirits that are appeased in this way are sometimes called *sekuru,* as if they belong to the category of family ancestors. Fear of the spirit, which remains a potent and unpredictable danger, activates regular family rituals, so that the offering of cattle and goats takes place much more frequently than in the case of families not threatened in this way. During such rituals the *ngozi* spirit will speak through its medium. The participants will endeavour to win its goodwill by acting as if they have come to rely on its 'protective powers'.

Relatives of an aggrieved or murdered person sometimes take the necessary measures to ensure that the spirit will arise against their enemies as *ngozi.* Such a person is buried with medicine in one hand. The corpse is told against whom to use the medicine, lest it starts troubling its own relatives. A black goat or fowl may be dedicated to the aggrieved deceased. After the funeral this animal will be addressed as if it were the deceased himself: 'You, X, if you rise, do not come to our house, but go to those people who have wronged you!' The purpose clearly is to deflect the wrath of the deceased, whose lust for revenge can lead to the affliction of its own family. Should the animal die after a while it is a sure sign that the spirit has moved to the guilty person's *musha.*[85]

The *ngozi* often starts afflicting the guilty party's relatives by causing severe illness. Mental disorder is one of the most frequent symptoms of *ngozi*-inflicted illness. Major disasters can be avoided if the people find out soon enough that a *ngozi* has turned against them, but in most cases, *ngozi* affliction is diagnosed only after the successive deaths of a number of family members.[86] Having selected one of the afflicted family members, the *ngozi* will reveal itself. It will first ask the people why they killed him. Then compensatory demands are made. Confirmation from a *nganga* is needed before the family will start negotiating with the relatives of the deceased. Only a specialized and powerful *nganga* will be willing to treat *ngozi* cases because if the *nganga* blocks the spirit's passage to the afflicted family, it may turn on his own relatives out of spite. Should the *nganga's* countermeasures prove to be inadequate in such circumstances he will be blamed for exposing his own relatives to the *ngozi's* onslaught.

85. Gelfand, 1962, p. 70.

86. The *ngozi* is believed to have *simba guru-guru* (great power) and it can wipe out a whole family if not properly appeased.

Once *ngozi* trouble has been officially diagnosed one or more of the following three types of protective measures can be taken:

1. Compensation is given to the *ngozi*;
2. exorcism of the vengeful spirit is effected by a *nganga*, and
3. preventive measures are taken to protect all the blood relatives of the afflicted persons against future attacks.

We shall briefly consider the major aspects of such protective treatment:

1. *Compensation.* The *ngozi* has a right to receive full compensation for the wrongful act which it seeks to avenge. *Mutumbu* must be paid to replace the complete physical stature of the deceased.[87] In earlier years the *mutumbu* usually consisted of a young girl and some cattle, sent to the *ngozi's* relatives after the *nganga* or *ngozi* medium had determined the 'fine'. Serious disruptions of family life may still, at present, be dealt with in this manner, although the tendency increasingly is to pay with cattle. Each of the ten or more head of cattle is supposed to replace a certain part of the deceased's body, from the feet to the head. Some informants maintain that only a living person can replace the head of the deceased. They say that a harassed family will start by sending the necessary cattle, and will feel compelled to present the *ngozi* with a 'wife' as soon as it shows signs of being dissatisfied.

As soon as the *ngozi's* 'wife' and cattle reach the village of its relatives, the spirit possesses one of its own descendants, who then gives directions about the procedure to be followed. If the spirit has not been *gadwa'd* at this stage, its future name-bearer will be pointed out and placed in charge of the *ngozi* cattle. Should he be too young the representative head of the family will take care of it for the time being. When the *kugadzira* takes place, one or more of the *ngozi* cattle will be offered to the spirit by way of pacification. If the *kugadzira* has already taken place when the *ngozi* compensation arrives, a special propitiation ceremony, with the ritual slaughtering of some of the beasts, will have to be conducted. The *ngozi* also reveals which of the males will act in its place as the *mhandara's* husband.

A special hut built for the *ngozi* will be swept by its 'wife' at regular intervals, to convince it of the family's remembrance. Similar measures may be taken by the afflicted family if the *ngozi* relatives are unknown or if they, as sometimes happens, refuse to receive the compensation. It seems, however, as if the *ngozi* hut is primarily erected for the spirit of an unmarried murdered

87. *Mutumbu*: 'the whole physical body'. The relatives of the vengeful spirit will claim the spirit's dues by saying: 'Since you have killed our relative, we demand a "whole body" in exchange (*zvawakauraya hama yedu tinoda mutumbu*).'

person, whose compensation consists of cattle only. When, for example, the *ngozi* cattle of a deceased young girl arrives at the village, her father will build her a small hut to dwell in. He will address the spirit as follows: 'Here I have built you a house to dwell in, my daughter. Leave those people you have come from in peace. I am giving your compensation cattle to your brother since you are his *chipanda* sister. He will find himself a wife with the aid of your cattle and in return he will keep you [*kumuchengeta*] at this house.'

Ngozi compensation, in whatever form, is always regarded as potentially dangerous. For this reason '*ngozi*' relatives sometimes refuse to negotiate with the members of an afflicted family, lest their *mudzimu* cause trouble in their own ranks. The *ngozi* is always 'near' to its 'wife' and cattle. Maltreatment of the *ngozi's* wife and misuse of this cattle can lead to severe forms of punishment. Once the spirit starts punishing its own relatives, and thereby becomes a pseudo-'*ngozi*' to them also, there is no end to the misery. All forms of misfortune in the family is then blamed on this spirit.[88] It is possible that under such circumstances the family members become so *ngozi*-conscious that regular rituals will have to be conducted for several generations to appease the spirit.

Conflicts sometimes arise between the *ngozi*-afflicted and '*ngozi*'-related families. If the latter family is reluctant to receive the compensation, or if the responsible members fail to propitiate their spirit in the proper way, the afflicted group will summon the aid of a *nganga* to try and direct the spirit against its own people. As soon as the spirit's relatives realize what has happened, they will try to redirect it once more. As a result the members of the opposing parties may, for some time, confine their ritual activities to efforts at directing the spirit against each other. But as soon as the toll in lives becomes too high, reconciliation may be sought by the representatives of each group.

88. In one of the well-known Rozvi families of Gutu, the mental derangement of two brothers and their sister, the lameness of another sister and the weak results in school of some of their children are all attributed to the mismanagement of the *ngozi* cattle of their *tateguru* by their eldest brother. The cattle had been paid some years ago by the members of an afflicted lineage, whose forebears are said to have killed this particular family's *tateguru* at a beer party in the distant past. The avenging spirit's grandchild, acting as head of the family, had slaughtered some of the compensatory beasts without the spirit's consent, and when an effort was made to appease the spirit, he sold the meat of the sacrificial beast instead of distributing it in the proper way. The experiences and beliefs of one of the afflicted family members, Miche Munyani, will be described in the following volume.

2. *Exorcism.* In the above-mentioned case of two families fighting each other, reconciliation can only be achieved through ritual exorcism. For the *ngozi* to leave the afflicted persons, both groups of people will be required to appear on the opposite banks of a river on an appointed day. A *nganga* will then kill and skin a black goat in the middle of the streaming water to 'cool down' (*tonhodza*) the angered spirit and to cause the ancestors of both parties that have become involved in the fight to return to their own group of descendants.

We have already mentioned the use of a fowl or black cow[89] for the purposes of exorcism. Kumbirai furnishes us with information about the symbolic meaning of certain trees during exorcistic actions. The *mushozowa* tree, he says, has a very hard wood which is never attacked by worms. It bears fruit which has a special attraction for goats. Thus the sacrificial goat is left at a *mushozowa* tree to make sure that it will not return with the spirit to the kraal. In this way the *ngozi* is cast out of the village. The hard wood of the tree itself symbolizes the ruthlessness and hardness of the *ngozi*, as well as the hoped-for 'hardness' of the family members against future *ngozi* attacks. After such an exorcism it is said: '*Vanhu vawoma*; *ngozi haichavagoni. Vawoma somushozowa*!' (The people have become hard; the *ngozi* will fail [to hurt] them; they have become as [hard as] the *mushozowa*).[90] On the other hand the *ngozi* may be exorcised at the *mukute* tree; a tree which grows in marshy places and bears soft, purple fruit. The idea is to make the *ngozi* as soft as the *mukute* in order to pacify it.[91]

3. *Preventive measures against future attacks.* As soon as the vengeful spirit is exorcised and its compensation paid, the *nganga* will take all the necessary precautions to 'fortify' the whole extended family group against future attack. Strong medicine (*mbanda*) is prepared and sprinkled (*kukusha*) over the bodies of all the family members to cleanse them from possible contamination caused by the spirit. Those members of the family who are not present at the time receive their own protective medicine as soon as they arrive at the village. Preventive measures differ according to the insight and experience of each *nganga*. In addition to the medicine sprinkled on the body, family members may be required to undergo a purification rite, which includes a detailed cleansing ceremony, or the *nganga* will furnish them with powerful amulets which they should wear under all circumstances. To prevent the *ngozi* from

89. Black presumably symbolizes the 'black' (destructive) intent of the *ngozi*.

90. Kumbirai, Unpublished Manuscript.

91. According to Kumbirai this tree is only used when a *ngozi* turns against its own relatives. A *mutorwa ngozi* (foreigner *ngozi* i.e. *ngozi* proper) can only by exorcised at the *mushozowa* because it is hard and merciless.

returning, the *nganga* drives magic pegs into the ground (*kupinga musha*: to peg the homestead) on all four sides of each homestead. Medicine will also be sprinkled at the doorstep and doorposts of such houses as a final precaution against the evil spirit's entrance.

It was noted that a *nganga*, and only a specialized one at that, plays a prominent role in most of the activities concerned with the elimination of the *ngozi's* destructive influence. No ordinary family member of the afflicted family group can perform this function. Neither is there much the afflicted group can do after they have paid the *ngozi* compensation. They therefore become dependent both on the *nganga* for protection and on the *ngozi's* relatives for the propitiation of their spirit. Their own family spirits who have also been roused by the *ngozi* against them, can only be pacified after the most essential measures of exorcism and the consequential separation of the *ngozi* from the family spirits have taken place. As the most dreaded spirit known to the Shona, the *ngozi* inspires nothing but fear. The punishment meted out often surpasses the wrong done, but the legitimacy of the *ngozi's* claim for restitution is beyond dispute.

That the bulk of Africans still believe in the possibility of *ngozi* attacks is convincingly borne out in the figures of tables 23 and 25. More than 90% of the ruralists and townsmen believe in the existence of such spirits, and nearly the same percentage of people attributed to the *ngozi* the power to kill (table 25). Relatively few families are in fact plagued by *ngozi* spirits but the general persistence of the belief as such forms at least the precondition for the practice of traditional ritual in times of crisis. Few Shona families, Christian or otherwise, will refrain from taking the appropriate, 'traditionally proven' action, once a *ngozi* threat has been diagnosed.

3. THE DIVINER-HERBALIST (NGANGA)

a) *Theoretical considerations*

The *nganga* is a religious professional whose activities include a wide variety of magical practices. Before we describe some of these practices the use in this study of the term *magic* and its bearing on religious activities – a subject of considerable controversy – needs some clarification.

In the first place magic can be defined as the achievement of a desired end through the correct, expressive and symbolic manipulation of power-laden objects and of spiritual forces; with or without the aid of spiritual beings. This type of action presupposes a specialized knowledge of and a certain control over the impersonal or personal forces set in motion. In the second place magic, as defined above, forms an integral component of religion.[92] The analytical distinction which is often made between religion on the one hand and magic (including the activities of 'magicians' and wizards) on the other, as if two well differentiated systems are involved, may be of some use to the observing outsider involved, but seems inconsistent with Shona beliefs and ritual. The Shona themselves do not make a clear division between the High-God and ancestral cult, and ritual activities involving magic. Some of the ancestral and alien spirit rituals are magical in character, and many of the objects used for curative or protective purposes are so closely associated with the *shavi* or ancestral spirit of the *nganga* who prescribes and supplies them, that the inherent power believed to be at work has distinctly personal attributes.

What then is the essential distinction in the wide religious continuum between magical and non-magical rituals? Tylor differentiated between beliefs and rituals involving reference to more – or less – 'personalized' spiritual beings, such as deities and spirits concerning tribal life, and those which imply the notion of an impersonal unindividualized power.[93] The latter, according to him, concerns magic. Another more recent definition also excludes the involvement of personal spiritual beings in magical rituals: 'In magic no appeal is made to spirits. The desired end is believed to be achieved directly by the ritual technique itself, that is, by the use of appropriate actions, objects or words. The action, formula or object is believed to have dynamic power *per se* or to be set in force by the volition of someone who has the necessary knowledge.'[94] Both definitions are valuable when it comes to distinguishing, in the broad sense of the word, between rituals solely directed at spiritual beings, and those concerning dynamistic forces of nature that can be harnessed for particular purposes if properly manipulated. But in terms of our own qualification of magic, which allows for the involvement of spiritual beings – as the force(s) symbolically manipulated or as the aiding power(s) behind the manipulator – neither of the aforementioned definitions are broad enough to allow for all kinds of magical ritual. Rites which do not presuppose

92. The term religion is used here in the sense as defined by Blauw (1968, par. 5): 'All ideas and those resultant patterns of behaviour, acts, practices, views and organizations concerning a reality "other" than that which is daily lived out and experienced by everybody; a reality which is considered to encompass and in many ways to permeate and influence ordinary reality, but which is also considered to be open to the influence of human beings.' – Translated from the Dutch text.

93. Tylor, 1871, quoted from Beattie, 1964, p. 212.

94. *Notes and Queries on Anthropology*, revised by a Committee of the Royal Anthropological Institute, 1964, p. 187.

spiritual beings may indeed be magical, but those that include such beings do not necessarily become non-magical.

Instead of qualifying rituals as magical on the grounds of the personal or impersonal nature of the force at work, it is rather the causal connection between the (supernatural or mystical) results achieved and the forces correctly unleashed by the active agent (the *nganga*) which is distinctive. In rituals involving spiritual beings, the recognition of and subjection to the overriding power of such beings, despite the effort to influence them, determines the action as non-magical. If the ritual is considered to control and have a compulsive effect on the spirit involved, it is magical. We are therefore in agreement with the distinction made by Pauw: 'Even when a spiritual being enters the chain of thoughts and is thought of as causing the effect the ritual may still be magical if it is thought of as *necessarily* resulting in that effect, as if the spiritual being is *compelled* by the ritual to react in a particular way. When it is believed that a rite or object *may* have a particular effect but that the outcome ultimately depends upon the decision of a spiritual being, in which that being decides according to its own free will, it is non-magical.'[95]

If this distinction is applied to the rituals already mentioned in this chapter, one can say that the approach of the High-God at Matonjeni and of the tribal spirits during a *mukwerere* ritual is essentially non-magical, compared to the distinctly magical character of a rite concerned, for example, with *ngozi* exorcism. Mwari and the tribal spirits may be moved to grant the pleas of ritual participants, but they are not controlled or manipulated. The *nganga*, on the other hand, 'orders' the *ngozi* spirit not to return to the afflicted when he places the fowl, representing the spirit, in the cave. He is not in the first place forwarding a request to and expecting an independent reply from the spirit, but doing away with it in a manner which symbolically expresses his intent. This part of the ritual bears a magical character in so far as the emphasis is on the correct procedure of the *nganga*, which of necessity drives the *ngozi* away. His actions are again of a magical nature when he prepares medicine and fortifies the village against future *ngozi* attacks. Some of the villagers may indeed regard the medicine as powerful and effective due to the *nganga's* ability to manipulate it correctly, or due to the 'impersonal' force at work in the medicine itself. The western observer deems the medicine symbolic and without any causal effectiveness as such, but the villagers believe that it is instrumental in keeping the avenging spirit away. The Shona *nganga*, for his part, will find it important to follow the correct procedure while doctoring the village and he may speak of his medicine as containing 'great

95. Pauw, 1960, p. 147.

power' (*simba guru*) both of which are essential aspects of magical ritual, but he will invariably ascribe this power to personal forces, i.e. to his healing *shavi* or *mudzimu*, the active agents within him when he performs the ritual. It is this aspect which the above-mentioned definition ('In magic no appeal is made to spirits') does not cover.

A certain amount of overlapping renders a straightforward classification of all rituals as magical or non-magical impossible. Especially rituals concerned with the lesser ancestral spirits, placed lower down in the spiritual hierarchy than the tribal spirits, are marked by magical trends. For, although these ancestors can be said, in the final analysis, to react to ritual out 'of their own free will', the tendency to exercise considerable pressure on them is unmistakably woven into the fabric of (family) ancestral rituals.

It should also be noted that the close relatedness if not partial identification of numerous charms and medicines, distributed by the *nganga*, with personal spiritual forces, does not exclude the belief in the inherent efficacy of medicines. Objects are often selected by professional 'magicians' and commoners alike, because of their appropriateness to the end sought. Because of this appropriateness objects are usually imaginatively endowed with an intrinsic magical power, so that the people using them think of them as instrumental in their effect and therefore capable of bringing about the desired end.

The practices of the *nganga* reflect the manipulation of objects or spiritual forces towards ends which are mainly regarded as socially constructive, as opposed to the antisocial machinations of the wizard (which and sorcerer). Both forms of magical action will have to be considered – the latter in the last section of this chapter – because they form the background to much of the prophetic activity of the contemporary Independent Churches.

b) *Types of nganga and their position in society*

There are mainly two different types of *nganga*: the diviner and the herbalist. The Shona make no linguistic distinction between the two, for any male or female 'doctor' may be called *nganga*, *murapi* or *chiremba*. In some districts the latter term is used exclusively for eldery female 'practitioners'. Few *nganga* who divine with wooden divining slabs (*hakata*), divining shells or through their *shavi* spirits, practise this art without distributing medicine of any sort, and many herbalists provide medicines without practising any form of divination. But it seldom happens that a *nganga*, whether he is a diviner-herbalist or merely a herbalist, claims to practise his profession without some kind of spiritual inspiration. His medical insight is never derived from his own talents;

it is the ancestors, *mashavi*, or a combination of both, who enable him to interpret the *hakata*, to 'read' the divining-mirror or to find 'strong medicine'.

Apart from the basic functional distinction of diviner (-herbalist) and herbalist, there are numerous varieties of *nganga*. Some specialize in curing barrenness, others in driving out evil spirits, curing chest or stomach ailments, detecting and curing an illness caused by witchcraft or simply providing people with the so-called 'good luck' charms. None of these varieties are mutually exclusive. A *nganga* who has built up a reputation for detecting the causes of death will, as a specialist in this field, receives a great number of people who seek information in this respect but also in connection with other troubles. There is actually no end to the scope of a *nganga's* activities. Gelfand aptly describes him (or her) as a 'kingpin' of African society, whose scope of activity embraces more or less everything affecting an individual or his family. 'European society', he says, 'has no one quite like the *nganga*, an individual to whom people can turn in every kind of difficulty. He is a doctor in sickness, a priest in religious matters, a lawyer in legal issues, a policeman in the detection and prevention of crime, a possessor of magical preparations which can increase crops and instil special skills and talents into his clients. He fills a great need in African society, his presence gives assurance in the whole community.'[96]

In everyday life there is little to distinguish the *nganga* from other villagers. They move around dressed in the same kind of clothes as their neighbours and are, as far as one can observe, treated as ordinary members of the community. Unless they are suspected of distributing destructive medicine on a large scale they are not feared but treated by their fellow-villagers as equals. Their important function in traditional society nevertheless gives them a potential social prominence or enhanced status, which one could not achieve in the tribal political realm without being favourably 'placed' by birth in the genealogical hierarchy of the distinguished leadership, for the positions of kraalhead, ward-head or chief. As long as the belief in the power of spirits and evil forces (sorcery and witchcraft) calls for the services of a *nganga*, his enhanced social status remains safeguarded.

It is difficult to assess the exact number of practising *nganga* in any one area. Nearly all family heads have some basic knowledge of curative herbs, a knowledge which is attributed to the family ancestors. They may even engage in minor divinatory practices in the case of less serious ailments within the family. Then there are a number of diviner-herbalists who practise periodically

96. Gelfand, 1964 (II), p. 55.

as the need for their services arise and who may cease operating once they are convinced that the 'healer' spirit which had called them, has been satisfied. Such persons nevertheless remain potential *nganga* and may start practising again when circumstances or the indwelling spirits demand it. Few *nganga* are full-time specialists, since the majority of them combine their professional activities with a certain amount of subsistence farming. In Chingombe with its 8 to 9,000 inhabitants, there are probably not more than three *nganga* who can be regarded as full-time practitioners, but there are well over twenty acknowledged and well-known 'doctors' periodically at work within the chiefdom's borders. In Chingombe North alone, within a two-mile radius of Zimbizi school, at least nine reputed *nganga* can be found amongst a community constituted by the members of six villages. All of these are diviner-herbalists who practise with the aid of a *mudzimu-shavi* combination or with one or more *shavi* spirits. Several of the women *nganga* act as the hosts of two or three *mashavi*, but their activities are never completely alike. The one *chiremba*, for instance, becomes possessed by one of her *shavi* spirits which she knows is the most suited to deal with the kind of illness or problem of the patient concerned, while another will become possessed successively by all three *mashavi* for each diagnostic and medicative spell. In the latter type of procedure the aid of an acolyte (usually a close relative) is not needed because the divining bones are thrown by the *nganga* while she is possessed by a *Chipuna shavi*; the interpretation of each throw is given at a later stage when the *Muzungu shavi* 'comes out' and the prescription for the right kind of medicine is given by her *Njuzu shavi*.[97]

Apart from an assisting acolyte, who is needed by some *nganga* to interpret the revelations of the possessing spirit (working through the *nganga*) to the patients, these *nganga* of the tribal areas mostly operate independently of each other. They meet annually during the *kutamba mashavi* dances, or when they themselves fall ill, or when a novice receives his or her basic training from one of the older *nganga*. There is an unwritten code of professional etiquette amongst them, such as the mutual respect for each other's practices and the recognition of the maximum time in which a *nganga* is supposed to treat a patient in order to achieve results. All well-known *nganga* have one or more spare huts at their homesteads where their patients can stay if necessary. Some of them will even accommodate patients who come from afar within their own private quarters.

97. This sequence of possession by different spirits was witnessed in the healing activities of *Mai* Masikati in the Bikita district. In Chingombe *Mai* vaGhoni and *Mai* MaMoyo follow practically the same pattern, with some minor variations.

In the urban environment the geographical factor enables the *nganga* to co-operate more closely with his colleagues than in the rural area. The founding of the 'African Nganga Association' in recent years reflects the attempt of urban *nganga* to establish a new form of joint action and control. In the 'Aims and Objects' of the Association's Constitution it is stated that every *nganga* must, for purposes of inspection and control, keep a record of all cases that come under his treatment. He must also keep a record of the kind of medicine he has prescribed. The traditional code is honoured in so far as it is the duty of the Executive to take disciplinary measures against those *nganga* who derogate others. Proof of 'inheritance' of their powers or of their apprenticeship (at least two years under a hereditary *nganga*) are the stipulated conditions for recognition.[98] Gelfand is of the opinion that the traditional *nganga* does not support this Association. He states that 'most of them [belonging to the Association] are herbalists, they neither divine themselves nor – as orthodox procedure demands – do they advise their clients first to seek a diviner to find out the spiritual cause of their illness. They are, in fact, nothing more than pharmacists who prescribe and sell herbs and charms over the counter . . . unlike the traditional herbalist, they charge for every herb they prescribe instead of waiting to collect their fees after a cure has been effected and the client's family is satisfied.'[99] This may be true in the bigger urban areas, but in Fort Victoria the situation is different: the ten officially recognized *nganga* of the Association in the Mucheke township are all diviner-herbalists and not just 'pharmacists who sell their herbs and charms over the counter'. None of the herbalists, some of whom come into town daily from the reserves to sell their medicines on the market, belongs to the Association. Regular contact exists between the members of the Association in the Mucheke township. Under the leadership of 'Dr.' Denis (plate 18) discussions are held at least once a month, besides the regular meetings by those *nganga* who are on friendly terms. Several of the town *nganga* are engaged in clerical or manual jobs. They therefore have to practise between working hours or at night-time.

It is obvious that both rural and urban communities have ample access to traditionalist diviners and herbalists. An accurate assessment of the extent to and the frequency with which Church members visit *nganga* can only be achieved through the regular attendance of healing ceremonies over a wide area. The impression one gets from occasional observations of *nganga* treat-

98. Under the heading: 'FUNCTIONS OF THE EXECUTIVE' in the Association's Constitution, it is stated that 'The Executive shall seek to know that everyone practising as a Nganga has inherited this practice from his ancestors or may have been trained by a hereditary Nganga for a period of not less than two years.'

99. Gelfand, 1964 (II), p. 117.

ment is that the majority of vaShona, both Christian[100] and non-Christian, visit the traditional doctors, especially during family crises. *Nganga* are so used to treating people from various denominations that they seldom take note of the religious affiliation of their patients. A great number of people make use of Western as well as traditional medical or prophetic (Independent Church) treatment. We shall discuss this trend when dealing with the healing activities of the Independent Churches. Mission Church members who consult *nganga* often state that they only obtain medicine (*mushonga*)[101] and that they ignore such parts of the prescription as necessitate 'ancestor worship'. Such statements, convincing though they may sound, do not necessarily imply the exclusion of all forms of traditional religious practices because, having been prescribed by the spiritual advisor *par excellence* and religious expert, few of the *nganga's* solutions are totally free from traditional religious implications. A Christian will perhaps refrain from full participation in a traditional ritual prescribed by the *nganga*, but he may very well make provision for the ceremony to be conducted by non-Christian relatives, and make use of such magical medicaments as will render him immune to the attack of angry *midzimu* or evil alien spirits. A symptom of the inherent acceptance of *nganga* practices, even in Christian circles, is the apparent lack of scepticism concerning the basic principles of interference and control in human lives, caused by ancestors, alien spirits, sorcerers and witches. Criticism will be directed at the individual *nganga*, but even then a patient will be reluctant to question the *nganga's* methods, since there is no way of disproving his professed powers .

Some form of spiritual endowment is always a prerequisite for a prospective 'practitioner' to become a *nganga*. With all the emphasis placed on the external, spiritual compulsion, the chances of this profession being exploited solely for commercial purposes are reduced to a minimum. Once the ancestral or *shavi* spirit[102] has made known its wish to operate through an individual,

100. The staunch supporters of the Spirit-type Independent Churches, whose prophets supplant *nganga* practices with parallel prophecies, as a rule do not visit *nganga*. It was evident, however, from the healing sessions which I have attended that nominal and active members of all the Mission and Ethiopian-type Independent Churches frequently visit the *nganga*.

101. The term *mushonga* can include any type of medicine with a causal effect, or magical preparations such as charms and amulets of a symbolic nature.

102. Hereditary *nganga* usually work under the guidance of the *midzimu* of the former family-*nganga* and its *shavi*. This category of *nganga* is regarded as the most skillful and powerful. The functions of the co-operating spirits differ. 'Dr.' Denis of Fort Victoria divines the causes of illness through the aid of his *midzimu*, who are called in by smearing medicine from an inherited calabash on his face. Medicative treatment is only given at a later stage when the 'doctor' is possessed by his healing *shavi*.

such a person stands under a moral obligation to fulfil the spirit's demands. There is no way of avoiding such a task without the dire risk of constant affliction by the spirit concerned. The first signs of such a 'calling' are the repeated healing dreams, followed by a spell of illness. Before a diviner is consulted, the afflicted person, in anticipation of his new task, will normally start treating others with the medicines he had 'seen' in his dreams. In families where the healing profession is passed on from one generation to another, the prospective *nganga* may reveal a wealth of inspired 'medical' knowledge even before a *nganga* is consulted. Confirmation by an acknowledged *nganga* is nevertheless needed before preparations are made for the acceptance ceremony by the relatives of the new 'doctor'. Once this ceremony, which includes the official welcome of the spirit(s) with a pot of *rukweza* beer, has taken place, the new *nganga* is fully installed in his new capacity and is free to continue with his practice under the guidance of his spirit(s). Most *nganga* spend a period of apprenticeship with another *nganga* before they become fully independent. Gelfand's detailed description of the ceremonies involved is also generally applicable to the Southern Shona and therefore needs no elaboration in this context.[103] Once this period has been carried to its ceremonial conclusion (*kugashira unganga*: to receive 'nganga-hood'), the new *nganga* will treat his 'teacher' and colleagues as equals and will invite them to the annual feasts in honour of the healing spirits. In Chingombe the teacher-*nganga* refer to their apprentice associates as doctors who have been *temerwa'd* (magically treated by means of bodily incisions) by them, which suggests that they have somehow conferred a form of assisting potency on their juniors.

c) *Divination and healing*

The diviner-herbalist's diagnostic and therapeutic treatment consists of three distinct phases: (i) detection through divination whether the ailment is caused by a spirit, wizardry (witchcraft or sorcery) or a combination of both; (ii) removal of the spiritual cause of illness by exorcising the spirit, or through prescription of the propitiatory rites to be conducted; and (iii) by treating the patient with the necessary medicine to cure the physical injury already sustained, or to protect the patient against future attacks. We will briefly consider each phase:

103. Gelfand, 1964 (II), Chapter 7. See pp. 60-61 for the *kugashira unganga* (to receive '*nganga*-hood') ceremony.

i) *Divination* (*kushopera*)

Before a diviner starts divining he must first of all make sure of the divining spirit's presence. The ritual involved (e.g. plate 15) is less elaborate than the rituals preceding the possession of an officially recognized medium by a *mhondoro* or lineage-guardian spirit. Manifestations of spirit-possession are normally much less spectacular than in the case of a senior tribal *svikiro*, but it is essential that the spirit indicates its presence through grunts, snorts, hissing sounds, monosyllabic cries, writhing of the body or high-pitched monologues. Not only does the trance-like state of the individual *nganga* vary from one healing session to the other, but among the different Shona *nganga* there is an unlimited variation of trances, from completely sober discourses with hardly any sign of a dissociated personality, to extreme forms of emotion-packed performances. A great number of *nganga* become possessed by merely dressing themselves, or being dressed, with the appropriate garments and ornaments, while others perform a simple cleansing ceremony (for the *Njuzu* spirits) or shake a rattle as an invitation to the spirits to put in an appearance. *Hakata*, ant-bear scales, divining shells or the divining mirror are the most frequently used tools of the Southern Shona diviners (plate 14 and 19). A subtle form of interrogation, depending on the *nganga's* knowledge of the patient's background, often takes place while the different throws with the divining tools are made. As a result the diagnosis is mostly based on information gleaned from the answer of the patient. Although the ideal diagnostic session is completed with a single performance, the *nganga* may suggest a continuation of treatment and will then elaborate on the first session in subsequent divinations, as his knowledge about the patient increases. The *nganga's* associates often supply him with the necessary information, or else he may learn much from gossip, especially in such cases where it is required of distant patients to stay at the *nganga's* homestead for a while.[104]

Because of the extension of kinship ties beyond the grave, the 'standardized' sets of obligations of living descendants to each related spirit are well known, and as an expert the *nganga* is of course familiar with all the details. He will soon learn from the patient if there are still some unfulfilled obligations concerning the family spirits, which will at least explain the withdrawal of their protective powers. Mention was made in the previous subsection of the most important obligations to the spirits in the form of dedicated or offered livestock and beer libations. A few remarks of the patient will give

104. The Shona people prefer to go to a distant *nganga* where they are not known. This factor does not really prevent the *nganga* from basing his diagnosis on the information indirectly or directly supplied by the patient him or herself.

the *nganga* an indication which family or extra-lineal spirit *has a reason* to feel offended or to opt for an outstanding sacrificial animal. On the other hand, the patient's own suspicions or mention of existing conflicts in his or her village may point at the possibility of witchcraft.

ii) *Removal of the cause of illness*

If ancestral spirits are diagnosed to be the sole cause of illness they are not driven off through exorcism, because such action would be contrary to the whole conception of the ancestor's protective function. The spirit in the bush must be brought home, the paternal spirit must receive his *gono guru*, the maternal grandmother her *imbwazukuru*, the mother-in-law her *ngombe youmai* and so forth. If all these basic needs have already been complied with, the ancestral spirits should be pacified through the dedication of minor articles such as blankets or pieces of cloth, together with the customary beer libation, as a sign of loyalty and remembrance. The *nganga's* therapy will vary from vague suggestions that the ancestors be placated, to precise prescriptions of how each propitiatory rite should be conducted.

As a rule *shavi* spirits cause illness when they select new hosts for healing or other purposes. Because of the beneficial talents bestowed on the host, the afflicted person will seldom request exorcism, and the *nganga* prescribes a rite of acceptance. Should the patient prefer to be rid of the spirit, the *nganga* may endeavour to exorcise it along similar lines as *ngozi* exorcism, or he may send the patient to a *nganga* who specializes in spirit exorcism. The basic idea is to divert or separate the spirit from the selected host and to 'send it away' by means of an animal dedicated to it. If the *shavi* is regarded as having established itself in the afflicted person, it will be made to *buda* (come out) in its host through the appropriate accompaniment of music and dancing, before the *nganga* drives it off; a ceremony which includes the sprinkling of fluid medicine on the patient and the symbolic waving movements of the *nganga* with his *muswe* (ox-tail used to drive off evil spirits). Exorcism of the *ngozi* spirit, as mentioned above, is regarded as one of the most dangerous tasks a *ngozi* specialist can perform, because of the chances of retaliation against the *nganga* himself or his relatives.

The technique of removing destructive medicines and evil spirits, if *uroyi* (wizardry) is diagnosed as the cause of illness, depends on the type of assault involved. Straightforward poisoning (*kudyisa*) which is also regarded as *kuroya* (bewitch or ensorcel), is treated with emetics. Other forms of wizardry (see below) mostly involve the transfer of evil, both spiritual and in concrete symbolic objects or animals, to the person or homestead of the victim. A favourite method of removing *uroyi* particles is for the *nganga* to

13. *Shavi* dance by two *nganga*, in honour of their healings spirits.

14. Urban *nganga*, Saidi, divining with the aid of dice and mirror; his customer, a prominent businessman of the Mucheke township, watches while he probes for the cause of an unsuccessful business-transaction.

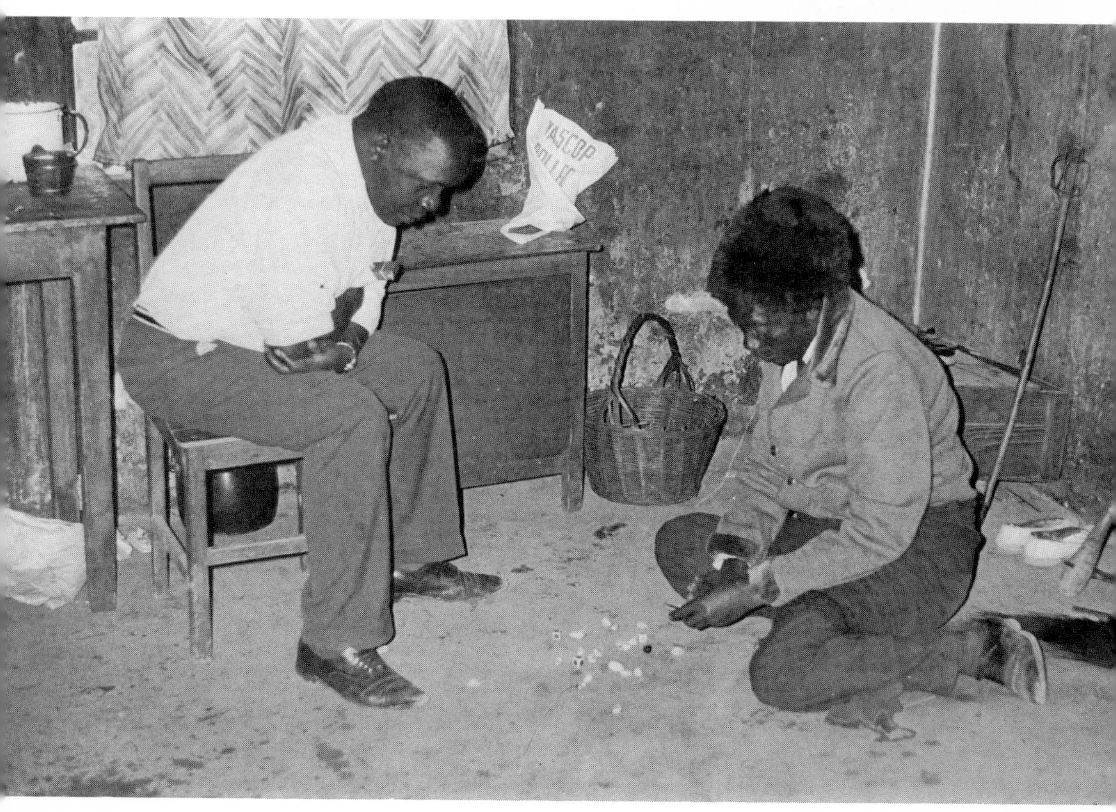

15. Urban *nganga*, Ndambakuwa, handing a pot of beer, with his *hakata* in it, to his father. Thus the healing ancestral and *shavi* spirits are invited to 'come out' and assist the *nganga* in treating his patients.

16. *Nganga* Ndambakuwa's patients watch while he invokes the healing spirits.

17. 'Dr.' Denis, one of the leading *nganga* in Fort Victoria, addressing the calabash of medicine which he uses to invoke the ancestral spirit from whom he has inherited his healing profession. His membership certificate of the '*Nganga* Association' is displayed on the wall behind him.

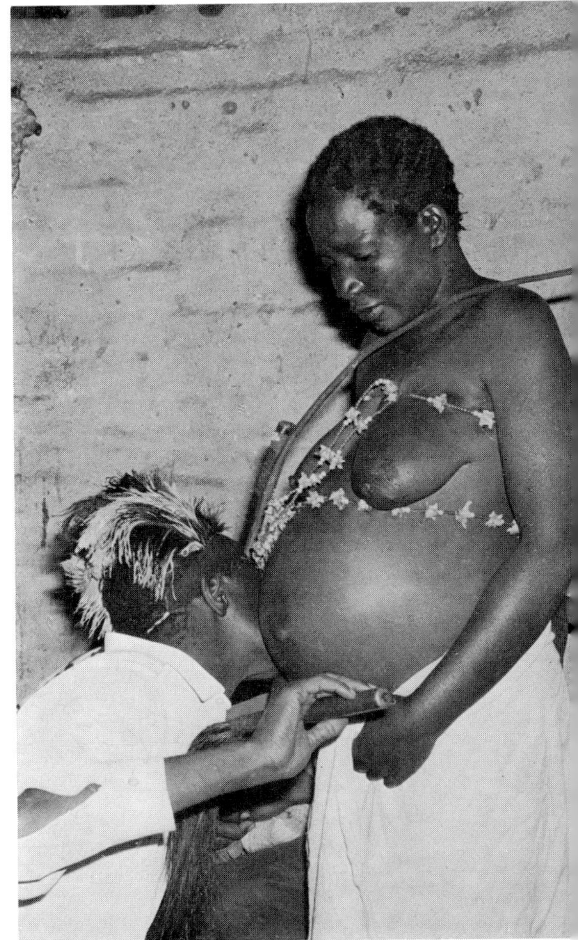

18. *Nganga* Ndambakuwa treats one of his female patients. With the aid of his *shavi*-prescribed 'medicine' (beads and snake-bones tied round the patient's body) and *muswe*, he drives away the evil spirits that threaten to invade the pregnant woman's womb.

19. Rural *nganga*, Maruta, divines with shells.

suck (*kuruma*: lit. to bite) such particles from the place where it is supposed to be lodged in a patient's body. Medicine will be applied to the appropriate spot before the sucking process starts. Having completed the operation the *nganga* will produce from his mouth odd pieces of bone, glass, teeth or hair, as proof that he has rid the patient of the evil objects implanted in his or her body by the sorcerer or witch. Polluted blood is drawn from the affected part of the body through cupping.[105] Destructive medicines are furthermore removed from the patient's hut, in the form of potent horns, teeth of wild animals, or any magical substance which is regarded as having been placed in the victim's hut by a witch or sorcerer. Through divination the *nganga* determines where such objects are, and then removes and destroys them himself. The most common procedure for the *nganga* is to move into such a hut and remove the *gona rouroyi* (horn of wizardry) from underneath the floor near the doorstep, or from the grass of the thatched roof. A purification rite is often conducted as a final means of getting rid of the contamination (*mweya wakaipa*: bad spirit, used here in the general, unindividualized sense of the word) caused by the witch or sorcerer. In addition to the patient himself, the whole interior of his house, including his clothes and cooking utensils, will be sprinkled with strong cleansing medicine.

iii) *'Medical' treatment*

Not all the *nganga's* medicines have magical properties. In spite of limited knowledge of anatomy and physiology, the symptoms of certain diseases are recognized and medicines of an empiric nature applied. The *nganga* is convinced that the medicine prescribed in such cases have a causal effect, and that it contains in itself the virtues to cure the specific disease. Gelfand estimates that 'the majority of his [the *nganga's*] remedies are administered purely empirically . . . so [that] we can hardly attribute all his treatments to a magical basis.'[106] But it is also maintained by Gelfand that relatively few herbs will prove to have much curative value when they are scientifically investigated.[107] He therefore stresses the importance of *suggestive therapy* in the medical treatment of *nganga*; a field in which the traditional mediciner has a distinct advantage over the European doctor. 'The whole setting creates a strong imprint on the patient, thus giving him faith and confidence in the *nganga*. His distinctive attire, his incantations, his collection of roots and

105. Cupping may be effected through the pressured application of one half of a tennis-ball over an incision, in such a way that the vacuum created draws blood from the cut. The real expert uses horns but the principle remains the same.

106. Gelfand, 1967, p. 137.

107. Gelfand, 1964 (I), p. 63.

herbs in full view of the patient, who knows his remedies have been handed down for generations, all give the impression of great magic and wisdom.'[108] The presupposed link with the spirit world serves to strengthen the belief in the mystical potency and therefore the effectiveness of the medicines used.

When the magical preparations of *nganga* are considered, it should be noted that the distinction between constructive and harmful magic is not always as rigid as observers tend to imply. Gelfand distinguishes between 'good' and 'bad' *nganga*; the former being the *nganga* proper who never administers harmful medicines, and the latter a *nganga* who misuses his talents to the detriment of others, and who is consequently called a *muroyi* (sorcerer) by his fellow Africans.[109] Such a clear-cut division seems inconsistent with reality. Although the Shona will refer to a *nganga* who makes exclusive use of, or distributes purely destructive medicine, as *muroyi*, they regard *nganga* who are primarily concerned with the improvement of society, but who also occasionally distribute harmful medicine, as 'good' and real practitioners. Such 'doctors' are not called *varoyi*. It is the *intention* of the *nganga* and the *frequency* with which he manipulates harmful magical preparations that determine whether he is regarded as essentially evil or not. If an element of retributive action that seems justified within the limits of customary law is involved, a 'good' *nganga* will often feel entitled to supply his client with harmful medicines or charms. Several such *nganga* who will, in the above-mentioned circumstances, provide their customers with bad *divisi* (a medicine that damages the crops of a neighbour) or *chitsinga*[110] medicine, are personally known to me. Suppose the future wife of a young man is unfaithful to him and he takes the *nhumbi* ('things') he has received from her as a sign of their agreement, to a *nganga*. The *nganga*, who realizes that justice is sought for a vow that has been broken, may use the *nhumbi* to cast a spell on the woman. This form of bewitchment is not fatal, but is believed to block the menstrual blood of the disloyal woman, with temporary barrenness as a result. Although destructive in its effect, such use of magical means has a positive function and is not sufficient reason for a *nganga* to be tagged as a *muroyi*.[111]

108. Gelfand, 1967, p. 139.

109. Gelfand, 1967, pp. 139-140; Gelfand, 1964 (II), pp. 28-29.

110. *Infra*, p. 165. This medicine is placed in a path to 'trap' victim, and it is therefore always associated with the sufferer's leg, which swells up when the medicine takes effect.

111. Crawford (1967, p. 105) correctly distinguishes between legitimate and non-legitimate medicines. He states that 'medicines which are used to capture thieves or exact vengeance where vengeance is justified are not . . . illegitimate even if they cause

Anthropologists usually differentiate between the rite performed, the spell cast and the object manipulated in magical practices. Amongst the vaShona the spell[112] (correct incantation) is not necessarily a prerequisite for magical action, since the power, whether personal or impersonal, is nearly always believed to centre in or to be closely associated with the object used. The ritual action in obtaining powerful medicine, e.g. the state of possession when a healer sets out in search of herbs, and the correct application of medicine are important aspects of the traditional 'medical' practice; but the basic potency is still in the first place associated with the medicine or charm itself. Most of the magical elements thus used in healing treatment are believed to act by way of *contagion.*[113] It is transferred to the body of the patient through sprinkling, inhalation, the rubbing of ingredients into small scars, or the wearing of amulets, by which process the required characteristics, associated with the magical objects, become part of the patient. Potent reeds supplied by a *Njuzu* spirit will, for example, symbolize fertility because of its connection with water, the place of its origin. To cure barrenness the (*Njuzu*) *nganga* will therefore, after having prescribed the necessary propitiation of the maternal ancestral spirits, treat the patient with such herbs. These are boiled in water and the vapour is inhaled by the patient, who has a blanket placed over her head to prevent the vapour from escaping.

Most amulets and medicine believed to act by way of contagion are *preventive* and *protective* rather than curative. This means that they are often distributed well in advance of the numerous afflictions that can be expected. In such cases the required medicines are of course forwarded to the clients, without the above-mentioned phases of the stereotype treatment taking place. Since the threat of evil spiritual forces always remains a reality to be reckoned with, many people take precautionary measures against possible assaults by obtaining *multipurpose charms* which they always wear on a string worn round the neck, arm or round the waist.[114] This strong medicine, consisting of a variety of magical objects bound together in a piece of cloth, is believed to fortify the body against intruding spirits. Of this type of charm

harm to the person against whom they are directed. The person who uses such medicine is not a sorcerer.'

112. Beattie (1964, p. 214) contrasts Melanesian magical practices, which are based on the spell, with that of Africa, where the emphasis is rather on the power of the rite itself and on the materials used in it, than on the correct form of the word used.

113. For a distinction between magic acting by *contagion* and magic acting by *association*, see *Notes and Queries on Anthropology*, 1964, p. 188.

114. For a description of the ingredients often used in amulets, see Gelfand, 1964 (I), Chapter 5, and Gelfand, 1967, Chapter 13.

the *sango*, carried round the upper arm, is the most popular. Pregnant women are regarded as highly vulnerable. If there is the least indication or mere suspicion of an interfering spirit who wants to cause damage to a pregnant woman through 'gripping her womb', all sorts of protective charms will be carried around the waist or upper parts of the body (plate 17). A different set of charms will be worn to *shandura jeko* (change the menstrual pain, i.e. change the sex of the coming child if the woman has previously born children of one sex only). Babies and young children are also regarded as vulnerable and prone to attacks from external forces. This attitude to some extent derives from the high incidence of infant mortality. To ensure a speedy closure of the baby's fontanelle, which exposes it unduly to harm, a piece of sheepskull is hung round his neck. Thus the hardness of bone, symbolized in the piece of skull, is conveyed to the baby in the effort to render the fontanelle impenetrable. Protective charms for young children are often strung around their necks, wrists and sometimes even around their ankles, as if to prevent evil from entering the body from all possible directions. Married women sometimes need mystical protection against the spiteful actions of former lovers. With burials those who have dug the graves or who have come in close contact with the body of the deceased, are ritually purified through the sprinkling of a cleansing substance. If this is not done the spirit of the deceased can find its way to such a contaminated person and cause affliction or death because it is dissatisfied with its untimely death, or with the sudden solitude imposed on it. In this way people seek to safeguard themselves through magical means.

But the use of magical objects concerns a much wider field than the prevention of illness or death. They are related to practically all kinds of activity in life: to ensure general prosperity, to guarantee the favourable outcome of an unusual venture, e.g. the search for a new job, to acquire certain skills, to be successful in hunting, fishing and agriculture or to win and retain the love of another person. We mention but a few examples. Suppose a woman notices that her husband is attracted by another woman. She will then go to the *nganga* to obtain the *muphuwira* love-potion which she adds to her husband's food. Once he has consumed it, his love and fidelity to his wife will be restored. A girl who wants to win the love of a boy washes herself with *zhangwa* medicine which is supposed to increase her attractiveness to the person concerned. Fishermen who are bent on catching an elusive type of fish prepare their hooks with medicine containing amongst other things the substance extracted from the boiled head of a *nengure* bird, for this little black bird is known for its ability to 'outwit' any eagle that tries to chase it or scare it off. In the effort to outwit their quarry the fishermen endeavour to harness the special quality of the *nengure*, which they need.[115] Numerous forms of magic can be used to ensure good crops. Before the seed is sown a *nganga* is called in to treat it. Once the green shoots start appearing in the fields, a special medicine (*divisi*) supposed to guarantee a favourable growth of the maize is applied by strewing it over the budding plants, or digging it into the ground. Destructive *divisi* is applied to a rival's maize by bringing potent sea shells, held in the palms of one's hands, in contact with the ripening maize as one walks along in the opponent's maize fields. To prevent such measures in one's own fields, pegs 'charged' with counteracting magic are driven into the soil at the corners of arable fields. A similar kind of treatment with counteracting pegs, called *kupinga musha* ('to peg the house') or *kugadzira musha nomushonga* ('to set the house right with medicine') is followed when a new house is built. A distant *nganga* is usually called in to perform this ceremony before the owner and his family move into a new house.

All the above-mentioned magical practices, and many more, are still to be found in Chingombe and other tribal areas inhabited by the Southern Shona. Western culture has not yet supplanted these activities, but has in certain ways indirectly stimulated it. Competition amongst schoolchildren cause many of them to make use of magic, in the effort to achieve favourable examination results. Subsistence farmers, some of whom are successfully applying Western forms of cultivation, make use of protective pegs and *divisi* to guarantee success, while outstanding schoolteachers are often suspected by their colleagues of using potent medicines. In town the scarcity of high-salaried jobs and the premium on specialized skills aggravate competition and intensify the need to achieve the necessary skills in the shortest possible time. Urban *nganga* therefore thrive on 'good luck charms' and on such magical devices as are supposed to impart to their bearers the talents sought. In the urban environment with its social insecurities and intensified suspicion of the practice of witchcraft amongst rivals, refuge is increasingly sought in the use of protective *mushonga*. Although the protective function of the *midzimu* is theoretically as valid in town as in rural areas, the absence of relatives and of large-scale rituals tend to undermine the sense of security otherwise provided by them. Consequently the increased use of protective magic partly compensates for the 'temporary loss' of the *mudzimu's* protection.

115. Crawford, (1967, pp. 104-106) lists several other examples of sympathetic magic, such as *mangoromera* a medicine which gives strength, and is obtained from the rhinocerus, elephant, crocodile and from electric wire; medicine obtained from the sluggish python serves to make a man patient and swiftness is obtained from the swallow killed in flight.

The manipulation of magical objects to achieve certain aims can be practised by any person. It is not the exclusive privilege of the *nganga* to supply such medicines. If a commoner finds any kind of object with an extraordinary shape, a certain potency may be attributed to it, perhaps because it symbolizes an attribute which is highly prized, or merely because its shape suggests inherent power. The value of such an object may increase in the course of time, if the successes of life become associated with it, but it may also be discarded in favour of stronger medicine if it proves ineffectual. Inherited possessions of the deceased often acquire a magical significance due to the connection they represent with the mystical power of the *midzimu*. Outstanding traits of character or special skills of the deceased are conveyed to the descendant who wears some of the inherited articles for this purpose. Finally, it should be stressed that, however wide the field of magical action, the *nganga* remains the generally recognized specialist whose magical preparations are used to acquire a wide variety of objectives.

4. WIZARDRY: WITCHCRAFT AND SORCERY

a) *The underlying principle*

Evans Pritchard's classic distinction between witchcraft and sorcery cannot be directly applied to the wizardry beliefs of the Southern Shona. Of the Azande, Pritchard states: 'A witch performs no rites, utters no spell and possesses no medicine. An act of witchcraft is a psychic act. They believe also that sorcerers may do them ill by performing magic rites with bad medicines. Azande distinguish clearly between witches and sorcerers.'[116] Such a clear-cut distinction between witchcraft as a purely psychic act and sorcery that involves the manipulation of destructive medicine does not exist amongst the Southern Shona. This has also been pointed out by other observers of Shona religion. Gelfand contends that the Shona people themselves do not accept this differentiation[117] and Murphree cautions us 'not to seek too close a parallel to the Azande model, with its rigid dichotomy between sorcery and witchcraft.' To Murphree 'the Budjga have only one word, *uroyi*, to cover a wide variety of mystically harmful techniques.'[118] Similarly, the term *uroyi* is used by the Southern Shona to indicate a wide variety of socially destructive

116. Evans Pritchard, 1937, p. 21.
117. Gelfand, 1967, p. 56.
118. Murphree, 1969, p. 56.

action, whether the mode of operation is purely psychic, involving 'black magic', or even if it concerns death through poisoning. Furthermore, the lack of a clear conception of the palpable apparatus used in certain forms of wizardry, renders a strict classification impossible. The so-called medicine used in certain instances, may be a really poisonous substance in a horn (*gona*) or other container, but it can also be an imaginary 'horn' or other form of medicine that 'moves through the air' to a physically remote victim.

Although the Southern Shona make no linguistic distinction between sorcerers and witches, there are distinguishable kinds of antisocial action which are differently evaluated by the people themselves. There is, for example, a difference between purely destructive acts executed to the detriment of others and to the disruption of the harmony of community life, and such harmful acts which are considered to have a 'constructive' end, since they concern the more or less 'legitimate' retaliation against a wrong done. For descriptive purposes we have chosen the term wizardry, as representative of the term *uroyi* in its widest connotation, i.e. to include both the destructive and constructive aspects of *uroyi* beliefs. Within this wide conceptual framework a distinction is made between sorcery and witchcraft, mainly on the grounds of modes of action and the nature of threat to society. This classification should not be interpreted in an absolutistic sense since each distinctive category involves a certain degree of overlapping and can only be applied with some reserve in this intricate field.

Unlike the Azande, both Shona witches and sorcerers are in possession of, and make frequent use of magical preparations (*mushonga*). The psychic act which distinguishes witches from sorcerers does not necessarily exclude the use of magical preparates. Whereas the Shona sorcerer's activities, like that of the Azande sorcerer, always include the use of medicines, the Shona witch, in addition to the use of medicines, is capable of working evil through a psychic act. This latter ability is acquired either through inheritance or intentional induction, which means that witchcraft cannot in all respects be contrasted with sorcery as involuntary versus intentional action. As will be indicated below the factor of heredity is important for a distinction made by the Shona themselves, not between sorcery and witchcraft, but between different types of witches.

Since the ability to work evil through a psychic act, and the use of familiars – which is closely associated to such action – is most commonly ascribed to female *varoyi*, we will refer to witches as predominantly female and sorcerers as male. This distinction serves descriptive rather than classificatory purposes for there are exceptions in both categories. Males, though rarely accused of it, are considered capable of the type of psychic action usually attributed to female witches, and female witches can make use of the physical medicinal objects – still to be described below – most frequently used by male sorcerers.

One cannot label the one category of wizardry as essentially evil in contrast with the other as not essentially evil, for the above-mentioned 'legitimate' retaliation in a conflict situation can be performed by either witches or sorcerers with or without the use of medicine. As a point of departure one could say that the perpetration of *uroyi*, witchcraft or sorcery, in so far as it involves harmful action, whatever the motivation of the active agent, and irrespective of whether it is regarded by the community as 'legitimate' or not, is fully 'bad' (*zvakashata*), and therefore potentially destructive. An important constructive aspect within the whole system of *uroyi* beliefs, on the other hand, lies in the aim of diviners to bring brooding social conflicts to a head through allegations of wizardry. Even if the solution of conflict situations through such allegations often involves a distinctly destructive act, i.e. the elimination or ostracism of the scapegoat, it aims at the maintenance of cohesion within society, and as such has a positive psychological function.

Having qualified both sorcery and witchcraft activities as generally 'bad', the next step would be to distinguish between the difference of threat posed to society by such activities. Whereas sorcery frequently involves 'bad' action which confronts the community with only an indirect threat, for instance, when a man uses *uroyi* medicine to improve his crops at the cost of another (or when he uses medicine against an agnate during a tribal political contest as a means of temporarily outwitting his opponent), witchcraft is nearly always associated with fatal illness or death and is therefore more readily disapproved of. Witchcraft, therefore, constitutes a more serious threat to the entire community. On the whole it is regarded as more dangerous than sorcery and women alleged to have indulged in such action are usually exposed to drastic punitive measures by the community which considers its well-being threatened. A sorcerer's acts can be as malicious and destructive as that of a witch, in which case the evildoer will be as severely punished. But it seems as if sorcery includes a wider range of less dangerous acts which arise from ambition, envy, or political strife and which are not necessarily punished by the community as a whole. Such action may be regarded as sufficiently countered by magical countermeasures undertaken by the sorcerer's opposing party.

The witch to some extent personifies the evil and disruptive forces in society. Crawford summarizes this personified image of evil as follows: 'Cannibalism is the most detested of all crimes, therefore she (the witch) is a cannibal; family ties are the most sacred of all ties, therefore she destroys members of her own family; medicine and magic are the forces with which one can control the environment in the interest of one's society, therefore they become perverted in the hands of the witch; animals such as snakes are dangerous because they can kill; owls are feared because they fly when all other birds sleep, therefore the witch has these creatures as her familiars. She is associated with all that is feared and that is detestable.'[119]

We have noticed that ancestral rituals, such as the *kugadzira*, have the distinct function of maintaining lineage unity. Not only does the participation of lineage members in such rituals serve to reinforce the family ties, but the unity of the spiritual order is also safeguarded through the accommodation of those spirits that are not yet officially installed in their rightful places in the hierarchical order. Ritual preservation consequently elevates lineage unity to a level where it becomes *sacrosanct*. This is part of the background against which beliefs in wizardry and accusations of *uroyi* should be viewed. Just as the unity of a lineage and, by implication, that of the nuclear village community is ritually preserved, forces that militate against it should be ritually dealt with. Beliefs in wizards enable the community to find answers to and deal purposefully with the mysteries and misfortunes of life.

The most serious threat to lineage unity is the successive deaths of members of one family. Such a situation inevitably leads to tensions and frustrations and the need for some action, since there is no disaster worse than the complete extinction of a family and hardly a greater need than the guarantee of its continued existence. The most likely suspects under such circumstances are the wives of the stricken lineage members, who, as *vatorwa* ('foreigners'), are not 'of the same blood' as their husbands, but have the most intimate contact with them and the other members of their households. It follows that this type of dilemma is sooner attributed to the dangerous acts of witchcraft than of sorcery. Only in the event of a lineage member being held responsible for such deaths is the accusation likely to be that of sorcery, because it is preferable not to accuse a blood relative of the type of action which may well be inherited and as a result cast a negative reflection on the entire lineage. The imputation of witchcraft convincingly carried out provides the lineage members of the deceased with the necessary sanction to take socially acceptable action against the person held responsible for such a threat. The resultant killing, ostracism or evasion of the witch has a cathartic effect, since evil of an antisocial nature is felt to have been effectively dealt with.

Death and illness are the most obvious disruptive forces in social life, but the social equilibrium can also be disturbed by the successes of talented in-

119. Crawford, 1967, p. 71.

dividuals, which may generate jealousy and lead to social friction. Such persons, like others who fail to conform to the accepted norms of community life, are the most likely to bring about change in the existing order. As a result they tend to be accused of wizardry, particularly sorcery. Beliefs in wizardry undoubtedly have the function of conditioning public opinion. It provides the representatives of the existing social order with a means to manipulate public opinion, because once an adversary is convincingly branded as a witch or sorcerer, his or her influence is, for all practical purposes, temporarily or permanently eliminated. Used as a device to discipline or expel the antisocial and nonconforming elements within society, wizardry beliefs and allegations in the past have formed one of the most effective conservative forces which maintain social cohesion and discourage change.

b) *Types of wizards and modes of operation*

An important factor is that of heredity. The *muroyi wedzinza*, says Gelfand, is the hereditary and therefore classical witch, who operates at night under the direction of an ancestral or *shavi* spirit, whereas the predominantly male *muroyi wamasikati* ('sorcerer of the afternoon', i.e. he whose medicine also works in day-time) acts of his own volition.[120] According to Crawford 'a "real" witch is a person possessed by an evil ancestral spirit (*mudzimu*) or an evil spirit of human or animal origin derived from outside the family circle.'[121] He stresses the hereditary factor in the making of a 'real' witch, which strengthens his argument that accusations of witchcraft are rarely made against near agnates, since it would imply a negative reflection on the accuser himself. It is tempting to accept this approach because it introduces the element of compulsion through an external spiritual force, which in turn explains the unpredictability of a 'real' witch's attitude in contrast with the sorcerer whose actions, motivated by envy, anger or jealousy, are directed at a particular enemy only.

Evidence from the Chingombe area suggests, however, that heredity does not necessarily feature prominently as a precondition to practise 'real' witchcraft. Here witches are classified as *varoyi vokumutsa murimo* (lit. witches who revive the medicine, i.e. continue the practices of their deceased forebears) and the *varoyi vokutemerwa* (witches who willingly accept their profession by having witchcraft medicine rubbed into their bodies by way of inci-

120. Gelfand, 1967, p. 27f.
121. Crawford, *op. cit.*, p. 74.

sions made by other witches). Both of these classes of witches are 'real' *varoyi*, capable of acting psychically and inclined to make use of animal familiars in contrast with the sorcerer who relies mainly on his ability to manipulate 'black magic'. Of the hereditary witches it is often stated that they are the most dangerous, due to the compelling force of the spirit which drives them towards destructive action. On the other hand, 'hereditary' does not necessarily mean 'incurable', at least not in Chingombe and the surrounding areas; for the evil ancestral or *shavi* spirit can still be exorcised under special circumstances. The witch who has been *temerwa'd*, however, has evil in her blood, and cannot get rid of it.

The terms *kumutsa murimo* (to 'raise' the medicine) and *kutemerwa* (to be incised) indicate the different ways in which a person becomes a witch of the one kind or of the other. A woman inherits the inclination to practise witchcraft from her maternal grandmother (*mbuya*) and the symptoms of such a spirit wanting to 'come out' (*kubuda*) are similar to those we have described in the case of the hereditary *nganga*. The difference lies in the content of the 'calling dreams' and the nature of apprenticeship. Instead of dreaming of healing the would-be witch dreams that she sees her grandmother, that she (the dreamer) eats human flesh, touches human blood and moves about at night in the nude. She recognizes the request of her grandmother's spirit to continue the latter's witch practices. As a sign of acceptance a black goat may be slaughtered in honour of the *mbuya's* spirit and a period of apprenticeship with other witches follows. By this time several other witches will have been attracted by the novice because they have noticed the familiar *bvute rambuya* (shadow of the grandmother who was a *muroyi*) 'on' this person. They deliberately set out to 'capture' (*bata*) the shadow of the new witch in order to ensure her joining their company. If the granddaughter fails to comply with her *mbuya's* request, pressure is brought to bear on her through misfortunes, temporary barrenness caused by the 'loss of menstrual blood' or through the tempting manoeuvres of other witches, who have been permitted by the *mbuya* spirit to enter her *muzukuru's* apartment 'through the door' at night. The *muzukuru* often complies under such circumstances, because female relatives who also experience the effect of the *mbuya's* wrath urge her to do so. To them a witch in the family is preferable to constant affliction and barrenness. The *muzukuru* who remains adamant will try to have the spirit driven away by a *nganga*. This practice of deviation is the same as with *ngozi* exorcism. A black fowl or goat is driven into the woods, once the witchcraft spirit has been ritually transferred to it.

Witches of the *kumutsa murimo* class are commonly referred to as persons who have a *shavi rouroyi* (*shavi* of witchcraft). This implies either that the *shavi* with which the deceased maternal grandmother operated is now also at work in the grandchild, or that the witch has 'inherited' her profession from an indwelling witchcraft *shavi*, which selected her as host independently of the express wish of an ancestral spirit. Females who become witches through their own free will associate with other *varoyi*, whom they allow to make incisions on their bodies, especially on the little finger or hips, in order to have the power of witchcraft literally rubbed into their bodies.

Descriptions of the nocturnal activities of witches seldom include a clear indication about the exact nature of the person who goes out to harm others. Gelfand correctly states that 'the Shona do not make it clear whether the witch moves around in person at night or whether her spirit leaves her body while she is asleep and then assumes her physical form.'[122] The majority of people seem to think of the nocturnal operations of witches in terms of a psychic manifestation, and it would be safe to say that they consider any female witch capable of such action. This means that the witch's *bvute* (shadow) can go out at night, while her body remains at home. The attributes of the *bvute* nevertheless remain vague. On the other hand, witches are also believed to move around physically at night. Several informants stated that they had actually seen single witches or companies of them moving around at night, naked, on foot or riding on hyenas. Whether in psychic or physical form, the witch uses one of her familiars when she has to cover big distances. The most frequently used animal is the hyena (*bere*), but a witch can also *tasva munhu* ('ride a person') with whom she will have sexual intercourse after the completion of her errand. If a man awakes at night and finds himself naked outside his hut, or if he awakes in the morning feeling thoroughly exhausted, he knows that he has been 'ridden' (*tasva'd*) by a witch. Apart from the hyena, the Shona witch makes use of snakes, *zvidoma* (small animals of psychic nature), owls, and crocodiles. She does not copulate with these animals but some of them are allowed to suckle at her breasts, which poisons her milk and endangers her own child. The smaller familiars such as the *chidoma*, snake and owl, are not used for transport. They convey the witch's evil potency to the victim. The *ndara* snake, particularly, is associated with witches; being bitten by one of them is a sure sign of planned witchcraft.

Evil magic can also be directed at the victim in an invisible form without the aid of a familiar. The *mushonga* is simply regarded as taking effect on the victim without the witch having come into contact with him or her. Another

122. Gelfand, 1967, p. 28.

method frequently used is for the witch to move to the victim's house and to plant the destructive medicine in or near it. Physical contact can only be achieved if the protecting ancestral spirits are persuaded to 'open the door' (*zarura mukova*) for the witch to enter the house. Needless to say, beliefs in witches stimulate the regular appeasement of the ancestors, since the favourable disposition of the family ancestors is one of the most reliable safeguards against witchcraft. For the witch to enter a victim's house she must know the *mutupo*, *chidao* and names of the deceased ancestors, otherwise she cannot approach them with her requests. Thus a close acquaintance between witch and victim is presupposed as an essential condition for the perpetration of such evil. Several informants suggested that if a witch is determined to 'pass' the guardian ancestors of her would-be victim, she would even singly conduct propitiatory ceremonies at the graves of such spirits in the effort to bribe them into permitting her access. Having entered the room of a sleeping victim, the witch may try to poison him or her by pouring a potent medicine into the sleeper's mouth. She may rub her medicines into the person's body through slight, hardly noticeable incisions, or she may 'remove' parts of the victim's organs. Should such a person fall ill and waste away, it is often said that he or she has been 'eaten' (*kudyiwa*) by a *muroyi*, which means that parts of the liver, lungs, intestines or other organs are believed to have been 'eaten' or removed for the purpose of making evil medicine.

A practice most commonly ascribed to witches is the eating of human flesh. Zionist prophet Potai's account is representative of this belief. He says: 'The shade of the witch goes out at night, leaving her body behind. She meets five or six other "shadows" with whom she goes out "on patrol" for the night's duty. These are the women who eat children. They each have a rib, taken from a child's body, which they use as whistles to call or warn each other. First of all they congregate, standing with their backs against each other, listening to the orders of their leader before they dispatch in pairs. They will ride on hyenas or on men to the graves. While the others keep watch, one of them will beat the grave which causes it to open and enables the witch to cut meat from the body of the deceased. Afterwards the grave is beaten again and it closes as if nobody had been there. The meat is now taken to the *varoyi's* special meeting-place where they keep pots to cook the meat. They do not eat all of it because some small pieces of meat are taken to their homes, so that they can use it against other people by throwing it into their food.'

It seems from Potai's account that he thought of the witch's eating of human flesh primarily as a psychic act,[123] because the women he described

123. See also Parrinder, 1958, p. 142.

were operating as 'shades' and not as physically represented beings. My informants are not in accord on this point. Many of them believe that a witch goes out in person to collect human meat and that a number of witches possess *mushonga* which they have prepared from such meat. Accusations of witchcraft often imply that the witch had used potions derived from parts of the human body. The confessions of a number of witches, prosecuted in Rhodesia under the Witchcraft Suppression Act, suggest that more than a mere psychic act of 'eating or using human meat' was involved.[124] In Chingombe one of the outstanding cases of witchcraft – it never reached the court or the administrative authorities, but was settled privately at the village court level – produced convincing evidence that the accused witch had at least severed, and was in possession of, the hand of the deceased infant of a co-wife.

The fear that witches would cut off parts of the bodies of the recently deceased also has a direct effect upon burial rites. The stone 'coffin' built into the grave, and the careful sealing of this 'coffin' with mud before the rest of the grave is filled up with loose soil, is believed by some to obstruct the witch's passage to the corpse. Sometimes the corpse is placed in a special cavity which has been dug to the side of the floor of the grave, so that eventually the mound of stones is not stacked up directly above the corpse. Thus the witch is misled about the actual locality of the corpse and when she 'opens' the grave she will find nothing. Relatives keep guard at the grave for the first few nights following the burial of the deceased. Gelfand states that these watchers will attack witches that dare come near the grave. He mentions the belief in a 'proper physical fight' and that those 'killed or injured may be identified afterwards by the marks of stones or blows on their faces or bodies as a result of the chase.'[125] Amongst the Southern Shona little mention is made of such physical fights with the witches, but it is regarded as essential, whether a new grave is watched or not, that the relatives should inspect the grave on the morning following the burial, or for several successive mornings, to see if there are signs of witches having tampered with the corpse. Should they detect such interference, trouble can be expected from the deceased's spirit and a *nganga* must be consulted.

As far as sorcery is concerned Gelfand distinguished between the *muroyi wamasikati* ('witch' whose medicines take effect during the day-time), i.e. the person who purchases the destructive medicine and uses it against another because he bears a grudge; and the 'black' *nganga* who distributes the medicine. As I have pointed out, a rigid classification into 'good' and 'bad'

124. Crawford, *op. cit.*, p. 114; Case of *R. versus Zalepi.*

125. Gelfand, 1967, p. 28.

nganga is impossible, because several *nganga*, dealing primarily with constructive medicines, also distribute 'bad' medicines under special circumstances. The implication of Gelfand's argument would be that the accusation of wizardry should involve, directly or indirectly, two *varoyi*: the supplier of evil medicine, and the person who uses it; but the fact that a 'witch-hunt' usually terminates as soon as the sorcerer, who is believed to have actually used malignant medicine, is 'found', seems to indicate that the personal source of the medicine used is not necessarily identified with *uroyi*. The fact that such an accomplice-*nganga* is not mentioned by the accused sorcerer may be due, in certain cases, to the fear that the *nganga* will retaliate should his name be mentioned, if indeed he is a 'bad' *nganga*; or that the *nganga* involved is simply ignored because he is not regarded as a *muroyi*. The so-called 'bad' or 'black' *nganga*, alleged to be *varoyi*, are so few and far apart that they cannot, in any case, supply all commoners in possession of destructive medicines, with such magical preparations.

There are mainly three types of *uroyi* that definitely include the use of magical objects, used by both witches and sorcerers. *Kudyisa* (to cause to eat, from 'eat': *kudya*), most commonly practised by women, concerns the application of real poison or medicine of a magical nature to the food of the victim. A witch who destroys people because she is driven to do so through the driving force within her, will add potions to beer during a beer party, without directing her onslaught against any particular person. She may also be motivated to *dyisa* a person with whom she stands in a conflict relation, in which case medicine will be flicked from underneath the fingernail into the *mukombe* of beer as it is presented to the victim, or else it will be added to the porridge given to the victim during a meal.

Chitsinga and *chiposo*, the two other forms of wizardry, concerns sorcery attributed to males. The former type concerns the leg-trap, and people who have been ensorcelled in this way always say: '*Ndatsingwa*', or '*Ndateyiwa gumbo*' ('my leg has been trapped'). A poisonous substance will be added to a sharp object, like a piece of bone or wire, and placed in the path known to be used by the victim, or else a magical substance, believed to penetrate the skin, will be strewn across such a path. The whole process of 'setting a trap' may involve an elaborate ritual, with the mention of the victim's names, *mutupo* and *chidao*, so as to prevent the medicine from affecting the wrong person. Once the medicine has penetrated the victim's footsole, it moves up the leg causing it to swell, and eventually reaches right up to the person's head or other parts of the body. Physical disorders diagnosed by the Westerner as rheumatism, 'water in the legs', or severe headaches, are ascribed by the vaShona to *chitsinga*. A person who treads on a thorn and suffers from infection afterwards, is bound to suspect *chitsinga*. It is not that the muShona is ignorant of the possibility of infection once a sharp object has penetrated his foot, but he is always inclined to ask first: 'Who placed it there?' and therefore to link the incident with a personal cause. The term *ndaposwa* ('I have been thrown at')[126] is sometimes used to convey the same meaning as the general term *ndaroyiwa* ('I have been bewitched or ensorcelled') but it mostly refers to the type of sorcery in which medicines are believed to be 'sent or thrown through the air' to cause damage to a distant victim. This brings us to the aspect of *associative magic*, which includes the use of material objects imitating the victim. The sorcerer using this method may 'kill' the victim's image he has made, by pricking it with a needle or 'drowning' it in water. He may also blow or throw the destructive medicines at the image of the victim, which action causes the desired effect to take place in the physically remote victim. The victim who has been *poswa'd* in this way attributes his physical disorder to visible objects (which can be sucked from his body by the *nganga*) or to an invisible substance that has 'travelled through the air' after the sorcerer has performed his evil-intended rite. There are numerous variations of associative magic. Not only the victim, but also the destructive object or 'agent', may be imitated. In Chingombe sorcerers are commonly believed to apply special medicines to a leather strip (*gashu*) which imitates a snake. The 'snake' is then sent to harm the victim.

We may summarize the broadly contrasting (but not absolute) characteristics of Shona witches and sorcerers as follows:

	Witch	*Sorcerer*
1. Sex:	predominantly female	predominantly male
2. Mode of action:	psychic and magical	predominantly magical
3. Time of action:	at night	during day-time
4. Motivation for destruction:	repetitive destruction attributable to the driving force of an inherited spirit or deliberately acquired medi-	generally less dominated by external spiritual forces; such antisocial action can be terminated by sorcerer

126. *Kuposa*, derived from *posha* or *potsa*, literally means 'to throw', which is descriptive of the act the witch or sorcerer is supposed to perform. The victim claims that the malignant medicine has been 'thrown' at him.

	cative power (through negative & antisocial traits of character) which has become part of witch's physique.	once the personally motivated aim is achieved.
5. Consequences & predictability of action:	mostly fatal and unpredictable, therefore dangerous to entire community.	injurious, occasionally fatal, predictable and therefore potentially less dangerous to the whole community.

The various types of wizardry having been distinguished, the question arises how strong these beliefs still are at present in the rural and urban areas. A comparison of the survey results in Chingombe and Fort Victoria shows that wizardry beliefs have persisted in both areas with equal tenacity. In reply to the question whether *uroyi* still exists at present, approximately 88-90% of the ruralists and urbanites replied in the affirmative (table 26). Only 2% of the ruralists and 6% of the urbanites were unsure, while 8% of the ruralists and 5% of the urbanites were prepared to state categorically that *uroyi* does not exist at all, in other words that one person cannot harm another through purely mystical, psychic or magical machinations. Townsmen distinguished the different types of wizardry more readily than the ruralists, especially the magical methods such as *chitsinga* and *chiposo*, adopted by male sorcerers. The fact that 85% of the townsmen and only 63% of the ruralists distinguished several forms of *uroyi* does not imply that the ruralists nowadays are less informed about the diversity of wizardry practices, but it does seem as if the use of a variety of magical means, particularly by males, in the field of economic competition in town, contributes towards a more constant awareness of wizardry (especially sorcery) practices and subsequently also a greater willingness of townsmen to enter into detailed discussions about this contentious topic.

An aspect which remains obscure in the statistical data is that, despite the general persistence of wizardry beliefs, individuals differ greatly about the effect of such beliefs in their lives. Some consider the threat of *uroyi* to themselves or their families only as a remote possibility – even though they may from time to time experience set-backs which others would have interpreted in terms of wizardry – and they are relatively free from the fear of bewitchment, while others, through circumstantial and temperamental factors, are much more dominated in their everyday lives by such fears. Table

27 gives us an impression of the extent to which individuals have personally experienced the effects of *uroyi*. Approximately 50-60% of the ruralists and townsmen claimed never to have been *roya'd*, while 15-17% of the people in both environments stated that they had observed the ill effects of such practices at close quarters, i.e. in the misfortunes, illnesses and deaths of close relatives. In contrast with the 21% of the ruralists, 31% of the townsmen stated that they themselves have been bewitched or ensorcelled. These figures in all probability reflect the tendency of an intensified preoccupation of townsmen with wizardry beliefs as a means of interpreting and explaining their often frustrating experiences in the urban environment. On the other hand, the considerable number of ruralists (6%) who professed to have been directly involved in wizardry, but who refused to give any further particulars about what had actually happened, seems to point at the more drastic punitive measures taken against wizards in rural areas and the subsequent secrecy in contentious cases in the effort to protect the accusers who may well become the subjects of prosecution under the Witchcraft Suppression Act if the details were publicized. Table 27 also illustrates a greater tendency among townsmen to diverge from the traditional patterns of curative treatment than among the ruralists. After being *roya'd* (bewitched or ensorcelled), comparatively more townsmen visited Independent Church prophets and Government or Mission hospitals in search of a cure, than the ruralists, of whom the majority, under similar circumstances, received treatment from *nganga* or the *muroyi* himself.

c) *Accusation of wizardry*

Certain outstanding features characterize the pattern of wizardry accusations. These have been highlighted by the recent analyses made by Crawford and Gelfand of a number of court cases[127] arising from such allegations in Rhodesia. Both of them point out that the majority of allegations take place between people who are well acquainted or closely related and live in the same or adjacent villages. In 68.8% of the cases studied by Gelfand the accuser and accused came from the same village.[128] Any kind of conflicting

127. Gelfand's percentages are based on his study of a number (35) of witchcraft court cases (1890-1930) in a number of Shona magisterial districts (Sinoia, Mrewa, Mtoko, Mt. Darwin, and Fort Victoria), as well as 90 records of charges made (1959-1963) under the Witchcraft Suppression Act. Crawford's analysis is based on 103 court cases (1956-1962) taken primarily from the Eastern Shona and a number of the Ndebele-Kalanga group.

situation caused by jealousy, misfortune or other factors causing social friction can lead to such allegations, but the circumstances that most often give rise to accusations of this nature are sickness and death (68.5% of the 1899-1930 cases: studied by Gelfand),[129] particularly if it concerns infants or young children. More than 45% of the cases studied by Crawford concerned the death of children.[130]

As to the reason why women are more frequently accused of *uroyi* than men, one should bear in mind the vital aspect of lineage unity and the necessity of rearing children to perpetuate the lineage. Any situation which endangers lineage unity and its perpetuation, such as a woman's failure to fulfil the essential obligations of bearing children for her husband's group, the successive illnesses and deaths of her children, strife between co-wives, etc., is bound to create tensions and distrust within the household and village group. Such situations easily give rise to witchcraft allegations and the natural inclination of lineage members is to suspect non-agnates, especially the wives of agnates, because they are the 'foreigners' most closely associated with their husbands' intimate household and other in-groups. Thus the majority of allegations against women in the rural village context are made against affinal females.

Crawford's case studies show that amongst the Eastern Shona relatively few accusations of wizardry were made by members of the same lineage against each other, and that the vast majority of accusations were made by lineage members against non-lineage members.[131] It follows that allegations of witchcraft are made at the expense of non-lineage females. Crawford convincingly argues that the relatively few allegations made against agnates arise from political rivalry, and mostly concern an accusation of sorcery, which is comparatively less dangerous than witchcraft. Lineage unity is therefore not threatened, since an accusation of sorcery need not lead to an irreparable breach, but, Crawford says, 'witchcraft is inherited, and to suggest that a lineage member is a witch, is to suggest that members of the lineage as a whole are witches. A witchcraft allegation against a woman who is one's own wife or the wife of an agnate may entirely disrupt the link between husband and wife; but the return of a woman to her parents does not affect the unity of the lineage and her children may be claimed by their father as soon as they are old enough to leave her.'[132]

128. Gelfand, 1967, p. 53.
129. *Ibid.*, p. 64.
130. Crawford, 1967, p. 156.
131. *Ibid.*, p. 140.
132. *Ibid.*, p. 142.

Conclusions about the frequency of allegations made against women cannot be drawn from an analysis of court cases only. Women have most to fear from such allegations since they are socially more adversely affected by the eventual outcome of an accusation than men. As a result the majority of cases reaching the courts inevitably concern the appeal of women whose social position have become unbearable due to such imputations; a great number of them concerning the criminal offences following the public naming of a witch. Many accusations actually made never reach the court. Therefore is it possible that the incidence of accusations made against females and of those made against males, is less divergent than a perusal of court cases seems to indicate.

Both Gelfand and Crawford have pointed out that by far the greatest number of cases reaching the courts come from rural areas.[133] Crawford suggests that this is attributable to the fact that infant mortality may be lower in urban areas where people are nearer to hospitals and to the different configuration of family units in the urban context. 'In town', he says, 'the family unit tends to be simple and not the extended family. Women do not normally have to live with their in-laws. It is, therefore, difficult for the traditional pattern of accusation to occur in the urban area.'[134] It does not necessarily follow that fewer allegations are made in the urban than in the rural areas. The friction caused by interpersonal rivalries, intensified competition in the economic field and problems of adaptation in an essentially 'foreign' environment would appear an ideal setting for accusations of wizardry. Accusations in town may have less serious repercussions for persons branded as sorcerers or witches than in the remote rural villages where the community – with a greater chance of escaping the notice of the European authorities – more easily resorts to drastic punitive measures against scapegoats. Because the accusations of individuals against each other in the field of economic competition are likely to be of a less serious nature than those made by agnatic lineage members against non-lineage members in the village context, fewer of the accusations made in the urban areas are brought to the notice of the authorities.

The procedure followed in the case of wizardry allegations varies from case to case. A distinction can be made between direct accusations without the consultation of a diviner and accusations following an imputation made during a spell of divination. The former type of allegations varies from the comparatively less serious accusation of *uroyi* made during a heated dis-

133. Gelfand, 1967, p. 83; Crawford, 1967, pp.169, 277.
134. Crawford, *op. cit.*, p. 169.

cussion, to the serious accusation publicly made by an individual who does so with the conviction that the person accused is really responsible for a particular malady or conflict. Such an accusation frequently follows a family crisis caused by the death of children, and the person likely or known to bear the accuser a grudge, is held responsible for the mishap. The accusation may be made face to face, or the accuser may strew some ash next to the doorstep of the accused. Such accusations carry less weight with the rest of society than those made by a *nganga* and they are sometimes ignored by the rest of the community. On the other hand it appears from an analysis of court cases that an increasing number of ruralists make serious accusations of wizardry without consulting a diviner. Gelfand found that in only 30.2% of the 1959-63 series a 'witchdoctor' was consulted before an accusation was made, in contrast with the 57.1% of the 1899-1930 series, and says that this may be attributable to the fact that 'Africans in the first few decades after European rule was established in Rhodesia still clung more closely to the correct procedure.'[135]

Tensions created in a village community through some unforeseen mishap or the successive deaths of villagers, which in turn give rise to suspicions or accusations of wizardry, often lead to the kraalhead taking a hand in the effort to restore the social equilibrium. He gathers a group of villagers, consisting of the complainant (accuser or accused), one or two court (*dare*) officials and a number of possible suspects, who must visit a *nganga*, as a single village delegation, to determine who the real culprit is. All the members of the group must contribute a small fee as token of their participation. Since refusal to participate is interpreted as admission of guilt, all persons nominated to the delegation by the kraalhead and his advisors will normally comply. On arrival at the *nganga's* quarters the token fees are handed over to him with the request that he should divine the cause of misfortune. Members of the delegation go into the *nganga's* hut separately or as a group. Some *nganga* maintain that they divine without questioning the visitors, but in the majority of cases questions will be directed at the various members of the party, and the *nganga* is often given a clear indication as to the identity of the suspected witch or sorcerer. Once he has determined who the witch is, the *nganga* has several methods of revealing his findings. He may shave the hair off the head of the guilty person, refuse to pour white flour on his or her forehead, as he does with the guiltless, return the token of the guilty, or if the wizardry concerns illness, command the witch or sorcerer to go and prepare the cure in *sadza* (thick porridge) and give it to the afflicted to eat. If

135. Gelfand, *op. cit.*, p. 77.

the guilty person is absent, the kraalhead sends someone to throw ash at his or her doorstep. According to the evidence given at court cases, it sometimes happens that the accused witch is stripped of her clothes and driven back naked to the village.[136] Soon after the arrival of the delegation, a *dare*-meeting will be called and the findings of the *nganga* made known in the presence of the whole village community. Thus we find that the tribal authorities are often involved in wizardry allegations in spite of the heavy penalties that can be incurred under the Witchcraft Suppression Act. This is understandable in view of the conflicting demands of the European and customary law. The latter regards the perpetration of wizardry as a crime punishable under the guidance of the traditional authorities. In spite of the risks involved, kraalheads therefore still take the initiative in a great number of allegations, regarding it as their duty to solve the conflicts arising within their villages.

Divination by ordeal,[137] commonly used in the past, and still used by the Kore-Kore in the north, is now seldom heard of amongst the Southern Shona. If an imputed witch is driven to desperation and wants to prove her innocence, or if a *nganga* forces a person, recourse will still be had to the ordeal. The accused will be expected to dip his or her hands in a pot of boiling water. If this can be done without burning the hands, it is an infallible sign of the person's innocence. Another method, and perhaps more often used, is to make the accused or a number of persons drink *muteyo* poison. The innocent will be aided supernaturally to get rid of the poison before it takes effect, whereas the guilty will suffer from an inflated stomach or constant illness, which may lead to an untimely death.

The consequences of witchcraft accusations can be very grave. In her despondency an imputed witch may commit suicide. What happens to her, once the *nganga's* verdict is made known in the village community, depends very much on her social status. If she was well loved and respected it is possible that no physical action will be taken against her but the pent-up emotions of the village community, once let loose, can lead to serious assaults and even death. People fear witches, and they will evade direct attacks once the first wave of reactions has passed, for fear of retaliation by the witch. There are other ways of bringing pressure on the accused, if the *dare* does not command ostracism, or if the witch refuses to move. Arson, or other forms of damage to the accused's property, will be committed

136. See, for instance, the case of *R. v. Jeka and Others,* as described by Crawford (1967, pp. 253-255).

137. For more elaborate accounts, see Gelfand, 1967, p. 74; and Crawford, 1967, p. 214f.

at night, so that the witch will be left with no doubts as to the wish of her neighbours, and at the same time will be unable to identify the attackers. A husband who is convinced of his wife's guilt will make life unbearable for her, thus forcing her to leave the village, rather than exposing his kinsmen to future assaults. Recourse may also be had to vengeance magic.

Crawford indicates that more than 50% of the cases of wizardry allegations amongst the Shona studied by him, concerned witches or sorcerers against whom punitive measures, both violent (attacks or damage to property) and non-violent (ostracism, divorce or general hostility of the community) were taken.[138] His findings clearly reveal that wizardry allegations in practice have a very real impact on society. An official divinatory imputation of wizardry sanctions a wide variety of punitive measures which the threatened members within a community consider appropriate for the unruly or mystically dangerous persons in their midst. Even in those cases where a community ostensibly ignores an accusation made against one of its members, it still remains a serious matter. Such a person, once stigmatized, remains suspect. She may become isolated in the course of time and at a later date be made the scapegoat of misfortunes befalling members of her village community.

The Witchcraft Suppression Act is obviously directed at the elimination, as far as possible, of the ill effects of such accusations on the persons accused. Under section 3 any person who accuses another of being a witch or wizard may be imprisoned for a maximum of 3 years, and section 4 provides that any accuser proved to be a 'habitual or reputed witchdoctor or witch-finder' is liable to imprisonment for a period not exceeding 7 years. (See Appendix I.) The persistence of the belief in *uroyi*, in both rural and urban areas, as shown in table 26, seems sufficient proof that the Act has had very little effect on the belief as such. It is possible that in the urban areas the absence of numerous imputations with serious consequence reflects a successful curb on allegations against named individuals. On the other hand accusations may occur with the same regularity as in the past, but with greater precautions by the diviner (*nganga* or Independent Church prophet) to avoid direct imputation and the increased restraint of those who take punitive action against a named witch or sorcerer. The subtle methods of witch-finding adopted by prophets will be discussed when I deal with Witchcraft in the Independent Churches. Nowadays diagnostic spells of both *nganga* and prophets leave no doubt that, in addition to the occasional direct imputations of wizardry, a great number of indirect accusations – sufficiently suggestive as

138. Crawford, 1967, p. 250.

to the possible source of trouble, yet couched in such terms as to safeguard the diviner against incrimination under the Witchcraft Suppression Act – are made.

d) *Cure of the witch and the bewitched*

The most typical Shona philosophy concerning witches is: 'once a witch always a witch'. As I stated before, a distinction is sometimes made between the curable hereditary witch and the incurable *muroyi wokutemerwa* (witch who was incised) who has an evil substance in her blood. Generally, however, most witches are considered incapable of even wishing to be cured.

I referred to the driving off of the evil spirit in the initial stages before the granddaughter has actually accepted to co-operate with the grandmother's spirit. Preventive measures of this kind are regarded as the most successful because the potential witch has not yet been corrupted by the *uroyi* spirit. Some *nganga* nevertheless try to cure an initiated witch. An essential condition is the request of the witch herself that she be cured, as well as the *confession of all her misdeeds*. The symbolic activities that follow are all directed at separating the indwelling witchcraft spirit from its host. An effort is made to arouse the spirit so that the host will become possessed. This may be achieved through dancing or other ritualistic activities. Then the spirit is given a black sacrificial beast or fowl which will be ritually killed. Gelfand provides us with a description of how a *nganga* places such a fowl on the head of a witch. He first of all tells the spirit that it will leave its host and enter the fowl. Then he gives the fowl, held on the woman's head, some medicine, 'calling out the name of the evil *shavi* until the patient becomes possessed.' The whole procedure will last about an hour until the fowl eventually dies. Death is a sign of the patient's cure.[139] Other frequent themes forming part of the symbolic activities of exorcism are the swimming of the *muroyi* through a river, the casting of the evil medicine into a deep pool, the *muroyi's* running away from the place of exorcism without looking back, as if to free herself completely from the evil spirit; and the burning of a grass hut above the head of the *muroyi*. The fact that such rituals are seldom performed, even by the *nganga* reputed for their exorcistic powers, and that a village community usually prefers to be rid of an imputed witch rather than try to have her reformed, is sufficient proof of the belief in the near impossibility of a witch's cure.

139. Gelfand, 1967, pp. 108-109.

For an ailment caused by wizardry, there are several alternative cures. If a person knows who has bewitched or ensorcelled him, he will send a go-between to contact the wizard in order to obtain an antidote or to persuade the person to come and effect a cure. Quite a number of the Chingombe inhabitants (about a quarter of all those who claim to have been bewitched – table 27) profess to have been cured in this way. It is commonly believed that an antidote exists for each evil potency and that the evildoer usually knows how to prepare it. In case of an emergency, a suspect witch will be threatened and even assaulted in the effort to procure an antidote from her. *Chitsinga* medicine sometimes 'traps' the wrong person. If this happens the *nganga* or sorcerers in the vicinity, known to make use of such medicines, will be requested to produce the antidote or to 'bite out' the medicine from the sufferer's body.

The *nganga* or prophet will be consulted for the treatment of ailments caused by wizardry. Although the figures of table 27 do not clearly reflect this tendency, it often happens that afflicted persons consult more than one *nganga*, or make use of both traditional and Western medical services. Gelfand was in the position to trace the case histories of 32 patients admitted to a Government hospital in Salisbury. He says: 'In all, 66 *nganga* were consulted about the 32 patients. Fourteen went to only one, but the rest consulted at least two or three and one visited at least seven different *nganga* before he came to hospital. Forty-one *nganga* attributed their patients' illness to a witch, 22 to their family spirits and three gave miscellaneous reasons for them.'[140] An increasing tendency to consult Zionist and Apostolic prophets in connection with wizardry is reflected in the high percentage of people (table 27) in Fort Victoria, who professed to have received such treatment. We will deal with this aspect at a later stage. Mention should however be made of an increasing number of prophets known as 'wizardry specialists'. They claim to effect cures through the power of the Holy Spirit and often state that they treat only members of their own Church. It was evident, however, that in practice a great number of people, Christians as well as traditionalists, regularly visit such prophets, in addition to *nganga* and hospitals.

The *nganga's* cure is based, as has been described, on the removal of the *muroyi's* evil medicine, by sucking, biting, and cupping it from the victim's body, or by removal of the evil substance from the patient's hut. The field of curative treatment is too vast to describe, but the emphasis on protection against future attacks is always evident. First of all the guardian *midzimu*

140. *Ibid.*, p. 86.

will have to be propitiated, an action which has at least the psychological value of creating a belief in the achievement of a greater degree of immunity against future attacks. Then the homesteads of the afflicted and close relatives are 'buttressed' with pegs (*kupinga musha*). This is followed by the communal purification rite of washing with *mbanda* medicine and rubbing protective medicine into incisions, made by the *nganga* on the bodies of the patient and other villagers. An illustration of the removal of witchcraft medicine and the treatment applied by a *nganga* is given in the account of a witness in the case of *R. v. Chemere alias Mahondoro*.[141] The accused, Chemere, was called to the village where Chiramwiwa, the alleged witch, resided. According to the witness:

'. . . accused had come to the huts of Chiramwiwa and he went into all the huts making a search for a snake and the head of my son who had died [which he had, at the divination, accused Chiramwiwa of possessing]. He found nothing. He dug and produced a bottle, he produced it from the ground. He kept the bottle. He poured liquid from the bottle on cuts in Chikwaiwa's head. He made cuts on the child's forehead with a razor blade. Accused said there was medicine in the bottle. Accused then went away. After this visit I saw the accused again. I said I wanted him to cleanse my hut with medicines. Accused agreed to do this. This happened a week after the visit to Chiramwiwa's kraal. He produced a horn from the grass roof of my hut. He just nodded at the roof and it fell down. I had never seen the horn before. This was in the hut where my son died. Accused said the horn had caused the sickness of my child. I then asked accused to treat my daughter who was sick. I wanted him to cure and protect her. Accused treated my daughter by making incisions on her forehead and another part of her body with a razor blade. He rubbed medicine on her forehead. He took this medicine from a small suitcase he had. This daughter is about four years old. After he had treated my daughter he said he wanted £1 for finding the horn and £3 for completing the treatment. I gave accused the £4 as requested. Accused accepted the money and then left.'

Another way of effecting a cure is by moving beyond the reach of the witch. It is believed that the witch will stop afflicting others once they have moved from the particular community. The cause of village fragmentation is at times ascribed to wizardry, although the real reason may be the struggle for power amongst agnates, disputes over land, and other factors that often give rise to 'kraal-splitting'. Those who hive off to settle in another part of the *dunhu*, ascribe their latest misfortunes to the threats and the use of evil

141. Crawford, *op. cit.*, pp. 268-269.

magic by the opposing party. They deem resettlement in another locality as the only and inevitable means of safeguarding themselves against the onslaughts of their *vavengi* (lit. haters, i.e. enemies); a kind of argumentation mostly used if other efforts to start with a new village have failed. Once the aim has been achieved, the temporary preoccupation with *uroyi* will fade into the background.

5. THE COMPOSITE PICTURE

A few summarizing and elucidating remarks should still be made about traditional religion. What Mbiti says about the traditional African conception of God also applies to the Southern Shona:

'The attribute of God's transcendence must be balanced with that of His immanence, since these two are paradoxically complementary. This means that He is so "far" (transcendental) that men cannot reach Him; yet, He is so "near" (immanent) that He comes close to men. Many foreign writers have gone astray here, in emphasizing God's remoteness to the exclusion of His nearness.'[142]

We have mentioned just this type of ambivalence in the conception of the Shona High-God, and pointed out that He is not primarily a remote deity. In fact, the popular Shona saying: 'God is far off' (*Mwari ari kure*) can have the connotation of spatial distance in the sense of Mwari being in the distant heavens, but it also, and perhaps more importantly, connotes the idea of a social relationship between man and God different from that between living men and their ancestors. It is another way of saying that man (the commoner) approaches Mwari indirectly, through his ancestors or through the messenger who speaks to Him at the cult centre. Unlike many other African tribes the Shona define the attributes of God fairly clearly through His many names. His oracular revelations indicate that He is a morally, economically and politically interested God. The reciprocity between Him and His people becomes manifest in His demands that His rest-days (*chisi*) and those of His deceased 'sons' (the tribal ancestors) be kept, in the demands of annual gifts for which He provides rain in return, His involvement in chieftain succession issues and in His guidance during periods of national crisis, such as the Rebellions of 1896-7. Mwari's moralistic involvement becomes evident in the direct retaliations of the ancestors against their living descendants for moral transgressions. The home-ancestors' temporary with-

142. Mbiti, 1969, p. 32.

drawal of their guardianship and the consequent exposure of their living relatives to the attacks of evil forces, are regarded as acts of retribution, sanctioned and inspired by Mwari. Even in the magical manipulation of the diviner, Mwari is not merely a distant observer, because He is the source of the forces at work. Should such forces become perverted in the hands of a sorcerer or witch and thereby pose a threat to the social cohesion of His people, it is on His behalf that punitive measures are undertaken.

I have pointed out that the High-God cult is still intact and that it functions as a centralized religious system. Its hereditary, ritual offices of priests, priestesses and keepers, and those of messengers, *mbonga* and *hosana* differ from the offices in ordinary ancestral rites since the actors are 'professionals' with clearly defined tasks. Whereas family rituals often deviate from the broadly conceived 'standard' pattern because substitute lineage members assume the position of absentees and improvisations of ritual procedure often take place, the ritual procedure of the Mwari cult follows the traditionally prescribed code more closely. Similarly, the local *mikwerere* (rain rituals), conducted under the jurisdiction of senior kraalheads, follow a more uniform procedure than the average family rituals.

The worship of Mwari waMatonjeni and of the ancestors correspond in that the approach and address of Mwari (during *mukwerere* rituals and at the cult caves), and of the ancestors, always coincide with the presentation of gifts. Basically the religious act of respect, the symbolic demonstration of loyalty and dependence, is an act of reciprocity. One does not put a request without simultaneously presenting the higher authority with a beer libation, other foodstuffs or whatever gift is appropriate to the occasion. This presentation of the gift, together with the actual address of the higher authority, which gives expression to a specific request, is the essence of *kupira* (derived from *kupa*: to 'give', i.e. to sacrifice or to offer). The term *kupira* is used in both types of rituals; the Shona speak of *kupira Mwari* as well as *kupira midzimu*. *Kunamata*, the nearest Shona equivalent for 'worship', and *kunyengetera* (lit. to pray) are terms seldom used by traditionalists in either ritual context.

Yet it would be wrong not to distinguish between the different manners of approach of the Supreme Being and of the ancestors. Perhaps theological presuppositions and an insufficient knowledge of traditional religion have prevented missionaries from distinguishing sufficiently between *kupira Mwari* and *kupira midzimu*. Once the ancestral rites had been qualified as (idolatrous) 'ancestor worship' a radical rejection of the African preoccupation with ancestral spirits seemed justified. But a careful consideration of the various connotations of the term *kupira*, under varying circumstances, clearly reveals significant differences. In everyday life the term is sometimes used when an important matter is brought to the notice of the tribal elders. A commoner will, for instance, say: 'I have "given" the matter to the elders (*Ndapira nyaya kuvakuru*)', after he has introduced an issue to some tribal dignitaries for their consideration. In the ancestral ritual context *kupira* has the connotation of *kukudza*, i.e. 'to show honour or respect'. In other words the ancestors are venerated. The honour shown them is more reverent than that which is shown to a living being because of their elevated position close to Mwari and because of their increased mystical powers. It is an attitude which in some respects borders on fear. Thus the sacrificial 'giving' to the ancestors, the show of honour, is somewhat different from the respectful 'giving' of a matter to a living person. Simultaneously, however, it is less than the honour paid to Mwari during the *mukwerere* rituals and Mwari cult. Indicative of the difference of approach is the 'scolding' of the ancestors and ordinary banter which is permitted in the address of these spirits, compared to the more reserved and resigned mood of the officiating priests and priestesses when they speak to Mwari at the cult cave.[143] Only at this juncture does *kupira* fully connote the idea of worship, in the sense of paying homage to the highest conceivable authority, the Creator of Mankind.

These distinctions should be borne in mind whenever mention is made in this study of ancestor 'worship'. Due to the chances of misinterpretation, some African theologians have totally discarded the term 'worship' in connection with the ancestors. Kumbirai, for instance, stated:

'If you mean respect by the term worship, it can be applied to the ancestors. If you mean the type of honour or homage we pay to God, then NO! We give our dead parents the same kind of respect and honour that we used to give them when they were alive; *nothing more than that*. We don't conceive of the ancestors as our creators. We say to them: "You people are now *with* God, you know better than we do, so we ask you to intercede for us . . ." The word worship is wrong, because to a Westerner it always gives the impression that the Africans are paying the *midzimu* the same kind of worship that they are paying to God – and that is not so (my italics).'[144]

Kumbirai correctly states that the term 'worship' has been wrongly applied to the traditional ancestral cults. But his identification of the respect paid to a living and to a deceased human being obscures the significant difference of approach, as we have pointed out above. Even the term veneration, fre-

143. See Daneel, 1970, pp. 76-81 for a description of an oracular session at the cult caves of Matonjeni.

144. Personal communication at Chikwingwiza College, 1967.

quently used instead, does not seem to bring out clearly enough this difference, viz. a respect for the ancestors which is indeed *more* than that shown to a living being, a respect which manifests itself by way of sacrifice, and an attitude which can border on adoration, even though it is always different from the homage paid to God. In this sense the term ancestor 'worship' seems an appropriate designation of the religious activities termed *kupira midzimu*.

The strong belief in the continued existence of man after death centres in the view of society with its unborn, living and deceased members all encompassed in a single whole. Life before and after death is conceived of as very similar; the ancestors have essentially the same needs as their living relatives. The living are constantly aware of the pervasive presence of the deceased, *they live with their ancestors*. Ancestor 'worship' therefore serves to maintain social cohesion and lineage unity, with mutual obligations between the living and the dead. Even the duties of ritual participants are determined by their positions in the kinship structure. In practice, however, group participation and a show of loyalty and right-mindedness is more important than precisely following the prescribed ritual procedure. As long as the standard ritual patterns – e.g. that the 'subordinated' *vakuwasha* and *varoora* of the deceased perform the ritual duties of slaughtering the sacrificial animal and brewing the beer, that a senior *muzukuru* takes care of the organization, and an agnate, in the case of a deceased male, acts as ritual officiant – are followed, improvisations according to the insights of participants are permissable. General satisfaction is usually obtained from the knowledge that the ancestor or ancestors concerned were given their dues and that participants in the ritual have done their best.

Features of regular communication between the living and the dead are the interpretations of hazards or success in life in terms of the direct involvement of spirits – ancestral and alien –, the visitation of ancestral spirits in dreams and the well-developed cult of spirit-possession. The latter type of spirit manifestation takes place on a non-lineage (e.g. the spirit-possessed *nganga* or *shavi* medium) as well as on a lineage (e.g. possession of a medium by a family's guardian spirit) or political (possession of a medium by a tribal *mhondoro*) basis. In turn, the living make known their wishes to the deceased through informal addresses in everyday life or through ritual addresses in which the use of symbols play an important role. Thus the *murevo* pot of beer and the *rushanga* construction around the trunk of a *muchakata* tree respectively symbolize the presence of the ancestral spirit and the dwelling place of the lineage ancestors. In this connection one should bear in mind that clear distinctions are not always made between symbolic objects and that which is represented. During ritual procedure the identification between the *murevo* pot or the ancestral blanket (*jira*), and the spirit represented, can be so close that the symbolic object for all practical purposes '*becomes*' the personal being with whom communication is established. Afterwards the symbol may again be treated just like any other ordinary object. This type of ritual identification is obviously directly related to the full identification between living host and visiting spirit during a spell of spirit possession.

Integrated into the religious system and making full use of symbolic objects and acts is the traditional diviner-magician. He is the professional who officially diagnoses the causes of social disruption and who prescribes the ritual restoration of social cohesion. At best he is a specialized preserver of lineage and family unity in so far as his therapy invariably includes instructions to troubled people that they propitiate their discontented ancestors. As a professional detector of wizards, and therefore of the antisocial forces in a community, the *nganga* provides the mystical affirmation and sanction for punitive measures. Since the system of wizardry beliefs is a means of consolidating the old order and of eliminating the elements making for social change, the *nganga* who rises to prominence can attain considerable socially manipulative power, usually of a conservative nature.

In conclusion one can say that group participation is one of the most prominent features of Shona traditional religion. Within the entire system, credal statements, lengthy incantations, a clearly specified 'liturgy' of ritual action and a detailed mythology are practically non-existent. *This religion is in the first place acted out, danced out, and in so doing all the participants become actively involved in ritual procedure.* People are generally less interested in rationalized explanations of religious action than in the actively enacted relatedness between the living and the dead. The activation of ritual participants through shared responsibilities for the provision and preparation of foodstuffs, for the conduct of the various stages of ritual procedure, for music and dancing, marks each ritual occasion. The dramatized presence of spirits through dances, whether it concerns the major annual rain ceremonies at Matonjeni, local *mukwerere* rituals, family rites, spells of *svikiro* possession or *shavi* dances, belongs to the heartbeat of this religion.

TABLES 21-27

TABLE 21. *RSS and CST – Benevolent powers of the midzimu*

Ability to protect *(rinda)* living descendants	Rural adults (M & F)*		Urban adults (M & F)	
	n	%	n	%
Ancestors can protect homestead	516	77	112	71
Ancestors cannot protect homestead	130	19	35	22
Can protect non-Christians only	2	0	1	1
Lost protective powers due to *chirungu* (Europeanism)	3	0	1	1
Don't know	19	3	8	5
Total	670	99	157	100

* M = males; F = females.

TABLE 22. *RSS and CST – Punitive powers of midzimu*

Midzimus' ability to harm (kill) relatives	Rural adults (M & F)		Urban Adults (M & F)	
	n	%	n	%
Ancestors can kill relatives	549	82	123	78
Ancestors cannot kill	97	15	24	15
Ancestors can kill non-Christians (only)	2	0	1	1
Lost punitive powers due to *chirungu* (Europeanism)	3	0	1	1
Don't know	19	3	8	5
Total	670	100	157	100

TABLE 23. *RSS and CST – Existence of shavi and ngozi spirits*

Existence of *shavi* and *ngozi*	Rural adults (M & F)		Urban adults (M & F)	
	n	%	n	%
Uncertain (Don't know)	6	1	7	5
Shavi and *ngozi* exist at present	634	95	142	90
Shavi and *ngozi* non-existent	25	4	6	4
Ngozi existent but not *shavi*	5	1	2	1
Shavi existent but not *ngozi*	–	–	–	–
Total	670	101	157	100

TABLE 24. *RSS and CST – Shavi activities*

The *shavi's* healing powers	Rural adults (M & F)		Urban adults (M & F)	
	n	%	n	%
Shavi spirits heal	549	82	124	79
Shavi spirits cannot heal	109	16	24	15
Shavi can heal dependent on God's will	2	0	–	–
Don't know	10	2	9	6
Total	670	100	157	100

TABLE 25. *RSS and CST – Ngozi activities*

Ngozi's ability to kill	Rural adults (M & F)		Urban adults (M & F)	
	n	%	n	%
The *ngozi* spirit kills outrightly	605	90	134	85
The *ngozi* cannot kill	53	8	14	9
Can kill dependent on God's will	2	0	–	–
Don't know	10	2	9	6
Total	670	100	157	100

TABLE 26. *RSS and CST – Uroyi (witchcraft and sorcery)*

Belief in existence of *uroyi*	Rural adults (M & F)		Urban adults (M & F)	
	n	%	n	%
Uroyi exists at present (unqualified)	180	27	5	3
Uroyi exists (distinguishes more than one form – eg. *Chitsinga*, *Chiposo*, etc.)	424	63	134	85
Uroyi non-existent	55	8	8	5
Don't know	11	2	10	6
Total	670	100	157	99

TABLE 27. *RSS and CST – Experience of uroyi*

Personal experience of witchcraft/sorcery		Rural adults (M & F)			Urban adults (M & F)		
		n	%		n		%
I have never been *roya'd**		375	56		86		55
My close relatives *(pamusha)* have been *roya'd* and I witnessed the consequences		116	17		24		15
Personally bewitched or ensorcelled	Was personally *roya'd*; medicine removed by *muroyi himself*	35	5	(21%)	4	(31%)	2
	Personally *roya'd*; went to *nganga* for treatment	71	11		15		10
	Personally *roya'd*; went to hospital	10	2		9		6
	Personally *roya'd*; went to prophet	12	2		17		11
	Personally *roya'd*; went to *nganga* and prophet	–	–		1		1
	Personally *roya'd*; went to *nganga* and hospital	6	1		1		1
Personal experience but refuses further information		43	6		–		–
Unanswered		2	0		–		–
Total		670	100		157		101

* *Roya:* used in the wide sense of the word (as the Shona use the term themselves); including therefore any form of bewitchment or sorcery.

European Missions amongst the Southern Shona

In the preceding chapter the nature and the persistence of the basic elements of the traditional religion were illustrated. Having obtained an idea of the *old*, we must now concern ourselves with the *new* religion, which was introduced towards the end of the previous century. Special attention will be given to Mission policy and practical strategy in the field. The differentiated nature of the impact of Protestant and Catholic Christianity on the customs and religion of the Southern Shona is of vital importance for an understanding of the Independent Church Movement. Only those aspects that have a direct bearing on the historical background and present nature of our subject, will be dealt with. There is therefore no pretence of an exhaustive treatment of the subjects broached.[1]

The main focus will be on the missionary enterprises of the Dutch Reformed (DRC) and the Roman Catholic Churches (RCC). Not only have these two Churches been engaged in the most extensive missionary work amongst the Southern Shona, as compared to other Churches and societies, but their contrasting methods seem to correlate with the higher or lower incidence of 'separatism' and therefore demand close scrutiny. Neither of these Churches has as yet experienced a major schism amongst the Southern Shona, in the sense of a whole group of affiliated Church members breaking away at approximately the same time; but considerable numbers of individual members and families have defected to the Independent Churches in the course of time. There is no doubt that the Protestant Churches have lost more of their members in this way than the Catholic Church. For comparative purposes the study had to be extended beyond the borders of the Chingombe chiefdom,

1. Several writers have remarked on the lack of detailed studies on the growth of Christian Missions in Rhodesia. See, for example, Shepperson, *Church and Sect in Central Africa,* Rhodes Livingstone Journal, 1963, and Ranger, *The Early History of Independency in Rhodesia,* in 'Religion in Africa', 1964. Due to a lack of comprehensive studies on the development of the two Mission Churches concerned, I had to rely on missionary periodicals, observations in the field and personal interviews with Church leaders. The chequered history of Christianity in Rhodesia still needs to be written.

because the people in this area have been subjected mainly to DRC influence, at any rate in the period of the initial rise of the Independent Churches during the second and third decades of this century. As a result Independent Church members in Chingombe who have defected from a Mission Church are mostly ex-DRC members, or people who have at least come into contact with the teachings of this Church through primary education. Unfortunately material available provides an insufficient basis for the accurate assessment of the incidence of secession from the DRC as compared to the RCC, but enquiries and observation in the field nevertheless yielded some clues on the reasons why more African Protestants defect from their Churches than African Catholics.

1. THE HISTORICAL PERSPECTIVE

In 1561 the first Christian martyr died in Mashonaland when Goncalo da Silveira, a Portuguese missionary of the Society of Jesus, was killed at the command of the Monomotapa ruler of that period. The efforts of Da Silveira, who baptized some 500 slaves, were followed up by missionaries of the Dominican Order. During the seventeenth century, the Catholic missionaries extended their work into various areas of the Monomotapa dynasty after having persuaded and baptized one of the Monomotapa rulers. But the decline of Portuguese military power brought an end to the efforts of these priests, so that hardly any trace of their work was left by the nineteenth century. Van der Merwe suggests that 'lack of education and thorough Christian instruction prevented Christianity from really striking root, however noble and self-sacrificing the efforts of some of the earlier missionaries may have been.' According to him 'the number of Africans who did receive an education were either severed from their people altogether, or were too few in number to exercise any lasting influence over the rest of their people. With the withdrawal of the Roman Catholic priests the deep darkness of African heathenism once more fell upon the land.'[2]

Robert Moffat's visits to Mzilikazi in 1829 and 1835 brought the Ndebele into contact with Christianity for the first time. In 1859 a Mission station was founded in Matabeleland by the London Missionary Society (LMS). This early effort hardly yielded any noteworthy results during the first years of operation, and the Mission station existed amongst the warring Ndebele by virtue of Moffat's remarkable relationship with the Ndebele monarch, rather than the success of the missionaries with the people.

2. Van der Merwe, 1953, p. 5.

It was only after the Pioneer Column had penetrated the country north of the Limpopo that Mission stations of a more significant nature were opened up by various Churches. Cecil Rhodes, working on the 'Leitmotiv' of 'Christianity and Commerce', made generous grants of land to Churches and Societies. He was convinced of the important role to be played by the bearers of Christianity in bringing Western civilization to Africa. Between 1891 and 1900 several Missions started work in Rhodesia. The *Church of England* was one of the first ecclesiastical bodies to commence work in the Eastern Shona districts, with St. Augustine's Mission station at Penhalonga as their main base. The LMS received land grants of 4,000 morgen both at Hope Fountain and Inyati, from where their activities expanded mainly into Matabeleland. Both English and American *Methodists* established Missions in the country. Under the leadership of Bishop Hartzell, the latter opened a station at Old Umtali on a large tract of land granted them by Cecil Rhodes. All six districts founded by the American Methodists are located in the Eastern districts near Salisbury and Umtali. In 1893 the *American Board of Commissioners* inaugurated work at Mt. Selinda, near the border of Mozambique. This station, together with Chikore, which was opened in 1895, became a centre of secondary education, teachers' training and medical work. The American Board missionaries directed their main effort at the surrounding Ndau people. In 1892 the *Berlin Missionary Society* commenced work in the Southern Shona districts. Mission stations were built at Gutu, Zimuto (near Fort Victoria) and Chibi, under the leadership of pioneering missionaries such as the Revs. Beuster, Knothe and Schwellnus. When this Society was forced to abandon its work in 1907, due to financial problems, the three Mission stations came under the control of the DRC. To the ranks of the pioneer missionaries also belong members of the *Seventh Day Adventists*, followed at a later stage by numerous other Churches, such as the *Church of Sweden* in Belingwe, the *South Africa General Mission, Evangelical Alliance Mission* and such groups as the *Southern Baptists, American Methodist Episcopal Church, Church of Christ, Full Gospel* and *Apostolic Faith.*

The Southern Rhodesia Missionary Conference was founded as early as 1903, with the majority of Protestant Churches affiliated to it. This Conference partly succeeded in eliminating unnecessary rivalry amongst the Protestant bodies by roughly delineating the 'spheres of influence' of each Church. The Roman Catholic Church refused at first to co-operate under such conditions. They were dedicated to their policy, expressed in 1948 by one of their Church leaders as follows: 'We shall always fight the Protestant Churches, try to prevent them from spreading... And any idea of recognizing any other church as sister church or the like, or happily or resignedly agreeing to differ, is quite out of the question for us.'[3] These words, though spoken by a Roman Catholic, nevertheless characterize the unrelenting spirit in which many missionaries in the field stood opposed to each other's work. It made co-operation in the spirit of true ecumenicity impossible and led to competition in the educational fields which was often not to the credit of either Catholic or Protestant bodies.

We shall now briefly review the development of the two Mission Churches which we have selected for comparative purposes, the Dutch (later African) Reformed Church of Mashonaland and the Roman Catholic Church.

a) *The Dutch (or African) Reformed Church*

During the Ndebele reign an attempt was made by the French missionary Coillard to start missionary work amongst the Banyai (Vakaranga). He was detained by Lobengula, who bluntly refused to have missionary work amongst the subjected Shona tribes, and the venture came to naught. In spite of Lobengula's prohibition, Rev. Stephanus Hofmeyr, DRC missionary at the Soutpansberg in northern Transvaal, sent some volunteer African evangelists to the Banyai. These courageous men paved the way for others to follow. In 1890, the Rev. S. P. Helm inspected the territory north of the Limpopo as far as the Zimbabwe ruins on behalf of the DRC. He returned with a favourable report but could find nobody willing to risk working amongst the Banyai, except the enthusiastic but frail Mr. A. A. Louw, a young man who had abandoned his theological studies at Stellenbosch due to bad health. Louw, a nephew of the well-known missionary statesman, the Rev. Andrew Murray, felt convinced of his call to Mashonaland, but his father was opposed to his plans. Amongst other things the old Rev. Louw wrote to his son: 'I cannot believe that it is the will of God that you should proceed to those parts at the expense of the Church to die there after a brief stay and be buried, whereas, humanly speaking, a longer and not less useful life was awaiting you . . .'[4]

But the young man never wavered once his decision was made. After five months of hardship, travelling by ox-wagon, he reached the mountain of Chief Mugabe in Southern Mashonaland (Sept. 1894) and there founded Morgenster, the main DRC Mission station, four miles from the Zimbabwe ruins. Instead of the predicted 'brief stay' Mr. (later Rev.) Louw was destined to lead the DRC Mission in Mashonaland for more than 40 years, during which

3. Louw, 1965, p. 187.
4. *Ibid.*, p. 55 (translated from the Dutch text). See also Van der Merwe, 1953, p. 13.

period he profoundly influenced, directly and indirectly, the whole missionary enterprise.

During the initial stages of work progress was slow and the first decade yielded hardly any visible fruits. In 1899 the first Karanga woman, Ishibato, was converted to Christianity. When Rev. Louw enquired about her wish to join the Church, she simply replied: 'The word has become so big in my heart that I cannot contain it any longer.' She was baptized together with two other Shona converts in 1901. In the same year a second Mission station was opened at Pamushana in the Bikita district. A few years later the three stations of the Berlin Mission Society – Gutu, Zimuto and Chibi – were added to the expanding interests of the DRC. In 1909 an Italian minister, the Rev. Orlandini, established a station in Chingombe, which was later called Alheit, in remembrance of the Rev. Alheit, whose congregation at Ceres in the Cape Province had taken a special interest in this station. Jichidza was founded by the Rev. J. F. Roux in the Zaka district to the south-east of Morgenster in 1908, Makumbe in the Buhera district by the Rev. P. A. Badenhorst in 1915 and Nyashanu, also in Buhera, in recent years. These Mission stations formed the main centres where evangelistic, educational and medical work was conducted and extended into the surrounding districts. The unhealthy climate initially claimed a heavy toll amongst the missionaries. Between 1903 and 1904 as many as 15 members of the staff had either died, or had to leave the field due to bad health.[5]

The Rev. Louw started with the translation of biblical passages into the vernacular as soon as he reached Mashonaland. Later he was assisted in his task by his wife and Dr. John Helm. In 1904 the Gospels and the Acts of the Apostles were first printed in Chikaranga,[6] and by 1919 the whole New Testament was translated. Several years of revision followed before the New Testament (1942) and ultimately the whole Bible (1950) was printed. The DRC missionaries contributed greatly towards developing Chikaranga as a written language. Mrs. Louw, an outstanding linguist, produced one of the first Shona manuals. In the course of time a Catechism, hymn book, religious literature and school books were printed in the vernacular at the Morgenster printing press. The Mission authorities ruled from the outset that all missionaries should master the vernacular.

At first the increase of converts was slow. In 1915 this Mission Church counted only 450 Christians and 691 catechumens. Ten years later the numbers had risen to 2,132 Church members and 3,593 catechumens. In the

5. Van der Merwe, 1953, p. 28.
6. *Ibid.*, p. 28.

1950's it counted more than 20,000 members, and 6-7,000 catechumens annually attended the confirmation classes. In 1967 the Church membership had risen to about 30,000.

In 1917, the Christian communities which gradually developed at and around the Mission stations were officially organized into congregations, each with its own Church council. The councils consisted of the local missionaries together with the African evangelists and a few elected elders. The local Church councils were responsible to the Mission Council in the field, and the Mission Committee in Cape Town.

This was the position until 1952, when the *Shona Reformed Church* (now called the *African Reformed Church*),[7] with its own synod and presbyteries, came into being. At present the 26 congregations are subdivided into the four presbyteries of Morgenster, Pamushana, Gutu and Bulawayo. The Church is affiliated as a Daughter Church to the Dutch Reformed Church in South Africa. A Federal Council of Dutch Reformed Churches is responsible for coordinating the functions of the various local Mother and Daughter Churches.

With the ideal of an independent, indigenous Church in mind, the missionaries started training local leaders at an early stage. Evangelist-teachers played an important role during the initial stages of expansion, but full-time evangelists were needed. Thus in 1925 the first evangelist school was opened at Morgenster, with the son of the Rev. A. A. Louw as the first lecturer. The Rev. H. W. Murray started with the first class of entrants for the ministry in the 1930's, and in 1938 the sixty-seven-year-old founder of the Shona Mission (who had meanwhile become renamed among the Vakaranga as '*sekuru*'-grandfather) ordained the Rev. Ezra Shumba as the first African minister. Since then the number of African ministers has risen to 20 in 1967; at which stage they were assisted by 13 European ministers, 53 African lay preachers, 16 African evangelists and 128 European lay workers.

b) *The Roman Catholic Church*

Two Jesuit priests, Father Andrew Hartmann and Peter Prestage, accompanied the Pioneer Column in 1890, when it penetrated the domains of Lobengula.

7. In the rural areas this Mission Church is still popularly referred to as the Dutch Reformed Church. For the purposes of this study I have given preference to this latter term, using it sometimes in abbreviation, i.e. DRC (this particularly applies to the headings of the statistical tables later to be presented in Volume 2). In this way the reader is prevented from mistaking the Mission Church for Zvobgo's secessionist group, which is also called the African Reformed Church; abbreviated to ARC in the text.

Catholic influence thus made itself felt from the earliest stage of European occupation. For the first six years the Church's organization fell under the jurisdiction of the Society of Jesus, after which it fell in charge of a Prefect Apostolic. In 1891, the first hospital at Salisbury was put up by the Dominican Sisters and in the following year the Jesuit fathers set up a Mission station at Chishawasha near Salisbury. 'Lacking financial resources, the Jesuits tried to make each one of their houses self-sufficient, and they developed a large 14,000-acre farm there [at Chishawasha]. The Fathers concentrated on agricultural and industrial rather than literary training, everyone, white or black alike, doing his share of physical labour . . . Chishawasha in fact resembled in some ways a kind of Paraguayan "reduction" in miniature; the Fathers governed with a firm hand and successfully resisted an attack during the Rebellions.'[8]

The work of the Jesuits at Chishawasha made a deep impression on the Administrator of Rhodesia, Lord Grey, in those early years. Having visited the Mission station after the Rebellion he commented on the Catholics' work, 'No work is too hard or too menial for them – manual labour in the fields as gardeners, farm labourers; the menial occupation of cooks, brewers, bakers, etc. . . . Before this order of the RC Church producing as it does the most admirable results, one must stand hat in hand; and when one contrasts with it the vulgar individualism of our Protestant churches one is obliged to admit that from the policy and action of these powerful and historical orders one has very, *very* much to learn.'[9] The impact of what he had seen at Chishawasha was afterwards portrayed in Grey's enthusiasm to experiment in the educational field. He wanted the Africans to be taught blacksmithing, carpentry, agriculture and domestic science. Ranger says that 'Grey's plan, in fact, was a revolutionary one in its context; nothing less than a Government attempt to emulate the Chishawasha approach and take the lead in the transformation of Shona society through education.'[10]

After the Matabele war in 1893 the Catholic field was extended to Bulawayo. It seems that Catholic endeavour during the first few decades was confined mainly to the Northern and Central Shona as well as to Matabeleland. Although Fr. Barthelemy, who had arrived in the country from St. Aidan's (South Africa), was sent to Fort Victoria as early as 1892, it took some time before the Catholic Church found a firm foothold in the southern regions.

8. Gann, 1965, p. 196.

9. Lord Grey to his wife, 23rd January, 1897, G R 1/1/1, quoted by Ranger, 1967, p. 314.

10. Ranger, 1967, p. 314.

Fr. Barthelemy's instructions were 'to organize the Catholic position in town and district; to discuss the question of a hospital with the local authority, to explore the country and prepare the way for missionary work among the natives.'[11] A small chapel-presbytery combination was erected and, under the guidance of four sisters from Salisbury, several huts were erected as a 'hospital' for Europeans and Africans. In 1893 Fr. Barthelemy explored the surroundings of Fort Victoria. He was offered the Mzondo farm, 10 miles to the north of Fort Victoria, where in time the Gokomere Mission station was established. Few converts were baptized in those years. Frey tells us that 'Gokomere's first baptism book contains three loose, rusty looking, rather small papers which seem to be torn from a small size of baptism book . . . According to that register Fr. Barthelemy baptized ten people during 1893; two of them "Militaris castris" + "Sub. cond." . . . Another two were baptized by Fr. Prestage. Probably all were Europeans to conclude from the names.'[12] In 1897, only four African baptisms by Fr. Ronchi, Barthelemy's successor, were recorded. The Dominican sisters were recalled to Salisbury. In the opinion of the Rev. Sykes, then Superior of the Zambesi Mission, 'the number of people at Fort Victoria and the foreseeable future of Fort Victoria did not justify to have several sisters there.'[13]

Catholic progress amongst the Southern Shona, i.e. in the Victoria, Chibi, Ndanga, Bikita and Gutu districts, was relatively slow for several decades. Here the DRC Mission dominated the field as far as education was concerned. But in 1938 the arrival of three Bethlehem Fathers (Boehi, Waldispuehl and Beckmann), whose Society was to assist the English Jesuits in south-eastern Shona regions, marked the beginning of rapid and vigorous expansion. In the following year several new Swiss priests and brothers of the Bethlehem Society arrived in the country. They took charge of the Gokomere (Victoria district) and Silveira (Bikita district) Mission stations in 1940. Together these stations counted only about 3,000 members at that stage.[14] Silveira was in poor shape with its *musha vedzimba dzakaipa* (village of dilapidated houses) when Fr. Waldispuehl took over from Fr. Swift.[15] At this stage Silveira had 7 village schools, but this number rose to 35 in the ensuing years. Soon after Dr. Boehi took over Gokomere from Fr. Gits, a small Church was built in Rupiri (1941) which marked the first extension of the Catholic Church into the Gutu district. After the Society had bought Mr. Vermaak's farm in the Gutu district, not

11. Johanny S. J., *Fort Victoria 1892-94* (A short study).
12. Frey, 1963, p. 165.
13. *Ibid.*, p. 165.
14. Michlig, 1963, p. 153.
15. *Ibid.*, p. 155.

far from the Chikwanda Native Reserve in 1944, Catholic activity intensified in Gutu. The shortage of staff and finance, caused by the second World War, was eased in 1945; Fr. Winterhalder, the missionary in charge, received assistance and Mukaro, as the new station in Gutu was called, was developed into a model Mission centre. Catholic village schools and out-stations mushroomed all over the Gutu district. Of these, Mutero in the Nyamande chiefdom was one. Following the method of building some of the out-schools into out-stations and then into Mission stations, the Catholics first turned Mutero school, which was opened in 1946, into an out-school and then staffed it with missionaries in 1956. Ten years later the missionaries were already administering 16 out-schools in the Gutu East region from the Mutero base (see map 2), with the prospect in the near future of elevating Makura, an out-station with Upper Primary school facilities in the Munyikwa sub-chiefdom, (in the eastern tip of Gutu) to the level of yet another Mission station in the near future.

Other Mission stations, such as St. Anthony's (Ndanga district) and Bondolfi (Victoria), were founded in 1949 and 1951 respectively. In 1966, the Church members belonging to these two new stations already numbered more than 10,000, a sign of the phenomenal growth of the Catholic Church in Southern Mashonaland during the past two decades. Up to 1947 European and African Catholics in Fort Victoria were ministered to from Gokomere Mission. Then the Prefecture Apostolic, with Mgr. Haene as its first prefect of Fort Victoria, came into being, and in 1955 the bishop's hierarchy was established in Rhodesia.[16] The Diocese of Gwelo, covering all of the Southern and Eastern Shona districts, came under the responsibility of the Bethlehem Fathers, while the Jesuits took charge of the Salisbury Diocese. Besides Gwelo and Salisbury, the three other Catholic Dioceses in Rhodesia are Bulawayo, Wankie and Umtali.

To get an impression of the expansion of the Catholic Church in the Gwelo Diocese[17] one need only glance at the statistics of this Diocese between 1959 and 1966. In this seven-year period the number of Catholics (approximately 2,000 Europeans and the rest Africans) grew from 70,176 to 120,053, thus showing an annual increase of about 7,000 members. In the same period 16 – 20,000 catechumens annually attended the Catholic catechism classes.[18] A statistical comparison between the RCC and DRC is complicated because of

16. Mulders, 1957, p. 476; Michlig, 1963, p. 158.

17. This diocese covers the districts of Gwelo, Que Que, Fort Victoria, Shabani, Mashaba, Chilimanzi, Bikita, Ndanga, Zaka, Chibi, Belingwe, Chiredzi, and Triangle. It has fifteen Mission and numerous out-stations.

18. Diocesan Statistics in Guti, Oct. 1965 and Oct. 1966.

the different standards applied in obtaining data. It does seem significant, however, that the DRC statistics over the same period show a fluctuation in Church membership of between 25,000 and 30,000, with hardly any overall increase in membership, and this in spite of a distinct numerical advantage in denominational schools in the Southern Shona regions.

High standards are set for the training of the indigenous priesthood. A preparatory course of four years is offered at three minor seminaries in Rhodesia (one of which is the Chikwingwiza seminary near Gwelo, for the Dioceses of Gwelo and Bulawayo). There is little difference between the curriculae of these seminaries and the ordinary secondary school courses leading to the Cambridge certificate or GCE, but as Niederberger says: 'The seminary differs from the secondary schools in *atmosphere*; it is more secluded, allows for more talks on the priesthood and also has more celebrations; the seminarians are on probation and are given a chance to decide.'[19] After completing Form IV the young seminarian can proceed to the Major Seminary at Chishawasha, where an 8-year course (3 years Philosophy and 5 years Theology) is taught, before ordination takes place. That the Catholic authorities have moved ahead cautiously with the ordination of African priests is clearly reflected in the low number of priests thus far ordained. In 1967 the Bethlehem Fathers employed only 6 African priests. This does not mean that African leadership is neglected in the Catholic Church. In addition to the 287 Europeans (84 priests, 61 brothers, 128 sisters and 14 lay workers), 73 African sisters, more than 50 novices and candidates and 109 African catechists were employed in the Gwelo Diocese in 1966, thus forming a strong missionary force.

2. MISSION POLICY AND STRATEGY IN THE FIELD

a) *The 'planting' of a Mission Church*

In his analysis of African Separatism in South Africa, Sundkler bases his argument on two value premises. *First*, Protestant denominationalism as the main reason for secession from Mission Churches. The application of the Protestant policy of 'independent', self-supporting, self-governing and self-propagating Churches stands in direct causal relation to Bantu 'Separatism'. 'My contention is', says Sundkler, 'that there has been altogether too much

19. Personal communication – 1967.

stress on the "*self*" and much too little emphasis on what the *Church* is. Without those "continuous principles" which have been delivered to the Church, "continuous life" is not to be expected.'[20] By way of illustration Sundkler mentions some examples of the consternation caused in the Mission field when leaders like John Kilner, secretary of the Wesleyan Methodist Missionary Society, and leaders of the Foreign Mission Boards of the United States began propagating a self-supporting Church in the field. A circular from the latter body to the Zulu Mission caused misunderstanding and resentment amongst the African Church leaders who thought that certain privileges were being withheld from them. This was 'one of the reasons for the formation of the Zulu Congregational Church in 1896.'[21]

Secondly, Sundkler mentions the 'impact of racial discrimination upon the life of the Christian Church.' He distinguishes the Calvinist claim of 'no equality' between White and Black in Church and State from the liberal proclamation of equal opportunity for all men regardless of race and colour. 'Neither of these policies, if left unhampered by any conflicting views, would seem to lead to secession. The problem arises when the more repressive view tacitly or openly becomes dominating in churches which in principle are equalitarian and liberal, but which by "practical necessity" – consideration for the race-conscious White membership of a particular church – have to conform to a general segregation policy within the church.'[22]

To what extent did these two factors play a role in the planting of the Shona Reformed and the Catholic Church? A detailed background study of the development of the Mission policy of these two Churches goes beyond the scope of this book, but a few outstanding features should nevertheless be mentioned. As for the DRC, the development of its Mission policy has always stood in direct relation to practical experience in the field, which has inevitably involved the racial problem. The decision of the Synod in 1857, for example – on the separation of races in services, catechismal teaching and observance of the sacrament – came *after* the creation of Mission Societies with separate services for the Bantu, and when the founding of separate indigenous congregations was already an established fact. That it was indeed a *practical necessity* and *not a matter of principle* that caused the 1857 motion to be carried by a large majority of Synod, is reflected in the wording of the

20. Sundkler, 1961, p. 17. His 'continuous principles' and 'continuous life' refers to Bishop Gore's statement at the World Missionary Conference held in Edinburgh in 1910. Gore said, 'We have got to put into all bodies of Christian the consciousness that continuous life depends on continuous principles.'

21. *Ibid.*, p. 30.

22. *Ibid.*, p. 17.

motion itself: 'The Synod considers it desirable and scriptural that our members from the Heathen be received and absorbed into our existing congregations wherever possible; but where this measure, as a result of the weakness of some, impedes the furtherance of the cause of Christ among the Heathen, the congregation from the Heathen, already founded or still to be founded, *shall enjoy its Christian privileges in a separate building or institution* (my italics).'[23] This decision was not aimed at the complete exclusion of members of different racial groups from each other's congregation. It envisaged separate places of worship without the prohibition of interracial communion of believers by Church law. The extent to which the DRC allowed itself to be led by practical considerations in the founding of separate Churches is clearly reflected in the interpretation of the Church's historic past by an ad hoc Committee for Race Relations. According to this committee the founding of separate Churches sprang from:

'A realization of the cultural and social needs of the non-whites and a sincere attempt to minister to them more efficiently and to train them for Church independence and leadership . . . [and also from] the fact that some white members preferred to attend separate communion services, and worship independently of the non-whites. Undoubtedly the motives there were grounded on social and hygienic considerations and on the racial attitudes of the nineteenth century . . .'

Furthermore, the Committee regarded the limitation of racial groups to the membership of their own Church as the result of:

a) the founding of indigenous Churches, each with its own interests and aspirations;
b) the cultural, social and other differences of the various ethnic groups;
c) the practice of ministering to the spiritual needs of the non-whites separately by specially trained missionaries (not ministers) because of the differences of language, and for other reasons;
d) the great social and political repercussions of the first half of the nineteenth century . . .[24]

After the important Synod of 1857, the first official Daughter Church to be constituted (1881) with its own Synod was the *Dutch Reformed Mission Church*, which comprised several Coloured congregations. When the Rev. A. A. Louw set out to do missionary work among the Southern Shona in 1891 an official Mission policy had not yet been fully developed. Nevertheless, at

23. *Statements on Race Relations,* Report of the Ad Hoc Committee for Race relations, appointed by the Federal Council of Dutch Reformed Churches, 1960, p. 4.
24. *Ibid.*, p. 6.

this stage he represented a Church that had accepted separate Churches as inevitable and had already started implementing this policy on the institutional and organizational level. It should be stressed, however, that with men like Louw and other pioneer missionaries of his time, the emphasis did not lie on creating *separate Churches* as an end in itself. These missionaries regarded the planting and organization of a local Church as the inevitable result of conversions in the field. Their primary aim was the winning of souls for Christ through the preaching of the Gospel.[25]

Louw's fervour for winning souls did not obscure his ideal for the founding and development of a Church in the Mission field. His summons to his co-workers at a missionary conference during the early stage of missionary pioneering, when hardly any Shona had yet responded to the Gospel, is revealing. 'The cause of expansion must be our primary concern', he said. 'Extension, now or never! We must achieve in Mashonaland now that which our Church expects – an outstretched, adjacent field of labour, where a great number of missionaries can exert their influence in a territory where thousands of natives are living. Yes, they [missionaries and African Christians] must form *their own Synod* – why not? It is not too late yet. Much, very much, if not everything depends on *us* here in the field. The Foreign Mission Committee listens to our advice and is completely led by us. The Committee trusts us and decides as we decide. If *we* have courage, so do they. Brothers, my watchword, our motto, must be: Onwards in the name of the Lord! *Deus hoc vult*.'[26]

Two things emerge clearly from Louw's words. He envisaged a large expansion that had to culminate in a Church with its *own Synod*, and he was fully aware of the fact that the Mission Committee did not dictate a set course to the missionaries in the field, but was actually to a great extent led by the experiences of those in the field.

Although there was no 'blue-print' on the exact nature of the Church to be planted in the Mission field, the influence of Anglo-Saxon and German-Lutheran Mission policies are discernable in the Shona Church that eventually

25. The official missionary policy adopted by the DRC Synod in 1932, confirms that the 'primary aim of all missionary endeavour of the DRC in the past concerned the preaching of the Gospel with the intent of gathering souls for God's Kingdom.' In the first two paragraphs under the heading 'Methods of Missionary Work', the gathering of souls for God's Kingdom and the 'founding of an organized Church' are closely linked. See *Acta Synodi,* 27th meeting, 1932. The Mission policy of 1932 was in fact an affirmation of the approach adopted by the pioneers in the foreign mission fields, such as the Rev. A. C. Murray in Nyasaland and the Rev. A. A. Louw in Mashonaland, as well as many others who have laboured in South Africa before them.

26. Louw, 1965, pp. 177-78 (translated from the Afrikaans).

came into being. German influence made itself felt locally through the 'inheritance' by the DRC of the three Mission stations of the Berlin Missionary Society, as well as through co-operation with the Swedish Lutheran Mission. Louw and his fellow-workers were also familiar with the ideas on Church indigenization as propounded by the distinguished German theologian, Gustav Warneck. Du Plessis, onetime secretary of Missions and then Professor of Missionary Science at Stellenbosch, had adopted Warneck's emphasis on the indigeneity of the Mission Church, on the respect of the missionary for the culture and customs of those to whom he preaches the Gospel, and on the building of a '*Volkskirche*' with its roots in the '*Volksleben*' (*Einwurzelung des Christentums in das Volksleben*).[27]

Van der Merwe indicates that the concept of a 'native' or 'national' Church, as envisaged by the academy successors of du Plessis, shows great affinity with Warneck's '*Volkskirche*'. 'The ideal', he says, 'was presumably: one Church for each ethic group.'[28] In the DRC's declaration of policy the phrase 'Christianity must not rob the native of his language and culture, but should ultimately permeate [*deurtrek*] and purge [*deursuiwer*] his whole Nationalism,'[29] clearly reflects a vein of thought similar to that found in Warneck and other German theologians.

In spite of the considerable influence of German scholars on the Mission Theology of the DRC, it should be noted that in the Shona Mission field the only real affinity with this approach can be found in the great emphasis on the study and use of the vernacular. Unlike missionaries such as Bruno Gutmann and Keysser, who propagated mass conversion (the tribe *is* the congregation – Keysser) and the retention of primordial social ties (*urtümliche Bindungen* – Gutmann) with the indigenous customs within the Church, Rev. Louw and his contemporaries were convinced of the necessity of individual conversion, which to them implied a radical break with customs and the religious practices of the past. 'Indigenous' to them meant effective communication of the Gospel through the vernacular and the training of an indigenous Church leadership. Yet the forms of worship and religious expression within the Church that they had introduced were little more than a replica of the sober forms within the Mother Church. Thus one can safely say that, as far as indigeneity of the Shona Church was concerned, the emphasis was not on *Shona* (incorporating Shona customs) but on the *Church*, the Church of Christ as understood by the missionaries. As will be indicated below, the emphasis within the emerging

27. Warneck, 1892, p. 22.
28. Van der Merwe, 1967, p. 53.
29. *Ibid.*, p. 52; with reference to Gerdener, 1951, p. 88.

Shona Church was that of 'discontinuity' with regards to the traditional past, as a result of which a double foreignness prevailed: that of the essential Christian position (*in* but not *of* the world), and that of a Westernized pattern of worship.

Of greater importance is the influence of Anglo-Saxon Missions. Venn's formula of the three 'selves' as the basis of 'independence' for the Mission Church,[30] which had left its imprint on the Anglo-Saxon Missions and especially the World Dominion Movement, was adopted, though in somewhat modified form, by du Plessis. According to him the Mother Church should welcome the independence of the Mission Church envisaged in this approach, as it would free her from duties which might well divert her from promoting the expansion of God's Kingdom further afield.[31] Through du Plessis and the experience of missionaries in the field, part of Venn's formula found its way into the official DRC missionary policy formulated in 1932. There it is stated that the founding of a Church in the Mission field in itself was not enough. 'Established congregations must be developed and become self-supporting and self-governing in the course of time.'[32] That the emphasis was on self-support is revealed in the declaration of policy: 'Where the Mother Church at first carried the whole *financial responsibility*, this burden should gradually be shouldered by the indigenous Church, until it ultimately becomes self-supporting, self-governing and self-propagating.'[33]

In the Shona Mission field the DRC missionaries came into regular contact with members of the Anglo-Saxon missions. The Rev. Louw had been one of the co-founders of the Rhodesia Missionary Conference. DRC representatives regularly attended the meetings and they also co-operated with English and American denominations in the production and distribution of literature in the vernacular. These contacts had a direct effect on the DRC strategy. Van der Merwe points out that with 'the Dutch Reformed Mission fields north of the Limpopo [Mashonaland and Nyasaland], the emphasis – as was the case with the World Dominion Movement – from the outset fell on self-support, self-government, their own disciplinary measures, and missionary action in the local congregations. Congregations in the Mission field accepted the respon-

30. According to Venn the principles of self-support, self-government and self-extension had to be sown by the missionaries with the seeds of the Gospel from the outset, if a healthy expansion of the indigenous Church was to be expected. For a discussion of Venn's views in connection with Church expansion in the mission field, see Beyerhaus, 1959, pp. 33-39.

31. Du Plessis, 1929, p. 255.

32. *Acta Synodi*, 1932, 11, no. 3; in van der Merwe, 1934, p. 261.

33. Gerdener, 1951, p. 87.

sibility for the support and accommodation of their own indigenous Church workers and the construction of their own Church buildings, since they were founded. The congregations were under the control of their own indigenous Church councils from the outset, without representation of the Mother Church, except that the white missionary took the seat of the chairman as long as non-white clergyman were not available. The Church councils in co-operation with the congregations took charge of disciplinary measures.'[34] As long as the Mother Church aided the Daughter Church with finance, the European missionaries continued to play an important role in its government and administration.

Coming back to Sundkler's first premise, which involves Venn's three-selves principles, it is evident that this factor played a less important role as a reason for secession during the development of the DRC missionary activities in Rhodesia, than was perhaps the case with some of the Protestant denominations in South Africa. For the emphasis in the Shona Mission field was never exclusively on the *Self* in the sense that the Mission Church was expected to become independent in the isolationist meaning of the word. Admittedly, the missionaries in the field worked towards a gradual transfer of the responsibilities to the indigenous leaders of the local Church, but the emphasis was also on the co-operation between the Mother Church and the Daughter Church, and the maintenance of inter-Church ties through co-ordinating bodies. The few prominent African Church officials who actually did break away from the Shona (African) Reformed Church – Evangelists Moses Ruwana, Tinos Chirashanye and Teacher Zvobgo –[35] did so as a direct reaction to the way Church discipline was applied. They resented the DRC prohibition of polygamy. What seemed unfair to them was a policy which attacked an age-old institution, woven as it was into the fabric of their society, and not in the first place the missionaries' concern for a *self*-governing and *self*-supporting Mission Church. Indirectly this factor may have played a role, in that the missionaries' efforts to foster a sense of independence among the indigenous Church leadership unintentionally stimulated the desire to found Independent African Churches. In the field of education the DRC policy that African communities should contribute to the provision of school facilities did sometimes create misunderstanding and resentment; but the evidence is insufficient to prove that this insistence on community responsibility (i.e. on the *Self*) directly stimulated Separatism. In the final analysis it was not the Mother Church's

34. Van der Merwe, 1967, p. 51 (translated from the Afrikaans).

35. See the historical development of the *Chibarirwe* and the African Reformed Churches in Chapter 5.

early emphasis on independence but the retarded process of evolution towards self-determination[36] and the resultant prolongation of European tutelage which generated dissatisfaction in certain circles and which stimulated the African's urge to organize his own religious life free from the ever-present European supervision.

This brings us to the position of the European missionary in the developing Church and the question whether the authoritarian system, inherent to the Catholic Church hierarchy, might not of necessity have created a more fertile soil for separatism than was the case with the DRC; aspects which will be discussed under the following subheading and which will throw some light on Sundkler's second premise concerning Separatism.

In contrast with the Protestant missionary policy, the Catholic aim is directed, as du Plessis puts it, 'at the establishment of the Church of Rome in the Mission field, and attaches chief importance to the incorporation of individual converts into the visible Church.' Du Plessis further states that 'both the Protestant and the Catholic missionary dwell on the necessity of faith; but with the Protestant, faith in Christ is the preliminary demand, and trust in the Church and its sacraments is subsidiary, while for the Catholic *faith in the Church and its saving power is the essential thing* and faith in Christ's mediation does not, in practice, receive its due emphasis (my italics).'[37] This difference of approach undoubtedly has its effect in the Mission field. Individual Catholic missionaries may in the past have stressed the personal faith in Christ's mediation, but their general concept of the essential function of the visible Church, backed by the fundamental Roman doctrine, *extra ecclesiam nulla salus,* largely determined their impact in the Mission field. The 'continuous principles' which make for 'continuous Church life'[38] are by the very nature of Catholic religious life presented much more forcibly right from the start of their missionary work. The intention of DRC missionaries, on the other hand, could never have been to separate individual conversions from the creation of a Mission Church. Their formulated policy, however,[39] the emphasis on evangelization, and the fact that the organization of congregational life in the field

36. The Federal Mission Council stated that the process of the Mission Church becoming independent would take a long time and that its full independence still lay in the distant future. See *Die Kerkbode,* Oct. 1953, p. 611, and Niederberger, 1959, p. 341.

37. Du Plessis, 1929, p. 340.

38. *Supra*, p. 195.

39. Durand (1961, pp. 121-122) has pointed out that the formulation of Church policy, e.g. in connection with the manifest unity of the Church, is in places marked by a certain vagueness which can give rise to misinterpretation.

sometimes followed several years after the first conversions took place, gave rise to criticism. Niederberger accuses the DRC of theoretically separating the two distinct spheres of individual conversion and the founding of a Church (*Kirchengründung*), which, he believes, leads to a '*kirchliches Vakuum*' between the Mother Church and the Mission Church, and therefore facilitates the founding of separate Churches.[40] He states that in so far as the Catholic Church conceives of its missionary task as *implantatio ecclesiae*, it differs in essence from the DRC approach. 'Here [in the RCC] no conversion takes place without incorporation (*Eingliederung*) in the Church. The Mission to the heathen is the continuing stream of the total revealed reality (*Offenbarungswirklichkeit*), as it finds its God-willed expression in the Church. Thus the heathen grows directly into the Church as the Church grows into the heathen world. As the Church becomes rooted in a specific country it can and will take on 'local colour' [*ein lokales Kolorit*] but she necessarily remains essentially one and the same Church everywhere.'[41]

Niederberger's argument is obviously based on the typical Catholic concept of Church unity, which emphasizes the external institutional unity and recognizes the local Church only as an incomplete component, fully dependent on the hierarchically structured, universal Roman Church. His criticism of the DRC's emphasis on both the mystical Church unity in Christ and on separate, independent local Churches (adapted to the socio-political situation) is not altogether unfounded. He makes no mention, however, of the inherent problem in the RCC concept arising from the effort to maintain external Church unity through the subordination of indigenous Churches to the curial leadership and Western Church law on the one hand, while following, on the other hand, a policy of accommodation which emphasizes the '*lokales Kolorit*' to such an extent that Catholic religious practices in some of the Mission fields verge on a syncretism which militates against the professed, external Church unity.[42]

Whatever the theological implications of the RC institutional Church unity, it has very definite advantages in the Mission field. Co-ordination of the massive missionary enterprise through the centralized '*Congregatio de Propaganda Fidei*' (now The Sacred Congregation for the Evangelization of the Peoples) provides missionary work with a united front and an effectiveness which the diversified Protestant denominations cannot achieve. In the Shona Mission field in particular one cannot discount the prestige value of a Church

40. Niederberger, 1959, p. 345.
41. *Ibid.*, p. 345 (translated form the German text).
42. See Gensichen (1961, p. 50) for a description of the '*akkomodationsfreudige Haltung*' of the Roman Catholic Church, and Durand's (1961, pp. 123-129) discussion of the papal encyclical *Humani Generis* in connection with Church indigeneity.

that claims to be a world Church, whose top-leadership is presented as being supra-national, and which, in contrast with the DRC, is freer from the kind of political associations which may be interpreted by local Africans as militating against the nationalist ideals of the indigenous population. Another very important factor is the financial advantage of a united front. After several Popes had declared the task of Missions to be the responsibility of the whole Church[43] there was a steady increase in financial contributions and Mission personnel. With growing financial support from overseas the Catholic missionaries were able to set up their work in an ambitious and imposing way. Thus there was less need for the Catholics to tax the material resources of the indigenous population; and whenever indigenous congregations were made co-responsible for ecclesiastical schemes, the principle of 'self-support' was less rigidly applied than some of the Protestant denominations found themselves compelled to do. Educational and other schemes could generally be undertaken in a spirit of co-operation less hampered by misunderstanding and subsequent reactions in connection with Church finance. Within the wide-reaching Church structure, Rome also intends her indigenous Churches to become financially less dependent on the Missionary Societies, but the pace is not forced.

The Church to be 'implanted' in the Mission field, according to Catholic doctrine, must be an indigenous one; indigenous in the dual sense of adapting to the local socio-religious background – to this we will refer later[44] – and also of developing a strong body of indigenous leaders. Since Benedict XV's missionary encyclical, *Maximum Illud* of 1919, there has been an ever increasing emphasis on the creation of an indigenous priesthood in the foreign fields. Cardinal Prefect van Rossum, in a circular in 1923, directed to the leaders of Missions, stressed that the Mission fields at one stage or another have to pass from the jurisdiction of the pioneers in faith into the hands of the indigenous priesthood, and that the indigenous Church leadership should under no circumstances be treated merely as an assistant clergy (*Hilfsklerus*) in the field.[45]

The most penetrating treatment of the problem of the indigenous priesthood is found in Pope Pius XI's encyclical *Rerum Ecclesiae* of 1926. He complains about the slow progress in training indigenous priests, warns against treating indigenous priests as if they held inferior positions, and demands the same philosophical and theological training for priests everywhere. In numerous statements Pius XI emphasized the need for a thorough training for the in-

43. Pope Benedict XV in *Maximum Illud* – 1919; Pius XI in *Rerum Ecclesiae* – 1926; Pius 11 in *Fidei Donum* – 1957, and John XXIII in *Princeps Pastorum* – 1957.

44. *Infra*, pp. 244. See Catholic approach to Shona traditional religion.

45. Freitag in Beckmann, 1950, p. 203.

digenous priesthood. Several distinguished missiological scholars, such as T. Ohm, Schmidlin, Beckmann and others, pointed out that the 'real missionary aim' was to build up an indigenous Church with its own leaders.[46] Freitag indicates that there is a great divergence of opinion in Catholic circles concerning this issue. Those who warn against a premature and one-sided promotion of the indigenous priesthood and who point out such obstacles as the indigenous leaders' inability to lead, their political activities and anti-European sentiments, are regarded as representatives of a pessimistic approach.[47] But these obstacles should not be allowed to retard real progress. Says Freitag:

'Gerade in unserer Übergangszeit vom vorwiegenden Europäismus in den Missionsländern zur *einheimischen selbständigkeit der Kirchen* gehört ausserordentlich viel Selbstbeherrschung und Gerechtigkeitsgefühl auf beiden Seiten dazu, soll nicht das herrliche Pionierswerk der ausländischen Missionäre bei seiner Schlusskronung empfindlich getroffen werden (my italics).'[48]

Thus we find strains of Catholic theology that show affinity with the Protestant ideal of 'independent' Mission (or Daughter) Churches. In the building up of an indigenous hierarchy a certain local autonomy (*Selbständigkeit*) is envisaged, which must come as '*Schlusskronung*' on the pioneering work done by European missionaries. Evidently the limits of such 'independence' are determined by the top leadership of the institutionally united Church, but even then the Catholic viewpoint inherently contains emphases similar to those found in Venn's 'three-selves' formula.

The main difference lies ultimately in the diverging approaches to the principle of Church *authority*. It is my impression, however, that in spite of doctrinal differences, the RCC and the DRC approaches to the founding of an indigenous Church, as they are manifested *in the field* – especially with regards to the training of an indigenous Church leadership – have so much in common that the DRC and RCC losses of Church membership would have been the same if this had been a major causative factor of Separatism. But, since the DRC lost so many more members or potential members than the RCC, the reason for Separatism in Mashonaland should be sought elsewhere and not, as Sundkler asserts for the South African Churches, in the emphasis on the *Self*.

In Mashonaland both Churches have moved cautiously with the training of Church leaders, as the low number of ordained priests and clergymen indicates. The Catholics have as yet no African bishop in Rhodesia. Although the theological training differs, both Churches have maintained high standards

46. *Ibid.*, p. 207.
47. *Ibid.*, p. 209.
48. *Ibid.*, p. 207.

from the outset, and except for dissenting laymen, neither of these Churches has – to my knowledge – so far lost any of their Shona *ordained clergy* through secession. Progress towards the delegation of full ecclesiastic responsibility to indigenous leaders in the Mission Church context, has in fact been slowed down in both by the very presence of European missionaries. Experiences in the field have led missionaries in both camps to the conviction that the 'coming of age' of the indigenous Churches would inevitably be a slow and long process. In spite of missiological theories and policies concerning Church independence, the presence of a substantial European missionary force in the field was therefore maintained, if not increased. In as far as the inevitable paternalistic attitudes of missionaries caused reaction and resulted in the dissent of Church members, it was bound to affect both Churches.

b) *The Mission station*

In recent years many of the denominations in Rhodesia have increasingly turned their attention to the urban areas. Both the DRC and the RCC now have substantial congregations in the major cities and a number of smaller towns. But their main influence is still felt in the rural areas where they exert their control over numerous schools and outposts from the various Mission stations. These stations are situated on large Mission farms, some of which were granted to the missionaries during the first few years of European occupation, while others have been erected on purchased European farms or on small tracts of land in the tribal areas.

When Louw arrived in 1891, he befriended Chief Mugabe, who 'gave' him a small patch of land to settle on. During the following year he undertook a three-week journey by ox-waggon to see Dr. Jameson, who on behalf of the BSA Company granted him a large tract of land. The 6,000 morgen stretched from near the Zimbabwe ruins to Mugabe's mountain. Reference has already been made to the large tract of land on which Chishawasha, the Catholic Mission station to the north, is situated, to Gokomere (formerly Mzondo farm near Fort Victoria) and Mukaro, formerly the farm of Mr. Vermaak. Important from the African point of view is that these Mission farms, whether granted by European authorities or bought from other Europeans owners, caused the missionaries to be closely associated with the land-divisioning and land-alienating power in the country. The new concept of private property in land, foreign to the African conception, was being introduced by both administrators and missionaries. Resentment about the division of land therefore had a direct effect on Missions. The attack on Chishawasha during the

Rebellion (1896-7) illustrates to what extent the Africans identified missionaries with the rest of the European community. The land issue in itself was one of the major causes of unrest in these years, as was stated by the rebel leaders during the peace talks, and it seems evident that the Chishawasha attack resulted from the antagonism generated by the introduction of foreign authority over vast stretches of land.

Another example of how the ownership of land interfered with the work of missionaries is the discontent caused in the Victoria tribal area by the Morgenster Mission farm. At first there was little indication of the underlying grievance, but as the population increased and land shortage became an acute problem, it became evident that the neighbouring Africans resented the fact that the Mission possessed so much land. It had been Louw's policy not to expand the Mission's farming activity beyond the needs of the station's community. He was outspoken about the dangers of secondary activities, such as trading and farming, obstructing the essential missionary task. When Cecil Rhodes offered him two more farms of some 3,000 acres each, for private use, he refused the offer because, he said, he had come to Mashonaland with the sole purpose of winning souls for the Lord.[49] The partial result of this approach was that arable parts of the Mission farm were allowed to lie fallow, which intensified the resentment of some of the Africans.[50] A further complication was that the particular territory where the farm was situated had been the cause of dispute between the surrounding Duma chieftaincies. This placed the missionaries, because of their educational work in all of the chiefdoms involved, in an extremely difficult position. In 1964 a large portion of the farm together with patches of fallow land were returned to the people in an effort to resolve their grievances.

The ownership of Mission farms gave the missionaries far-reaching powers. They could eject individuals or villages on the grounds of bad conduct, persistent poor cultivation of the land, or the refusal to educate their children. Missionaries never forced people living on Mission lands to attend Church services, but the communities as such were naturally subjected to Westernized Christian ideals of orderly behaviour. To the Africans the missionary must at first have seemed like a new type of chief, with powers and privileges far beyond the purely religious realm. It was only too obvious that the power of missionaries depended on, and was part of, colonial rule.

Grievances about land tenure thus had repercussions on the Mission field, and in a major case like the Morgenster farm it is highly probable that this

49. Louw, 1965, p. 183.
50. Aquina, 1966, p. 5.

factor contributed considerably towards the defection of individual Church members living in the Victoria tribal area. On the other hand, land ownership could hardly have played a similar role as a background factor to fission in places like Gutu East, where both the Mutero (RCC) and Alheit (DRC) Mission stations comprised only a few acres each. What did play a role was the different ways in which individual missionaries exercised their powers. To mention but one example: at Alheit, more than 100 miles away from Morgenster, Rev. Orlandini for the first two decades of Mission work 'ruled' with a relatively free hand. Sporadic visits from the main Mission station could not alter the independent character of the work done at this isolated station. In his enthusiasm to expand Church and industrial activities on his station, the Italian minister often acted independently ahead of the program stipulated by the Mission Council. He relentlessly drove himself as well as the Africans who worked for him. Despite his dedication and good intentions, his behaviour sometimes caused friction between him and the local Africans. Although he may have been an exception to the rule Orlandini's autocratic behaviour and mental make-up helped to create a certain image of the Mission in Chingombe, which contributed more directly to the formation of independent congregations than was the case with other DRC Mission stations that were for many years more directly under the control of *sekuru* Louw.

For a comparison between RCC and DRC Missions, the eccentricities of individual missionaries are less important than the different approach to racial relations. Ideologically of course, the two Churches stand diametrically opposed to each other in this respect. Fairly recently the Catholic bishops of Rhodesia published a pastoral instruction ('Peace through Justice' – 1961) emphasizing the unity of the human race. On racial harmony it says: 'Though many fail to see it, or refuse through sheer selfishness to acknowledge it, the doctrine of racial superiority, as taught and practised by many in this country, differs little in essence from that of the Nazis, whom Pope Pius XI strongly rebuked in these words: As God's sun shines on all that bear human countenance, so does His law know no privileges or exception . . . Only superficial minds can make the mad attempt of trying to confine within the boundaries of a single people, within the bloodstream of a single race, God the Creator of the world.'[51] Further south, the Catholic authorities denounced *apartheid* as far as separate worship and unequal employment were involved. In 1959 Archbishop Denis Hurley of Durban publicly declared that *apartheid* was impossible and that the only solution of the racial problem was integration.[52]

51. *Peace through Justice,* Pastoral Instruction of the Catholic Bishops of Southern Rhodesia, 1961, pp. 10-11.

52. Latourette, 1963, p. 453.

In its declaration of policy the DRC also accepts the unity of the human race,[53] but relating it to the political policy of separate development, it simultaneously emphasizes the diversity of the human race, and the possibility of the one true Church being embodied in separate independent Churches. On racial relations the declaration of 1932 reads as follows:

1. In all its missionary activities the DRC envisages above all the conversion and spiritual elevation [*opbou*] of the Coloured and Native, in conjunction with their well-being in all other spheres of life.
2. The DRC furthermore is of the opinion that this well-being is not promoted by way of *racial integration* and *social equality* . . . but by way of the preservation and development of their national character, sanctified by the blessed influence of the Gospel, so that both Coloured and Native can increasingly in every sphere take their legitimate place in society.[54]

To these basically different aims in respect of racial integration, one can still add that the position of missionaries in the developing Mission Churches are different from a Church law point of view. Catholic missionaries and African converts belonged to the same local branch of the *one* Roman Church answerable, theoretically at least, to one authority. The DRC missionaries on the other hand enjoyed a kind of double membership in both the Daughter and Mother Church. This meant that in disciplinary cases involving missionaries, a preliminary investigation could be conducted by the leaders of the Daughter Church, but that the final measures were to be taken by the Mother Church, thus safeguarding the European missionaries from the control of indigenous leadership.[55] To this must be added the fact that the RCC and DRC missionaries came from essentially different backgrounds: the former from Europe, where the Churches have become increasingly aware of and sensitive to all forms of discrimination after two world wars; the latter from South Africa, a milieu marked by, and to a great extent accustomed to, racial separation. DRC missionaries, by common descent and destiny, have much more in common and are therefore more closely identified with the Afrikaans-speaking people in their neighbourhood, who are predominantly in favour of racial segregation. If, then, racial attitudes are a cause for African separation, the odds seem heavily stacked against the DR Mission Church.

53. *Statements on Race Relations,* p. 8. 'The Dutch Reformed Church accepts the unity of the human race, which is not annulled by its diversity. At the same time the Dutch Reformed Church accepts the natural diversity of the human race which is not annulled by its unity.'

54. Mission Policy – *Acta Synodi, 1932* (translation from the Afrikaans text).

55. Van der Merwe, 1967, p. 73.

In practice, however, the positions of both Churches are closer than official policies and ideological statements would reveal. For all practical purposes the DRC missionaries and the African members on their Mission stations belong to the same Church, the juridical difference in membership having remained a measure applicable only in exceptional circumstances. They worship, have their children baptized and participate in Holy Communion in the same Church building together with their African brethren. As far as social ties are concerned, day-to-day activities in the educational, medical and other fields are generally marked by a cordiality of relationship, with some reserve in their private social lives. In this respect there is a difference in social structure between the DRC and the RCC Mission communities. Catholic priests, both African and European, have their living quarters in the same building, whereas the DRC African and European ministers have separate living quarters and lead segregated family lives. This difference was not of crucial importance during the rise of Southern Shona Church independency, when the training of an African priesthood and clergy had hardly begun; at present it is of course becoming an increasingly important factor. The point is, however, that, apart from the clergy, present-day social patterns at both DRC and RCC Mission stations are very similar. A certain degree of '*social distance*' exists in both camps. When, for example, European priests or ministers want to contact African teachers, they have a special office for such occasions, or else they visit the teachers at their houses; whereas teachers, pupils and commoners do not normally enter the living-rooms or common rooms of priests and ministers. In the final analysis both the RCC and DRC missionaries in the eyes of the majority of Africans belong to the privileged class. The missionary is the 'land-owner', the one who rules the Mission station, the supervisor who always retreats into a higher commanding position as the African rises in status. He is the controller of funds and finance, the man with the 'nice house' and a higher or at least different standard of life; in short, the man of power (*simba*) who holds the reins.

c) *Auxiliary services*

As in the case of all the major denominations in Rhodesia, the DRC and RCC made use of a comprehensive missionary approach. It was realized that if the Gospel was to have any lasting effect, the whole of African life had to be influenced; the 'head and the hand had to be trained together with the heart.'[56]

56. Van der Merwe, 1953, p. 42.

In the wide scope of Mission activities, ranging from elementary education to vocational training in Agriculture, Handicraft, Domestic Science and other subjects, the basic educational and medical services are the most outstanding. The growth of the Mission Churches greatly depended on the provision of facilities in these two sectors, to which the following discussion will be confined.

i) *Education*

Under the heading 'Methods of Mission work' in the official DRC Mission policy, it is stated that the preaching of the Gospel is the primary and main means through which the Mission works towards the expansion and consolidation of God's Kingdom. It is added that the 'General Mission Committee is convinced that there are justified and proved auxiliary aids which can serve, through God's guidance, to achieve the envisaged aim. The Mission had found such proven aids through years of experience, in the educational, medical, industrial and such like services . . .'[57]

The Catholic policy differs from that of the DRC in being more explicit about the central position of education in the total missionary endeavour. 'It has been the policy of the [Catholic] Church to give first priority in the disposal of personnel and funds to the establishment of Catholic schools. In the whole build-up of these African Missions, missionary method simply meant *missionary school method*.'[58]

In the field the missionaries of both Churches found themselves confronted with a situation which demanded rudimentary school work as a prerequisite to successful evangelization. They simply had to give the African some form of education in order to impart the teaching of the Bible to him, or to enable him to read it in the vernacular. Statements of missionary leaders reveal to what extent they soon came to rely on their educational work as a means of reaching the people. Reflecting on the educational work of the Bethlehem Fathers since 1946, Boehi writes: 'The missionary methods in our early days were not much different from what they have been ever since. *We found our way to the people and the people found the way to the Church through the schools* . . . the people were generally very keen on schools and so we spent most of our time building out-schools, much of it with our own hands, and supervising them (my italics).'[59] As far back as 1910, Louw commented: 'Of

57. Missionary Policy, Van der Merwe, 1934, pp. 261-262 (translated from the Afrikaans text).

58. *Memorandum of the Missionary School Policy in the Diocese of Gwelo,* in *Guti,* May 1966, p. 100.

59. Boehi, 1963, p. 152.

singular importance are our schools, where religious instruction – and not mere education – is placed in the forefront, with nothing less than the *conversion of children as its aim* . . . Our hope for the future are the children. As is the case with Christian nations, it is indeed easier to positively influence the children than the adults who grew up in sin and bad ways.'[60] Louw's words reflect the awareness of the importance of schools at an early stage of development in the field, as well as the primary motivation for such schools, which was pastoral rather than academic.

For our purpose we can distinguish three separate phases in educational history among the Southern Shona, each with its particular bearing on the problem of Church Separatism. They are: 1. the initial pioneering stages by Missions, from 1900 to 1927 (when the Native Education Department was founded); 2; stagnation during the economic slump, increased governmental control and the marked rise of teaching standards between 1927 and 1947; and 3. the intensification of denominational rivalry in the educational field coinciding with the rapid expansion of the Catholic enterprise in the Southern districts after 1947.

1900-1927. During the initial stages of the Colony's development the missionaries encountered serious obstacles when they tried to introduce schools. Of his first unsuccessful attempts to get pupils for his schools at Morgenster, the Rev. Louw reports: 'When the children discovered that they did not receive "regular pay" for their work (!) of walking to the school each day, and learning texts or listening to Bible stories to please *us*, they simply stayed away.'[61] In addition to the foreignness of the whole idea of education in the eyes of the children, the missionaries met with stiff opposition from the traditional authorities. Amongst the Shona the expectations of being freed from the yoke of the settlers that had risen during the Rebellion still manifested themselves in the stubborn refusal of chiefs to have schools in their chiefdoms. Missionaries were often prevented from building schools until some incident happened to change a chief's mind. Thus one of the first DRC out-schools was granted by Chief Chitsa in the Gutu district, only after Rev. Orlandini had driven the 123 miles from Alheit to Morgenster by horse-cart to take the chief's son, who was then critically ill, to hospital.[62]

Even after the initial prejudices against education had broken down, the

60. Louw, 1965, p. 181.
61. *Ibid.*, p. 145.
62. Van der Merwe, 1953, p. 40.

missionaries were for many years beset by serious handicaps. I mention one example to illustrate how the philosophy of a subsistence-farming community actually hampered the attendance of pupils at out-schools. Father Winterhalder vividly describes his experiences as a school superintendent in the 'early years' as follows: 'Attendance at school was very poor. It was practice at every school that after religious instruction *and* register calling the teacher asked: "Who must go for herding?" and always a large number, up to one third, left the classroom. To stop this I had to do plenty of "Blitz" visits, often doing three or four schools in the same morning. At Guramatunhu I once found 30 of the 80 children absent although most were entered as present in the register.'[63] When the headman was called in, he countered Winterhalder's exhortations with the most revealing reply: 'Why did you not notify us that you were coming; I certainly would have sent for all the children. Father Hector used to call out his visits in church the previous Sunday. If you would have done the same you would see a full school. It's your mistake; only you are to be blamed for having so many children absent.'[64] This was just one of the many difficulties encountered by missionaries, due not only to the traditional outlook of ruralists, but also to the problems caused by a system of remote control of widely scattered out-schools.

The DRC practically dominated in the Southern Shona districts during this period, and continued to do so up to the late 1940's when the Bethlehem Fathers began expanding their work in this field on a large scale. Characteristic of the DRC approach at this stage was the concentration on the development of out-schools in the rural areas. Between 1910 and 1926 the most rapid expansion took place when the number of out-schools was increased from 10, with 2,300 enrolments, to 362 with 21,149 enrolments.[65] The schools were classified into three main divisions: boarding-schools on Mission stations (first class), day-schools under European care (second class) and vernacular or out-schools staffed with African teachers only (third class). According to the 1924 statistics the RCC had slightly more first and second class schools in the whole of Rhodesia than any other denomination, but the DRC was then already clearly in the lead with 285 out-schools, compared to the 177 of the Anglican and the 109 of the Catholic Church.[66] The majority of the out-schools provided only lower primary courses, Sub A to Std. 3, and acted as feeders for the Central Primary or Boarding schools on the Mission stations. In the course of

63. Winterhalder in *Guti,* Sept.-Oct. 1963, p. 160.
64. *Ibid.*, p. 160.
65. Van der Merwe, 1953, p. 40.
66. Smith, 1928, pp. 154-155.

time these Central Primary schools were developed to provide courses up to Std. 6. It is important to note that the main need during this period was to supply the African youth with rudimentary education. Relatively few of them passed beyond the Lower Primary level, with the result that the imbalance of a system which provided disproportionately few facilities at the Higher Primary, compared to the Lower Primary level, was not felt at this stage. With its numerous out-schools the DRC therefore had the advantage of making its influence felt in a very wide field. But once the demand for higher education increased as a result of the growing awareness among Africans of its necessity, this Mission was bound to be the most hard hit by the African's reaction to the lack of sufficient facilities. The full impact of this reaction was only felt after the 1930's, since the second decade of this century was still marked by the struggle against such barriers as prejudice against the education of girls.

A marked feature of this early period of education was the relative freedom of the Missions. The Education Ordinance of 1899 provided for some grants to Mission schools. These grants were gradually increased but the Missions themselves by and large provided the funds that were needed and consequently kept the initiative in the development of their institutions. In 1913 a Committee, representing the Government and Mission officials, drew up a guideline for co-operation, which subjected Mission schools to governmental inspection. The main decision-making power nevertheless still lay with the larger Mission bodies, who actually shouldered the responsibility of the entire educational system up to 1920, when the first two Government centres at Tjolotjo and Domboshawa were opened for the training of agricultural and industrial teachers. Rhodesian Government officials took a greater interest in African education after the first world war. They were partly activated by the reports brought out by the Phelps-Stokes Commission of 1919 and 1924, as well as the Ormsby-Gore Commission of 1924. And yet the Government before 1927 'still took no direct part in the main field of native education; mission schools were given increasing grants, but they received relatively little attention from officials in the Education Department, who were primarily concerned with the work of European and Coloured schools.'[67]

Other outstanding characteristics of the educational field concern the low qualifications of teachers, and the nature of the curriculum. Up to 1927 more than 75% of all the 'teachers' employed did not have higher qualifications than Std. 4. Since the schools had for some time been little more than 'evangelization centres' – the missionaries' interests not being directed primarily at developing an academic system – and since there were hardly any highly

67. Gray, 1960, p. 132.

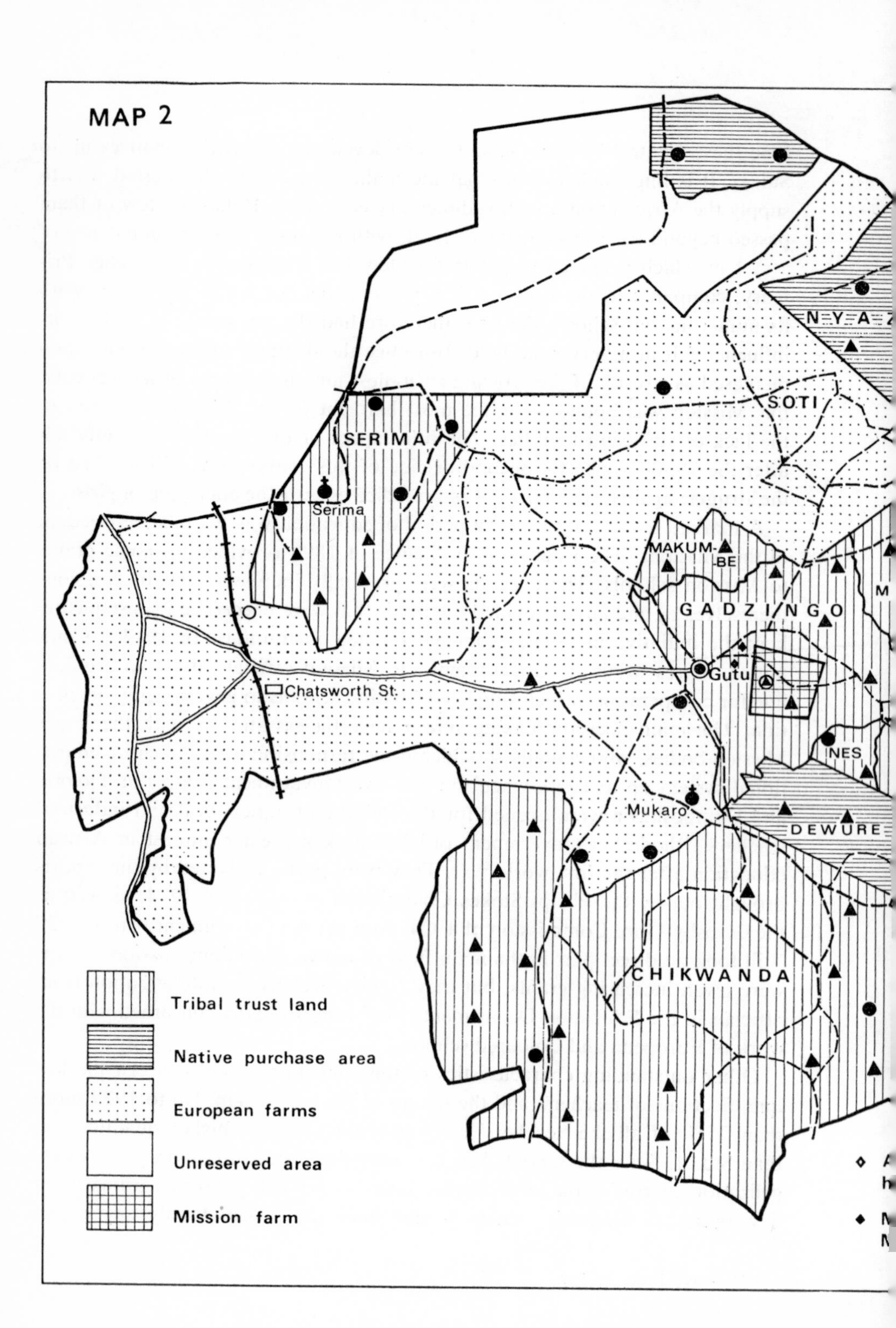
MAP 2
N Y A
SOTI
SERIMA
Serima
MAKUM-BE
GADZINGO
Gutu
Chatsworth St.
NES
Mukaro
DEWURE
CHIKWANDA
Tribal trust land
Native purchase area
European farms
Unreserved area
Mission farm

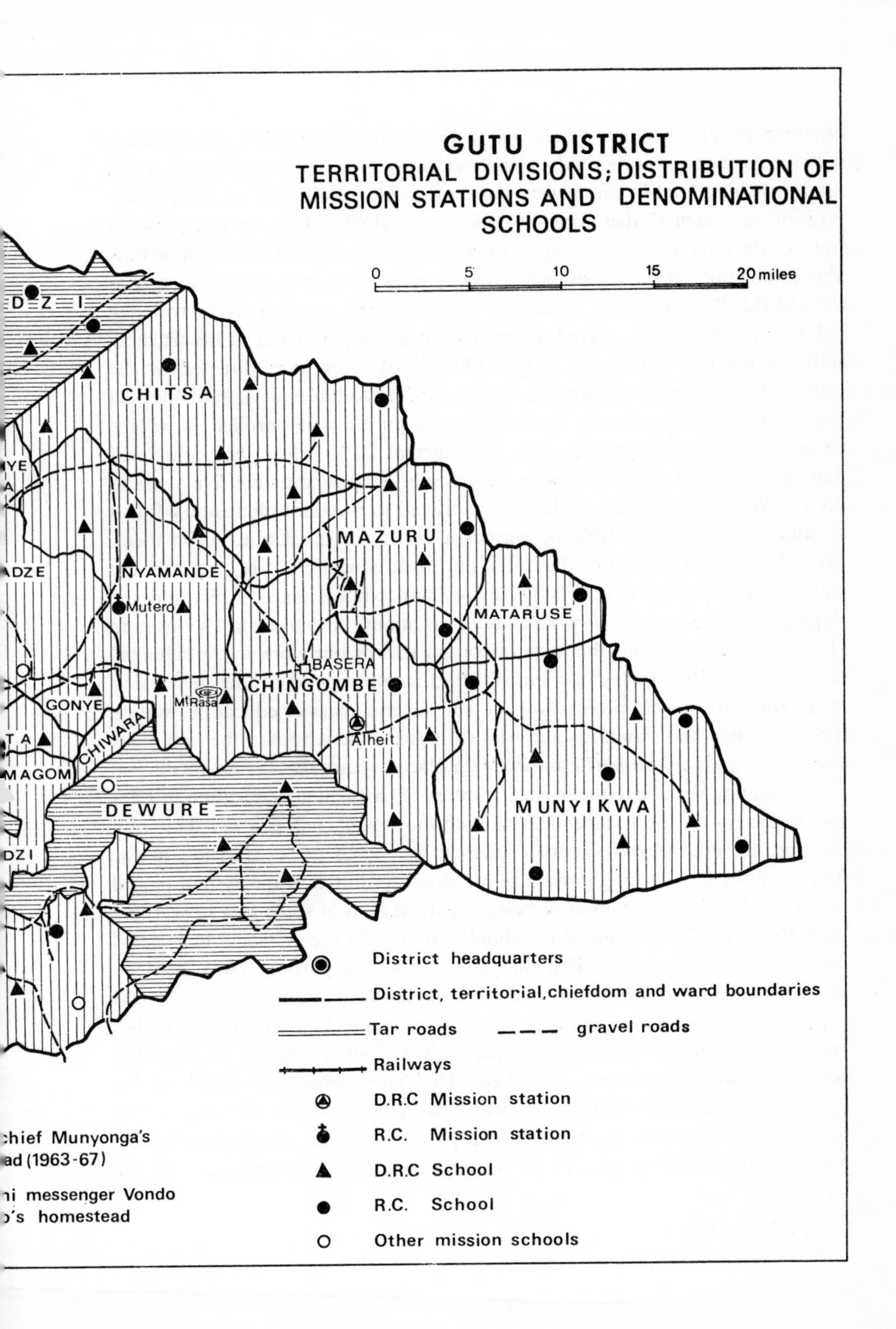
GUTU DISTRICT
TERRITORIAL DIVISIONS; DISTRIBUTION OF MISSION STATIONS AND DENOMINATIONAL SCHOOLS
0 5 10 15 20 miles
CHITSA
MAZURU
NYAMANDE
Mutero
MATARUSE
BASERA
CHINGOMBE
GONYE
Mt Rasa
CHIWARA
Alheit
MUNYIKWA
DEWURE
District headquarters
District, territorial, chiefdom and ward boundaries
Tar roads
gravel roads
Railways
D.R.C Mission station
R.C. Mission station
D.R.C School
R.C. School
Other mission schools

qualified people available, there was a premium on reliability of character, willingness to co-operate, and an inclination to give religious instruction, as far as teaching qualifications were concerned. The attainment of the prestige position of 'teacher' therefore depended to a great extent on the personal traits of the African, and the extent to which he succeeded in making a favourable impression on the missionary. Consequently subjective elements, such as the individual missionary's discretion and his personal relationship with the indigenous community, played a vital role in the appointment of his teaching staff. In the out-schools the major educational effort was directed at the rudiments of reading and writing. This is understandable in view of the fact that even in 1937 as many as 60% of the public who enrolled in village schools left before completing Sub. A, a further 20% before they completed Sub. B and that it took those who passed Sub. B approximately five years to do so.[68] With the majority of children restricted to the most elementary forms of education, there was little by way of a variety of subjects to teach them. From Louw's description of the initial efforts at education, it is clear that the children were mainly taught Bible history and biblical texts. 'This, and the singing of songs, some of which are translations of our own Psalms and Hymns [*Gesange*], forms the most important part of our work in the schools,' he wrote in 1910.[69] Today one can still find members of the older generation in the rural areas, who profess to have had several years of education, stating that they passed no standards and who still regard the school in the first place as *nzvimbo yokudzidza maTestamende* ('a place to learn the Testaments').

Considering the above-mentioned features of early Shona education in relation to the rise of the Independent Church movement, one can say that from the start the educational system contained the 'seeds of separatism'. In the first place the far-reaching powers of Missions permitted in the system placed the missionary in the position of being regarded, and in some cases regarding himself, as the final authority in school matters. To the Africans in isolated rural areas, the European missionary, for all practical purposes, was the decision-making power. *He* had introduced a foreign system and therefore it was expected of him, for some time at least, to maintain the initiative, to advise, guide and control. In the report of the Judges Commission the missionary's position in the past is aptly described: 'He "knew what was right" for his people. On matters of discipline he was both judge and jury. *Of necessity he was an autocrat*; for he was dealing with primitive people who had no knowledge of educational systems or of Western concepts of discipline . . . In the

68. *Ibid.*, p. 140.
69. Louw, *op. cit.*, p. 181.

past this attitude was perhaps the only one possible. African children came from a society in which the fiat was given by traditional authority. When the child entered school, the missionary took the place of the chief as law-maker and judge.'[70] There are indications that the Independent Church movement to some extent developed as a reaction, and as a direct challenge to this paternal control of the missionaries in the educational field.

Secondly, the subjective and arbitrary criteria that were applied to the appointment of 'teachers', at a stage when Government control had not yet established a standardized pattern, had an adverse effect on missionary work. With the increase of Government control and the rise in teaching qualifications some of the 'teachers' and 'teacher's assistants' found that their services were no longer indispensable. It was only natural that the resentment and reaction of those who depended on the missionary for an elevated status was partly directed against that same missionary – and by implication the missionary's Church – when they came to be dismissed. It is no coincidence that some of the most influential contemporary Independent Church leaders claim to have been 'teacher-assistants' in the past.

In the third place, the preoccupation of missionaries with schooling, and the evidently central position of religious instruction in the school program, caused a certain degree of confusion in the African community about the exact nature of the Church. *Kereke* (Church) and *chikoro* (school) to many Africans were either inseparably linked, or meant one and the same thing. Nowadays rural Africans still refer to their religious affiliation when they speak of *chikoro changu* (my school) and they add the qualification *chikoro chamabuku* (school of the books) when they speak of the educational institutions. The early example set by the missionaries inspired future 'Separatist' Church leaders to establish their own Missions with schools under their own supervision. In addition to the generating of a spirit of independence by the isolation and remoteness of some of the out-schools, the identification of Church and school also contributed towards a misunderstanding of the 'continuous principles'[71] essential to Church life. To some secessionists the foundation of a new Church must have seemed as simple as, if not synonymous with, the building of an out-school!

1927-1947. The two decades following the initial development of the Native Education Department in 1927 are marked by the successful attempt to im-

70. *Report of the Southern Rhodesia Education Commission* (A. V. Judges and Commission), 1962, p. 141.

71. See Sundkler, *Supra*, p. 195.

prove the overall standard of teaching qualifications. Within a few years the number of teachers with qualifications below Std. 4 was drastically reduced. In 1934 only about 30% of all the African teachers still belonged to this 'minimum-qualification' category.[72] In the same year the required standard for a three-year course in teacher's training was officially set at a minimum qualification of Std. 4. During the early 1940's the first 55 teachers with PTL qualifications (Std. 6 + 2 yrs. training) started teaching.[73] The pattern of co-operation between the African parents, the Mission bodies and the Government became firmly established in this period as well. Generally speaking the parents in rural areas were responsible for building primary schools and buying books and other equipment needed for the classrooms. The Missions covered part of the costs for the buildings and contributed the management and supervision, while the Government determined teaching establishments for schools, paid salary grants for all approved teachers, controlled the syllabi and provided the school inspectors.

Despite the higher level of teaching qualifications and the improved organization of the whole educational system, a set of negative factors were operative, especially during the 1930's which caused misunderstandings and even dissent between missionaries and members of the indigenous population. It should be kept in mind that we are now dealing with the period of a major upsurge of the Southern Shona Independent Church membership! The irony of the situation during the early 1930's was that just at a stage when the Africans were awakening to the challenge of education the Administration and Missions seemed to curtail financial aid. At a time when the opportunities of developing ecclesiastic and educational leadership, when the realization of the dignity of responsibility sent a wave of enthusiasm through the ranks of the Africans, the effects of the economic slump made itself felt in the country. The decrease of financial resources from overseas, together with the reluctance of the Rhodesian Legislative Assembly during the 1930's to supply funds for African education meant a serious handicap for the educational program. Between 1930 and 1936 a total of more than 130 schools were closed down in the rural areas. In the same period (1932 to 1937) revenue collected directly from Africans increased by £60,000, whereas Government grants to Missions increased by only £3,000.[74] This state of affairs had a direct negative influence on the work of the DRC. Government grants to this Church which had risen from £4,437 in 1925 to £7,387 in 1930, were raised to only

72. Gray, 1960, p. 142.
73. *The Economics of African Education* – Gvt. Publication, 1967.
74. Gray, *op.cit.*, p. 143.

£8,685 in 1935. Between 1930 and 1935 more than 30 DRC out-schools were closed down and the number of teachers was drastically reduced from 548 to 334.[75] The decrease of educational facilities together with the strain of the slump on the financial resources of the indigenous population provided fertile soil for discontent.

The financial problem was complicated by the great difference in living standards between missionaries and the average rural African. This made it difficult for Africans to understand why all the necessary funds were not forthcoming from the 'rich' Mission at a stage when the advancement of the system, which they (the missionaries) themselves had introduced, seemed imminent. Instead of receiving the longed-for aid the African found that 'he was continually being badgered by the "rich" who pose as his benefactors for endless subscriptions and fees.'[76] That the financial issue has remained a missionary problem up to present times appears clearly in the Judges Report which states that 'the African public whom they [the Churches] serve certainly has no notion of what has come into the school system by way of gifts from subscription sources, or investment income, or grants from overseas societies and mother churches. *Local communities often half believe that they themselves are misled and even cheated* (my italics).'[77] If ever there was a period during which the Africans did feel cheated, it must have been during the early 1930's when progress from the village school to a higher primary school became increasingly dependent on the ability of the parents to pay school fees, when the Churches for reasons not always understood by the Africans, started closing down schools, and when large numbers of teachers were dismissed. At the personal level numerous ex-teachers must have felt themselves thwarted in their ambitions. It stands to reason that the DRC which virtually 'monopolized' education in the Southern Shona regions at this stage, was bound to suffer most, directly and indirectly, from the conflicting and reactionary emotions generated in the educational field during this troubled period.

Another source of discontent which became increasingly evident during the 1940's was the apparent lack of facilities for secondary education. For a long time Std. 6 and a course in teacher's training was about the highest possible attainment to which an African could aspire. Only the privileged few were able to reach a higher standard of education by studying in South Africa. Towards 1947 only a handful of secondary schools had been opened. From the

75. See *Statistiese Opgawe 1924-1955*, of the DRC.

76. Grimston, *Survey of Native Educational Development*, 1937, in Gray, 1960, p. 146.

77. Judges Report, 1962, p. 156.

rural African point of view the main problem at this stage, however, was not so much the lack of secondary education, because to most of them Std. 6 in their own community still had the same prestige value as matriculation to the European. It was the bottle-neck at Std. 3, caused by the disparity between lower and upper primary facilities, which was beginning to make itself felt. Towards the end of this phase the general picture in Rhodesia was that the 2,000 primary schools had as many as 190,900 lower primary, compared to a mere 14,600 higher primary enrolments. The dissatisfaction caused by such drastic limitations after Std. 3 had a direct influence on Church membership and the nature of denominational rivalry, as will be shown in the following section.

After 1947. Generally speaking the two decades following 1947 were characterized by continuous expansion in the whole educational field. Between 1947 and 1966 the primary school enrolment increased from approximately 200,000 to well over 675,000; secondary schools increased from 4 to 88, with an intake of more than 13,000 pupils per annum. The average expenditure on African education had risen from 3.1% to 9.5% of the National Budget, which meant that well over £6,000,000 was spent on education for the period 1966-7. From 1947 onwards the Government accepted full responsibility for paying the salaries of all qualified teachers in Mission schools, which meant that the first steps towards uniform conditions of service were taken. Complete uniformity in salaries was only achieved in 1960 after the promulgation of the African Education Act. The standards required for qualification as teacher were continually raised, and the primary system at present is served by a large number of qualified PTL (std. 6 + 2 yrs. teacher's training) and PTH (Junior Certificate + 2 yrs. teacher's training) teachers.

The awakening of Africans to the benefits of education and their increasing demands for more and more schools presented the Mission with the challenge of expansion. Simultaneously the Mission bodies found themselves being subjected to the highly organized control of a re-organized Government inspectorate. The more the Missions started relying on material aid in the form of salaries, boarding and other grants provided by the Government, the more they were tied to a system of administration, which laid down rules concerning buildings, syllabi, management and inspection. In this complicated 'partnership' the Government tried to steer clear of denominational competition. It introduced the principle of limited geographical distribution of educational facilities, through which each rural school was supposed to have its own 'autonomous educational sector' with a 3-mile radius. The Missions had to accept limitations, for example, in the time allowed for religious instruction.

School management became a costly and specialized affair. Well-trained, full-time school managers (European and African) were gradually replacing the ministers of religion who in earlier years, in addition to their pastoral work, had to act as school superintendents for numerous out-schools. In so far as European missionaries still acted as school managers, they found themselves so preoccupied with administration that little time or energy was left for pastoral work.[78]

This period is particularly marked by the intensification of inter-denominational rivalry. In 1937, Brian Grimston reported on what he called the 'deliberate stifling of the DRC missions by RC missions,'[79] and in 1960 Rea (a Methodist minister) complained that 'in the religious scramble for Africa, she [the RCC] never hesitated to bid for the loyalties of villages already committed to other denominations by offering to build their schools free of charge.'[80] In the Southern Shona regions the rising conflict concerns primarily the DRC whose religious dominance (in Gutu, Victoria, Zimuto, Chibi, Ndanga and to some extent Bikita) was threatened by the rapid expansion of the RCC which started building schools on a large scale in these territories.[81] Compared to the DRC, the RCC had the distinct advantages of increased numbers of Swiss personnel after 1947, and of material resources which enabled them in certain instances to cater more rapidly than the DRC for the ever increasing African demand for schools. Material resources enabled the RCC to adopt an approach to the erection of schools differing from that of the DRC. Instead of making the local community directly responsible for the building of the school from the outset, as the other denominations were doing, the Catholics started by providing building material and builders, so that there was no undue delay in the procurement of the much needed facilities. The costs of building were then repaid to the Mission by the local community in the course of time by way of school fees. Rea's charge that the Catholics offered to build schools free of charge does not fully apply to the Southern Shona situation. What did happen is that the Catholic Mission, without shouldering all the costs, contributed more than most Missions could afford towards providing building material, and this fac-

78. The DRC has advanced more rapidly than the RCC with the appointment of African school managers. Few European missionaries in this Church still act as full-time school managers.

79. Grimston Report, 1937, p. 56.

80. Rea, in IRM, 1960, pp. 197-198.

81. According to the *Memorandum on the Mission's School Policy* (in *Guti,* May, 1966, p. 100), the influence of the Catholic Church in 1947 was still negligible in Gutu, Ndanga, Fort Victoria, Chibi and the southern districts of Nuanetsi, Shabani and Belingwe.

tor, added to the speed with which a new school could be erected, obviously made the RCC offer, compared to that of the DRC, more attractive in the eyes of the Africans.

Where they entered DRC-occupied areas the Catholics were in a position to capitalize on the misunderstanding and disaffection that had arisen between some of the rural inhabitants and the DRC missionaries, partly as a result of the closing down of schools during the 1930's. By providing higher primary facilities in areas where the DRC, due to its numerous lower primaries, could not possibly provide higher primary accommodation for all its lower primary pupils, the Catholics were able to meet a deeply felt need. DRC pupils in the lower primaries who were unsure of enrolment in DRC higher primaries started joining the Catholic Church in the effort to safeguard their educational careers. The DRC thus found itself confronted with a dilemma. Sticking to their standard of not catechizing children under 14 yrs. of age (due to the emphasis on conversion) they were hardly drawing any of the lower primary pupils, apart from the odd exception, into the fold of their Church.[82] Once the Government set the age limit of those pupils who could proceed to the upper primary at 14 years and the numbers of older pupils in the lower standards started dropping, the value of the lower primary as a 'catchment area' for Church membership was partly lost to the DRC.[83] Due also to the large number of applications from the DRC lower primary schools for the relatively few DRC upper primaries, the DRC had to stress performance in school, rather than Church membership, as a qualifying criterion for promotion of children to the higher standards. The Catholics, who allowed children to join the catechism classes at a younger age, were organizing catechist centres near DRC lower primary schools, thus attracting DRC pupils who did not stand a chance of qualifying for a DRC upper primary school, and simultaneously winning them for the Catholic faith. There is no doubt that the motivation of pupils joining the Catholic Church under such circumstances was influenced by their ambition to get the highest possible education.

For the pupil in the DRC school Church membership starts playing a decisive role at a later stage when he seeks enrolment for secondary education. Whatever the actual criteria applied by the Mission educational authorities, the general consensus amongst members of the African community is that

82. It sometimes happens that Std. 3 pupils who are older than the prescribed age limit, start attending catechism classes in the hope of being considered by the DRC school authorities for promotion to a higher class.

83. In earlier years, the presence in the lower primaries of numerous young people above 14 years of age, enabled the DRC Mission to win more people for the Church at a lower educational level than is the case at present.

'Church membership gets preference' if a choice has to be made between applicants with approximately the same school rating. Considering the far greater numbers of pupils in lower primary than in upper primary schools, as well as the difference between the Catholic and the Reformed Protestant approach to the qualifying age for catechism, it is evident that from a purely pragmatic point of view the Catholics were 'profiting' more than the DRC in terms of increased Church membership because of the African need for education. Small wonder that the DRC officials, who in the past worked on the principle of acknowledging the predetermined 'spheres of influence' of other Protestant bodies,[84] regarded the Catholic missionaries as intruders in those areas where they themselves had been labouring, free from competition, for many years. Realizing that there were certain advantages in having two or more competing educational agencies in their chiefdoms, several African headmen, whose first concern was to acquire more school facilities for their children at the most feasible cost, regardless of any doctrinal differences of a foreign faith, requested the authorities to allow Catholics to build schools at their villages.[85] And so, in spite of attempts by the DRC missionaries to keep the Catholics out of 'their areas', the RCC soon gained a foothold in most of the Southern Shona districts.

Rivalry in education mainly concerns the rural districts. After the recommendations of the Kerr Commission (1952) that the Government should assume responsibility for African education in the urban areas, and the Missions in the rural areas, the Protestants surrendered their urban schools to the Government. The Catholics, on the other hand, retained some of their urban schools, of which the Don Bosco Primary school with its 600 pupils (in 1966) in the Mucheke township (Fort Victoria) is an example. The 30% Catholic Church membership of this school in 1966[86] points to a somewhat limited value of the urban school as a 'campaigning institution' compared to some of the rural schools.

Turning now to Gutu East with the Alheit (DRC) and the Mutero (RCC)

84. Through the Missionary Conference the majority of Protestant bodies were able to determine the approximate boundaries of such spheres of influence. Unnecessary rivalry was thus excluded. A working agreement was achieved, for instance, between the American Board and the DRC leaders in some of the south-eastern districts where both Missions had vested interests.

85. Before a new school can be erected an agreement between the local headman and the Mission authority must be achieved. The request then goes from the Mission's school manager, District Commissioner and Provincial Commissioner to the Circuit Inspector.

86. *Statistics of the Gwelo Diocese,* in *Guti,* June, 1966.

Mission stations, each ministering to several out-schools[87] in that part of the district, we must consider the extent of Church rivalry. Teacher Mutero, who witnessed the growth of the Mutero Mission station from the start, provides us with an interesting narrative of the background of this station.

'My grandfather', he says, 'joined the RCC in Johannesburg while working there as a labour migrant. When he returned he found that Rev. Orlandini of the DRC had closed down 5 schools without replacing them. He therefore decided to request the chief to allow the RCC missionaries to enter this chiefdom [*nyika*] and build schools. I myself attended school at Gokomere (RCC) because we did not have sufficient facilities here in Nyamande. Dzoma, the DRC school which stood near the site where the Mutero station now stands, was closed down. The number of pupils at the time had dropped to below the required total. Having studied at Gokomere up to 1944, I returned, and we decided to request the Catholic fathers to open a school near our village. Father Winterhalder came out here during the holidays. My father, who was then acting as kraalhead, Fr. Winterhalder and I went to Chagwiza, who was then the acting chief Gutu. The chief was pleased with the request because the children in our area had to go long distances for their education. Both my father and the chief favoured the Catholics, although they were then for the first time entering this area. The missionary who was then at Alheit mission tried to persuade the chief to stop the Catholics from entering the *nyika*, but Chagwiza said to him: "I have had enough of the DRC missionaries because many of my children [i.e. "children" of the chiefdom] are not now attending school. They have not attended for a long time because you have closed down the school". The chief also said that he was not satisfied with the way in which the schools were managed. He and his people were under the impression that the DRC missionaries did not care much about this particular problem. *They were not sure whether the renewed interest of the* DRC *derived from real concern for them, or merely from their efforts to keep the Catholics out of the district.*

After the chief's approval negotiations started with the District Commissioner and in 1946 the first RCC school was opened here at Mutero. The RCC missionaries, financed from Gokomere, brought in building material and builders. Bricks were made by the members of the local community, but the fathers supplied building materials such as the iron sheets for roofing, and they covered the cost of building. We could repay the Church with school fees. We found that in this way the RCC schools would grow much faster than the DRC ones. Look at Jarawaza and the other DRC schools around us! They

87. See map 2.

do not achieve much and are not progressive enough. If you make the community fully responsible for the building of the schools, it has a retarding effect on educational development. At times school fees can hardly be found . . .

There was much in-fighting and arguing at first. The staunch DRC members refused to send their children to a RCC school and few pupils enrolled. Later, the old people without Church affiliation sent their children, and then the DRC members followed suit. The DRC people thought that there was only *one* true Church. They had no idea about Catholicism. Gradually they realized that Catholics also worship God, that the Catholic religion was just as good and that this Church could help them as a "trustworthy Church". All is now all right; there is no real difference between a Catholic and a DRC member. The denominational antagonism has vanished. We mix freely with the DRC teachers and help each other (my italics).'[88]

Teacher Mutero's account clearly reveals the dissatisfaction that had arisen in this area due to the closing down of the DRC schools. It is obvious that much of the resentment arising in an unfortunate situation – to some extent beyond the control of the Mission itself – was directed against the DRC, and in a situation where this Church was being branded by a section of the community as a scapegoat, responsible for the lack of educational facilities, the RCC, with its ambitious school program, could step in as the benefactor of a 'neglected' community. The difference between the facilities offered by the two Churches was soon noticed by the rural inhabitants; although they were proud of the old schools they had built themselves, the dilapidated class-rooms at Jarawaza (to which Mutero refers), for example, contrasted sharply with the modern buildings at Mutero, Additional factors, such as the RCC school fees in certain instances being just below those of the neighbouring DRC schools, the provision of maize in villages stricken by drought and a more lenient attitude to the teacher's consumption of native beer, all added to the attraction of this new Church.

Mutero's views of the present-day lack of denominational antagonism are indicative of what one can call 'denominational relativism'. The initial antagonism of a predominantly DRC-influenced community soon broke down once the advantages of the new Church became noticeable. To the majority of African commoners the trustworthiness of the new Church was determined by its ability to offer educational aid. The doctrinal differences between the DRC and the RCC were and still are of only relative significance to most Africans, for, although they are fully aware of the differences in ritual, the cleavage between Catholicism and Protestantism does not have the same historical

88. Personal Communication at Mutero Mission, 1967.

meaning for them as it has for the European members of these Churches. This does not mean that the two Churches are co-existing peacefully in the same district, for, especially at the levels of school administration, where the representative officials are more keenly aware of the conflicting strategies of two competing groups, bitter comments can be heard. Mr. Gopoza, an African school manager of the DRC at Alheit, commented on the Catholic activities in the eastern sector as follows:

'In our area the Catholics do not co-operate in school building projects as do members of the Independent Churches. They deliberately work towards the breakdown of the whole system in order to get their own people, the Catholic fathers, to come in and start their schools. Since the Catholics have more vacancies for pupils coming up from the lower standards they get the DRC pupils on condition that they turn Catholic . . . The fathers mix freely in African society and go further in associating with people at the village level than I myself would go. They go into the reserves and befriend people by drinking beer with them. That is something we as DRC's cannot do, and to some extent it is a pity, because at a beer party there are only two possibilities: making friends or making enemies, and *when you are in, you're in*!'

It seems significant that a prominent African should point to the Catholic participation in beer drinking as a way of winning the confidence of the rural inhabitants. He is fully aware of the effectiveness of this approach especially against the background of discontent that had been caused by the rigid disapproval of beer drinking by the DRC missionaries. In his final comment there is a sign of frustration because this DRC attitude prevented him as educator from competing with the 'intruder' on even terms.

A comparison of the statistical evidence of the DRC and RCC of the past few years bears out the difference in correlation between control of the educational system and the influx of Church membership (table 28). Since 1960 Alheit has had 24 schools with a total of nearly 5,000 pupils each year. Unfortunately the figures on Mutero are incomplete. But judging from the number of teachers employed by them in 1960, they had considerably less schools than the DRC at the time. By 1966, however, they had 16 schools with 4,252 pupils. Despite its numerical advantage in pupils and teaching staff the DRC was recruiting far fewer of the pupils enrolled in its schools, than was the RCC. If anything, this Protestant Church was losing ground rather than attracting a stable or increasing number of Church members each year through its schools. The number of DRC catechumens in this circuit actually dropped from 806 in 1960 to 239 in 1966; the number of confirmations which was well above 100 per year from 1960 to 1964, had dropped to 51 in 1966. During the same period – 1960 to 1966 – the Catholics maintained a fairly stable average of approximately 1,400 catechumens per year and a high annual rate of confirmations vacillating between 500 and well over 1,000. Moreover, the total Church membership of Alheit had dropped from 3,120 in 1960 to 1,713 in 1966, whereas Mutero's membership showed a sharp rise from 3,824 to 7,995.

A factor which influenced the DRC's work at Alheit and which contributed towards a loss of adherence was the political disturbance between 1962 and 1965. The refusal of the African Church leaders at Alheit to co-operate with the local political leaders of the extremist nationalist party, ZANU (Zimbabwe African Nationalist Union), who had their headquarters at the Basera township near Alheit, undoubtedly caused antipathy against the Mission among some of the rural inhabitants. Yet, one of the main reasons for the discrepancy in the statistical figures between the two Mission Churches lies in the application of different criteria for entry into catechism, such as the above-mentioned age rates, which enables the Catholics to utilize the schools under their jurisdiction as 'recruitment centres' for Church membership more effectively than the DRC. In addition, the Catholics make use of a more efficiently organized and partly salaried lay Church leadership. This is clearly reflected in a survey of the educational and ecclesiastic situation in the Chingombe chiefdom:

In 1966 there were 1,614 pupils (1,121 in lower primary and 493 in higher primary schools) in the chiefdom's 7 DRC schools and 165 pupils in the single Catholic school at Makamure. Of the 51 confirmations at Alheit in that year, only 11 were Chingombe inhabitants attending the upper primary classes, which means that of a vast school-age community only a few upper primary students were in fact introduced as communicant members into the ranks of the Church. Except for a few pupils, none of the thousand and more lower primary pupils in the DRC schools were attending DRC catechism classes – the majority of them being too young according to DRC standards – whereas 19 of the 39 Std. 2 pupils in the solitary Catholic school[89] had already entered catechism classes. In the same year Mutero had employed 40[90] lay catechists, one for each of their own, *and one for each of the* DRC *schools* in the eastern sector of Gutu. There was no secret about the Catholic catechetical centres near each DRC school being there to cater for the 'educational' needs of those pupils who were unlikely to qualify for the DRC upper primary schools as well as for the instruction of children of Catholic parents. Of the 1,114 Mutero

89. In 1966 the RCC school at Makamure, which was opened in 1962, only had facilities up to Std. 2.

90. See Church Statistics in *Guti,* June, 1966. Some of these catechists receive a part-time or full-time salary.

confirmations in 1966 a great number must have come from Chingombe. This 'educational stronghold' of the DRC therefore proved fertile soil for the missionizing activities of the Catholic Church.

If one considers that the bottle-neck at Std. 3 in Chingombe and the surrounding areas affects the DRC more directly than the RCC, that the Catholics in 1966 had far fewer lower primary pupils, some of their schools, such as Makamure, not having reached Std. 3 level yet; and that the higher primary intake at Mutero alone was at least double that of Alheit, it is understandable that the whole educational set-up of comparatively more Catholic upper primary vacancies enables the Catholics to attract numerous DRC pupils. One of the traditionalist spokesmen in Chingombe aptly summarized the situation: 'We suspect the DRC people of favouring their own children when there are so many applications for so few vacancies, so we make our children join the RCC, in order that they might have a better chance of reaching the higher classes.' Representative of the image of the Catholic Church in the educational field was the comment of a traditionalist near Mutero: 'Why should we build our own schools and take all the responsibility ourselves? The DRC, who favours this policy, cannot provide us with all the necessary facilities up to Junior Certificate, but the *vaRoma* [Roman Catholics] can do so for most of their pupils.'

The overall figures of these two Mission Churches in the Southern Shona regions seem to support the argument that the RCC draws more of its pupils into its religious fold each year than does the DRC. In 1966 the DRC, with 429 schools, 72,951 pupils and a staff of 2,232 teachers, had only 4,805 catechumens compared to the 18,310 catechumens of the RCC in the Gwelo diocese, drawn primarily from its 265 schools, with 50,778 pupils and 1,322 teachers.

Although the extent to which the two Mission Churches 'utilize' the educational system for purposes of Church expansion differs, it has become an established fact that both institutions attract substantial numbers of their adherents while they are at school, and that the history of Missions in this field is to a large extent the 'history of Education'. This close association between Church and school, and the general impression of Africans – undoubtedly fostered by denominational rivalry – that *Church membership implies educational benefits* led to superficial forms of christianization. The drift of post-educational Church members away from both Mission Churches reflects the ulterior and pragmatic aim that motivated many pupils to join one of the Churches. In 1964 some warning notes were sounded in Catholic publications. Frey wrote: 'Notably high is the fall-away among the young people who were baptized while attending our schools. On some Missions school-aged children are probably baptized who are not sufficiently instructed in the Faith. Much worse is the fact that many of them had little or no introduction into the Christian way of life.'[91] Shortly afterwards Winterhalder responded in the same vein: 'I am suffering from the same nightmare as Father Frey: In a great number of our Christians, Faith only penetrated skin deep. *The leakage after school is great* especially amongst girls, falling away to Sabbatists and indigenous sects (my italics).'[92]

In Chingombe part of the 'leakage' actually starts before pupils attending Church schools have become affiliated to the Church. Commenting on this trend, Rev. Shiri, DRC minister at Alheit, stated that the drop in Church membership is due to the loss of interest among schoolteachers, who no longer honour the Church [*kudza kereke*] and therefore do not inspire the pupils to join the Church, as they used to do. Shiri's comment, although not covering the whole complex of factors involved, has a large element of truth in it. It also shows clearly how dependent the Church has become on its schools as 'evangelistic agents' and sources of Church membership. It is a pointer to the waning prestige of the Churches which the Judges Commission report mentions: 'We have become increasingly aware', it is stated, 'that the "missions" are not now held in as high esteem by local communities though their services as "providers" appear to be more massive than ever before.'[93]

The teachers' lack of interest in the Church's religious affairs is only part of a much wider reaction in the African community to the adverse effects of denominational competition in the educational field. In Chingombe this reaction affects the DRC membership more than that of the RCC, partly because the Catholics still represent the interesting 'new group' that came in to 'correct the mistakes and offer more' than the familiar and locally older institution. There are, however, members of the African community who are becoming increasingly critical of Catholic activities in their chiefdom.

Although denominational rivalry did not play an important role as a background factor during the rise of the Independent Church movement in a place like Chingombe, where there was only one major Mission Church at work during the initial growth of this movement, it became increasingly important after 1947, as an additional force which started to condition the fluidity[94] of Church membership between the numerous religious groupings. Does the authoritarian control of education by the two 'European-directed' Churches stimulate dissent? What happens to the children of 'Separatists' in Mission

91. Frey, 1964, p. 98.

92. Winterhalder, 1964, p. 121.

93. Judges Report on Education, *op. cit.*, p. 154.

94. By fluidity is meant the constant process of religious change, people defecting from one Church and joining another. This aspect will be dealt with in Volume 2.

schools? Do they join or feel compelled to join the catechist classes? In what way is the religious life of school-going children of 'Separatist' or Mission Church parents influenced when they leave school after completing Std. 3 or Std. 6? An effort to answer these questions will be made in a following volume by presenting the information obtained from school leavers in Chingombe.

ii) *Medical service*

As closely associated as the educational institutions had become with the whole missionary enterprise, so closely did hospitals become linked to main Mission, and clinics to minor Mission stations. The medicine chest, stethoscope and scalpel accompanied the Gospel and were often of the most important aids in winning the confidence of people who were relucant to permit the missionary's entry. Numerous were the occasions when the suspicions or antagonism of traditional authorities were overcome after medical treatment. Successful medical treatment often preceded and paved the way for schools, as we mentioned earlier in the case of Chief Chitsa. Even in recent years the medical service provided by Missions has proved to be of great importance in conditioning the attitudes of Africans towards the work of missionaries as a whole. When emotions ran high during the land dispute over the Morgenster Mission farm during the early 1960's and there were threats of burning down buildings on the Mission station, the person to pour oil on troubled waters was a chief who had previously become converted in the Morgenster Mission hospital.

The pattern followed by both Mission Churches under survey was to establish one or two fully equipped medical centres on main Mission stations, staffed with several qualified doctors and African personnel, with smaller hospitals and clinics at outposts in the rural districts. Qualified male medical assistants or sisters were placed in charge of the clinics. Whereas these outposts acted as feeders of patients with serious ailments to the main centres, regular visits of doctors kept the clinic staff and patients in touch with the medical and evangelistic activities of the Mission stations. Healing of the sick was accompanied as far as possible by the proclamation of the Gospel, which meant that regular morning prayers and special services were conducted at the hospitals. At the DRC Mission hospitals at Morgenster and Gutu special evangelists were appointed to tend to the religious needs of patients. At present Sunday services are relayed into the wards and doctors testify to the faith when they treat patients; they pray regularly before operations and pay special visits to some of the bed patients.

At Morgenster Dr. John Helm laid the foundations for medical work during

20 years of loyal service (1894-1914). As a linguist he contributed to the translation of the Bible. Concerned with both the spiritual and physical needs of the Vakaranga, he not only gave them medical treatment, but regularly held services in the Church and instructed his own catechism class. Dr. M. H. Steyn arrived in 1924. Under his supervision the John Helm Memorial hospital (1930) and the Cinie Louw Memorial hospital (1934) were erected at Morgenster and patients started flocking from all over the country and even beyond its borders to this popular centre.[95] Steyn, one of the most outstanding characters in the Southern Shona Mission field, spent many years of dedicated work at Morgenster. In recognition of his services he was awarded the MBE by the Governor of Rhodesia in 1951. More important, the Africans in the rural areas honoured him with the title '*nganga huru yenyika*' (the great 'diviner' of the country). At Gutu Mission another medical centre was erected which at present accommodates nearly as many patients as the one at Morgenster. Four regular doctors, assisted by 15 orderlies (male medical assistants) and over a hundred trained and trainee nurses attended to more than 19,000 registered patients in 1966 and performed 1,826 operations. In the same year each of the four clinics had approximately 3,000 patients and gave more than 25,000 treatments.

The medical service of the Catholic Church in the Gwelo Diocese was developed mainly at the Driefontein Mission station, where two regular doctors attended to more than 2,400 patients in 1966. There are at present 11 medical centres at the various Mission stations, with accommodation varying from 400 beds (Driefontein) to 19 beds (Gokomere). In 1966 as many as 17,080 patients were treated.[96] In contrast with the DRC which trains male medical assistants, this Mission is especially noted for the employment of great numbers of European and African sisters.

The close association of the Mission's medical and religious work was not entirely foreign to the Shona people. Like the traditional diviner the Mission doctor was a specialist who attracted people to his home base for regular treatment. Both were specialists whose therapy had medicinal and spiritual implications. Because of this therapeutical combination the Mission Church acquired for some the image of a healing institution – a factor which indirectly stimulated the healing activities of the Spirit-type Independent Church leaders. For, although the prophetic Church leaders did not agree with the

95. Patients arrived from Portuguese East Africa, Northern Rhodesia, Nyasaland, Bechuanaland and the Transvaal.

96. I presume that these are only bed patients. Together with the out-patients the total attendance will probably be much higher.

use of medicine (*mushonga*), they, too, gave the ministry of healing such a prominent place in their religious activities that it became a means of attracting large numbers of people to their Church centres. Especially the Mutendi Zionists and Maranke Apostles came to regard proper Church headquarters (or a 'Mission station' in their conception) as incomplete without a healing centre. The terms '*hospitara*' and 'maternity' are applied to some of these healing centres with a sense of pride as if to convey the impression that such centres are as important and attract as many people as the medical institutions at Mission stations. The lesser prophetic officials became 'healers' (*varapi*) to small groups of patients, while the more popular healers had clusters of huts built at their homesteads, at which '*hospitara*' their own assistant prophet-doctors could tend to the sick.[97]

The *nganga*, with his intimate knowledge of the spirit world, has been discussed in the previous chapter. As will be indicated, the prophetic healers also have a distinct advantage in the psycho-therapeutic fields, based on their preoccupation with the spiritual causes of disease, minor ailments and psychic disorders. Thus both traditional and prophetic healers cover a gap which the European medical worker was either unaware of, or, by the very nature of his Western disposition and working program, could not cope with. One can only admire the efficiency and high standard of medical treatment in Mission hospitals, but the great number of patients makes it impossible for the medical staff to occupy themselves with the detailed background, history and beliefs of each patient.

Despite the sincerity with which many African patients accepted the Christian faith, the New Message which they heard was often insufficiently related to the (for the African) immensely real powers of the ancestors and of wizardry. Aware of the missionary's disapproval of ancestor 'worship' and *nganga* practices, patients often removed amulets or other signs of having visited a *nganga* when they went to Mission hospitals. To the Mission doctor working against time, much of the inner fears of patients therefore remained concealed, and it is hardly likely that patients would – without careful and patient probing – reveal to him many of their own ideas about the mystical forces which they held responsible for their ailments. Thus the Mission doctor's testimony about the salvation of man through the work of Jesus Christ did not always sufficiently emphasize the real liberation from the spiritual forces believed by the patient to be operative in his or her life. In short, the Mission doctor's method all too frequently implied a negation of the *midzimu*, *shavi* and *ngozi*

97. Examples of these healing centres will be given in a chapter on faith-healing, in Volume 2.

spirits or of the *uroyi* beliefs. Or else he told the African that these had become powerless through Christ, without really exorcising the spirits through the type of vividly enacted, symbolic action on which much of the African's religious life depends. The Independent Church leaders, to whom the afflicting spiritual forces also represent a grave reality, responded to the need for a visual, exorcistic manifestation of the victory, in Christ, over such binding powers.

d) *State and Church*

Officially the DRC policy stipulates that representatives of the Church should co-operate with Government and Government officials, if, by so doing, they *promote the cause of Christ.*[98] The State as a God-given authority should be honoured and should receive its due from the missionary in so far as its demands are not in conflict with the calling of the Church. It can be said that the DRC approach was generally in line with the statement of the World Missionary Council at Tambaram. 'Our basic conviction', it read, 'is that the attitude of the Church . . . towards the State should be positive and constructive, and not merely negative and critical . . . sincere loyalty and willing obedience should be the Church's normal attitude.'[99] Co-operation with State authorities, however, could never imply compromise on principles, lest the Church should lose its prophetic task. The decision of the Synod of Middelburg in 1896 concerning the Church's use of Government grants illustrates the awareness of Reformed Church leaders that the Church should maintain its own identity and independence in relation to the State. It was stated that the Church could request and use governmental grants for education and medical service, but not for the actual 'sending out' of missionaries.[100] Church leaders from time to time stressed that the Church should not become closely associated with party politics,[101] and at the Reformed Ecumenical Synod of 1963 the belief was expressed that the Church has a definitely critical function concerning the practical application of Biblical principles. The Synod declared that 'where there is a violation by the civil Government of the teaching of God's Word, it is the duty of Christians, unitedly and individually, to address the necessary admonition to those in governmental authority. It is the respon-

98. Van der Merwe, 1934, p. 263.
99. Van der Merwe, 1967, p. 179.
100. *Ibid.*, p. 179.
101. *Ibid.*, p. 173; see also du Plessis, 1929, p. 269.

sibility of the Church to instruct its members in the application of God's Word to every sphere of life and, where necessary, to address the Government concerning such problems as may arise.'[102] The 'partnership' between State and Church, as viewed by Church leaders of the Reformed tradition, was therefore qualified some very definite conditions.

Similar qualifications are to be found in the Catholic tradition. Both State and Church are regarded as 'perfect societies', drawing their authority from God. Mutual respect and co-operation are required, but 'the Church does not prefer one country to another, does not love one people more than another; is not concerned with upholding one form of Government rather than another.'[103] The missionary should occupy himself with his primary task, which is the salvation of souls, and he should avoid too close an identification with any political party, since 'the legitimacy of power is not bound up by Providence with any one form of government, or with any political party.'[104] Characteristic of the instructions to missionaries are the words of Pope Benedict XV in *Maximum Illud* (1919): 'Forget your people and your father's house, remember that you are not to propagate the kingdom of men, but that of Christ; that you are not to enrol citizens into any country of this world, but that of the next. It would be regrettable indeed were any of the missionaries so forgetful of their dignity as to think more of their earthly than of their heavenly country and were too much bent upon extending its earthly glory and power.'[105] Missionaries are reminded that they are ambassadors of Christ and not of their own countries.

During the initial stages of development in the colony the representatives of both Churches were on friendly terms with the officials of the Chartered Company. The Rev. Louw had to be diplomatic in his dealings with Jameson and Rhodes because he was representing the 'National Church' of a people who was fighting the British. Jameson nevertheless permitted his entry into the country after their first meeting on the banks of the Limpopo, and shortly afterwards he granted him the large Mission farm at Morgenster. The relationship between Louw and Rhodes was one of cordiality and mutual respect. The latter was impressed by the work done at Morgenster. As a sign of appreciation he donated money to the Mission and sent Louw some blue-gum seeds for plantations on the Mission farm. When Louw's parents approached Rhodes at Cape Town for permission to send some supplies to their son, he

102. *Acts of the Reformed Ecumenical Synod,* 1963, p. 39.

103. *Peace through Justice,* Bishop's Pastoral Instruction, 1961, p. 28.

104. *A Plea for Peace* – Pastoral Instruction of the Catholic Bishops of Rhodesia, 1965, p. 3.

105. *Maximum Illud,* in *Peace through Justice,* 1961, p. 29.

promptly sent a telegram to Fort Victoria with an order to have local supplies forwarded to the Mission station, because, as he said to the old minister: 'Your son amongst the natives is worth as much to me as a hundred of my policemen.'[106] This, then, was the kind of appreciation that statesmen had for the work done by missionaries of the larger denominations. Mention has been made of Lord Grey's enthusiasm to experiment in the educational field after he had paid a visit to the Catholic Mission station at Chishawasha.

The friendly relations between missionaries and European rulers did not, of course, escape the notice of Africans. To some of them the Churches with their large Mission farms represented 'Government agents'. But the association of Church and State was also a relatively loose one during the first two decades of Company rule. The missionaries were then still 'educators in their own rights', free from governmental pressures and less directly linked with administrative officials in the eyes of Africans in remote rural districts. During the inter-war period, however, the development of the educational system contributed towards a much closer link between State and Church. Mission schools were subjected to inspection, they had to be adapted to the circumstances according to prescribed rule and the Church's increasing dependence on the financial grants of the Government jeopardized some of its essential functions. In both the Dutch Reformed and the Roman Catholic circles there was an awareness of the danger involved in this type of 'partnership' with the Government, but it was only remarkable individualist missionaries, like the Anglican Arthur Shearly Cripps, who was radical enough to accept the consequences of an uncompromising refusal of governmental grants for his schools. He was greatly alarmed at the danger of the Church losing its independent character, and by implication also its testimony concerning the rights of the African people.[107]

Cripps and White, two outstanding missionary leaders respectively representing the extreme left wings within the Anglican and the British Methodist Churches, were alert to the misunderstandings that could arise among Africans if Missions became identified too closely with the Government or with the European settlers. White was of the opinion that 'some missionaries brought a stain on the name of Christ by their weak acquiescence and dependence upon Europeans who had all the power in their hands . . . thus they seemed to the Africans themselves to be taking sides against them. The actions of missionaries ought to be free from suspicions of this kind. Their motives, from

106. Louw, 1965, p. 138.

107. Ranger, *State and Church in Southern Rhodesia (1919 to 1939)*, Unpublished Article, pp. 8-11.

the African side, ought to be entirely above reproach.'[108] Through White's influence and under his leadership the Rhodesia Missionary Conference outlined its program of specifically representing the interest of Africans, who were still politically inarticulate, and of co-operating with them when there was no longer any need for such ideal paternalism. In his presidential speech of 1928 White told the Missionary Conference that its members had to speak out on behalf of a politically inarticulate people, that 'it was not in accordance with fact to say that the Prime Minister, who is Minister of Native Affairs, represents the native people', because the Prime Minister was responsible to the purely white constituency who had elected him. 'But even if there was the slightest chance', he continued, 'of such an adjustment of the franchise, that they [the Africans] could take part in electing their political representatives, they are unaccustomed to deal with intricate political questions, the issues of which are far beyond their range of vision. At present someone must think out these things for them: someone must speak on their behalf . . . In the order of God's providence it does seem that this duty falls to our lot.'[109]

White's concern for the Africans was not unfounded. During the inter-war period there was hardly any continuous representation of African interests at a national level. There were no representative bodies demanding political rights on a large and nation-wide scale. The incorporation of Africans in leading governmental positions was still something of the future. At that stage the African intelligentsia had limited opportunities, with the result that those who were employed as teachers, clerks and messengers were reluctant to take political initiative, lest they prejudice their positions and lose their jobs. Communications in the rural areas were still ineffective and therefore hampered concerted political action. Through isolation, great numbers of Africans in the rural areas were still thinking, in the first place, in terms of tribal and not national politics.

Thus the Missionary Conference assumed the role of 'watchdog' of African interests. Ranger indicates that the Missionary Conference was a *political power* during the 1920's. 'Its deliberations', he says, 'were attended by large numbers of officials and politicians and copiously reported in the local press... At the 1922 conference... resolutions were passed welcoming Government action against excessive judicial sentences; recommending the creation of Native Purchase areas; recommending the establishment of native councils with power to elect parliamentary representatives; and urging that Imperial guarantees be

108. *Ibid.,* p. 12; with reference to C. F. Andrews, *John White of Mashonaland,* 1935, pp. 175, 199.

109. *Ibid.,* p. 14-15. *Proceedings of the Missionary Conference,* 1926-28.

built into the new Constitution.'[110] The clearest sign of the Conference's direct influence in political matters was its rejection of a draft bill on the control of native preachers in 1924.[111] This Native Preacher's Bill was designed to control the movement of 'Separatist' Church leaders – a measure which the Native Department had urged for many years. On this issue the missionaries were divided, but the White-Cripps faction, which contended that the bill implied an infringement of religious liberty, carried the vote. The result was that the Government dropped the bill, as it was unlikely that the British Government would approve of it after its rejection by the Missionary Conference.

On the issue of segregation there was little difference between the representatives of the various Missions. Nearly all of them favoured *territorial separation* as the most practical policy to enhance progressive development. 'Very few theorists of those days', says Gann, 'thought in terms of cultural assimilation . . . The Premier accordingly met no serious opposition from local clergymen, and when he presented his case to the Southern Rhodesia Missionary Conference the reverend gentlemen congratulated the Government and the members of the Legislative Assembly on the fact that the principle of land segregation, as enunciated in the report of the Morris-Carter Commission of 1925, was accepted with such practical unanimity.'[112] The motives behind this general acceptance of the principle of land segregation must have varied considerably in the different ecclesiastic circles. Cripps, to whom Gann refers as an 'Utopian Socialist',[113] presumably was of the opinion that, ideally at least, Africans should be allowed to purchase land in any part of the country, but realizing that such a viewpoint had no chance of acceptance, he supported the native purchase scheme, and propagated an equal division of unalienated land. It is likely, on the other hand, that the more conservative missionaries of the DRC supported this principle of land segregation because they regarded it as a natural trend, in line with the situation in South Africa, and favourable to their own policy of Church indigenization, which excluded racial integration and social equality. Simultaneously, however, all the missionaries realized that a policy of separate development could only succeed if generous land grants were made to the Africans. DRC missionaries had started moving on the matter of land purchase for Africans at an early stage. A memorandum on the reserves, drawn up in the Administrator's office in 1920, makes mention,

110. *Ibid.*, p. 15.

111. *Ibid.*, p. 16. See also the letter of the Chief Native Commissioner to Premier, 10 April, 1924, National Archives, File 584/A/259.

112. Gann, 1965, p. 275; with reference to the S. R. Missionary Conference Proceedings, 1928.

113. *Ibid.*, p. 275.

amongst other things, of the pressing land problem in Gwanda, where the Native Commissioner could not find sufficient land for people coming in from alienated areas. It states that 'the local missionary of the Dutch Reformed Church is already moving in the matter, and urges that natives who are compelled to move should be allowed to purchase land in the vicinity if they desire to do so.'[114] In the Missionary Conference Cripps and White took the initiative in urging a fair division of the available land and it was recommended by the Conference that Africans should receive their share in land on a 50-50% basis. When the Morris-Carter Commission ignored this recommendation in favour of a division on the basis of 37% to the Africans and 63% to the Europeans, Cripps suggested that the Conference reject the Commission's report, but the majority of Conference members refused to do so, on the grounds that they would be playing into the hands of those opponents of the Government who completely rejected the principle of Native Purchase Areas. Cripps's withdrawal from the Conference, soon afterwards, marked the turning point in the role of this body in directly influencing Government policy on the land issue. White's efforts to obtain modifications of the Land Apportionment Act led to a repudiation of his views by his own Church authorities and to direct clashes with the 'establishment' which put an end to his career as president of the Mission Conference. He was sharply attacked by the Prime Minister who accused him of saying that 'white people could not act fairly towards native peoples'. The Prime Minister referred to him (White) and Cripps when he spoke of 'some missionaries' who thought they had a monopoly on Native policy, and in whose eyes the Government could do no right.[115]

As affiliated members of the Missionary Conference, both the DRC and the RCC participated in a program which, during the 1920's, aimed at 'political' representation of the African's point of view. Cripps thought that Burbridge, the Roman Catholic member of the Conference Executive, was 'throwing himself into the Native's Up-Hill cause in a very exemplary manner'. The DRC members, though politically more reserved, pressed for a fair solution of the land problem. But up to 1930, the main drive to speak out publicly on behalf of the Africans, came, as we have seen, from Anglican and Methodist quarters. On occasion White even went so far as to appeal to the British Government over the heads of the Southern Rhodesian Government, which provoked opposition in governmental and Mission circles. It was this possibility of appeal to the British Government and the British public which placed the Missionary Conference in a position to bring some pressure to bear on the

114. Ranger, *State and Church,* p. 18.
115. *Ibid.,* p. 22.

policy-forming agents of the local Government. At times the efforts of the missionaries yielded meagre results, but the image of the Conference as a body willing to take a radical stand on behalf of Africans was firmly established in this early period.

The absence of White and Cripps after 1930 had a marked effect on the Missionary Conference. Its significance as a political force waned. This trend was also due to the change of circumstances, such as the founding in 1928 of the *Southern Rhodesia Bantu Christian Conference* (SRBCC) as a representative organization for the African clergy. It can be said that the Conference to some extent failed to obtain the co-operation of African leaders, which objective, under the influence of White, was to be the second phase of its program. The ingrained paternalistic attitude proved to be a serious handicap of which the missionaries could not rid themselves overnight. Consequently the majority of Conference members regarded the African clergy as not fully capable of representing the social affairs of their own communities. According to their judgment the emergence of the SRBCC was somewhat premature, and a system was therefore devised whereby resolutions of the new body had to be submitted to the Missionary Conference for approval before they were forwarded to the administrative or other authorities concerned. Thus, in the effort to curb the political preoccupation of the SRBCC members, a significant change of function took place. As Gray correctly remarks, 'The Missionary Conference found itself not acting as the political spokesman of the African people but as a kind of censor of their political aspirations.'[116] The 25 years that lapsed before the two Conferences were merged must have seemed to some of the African Church officials as a delay of recognition of their legitimate positions as partners of the European organization. The Mission Churches, that had emerged before 1930 as champions of the African cause, to some extent seemed to obstruct the way to political expression during the next two decades.

As far as the differences between the various Church policies on State-Church relations are concerned, much remained obscured to rural Africans before, and even long after, the foundation of the SRBCC. Especially in the Southern Shona districts, far removed from Salisbury and Bulawayo, much of what was being said and done at the Conference escaped the notice of ruralists. The image of Christianity in the remoter parts was being conditioned by the direct contact with missionaries engaged in education, and not through newspapers. Africans may have been aware of the concern of individual missionaries with the land problem and they may have had some confidence in the

116. Gray, 1960, p. 30; Central African Archives 1/1/3, pp. 107-109.

promises of missionaries who openly tried to use their influence in the African struggle for more land, but they were also aware of the growing 'partnership' between the Government and Missions, and of the fact that missionaries were increasingly hamstrung by their obligations to the Government, on whose financial subsidies they became dependent. Although it must have been evident that the missionaries and Government officials were generally inspired by a different motivation in their work, the 'people of God' still belonged to the ruling class, they were still Europeans and they did, at best, only indirectly represent African interests in their dealings with the Government.

There are sufficient indications of the cordial relations and mutual respect between Mission leaders and State officials. The DRC leaders, in particular, had an outstanding record. Stanley, the Governor of Rhodesia, wrote to the Rev. Louw in 1941: 'It is a great satisfaction to us to know that we stand well in your regard, for there is none whose good opinion we could value more highly than that of a man who has devoted his life with such splendid success to bringing the light of the gospel into the darkness of the land . . .'[117] Charles Bullock, well-known Chief Native Commissioner, expressed his appreciation in a letter to Louw, for the 'incalculable effect your altruism and personality have had on the relationship of all people in this country.'[118] George Stark, Director of Native Education, mentions the very high regard his Department had for Louw's judgment in matters pertaining to the Dutch Reformed Church relations in the country. He wrote to Louw: 'You are bequeathing a legacy of which any man must feel proud, for it is a legacy which has been built up and made possible only through a life lived in close communion with God and in service of the people.'[119] At the request of the Queen-mother of England, who visited Morgenster in 1953, the old veteran was awarded the OBE in 1954. Louw was then 91 years old.

The example set by Louw was followed by the successive Mission leaders, with the result that the impression made on outsiders was increasingly that of a close link with the Government. DRC criticism of Government policy took place by way of personal contact or through correspondence. No public attacks were made on Government policy. On the issue of Federation, for example, the DRC took no official stand. It was a different matter altogether as far as matters of a strictly religious nature were concerned. When, for instance, the Government's Information Service published a pamphlet ('How you can help Government and Yourself') in 1962, with the words: 'By your fathers' spirits you

117. Louw, 1965, p. 273.
118. *Ibid.*, p. 274.
119. *Ibid.*, p. 275.

can now do what is right', the Dutch (now African) Reformed Synod was provoked to raise a sharp protest. On behalf of the Synod the Rev. G. Murray wrote to the Prime Minister that 'this sentiment is in direct conflict with the Christian Gospel which we as Missions and Churches have been proclaiming in this country for the past seventy years and . . . we have no option but to express our strongest disapproval in this connection.'[120]

The deliberate effort in recent years to maintain as politically neutral an attitude as possible, prejudiced the position of DRC missionaries to some extent. Africans, having previously noticed the reservations and aloofness of most missionaries on the social level, are now becoming increasingly suspicious of the Mission's position in relation to the Government. A prominent DRC African schoolmaster in the Gutu district stated in this connection:

'The people and many of the DRC teachers say that the DRC should take a clearer stand in politics. *The Church should not remain quiet* on some of the political issues, but should demonstrate clearly what is right and what is wrong – which does not necessarily imply their withholding their support from the existing Government.

Most of the people are convinced that the DRC takes a fairly neutral stand, but a great number of them feel that by remaining silent, the DRC might be siding with the Government completely [i.e. without criticism] . . .

I personally think the Church is perfectly correct in remaining as neutral as possible . . . but the Church should make a deliberate effort to explain its position in relation to the Government, to the people, in order to avoid already existing misunderstanding.'

In recent years the Catholic Church has been much more explicit in its criticisms of the Government than the DRC, and demonstrated a closer indentification with the nationalist aspirations of the indigenous population. Educational 'partnership' and efficient co-operation with the Government at the administrative level was maintained, but at the same time Church authorities published pastorals that spoke of the urgent need of a thorough land reform,[121] of the 'scandal of those working conditions in which normal family life is made impossible, the often inadequate wages paid to servants, the humiliations of discriminatory legislation, [and] the inequalities of opportunity in education.'[122]

The implementation of the Government's Community Development pro-

120. Letter extract 3/11/1962 (GMM/WDE), Murray to Premier. See also *Acta Synodi*, Morgenster, 1962.

121. *Peace through Justice*, 1961, p. 14.

122. *A Plea for Peace*, 1965, pp. 10-11.

gram led to serious opposition by Catholic leaders, who felt that new schemes were initiated by the Government, and not coming from the people themselves.[123] They also urged that Community Development should not be used as a means to promote separate development.[124] As for race relations, they recommended that 'the stigma of segregation' be removed from Catholic schools, and in order to spare the children concerned the least possible hardship 'such integration might at least begin with the higher classes, where pupils have already proved their ability and where the language barrier is less likely to present difficulty.'[125]

From the warning remarks of Kilchmann in the Missionary Periodical of the Gwelo Diocese, *Guti*, it can be deduced that individual Catholic missionaries have identified themselves with the African Nationalist cause to a degree beyond the missionary's essential task. Kilchmann states that missionaries are not ruthless diplomats who must achieve their ends at all costs. 'Yet even among missionaries', he says, 'desultory remarks on Government action to keep peace and order can occasionally be heard. Some are even known to rejoice whenever property of Europeans is attacked. The tendency is to regard any Government action as misguided and wrong. African nationalist moves of violence are condoned. Plainly put, this is sheer opportunism which is unworthy of dispensers of truth . . . we are not here for political ends, only for the unwatered Word of God. We have to foster whatever is good and condemn whatever is morally bad. It is not the missionary's business to work against the other "perfect society", the State. Neither now, nor once majority rule is achieved.'[126]

On the other side of the scale one finds Catholic Father Rutishauer who, in a thought-provoking article, warns against the temptation the Church continually faces to come to terms with those in power, the temptation of power itself. According to him the missionaries in Rhodesia are about to give in to this temptation, as the 'good men' – the clergy and liberals, who have come to terms with Apartheid in South Africa – have done. Security and order, he says, is promised by the Rhodesian Front 'at the cost of higher goods – justice and charity towards the African majority. And therefore it is a rotten security and a false peace. You can't condemn a resident people to permanent bondage and servitude, in order to guarantee and perpetuate the security of a white minority.' Rutishauer rejects any form of compromise in the present political

123. *Problems of our People* – Pastoral Instruction of the Catholic Bishops of Southern Rhodesia, Gwelo, 1963, p. 11.

124. *Ibid.*, p. 7.

125. *Peace through Justice,* 1961, p. 18.

126. Kilchmann in *Guti,* June, 1964.

situation. 'To accept racial discrimination within the body of Christ, within the unity of the Church, is not only a contradiction of the nature of the Church but a blasphemy against the Holy Spirit of God Himself. The dilemma of the Christians and missionaries is that they are confronted with this temptation. In order that we may be unmolested, in order that we may be free to administer to our people – in order that somehow we may retain control of our schools, our institutions and our buildings, we are tempted to be diplomats and to say yes to the State, even to an illegal state [this was written after UDI] . . . That is our peril today – for life and freedom (i.e. our own freedom); the right to possess what we have built at such great cost is too high a price to pay for the life of our soul.'[127]

In these passages one notices a spirit similar to that of the uncompromising Anglican, Cripps, and the unwavering Methodist, John White. The notably intensified struggle in Catholic Mission circles to determine what the missionary's attitude towards the Government in a complicated situation should be, deserves credit. This concern with the rights of Africans, manifested in the sympathy of Catholic missionaries with the African cause and expressed in the pastoral letters of the bishops, has had a definite influence on the image of the Catholic Church among Africans. In contrast to the seemingly evasive attitude of the DRC missionaries, the Catholics have been outspoken in their political convictions. The Africans must also have been aware of the generally different patterns of identification of Catholic and DRC missionaries with the European 'settler' community. The former missionaries were foreigners and therefore politically more detached from the sentiments of the white authority, whereas the latter, of whom an increasing number were second-generation missionaries who regarded Rhodesia as their mother country, were more bound to the European community and therefore less inclined to champion the African cause in radical political terms which could prejudice their own social standing.[128]

Finally, one may ask in how far the difference between the RCC and the

127. Rutishauer in *Guti,* June, 1966.

128. In the DRC missionary circles the divergence of political opinion has remained more obscured than in the Catholic camp, partly because of the lack of publications. The struggle for greater clarity as regards the pressing problems of identification with the political aspirations of the Africans and of interracial contact in private and public social life, has nevertheless caused considerable friction amongst the 'liberal' and 'conservative' DRC missionaries. It seems af if a number of missionaries left the field in recent years due to the growing conviction of several of the prominent missionary leaders (in the field) that some of the former social barriers should be dropped and that special 'social meetings' for the African and European staff members be arranged.

DRC in their attitudes towards Administration and Government policy, especially as regards social relations, had an effect on Separatism. I believe that this difference, being barely noticeable during the 1920's, was of little consequence during the early stages of Separatist development. In fact, Louw's fearless spirit and great influence did much to create bonds of mutual trust between Africans and missionaries, which in practice were as sound as, if not better than, those existing in many other missionary communities. With regard to social problems, for instance, Louw 'never shared the fear with some of the other missionaries, that the native would gradually achieve the same status and push them aside.'[129] During the past two decades, however, the diverging attitudes – the DRC largely maintaining its 'neutrality'; the RCC becoming outspokenly critical on racial issues – have become increasingly manifest to the African public at large. Yet, by this time, the potential effect of this difference was largely lost because Separatism and the spread of Independent Church movements all over the country had already become a massive fact.

e) *Attitudes towards traditional customs and religion*

The great discrepancy between the Roman Catholic and Reformed approach to the culture and religion of the people in the Mission fields lies rooted in their basically divergent theological traditions. In contrast with the 'total corruption' (*curruptio totalis*) of human nature taught by the Reformers, Rome maintained a Natural Theology, which involved the ontological analysis of human nature, and held that the 'rational soul' (*anima rationalis*) has escaped the corruption of sin, thus enabling the uncorrupted human reason to obtain true knowledge of God from nature itself. Calvin admittedly recognized a remnant of the *imago Dei* in man and spoke of a *sensus divinitatis* in human nature, but then only in acknowledgment of the inescapable impression[130] caused by an almighty God in His relation to man, and not in the sense of an 'ontological human organism' escaping from the effects of sin. The Dutch Confessions of Faith (NGB), the Canons of Dordt and the *Confessio Belgica* mention the *vestigia* (remnants) of the gifts of God, and the light of nature that has remained in the human being after his corruption by sin. As with Calvin, these distinctions were made in recognition of God's general revelation as referred to in Paul's epistle to the Romans. It did not imply a qualitative reduction of the totality of corruption and was therefore no concession to

129. Louw, *op. cit.*, p. 191 (translated from the Afrikaans).
130. Berkouwer, 1951, p. 125.

Natural Theology. The *vestigia* did not eliminate part of the corruption but underscored the urgent nature of the accusation that all light within us had become darkness.[131]

From the Roman Catholic viewpoint the Reformers held an unduly pessimistic view of human nature. The emphasis on *sola gratia* (mere grace) did not necessarily and indeed should not lead to the doctrine of *corruptio totalis.* It was conceded that sin had brought about a certain perversion of human nature, with the loss of supernatural gifts (*vulneratio naturae*),[132] but the powers of human reason were not eliminated, so that man could still achieve a true (but admittedly incomplete) knowledge of God based on the reality of creation. Due to the *analogia entis* between God and man, it is possible for the human being to obtain rational knowledge of the first cause (*prima causa*) of creation, i.e. of God, independent of supernatural Revelation.

As a result of these basically different points of departure concerning the corruption of human nature, the official policies of the two Churches on the possible adaptation to indigenous cultures vary considerably. Both Churches envisage the founding of indigenous Churches, but in the Reformed tradition this did not imply the *assimilation* or *absorption* of any indigenous customs or religious practices as if these had escaped the effects of sin and contained an inherent quality of goodness which made its incorporation acceptable. The emphasis was rather on a radical break with heathenism and hence with traditional custom. Though traditional religion was viewed as a particular manifestation of God's general revelation, its institutions had been contaminated by the inevitable *corruptio totalis*, so that traditional practices could only be incorporated in the Church if these were totally renewed in Christ. From the Reformed missiological point of view it is hardly possible to speak of a process of 'adaptation' or 'accommodation', for Mission work can only 'make use of' or 'possess' indigenous cultures. As Bavinck states: 'The Christian life does not adapt itself to the heathen forms of life, but takes it into possession, and by doing so, renews it.'[133] Bavinck compares renovation with the renewal of a national language: 'What Jesus is doing with customs and laws', he says, 'is comparable to what He is doing with languages. He takes the old words and renews them . . . He does this with customs also.'[134] Similar trends of reasoning can be found in the works of Reformed theologians and missiologists in South Africa. On the one hand missionaries are warned not to rob the

131. Berkouwer, 1957, p. 131.
132. Berkouwer, 1951, p. 53.
133. Bavinck, 1954, p. 181 (translated from the Dutch text).
134 Bavinck, 1949, p. 75.

natives of their language and culture, and missionaries are urged to show respect to indigenous cultures. On the other hand we read that the native's 'whole nationalism should be purged and purified',[135] that 'Christianity is never against nature so as to destroy it, but works towards the purification of the natural from the pollution of sin.'[136]

Rome's Natural Theology enables her to take a completely different view of indigenous Christianity. In creation uncorrupted *semen* (seeds) of the divine *Logos* are found.[137] Indigenous and inherently good customs are found amongst all nations, and to these the Catholic Church lays claim in the name of the Son of God. Catholic missiologists speak of 'building bridges' between Christianity and indigenous cultures, of a synthesis between heathen and Christian truth, of a 'reverent gathering of the "*Bruchstücke*" that are to be built into the new building of revelation and redemption, so that in Christ both parts may become one (Eph. 2 : 14).'[138] Both processes of *accommodation* and *assimilation* are fully justified in this theological framework. The former process recognizes the adaptation of the missionary and the contents of his message to the customs of the heathen. The latter implies the incorporation of such customs into Christianity. Warning notes have from time to time been sounded in missiological circles, such as that of Väth who opposes Thauren's and other Catholic missiologists' conception of accommodation. He emphasizes that Christianity is a revelatory religion (*Offenbarungsreligion*). He rejects all forms of synthesis and urges the need for a complete breach between Christianity and the heathen background.[139] As we shall point out later, the main concern of some Catholic missionaries in the Rhodesian field is also to baptize, to purge and to Christianize heathen rites that are assimilated. Generally speaking, however, Catholic accommodation lends itself to a flexibility and leniency totally different from the more rigid Reformed approach. In contrast with the 'principle of discontinuity' that characterizes the contact between Protestant Christianity and pagan culture along the whole front, Catholic popes view their Church as the preserver of the natural culture of pagans. Thus we note Pope Pius XII's comment in *Summi Pontificatus*: 'Anything whatever that has found acceptance in a people's way of life, provided only that it be not inextricably bound up with superstition and error, is at all times

135. Gerdener, 1951, p. 88.

136. Van der Merwe, 1967, p. 154; with reference to A. B. du Preez, *Eiesoortige Ontwikkeling tot Volksdiens*, p. 114.

137. *2nd Apologia of Justin*, Chapter 13, in Bühlmann, 1950, p. 62.

138. Bühlmann, 1950, p. 62.

139. Väth in *Zeitschrift für Missionswissenschaft*, 1927, p. 171; Bühlmann, *op. cit.*, p. 60.

weighed sympathetically and, if possible, *retained intact and unmarred* (my italics).'[140] In the encyclical *Evangelii Praecones* Pius XII elaborates on this theme: 'When the Gospel is accepted by diverse races, it does not crush or repress anything good and honourable and beautiful which they have achieved by their native genius and natural endowments . . . Rather she [the Church] acts as an orchardist who engrafts a cultivated shoot on a wild tree so that later on fruit of more tasty and richer quality may issue forth and mature.' He furthermore remarks on the human nature's 'retention of a naturally Christian propensity' in spite of the 'hereditary blemish of Adam's sin' which can be raised to 'supernatural activity' if it is illuminated by divine light and nurtured by divine grace.[141] Terms such as 'engraft', 'raise' and 'illuminate' leave scope for the element of renovation and transformation, which undoubtedly characterizes assimilation of certain pagan practices in the Church; but there is a vast difference in the theological climate between this grafting upon old foundations in a more or less continuous line of grace, and the Reformed emphasis on the drastic change of all traditional practices 'possessed' and assimilated in the Church.

Turning now to the Shona Mission field it is of interest to note that the difference in the theological background had little effect on the Protestant and Catholic approaches to heathenism during the pioneering phase. There was no adequate knowledge of traditional religion and thought on which a similar synthesis as that of, for example, the Jesuits in China, could be attempted. As Gann correctly states, 'an analytical frame of mind and a permissive outlook do not flourish on the frontier . . . Early evangelists – black or white – took their lives in their hands by going out to the far North; they did not go to analyze, synthesize or apologize, they went to fight Satan and all his works; they took risks because they believed they were fighting evil, and evil brooked no compromise.'[142] Mission leaders in both camps found little or nothing in heathen customs that could be assimilated or used. Even Fr. Prestage, who deliberately tried to penetrate into the indigenous system of thought and religious beliefs, was of the opinion that the dominant fear of the ancestors and the concomitant power of the spirit mediums eliminated any possibility of building on these foundations.[143] Louw's emphasis on personal conversion – which implied a radical break with the past – has already been mentioned. To him the only real 'point of contact' between Christianity and Shona culture

140. *Summi Pontificatus* in Burke, 1957, p. 57.
141. *Ibid.*, pp. 56-57.
142. Gann, 1965, p. 206.
143. *Ibid.*, p. 206.

was in the use of the vernacular, but even there all the old concepts had to be filled with new meaning in the essentially different context of the New Message. All forms of heathen dances and drumming, which were inseparably part of traditional religious expression; all forms of ancestor 'worship', consultations with the *nganga*, all forms of polygamy and succession marriage, had to be abolished. In his opinion these could not be purged or renewed. But even then it is significant to note that 'he [Louw] never overturned or kicked a beer pot to pieces, that he never insulted or confiscated the divining bones of the witchdoctor, never mocked their superstition. He believed rather in the exorcising power of a new, substituting love.'[144]

Gradually, as the indigenous congregations grew and their organization demanded a detailed policy towards traditional customs, the divergent lines of approach adopted by the leaders of the two Churches emerged more clearly. The attitudes towards some of the more important customs and religious practices need a more detailed scrutiny as we are here dealing with *one of the direct causes of dissent of African Church members*, and to my mind, *the most important reason why the* DRC *loses more of its members than the* RCC:

i) *Church discipline and customary forms of marriage*

Bridewealth (*Roora*). The custom of contracting a marriage by paying bridewealth has proved to be one of the most tenacious and deeply rooted of all customs in this (patrilineal) type of African society. Even today practically all African marriages still maintain – in addition to requirements stipulated by State and Church – this *roora* custom. Among the Southern Shona only a few exceptional cases were found of people who have completely and publicly abolished the use of *roora*.[145] In traditional Shona law a legally valid marriage could be contracted also without *roora*. Its almost universal usage, however, and the tendency in European courts to regard *roora* as one of the 'essentials' of customary marriage, caused it to be associated with the validity of marriage itself, instead of being, strictly speaking, the means whereby the husband's family obtained the right to the children born of this marriage. Another thing to remember is that customary marriages are contracted by the respective families and not the individual parties, however desirable the assent and cooperation of the latter may be. A lawful customary conjugal union between man and wife should therefore be seen as the result of a valid agreement between their families to establish lasting and mutually beneficial ties of affinal

144. Louw, 1965, p. 191 (translated from the Afrikaans text).

145. One of these exceptions is Rev. Shiri at Alheit Mission, who married off his two daughters without any *roora* arrangements.

relationship between them. Social and economic changes have affected the evaluation if not the function of *roora*, and opinions about this payment vary. Certain aspects about its function clearly emerged, however, from the answers of Africans, rural as well as urban, who were interviewed (see table 29). It is still recognized that the payment of *roora* establishes a right to the procreative powers of the woman. But even more explicitly voiced was the opinion that it constitutes a general compensation to her parents (*uredzi hwavabereki*), and that is strengthens the relations between the two families (*kuumba ukama*).

These latter two aspects were considered to be the most important functions of *roora* by 62% of the urban and 66% of the rural inhabitants. In Chingombe the emphasis is increasingly on its being a compensation to the in-laws, in the sense that the wife's parents have earned the right to it by having properly raised their daughter. This view can be partly attributed to the general rise in the educational standard of girls. The higher the standard achieved by a girl the higher her '*roora* value' becomes and the stronger the demand by a great number of parents to have at least some form of compensation in return for the relatively high cost of education. The emphasis in the urban area on the reinforcement of inter-family ties – and not in the first place on the ties between husband and wife – through *roora*, may result from a need to curb marriages based solely on the initiative of the partners concerned and to restore some of the traditional sanctions in the urban community. In urban areas *roora* arrangements are becoming more commercialized and it is misused by quite a number of people, but it still remains an integral part of most African marriages.

Generally speaking, the attitude of Protestant missionaries, in the 19th century, was marked by an inclination to condemn the *roora* practice outright. This was resented by the Africans and caused some of the newly converted Christians, also of the DRC, to leave the Church. But the indigenous officials of the growing Mission Churches successfully pressed for moderation. In 1923, the Missionary Committee of the DRC in the Cape Province still repudiated *roora* as a sinful custom. Two years later, the General Missionary Committee decided that *roora* was to be viewed as a custom which could be purified of its heathen features.[146] Later the Missionary Council in Mashonaland suggested that *roora* should be temporarily tolerated in the hope that members of the indigenous Church might themselves in time adopt more drastic measures to control or reject it. Payment of *roora* was not subjected to Church discipline, but a plea was incorporated in the African Reformed Church law, that:

'a) believers must be urged not to raise the *roora* payment unduly, and

146. *Die Kerkbode, Acta* ASK 1925.

b) girls and boys should be taught at their meetings not to be greedy [for money] when making marriage arrangements.'[147]

The tendency to repudiate this customs nevertheless remained, for it is clearly stated in the DRC catechism book (*Katekisma*) that *roora* should be regarded as one of the bad customs of the fathers, fit only to be 'thrown away' (*kurashwa*). In view of the continuation, and for all practical purposes, full recognition of this practice by Africans, the disapproval of the DRC missionaries is obviously a sore point with some of the African Church members. Rome's early acceptance of this system included the presupposition and hope that this custom would, in time, disappear. In so far as the custom was opposed it was a much less overt attack than was the case in DRC circles.

Polygamy. According to customary law any marriage is at least potentially polygamous. We have already taken note of some forms of succession or substitution marriage.[148] In practice the incidence of polygamy seems to be decreasing. Of the total adult population in Chingombe approximately 15%, and of the adults interviewed in town about 9%, belonged to polygamous households. Moreover, the number of Church members disciplined for polygamy is relatively low in comparison with the numerous cases of adultery which demand the constant attention of Church authorities. An analysis of disciplinary measures taken by the DRC over a period of nine years (1958-1966) at Alheit reveals that only 12 out of the 519 cases concerned males who had taken a second wife (table 32).[149] Although the complex problem of disciplining polygamy remains, its dimension has diminished considerably.

As regards polygamous marriages, both Mission Churches have adopted a similar line of approach. In Catholic tradition the Council of Trent anathemized those who even suggested that 'it is lawful for a Christian to have more than one wife.'[150] Calvin rejected this practice and urged the necessity of breaking the bonds with a second wife as a prerequisite for proper Church membership.[151] In 1909, the Cape Synod moved that polygamists who wished entry into the Church should be allowed Christian instruction, but could not be

147. BUKU YEMIRAIRO – *Rules and Regulations of the African Reformed Church* (DRC) Morgenster Mission, p. 40, No. 14.

148. *Supra*, p. 50.

149. Disciplinary statistics, admittedly, cannot be used as an accurate index of defections from Mission Churches because of polygyny. The incidence of polygamists or prospective polygamists actually leaving Mission Churches because of this practice is higher than the number of disciplinary cases entered in Church records.

150. *Survey of African Marriage,* p. 336, in Van der Merwe, 1967, p. 161.

151. *Ibid.*, p. 161; with reference to Esser, *Zending en Poligamie,* p. 172.

baptized. The Federal Missionary Council in 1945 once more decided against the baptism of polygamists. Only under exceptional circumstances did the DR Mission Churches of the Transvaal and Natal allow polygamists to be baptized. The Shona Church, however, followed a stricter line than most DR Mission Churches by not only refusing all male polygamists to become baptized, but by also adding the qualification that only those wives of polygamous males who had entered this type of matrimony without any knowledge of the Christian ideal, could acquire full Church membership.[152] A male polygamist who becomes converted is not allowed to attend catechism while he has two or more wives, but he should be encouraged to attend Sunday services.[153]

Other regulations determine, for example, that a Church member is not allowed even to act as a go-between (*munyai*) in marriage transactions involving a second wife,[154] nor can he marry off his daughter to a male who already has a wife.[155] A female catechumen who becomes the wife of an already married male will be debarred from catechism and forfeits all qualifications already acquired.

The Catholic Church also debars polygamists from participation in the Sacraments. Whereas the Catholic schoolteacher is normally subject to more lenient rules concerning adultery than the DRC teacher, the addition of a second wife to his household is the one offence which leads to unconditional discharge. Yet the Catholic approach to polygyny generally seems to be marked by a certain operational leniency not found among Protestants.[156] To

152. *BUKU YEMIRAIRO – Rules and Regulations* . . . p. 50 (translated from the Chikaranga). DRC law no. 179 reads as follows:
'a) The Church is convinced that a marriage concerning two or more wives, diverges from what the Word of God teaches us about true marriage.
b) Women who had no knowledge [who were unenlightened] about this matter when they were married, are allowed by the Church to be baptized and become Church members - the Church Council first having properly investigated such cases - and having acquired permission from the Church Conference (*Rangano Huru*).
c) A polygamist male will be allowed to attend Sunday services after his conversion, but he will not be allowed to attend catechism classes.'
It is of interest to note that the Reformed Ecumenical Synod, held at Lunteren in 1968, adopted the following motion on polygamy:
'That Synod sees no scriptural obstacle to the baptism of those who before conversion were polygamists and have come to repentance, though the biblical norm must continue to be proclaimed, and the polygamist must be earnestly counselled concerning the matter.' See *Acts and Reports of the Reformed Ecumenical Synod,* Amsterdam, 1968, p. 39.

153. *BUKU YEMIRAIRO,* No. 181, pp. 50-51.

154. *Ibid.,* No. 137(13), p. 40.

155. *Ibid.,* No. 137(10) and No. 177.

my knowledge wives of polygamists are allowed to become fully participating Catholics whatever the state of their 'enlightenment' at the time of their marriage.

Elopement (kutizisa) and other forms of traditional marriage. The one traditionally recognized marriage procedure acceptable to both Churches is the regular proposal marriage, called *kumema* (to call) or *kukumbira* (to ask). Holleman gives a detailed record of the various stages in the negotiation between the wife-receiving and the wife-providing families, such as the first proposal payment (*ruvunzo*: to ask) by the intermediary, leading to the *rutsambo* and the affinition agreement between the two families; the *chiuchiro* (to clap hands) gifts given to the prospective bride's father by the son-in-law as a sign of his respect and social subordination; the selection of marriage cattle at the son-in-law's (*mukuwasha's*) kraal; the *kuperekedza* (escort) ceremony, when the bride's *vatete* (father's sister) escorts her to the groom's village and finally, the 'unbinding' of the bride by the groom's father, before the actual consummation of the marriage takes place.[157]

The majority of Mission Church members inform their local Church leader of their intentions to marry, soon after an affinition agreement between the two families has been reached, but the *tezvara* (bride's father) usually delays his permission for a Church marriage until the first selection of marriage cattle has taken place. Then the bans can be called in Church, after which the ultimate Church ceremony and civil registration takes place. In accordance with the Christian ideal members are urged that cohabitation should take place only after man and wife have had their union blessed in the Church. All forms of customary marriage that militate against this ideal are condemned by the DRC.

As regards elopement (*kutizisa*), the DRC rules determine that a believer who participates in this procedure – which is even more common than the proposal marriage – will be disciplined for adultery. Catechumen boys and girls who elope are excluded from the catechism classes and must start at the beginning if they rejoin the classes after a disciplinary period. Credit marriage (*kuzvarirwa*)[158] which implies child betrothal or forced marriage is opposed by a

156. For an example of such leniency, see Murphree, 1969, pp. 137-138.

157. Holleman, 1952, pp. 99-108.

158. *Kuzvarirwa,* which is identified by the Administration with 'child betrothal' is prohibited by statute law. Holleman (1952, p. 116) uses the term 'credit marriage' for two reasons. 'Firstly, to avoid the implication of child betrothal which – although certainly not uncommon – is not necessarily an element of this type of transaction; secondly, because such transactions are almost invariably the result of a state of

Church rule which states that Christians can only give their children in marriage when such children have come of age; the minimum age-rates being 17 years for boys and 16 years for girls. Christians involved in the traditionally acknowledged seed-raising procedure, which involves the assistance of a third party (male or female) in a childless marriage to raise children, are disciplined for adultery. A female who is inherited (*kugarwa nhaka*) after her husband's death, can only be accepted as a fully participating Church member if she is the inheritor's first wife and if they are married according to Church regulations. A female believer who marries a heathen through civil registration without the official escorting (*kuperekedza*) ceremony, or a woman who, through *chimutsa mapfiwa* arrangements, becomes the substitute wife in the place of a deceased or barren relative, is disciplined for a year or debarred from catechism classes.[159]

All the above-mentioned offences are regarded by the DRC as forms of adultery, punishable, unless otherwise specified, by exclusion from the sacraments for a set period (usually one year, according to rule 167) or unconditional restriction (*shamhu isingatarwi*), or even excommunication. A special clause determines that schoolteachers who commit adultery will not only be placed under Church discipline, but will also be discharged from their posts.[160]

The DRC concern for high marital standards among its members, and the strictness with which its Church laws were applied, are reflected in tables 32 and 33. Approximately 76% of the 519 Church members disciplined at Alheit during the 9-year period of 1958-1966, were charged with adultery (*upombwe*). Unfortunately the records do not include complete descriptions of each case, so that the majority of cases were simply recorded as 'adultery'. It can nevertheless be taken for granted that quite a number of the unspecified cases concerned vaiiations of customary marriage, prohibited under the above-mentioned rules. It is significant that, in spite of incomplete records, a large number of disciplined men (73) and women (106) appear to have participated

---

economic emergency in the girl's family, forcing her father to procure cattle or essential food against the promise that one of his daughters will eventually be married to a creditor or a member of his family. To the Shona the characteristic feature of *kuzvarirwa* is that the agreement is reached between the families without the prior knowledge of the girl concerned.'

159. See *BUKU YEMIRAIRO;* Elopement; rule 162, 175; Credit marriage: rule 137; Seed-raising: rule 151; Inheritance of wife: Rule 163; Marriage between Christian female and heathen male: rule 161; *Chimutsa mapfiwa* (substitution): rule 182.

160. All DRC teachers have to sign a contract which subjects them to termination of service according to the discipline of the African Reformed Church, should they be found guilty of sexual misconduct (point 3 of the *Teacher's Employment Contract).*

in *kutizisa* (elopement) procedures. Holleman convincingly shows that this form of marriage is more popular than the regular proposal marriage, and that it is a fully recognized procedure in customary law, provided that the two partners – as generally happens to be the case – refrain from cohabiting before the bride's parents have been notified and have shown signs of agreement. Young people prefer this shortcut to the long drawn-out procedure involved in the *kumema* arrangements.[161]

One of the main reasons for the high incidence of *kutizisa* disciplinary measures by the DRC is the lack of an effective penetration of the Christian ideals of preparing for marriage even within the ranks of the Church. Tables 30 and 31 reveal how persistently the customary approach has been maintained within and without the Churches, in spite of many years of Christian teaching. Both in Chingombe and the Mucheke township the great majority of people (86% ruralists and 74% urbanites) stated that either *roora* payment or agreement with the groom's father-in-law is the essential precondition for official recognition of the union between husband and wife. A great difference of opinion concerning the payment of *roora* itself exists. Some hold that the whole payment must be completed before a woman legally belongs to her husband, while others state that once the *tezvara* has declared himself willing to negotiate, or once the first marriage beasts have been transferred, the community accepts the couple as husband and wife. The percentage of people (5% ruralists and 18% urbanites) who considered the Church rite as an essential precondition for a valid marriage was remarkably low. The members of the DRC and the RCC included in the Chingombe random sample survey did not differ significantly in their opinions from the rest of the community. Only a small minority (16% DRC and 1% RCC members) considered a Church ceremony essential. Perhaps the divergence of opinion in the DRC and RCC ranks may be ascribed to the much greater leniency of the Catholic officials towards *kutizisa* and other types of customary marriage arrangements (apart from polygamy).

Similar trends of opinion mark African views on sexual intercourse (table 31). Very few of those interviewed, Christian and non-Christian alike, considered the Church marriage to be a prerequisite for sexual intercourse. What mattered in the first place was the agreement between the respective families and the payment of *roora*. These were still the premises for lawful sexual intercourse rather than the prescribed ideals of the Christian Church. In view of these results it is hardly surprising that by far the greatest number of disciplinary measures of the DRC concerns adultery (*upombwe*).

161. Holleman, 1952, p. 109.

Of the 519 Church members disciplined at Alheit between 1958 and 1966 – see table 33 – only 189 (37%) were fully re-accepted in their former positions as Church members. Comparatively more adulterers (39%) than beer drinkers (36%) and members defecting to Independent Churches (22%) were re-accepted during the nine years surveyed. Yet the fact remains that the largest number of those who had permanently left the Church were members who had been 'beaten by the Church's adultery-cane (*shamhu youpombwe*)'.

A perusal of the DRC statistics from 1923 to 1966 (table 34) also reveals a great loss of membership through disciplinary measures. Very often the number of Church members re-accepted per year drops to less than 50% of the number of persons disciplined. Considering that, since 1950, the African Reformed Church (DRC) as a whole disciplined from 500 to 800 and more members per year and that only 40 to 60% of these members were officially re-accepted, then the loss of membership must run into several thousands during the past two decades. Judging merely from these figures, the European and African officials of this Church have tried to maintain a high standard of Christian morality at a singularly high cost. In some of the Presbyteries the number of disciplinary cases in 1966 even surpassed the numbers of the new Church members confirmed.

As we are here dealing with one of the primary causes of individual secession, the reasons for disciplining DRC members are of importance at this juncture. They are fully described in the Shona catechism book, which states that 'if the Church disciplines a person it "beats" with tears and not with harshness.' The intention therefore is not to drive people away. It disciplines: 1) to honour God, 2) because of the bad influence (of sin) on other Church members, and 3) to make the sinner return to the congregation of God's people.[162] Church rule no. 148 furthermore has it that 'if a Church member has sinned, he must be called to have his offence judged by the council (*dare*). If he cannot come he will state his case to the overseer (*mutariri*). But if he completely refuses to come to the *dare*, his case will be judged in his absence.'[163] In practice, however, the good intentions of the Church are not always as manifest to the Church members as the officials-in-charge prefer to believe, and the figures indicate that the opposite of the aim 'to make the sinner return' is in fact being achieved. It is true that DRC members are often proud of their Church and speak with appreciation of the maintenance of a strict code, but it is equally true that the legalistic way in which the Church

162. *KATEKISMA* (Catechism) – *neDudziro yeDzidzo dzeDutch Reformed Church*, 1966, p. 78 (translated from the Chikaranga text).

163. *BUKU YEMIRAIRO - Rules and Regulations*, p. 42.

sometimes metes out its punishment contributes towards the breaking away of its members.

The essential features of a whole Church council session, held at Pamushana Mission in the Bikita district in 1967, are included in Appendix II, to illustrate the disciplinary process. The most outstanding feature of the whole procedure was the absence of every one of the eleven members who were disciplined or re-admitted. This is not a fully representative picture of all DRC disciplinary sessions because accused members sometimes do appear on such occasions, but generally speaking the divergence between the ideals expressed in Church law and catechism books, and the procedures adopted in practice, is only too obvious. To the majority of disciplined sinners the discussion of their case at the Church council remains an unhappy issue which they are ashamed to attend. Thus, many of those disciplined, through their absence at the official 'trial', do not notice the sympathy and concern of Church leaders for their flock, which does come out in the discussion (see Appendix II). It is also evident that in most cases the only factual evidence on which the verdict is based, was presented by the particular overseer (*mutariri*), which means that the *mutariri's* interpretation and application of Church rules is an important factor in the local congregation. Much depends on his own discretion and his relation to the members disciplined. According to Rev. B., the European missionary at Pamushana at the time, the follow-up by *vatariri* of those debarred from Holy Communion is poor: 'Usually a *mutariri* or elder merely informs the person concerned of the Church council's verdict, after the meeting. But by that time the disciplined member feels ousted, and for all practical purposes does not belong to the in-group any longer. If – as often happens – members of the Church council do not visit him or her again, such a person feels neglected and will eventually join another Church.'[164]

In *shamhu* procedures this lack of continued contact by Church officials is an important factor which causes Church members to defect to other Churches. On the one hand the awareness of the loss of Church membership through *shamhu* was apparent during Council (*Rangano*) discussions. In one case[165] *Mutariri* Z., for example, pleads for the woman under discussion: 'We should punish her but not "throw her away" completely.' On the other hand, a noticeable determination to judge fairly deserves merit. The question is, however, whether the deliberate intention to 'make examples of such cases' – as was explicitly stated during the discussion – does not introduce an element

164. Rev. A. B. – Personal communication after *Rangano* session at Pamushana Mission, 1967.

165. See Appendix II, Case 2.

of cold formalism which is foreign to the Christian concept of understanding love. The precision with which judgment was passed on the adultery (*upombwe*) cases gave the impression of strictness and inevitability, which presumably accounts, to some extent, for the absence of the 'accused'.

From the discussions it is clear that the European missionary, Rev. B., and the African minister, Rev. M., did not dominate the proceedings and that enough scope was left for the *vatariri* to express their opinions. Nevertheless the presence of a European missionary seems to have a subtle steering effect on the proceedings. This tendency is reflected indirectly in the African minister's emphasis on strict consistency in the application of Church law.[166] A comparison of disciplinary measures taken during the absence or presence of a European missionary bears out this point. At Alheit Mission, for example, the introduction of an all-African Church *dare* has favourably influenced the incidence of *shamhu* cases. In spite of Rev. Shiri's reputation for strictness in the application of Church law, there has been a notable decrease in the annual number of disciplinary cases since his arrival in 1963, in contrast with the preceding period, when the Mission station stood under the direct control of a European minister (see figures in table 32).

Finally it should be noted that during the *Rangano* session at Pamushana, eight of the eleven cases were treated as adultery offences. Of these, only three concerned straightforward charges of adultery, in which evidence of unlawful sexual intercourse seemed established. The other five charges all concerned forms of traditional marriage – polygamy, elopement and inheritance – which only by implication constitutes *upombwe*. The absurdity and danger of a formalistic approach is illustrated in the sentence passed on Bettina Shoko[167] for eloping with her boyfriend. It was explicitly stated by the *mutariri* that Bettina was not yet pregnant. Since the first phase of elopement normally includes a strict prohibition of sexual intercourse, it is possible that Bettina was not guilty of the offence she was actually charged with. A realistic solution may have been to try and persuade Bettina and her prospective husband to marry in Church before the 'unbinding' ceremony, as prerequisite for sexual intercourse,[168] took place. But because *kutizisa* had become synonymous with adultery, in Church law, Bettina was given a year's punishment at the risk of alienating her from the Church, and also some others who might react to such measures.

The Catholic disciplinary system is marked by much greater flexibility than

166. See Appendix II, Case 2.
167. See Appendix II, Case 11.
168. *Supra*, p. 252.

that of the DRC. *Shamhu* in the DRC sense of the word does not exist in the Catholic Church. In earlier years it was expected of Church members who had trespassed against Church laws to do public penance. This amounted to the performance of light labour such as working in the gardens of the Mission station for a set period. Disciplinary measures of this nature were abolished in the early 1960's for political reasons, but it had never cost the Catholic Church a loss of Church members, comparable to that of the DRC. Niederberger, who worked on Mutero Mission station for several years, says in this connection: 'We did not lose many people through public penance. People on the whole appreciated it.' He also states that Church members were never excluded from Holy Communion for longer than a few weeks at a time. African women of their own accord tended to stay away from Holy Communion during pregnancies of 'illegal children'.[169]

An accurate comparison of the disciplinary systems of the DRC and the RCC, based on figures, is impossible, as earlier public penances and confessions are not on record. The difference in approach can nevertheless be gauged from some of the comments of Church leaders at Mutero Mission. Father Haag, head of the Mission station, states that:

'Church members are not disciplined for *kutizisa* (elopement), but are urged under such circumstances to get married in Church. People are expected to confess adultery and some of them do so, although teachers who "despoil" schoolgirls are reluctant to confess. When I listen to confessions I am not expected to know who the people are . . . We do not necessarily investigate adultery cases. If the matter becomes public through a village *dare* or through rumours, the priest intervenes, but if the guilty party shows a penitent spirit and confesses, it is all right.'

Father Urayai (an African priest) stated that they are aware of many young people actually living together before the Church wedding but no special effort is made to investigate such issues. 'People who commit adultery', he says, 'know that they must come to confession first, because they cannot receive Holy Communion in that state.'

Teacher Mutero, after more than 20 years' service in the Catholic Church at Mutero Mission, comments on the position of trespassing schoolteachers as follows:

'A schoolteacher is not disciplined if he *tizisa's* and his wife becomes pregnant before his Church marriage. If he spoils a girl but has no intention of marrying her, he is called in by the priests to discuss the matter. He must confess and also pay "damage" according to the finding of the local [village

169. Personal communication, 1967

or ward] *dare*. He may be transferred to another school *but he does not lose his job*. Discharge of teachers guilty of adultery only takes place in exceptional circumstances when the Church is publicly scandalized.'

These comments clearly reflect the totally different attitude of the Catholic Church. Unlike the DRC's subjection of Church members to the scrutiny of *vatariri* and the ostentatious control of a Church council functioning as a tribunal, the Catholic system of discipline confines much of the weaknesses of its members to the face-saving privacy of the confession box. To many of the Shona people whose moral code and understanding of the Biblical concept of sin is still conditioned by traditional notions of proper conduct, this approach is more acceptable than the public – and therefore often humiliating – strictures of the DRC. Of particular importance, too, is the different Catholic treatment of defaulting schoolteachers. The separation of the religious and moral issue from the teacher's professional position seems to cause less resentment than the temporary loss of a job, which for the DRC teacher is the inevitable result of Church discipline. The friction caused in DRC circles by the investigation of a *mutariri* into the private (and by implication professional) affairs of a teacher, who usually feels superior to the less educated overseer, is therefore avoided by the Catholic Church. DRC teachers disciplined for sexual misconduct[170] not only defected to the RCC, but several of them joined and became leaders in African Independent Churches. An outstanding example is a certain DRC teacher who had taught in DRC schools for 7 years, before he and his wife – who was also teaching in a DRC school at the time – were disciplined and temporarily discharged on account of a pre-marital pregnancy. They afterwards joined the *Chibarirwe* (African Congregational Church) of which this man today is the well-respected General Secretary. Such cases clearly illustrate the consequences of a strict and uncompromising application of Church law to cases of 'sexual misconduct' which are often based on traditionally sanctioned customs.

ii) *Beer drinking*

The close association of beer drinking with ancestral rites and with the evil

170. In earlier years DRC teachers who were discharged from their positions on the grounds of adultery, were often employed in RCC schools. That this was a common practice is reflected in the Regulations of the DRC (ARC), where a special sub-section stipulates the procedure to be followed by the Church officials if 'a teacher who was employed by the Catholic Church while under Church discipline, asks to be restored (rule 174, c).' According to Mr. T. H. Barnard, DRC Secretary of Education, this practice is not now as common as in the past due to the availability of a larger number of Catholic teachers who were trained at Catholic institutions.

that sometimes follows its excessive consumption has led the DRC missionaries to take a radical stand on this issue. It was recognized that women, being subordinate to their husbands, are sometimes forced to brew beer. Special provision was therefore made to exclude these women from restrictive measures, but it was also stipulated that female Church members are not allowed to arrange the traditional beer-work parties (*nhimbe*) in their fields, even if they do not drink themselves.[171] All Church members are prohibited from attending beer parties, which of course include the above-mentioned *nhimbe* parties.[172] Realizing, however, that such prohibitions have direct economical implications for the rural subsistence farmer, the Church allowed its members to use *mangisi* (unmalted sweet beer),[173] so that they could at least take measures to acquire a labour force for the work in their fields. Schoolteachers are bound by contract to abstain from intoxicating liquor.

In the course of years there have been widely different interpretations regarding the application of beer laws by DRC missionaries and overseers (*vatariri*). Some preferred to turn a blind eye to the participation of Church members in beer parties, especially when these concerned collective agricultural activities in the field; or *vatariri* simply refrained from determining whether Church members were in fact brewing sweet beer (*mangisi*) or real strong beer (*doro*). In exceptional cases some even went so far as to overturn the odd pot of beer. Yet the general trend was to confine the application of restrictive measures (*shamhu*) to those who indulged in excessive drinking. This especially applies to schoolteachers, of whom increasing numbers are now moderate consumers of European liquor. DRC education officials estimate that at least 80% of the African teachers employed in their schools occasionally take alcoholic drinks and they admit that a strict application of the Church's laws has become impossible. In spite of a greater flexibility during recent years the DRC had nevertheless retained the reputation for dealing severely with its beer drinkers (*shamhu* for beer drinking usually involves a period of 6 months restriction from Holy Communion). Ruralists often think

171. Rule No. 164 reads as follows: 'As regards female members who are ordered to brew beer *(kubikiswa)* by their husbands: The Council must investigate such matters. If it finds that such a woman is forced it will allow her to participate in the Sacraments, but she is not allowed to use beer for the work on her (own) fields even if she does not drink it herself.'

172. Rule 166 reads: 'Feasts that do not bring about Church discipline are feasts: (a) without beer, (b) . . .' For the *nhimbe* party see Chapter 1, p. 35.

173. Rule 165 determines that 'sweet beer *(mangisi)* without malt [which is used for the second stage of beer brewing], which is kept for a day only, is permitted by the Church'.

of the DRC in the first place as '*vaDutchi havadi doro*' (the people of the DRC who reject beer).[174]

Table 32 illustrates the validity of the assumption that the influence of individual missionaries makes a great difference in the application of restrictive measures. In 1958 more males (23) and females (9) at Alheit were disciplined for beer drinking than in any of the following years. The European missionary at Alheit was succeeded by another in the following year, which shows a marked drop in disciplinary cases for beer drinking. These could not have been such a sudden decrease in numbers of beer-drinking Church members, or in beer drinking generally, to explain such a sudden drop in numbers. The most likely explanation, therefore, is the different approach of the new missionary and his influence on the overseers. Far fewer beer drinkers than 'adulterers' (13% v. 76%) appeared before the Church *dare* from 1958 to 1966, and of those disciplined the majority were men. Such measures seem to have a different effect on men than on women, because of the males only 25% were re-accepted, while 50% of the women were officially re-accepted after their period of 'punishment' had lapsed.

The importance of the different attitudes of the two Mission Churches on the beer issue is clear from the common reply of rural Africans to the general question: '*Siyano huru pakati pavaDutchi navaRoma ndeipi*?' (What is the big difference between the DRC and RCC?) Invariably the reply is quite pointedly: '*vaDutchi vanoramba doro, vaRoma vanoritendera*' (the 'Dutch' prohibit beer, the 'Romans' allow it). School manager Gopoza's already quoted comment[175] on the Catholic priest's attendance at beer parties reflects this difference between the two Churches. The one group repudiates the consumption of beer and, even more important, evades or dissociates itself from people when they are drinking beer, while leaders of the other group accept the occasional calabash (*mukombe*) of beer and attack excessive beer drinking only; in short, they identify themselves with Africans when they are enjoying themselves in a traditionally accepted and respectable way. Small wonder that a DRC educational leader like Gopoza, who has noticed the advantages of the more diplomatic Catholic approach, finds it 'a pity' to be bound to Church rules when it comes to countering – in the competitive field of education – the 'intruding' Catholics, who make friends at beer parties.

Catholic teacher Mutero is correct in stating that 'the DRC contract for teachers makes very little difference to the conduct of teachers, in practice'

174. Such associations derive from the DRC prohibition of beer drinking for its members and also from the general evasion of beer parties by its European missionaries.

175. *Supra*, p. 226.

and that 'we teachers of both Churches drink beer together', but there still remains a vast difference between the one Church which continues fighting the consumption of *doro* with a figurative 'cane' designed for this purpose, and the other which blesses beer to be used for ancestral rites and allows Church members to brew large quantities of beer even for the opening ceremony of a new Church.[176] The result of this difference shows up in the composition of the membership of the defiantly beer-drinking *Chibarirwe* (ACC): numerous former DRC members and hardly any Roman Catholics!

iii) *Religious practices*

Traditional forms of religious expression. In Chapter 2, I mentioned the vital importance of singing, dancing and drumming in traditional rituals, such as the *kugadzira* and *kutamba mashavi* ceremonies, especially as a prelude to spells of spirit-possession. The initial attack of missionaries on pagan ritual inevitably led to the negation if not complete exclusion of indigenous forms of religious expression.[177] Dancing and drumming were not permitted during Church services. Imported music was used and strict measures were applied to avoid the kind of rhythms that could lead to ecstatic emotionalism. When missionaries started thinking of introducing traditional music and instruments they often encountered opposition from African Church leaders who felt that the association of such items with pagan rituals was still so close that they could not be incorporated into Church life.

In the DRC, especially, the liturgy is characterized by its soberness and a minimum of symbolic action. The only indigenous custom that has been deliberately incorporated into the Church service is the sitting or kneeling with hands held together, as a sign of respect during prayer. This practice corresponds to the way in which a Shona commoner expresses respect in the presence of a dignitary. Most of the DRC hymns are sung to Western-type tunes, although it is true that the typically African way of singing has given this foreign Church music an unique 'indigenized' quality. At Gutu Mission the possibility of incorporating small drums for special Church meetings was discussed, but the idea was rejected at the request of African Church leaders. Musical instruments are hardly ever used in a DRC service. In the section of DRC law dealing with liturgy, it is stipulated that 'the Church believes that a musical instrument in itself is not bad, but because some may

176. In 1967 the Member in Charge of the BSAP at Gutu had to take a hand in limiting the beer brewing at Basera township, which formed part of the preparations for the opening of the new Roman Catholic Church nearby.

177. Tracey states that 'the condemnation of the Mashavi cult has done more to destroy local culture than any other influence.' (in NADA, XII, 1934, pp. 29-52).

cause the believers to stumble, the Synod says that if someone wants to use any kind of musical instrument during any service, he must first ask the Church council. The Church council will consider the committee's opinion on the investigation of [the use of] musical instruments . . . The Church refuses the use of *hwamanda* [musical horns] in whatever kind of worship, even when the people are called together for a service . . . To ululate [*kupururudza*] and to dance joyfully [*kupembera*] is not allowed during a service . . . It is not allowed to use tambourines during Church gatherings.'[178] Thus, for the sake of good order and proper conduct and also because of the emphasis on preaching during services, the typical Shona expressions of joy (*kupururudza* and *kupembera*) were discarded.

The RCC from the outset had the advantage of a much more colourful and therefore, to the African, more appealing Church ritual than the DRC. During Mass there was the striking attire of the priest, the central role of the sacraments, an emphasis on symbolic action and comparatively less time spent in preaching, which corresponded more to the brief addresses to ancestors in traditional ritual than the often lengthy DRC sermons. There was also the peculiar attraction of the Gregorian chant, in respect of which one can agree with Inauen, that the 'Gregorian chant is equally strange and equally appealing to European and African ears; it is strange because it is neither European nor African and it is at the same time strangely familiar because it is the only universal religious music mankind has; universal because in it we find the ancient musical traditions of Africa, Asia and Europe.'[179] In recent years the Catholics have made special efforts to indigenize Church music. After experiments with drumming it was decided that the use of drums in Church should be made optional. Urban congregations, whose members regarded the introduction of drums as a retrogressive step, were therefore free to discard it, while rural congregations were allowed to make use of it. At Mutero Mission drums are only used on special occasions. The general consensus is that the controlled use of drums greatly contributes to the attraction of Church services. Rhythmic clapping of hands, but no dancing, is allowed in the Church building. At Bondolfi Mission, near Fort Victoria, African teacher Ponde was appointed by the Church as full-time composer of Church music in an entirely African style. Much of his work can now be heard in Catholic congregations all over Rhodesia.

In view of the regular use of indigenous musical instruments and tunes in the African Independent Churches, which illustrates the need for less foreign

178. *Rules and Regulations,* p. 34, rule No. 132/10 (b) (c), and 11.
179. Inauen in *Guti,* Aug. 1962, p. 99.

forms of religious expression, it is understandable that the Catholic Church's efforts to accommodate its ritual to Shona tradition have met with success. According to Mr. Barnard – DRC secretary of Education – who had been working in Rhodesia as a missionary for more than 40 years, several African leaders have told him that the way in which the Catholic faith is presented to the African people is more *interesting* and more *acceptable* than that of the DRC. Due to the liturgical differences between the DRC and the RCC, the attraction of ritual proceedings in present-day Independent Churches probably has a greater appeal to members of the former than the latter Church.

High-God and ancestral rites. The Matonjeni cult came under direct attack from missionaries and settlers during and immediately after the Rebellions of 1896-7. In subsequent years the immediate problem facing missionaries was that of the more evident ancestral and *shavi* cults, and the potent influence of the *nganga.* The secretive character of the High-God cult and the obscured influence of the Matonjeni messengers contributed towards a less direct confrontation with this institution on the part of the missionaries. In the DRC 'Katekisma' it is stated that those who request rain from 'the rainmakers' (*vanisi vemvura*) are breaking the first commandment because rain can only be sent by the Christian God.[180] The practice of rainmaking is, moreover, condemned as one of the 'bad customs' of the forefathers that should be 'thrown away'.[181] Significantly, however, the Matonjeni cult is not explicitly mentioned in the DRC 'Katekisma', despite the fact that the old High-God's name, Mwari, is used for the Biblical Elohim. When, for example, the attributes of God are explained in the 'Katekisma', one finds a good description of the Biblical God (who is One, Spirit, Omnipotent, Eternal, Love, Holy, etc.),[182] but no deliberate confrontation with Mwari waMatonjeni to clarify the conceptual differences between the Christian and the traditional deity. Missionaries must have been either unaware of the possibility of conceptual confusion (hardly surprising in the light of the assumed remoteness of the Matonjeni deity in everyday rural life), or they may have felt that their rejection of rainmaking activities, together with a positive doctrine and the teaching of the Biblical God, would be sufficient to counter the dangers of syncretistic thinking.

The Catholics also made use of the term Mwari for the Biblical God. They actually relied on the DRC translation of the Scriptures for many years before a Catholic version of the New Testament came into use. It is my impression

180. *KATEKISMA,* p. 8.
181. *Ibid.,* p. 92.
182. *Ibid.,* p. 36.

that God the Father (Mwari *Baba*) has generally received primary emphasis in Catholic teaching, in contrast to the great Christological emphasis of the DRC. This would fit the customary thought-pattern, based on the seniority principle, more readily than a propagation of salvation which centers on and more or less 'elevates' the Son above the Father.

DRC missionaries have expressed concern at the possibilities of confusion in the African mind, due to the central position of Christ in the preaching and doctrine of their Church. One of them quoted an African as saying: 'Since the [DRC] preachers came, they have been telling us that the Messiah would come again, but He has not yet arrived, so we don't believe any longer. The *vafundisi* [ministers] do not tell us the truth. Why does the Messiah not come?' These words give one an impression of the way in which a strong Christological and Eschatological emphasis in preaching can be interpreted by some Africans. It is quite possible that the very nature of Protestant evangelization in a politically turbulent African setting has helped to create a religious climate favourable to the growth of 'Messianic' movements.

There has been no deliberate attempt by the DRC to supplant the Matonjeni cult with a Christianized rain ceremony other than special prayer meetings with concerted requests for rain in times of drought. The Roman Catholics, on the other hand, have adopted an elaborate rain ceremony 'We pray for rain' (*Tinonamatira mvura*) – first printed in 1962 – which includes relevant Biblical passages such as Judah's lament in a time of drought in Jeremiah 14. It is conceivable that phrases such as 'they come to the pits and find no water; they return with their vessels empty' (verse 3) and 'because of the ground which is chapt, for that no rain hath been in the land, the plowmen are ashamed, they cover their heads . . .' (verse 4) if read out loudly to an agrarian community during a period of drought, will be regarded by its members as a profound expression of their own most urgent need. In the prescribed liturgical prayers the main theme is the oft-recurring plea: 'Bless our fields, our seeds, our cattle – grant us sufficient rain, hear us, Lord!' More important still, from the African point of view, is the ritual blessing by the Catholic priest of the fields, the grazing areas, the seed to be sown and the livestock. Such action serves as an understandable substitute for the magical treatment of fields and seed to be sown, by the *nganga*. Prayer is followed up by symbolic action, in other words, the request for rain finds expression in concrete action and God's power is demonstrably related to the objects requiring His aid.

The difference between the two Churches is further illuminated by the constant depreciation of all ancestral rites by the DRC, in contrast to the more accommodating attitude of the Catholic Church. In the former Church al/

forms of ancestor worship and divination practices are regarded as trespasses against the first commandment.[183] In respect of the fifth commandment it is held that children should honour their parents, but if these are heathens and demand of their children that they *shopera* (attend divination) and participate in *pira midzimu* (ancestor worship), the children may ignore their parents' wishes.[184] Amongst the evil practices directly ascribed to Satan, through which he tries to tempt and divert the believer from the Christian way of life, are listed: Ancestral and *shavi* rituals, divination practices, belief in *ngozi* spirits, witches, witch mediums, such as the hyena and other animals, the perpetration of evil through the bones of snakes (and by implication all magical practices), the treatment of the fields with magical medicine (*divisi*), and the preoccupation with *shurire* (bad omens).[185] Christians are warned to avoid all these practices. Furthermore DRC law determines that a believer who visits heathen *nganga* must be disciplined by the Church.[186] Cases of ancestor worship are treated under this Church law because of the close link with the work of *nganga*. If one considers these strict rules together with the DRC repudiation of beer drinking, it is obvious that the DRC stands diametrically opposed to all forms of traditional religion. As a result European missionaries and African ministers hardly ever attend traditional rituals. Yet the frequency with which DRC disciplinary measures for participation in traditional ritual are applied suggests that usually a more permissive attitude prevails at the local congregational level than the rigid strictures of Church law seem to imply. During the 9-year period surveyed at Alheit (table 32) only *one* Church member was officially debarred from Holy Communion because of a visit to a *nganga*, in spite of the common knowledge that many Church members from time to time do participate in traditional rituals. Rev. Shiri says that he is aware of the fact that Church members visit *nganga* secretly when they suspect bewitchment of themselves or of one of their relatives, but that such cases are never reported to the Church *dare*. He himself makes no special effort to find out who such Church members are. He contends that the *vatariri* are afraid of magical countermeasures against themselves, should they report members who secretly visit *nganga*. Mr. Gopoza, the school manager, suggests that the '*vatariri* are afraid to report people who *pira* privately because even the

183. *Ibid.*, p. 8. The ancestral spirits are equated with idols. Amongst other things it is stated that 'a person who divines breaks the first commandment because he deviates from his [true] worship by inquiring from the *hakata* [divining bones] that which is only known by God.'

184. *Ibid.*, p. 8.

185. *Ibid.*, p. 92.

186. *Rules and Regulations*, p. 43, rule No. 151f.

teachers side with them [i.e. with those who still *pira midzimu*]. The teachers dominate the *vatariri* because the *vatariri's* children or relative's children, whose progress can be barred by the teachers, attend the schools.' The discrepancy between the letter of the Dutch Reformed Church law and its application seems to derive from the leniency of Church officials low down in the leadership hierarchy – officials who are more directly in contact with Church members still living under the sway of the ancestors. But the reason why Church officials – and especially those at the top of the leadership hierarchy – 'turn a blind eye' to traditional religious practices should also be sought in the thorough identification of such officials with the policy initially inspired by the European missionaries; a policy which was directed at the elimination and negation of (as can be read from the Church laws) rather than at confrontation and dialogue with the Shona spirit world.

The influence of evangelistic and fundamentalist minded Mission leaders was bound to make its deepest imprint on African ministers who closely cooperated with them. Thus the missionary's disapproval of traditional religion was taken over by the African Church leader. To underscore this point a few poignant remarks made by Rev. Shiri are worth mentioning:

'Mwari waMatonjeni', he says, 'is the God of untruth; Matonjeni and ancestral rituals are not the signs of the Christian God's involvement with the Shona people before Christianity came. Worship of the ancestors is completely wrong. It nevertheless gave the people an idea of how to pray . . .

The *midzimu* are powerless; the *ngozi* spirits are nonexistent, and therefore cannot kill . . . I have last seen a *shavi* dance when I was a boy, many years ago . . . I do not personally know any of the *nganga* here in Chingombe – I do not particularly look for them!

I have never tried to exorcise a *shavi* spirit. The Church members never come to me with complaints of *shavi* or *ngozi*, because they know they will be sent away [note the intolerant attitude towards any preoccupation with the traditional spirit world]. They know I am an African who really believes in the DRC way, that I know all about the *midzimu*, and that I am strict about it. So they hide these things from me . . . The people say I am a black man who is very strict because I live with the *shumba* [lit. lion; but the term refers to the European in this context].'

These remarks reflect the unwavering spirit of a man who is convinced that the Christian life must imply a radical break with pre-Christian religious practices, a man who is known to have publicly challenged more than one reputed *muroyi* (sorcerer) to use his mystical powers against him, and a minister who was entrusted with the leadership of the first all-African Mission station of the DRC. The personal testimony of such a Church leader can only be admired. Yet it remains doubtful whether this approach leaves any scope for an understanding and effective pastoral treatment of the hidden but persistent belief in the ancestors and alien spirits among Church members. In the face of such a strict dismissal of traditional institutions Church members are bound, as Shiri himself says, to hide their problems concerning the ancestor world from him and, sadly enough, turn for a solution elsewhere.

Shiri's remarks do not reflect the approach of all the ministers and officials of the DRC. Van der Merwe has brought to my attention that during his period of service as a missionary in Masonaland he and other missionaries have come across, and successfully dealt with, several cases of spirit-possession.[187] It is also known of some woman missionaries of the DRC that they have taken a special interest in the traditional spirit world and have developed their own spiritual 'techniques' of exorcising troublesome spirits from afflicted Church members. In '*The God of the Matopo Hills*' I describe the efforts of one of these missionaries to exorcise a Matonjeni spirit from an African woman who was formerly dedicated to the Shona High-God.[188]

Despite the variety of attitudes found amongst the clergy and lay workers of the DRC, there remains a vast difference between the approach of this Church and that of the Catholics to the traditional ancestral rites. Far from condoning it, Catholic priests at first attacked *pira midzimu* rituals. But subsequently, as Haag says, 'the Fathers started attending rituals and blessed the sacrificial meat and beer with holy water to dedicate it to the Mediator', and nowadays 'experiments' are being conducted in an effort to incorporate 'Christianized' Shona rituals in the Church's liturgy. Whereas the DRC condemnation of ancestral rites has been maintained through the years and has led to an official evasion rather than a preoccupation with these rites, the Catholic disapproval gradually changed to a more flexible approach – in accordance with their theological premises – which increasingly concerned itself with the selection of what is 'good' in the traditional system for assimilation into the Church. This concern with the traditional religion and the attendance of rituals made the Catholics aware of the persistence of traditional beliefs and practices. It also led to such subtle distinctions as that of the *nganga* as diviner, to whom Church members are not supposed to go, and of the *nganga* as a herbalist to whom Church members are allowed to go to collect medicine. *Shavi* dances, again, are not officially condoned, but there are, to my knowledge, no strictures comparable to those of the DRC to prevent Church members from attending such occasions.

187. Personal communication (correspondence) with Prof. W. J. van der Merwe.
188. Daneel, 1970, pp. 63-64.

This main interest was directed at the African's great concern with his *midzimu*, during burial, *kugadzira*, *mukwerere* and ordinary family rites. Kumbirai, the leading light among the Shona priests, has been engaged in this field for several years. 'He was the one', Niederberger, dean of Chikwingwiza seminary, remarked with approval, 'who made us aware of the fact that *kurowa guva* [i.e. *kugadzira*][189] is done by the Shona people for everybody. We, as missionaries, were not aware of that at all and it underscores the fact that we have not yet achieved a full conversion.'[190] Kumbirai, who professes to have been greatly stimulated in his work by the ideas of the Catholic theologian, Hans Küng, sees his task as that of finding out just what is adaptable to Christianity in the traditional rites. Is there anything in Shona religion that can make a contribution to Christianity? 'It is not a matter of compromising, but of adapting what is good in Shona religion', he said. A train of thought totally different from that of a DRC leader like Shiri can be detected in Kumbirai's theological evaluation of Shona traditional religion. To the question whether Shona religion can be seen as part of God's general revelation or as *preparatio evangelica* he answered:

'Yes, traditional religion is the sign of God paving the way for the vaShona to accept the Gospel of Christ. Christ came to perfect this religion. All along it was debased, just as happened in Old Testament times, as was the case with Moses and the calf. There were always abuses, but basically it was God's preparation of His people for the Gospel.'

Q.: Do you make a qualitative distinction between the Jewish religion of the Old Testament as *preparatio* for the revelation in Jesus Christ, and the Shona traditional religion?

K.: 'There is a distinction, but whether it is of *kind*, I do not know; it is probably of *degree*. It was revealed to the Jews that Christ was coming but to the Shona it was *implicit*. The Jews led [the religious field] because they knew He was coming; the others [i.e. the Shona] practised religion more blindly but it was all the divine Providence.'

Q.: And yet the Shona religion must be christianized and changed?

K.: 'It must be elevated!'

Theological premises that allow for a distinction of degree rather than kind between the Old Testament and traditional religion, that see the aim of christianization as fulfilment, perfection or elevation of the traditional religion, must of necessity arrive at a completely different appraisal of the ancestral rites than the Reformed emphasis on the satanic, and consequently on the

189. *Supra*, p. 101f.
190. Personal communication, 1967.

radical break (discontinuity) with ancestral rites after conversion. Kumbirai therefore strongly criticizes the use of the words 'ancestor worship' when speaking of the *bira* (ancestor propitiation) as an institution. In contrast with men like Shiri, Gopoza and other DRC leaders who hold that *kupira* includes an element of worship next to the main connotation of honouring the spirits, Kumbirai emphatically states that 'the muShona is not deifying his ancestors at a *bira* . . .' As has already been mentioned in Chapter 2, Kumbirai regards the respect and honour given to the ancestors as the same as that shown to the living; 'nothing more than that'. His rejection of the term worship in connection with ancestral rites is based on his distinction between the different attitudes of respect and homage, paid to the *midzimu* and Mwari, respectively.[191] Such a lenient and positive evaluation of the address to the deceased family spirits fits the Catholic custom of honouring the saints, with the result that the process of adaptation is not unduly hampered by official hesitation or objection. To be more concise we will briefly trace the pattern of Catholic adaptation in connection with a few rites:

Burial rite. Kumbirai's proposal for a new burial rite was officially accepted by the Bishop's Conference in 1966. It includes the address of the ancestral spirits of the person who is buried, by the priest and the Church members who attend the proceedings, before the coffin is lowered into the grave. The order of address is as follows:

Priest: Holy Mary, here is your son, N. [the deceased] –

All participants: Go with him to Mwari [*endai naye kuna Mwari*]!

Priest: You, his saint, and you, his angel and keeper, there is the person, who belongs to you –

All: Go with him to Mwari!

Priest: All of you, angels and saints, this is your relative –

All: Go with him to Mwari!

Priest: You, of his father's *chizvarwa*,[192] here is your child –

All: Go with him to Mwari!

Priest: You, his fathers and all his forefathers [*madziteteguru*] and all of his father's *rudzi* [tribe] who have died, this there is your child –

All: Go with him to Mwari!

Priest: You, of his mother's *chizvarwa*, who have died, this is your child –

All: Go with him to Mwari!

191. *Supra*, p. 179.

192. *Chizvarwa:* lineage segment, embracing several generations.

Priest: You, his *madzisekuru* [maternal uncles] and his *madzimbuya* [maternal grandmothers] and all of his mother's *rudzi* [tribe], who have died, this is your child –

All: Go with him to Mwari!

Priest: You, all his relatives and all his friends who have died, this is your relative –

All: Go with him to Mwari!

When he sprinkles the coffin with holy water the priest says to the deceased: 'I sprinkle you with the water of appeasement so that you may be "cooled" [*utonorerwe*] with the blood of Christ, in the name of the Father, the Son and the Holy Ghost.'

During the incensation he says: 'I incense you (*ndinokupfungaidzira*) with the smoke of heaven. Let the pleasant smell drive your enemies and the evil spirits away, in the name of the Father . . .'

In the concluding prayer the priest first addresses God with the words: 'Father, we have escorted our relative, let him stay with Thee. He is now Yours; ours [i.e. our task] is now finished . . .' and then the deceased is exhorted to ask God on behalf of his family to divert hardships from them: 'Constantly intercede for this family of yours, N., so that it may be free from the troubles of this world, as well as from the things that despoil spirit and body. On the day of their death, you must meet them and escort them to heaven, to Mwari, to eternal joy.'[193]

The retention of the mediating function of the *midzimu*, as is clearly revealed in this ritual, creates no problem to the Catholics in the light of their doctrine that those ancestors who have kept the natural law are *with God* in heaven and can accompany the deceased relatives to Him. As Fr. Urayai (at Mutero) states: 'These ancestors are saints, as all those deceased who had gone to heaven.' Kumbirai maintains that a distinction is made in the Church between the mediating function of the *midzimu*, who form the direct bridge between God and man for the non-Christian muShona, and that of the *midzimu* who pray to God through Christ for the Christian. In connection with the address of *all the midzimu* of the recently deceased, during the burial rite, he states: 'I place the *midzimu* as a category in heaven; who are there and who are not there is not my concern. If they are not in heaven, God knows about it.' Kumbirai also says that the inclusion of the phrase 'Go with your relative to Mwari!' has met with tremendous response during the experimental stage. Long before its publication Kumbirai had already begun to use the abovementioned liturgy, and elderly men had told him afterwards: 'Father, now we

193. See *Kuvigwa kwomunhu*, 1967, pp. 6-15.

understand what the faith is', and, 'This is the way in which we understand.' Such reactions are to be expected from people whose religion centres in the address to and the mediating function of the ancestors.

As for burials, the DRC law determines that Christians should be buried with 'reading from God's word, singing of Church hymns and prayer.' Heathen customs, such as the killing of sacrifical beasts, are prohibited and Christians should try to console all those who 'cry with a loud noise (*vachiita mhere-mhere*)' – as is customary during Shona burials.[194]

The kugadzira ritual. Catholic priests have for several years been trying to 'christianize' the *kugadzira* (or *kurowa guva*) ritual. Some of their efforts, which amounted to little more than the 'consecration' of the sacrifical beast and the beer with holy water, were highly superficial. Such procedures were called *musande*, which more or less meant the sanctification of the traditional ritual. But these efforts did not really change the traditional connotations of the rite. The ritual was given a Christian cloak and no thorough confrontation between Christ and the *midzimu* took place. The result was that some of the rural Africans interpreted the Catholics' efforts as a vindication of practices which missionaries of other denominations condemned.

Kumbirai in recent years worked out a detailed Church ritual based on the various stages of the *kurowa guva* ceremony. His was a more penetrative attempt to christianize this key-ritual than any previous effort, but the incorporation of nearly all the procedures of the old rite nevertheless gave rise to doubts in Catholic circles. Consequently his '*Magadziro echiKriste*' (Christian ceremonies for accommodating the spirit of the deceased – see Appendix III) was circulated to the leaders of Mission stations for 'experiment' and comments, without the Bishop's Conference, as yet, having officially approved of it.[195] We are here dealing with a controversial issue, which has provoked the more conservative priests into writing strong-worded, polemic letters. Others, especially in the Chilimanzi reserve where Kumbirai conducted much of his research work, have actually carried on with the process of accommodation through the incorporation of some of Kumbirai's suggestions into the patterns of *musande* previously adopted.

The proposed rituals are regarded as supplementary to the burial rites and start off with a sprinkling of the deceased's house with holy water. God is

194. *Rules and Regulations*, p. 35, rule No. 133.

195. Kumbirai (personal communication) comments on the Bishop's Conference as follows: 'The bishops are interested and would like to see a good deal of adaptation being done, but they are conservative and afraid that people would rush ahead and produce something contrary to Christian principles.'

asked by the priest to 'drive all evil from within the house with the blessed water.' (See Appendix III, No. 1.) When the grain is produced for the beer brewing preparations of the *kugadzira*, the priest blesses it with *mvura yedonhodzo* (appeasing water) after the relatives of the deceased have 'prayed' to the deceased and other *midzimu* – in front of the pot-shelf (*rukuva*) in the house of the deceased as follows:

'N. [deceased], if you have not yet reached Mwari, where your relatives and all the saints are; if you are still in Purgatory, see this grain which we have brought so that we may gather the people who intercede on your behalf before Christ [*vanokunamatira kuna Kriste*] who has delivered you in order to call you to Himself in heaven where your relatives, the saints and the everlasting joy of heaven are. . . . N. and N. and N. [mentioning the dead relatives], this is the grain with which we have gathered the people so that they may cause your child to reach [*vasusukidze*] Mwari, where you are. If he is not there yet, ask Christ, his Redeemer, to take him out of Purgatory and to place him in heaven.' (Appendix III, No. 2 '*Kuburitsa zviyo*'.)

When the main ritual starts, the priest blesses the sacrificial animals (ox and goat) as well as the sacrificial beer. With each blessing he qualifies the specific object as symbolic of Christ's blood and its redeeming function. When, for instance, the sacrificial goat is sprinkled with holy water the priest prays to God: '. . . Let the blood of this goat be a sign of Your exoneration and deliverance of him [the deceased] from all his sins of fighting, of angry hatred, etc. . . .' (App. III, No. 3, 4 and 5.)

At the grave the deceased is told that his Christian friends have come to guide him to Mwari where all the others are. Once more the grave is sprinkled with water and incensated by the priest, after which a short Mass is conducted. (App. III, No. 6 and 9.)

During the name-giving ceremony the *muzukuru* or ritual officiant sprinkles holy water instead of beer on the future name-bearer, who is seated on a mat. He addresses him by the hereditary name of the deceased. The spirit of the deceased is told that it is he who has risen (*ndiwe vamutsiwa*: it is you that has been caused to rise). He is asked to take care of the new name-bearer so that he in turn may look after the affairs of the family for whom he has accepted the responsibility. When the deceased's *tsvimbo* (walking or hunting stick) is handed to the name-bearer, his sister's son says: 'Let this stick (or sticks) be symbolical of the stick of the cross with which you fight Satan.'

If inheritance of the deceased's wife does not militate against the Church law that prohibits a male from taking his *muramu* (wife's sister) as wife, the *nhaka* (inheritance) ceremony is allowed to take place. Before the *kudarika uta* (crossing the bow) ceremony the woman concerned states: 'In the name of God I jump over this bow to prove that I have not burnt the grave of my husband [i.e. I have not cohabited with another man]'. She then jumps across the bow saying: 'In the name of the Father [jump] and the Son [jump] and the Holy Ghost [jump].' Allowance is made at this juncture for the customary *pururudza* (ululation) and joyful dancing by the other participants. The *sendekauta* (acceptance of the inherited wife) part of the ceremony includes the dedication of beer to God and the deceased male by the person inheriting the widow (*mugari wenhaka*) with the words:

'With this beer I demonstrate to You, my God, and you, N. [the deceased], that I have become the guardian of your wife and of everything relating to your family. N., keep on being our intercessor before God that He may shield us from all spiritual and physical danger! Christ our Lord, teach us to bear our cross . . .' (App. III, No. 10: *Nhaka.*)

Considering the original function of the *kugadzira* ritual it should be kept in mind that two of the most prominent spiritual considerations were, firstly: the accommodation of the deceased's spirit, from a state of 'being in the bush' (*mudondo*) into the spiritual hierarchy of the ancestors; and secondly: the 'bringing back home' of the now officially recognized spirit to the living family, to act as its protector. It is clear that both these considerations still play a central role in the 'christianized version' of the ritual proceedings. The spirit of the deceased is now introduced into the Christian community of the deceased saints. God is asked to accept the deceased and the saints (including the *midzimu*!) are asked to accept and accompany the deceased person's spirit. Thus the spirit is officially incorporated into the divine spiritual hierarchy, which encompasses, so it would seem, the whole traditional hierarchy. The protective function of the deceased's spirit is also upheld, although the emphasis is now on his mediation, through a more direct contact with God than was the case in his traditional role as *mudzimu*, a mediation that paves the way for eternal life. In this way the traditional concept of *kurinda* (to protect or guard) acquires new meaning because the guardian spirit, 'standing at the door' to ward off evil, is now in the first place regarded as an intercessor. The analogy between the traditional six or more months of 'wandering in the bush' before the spirit was *gadzwa'd* and the Catholic concept of Purgatory has not escaped Kumbirai. He is convinced that this analogy can be used to elevate the concept of *ari mudondo* ('he is in the bush') to the Catholic version of temporal punishment.

Kumbirai emphasizes that such rituals cannot take place without the necessary explanation to the participants. 'If I perform the burial or the *kugadzira* rite according to the new ceremony', he says, 'I first of all give the people some explanation, some reason for adaptation. I tell them that Christ came not to destroy but to rebuild. I tell them that the Church says: "All good elements in any culture can make a good contribution to Christianity because we know that Christianity has been built on Hebrew, Greek and Roman cultures . . ." '

These efforts to assimilate traditional rituals met with great approval from Church members in the rural districts. Teachers Mutero and Paradza, two of the leading figures of the educational staff at Mutero, expressed their appreciation for the 'experimenting' work of the priests. The former holds that the old religion is on the way out 'but it nevertheless remains of the utmost importance, and it is safer for Christianity to be *related to* the African ways, because the Africans would otherwise feel that it is simply a European religion and that God belongs to the European.'[196] A clear indication of the variations in the appreciation of Africans for the newest forms of Catholic accommodation can be found in the remarks of these two teachers. Whereas Mutero spoke of *relating Christianity to* the African way of life, Teacher Paradza, who was more sensitive to the dangers of syncretism, emphasized that traditional rituals could only be incorporated into the Church in a *fully transformed state*.

In the clerical ranks an even wider difference of opinion was apparent. Rubio, a Spanish priest representing a small group of highly critical Church leaders, voiced his protest against a too lenient approach of the *mudzimu* cult: 'I came to the conclusion', he writes in Guti, 'that wherever there is a real [spirit] possession . . . it is the devil which possesses, not the soul of the departed person, and therefore the cult directed to it, is *devilish*.

. . . The *mudzimu* cult is not a mere honour . . . but the highest act of worship which the Africans can think of . . . it has been proved that such a cult is never referred to God [he deduces this from Gelfand's works] but it is directed to and ends in the *midzimu* themselves. A thing that is, of course, *idolatry*.'

Of Kumbirai's work he says: 'I was shocked to see that there is a strong tendency to baptize the system of *midzimu* almost by all means. The intention is good but the results may be very pernicious . . . the system itself cannot be baptized unless we want to make the devil himself a christian.'[197]

Hannan denies Rubio's allegation that the cult bears no relation to God. He suggests that it would be consistent with the whole traditional idea of mediation – also seen in the judicial process where the *muguri wemhosva* ('judge') is always addressed through a go-between – when Mwari is not approached directly but through an intermediary, and such intermediaries might very well be spirit elders of family or tribe, who are expected to transmit the

196. Teacher Mutero – personal communication at Mutero Mission.
197. Rubio, in *Guti*, June 1965, pp. 92-93.

requests of the living to God.[198] Also the reaction of Kuehne to Rubio's statement that the ancestral rites are idolatrous, represents the opinion held by a great number of priests in the field:

'... It is just as wrong to accuse wholesale all sacrifices in Bantu religion as idolatrous as it is wrong to accuse us Catholics of adoring saints and saintly objects. Just as a Catholic never adores a saint ... because he knows a saint is not God, so a Bantu always knows that a *mudzimu* is not God. This is, as I see it, the fulcrum to the solution of this problem.

Therefore, to my mind, we should not fight a negative fight against honouring the *midzimu*, but show them positively how to do it, e.g. replace their sacrifices with Holy Mass, *give them suitable prayers for and to the midzimu.* The latter may be heresy in your ears, but I do it all the same when I pray with our trainees before religious instruction: "*All our dead relatives, pray for us and help us to become good teachers* (my italics)." '[199]

In Kuehne's remarks we note once more the permissive and flexible spirit behind the Catholic idea of accommodation. On the basis of a 'positive' evaluation of the pre-Christian *mudzimu* cult – an evaluation which is justified in Catholic theology – it is consistent to arrive at a point where it becomes feasible to speak of '*suitable prayers* for and to the *midzimu*' and eventually to introduce such suitable prayers into the classroom.

The Catholic search for reconciliation contrasts sharply with the unyielding firmness of the Reformed Church. Far from allowing any communication (not to speak of prayer) with the ancestors, the DRC abolished *runyaradzo*, the one ceremony in their Church which aimed at adaptation to the traditional post-burial procedures, as soon as it became apparent that the ruralist members were turning it into a glorified *kugadzira* rite. Shiri himself was dissatisfied with the way in which the *runyaradzo* – initially intended to be a consolation ritual for the relatives of the deceased – was being conducted. According to him it began to resemble the *kugadzira* ritual. So it was abolished by the *Rangano Huru* (Church Conference) in 1965. Shiri's remark that the Church members at Alheit Mission were greatly dissatisfied when they heard

198. *Ibid.*, p. 97; also Hannan to Rubio.

199. *Ibid.*, pp. 116-117; Kuehne to Rubio. A more moderate critic of the newest trends of adaptation is Dr. Oskar Niederberger, who judges that the adapted *kugadzira* ceremonies go a bit too far. According to him there are two grave dangers involved: Firstly, that of misinterpretation from the traditional side: 'people will just interpret it in their own way if proper instruction is not given', and
Secondly, the danger of the Church, generally, being insufficiently aware of the absolute necessity of instruction to prevent misunderstanding (personal communication, 1967).

of this resolution reveals the reaction of a great number of people to the unyielding attitude of the DRC.

Ultimately it is not a matter of the one Church only repudiating and the other simply condoning what is left of the traditional religious past. In the foregoing pages I have tried to show that there are variations of approach, especially in the Catholic Church. It would be fair to state that there is also a number of DRC missionaries who are greatly interested in the problem of adaptation and indigenization (although few articles on traditional religion find their way into print, e.g. in the monthly DRC news bulletin *Munyai waShe* – Messenger of the Lord). These, too, are more flexible and tactful in their approach to traditional rites than their strict Church laws would express. It is also true that some of the African members of the DRC (African Reformed Church) themselves are in favour of the Church's policy of disallowing traditional rites, especially those who succeed in enduring the trials of life without visiting the diviners or resorting to ancestor worship. On the whole, it nevertheless appears that the DRC rejection of all that savours of *kupira midzimu* has done much to generate discontent. Although very few members are actually disciplined for their participation in traditional rites, the fact remains that DRC leaders attack such rites in public, and usually avoid contact with Africans when they are feasting in honour of the spirits. Some Africans therefore feel that the rejection of their old religion is another manifestation of the European's attitude of superiority, because it means the rejection or deliberate negation of something that was their very own, something that bears a direct relation with their very identity. This factor may not always be directly associated with the reasons for fission in the Churches, partly because it is less obvious than other causes of discontent, but it is nevertheless a potent source of separatism. That the DRC was bound to lose more of its members or potential members than the RCC because of a lack of dialogue with the 'traditionalist' – as pagan, sympathizer of Church member – needs no further elaboration.

TABLES 28-34

TABLE 28. *Figures on educational facilities and Church membership of Alheit (DRC) and Mutero (RCC) Mission stations*

Item	1960		1961		1964		1965		1966	
	Alh.	Mut.	Alh.	Mut.	Alh.	Mut.	Alh.	Mut.	Alh.	Mut.
Number of schools	24		24		24		24	16	24	16
Children in schools	4695		5240		4955		4815		4800	4252
Teachers	111	57	128	64	133	91	135	97	270	102
Catechumens	806	1470	500	1580	220	1200	204	1500	239	1400
Confirmations	110	1258	175	686	113	923	89	527	51	1114
Total Church membership	3120	3824	3360	4657	1200	6538	924	7235	1713	7995
Catechists									8	40

TABLE 29. *RSS and CST – What is the meaning of Roora (bride-price)?*

Opinions expressed by rural and urban adults on *roora*	Chingombe adults n	Chingombe adults %	Fort Victoria adults n	Fort Victoria adults %
It safeguards claims of male's lineage to married female's procreative powers *(kuwana chibereko:* to have children)	80	12	20	13
Token of appreciation to in-laws	51	8	25	16
Compensation to in-laws for upbringing of child (*uredzi hwavabereki*: comp. of in-laws)	293	44	32	20
Kuumba ukama: To strengthen the ties (between the families of husband and wife)	151	22	66	42
Secures wife's obedience	29	4	7	5
Enforces husband and wife's responsibility for children	5	1	–	–
Strengthens bonds between husband and wife	26	4	1	1
It is a means to put pressure on husband to keep wife well	4	1	4	3
No answer	31	5	2	1
Total	670	101	157	101

TABLE 30. *RSS and CST – Marriage: When is the union between two individuals officially accepted by the community?*

Opinions expressed by rural and urban adults	Rural adults (Chingombe) n	%	Urban adults (Fort Victoria) n	%	Rural DRC members n	%	Rural RCC members n	%
After *roora*	449	67	67	43	72	60	67	78
After agreement with father-in-law	124	19	48	31	17	14	10	12
After Church rite	34	5	28	18	19	16	1	1
After civil registration	4	1	–	–	1	1	–	–
When two individuals have agreed	23	3	11	7	3	3	3	4
After exchange of gifts	1	0	–	–	–	–	–	–
After *vatete* has officially handed over (*perekedza'd*) bride	1	0	1	1	–	–	–	–
Unanswered	34	5	2	1	9	7	5	6
Total	670	100	157	101	121	101	86	101

TABLE 32. *Shamhu (disciplinary) cases treated by the Alheit Church Council from 1958 to 1966.*

	European ministers					African ministers					
Nature of transgression	1958	1959	1960	1961	1962	1963	1964	1965	1966	Total	
Polygamy: men who took 2nd wives	5	5	2	–	–	–	–	–	–	12	170 (33%)
Adultery: males who 'damaged' young girls, etc.	6	15	12	11	6	4	9	15	7	85	
Males who *tizisa'd* (eloped) with their wives	17	8	3	16	5	7	6	1	10	73	
Females who were *tizisa'd* (eloped with husbands)	32	14	5	16	7	10	12	2	8	106	224 (43%)
Females who were *gargwa nhaka* (inherited)	2	–	1	–	–	–	1	–	–	4	
Adultery: Females (without intention of marriage)	8	28	19	17	16	4	5	10	7	114	
Beer-drinking males	23	6	3	–	2	–	1	4	1	40	66 (13%)
Beer-drinking females	9	6	7	1	1	–	–	1	1	26	
Men who attended Indpdt. Church activities	5	2	1	–	–	–	3	2	–	13	58 (11%)
Females who attended Indpdt. Church activities	1	3	13	1	–	–	9	6	7	40	
Males and females who visited prophets for healing	1	1	–	–	1	–	2	–	–	5	
Males and females who visited *nganga* for healing	–	–	–	1	–	–	–	–	–	1	
Total	109	88	66	63	38	25	48	41	41	519	100%

TABLE 31. *RSS and CST – When is sexual cohabitation permitted?*

Opinions expressed by rural and urban adults	Rural adults (Chingombe)		Urban adults (Fort Victoria)		Rural DRC members		Rural RCC members	
	n	%	n	%	n	%	n	%
After agreement by two individuals	43	6	11	7	4	3	6	7
After *roora*	403	60	57	36	67	55	59	69
When *roora* has commenced	8	1	–	–	1	1	1	1
When *tezvara* has agreed	112	17	29	19	13	11	10	12
After Church ceremony	52	8	35	22	22	18	3	4
After *vatete* has officially handed over (*perekedza'd*) bride	4	1	23	15	–	–	–	–
After civil registration	2	0	1	1	–	–	–	–
Unanswered	46	6	1	1	14	12	7	8
Total	670	99	157	101	121	100	86	101

TABLE 33. *Alheit: Disciplinary measures withdrawn 1958 – 1966*

Members restored	1958	1959	1960	1961	1962	1963	1964	1965	1966	Total	
Male beer drinkers	3	4	2	1	–	–	–	–	1	11	24
Female beer drinkers	2	–	9	1	–	–	–	–	1	13	
Adultery cases: males	5	11	9	6	7	6	8	4	4	60	152
Adultery cases: females	2	14	17	11	14	8	11	12	3	92	
Return from Indpdt. Church: males	1	–	–	1	–	–	–	–	1	3	13
Return from Indpdt. Church: females	1	–	7	–	–	–	–	–	2	10	
Totals	14	29	44	20	21	14	19	16	12	189	

24 out of 66 'beer drinkers' restored = 36%
152 out of 391 'adulterers' restored = 39%.
13 out of 58 'Separatists' restored = 22%.

TABLE 34. *Overall survey of DRC disciplinary measures, 1925–1965*

DRC – All presbyteries	1925	1930	1935	1940	1945	1950	1955	1960	1965
Members disciplined	62	96	85	93	224	467	503	851	685
Members restored	36	41	82	60	107	271	341	415	298

Part 2

The rise of the Southern Shona Independent Church movement

4

The Spirit-type Churches

For descriptive purposes the term Spirit-type or simply *Mweya* (Shona for Spirit) Churches will be used to distinguish prophetic movements which emphasize the inspiration and revelation of the Holy Spirit, from the non-prophetic Church groups. A wide range of prophetic groups, varying from semi-Messianic[1] to simple Zionist or Apostolic Churches – where the Church leadership does not usurp the mediating function of Christ – is included in this category. In order to present a coherent picture of the growth of a complex and widely proliferated phenomenon, the historic account will centre mainly on the experiences of the outstanding leaders of the Zionist and Apostolic movements. The development and nature of group leadership and group ideology has a direct bearing on the ultimate classification of each movement. The full details of leadership and doctrinal differences, however, are not included in the historical account so that, in the first place, a broad picture is obtained of the general trends of development and geographical spread.

It will be noted that Zionism among the Southern Shona only started spreading in the 1920's and Johane Maranke's Apostolic movement in the early 1930's. Ranger provides us with an interesting account of the early rise of what he calls 'Independency' in Southern Rhodesia.[2] His study, which is based on archival material, reveals 'that not a very great deal happened before 1930. There was no development of a strong and widely based Shona Independent movement [before 1930].'[3] The comparatively late rise of Independent movements among the Shona derives from a complexity of factors, such as the strict control by the Government on the movement of sectarian preachers – to which we refer in Chapter 6 – the conservative and inward-looking nature of Shona society, and the more limited initial contact with the South African

1. The term 'semi-Messianic' is used to indicate groups with Messianic tendencies. None of the surveyed groups can be classified as proper Messianic movements on the basis of the information accumulated. This subject will be dealth with in greater detail under the heading 'Church Leadership' in Volume 3.

2. Ranger in *Religion in Africa,* 1964, pp. 52-74.

3. *Ibid.*, p. 54.

Independent Churches through labour migration than was the case, for instance, with the more mobile Ndebele labour migrants. In so far as movements of a pentecostal nature did spread among the Shona before 1920, very little impact was made on the tribes surveyed in the southern districts. The *Original Church of the White Bird* (*Shiri Chena*) founded by Matthew Chigaga Zwimba in 1951 was a tribal Church 'the membership of which never extended beyond the Zwimba reserve.'[4] Zionism spread to Rhodesia only after the first World War when two Ndebele labour migrants, Mabhena and Petrus Ndebele, who had joined Mabilitsa's *Christian Apostolic Church in Zion* in South Africa, returned to Matabeleland and started propagating the new faith in the Insiza district.[5] If this early Zionist movement did expand beyond the borders of Matabeleland there are at present no significant traces left of such expansion in the Southern Shona districts. The *Apostolic Faith Church* was introduced in Rhodesia in 1918 by a certain Luttig, who had joined this pentecostal Church in South Africa. He employed Dingiswayo, a Nyasa by birth, whom Ranger describes as 'a man of real ability, and an effective preacher and teacher'[6] who had been educated at Livingstonia. Together they propagated the pentecostal message in the vicinity of Gatooma. Dingiswayo was soon fired by Luttig because of alleged misuse of Church funds. He then became overseer of the *Christian Catholic Apostolic Church in Zion* in Southern Rhodesia, after negotiations with this movement's representative in Johannesburg, but in 1923 he was deported to Nyasaland when the authorities became alarmed at the effect of pentecostalism on rural Africans. Luttig, in turn, was debarred from entering the Shiota reserve when he tried to reclaim the former members of the AFC who had followed Dingiswayo. In spite of these clashes with the Government both pentecostal movements survived and added more members to their numbers in the central and northern Shona regions. The AFC actually became well established and at a later stage undertook extensive evangelistic work among the Southern Shona from their base at Rufaro Mission. Apart from a virile congregation in the Mucheke township the AFC, which is still dependent on European leadership, was not represented in great numbers in the Gutu, Bikita, Ndanga and Chibi districts. In these regions its

4. *Ibid.*, p. 54. Ranger says that the very name of the Church (*Shiri Chena*) contained a double reference to Christian and traditional sources of authority. The white bird stood both for the dove of the Holy Spirit and for the traditional messenger of the High-God, Mwari, to mankind. This Church was effectively related to the then still vivid memory of the Shona Rebellions, by listing those martyrs who had been killed during the risings as martyrs in the Church.

5. *Ibid.*, pp. 63-64.

6. *Ibid.*, p. 64.

growth cannot be compared with the spectacular rise of the all-African Zionist and Apostolic movement we are about to describe. It can safely be concluded that this specific type of pentecostalism did not have a direct determining influence on the principal Southern Shona leaders of the Spirit-type Churches with which we are concerned. These men were in the first place attracted by the 'purely' African and Africanized version of pentecostalism which they encountered in South Africa.

1. THE RISE OF THE SOUTHERN SHONA ZIONIST MOVEMENT

The five principal characters around whom the Zionist movement developed in Rhodesia in the early 1920's are Moses Makamba and Mtisi, both vaNdau from Bikita and Melsetter respectively, David Masuka, a mu-Duma from Bikita-East, Andreas Shoko, a muMbire from Chibi, and Samuel Mutendi, a muRozvi from Bikita. Mutendi's Rozvi descent is of importance. This particular tribe, as we have seen in Chapter 1,[7] was superior to the other Shone tribes from a military and a tribal political point of view, since it was the only tribe which succeeded in establishing a centralized dynasty among the widely dispersed Shona tribes before the arrival of the powerful Ndebele. The Duma and Ndau tribes have the same totem, *Moyo* (heart), and are closely linked to the Rozvi tribe, but in the past they were of lesser significance as politically centralized groups. Mutendi's eventual wide influence and the acceptance by other Zionist leaders of his unwavering leadership in the face of much opposition in the initial stages of development, have at least some roots in his being a muRozvi of stature. He traces his descent through the royal houses of Makuwa, Mudengedzerwa and Chiruma Mushavi to the famous Rozvi *Mambos* (kings), Dyembewu and Chirisamuru.

Andreas Shoko, on the other hand, belongs to a much less powerful tribe, but the vaMbire are still known and highly esteemed for their priestly function in the Shona High-God cult,[8] a position which they have held for many generations. Of these initial leaders Mtisi's sphere of influence is primarily limited to the Melsetter and other eastern districts. I met only a few of his followers and made no special effort to reach his headquarters. David Masuka Sr. has died, and Makamba only starts playing a more prominent role as a secessionist leader at a later stage of Zionist development. Thus particular attention is

7. *Supra*, p. 18f.
8. See High-God cult; Chapter 2, p. 86.

directed to the experiences of Mutendi and Andreas Shoko, especially where it concerns the early beginnings of the Zionist movement.

a) *Contact with Mission Churches*

Apart from Mtisi, all these leaders had contact with the Dutch Reformed Church before they left for the Union of South African as labour migrants They all had two years of training at an early stage of missionary educational development when the basic effort was still directed at Bible study and the rudiments of reading and writing. They had therefore attained some reading ability and Bible knowledge from the Protestant angle. Masuka, Makamba and presumably Mtisi had no Catechetical training and never joined the DRC as full Church members. Makamba regards himself as having been converted to Christianity for the first time in 1921 when he was baptized as a Zionist. Their joining the Zionist movement, as such, therefore did not imply an actual breakaway from a Mission Church.

With Mutendi and Andreas it was different. They had become much more involved in the Mission Church life before leaving Rhodesia, since both of them had by that time served as 'teacher assistants' in the DRC rural schools at Gumunyu and Zunga respectively, and both were full communicant DRC members. Mutendi even acted as a preacher for a while. In the personal accounts of both leaders there are no direct traces of thwarted ambitions in the context of the Mission schools, but Andreas Shoko's employment as herd-boy on the farm of the District Commissioner at Chibi, before leaving for South Africa, suggests that he might formerly have been demoted as 'teacher assistant' and that his contact with Missions was then less direct than at first. Mutendi himself, as an ex-policeman with low educational achievements, did not have bright prospects in the educational field, and for a man of his ambition it was hardly likely that he would remain working in a position which offered so few possibilities. While 'teaching' at Gumunyu he already had visions of establishing his own African Church. Nevertheless he remained in contact with Rev. Malan of Pamushana Mission, under whose supervision he was working until he departed.

b) *Labour migrants meet the South African Zionists*

Mtisi, Makamba and Masuka were the first of the Shona leaders to join the South African Zionists in 1921. They worked in the vicinity of Pietersburg in the Transvaal, where they met Bishop Mhlangu, the founder of the *Zion Apostolic Church of South Africa.* This Church was newly founded after the *Zion Apostolic Church*, founded by Rev. le Roux and some African leaders in 1908, was subdivided into several schismatic bodies.[9] Makamba still remembers having met Rev. le Roux while working at Pietersburg. He particularly mentions Mhlangu's impressive personality and the Zionist ideology, based on a direct application of Biblical texts concerning Zion on the African Church, as the main factors which attracted him to this Church. Mhlangu was a man after their own hearts and he convinced them that the only way to real salvation was baptism in 'Jordan'. Thus they were all immersed in 'Jordan', a countryside river, and afterwards returned to Rhodesia, Mtisi in 1921, Makamba in 1922 and David Masuka in 1923.

Although Mtisi was the first to return, it is acknowledged that Masuka was appointed as 'minister' and therefore as senior representative of Mhlangu in Rhodesia. Mtisi and Makamba were appointed as evangelists. Since these leaders were engaged as labour migrants their original intentions were to return home after their economic aims – which invariably included the acquisition of sufficient money for bride-price (*roora*) purposes – had been achieved. Their return to Rhodesia at different periods seems to have been due to their financial achievements, rather than to competitive religious aims.

Mutendi reached the Transvaal at a later date than the above-mentioned leaders. He is the only leader who claims to have had a special calling to become a leader of a purely African Church, before meeting the South African Zionists. Several of the dreams which form the basis and justification of his calling are therefore referred to in the *Zion Christian Church Rungano*,[10] the handbook of Mutendi's Church. The events here recorded in Biblical verse form represent 'canonized history' with strong moral directives for the members of this Church. In Chapter 9 : 1[11] it is stated that Mutendi had his first significant dream in 1919 whilst working in the BSAP (British South African Police). An angel appeared and said: 'Look, I inform you that you will have your own Church in this country.' This dream both frightened and inspired him. As a result he started 'praying powerfully' and on occasion took the prisoners under his care to Church services. Shortly afterwards he dreamt that he possessed a house on an open plain where many children came to place their sheaves of hay around his own. The Biblical theme of Joseph

9. Sundkler, 1961, pp. 48-49.

10. *Rungano* literally means 'tale', but in this context conveys the meaning of 'Church History'.

11. *Zion Christian Church Rungano,* Salisbury, p. 9.

called to an important task is thus clearly reflected and the underlying ambition is evident. The interpretation of these dreams by a fellow policeman, one Rarimoni Mutevi, is canonized as follows: 'Your dreams indicate that you will become the leader of a big group of people, which is a Church, and you will gather in it very many people.'[12]

Soon the dreams were followed by spells of spirit-possession and speaking-with-tongues. These phenomena, apart from being frowned upon by the missionaries, were interpreted by fellow DRC members merely as forms of *shavi*-possession. Mutendi admits to having been confused by these spells at first because the nature of such seizures were similar to the traditional *shavi*-possessions; but once he had had similar experiences in the Zionist Churches in South Africa, he became convinced that it was not the 'spirits of this world' that visited him, but the Spirit of God. Mutendi bases this claim on 1 Corinthians 2 : 12-15. He furthermore saw (and still sees) his calling as similar to that of Moses (Exodus 3) and Isaiah (Isaiah 41 and 55).[13]

The dreams and spirit-possession continued during his stay at Gumunyu school and eventually culminated in the third canonized dream which occurred in 1922 when he and some friends were sleeping in the low-veld, on their way to the Transvaal. They had had a heated discussion about the doctrines and laws of the various Mission Churches before they went to rest. It was then that Mutendi dreamt once more of an angel coming to him. The 'Messenger' was draped in white and said to him: 'The Church about which I have been visiting you in the past is the Zionist Church. It is a good Church to stay in.' When he recounted the dream to his friends the following day they all commented that it was markedly similar to the dream Jacob had when he was on his way to Laban. By this time Andreas Shoko had already joined the group of travellers. As the junior of the group, he acted as the cook, a fact which had an important bearing on the eventual choice of Church leadership in South Africa and on the eventual inter-Church relations in Rhodesia. Of the canonized dreams the description of the third one contains the first explicit reference to a Zionist Church. It indicates that Mutendi had already taken note of the newly converted Zionists, who by that time had just started returning to Rhodesia. Convinced that God himself had called him to Zion, he continued his journey to the Transvaal. But in spite of his religious convictions the principal motive for this journey was 'to work in order to obtain cattle' (*kusevenza agotengawo ngombe*).[14]

12. *Ibid.*, p. 11.
13. *Ibid.*, p. 15.
14. *Ibid.*, p. 13.

After working for a year on a farm at Bronkhorstspruit, Mutendi and Andreas moved to Pretoria where they worked as bricklayers. In the African township where they lived they met members of the *Zion Apostolic Faith Mission* under the leadership of Eduard of Basutoland.[15] Having tried at first to conduct their own services in DRC fashion, they were soon attracted by the preaching of Enginasi Lekhanyane, the local leader of the ZAFM (Zion Apostolic Faith Mission). Apart from the tremendous personal influence of Lekhanyane and their pleasant surprise at the efficient way in which Africans could run a Church of their own, there were other aspects which appealed to the Rhodesians:

First, this Sotho Church had found a *mythical charter* in the Bible. Andreas Shoko relates that the Sotho Zionists used to ask them whether they could find 'Dutch Reformed Church' in the Bible. Apparently the historical background of the Mission Churches, such as that of the DRC with which they were familiar, could hardly have had any direct existential value in these circumstances and the direct link of an African Church with the Primitive Christian Community of the New Testament, based on the literal interpretation by Africans of such texts as Rev. 14 : 1, Rom. 11 : 26 and John 12 : 12, was most appealing. Against the traditional background of the importance attached to a name – as we have seen, for example, in the case of a deceased father's name devolving upon his senior son as the representative of the dead man's status – this preoccupation with a charter, through the name of the Church itself, is understandable. Jesus Christ, the Lamb of Mt. Zion (Rev. 14 : 1), seemed to be closely related to them now. His presence was 'extended' more directly through the name 'Zion' – and thus with a movement of Africanized

15. See Zionist Genealogical table. Sundkler (1961, p. 48) says: 'The initial force behind this [Zionist] movement was an apocalyptic Church in the United States, the Christian Catholic Apostolic Church in Zion, founded in 1896 by John Alexander Dowie, the 'First Apostle and General Overseer'. The main teaching of the Church was 'divine healing', 'triune immersion' and the conviction that the second coming of the Lord was 'near at hand.'
Bishop Bryant of the CCAC in Zion visited South Africa in 1904 and baptized the first group of Africans into the Church at Johannesburg. A European, Rev. P. L. le Roux, also joined the movement. Through the influence of Pentecostal and Apostolic Faith missionaries the 'Baptism of the Holy Spirit' received a strong emphasis and in its modified form the Church of Rev. le Roux and the first grouw op African adherents were called the *Zionist Apostolic Church*. From this initial body a great number of Zionist offshoots emerged. Mhlangu, a Zulu, started with the *Zion Apostolic Church of South Africa* and Eduard of Basutoland branched from him to form the *Zion Apostolic Faith Mission*. It is with these two Zionist Churches that the Rhodesians first came into close contact.

worship – than it would have been if His presence became tangible only through a haze of foreign and European impregnated history. Through this new name, and because of the charter they derived from it, the identification with the Lamb of Mt. Zion was both simplified and much more direct for God's black children of Africa.

Secondly, this Church had *Mweya* (Spirit). Whereas in DRC circles Mutendi had found opposition and criticism of his spells of '*shavi*-possession', he now found appreciation and encouragement. Once his charism of speaking-with-tongues was recognized by the new group as being derived from the Holy Spirit, he was virtually qualified to be a future Church leader. Furthermore, the Zionist prophetic activities with their revelatory spells of Spirit-possession were familiar against the background of Shona divination. The inclusion in the Church of these indigenized practices – syncretic, yet felt to be truly Christian – fulfilled a basic religious need and was to become one of the main pivots of Mutendi's popularity in Rhodesia.

Thirdly, it was explained by the Sotho preachers that Baptism could only have its fullest meaning when Jesus Christ was 'followed into Jordan'. Conversion and Rebirth would otherwise remain incomplete. This literal interpretation of the 'law' of the New Testament somehow corresponded with the strict application of tribal laws as a condition for social well-being in the past, and the baptismal ceremony itself resembled a purification rite.

Mutendi and Andreas's isolation from the Missionary Church had at this stage become complete. Mutendi recalls that two letters, written by his friends during this period to Rev. Malan to find out whether he was allowed to continue preaching in spite of his '*shavi*-possessions', were never answered. Emotionally and spiritually he and Andreas had come to rely on their Zionist friends. They had a growing conviction that conversion in the Dutch Reformed Church was as yet incomplete. Had they not received divine guidance through dreams that they should join the Zionist Church? In 1923 they were therefore led to the Zionist 'Jordan' – a small river outside Pretoria – and baptized by Enginasi Lekhanyane as Zionist members of the ZAFM. Andreas relates of this great event: 'We went into the river together after we had confessed our sins. Mutendi was possessed by the Holy Spirit that same day and he spoke with great power. I had to wait a full year before the Spirit entered into me. I often dreamt that I was filled by the Spirit, but it would not "come out" [*buda*] properly.'

Whereas Mutendi had several directive dreams before joining Zionism, Andreas began to have them shortly afterwards. The most important of these he recalls as follows:

'I dreamt that I was climbing a high mountain. When I reached the summit

I suddenly came across a lot of baboons. These were so terrified when they saw my white face that they all fell over a ledge. When I later arrived at the foot of the mountain I found the baboons lying there, dead. When I told the prophets of my dream they said that I would become filled with the Holy Spirit – hence the white face! – and then drive the evil spirits out of many people.'

The dreams of both Mutendi and Andreas reflect their aspirations at certain periods: the former wanting to become the leader of his own African Church, and the latter wanting the charismatic powers of exorcism, which, in the new movement, was one of the most important qualifications for Church leadership.

Mutendi was chosen as 'Zionist emissary to Rhodesia' at a special Church meeting shortly after his new conversion. He was nominated by Andreas Shoko because of his seniority and possibly also because he was a muRozvi. Andreas is said to have stated, 'You must all vote for Mutendi because he is my senior [*mukuru*] for whom I have cooked food during our journey from Rhodesia.'[16] Towards the end of 1923 Mutendi returned to Rhodesia in his new capacity as a Zionist preacher. He was urged by the South African Zionist leaders to contact David Masuka in Bikita, and one of the Zionist prophets instructed him to start his preaching activities by reading Luke 3, which refers to the work of John the Baptist. In the *Rungano* it is stressed that he was sent back to Rhodesia with a definite religious assignment. It was not the mere home-coming of a commoner labour migrant, because 'Samuel came here carrying the Word only, without blankets or extra clothes . . . As Moses was afraid when he was sent, so he [Mutendi] was very much afraid.'[17] Andreas stayed behind in the Transvaal for another nine years before he, in turn, started his campaign in the Chibi district in 1931. Mutendi's spiritual life had therefore undergone an earlier and more radical change than that of his friend, in that he regarded himself as a Gospel messenger, charged to return to his country with a full-time Church assignment.

c) *Initial growth of the Zionist movement in Rhodesia*

Mtisi, the first of the Zionist evangelists to return to Rhodesia, started preaching in the Melsetter district. The homestead from which he operated was called 'Zion City'. Makamba and Masuka, who lived in adjacent chiefdoms in the

16. *Rungano*, p. 14.
17. *Ibid.*, p. 15.

Bikita district, could co-operate with one another closely, but Mtisi, although he acknowledged Masuka's senior leadership in Rhodesia, was from the start only loosely affiliated. These three leaders at first caused unrest among the ruralists as they moved about in the reserves on their preaching tours. Their activities proved to have a special attraction for females, as a result of which some suspicious male traditionalists accused them of disrupting family life. They also met strong opposition from the tribal authorities, who kept administrative officials informed about their movements. Consequently both Masuka and Mtisi were detained for a short period at Buhera. Without appropriate legislation the administrative authorities could not fully restrict the movements of roving preachers, but they could prosecute religious leaders on the grounds of seditious preaching (a matter which will be dealt with more fully in Chapter 6). Investigations were therefore conducted into the nature of the new Church's evangelistic activities, which resulted in some detentions.

The opposition from Missions, Administration and chiefs dampened the first wave of enthusiasm among both leaders and followers. It was even rumoured att he time that Mtisi and Masuka had backslid (*kuheduka*) and had reverted to the traditional forms of worship. When Mutendi arrived late in 1923, he visited Masuka who, according to the *Rungano*, was like a man who 'had fallen back onto the world because of his fear of imprisonment.'[18] Masuka took heart again and for some time accompanied Mutendi on preaching tours. It must be noted that, although they belonged to the different Zionist Churches of Mhlangu and Eduard of Basutoland, the Rhodesian Zionists at this stage felt their Church to be one.

Mutendi's first important sermon was delivered soon after his arrival, when he attended a DRC Sunday service at his old school at Gumuyu. The teachers requested him to tell them of his experiences in the Transvaal.

'He stood up and preached with great power from Luke 3, as he was told to do by the prophets. He preached at length and only from that chapter. Many believers were possessed by the Spirit. The people present got frightened and some of them ran away, saying: "That man arouses *zvitebwe*" [vengeful spirits which cause destruction to the cattle of their enemies by entering a maneless lion and then proceed to kill] . . . Some people laughed when they saw the others getting possessed by the Spirit . . . From that day, when he had preached and the people had laughed at the Spirit, he never stopped preaching the Word of God, and was greatly strengthened by that same Spirit.'[19]

In this first public appearance the theme that stood central in Mutendi's

18. *Ibid.*, p. 19.
19. *Ibid.*, pp. 17-18.

sermon was the work of John the Baptist. The accompanying manifestation was Spirit-possession. These two typically Zionist characteristics, in addition to faith-healing through the laying-on of hands, at that time indicated the new 'Church program' on which this 'man of God' could be expected to elaborate in the future.

i) *Campaigning methods*

At first the simplest way of spreading the new message in the rural areas was by travelling on foot from one village to another, preaching and baptizing new converts. Farm life in the reserves permitted short spells of absence of males from the main agricultural activities. Villages in the immediate vicinity of the leader's homestead could be reached throughout the year. Longer trips could be afforded during the slack months before the coming of the rains. As soon as his own polygamous household was established the leader was able to relegate farming responsibilities to wives and children, which in turn freed him for evangelistic activities.

The initial efforts to obtain a following seem to have been directed at the family and extended family groups. It is not incidental that Mutendi concentrated first of all on close or distant relatives in the Rozvi sector of Bikita, and that the first mass baptism of 25 members took place in the predominantly Rozvi village of Mupamawonde. In this way the senior members of the new movement were almost without exception recruited from among relatives. These close associates formed a nuclear body of followers, from whose ranks appointments to the key-positions in the leadership structure could be made, when the growing movement made it necessary to delegate control over distant congregations. It would be wrong to assume, however, that the Zionist Churches developed along purely mono-tribalistic lines. The rural population in Chingombe had become, as we have seen, so diversified that even at an early date these Church groups could not have been referred to as purely Rozvi, Duma or Ndau. If, on the other hand, the term 'tribe' is used in the sense of all the inhabitants living within a chiefdom (*nyika*), one may say that the Shona Zionist movement, in the initial phase, represented 'tribal Churches' because the main groups of followers lived in the same chiefdom as did their leader. As soon as substantial numbers of people living in other districts started joining the different Zionist Churches, however, the movement, having outreached the limits of kin-group, local ward and chiefdom, took on a multi-tribal character.

The fact that Masuka and Mtisi were already detained in Buhera (a reserve a long way from where they lived) before the arrival of Mutendi shows that from the start the activities of these leaders went beyond the boundaries of their district and chiefdom. Bishop Masuka Jr. states that his father started working in Bikita, Zaka and Buhera, but that he soon went on longer eastward journeys, past Fort Victoria to Mashaba, and southward as far as Belingwe and Nuanetsi. On such trips the leader would be accompanied by fellow Church members, singing, dancing, preaching or bearing witness to the leader's healing powers. On special campaigns his whole family came along to attract people to the services by clapping hands and dancing. The incentive for such journeys was quite often that sick people, who had heard of Zionist healing, had requested the leader's help. Therefore, the more evident the mystical power and the charismatic qualities of the prophetic leader became, the greater his popularity and the more rapid the expansion of his Church.

In this respect Mutendi became the outstanding figure. He was believed to have the mystical powers of healing, exorcising evil spirits, granting fertility to women and of making rain. The *Rungano* records several miracles performed by him. At Magara he healed the first patient through the laying-on of hands, at Mupamawonde he laid hands on a woman who had been barren for 10 years, thereby making it possible for her to have a child, and at Rukuni he is reputed to have raised a young girl of the chief's house from the dead. In Chapter 18 of the *Rungano* we find the following description of the great miracle at Rukuni's village:

'(Verse 2) On a certain day a messenger reached Mutendi with a message that Miriam, one of his Church members, had died after falling from a tree. He then said, "Come and bury our Church member who has died!" Both of them departed.

(Verse 3) When they reached Rukuni the coffin had already been made, but the prophet Petro Mamvura had ordered them not to bury the deceased as she would be raised from death. He told the people, "Mwari revealed to me that He wants to demonstrate His power to the people in order to assure them that He is God and that He has sent His Messenger [Mutendi] to proclaim His Kingdom."

(Verse 4) Samuel Mutendi then said to the child's parents: "We cannot bury this child, because she has not really died." Thereupon the elders [*vakuru*] answered angrily, saying, "You are an impostor. How will you raise a child who has been dead for quite a while?" They then threatened him with guns and said that they would shoot him if he did not succeed in raising the child. But he, Samuel Mutendi, entered the house where the corpse lay to pray for the child while the others waited outside. Since she was the daughter of Chief Rukuni there were guns to fire the customary shots at the funeral.

(Verse 5) The men with the guns repeatedly threatened, "If you do not succeed today in raising the child, we will shoot you!" The believers outside also prayed until Mwari performed a mighty deed by raising the child. This is proof of the complete power of God. Samuel then returned the child to her parents. All the people, heathens and believers, praised the Lord.'[20]

From this narrative it is evident that Mutendi places primary emphasis on the *power of God* and the *honour of God*, when it comes to healing or performing other miracles. Such deeds are amplified with Biblical texts such as James 5 : 14, where the ill are exhorted to go and be prayed for by the Church elders. It is often stated that the God, Mwari, did all these things through the hands of Mutendi. The explanation usually attached to the great preoccupation with healing is that Jesus Christ would never have had such a great following if he had not healed people. *Rungano* 46 : 6 reads: 'It has not been written [in the Bible] that now that Jesus had preached with great force many people became converted because of His preaching, or that they followed Him because they wanted to hear the teaching of Mwari, but that many people followed Him because they wanted to be healed;' and verse 10 has it that 'God knew that even if Jesus preached, knowing everything, the people would not believe in Him, but if He was given the power to heal the sick, the people would accept His teaching, because, no matter who the person is, everybody wants to live.' *Healing therefore became a recognized method of convincing the people of this man's mission.*[21] From all over the country people with ailments started flocking to Mutendi's homestead (see map 3), so that a whole compound of huts had to be built for these patients.

ii) *The first major schism*

In 1925 Minister Lekhanyane summoned Mutendi and other Zionist leaders to come to the Transvaal because of a threatening schism between himself and Eduard. The problems were twofold:

1) From an administrative point of view Eduard's Church had grown to proportions beyond his own immediate control. Supplying all the newly appointed ministers and evangelists with certificates from Basutoland posed a problem. Lekhanyane, who had become the most influential leader in the Transvaal, sensed that reorganization of the ZAFM Church was imminent, and he intended doing it himself.

2) Lekhanyane's relationship with Eduard had suffered because Lekhanyane had breached the ZAFM constitution by taking a second wife. Al-

20. An analysis of Mutendi's healing and other miracles will be presented in Volume 2.

21. Prophetic healing activities prove to be one of the strongest attractions of the Zionist and other Spirit-type Churches.

though the ZAFM took a more tolerant view on the issue of polygamy at a later stage, this offence was a serious one at the time. But these issues may very well have been secondary to the driving powers of leadership ambition. If one considers the phenomenal growth of Lekhanyane's Church after the schism, as well as the remarks of Masuka Jr. and Makamba that the central issue was that of leadership (*ukuru*), it seems that the primary cause of fission was indeed that a sub-leader wanted to take control of what he sensed was rapidly becoming a mass movement.

A delegation under the leadership of Mutendi set out on foot for the Transvaal. Makamba was sent as the representative of Masuka's Church, its leader being ill at the time. Joram Gwai, Mutendi's nephew and future secessionist leader, together with several other men and two women, accompanied Mutendi. At Messina Joram was detained and stayed behind; at Pietersburg Makamba left the group to go and see Mhlangu, and so the party grew smaller until eventually only Mutendi and the two women reached Pretoria. There they participated in a big Zionist conference with representatives from other Independent Churches. On this occasion, Lekhanyane presented the new Constitution of what was to become the *Zion Christian Church*.

Andreas Shoko, who was then still working in the Transvaal, refused to join Lekhanyane, but, together with Pietros (Lekhanyane's younger brother) and Majaula, two prominent South African leaders of the ZAFM whom he had meanwhile befriended, remained loyal to Eduard of Basutoland. Makamba's absence was sufficient indication of his disinclination to join the new movement. Masuka had probably instructed him to seek Mhlangu's advice on the latest developments of the Zionist Churches in South Africa and on the advisability of following Mutendi into the new Church. Thus Mutendi knew that, of the Rhodesia Zionist leaders, he would stand alone if he joined Lekhanyane. He states that he himself had been uncertain until one night, when he had a dream which made a decision possible. He dreamt that he saw two white-washed houses, one belonging to Lekhanyane and the other to Eduard. Then he heard a voice asking: 'If many people in Nyasaland were to be converted and baptized, would they then have no God?' He replied: 'They would indeed have a God!' The next day he was 'surprised' to hear Lekhanyane's interpretation of the dream, revealing that he, Mutendi himself, was the man of Nyasaland and that his God was the true God. With this prospect of further Zionist expansion beyond the borders of Rhodesia in which he himself would take an active role, and with the conviction that the dream was God's revelation to him, Mutendi felt guided to join Lekhanyane. This step had its rewards. Mutendi was immediately ordained as a minister, which meant that he then had the same status as David Masuka, the highest ranking

Rhodesian Zionist of those days. He also accompanied Lekhanyane to the Government Buildings in Pretoria to have the name of their Church registered in the 'books of the Government'. About this occasion he commented: 'The Europeans were greatly surprised that Africans could run a Church themselves and "make it stand".'

Apart from some superficial changes, such as the wearing of uniforms instead of the colourful Zionist garments, the adoption of different dances and special drums for worship and other minor matters of form, the new Church hardly differed from the other Zionist groups. Healing, Spirit-possession and Baptism remained the characteristic activities. What did make a difference was that Mutendi returned to Rhodesia with more prestige than he formerly had and with less binding obligations to the other Zionist leaders. He had, in effect, come back to build his own Church!

iii) *Growing autonomy of the Rhodesian Zionists*

During the early stages of development, the Zionist leaders tried to keep regular contact with their superiors in South Africa. Correspondence was sporadic but regular visits took place by the leaders themselves or by delegations. Mutendi made several trips to see Lekhanyane, he modelled his Church along lines similar to Lekhanyane's and remained loyal to him until the latter's death in 1948. At this time it had become difficult to obtain a pass to travel to South Africa. Mutendi was actually refused permission to attend Lekhanyane's funeral. With this personal link between the two founding leaders of the ZCC gone, and with the stiffening control of Zionist movements by the Rhodesian Government, the gulf between the ZCC in the Transvaal and its branch in Rhodesia inevitably widened. In 1953, Eduard Lekhanyane, who had succeeded his father, paid Mutendi a visit to strengthen their ties, but this was the last personal contact they had. Mutendi had become a powerful leader in his own right. He still acknowledged the link with the Transvaal Church, but his Church had in fact become fully autonomous. Was he not one of the founders of the Church and senior to Eduard? To him the successor of Lekhanyane represented a 'young one' (*muduku*) whom he respected as the son of his friend, but who had no real authority over the Church in Rhodesia.

This pattern of gradual severance of direct relations with the South African Zionists also applies to the other Rhodesian factions. Andreas Shoko, for instance, returned twice between 1931 and 1940 in order to report to Eduard of Basutoland on the growth of the ZAFM in Rhodesia. But after Eduard's death and the succession to his position by Bishop Johane, his eldest son, Andreas had no personal contact with his superior in South Africa. Andreas's recognition of the new leader in the Transvaal had no direct consequence for the organization of his Church.

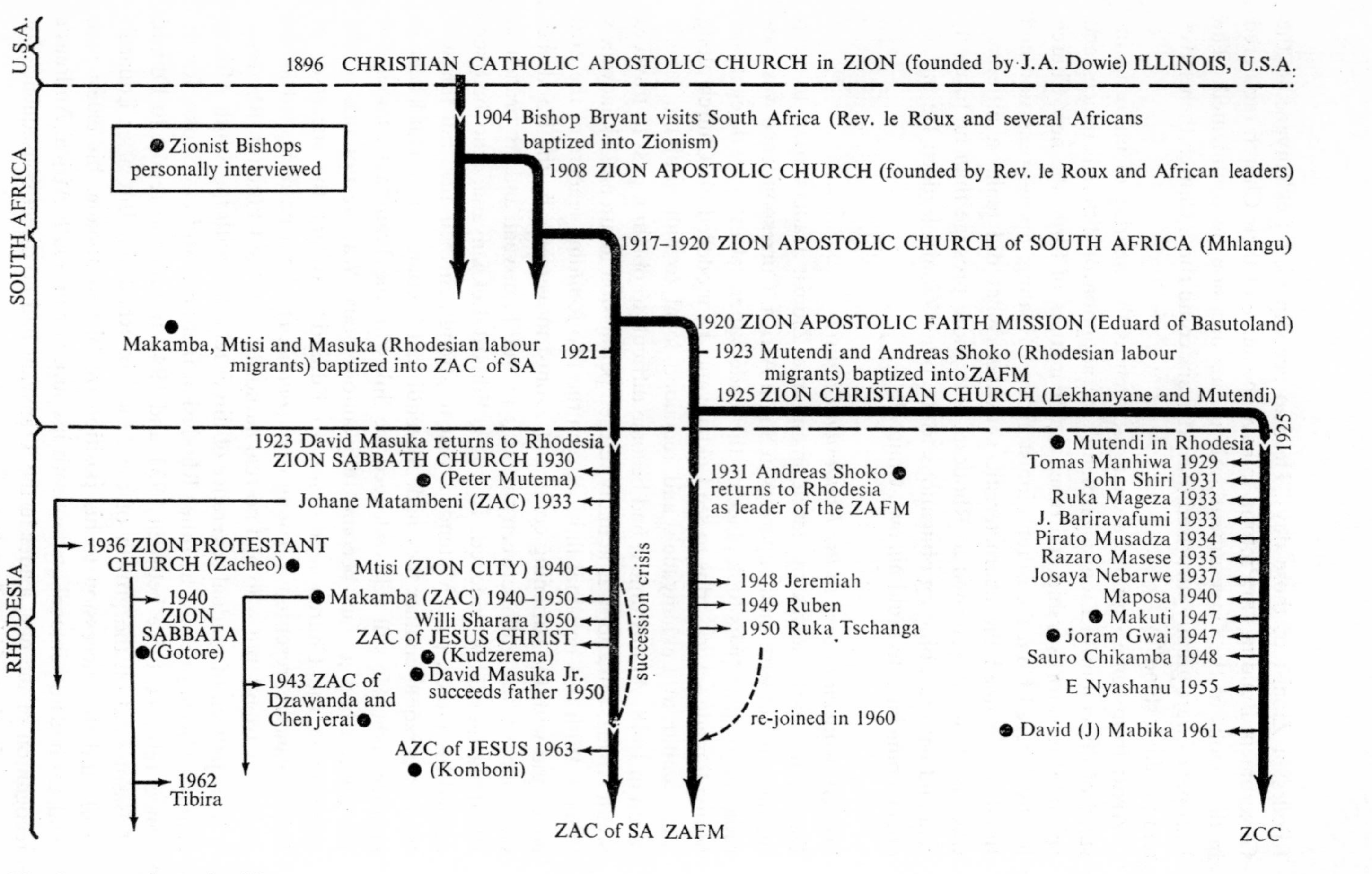

Zionist genealogical table

Both Makamba and David Masuka visited Mhlangu regularly during the first years of building their Church, but this did not mean more than Mhlangu's having some 'advisory control' over his congregations in Rhodesia. At an early stage of development Mtisi, Makamba and Masuka considered themselves independent enough to consecrate each other as bishops. In times of schismatic crises, however, advice and recognition were sometimes solicited directly from the Transvaal leaders by the contending secessionist leaders. Thus it happened that Makamba, who had become semi-independent of Masuka since 1940, sought to strengthen his ties with Mhlangu's leaders at a time when a radical severance of ties with Masuka seemed imminent. He therefore visited the Transvaal in 1949 when Mukwenya was installed as President of the *Zion Apostolic Church of South Africa* in the place of the late Mhlangu. In 1950, when Masuka died, Makamba based his bid for future leadership of the Rhodesian branch of this Church on his own reordination as a bishop, which had taken place at the hands of Mukwenya during his (Makamba's) visit to South Africa. This claim that his own leadership was being recognized by the 'Mother Church' in the Transvaal enhanced his prestige in the eyes of local members and enabled him to complete the schism in which the majority of Masuka's followers supported him. David Masuka Jr. had to fall back on the assistance of Mutendi for his consecration as a bishop and successor to his father. He nevertheless claims that the Mhlangu leaders in the Transvaal recognized his leadership by letter.

At present, and from the point of view of organization, these ties have become completely severed. As we have seen this severance was due mainly to the fact that loyalty among these Church leaders was experienced primarily as a personal matter. Once the Church's founder had fallen away, the Rhodesian leaders felt less bound by the link to the Mother Church. Additional complications were the geographical distance, which made regular contact difficult, and circumstantial factors such as the curtailment of the movement of certain Zionist leaders to and from South Africa. The maintenance of these ties could have a pragmatic value, as we have seen in Makamba's case. Ideologically, however, identification with the South African Zionists still remains of the utmost importance because it represents the immediate link with the Primitive Christian Church. The vital question for a Zionist leader still is: Who laid hands on you when you were ordained? If the answer is: Lekhanyane, Mhlangu, or any of the other recognized leaders in South Africa, the status of such a leader is accepted as legitimate and of a higher order than that of those who were ordained by local sub-leaders. In the *Rungano* Mutendi traces the origin of his Church through Lekhanyane and Eduard, whose roles he emphasizes, to the Zionist Churches in America, and from these through the early Churches in Europe right back to the first Christian congregation in Jerusalem.

d) *Schisms and the geographical distribution of the Separatist bodies*

i) *The Zion Apostolic Church of South Africa*

This Church, under the leadership of David Masuka, suffered its first schism as far back as 1930. Peter Mutema, a muDuma of Bikita who had joined this Church only a year before, decided that it was of great importance to worship the Lord on the Sabbath Day. According to his interpretation of the Bible the Sabbath was the only proper day of rest. Doctrinal issues therefore in this case seem to have been the main reason for fission. Bishop Mutema himself states that he had several discussions with Masuka on this matter. When they could not agree they decided to part in friendly fashion, and as a result the *Sabbath Zion Church* (see Zionist genealogical table) came into being. The continuation of a cordial relationship between the leaders of the two Churches up to the present day and the fact that Masuka even consecrated Mutema as an independent bishop when they separated suggest that the leadership issue as an end in itself was not a primary cause for separation. The membership of the SZC has grown to approximately 700 members – women and children included – with 4 bishops, 15 ministers, 9 evangelists and several junior officials. Members are to be found in the tribal areas of Bikita, Gutu and Buhera, each district having its own centre for the celebration of the annual *Paseka*.[22]

In 1933, Johane Matambeni, a muNdau from Chipinga, broke away from the *Zion Apostolic Church of South Africa* with several other Ndau Church leaders. They retained the same name for their Church as before. As reasons for this schism mention is made of the misbehaviour of Bishop David Masuka who breached the Church law in taking a second wife and in giving way to the pressure of a number of subordinate leaders who had pressed for a more lenient approach to the use of beer by Church members. Important as these factors might have been in terms of Church law, the decisive reason for the rift seems to have been *tribalistic*. Matambeni not only shifted the headquarters of his faction to Chipinga, which is Ndau territory, but he also managed to persuade a number of the most influential Ndau Church leaders to follow him. Of these Zacheo was one. Zacheo explained: 'I favoured Johane Matambeni

22. *Paseka:* 'Passover'. This term is used for the three major Church festivals each year. The general procedure of such festivals will be described in Volume 3.

20. Rev. Samuel Mutendi listening to a sermon of one of his subordinate Church officials.

21. At Zion City chiefs from Gutu, Ndanga and Bikita listen attentively while the 'man of God' (Mutendi) preaches.

22. Zionist bishop, Andreas Shoko, attending a Sunday service near his homestead in the Chibi district.

23. Bishop Andreas Shoko at work in plain clothes.

above David Masuka because he spoke chiNdau fluently and we could therefore understand him better.'[23]

When Matambeni died in 1936 a *leadership-succession crisis* arose, with Zacheo and Juwere as the main contestants. As was the case with Makamba, direct assistance was sought from the South African Zionists while by-passing other senior Zionist leaders in Rhodesia. Several letters were written to Mhlangu of which the outcome is not fully clear, but Zacheo claims that Mhlangu favoured him as the leader. An additional factor, migration from one tribal area to another, which played a role in several of the minor schisms, came into play at this stage. Zacheo migrated to Nyamande in the Gutu district, consolidated his leadership amongst the Church members to the west of Chipinga and then founded what he prefers to call the *Zion Protestant Church.* The name signifies the protest of a rather fanatical character against the lax application, by some of his Zionist predecessors, of the Church laws on marriage, beer drinking and his own 'law' on education. In the years after 1936 he stiffened his opposition to the education of the children of his followers in Mission schools. This move led in turn to a further schism, when the more lenient leader, Tibiria, broke away in 1962. It had obviously become precarious to follow a leader whose uncompromising attitude in the field of education led to head-on clashes with the Administration which embarrassed the position of his followers in relation to the authorities. Zacheo's following consequently dwindled away. At present his Church members, some 300 to 400 people, are widely dispersed in the Gutu, Zaka, Bikita, Chilimanzi and Buhera districts. He claims to have a congregation in both Bulawayo and Salisbury. He has only one minister (an elder full brother) apart from two evangelists working in each of the districts mentioned.

Nehemia Gotore, a Rufura kinsman of Gutu, founded his own *Zion Sabbath Church* in 1940. After two years of catechism in the DRC he joined Masuka in 1934, then followed Zacheo for a few years before he decided to organize his 'own' Church. Like Peter Mutema he gives *doctrinal reasons*, concerning the Sabbath day, for his secession. Having started with only four other Zacheo-followers, he gained a considerable following in the Gutu, Bikita and Buhera districts. The majority of his followers are living in the Munyikwa sub-chiefdom in the eastern tip of Gutu where the bishop himself resides. His Church membership amounts to approximately 1,000 people with a well-organized leadership structure of 5 bishops, 15 ministers and a whole group of representative sub-leaders.

Between 1940 and 1950 Masuka's ZAC of SA experienced a major setback.

23. Personal communication, 1966.

The trouble started in 1940, when Masuka was accused by his fellow Churchmen of a serious breach of Church law by allowing his third wife to be taken by his eldest son.[24] Whatever the true state of Masuka's domestic affairs, the three most influential bishops, representing the nuclear Zionist congregations in the Bikita, Buhera and Melsetter districts, regarded it as sufficient reason to dissociate themselves from their leader. To Bishop Mtisi of Melsetter it merely meant the final severance of an affiliation which had been a loose one from the outset. He had been directly responsible for the conversion of the majority of Melsetter Zionists and felt entitled to an independent leadership in his own district. In practice the schism meant the continuation of ordinary Church life for the Melsetter members, under the same name (also referred to as the *Zion Apostolic City*) – to which the additional distinction 'Zionists of Mtisi' (*vaZioni vaMtisi*) was added – and the administering of the Sacraments during the annual *Paseka* ('Passover' feast) by the local leader, Mtisi, instead of David Masuka.

The relationship of Bishop Makamba (Bikita) and Bishop Willi Sharara (the most influential Zionist bishop at the time in Buhera) to their leader had been of a different nature from that of Mtisi. In spite of their complaints they remained loyal to David to the extent of attending the annual *Paseka* at his headquarters until he died in 1950. Only then did they finally break away. It must be noted that a major crisis usually arises in all these Churches at the death of the founder leader, around whose person the movement had started. Makamba is a typical example of the senior leader who, having converted many members in co-operation with the principal leader, claims the leadership of those whom he feels to be 'his own followers' when the senior son of the deceased leader inherits his father's position and starts exerting his influence over the widely dispersed congregations. Through the new status, achieved by reordination in 1949 in the Transvaal, in addition to his role as co-leader in the initial period of Church expansion, Makamba became the favoured successor of David, especially in Bikita. Several junior officials with their congregations from other districts joined him in the course of time. The numerical strength of his followers can safely be estimated at 4,000 to 5,000. The main spheres of his influence lie in Bikita, Buhera and Gutu, with smaller groups in the Zaka and Victoria districts. He has 30

24. It was alleged that after having paid full *roora* for this woman, Bishop Masuka – hampered by old age and therefore incapable of impregnating his new wife – allowed her to cohabit with his son. This is not an unknown custom, though practised with great discretion to avoid undue publicity. Under such circumstances the woman concerned does not really become the son's wife.

junior bishops, called *vaongamiri*,[25] each of them assisted by evangelists, keepers and councillors (*vatongi*).

Willi Sharara would still have accepted David Masuka Jr. as leader had the latter consented to his consecration as archbishop at the hands of the junior bishops of his own Church. This, however, would have prejudiced the position of the new leader, because Willi Sharara and the other bishops had all been subordinate to his father. How could the son of Masuka as representative of his father and as the actual 'embodiment' of the deceased – and being so closely identified with his father's spirit from the traditional point of view – accept ordination from his junior? He chose the less embarrassing way of asking Mutendi of the ZCC, a close friend of his father's, to conduct the ceremony. Sharara refused to recognize this procedure. He resented the fact that during sermons Mutendi used to harp on the weakness shown by the deceased Masuka in those first years of trouble with the Administration, thereby emphasizing his own leading position in the Zionist camp during the 1920's and 30's. He also resented the foothold Mutendi had gained in the circles of the Ndaza Zionists, of whom he sometimes patronizingly spoke as 'my children'. When Willi 'walked out' in 1950 he had the Buhera congregation behind him. His influence also spread to Zaka and Gutu. The more than 2,000 'Willi Zionists' are at present led by Bishop Amos Sengamai, whose headquarters are in the Buhera district.

The *Zion Apostolic Church of Dzawanda* was founded in 1943, when two *vaongamiri* under guidance of Bishop Elijah Dzawanda seceded from Makamba. Each of them was supported by most of the family congregations under his care: Dzawanda in Buhera, Machamba in Melsetter and Nehemia Chenjerai in Gutu-East. Chenjerai gives the reasons for their siding with Makamba against Masuka as follows: 'Firstly, Masuka disgracefully hit a Church member in public, and secondly, David collected tithes from Church members and used it for his private purposes. We argued', he said, 'that Church funds could only be collected for the purpose of supporting the celebration of the Holy Communion.'

In turn, the secession from Makamba was sparked off by a dispute about Dzawanda's powers as a bishop. Makamba found himself confronted with the same kind of proposition as the one from which he profited when he finally broke away from Masuka's group. Dzawanda, he discovered, was appointing Church leaders in Buhera without consulting the Church council beforehand.

25. The term *muongamiri* is possibly derived from *unganidza*: 'to gather or call together'; *muongamiri* from *muonganidzi* will then designate 'the leader who calls others together'.

When Makamba opposed this action. Dzawanda pointed out that he derived his powers and freedom of action from the South African Zionists, who had ordained him while he was working in the Transvaal as a labour migrant. Chenjerai and Machamba joined Dzawanda, knowing that this was the safest shortcut to promotion in the leadership hierarchy, unless they were prepared to set out on their own at the risk of losing their followers if their initial efforts proved to be unsuccessful, as often happened to seceding leaders. This continual shuffling of power actually still takes place in these separatist bodies. Bishop Chenjerai, who has consolidated his own position among the congregations in Gutu-east, is at present becoming increasingly independent of Dzawanda. His work as a 'master farmer'[26] makes it difficult for him to visit his superior regularly, and it would hardly be surprising if he were to proclaim himself soon as the archbishop of the Gutu congregation, summoning the Church members of his district to celebrate the *Paseka* at the Church building on his farm, rather than having to undertake the regular long journey to Dzawanda. At present he leads five congregations, each comprising 50 to 100 members, with a minister, an evangelist and several sub-leaders in each Church unit.

Bishop Kudzerema's formation of the *Zion Apostolic Church of Jesus Christ* was the natural outcome, in 1950, of a situation that had developed without noteworthy conflict. Masuka befriended Kudzerema and delegated more powers to him than to the 'ordinary' bishop. He was allowed to conduct Communion Services for those members in Gutu who found it difficult to travel to Bikita for the annual *Paseka* festivities. More important still was the freedom which Masuka allowed him in the handling of part of the collected Church funds. In this relationship of mutual trust there was no manifest struggle for power. Kudzerema simply gained more control of the Gutu congregations in the vicinity of the Devure Native Purchase Area, as a result of which he was virtually left in charge of these when Masuka died. Several factors led to the growing autonomy oft hese congregations: first, the centralized control of Masuka's Church slackened in the years preceding his death, due to his bad health and fading popularity. Secondly, Kudzerema and several Zionists under his leadership had become 'master farmers', and having purchased small farms in the Native Purchase Area, their new agricultural preoccupation necessitated a new routine of life which rendered frequent visits to the Church headquarters in Bikita impossible. Thirdly, when Pauros Kudzerema (Jr.) succeeded his father as Church leader he had become so accustomed to the independent way in which local Church life had been organized, that he continued ministering

26. For 'master farmer', see Chapter 1, p. 62.

to his father's congregations without visiting David Masuka Jr. Pauros Kudzerema regards both the younger Masuka and himself as bishops, each in his own right, each having inherited what was due to him. Kudzerema's followers at present amount to about 700 members, some of whom stay beyond the borders of Gutu, in the Zaka and Bikita districts. The various congregations are tended to by 10 ministers, who act as junior bishops.

The most recent secession in the *Zion Apostolic Church of South Africa* occurred in 1963, when Bishop Komboni Vambire formed the *African Zion Church of Jesus* in the Mucheke township at Fort Victoria. He is one of the few Zionists who joined the ZAC while working in town. Having joined Masuka's Church in 1944, he started preaching and baptizing in town and at Mupata, his home village in the Gutu district. His success as an evangelist caused considerable jealousy among the other Zionist leaders, leading to friction with Masuka's Church officials in town. Promotion as Church leader within this fold was therefore out of the question for Komboni, who became isolated from the main body of urban Zionists. For seven years he remained in the Church without attending the usual Zionist meetings, but instead conducted regular services for a small group of relatives and friends. In 1963 he met a certain Bishop Mpofu from South Africa who was travelling through Rhodesia on his way to Zambia. Inspired by the latter, Komboni formed his own Church, drafted a constitution and presented the District Commissioner at Fort Victoria with a list of names of 250 followers. These were the names of people whom he had baptized in the course of years during his weekend visits to his home village at Mupata. He was granted official recognition by the Administration and he was 'officially' ordained as a full bishop by several other Zionist secessionist leaders, among whom was Bishop Chenjerai, whom he had invited for this first major ceremony of the new Church. The outstanding constitutional differences between Komboni's and Masuka's Church were Komboni's return to monogamy and his compromise between faith-healing and medical treatment in European hospitals.[27] Both these aspects are directly related to the divergent living conditions of townsmen and those of people in the rural areas. In spite of the 'town-orientated' Constitution of his Church, Bishop Komboni now has only five adult male Church members with their families living in the township, while the rest of his approximately 400 members live in the Gutu tribal areas. He claims to have 12 ministers and 50 evangelists, which means that nearly every adult male member in his Church must be an office-bearer.

27. See his constitution, in Appendix VII.

All the above-mentioned Churches still have this in common that the members refer to themselves as 'Zionists of the Cord' (*vaZioni veNdaza*) to distinguish them from the Mutendi Zionists. On the level of the local congregations in Gutu, Bikita and Zaka, the schismatic tensions between the leaders are not always evident, as the ordinary Church members on the whole still feel that they belong to 'father' David, whom they recognize as the forerunner who introduced the Ndaza Church in Rhodesia. When speaking to outsiders they minimize their differences and refer to the 'one Church of David'. The secessionist leaders vary in their attitudes to David between the extremes of being either well disposed or critically opposed to him. Bishop Zacheo is of opinion that David is leading the people astray by permitting polygamy and being lax about other Church laws. He prides himself on standing alone as a radical representative of a small but 'true' Zionist Church, which does not associate with so-called backsliders. Chenjerai, again, is bitterly opposed to such practices as the mismanagement of Church funds of which he accuses David, while Komboni severed all ties with the Masuka group because of personal prestige conflicts. Makamba remains non-committingly aloof of David Jr., 'this apparent late-comer in Zionism.'

On the other hand, Bishop Mutema and Kudzerema are both well disposed towards David. The former attends David's Sunday services and occasionally participates in his Holy Communion services. Both he and Kudzerema have frequently sent contributions for the building of a Church at the old Church headquarters in Bikita. They refer to this building as 'our Church of Zion' which shows that their loyalty to David has not faded completely.

David himself admits that he has lost contact with Mtisi and Willi Sharara's groups. He nevertheless maintains that *all* the secessionist leaders and their followers are 'his children'. People like Makamba, he says, have submitted to the temptations of this world by aspiring to Church leadership (*ukuru hwekereke*) and they are tragically misleading many Church members. He bases the legitimacy of his assertion '*my Church is the true Zionist Church in Rhodesia*' on the historical fact that his father was the first high-ranking Zionist leader in the country (at least in that part of the country known to him). In his reference to all Ndaza Zionists as 'his children' lies the wish and fervent hope to re-unite the splintered groups into one solid movement.

At present the numerical strength of David's own following lies between 2 and 3,000 members. Apart from a strong concentration in the immediate vicinity of the Bikita Church headquarters (map 3), members are also to be found in the Zaka, Gutu, Belingwe, Nuanetsi and Victoria districts, with several congregations in the major towns and cities. Some congregations are reported to be in Portuguese East Africa. David has more than 50 ministers, the majority of whom regard themselves as 'bishops' in relation to those Church members under their jurisdiction.

ii) *The Zion Apostolic Faith Mission*

The ZAFM under the leadership of Bishop Andreas Shoko suffered only three schisms. In 1948 Jeremiah parted from Andreas with about 200 Church members. His main complaint was that 'father' Andreas had introduced polygamy into the Church. But he had hardly formed his own ZAFM near Chief Shindi's place in the Chibi district, when he himself took a second wife. In this case the stated reason for fission was clearly secondary to other motivations. As so often happens with these Independent Churches, a doctrinal conflict only serves as a camouflage for the ambition of Church leadership, which is usually the most potent source of separation. Andreas has kept close contact with Jeremiah since 1948 in a constant effort to win him and his followers back to the original fold, but up to 1965 his efforts were in vain.

Of Ruben, the next secessionist, little is known. He left the ZAFM in 1949 in order to join the *Members in Christ Assemblies* which has its headquarters, under European control, in Pretoria. He lives near Andreas at present but hardly has any followers.

Ruka Tschanga caused a major schism in 1950 when he broke away with hundreds of Church members living in the Belingwe area. He was, however, unable to maintain his position because his followers flocked back to Andreas. Eventually he admitted defeat and rejoined the ZAFM himself. Characteristic of this kind of manoeuvre by Church leaders is the confusing effect it has on the ordinary Church members in the remote areas. These members are not in constant contact with their principal leader, and when their local leader breaks with the founder of the Church they are at a loss as to whom they should follow. When Zionists in the Belingwe area were interviewed by me in 1965, they were uncertain whether they should mention Tschanga or Andreas as the main leader of their Church.

It must be said to Bishop Andreas's credit that, as a result of his strong yet flexible character, he has been able to avert fission on a large scale. Due also to a patient and persuasive determination, he even succeeded in winning back many of the subordinate officials who had broken away under the main secessionists. During a Church service in the Chibi reserve on the 16th of May, 1965, Andreas clearly demonstrated his personal involvement in the 'home-coming' of one of these stray leaders, a certain Simon Tawanda. On this occasion he announced that Simon, having been lost, had 'returned to his father' for a common act of joint worship. This announcement was followed by loud cheering as the members present watched Andreas leap jubilantly in the air with loud 'Hosannas' and 'Hallelujahs'. The humility of this leader, which accompanied this vivid expression of joy, must have been one of the important personal contributions towards the cohesion of the leadership of this Church.

At present Andreas has about 5,000 followers, most of whom live in the Chibi and Victoria tribal areas. Some are in the Belingwe and Nuanetsi areas, as far south as Beit Bridge, and several are in the main urban centres. Andreas has organized his followers into smaller congregations than most of the other Ndaza leaders have done. Consequently, he has 54 ministers living in the chiefdoms of the Chibi district, 45 ministers in the Victoria district, 10 in Belingwe, 3 in Umvuma township and one in each of the larger towns and cities, Salisbury, Bulawayo, Gwelo and West Nicholson.

iii) *The Zion Christian Church*

Between the years 1929 and 1961 Mutendi's *Zion Christian Church* has suffered no less than 13 schisms. Unlike David Masuka's Church this group has not yet experienced the major crisis which threatens a Church when its founder falls away. This may be one of the reasons why none of the ZCC secessionist leaders has as yet succeeded in gathering a following exceeding 150 to 200 members. In most cases a leadership struggle with Mutendi resulted in a total failure on the part of the secessionist leader. To his followers Mutendi, with his beneficial mystical powers, is not only the leader of the Church, but he *is* in a certain sense the Church itself. The whole movement was built up round his person, which to some of his followers was something akin to a black Messiah. As a result those members who did not feel themselves directly involved in any secessionist's action could hardly be expected to have confidence in someone with much less power than the most influential Zionist leader in the country.

In 1929, Manhiwa was followed by two sub-leaders, Jarnos Shuro and Munyengedzwa, when he dissociated himself from Mutendi. The basic reason for this secession was the tension in the inner circles of the ZCC when Mutendi met with mounting opposition from both tribal and Government authorities. They broke away when Mutendi was arrested for having unlawfully opened a 'school' in the Gutu district. Manhiwa in particular thought that too close an association with Mutendi at that stage could jeopardize their own positions and that it might be safer for them to continue their religious activities with smaller groups, in order not to attract undue attention. Afterwards both Manhiwa and Shuro fell back on traditional forms of worship. The former established himself as a spirit medium (*svikiro*), while Munyengedzwa and what was left of his secessionist followers joined Masuka's Ndaza Zionists. In the

ZCC *Rungano* Mutendi quite 'appropriately' compares Manhiwa with Theudas, who, according to Acts 5 : 36, 'asserted himself to be a person of importance. With him a number of men allied themselves, about four hundred, but they were killed and all who had listened and adhered to him were scattered and brought to nothing.'[28] This reference to Theudas in Acts 5 concerns a pharisee's argument in the Sanhedrin about the possible disintegration of the work of Christ's Apostles, if their undertaking proved to originate from purely human motivations. Mutendi's application of the text indicates that he regarded Manhiwa's failure as a direct result of the lack of divine guidance.

Another leader who played an important role in the traditional religion after seceding from Mutendi was one Maposa of the Gutu district. He reacted strongly, in 1940, when the Church council disciplined him for a full year after they had found him guilty of committing adultery. For some time he managed to operate independently as a Separatist leader, but his movement disintegrated when he turned to full-time divination by establishing himself as a *nganga*.

Johannes Shiri was the only leader to break away (1931) on explicitly tribalistic grounds. He stated that, as a muDuma, he preferred not to remain in a Rozvi-controlled Church. The crisis leading to this fission was probably aggravated by the Rozvi-Duma boundary conflict, which had caused much bitterness and discontent among the members of the two tribes since the beginning of this century. Johannes still acts as the leader of a small following in the Nyahunda Purchase Area.

When Mutendi was imprisoned as a result of the school issue, Pirato Musadza found himself in 1934 in the invidious position of being branded as the scapegoat for Mutendi's misfortunes. It was alleged by some of the other ZCC officials that he had drawn the attention of the police to the ZCC religious activities which continued to take place in caves at night, after the Administration had officially proscribed them. As a result he broke all connections with Mutendi's group and continued to minister to a small group of followers in the Gutu district.

The causes of at least seven of the ZCC schisms can be traced directly to discontent arising from frustrated leadership ambitions. Ruka Mageza (1933), from the Zaka district, complained about the delay of his promotion from the position of evangelist to that of minister. Johannes Bariravafumi (1933) waited until the Government showed a more tolerant attitude towards Zionism and then became the self-appointed 'bishop' of a few Nyashanu congregations in the Buhera district. Rasaro Masese (1935) wanted to take the initiative in

28. *Rungano*, pp. 72-80.

introducing new forms of worship, parallel to those of the Ndaza Zionists; but when he separated from Mutendi only a few close relatives followed him. Josaya Nebarwe (1937) claimed the right to act as a marriage-officer on behalf of a few distant congregations in Bikita. Some of the members of these congregations had requested that marriage rites should be conducted at different places in order to avoid the inconvenience of the parties having to travel to Church headquarters for this purpose. When Mutendi refused, Josaya seceded. Sauro Chikamba (1948) requested independent Communion services for his congregations in Ndanga South. He stated that it was impossible for Church members living far away to undertake the long journey to Moriah for the quarterly *Paseka* festivities. When his request was refused he sent an application for recognition to Joseph Lekhanyane in the Transvaal. By this time, however, Joseph had branched off from Eduard, his elder brother and actual successor to their deceased father Enginasi Lekhanyane. Sauro Chikamba thus became affiliated with a leader who was, geographically speaking, much further removed from him than Mutendi, which left him with a relatively free hand among the Church members who had followed him. Eduard Nyashanu (1955) claimed the leadership of the Nyashanu congregation on the strength of his direct consultations with, and ordination by, Transvaal leaders; and David Mabika (1961) is said to have forged a minister's card in an effort to gain greater control over the Zionist congregation in the African township at Fort Victoria.

Of the above-mentioned leaders the 'Churches' of Manhiwa, Masese and Maposa have become practically defunct. The others are still operating on a small scale. At least four of these secessionist leaders have died and have been succeeded by their sons. None of them actually adopted new names for their Church groups, but kept operating under the name *Zion Christian Church.* Most of them introduced new forms of worship as well as Ndaza Zionist garments, in an effort to distinguish themselves from the Mutendi group, without, however, dissociating themselves from Zionism as such.

The two major schisms of the ZCC in 1947 were the result of a serious crisis in Mutendi's domestic affairs. He was accused of having impregnated the wife of Nison, one of his evangelists, during one of his country-wide evangelistic campaigns. Athough Mutendi denied the charge during sessions of the Church council held at the request of the complainants, he eventually took the woman concerned under his care, after she and her husband had parted. When she gave birth to a child, Mutendi was falsely accused of murder, for it was reported to the police that twins had been born and that one child was missing. The inference was clear: Mutendi was accused of having done away with the one child in accordance with the old Shona practice of killing one twin. Mutendi was acquitted by the High Court, but not after he had suffered six months' detention as the result of this assusation.

The principal movers in the conflict concerning Nison's wife were Joram, Mutendi's cousin, Rukuni and Furanai, both agnatic kinsmen, i.e. 'brothers' of Mutendi – all of whom had achieved leading positions in the Church at the time. They belonged to the royal Rozvi houses that had rival claims to the Rozvi sub-chieftainship. Mutendi himself was not only Church superintendent and kraalhead, but he also claimed seniority in the Rozvi house of Makuwa, which was to provide the next incumbent to the Rozvi sub-chieftainship. Holding considerable power and authority as a Church leader over the very persons who were his rivals in the struggle for tribal political power proved to be too much of a paradox in a society whose customary laws had not yet been sufficiently adapted to such new forms of authority. Envy in the inner Church circle turned into bitterness as external political forces came into play. Therefore some means had to be devised to remove the 'big man', but conclusive evidence could not be produced and the conspiracy came to naught. Mutendi publicly reprimanded Joram for the role he had played in this action, after which a schism became unavoidable and several discontented agnatic relatives left the Church.

Joram managed to hive off with some forty of Mutendi's followers, including several of the Church's prominent evangelists. He wrote a letter to Lekhanyane, whom he had met in 1925, requesting permission to continue working as a minister of the ZCC, independently of Mutendi. This permission was granted and he erected his own Church headquarters only a few miles from Mutendi's 'Jerusalem'. From this base he ministers to his followers – about 150 Church members, including 4 ministers and 4 evangelists – in the Nyahunda Native Purchase Area (Bikita) and the Gutu district. Eduard Lekhanyane, during his visit to Rhodesia after his father's death, tried to reconcile the two opposing leaders, but his efforts proved fruitless.

Makuti, from Chingombe in Gutu, sided with Joram in 1947 in the matter of Nison's wife. He used Mutendi's temporary predicament and loss of prestige to induce the subordinate leaders under his own care to help him with the formation of a separate branch of the ZCC. After his death Matthew Zungura succeeded him as leader and introduced Ndaza-type customs when closer cooperation was sought with the congregations of David Masuka and Willi Sharara in Chingombe. Zungura, better known as Forridge, at present has 5 ministers, 6 evangelists and 4 preachers who assist him in tending to a Church membership of about 200 people, resident in the Munyikwa and Chingombe sub-chiefdoms in Gutu and in Buhera.

Mutendi's own following at present amounts to some 8,000 to 10,000 people. The main concentrations are in the Southern Shona districts, such as Bikita, Zaka, Ndanga, Victoria, Chibi, Belingwe, Nuanetsi, Gutu and Buhera. In each of these areas there are several congregations, well organized by local Church officials under the direction of a single Zionist minister who controls the local hierarchy. ZCC congregations are also to be found in all the cities and main towns – to the east as far as Chipinga, Melsetter, Umtali (with small factions in Portuguese East Africa), to the west as far as Plumtree and Bulawayo, to the south as far as Beit Bridge, and as far north as Livingstone in Zambia, Sinoia and Mt. Darwin north of Salisbury, while there is a single congregation in Malawi.

Mutendi's attitude towards the secessionist leaders is explained at length in the *Rungano*. Chapters 36 and 37 deal with the trouble caused by Joram Gwai. It is recorded that he wrote a letter to Lekhanyane with the purpose of causing disunity between the top leaders of the ZCC. Lekhanyane returned the letter to Mutendi, who made Joram read it out aloud in public. When Joram still refused to admit his guilt, Mutendi retaliated by calling down lightning and thunder from heaven. He (Mutendi) is reported to have said during a meeting: 'If God is with me I will have Him send down lightning so that you [potential dissenters] will be thrown to the ground because you do not listen!'[29] The rain and lightning came directly after the meeting. It was of such force that one of the discontented leaders ran to Mutendi's house, begging the 'man of God' to come to their aid. Mutendi then pointed his staff at the clouds and with a loud 'Amen!' caused the storm to subside. All were filled with great fear and went to Mutendi to confess the evil thoughts they had harboured about him. Thus, by successfully making use in a period of crisis of the general belief in his powers to manipulate mystical forces, Mutendi succeeded in averting a major schism. To this event the same significance is ascribed as to the one related in 1 Sam. 12 : 16-20 in the Old Testament, when the prophet Samuel called down rain and thunder to subdue the Israelites when they wrongfully clamoured for a king.

In the *Rungano*, Chapters 49 to 52 all deal with disunity in the Church. Mutendi addresses his followers in the first person, entreating them to co-operate in a spirit of unity, since *ukuru* (leadership ambition) had become a disease which 'pulls the Church apart'. He compares the African Church with a dish which had been left by a father for the use of his children. The dish is a symbol of love to keep the children together. Unfortunately they fail to perceive this meaning, and try to snatch the dish from one another until it breaks into pieces. Then follows the application in chapter 48 : 8, 'Don't you

29. *Ibid.*, p. 48.

[leaders] agree that you are today snatching the dish which you have received as an inheritance from your father, from which you were ordered to eat together?' This rebuke is then countered by the direct assertion in verse 10: '. . . but I [Mutendi] carried your dish safely without breaking it until I arrived and gave it to you, so that you could all eat from it.'

In Chapter 51 the exhortation to follow Jesus Christ's new law to love one another is related directly to the secessionists. In so doing all the Zionists must remember that 'you come from one womb' (*makabva mudumbu rimwe*), i.e. the 'womb' of the *Zion Christian Church*. 'This I say', Mutendi continues, 'because a child may forsake [*rasha*: lit. throw away] his father, but the father cannot throw away or forget his child.' (Chapter 51 : 9) The names of those who had 'thrown away their father' are then listed, each with a Biblical verse opposite his name to indicate that such things have happened before. The secessionist leader Maposa of Gutu, who had become a *nganga*, is likened to Simon the wizard of Acts 8; Sauro Chikamba is compared with Absolom (2 Sam. 15), the son of David, of whom the Zionists believe that he 'changed headquarters' because Jerusalem was too far off; and Joram Gwai, the main culprit, is compared with Jerobeam (1 Kings 12) who became king of Israel at a period when Rehabeam, Solomon's son and legal successor, fell into disfavour. Of Joram, Mutendi says: 'His bid for leadership in the Church was unfounded in the same way as that of Jerobeam, who could not become the true king of Israel. Both of them were councillors [*makota*] and respected visitors who, however long they had stayed as foreigners [*vatorwa*] among them, were not of the same clan [*mutupo*] as the leading party, and this disqualified their leadership.' Mutendi furthermore warns the secessionist leaders that their gravest mistake is diverting ordinary members of the true faith and then leaving them in a state of confusion. He concludes in Chapter 52 : 5: 'You [true believers] belong to me. You have been chosen as such by God, and I know that those who have been chosen by God will not go elsewhere.'

2. THE AFRICAN APOSTOLIC CHURCH OF JOHANE MARANKE (AACJM)

a) *Johane's calling*

Johane, the founder of the largest Independent Church in Rhodesia, was born in 1912 in the Maranke tribal area (see map 3). His father, Momberume, is of royal Sithole blood – the *mutupo* being *Moyo* (heart) – and his mother was a daughter of Chief Maranke. He was the youngest of three brothers, Conorio and Anrod being his seniors. Anrod, who was still alive during my research period in the Maranke area in 1966, was able to give first-hand information about the visions Johane had as a child. From the age of six Johane regularly spoke to him about the 'many people he saw on a cloud in the east'. He used to ask Anrod if he, too, could see these people.

Some of the visions and dreams were told to the missionaries of the American Methodist Mission. They thought that Johane would one day become a minister in their Church, so they tried to stimulate his interest in this direction. After completing Std. 2, however, Johane left school and went to Umtali as a wage-labourer. By this time he had completed the Methodist catechism classes and was baptized – under the name of Roston – in the Mission Church. The Biblical knowledge he had attained at that stage was therefore of Methodist missionary orientation.

Johane's important visions are all recorded in the Apostolic Book called *Umboo utsva hwavaPostori* (*'The new Revelation of the Apostles'*) which is regarded by the Apostles as a canonical addition to the Bible. Chapter 1 to 11 deal with early visions before the outpouring of the Holy Spirit on Johane in 1932. Biblical influence is clearly noticeable in these chapters and the Joseph theme often recurs. In Chapter 1, for instance, Johane speaks in the first person: 'I was surrounded by a white cloud and the Holy Spirit descended on my head . . . I was singing the new song, "Hallelujah! Hallelujah!", and when I walked up an anthill a book was given me. Then my father and brothers came. They knelt before me and started worshipping God . . . That is how the Holy Spirit first came to me.'[30] The seventh chapter contains a narrative even more closely related to the Biblical Joseph:

Verse 1: 'I looked up into the sky while I was herding cattle one afternoon and saw a star falling down. It landed in front of me. Then came three more and fell on top of it, whereafter a voice ordered us to make sheaves of cut grass.

Verse 2: The others [future followers] made big sheaves, while mine was very small. When we went to the judge we threw down our sheaves, mine going underneath those of the others. The judge demanded that the sheaves be brought closer to him so that he could see whose was the biggest. The others took theirs and left mine lying on the ground. Of its own accord my sheave then started growing until it became much larger than those of the others. The judge then told them that since mine was the biggest I was to become the

30. *Umboo utsva hwavaPostori* ('The new Revelation of the Apostles') by Johane Maranke the Baptist, p. 1.

leader. He said, "You must listen to whatever Johane tells you and do the good works he is doing".' Johane concludes, 'Since that day I became their jugde [mutongi].'

In this chapter one finds that Johane is given divine authority by the Judge, who can be no other than God. Authority achieved in this manner is regarded as authentic and indisputable in Apostolic circles.

An interesting feature in these chapters is the mention of two books, one for each hand, which had been given him during one of these visionary spells. These books were written in a foreign language which he could understand through the inspiration of the Holy Spirit and not through the education he had attained at the Mission station of the Europeans. The contents of these books hold the message of eternal life (*sadza risingaperi*: porridge, i.e. food of eternity). To Johane these books must have signified a special message concerning eternal life. Of great psychological value is the belief that his ability to interpret this message was independent of the knowledge he attained from missionaries and Mission schools, a fact which clearly reflects the urge to propagate the Christian message free from European supervision.

Chapters 5 and 6 relate encounters with Jesus in heaven, Jesus being presented as a person with a long white garment and eyes aflame. A voice told Johane that he was blessed forever, and directly afterwards he saw himself walking through many countries with a large following. He was leading his followers with a staff (*tsvimbo*) which enabled him to protect them from being burnt when they passed through fire, and to prevent them from being hurt when they passed through hostile countries. Here he features as a Moses who leads his 'Israelites' to some better destination. The staff is used in similar fashion – to perform miracles, and to direct the chosen people. Says Johane, 'I was flying with the Apostolic staff and all the people of the country followed. Whenever I held the staff upright the people would stop as I did.'[31] The great number of followers are like the grains of sand on the shores of lake Nyasa in Malawi.

Chapter 8 gives an account of Johane's encounter with the beings in the temple of heaven to which he was summoned. There were angels as well as men with garments and long beards.[32] In this chapter the calling of Johane comes in the form of a clear and exclusive command:

Verse 3: 'The one in heaven told me to go back to earth and to do the work of Jesus.

31. *Ibid.*, pp. 2-3.

32. The white garments, staffs and long beards were to become the distinguishing sings for male Apostles, in contrast with the regalia of other religious bodies.

Verse 4: The voice said, "If you go back to the earth and do the work of your Lord, anybody who does not obey you will not be allowed to enter this temple . . ."

Verse 6: Says Johane, "Everybody who turns away from me, has refused salvation [*ruponeso*] . . . such a person will not be given a chance to cheat other people and have them form a separate association [*sungano*]." '

The exclusiveness of his task is therefore directly linked with the promise of eternal life. It reflects the need of safeguards against future schisms which were anticipated at this stage, and the first signs of which had already appeared when the 'New Revelation' was written.

Shortly before returning to the Maranke tribal area from Umtali, Johane had prophetic visions, accompanied by physical symptoms similar to the 'deaths' experienced by other African visionaries, such as Alice Lenshina of the Lumpa Church and the Shona Messiah, Johane Masowe.[33] These visions were accompanied by lightning, thunder and a strong wind. 'The thunder', Johane relates, 'was in my heart, and I sat down thinking that I was about to die . . . a strong wind started blowing through the house and I fluttered around like a leaf . . . I became dizzy . . . began to forget.' While he was in this state the voice of God came to Johane, telling him to go back home to start His work. On another occasion a voice said, 'I am the priest of God. When you receive the Holy Spirit in July, I shall meet you plainly. When I meet you, you shall have the congregation of Jesus and its name shall be "Apostolic Church".'[34] Before he left him, the priest of God gave him garments, a staff and a book as an additional sign of his ordination.

The visions recorded in the *Umboo utsva* may not have been generally known before Johane's inspiration by the Holy Spirit in July 1932. These may therefore have been partly construed and elaborated on at a later stage for the purpose of clarifying moral directives and to impress upon the followers the uniqueness of his calling. The calling may in fact have been much less vivid and clear than this 'Apostolic Bible' portrays. It nevertheless reveals the African's need for a clear charter for the new Church and the importance attached to a direct calling from God, in much the same way as the Biblical prophets of old.

33. For the Lumpa Church, see Taylor and Lehmann, 1961, pp. 248-249; and for Masowe, see Sundkler, *op. cit.*, p. 324.

34. *Umboo utsva* (The New Revelation), Chapter 11 : 2 (p. 8).

24. Zionist bishop, David Masuka (Jr.), in official attire, preaching to a group of followers at Church headquarters in the Bikita district.

b) *The birth of a new Church*

i) *Outpouring of the Holy Spirit*

On the evening of the 17th July, 1932, Johane was on his way home, having visited his in-laws. Near Mt. Nyengwe he suddenly noticed a strong light falling on him. He heard a voice saying, 'You are John the Baptist, an Apostle. Now go and do My work! Go to every country and preach and convert people! Tell them not to commit adultery, not to steal and not to become angry! Baptize people and keep the Sabbath day!' Johane described this experience as being awesome, his soul 'becoming very small' while the light was on him.[35]

His older brother, Anrod, relates this memorable occasion as follows: 'That evening when Johane came home he had a strange look on his face and he kept saying, Amen! Amen! My parents thought that he had gone mad, but our uncle, Peter Mupako, who was a Zionist at the time, knew better and assured us that it was not madness but the Holy Spirit that had taken hold of Johane. Mupako also fell down and was filled by the Spirit.'[36] Gwati, Johane's maternal cousin, says of the event, 'Peter was a Zionist, and when he saw Johane he was filled by his [Johane's] spirit' – as if to say that the Apostolic Spirit of Johane and the Zionist Spirit of Peter were different. As the stereotype phrases used by Zionists and Apostles differ while they are speaking with tongues, Gwati's statement may have been another way of saying that Mupako was adopting the same kind of Spirit manifestation as he was observing in Johane.

35. Note the similarity with the experience of St. Paul when he received his divine call on the way to Damascus.

36. Personal communication, February, 1966.

On opposite page from left to right and top to bottom

25. *Mupristi* (high priest) Johane Maranke (left) founder of the African Apostolic Church, and his maternal cousin, Prophet Simon Mushati, who acted as second-in-charge on *Paseka* rounds.

26. *Mutongi (judge)* Momberume, Johane's father, who was one of the first converts of the Apostolic movement.

27. *Mupristi* (high priest) Abero, Johane's senior son and successor, observing his followers celebrating the Lord's Supper.

28. *Murapi* (healer) Anrod (back row, second from left), Makebo (front left) and Judah (front right) – the deceased Johane's brother and two sons – together with other relatives who also hold high office in the Apostolic Church's leadership hierarchy.

29. Apostolic *Pendi* meeting held in 1966 near Church headquarters in the Maranke reserve.

Those present when Johane arrived were his parents, his uncle Peter and his two blood brothers, Conorio and Anrod. They started singing the song: 'Lord, we are gathering here in your house'. Johane did not join in the singing because he was again 'caught by the Holy Spirit' and started speaking with tongues. In Chapter 12 of the 'New Revelation' Johane narrates the vision he had on this occasion. 'I was in a house which had been divided in two by the Holy Spirit. In the house there were many ministers of the various Churches. Suddenly there was a flash of lightning and a voice ordering me to shout out loudly to the people that the Kingdom of God had come, and that they had to accept God. The voice also said: "You are blessed, son of Africa". I then shouted loudly to the sleeping ministers of the Churches, but they remained fast asleep.' This vision implies an accusation against the leaders of Mission and other Churches. It is undoubtedly interpreted as a divine justification of the new leader's mandate.

The same chapter continues with many directives given by the Holy Spirit in connection with the organization of the Apostolic Church. The mystical powers bestowed on Johane are mentioned in verses 9 and 10: 'You will have power to cure the sick by laying hands on them and by consecrating water for them to drink; you will be able to drive away any kind of *shavi* through the laying-on of hands. Take the long staff, wherever you go, for healing purposes! Through your hands fertility will be conveyed to the barren and when you step in fire you will not be burnt . . .'

V 13 'When you want to lay hands on a new convert so that he can perform miracles, so be it. If you want him to have the Holy Spirit, so be it. If you want him to heal others, he will do so. If you want him to prophesy or preach, it will be so.'

V 15 '. . . Those who die after you have pardoned [*sunungura*] them, will be saved, but those who die before you have done so, will be judged by God . . .' [Johane therefore understood his task to be a mediating one, with direct implications for life after death.]

V 25-26 '. . . When you want to baptize people or when you want to preach and pray for them, you must always start with the song:

> Everywhere we see people who do not know Christ,
> They are lost, that is why they sin,
> Our mighty God send the Holy Spirit to those who do not have it . . .
> God bless Africa and hear our prayers, God bless it!
> Come Holy Spirit, come Holy Spirit, come Holy Spirit!
> Bless us, your servants.'

Thus Johane received his full charter for the new Church, which was about to come into being, directly from the Holy Spirit. The emphasis on the Holy Spirit is important for an understanding of the ideology within the Apostolic movement. All the laws and customs within the Church are justified with direct references to the inspiration and command of the Holy Spirit. It provides the Apostles with an authority whose authenticity they accept without question, and as something that lies beyond the interference by missionaries. They actually accuse the missionaries of having deliberately denied the Africans the spiritual benefits of the Holy Spirit. Another great advantage of the emphasis on divine inspiration is that the Apostles can comfortably minimize Johane's early training by Methodist missionaries. Leaders such as Chakaza, Johane's son-in-law and one of the most influential Apostolic leaders in the Maranke reserve, fondly states that the parallels between Johane's visions and Biblical themes were only discovered *after* God had personally manifested Himself to Johane. This attitude reflects the need to emphasize the authenticity of Johane's calling as well as the uniqueness of his contact with God, apart from and superior to the influence of European missionaries. This movement was, from the outset, conceived of as something unique, something typically African. It was going to meet the needs of people who were unaware of the Kingdom that was at hand, needs which the Mission Churches – such seems to be the implication of the reference to the sleeping ministers – had failed to recognize.

ii) *The first converts*

The initial growth of the Church took place within the inner and extended family circles. That first night Johane's relatives hardly slept. Spells of Spirit-possession and intermittent singing continued until the next morning. Conorio, Anrod and Peter, the two blood brothers and their paternal uncle, then went out to tell the people in the neighbourhood what had happened. Johane first of all went to Ruka Mataruka, his wife's sister's husband, to tell him of the new Church. Ruka became the first official convert of Johane and was duly filled with the Holy Spirit. He was to become the first evangelist of the new movement.

From Ruka, Johane went to Mushati, his maternal cousin (*hwanamai*). Their mothers were both daughters of Chief Maranke. Mushati stayed at the Mazodza village and was reading the Bible when Johane arrived. His first impression was that Johane had gone mad, since he kept on speaking with tongues. When Johane asked him whether he understood what he was reading and he answered in the negative, Johane started explaining certain portions of the Bible to him. Mushati, at this stage, was a 'potential' Methodist Church member who had passed Std. 2, but, like Johane's brothers, had not yet been baptized into the Mission Church. On this occasion Johane surprised a party of beer drinkers at Mazodza's village. In an effort to convince them of his calling he stepped into a fire, and did not get burnt.[37] He then turned to Mushati and said, 'God has sent me to call you. Follow me!' Mushati accompanied Johane to an anthill where more speaking-with-tongues took place before Johane concluded with the following summons to Mushati: 'Your name from now on will be Simon and you will be a prophet. Follow me!'

As the news of the new Church spread, people started coming from all over the Maranke reserve to the Momberume homestead to be taught by Johane. Together with Johane the initiative was taken from the movement's inception by his closest relatives. Conorio and Anrod became convinced in those first exciting days. Gwati, another maternal cousin, was soon to follow and he became the movement's secretary (*munyori*). Simon Mushati had his first experience of the Holy Spirit on the 14th of July, after he had been discussing Church matters with Johane and some other relatives. They had studied certain passages in the Bible, some of which Simon still remembers, such as Mark 16 : 15 (the great mission command), Romans 8 : 1 and Galatians 5 : 1. It was during these discussions that Simon, as he himself states, 'found his heart accepting and responding to the message of Johane'. The discussions were carried on until late at night. Simon and Grace, his girlfriend, left the homestead in the early morning hours. They were discussing the work of the Holy Spirit when they approached the rivulet, Dambakuzara. 'I then saw a movement as if someone was moving very slowly', related Simon. 'My heart started boiling as hot water would boil. I fell to the ground because the Holy Spirit had taken hold of me, and I found myself shouting, Amen! Amen! Grace was sobbing with anxiety because she thought that I had fallen seriously ill. After a while I moved to the nearest cork tree [*muchakata*] and began to worship the Lord. The Spirit stayed with me the whole night. Back home the people thought that I was mad. While I was praying the next morning, I saw something white and shining like a star descending from heaven and settling on my head. It covered my hair before it started running down my face like water. Afterwards I went and told Johane what had happened. He agreed that the Holy Spirit had also come to me.'[38] This manifestation of the Holy Spirit to Simon was interpreted as a super-

37. Fire-walking was to become an established practice of the Apostolic movement. See also Murphree, 1969, p. 104.

38. Personal communication by 'St.' Simon in the Maranke tribal area, 1966.

natural confirmation of the summons he had received from Johane. It enhanced his position at an early stage as the first prophet of the movement.

The chief was informed of the new movement and he wisely stated that he had no objection to it, provided the leaders behaved well and refrained from stirring up trouble. He thought that the movement would 'die' of its own accord if it was not inspired by God Himself. But not all the tribal authorities were as well disposed towards the Apostles. Some of the kraalheads refused to give permission to these fanatics to enter their villages. They regarded them as representatives of the spirit of madness. When the Apostles came across this kind of resistance they would sing near the village to attract the well-disposed inhabitants. Many of these were converted and became filled by the Holy Spirit. Some resistance was also met from the Methodist missionaries who were concerned about the loss of their Church membership. Especially the African Methodist ministers sharply criticized the Apostles and accused them of having a false spirit. They predicted that the movement would not last long. At a later stage, when official recognition was sought for the movement, Johane turned towards the chief, his maternal grandfather, who took him to the District Commissioner at Umtali. Recognition was granted after it had been ascertained that Johane had a substantial following and that, as a person, he was of good repute. Permission to conduct evangelistic campaigns was granted on the condition that the Apostles should not interfere with the work of the established Mission Churches.

On the 20th of July the first big Sabbath day was celebrated. All the newly converted followers had to be baptized in 'Jordan'. The Murozvi river was selected for this memorable occasion. Gwati, the *munyori*, explains that '*takaita Jordani paMurozvi* (we "made" Jordan at Murozvi).' Estimates made by various leaders on the number of people baptized during this first mass baptism vary, but since Gwati was the secretary from the beginning and as it was his task to count people during Passover and other ceremonies, one can probably take his estimate of roughly 150 people as being fairly accurate. It is understandable that no accurate reports were written at the time. It is important, however, to note the successive order in which the people were baptized, because this factor has become the point of reference for present-day secessionist leaders when they argue about the seniority of Johane's fellow leaders.[39]

39. After the death of Johane, many years later, his brother Anrod and cousin Simon became the main contestants in the bid for power in the Church. Those who sided with Simon often refer to this baptismal ceremony to indicate Simon's seniority over Anrod.

When everybody had gathered at the side of the pool at Murozvi the Holy Spirit caused Ruka Mataruka to 'fall in the pool' (*putsika mudziva*). He baptized Johane who, in turn, first baptized Simon and then Ruka, before the others followed. Johane's father on this occasion threw away his bag containing medicine and underwent the laying-on of hands to 'bring on' the Spirit. Simon remembers that there was much lightning and thunder during the whole procedure. The earth 'thundered and trembled' as the surroundings seemed to turn blue. In Chapter 15 of the 'New Revelation' it is recorded that everybody who had come to the pool was shouting that the Kingdom of God had come. It is also mentioned that Johane drove out many evil spirits as the people passed through 'Jordan'. Through visions he received instructions about the way the whole rite had to be conducted. Evangelists had to stand on the other side of 'Jordan' to 'receive' the new converts as they emerged from the water on the opposite bank, while prophets had to guard the pool lest someone committed the grave sin of entering the holy water before he or she had confessed his or her sins. The whole ceremony came to an end with the singing of the well-known song: 'God bless Africa' (*Ishe komborera Afrika*).[40]

After the baptism there was the laying-on of hands on some of the new members, consecrating them for the various tasks the Holy Spirit had assigned to them. The key positions were all taken by Johane's relatives who already at this stage formed the nucleus of the new Church, and who were in due course promoted to the highest leadership positions as the hierarchic order developed more fully. Ruka (brother-in-law) was made 'first evangelist' and was later to become *Rabaumah* evangelist[41]; Simon (maternal cousin) was made 'first prophet' and was later to become *Rabaumah* prophet; Anrod (elder blood brother) was made a junior prophet (with three lines)[42] – subordinate to Simon; Conorio (eldest blood brother) was made 'first healer' and became *Rabaumah* healer (*murapi*); Gwati (maternal cousin) became the first secretary of the Church and Momberume (father) was consecrated as a 'judge' (*mutongi*), and given the task of settling domestic disputes of Church members in the Maranke reserve and surrounding areas. Positions of leadership were also bestowed on Beremauro and Mudara, distant agnatic relatives of Johane's. They started playing a more prominent role only after the death

40. At present many Africans consider this song to be their national anthem.

41. The term *Liebumah* (which is the spelling generally used by the Apostles) is pronounced *Rabaumah* or *Liebauma* and indicates the topmost ranks in each of the major Apostolic offices (a diagram of the Apostolic leadership hierarchy will appear in Volume 3). The derivation of this term is not fully clear.

42. This is the prophetic rank immediately below that of Liebaumaship.

of Johane. At this early stage the leadership structure had not yet been properly worked out. It was only with the gradual expansion of the Church that the demand for a clear delineation of the powers, attributed to each position, arose. The design for this leadership structure, as it took shape in the course of years, is said to have been revealed to Johane through repetitive visions.

iii) *The fight against traditional religious practices*

Although one can detect signs of cultural nationalism and forms of religious indigenization in this movement, it is true to state that from the outset there was an acute awareness of the necessity to eliminate certain pagan practices. In the 'New Revelation' there are several references to the *shavi* spirits (used here in the general sense of including all spirits other than *Mudzimuneira* – the Holy Spirit – whether malevolant like the *ngozi* or beneficient like the *manyahana* healing spirit) which were exorcised by Johane and his followers. The Apostles also attacked ancestor worship (*kupira midzimu*). Anrod describes the meaning of the new movement as an immense relief from the old binding practices which were often exploited by the *nganga* to serve their own ends.

This Church did not concentrate on the removal of medicine and 'horns' from the homesteads of those who were considered to be bewitched, as did another Apostolic group, the *Shinga Postora* (The Courageous Apostles) which, branched from Johane Masowe, popularized this practice in order to attract people.[43] In the 'New Revelation' mention is made of only one occasion when Johane entered a hut and removed malignant witchcraft articles from beneath the floor before he baptized the people living in the hut. The present leaders of the Church, Abero and Makebo, Johane's elder sons, object to such practices. They probably realize that the removal of medicinal horns from houses often leads to direct accusations of wizardry which, if pursued and punished under the Witchcraft Suppression Act, would prejudice the position of other Apostolic prophets. What they did do from the start, however, was to burn the personal charms and other objects used in traditional religion of those wishing to be baptized. New converts were not allowed to enter 'Jordan' before they had produced all their possessions of magical significance. Revelations by the Holy Spirit were believed to enable the prophets to detect those who had hidden this sort of medicine at home.

Johane's parents, both of royal descent, were well versed in the traditional religious practices and both had been active in this respect. Johane's mother

43. *Infra*, p. 340.

was a well-known spirit medium, and his father had already dedicated a bull (*gono guru*)[44] to his deceased ancestors for future worship. This particular bull had the ancestral house name, Momberume. Anrod's account concerning this bull runs as follows: 'The Holy Spirit, having reached Johane, said, "Remove that beast, for if you do not, you will have endless troubles with the demons at this homestead". In order to remove the demons the beast was killed.'[45] Demons and ancestral spirits thus being directly associated with each other, there could be no affinity between Holy Spirit and ancestors. The bull was burnt and none of the meat was used for sacrificial purposes. This episode marks the most radical break with the ways of his forefathers, and the public recognition by the father of the spiritual authority of his own son.

Johane's mother, who had inherited such regalia as blankets and drums to act as spirit medium for one of the senior tribal ancestors, had to burn all these articles. She did so, and all the demons were believed to have fled from the Momberume homestead. But this happy state was of short duration. The rules of the Bocha tribe – which are that a *svikiro* should comply with the will of the ancestral spirits or forfeit her privileged position – became too much for the mother. She yielded and once more started attending beer parties, while secretly acquiring new blankets for the spirits, which she would use when she was away from home. It was then that her son Anrod fell gravely ill. While lying in one of the huts he had a revelation from the Holy Spirit, indicating that the return of demons had come about as a result of his mother's secret practices. When she came back from one of the beer parties he spoke to her, saying, 'Mother, you have returned to the world . . . I see the blanket you wear when you go to the beer parties. The Holy Spirit has spoken to me asking what it is that attracts you to the beer parties, because the result of this is that we, your children, are under the threat of death.'[46] Hearing this, Anrod's mother was overcome with grief because she realized that her son might indeed be killed by *vademoni*. She handed over the blanket which she used as a medium of her deceased 'brother' and it was burnt. Anrod recovered from his illness soon afterwards.

But in spite of repeated reprimands from Momberume, who had meanwhile become a staunch Church member, Anrod's mother eventually broke with the Church and continued her divinatory practices. Anrod explained her dilemma by pointing out that, being the daughter of a chief, it was particularly difficult for her to abandon the ways of her fathers. This reveals the inner

44. *Supra*, p. 113f.
45. Personal interview with Prophet-healer Anrod, 1966.
46. Personal interview.

conflict which can arise when a person is faced with the choice between status and prestige (which in this case involved a considerable sphere of influence) in a tradition-orientated society, and an uncompromising form of Christianity, for within her son's Church this woman would undoubtedly have lost much of the authority she wielded in traditionalist circles.

The fight against traditional worship, magical practices and witchcraft still continues in this Church and can be observed best at baptismal ceremonies and *Paseka* meetings. Case studies in the Maranke reserve reveal that the pull of the ancestors remains a powerful factor, and that many of the Church members leave the Church temporarily or for good, when pressure is brought to bear on them by relatives still participating in ancestor worship.

c) *Expansion of the Apostolic Church*

The initial growth of Johane's movement took place in the Maranke tribal area, especially in the Mufararikwa and Masvaure wards where most of Johane's relatives resided. It did not take long before some of the leading figures moved or were posted to other areas as advisors and guides to distant congregations. Ruka Mataruka settled in Buhera; Moses, one of the leading evangelists, was made responsible for the Manyika territory in the vicinity of Umtali; and Simon the prophet worked amongst the Shangaan people near the border of Portuguese East Africa.

Johane's father and his two brothers hardly ever accompanied Johane on his country-wide tours. They rather formed what one might call the 'Consolidating and Advisory Board' at home, during the long spells of Johane's absence. Conorio tended the sick through prayer and the laying-on of hands. A small colony of patients gradually grew at his homestead. Those with serious complaints had to stay for long periods, and huts were built to accommodate them. Anrod advised Church officials, who came from faraway congregations to discuss organizational or other Church matters. Momberume, again, with a selected body of *vatongi* ('judges') settled disputes and disciplinary cases concerning adultery, wizardry and other offences among Church members. Conorio died without having sons to continue his work. His position was therefore 'inherited' by his brother Anrod, who then held the dual function of healer-prophet. Anrod himself states that he had little to do with the expansion of the Church beyond the boundaries of the Maranke reserve. He accompanied Johane on only one tour to Zaka and Fort Victoria. He regarded his main task as that of 'the one who stays at home' (*mugari wapamusha*), or of the 'keeper of the belongings at home' (*muchengeti we zvavapamusha*).

Cousin Simon, on the other hand, was the first prophet to attain Liebaumaship, the highest rank of prophetic leadership. Compared with Anrod he was of higher standing, since Anrod, before he attained Conorio's Liebaumaship as a healer, was of the lower prophetic ranks. Simon accompanied Johane on most of his tours and came to be regarded as the movement's 'second-in-charge'. He helped Johane to administer the sacraments and to ordain leaders whom the Holy Spirit deemed worthy.

Shortly after starting his own movement Johane considered joining Mutendi's Zionists, or at least obtaining Mutendi's benediction for the continuation of his own Church work. A delegation of Church leaders was sent on foot to Mutendi. Those who went still remember the encounters they had with wild animals on the way. They came across lions and leopards in the Sabi valley, which they believed to represent evil beings which had to be driven off through the power of the Holy Spirit. They passed from one village to another, preaching that the Kingdom of God would come within three years.[47] All those who accepted the message were baptized and left to form new congregations. Newly appointed leaders were told to contact the founder of the Church at his headquarters at Maranke. Simon relates that they baptized up to 52 people on a single day as they moved along, which indicates that even at an early stage of its development the Apostolic Church had gained impetus beyond the borders of the Maranke area.

But an agreement between Mutendi's Zionists and the Apostles proved to be impossible. 'During the discussions the Spirits of the Zionists and of the Apostles came out', says Simon, 'and they were seen to be different.' (*Ndipo pakabuda Mweya yavaZioni neyavaPostori, ndokuona kuti Mweya yakasiyana*). Mutendi's reference to this episode is interesting. He claims that the Apostles 'belong' to him, and he bases this claim on the fact that they had undertaken such a long journey to see him. To him the important thing is that the Apostles set out to Zion City to 'receive hands' and therefore also the Holy Spirit through him. He does not state that they never came to an agreement, but even suggests that the Apostles were diverted on the way and never actually reached his headquarters.

David Masuka Jr. also claims seniority and some sort of affiliation to the Apostles. He says that Johane came to his father to be ordained. It is possible that the Apostles, after they had failed to come to terms with Mutendi, went to Masuka to seek some compromise solution, because they had made a long journey and they felt the need of at least some sort of 'recognition' of their

47. Note the strong eschatological emphasis during the first period of Church expansion which is characteristic of most Spirit-type Churches.

Church by another African leader of a Spirit-type Church. Having succeeded in organizing the largest Independent African Church in Rhodesia, the Apostles themselves prefer to ignore this early effort to link up with the Zionists. Masuka's claim, however, is acceptable in the light of the general need of Independent Church leaders for some form of affiliation with the historical 'Church of the Spirit' which traces its descent back to the first congregation in Jerusalem. This effort at affiliation with another '*Mweya* Church' is also important in that it reflects, in spite of the continued distinction between the Zionist and Apostle Spirits, the closer identification between the Spirit-type Churches than, for instance, between the Spirit-type and Ethiopian-type Churches. At present the majority of common Apostles and Zionists will be satisfied with unqualified references to the Spirit of Zion or the Spirit of the Apostles. Only the more sophisticated leaders recognize one and the same Christian Spirit but distinguish its diverse activities within the context of different Church groups.

The 'New Revelation' gives very little factual data on the growth of the Church. Chapters 13 to 26 deal exclusively with the personal experiences of Johane. The scattered references to activities in tribal areas are all directly related to the founding leader's personal experiences. In Chapter 14:2 Johane says: 'I went around to all the villages, preaching, speaking with tongues and driving out *shavi* spirits. I healed people, performed miracles and even walked on fire.' Chapter 15 consists of a narrative of a big meeting, held on the 15th of August, 1932. On this occasion Johane took the people to a 'Jordan' where he fell into the water and proclaimed to them that the Kingdom of God was at hand. Verse 13 has it that 'many people who had just come from beer parties were rid of evil spirits; everybody received the Holy Spirit and 160 persons in all were converted.'

The first *Paseka* or *Pendi* (the Apostles frequently use the word *Pendi*, presumably derived from Pentecost, to indicate their annual festival) was held on the 24th of August, 1934. The Holy Spirit showed Johane that there should be an annual 'eating of bread and drinking of wine' in commemoration of Christ's death for those who wanted to go to heaven. This occasion even grew in importance in the course of years. After Johane's death in 1963 the *Paseka* date was shifted to the 17th of July, in commemoration of the Apostle leader's calling by the Holy Spirit. Each year in July, thousands of people flock from all over the country and beyond its borders to the Maranke reserve for this big occasion. Participation in this outstanding event is coveted by every zealous Apostle.

Phillip and Munyonga were the first patients to arrive at Maranke from as far afield as Salisbury for treatment. Both of them complained of having been bewitched and they wanted Johane to drive the evil spirits away. After staying at Johane's homestead for a few weeks they returned to Salisbury where they began to preach and convert others. Their testimony of Johane's healing abilities became a powerful attraction. It was part of Johane's expansion strategy to heal people, and then to ordain them as leaders in the new movement before sending them home to win new converts.

In the late 1930's Johane was requested to visit some of the reserves in the vicinity of Salisbury, where the first 'patients' had meanwhile succeeded in converting many new members. He and Simon set out on foot, travelling from one village to another with their apocalyptic message. Simon interpreted to the people what Johane said when he had spells of Spirit-possession. Healing featured prominently in all their activities. Their attitude concerning the 'things of this world' was radical and prohibitive, modelled to a large extent on Old Testament laws, especially as regards the use of certain types of food. Amongst the new converts the natural leaders were sought out and ordained – always, of course, with the sanction of the Holy Spirit. These leaders were then left behind to organize and extend the new congregations. They were also expected to report back at Maranke headquarters (map 3) from time to time on the progress of their work.

As the Church grew, the local congregations gradually became 'top-heavy' with leaders. The procedure was that the local officials appointed nominees – mostly close relatives – as assistants to help them with the work of the Church in the rural areas. These nominees were expected to come to the annual *Paseka* festival, where the Church council could discuss their nominations, and, if approved, ordain them officially as leaders. In this way a strong motivation was created for men with leadership aspirations to attend the annual *Paseka*. Leadership disputes ensued, and in 1940, Johane introduced a differentiated leadership structure to cope with rising leadership conflicts. This system comprised a hierarchical structure of five different offices of leaders – baptists, evangelists, healers, prophets and judges. Each category of leadership was subdivided into five ranks. Promotion from a lower to a higher rank depended on the death or disqualification of a senior official, or on inheritance.[48]

In eight years' time a phenomenal growth of the Church had taken place. Simon, who kept a record of all the places in the various tribal trust lands where they had established *Paseka* or *Pendi* centres for the local Church members, estimates that by 1940 they had well over 100 such sites which they had to visit annually to conduct Communion services for Apostles scattered

48. The patterns of leadership succession will be described in Volume 3.

all over the country. These journeys were undertaken on foot, on bicycle and by ox-cart, until 1950, when a big meeting of Church leaders at Musengezi decided to contribute money for the purchase of a motor vehicle. In the following years enough money was collected to purchase two Land-Rovers, for the exclusive use of Johane, Simon and other leaders on *Paseka* journeys. Whereas Johane and Simon at first used to stay one week in a tribal ward before conducting a *Paseka* ceremony, they were later forced to conduct up to four or five such ceremonies per week in the wards of the more densely populated areas. In 1957, Abero and Makebo, Johane's eldest sons, who had meanwhile been consecrated as baptists, were given the responsibility of touring the central and southern districts of Rhodesia to conduct *Paseka* services.

Johane's travels took him southwards as far as the Transvaal and the Orange Free State, where he is reported to have baptized many people. His main drive was towards the north, however, and on one of his several campaigns beyond the boundaries of Rhodesia, he reached the central parts of the Congo. Especially amongst the Kasai he founded a strong following. When Abero visited the Congo in 1964, having by that time succeeded his father, he stayed in the country for more than a month and conducted 8 *Paseka* ceremonies in the vicinity of Elizabethville and Chingulu. The total count of their followers in the Congo was then 10,700 and it is reported to be still rising.[49] In 1965 more than 10,000 were reported to have received the Sacraments at places such as Ndadya, Blantyre and Port Herald in Malawi. Apart from a substantial membership in Malawi, Zambia, Congo, Mozambique and Botswana, this movement at present has spread to all the cities, major towns and tribal areas in Rhodesia, with, for example, eight large *Paseka* centres in the Gutu district alone. In Rhodesia there are approximately 50,000 Church members, with crowds up to 20,000 annually visiting the Maranke reserve for the main festivities.

d) *Minor and major schisms*

Between 1940 and 1950 only two schisms worth mentioning took place in the Apostolic Church, neither of which resulted in heavy loss of numbers to the parental body. The first schism occurred when *Ruka Mataruka*, Johane's brother-in-law, refused to worship with the founder of the movement any longer. Ruka had gained a considerable following through his evangelistic

49. Barrett (1968, p. 296) estimates the Apostles of Johane to amount to 40,000 in the Congo.

activities and he wanted to assert full authority over these members. He maintained a loose affiliation with Johane for several years, but led his followers up into the mountains for worship. Yet his followers attended services in both camps until the schism became complete. During one of the big conferences, Ruka publicly challenged Johane's authority as the leader of all Apostles. There then followed what one can best call a 'fire-competition'. Ruka is said to have 'made a fire on his head' while preaching in order to demonstrate his superiority over Johane. The latter countered the challenge by placing his Bible and garments in a fire while preaching, without their being burnt. Those who were present were satisfied that Ruka's bid for leadership of the group had failed, and many of his followers rejoined Johane. Ruka's prestige finally dwindled when Johane and Simon staged campaigns in Portuguese East Africa and some of the south-eastern territories in Rhodesia, where Ruka had his main following. They stressed that Ruka had gone astray as a leader and that eternal salvation could not be obtained by following him. As a result Ruka was left behind with only a handful of loyal followers. It was afterwards reported that he had completely fallen back on traditional forms of worship.

Joshua, Johane's first convert in the Gutu district (at Vunjere near Chingombe), and at the time of secession the most important Liebauma prophet-healer in that area, broke away in the early 1940's. He took a considerable number of the Gutu members with him, many of whom soon returned to the original fold. The cause of this fission is difficult to assess accurately, beyond the fact that a dispute arose between some of the Gutu Apostles and their local leader Joshua, because of an alleged misappropriation of Church funds. The issue was Joshua's purchase of a bicycle for Church work, with Church funds. When the matter was sorted out to Joshua's discredit by the Church court in Maranke, he decided to carry on independently with as many members as would follow him. Since then he has managed to gain new followers in Gutu, but these form what one might call a 'floating membership' with members coming and going between his and Johane's groups as their personal preferences dictate from time to time. In recent years Joshua has become one of the most popular 'witch-hunters' in the South-Eastern districts, modelling his practices on the traditional witch-hunts. His popularity as a witch-finder resulted in his becoming very much of a roving prophet with insufficient stability at his Church headquarters to organize his followers into a cohesive group.

The major schism in the Apostolic Church took place in 1963, shortly after Johane's death. Johane, Simon and Obed Chanakira were out on one of the *Paseka* rounds when a prophet told Johane at Gwelo to return home, lest he fall grievously ill while continuing the journey. Johane refused to heed this advice, saying 'I must die whilst doing evangelistic work (*Ndinofanira kufa pabasa rouvangeri*).' The Apostles at Sanyati found their leader too ill when he arrived there to conduct the *Paseka*. At Karoi, further north, his condition became critical and he was driven back home while Simon and Obed were ordered to continue the trip into Zambia. When Johane died shortly after reaching home, Simon was summoned to return to the Maranke reserve immediately because he was the only Apostle leader who 'knew how Johane had to be buried'. When he and Obed arrived at Johane's homestead they found that the seeds of suspicion concerning the cause of Johane's death had already been sown. It was suggested by some of Johane's close relatives that these two leaders, who had accompanied him, had ensorcelled him by adding some deadly potion to his food, in order to succeed to his leadership after his death.

In the struggle for power that followed, Johane's maternal cousins (Simon and Gwati) and some of his more distant relatives (Beremauro and Moses), who had all achieved leader positions in the Church, sided against Johane's blood brother, Anrod, and partly against Johane's sons. Anrod was in a strong position. He could claim seniority of Church membership over Simon because he had been converted – although not baptized – by Johane before Simon. At the same time, and even of greater importance, there was the fact that he was Johane's full brother, which enabled him to invoke the traditional Shona law of succession on behalf of Abero, Johane's senior son and legal successor. Simon argued that in the hierarchic order of the Church he had always been second to Johane, and that the Church founder's wish before his death was that he, Simon, would continue to act as the leader on *Paseka* tours. It is common knowledge that Johane had ordered Abero to succeed him as the Church's leader, but it is dubious whether there were clear instructions concerning the future positions of the junior sons. Anrod knew, however, that the only way to prevent Simon from consolidating his already powerful position in the Church, was to relegate all the really significant leadership positions to Johane's sons on the basis of customary law. In this way he, as *babamukuru* of Johane's sons, could maintain his influential position in the Church without interference by his maternal cousins. Factors to Anrod's advantage were, firstly, a social setting which favoured the inheritance of leadership, and secondly, a Church membership which still accepted the *kugadzira* ritual in its Christianized version. As superordinated kinsman and advisor of the successor to Johane's name and house (*imba*), he was in a position to exploit these factors to the full. On occasion he himself commented on the retention of some of the *kugadzira* procedures by Apostles as follows: 'The Holy Spirit did not rule out [*dzivisa*] the customs introduced by our forebears; He only refused our worshipping the ancestors.'

On the day after Johane's burial, after it had been ascertained by a delegation that witches had not tampered with the grave, all the relatives assembled at Johane's homestead for the *kugadzira* proceedings. It should be noted that the traditional *kugadzira* ritual is conducted by some of the Manyika tribes directly after the burial ceremony, in contrast with the Karanga tribes who conduct it at a much later stage. The ritual as conducted by the Apostles is said to be devoid of ancestor worship (*kupira midzimu*); traditional beer is not used and the ritual in the Church mainly signifies the transfer of the name and responsibilities of the deceased to the senior son. Anrod started the proceedings by saying, '*Yabara yafa*' ('That which dies gives birth', meaning that Johane had left descendants when he died). He then asked Abero, Johane's senior son, to take place on a sleeping mat (*rupasa*) for the name-giving ceremony to take place. Abero received his father's hereditary name and his staff, which signified his acceptance of responsibility for his father's family as well as his installment as 'first priest' of the Church. When Anrod proceeded by giving Johane's other two Church staves to Makebo and Judah, Abero's younger brothers, with the clear implication of conferring the second and third leading positions to them, Simon stood up to complain. He said, 'The inheritance of the Word of God is not inherited by children! (*Nhaka yeShoko roWedanga haigarwi nhaka navana kwete*).' Anrod then told Simon that he, as a distant relative, had no say in the matter. He also stated that, before his death, Johane had ordered that Simon should be told to 'rest' after his return from the north, and to cease his *Paseka* activities. This, then, was Anrod's trump card. He claimed to have privately received Johane's last instructions. During this family ritual Simon, as a distant relative, was not entitled to interfere drastically with the proceedings. Realizing that he had been bypassed in a family ritual, which nevertheless held direct consequences for the entire Church, he sat down and remained silent.

During the part of the ceremony called *kugova nhaka* (distribution of the possessions of the deceased),[50] Anrod sat down on the sleeping mat to receive his inheritance in traditional fashion. There being no other full brother to inherit the 16 widows left by Johane, Anrod was the legal claimant, according to customary law. The practice that the women of the deceased 'cross the bow' (*kudarika uta*) in order to detect those who had committed adultery, had been discontinued in the Church, because the acceptance of the all-knowing Holy Spirit, as 'sin-detector', made this practice superfluous. All that was expected of the women on this occasion was to offer Anrod some drinking water in a gourd if they were prepared to accept him as their future hus-

50. *Supra*, p. 109.

band and guardian. Thirteen of the sixteen women complied, while the other three decided to return to their home villages. It was decided that the 40 head of cattle left by Johane would be taken care of by Anrod together with Abero and Makebo. Since the three eldest sons had already completed the *roora* payment for their first wives, the cattle had to be kept for the future *roora* arrangements of the junior brothers. Decisions concerning the cattle could not be taken individually by Abero or Anrod, but Anrod in his capacity as *babamukuru* (father's elder brother) had the final word in such matters.

The two Land-Rovers were on this occasion regarded as part of Johane's personal *nhaka*-estate – and because these motor vehicles had been purchased for the purpose of visiting outlying *Paseka* centres, it was agreed by the relatives that Abero and Makebo now, being first and second priests, should have the new and older model respectively. Had Johane not wished his sons to continue the *Paseka* rounds, Abero in northerly and Makebo in southerly direction? Simon's supporters later bitterly opposed this arrangement. To them the Land-Rovers represented Church property, purchased with Church funds, which should not have been disposed of in the same way as Johane's personal possessions. They felt that this issue should be resolved by a Church council of elders, and not by the close relatives of the deceased. But Simon's complaints were never heard in a full Church council. His public statement that Church leadership could not be inherited, and his refusal to accept what he called 'the leadership of children', was immediately used against him by Anrod's faction to brand him as a rebel.

With the *kugadzira* ritual Anrod had played his trump card. He had become the prime mover in Church affairs by entrenching the key positions within Johane's agnatic line of descent. Abero, the successor in name, acknowledged the paternal authority of his *babamukuru* not only in domestic but also in important Church affairs. It is generally acknowledged in Church circles and also by Anrod himself, that important matters (*mhosva huru*) cannot be judged without consulting Anrod. He had furthermore succeeded in eliminating Simon's claims by virtually confronting him with the choice between staying in Johane's Church as a 'resting member' – for which he vouched Johane's sanction – or breaking away and forming a Church under his own leadership. As rumours had already been spread about Simon as a possible sorcerer (*muroyi*), who in one way or another had a hand in Johane's death, the additional suggestion by Anrod's faction that Simon was the one who had all along been planning to break away and organize his own Church found fertile soil. At a later stage, when Simon began organizing his own Church, *after* he had failed to gain the support of the Church council against the arrangements made by Johane's close relatives, Anrod ingeniously posed as the champion of Church unity.

In the ensuing conflict Gwati, the secretary, and a maternal cousin of Johane, who found his position in the Church to be in the balance, publicly sided with Simon. More distant relatives, like Moses and Beremauro, steered a safer course, although a number of oral reports suggest that they did not agree with Anrod's actions at the time. The only way the opposing parties could publicly vent their feelings was during Church services, when they could preach against each other. Anrod is reported to have called Simon a heathen for trying to cause a rift in the Church. Simon countered by preaching that Anrod had illegally grabbed the power in the Church. He said that Anrod had inherited his Liebaumaship from Conorio, meaning that he (Anrod) was actually only a junior leader, without jurisdiction in matters of Church leadership. 'Is it not I who had helped Johane by laying hands on new leaders when they were consecrated?' he asked. Simon stated that he had no objection to Abero's inheriting his father's position, but he could not agree with the ordination of the 'young ones' (Makebo and Judah), which implied his own expulsion and that of his son, Lishon. He reminded his audience that at Johane's request Lishon had accompanied Abero on *Paseka* tours in the past, in the same way as he, Simon, used to accompany Johane. After Johane's burial Lishon had been abused and chased away by Johane's relatives.

Gwati gives a lively account of the 'fighting sermons' at Chikozho, one of the places where the Church had a monthly meeting. 'Anrod scolded us and said that God had given the Church to Johane's children. Simon then severely scolded Anrod, after which I stood up and preached forcefully from 2 Kings 2 : 15. I told them that the prophet Elijah was not succeeded by a son, but by Elisha, which proved that the leadership of this [prophetic] type of Church cannot be inherited. That day we "hit Anrod so hard" with Biblical verses that he remained quiet and refused to eat porridge [*sadza*] for the rest of the day.'[51]

The final crisis came when Anrod announced a change in Church program. It had become a routine practice for the Apostles living in the Maranke tribal area to have an annual meeting at Mt. Nyengwe, where Johane was first 'filled' by the Holy Spirit. On these occasions Johane used to lead his followers up the mountain and prophesy for them on personal and Church matters. All the great prophecies of the past were therefore associated with Mt. Nyengwe. It was believed that on this mountain the Spirit revealed itself with particular power. But Anrod called a meeting to tell the people that Johane had not authorized (*simbisa*) anyone else to lead the Apostles up the

51. Personal interview with Gwati, 1966.

mountain, so that this practice would be discontinued. Instead, he said, there would be meetings at Mufararikwa, an area much closer to Abero's homestead. This move was a final blow to Simon. Mt. Nyengwe is near his homestead and the homesteads of those relatives or Church members who were likely to remain loyal to him. Elimination of this important meeting meant that large-scale meetings were no longer to be held in a place where Simon could take the initiative, and where he still had a chance of asserting his influence through his prophecies on the mountain. Had this practice been continued, Simon, as first prophet of the movement, might well have been considered the only competent person, for the first few years at least, to lead the Apostles up the mountain. Ironically enough, both parties based their arguments on Johane's alleged instructions: Anrod by referring to Johane's last wish before he died; and Gwati, by referring to his dreams after Johane's death, in which Johane was said to have urged that the Mt. Nyengwe prophecies be continued.

At this stage Simon and his supporters announced that they would continue to worship at Mt. Nyengwe, regardless of Anrod's new arrangements. They notified the chief and requested him to try and settle the dispute at his court. The chief reluctantly called a meeting to see if he could resolve the conflict and the growing unrest. A delegation of 42 senior leaders of Johane's Church attended this *dare*. Simon's main complaints comprised: first, the 'illegal' ordination of Makebo and Judah, who had not been anointed by the Holy Spirit; secondly, Anrod's abolition of the meetings at Mt. Nyengwe, and thirdly, the inheritance of both Land-Rovers by Johane's sons. It should be stressed that up to this stage Simon had repeatedly stated that he did *not* want to form a separate Church, but that he could not accept Anrod's reasons for ousting him and his son from the leading positions they occupied prior to Johane's death. The *dare* neatly circumvented the real issues by proposing that Simon be allowed to form his own Church and have it registered in the District Commissioner's 'book'. In this way a direct judgment concerning Anrod's manipulation of the succession issue – which involved conflicting traditional and Christian values – was avoided. Acceptance of these proposals, however, would give Simon – contrary to his own wish – the green light to organize his own Church without interference, and this would, temporarily at least, ease the tension. Moreover, the proposal at the *dare* had the advantage of compromise, which saved the senior Church leaders the embarrassment of taking a public stand for or against Anrod, who was certain to maintain the central leadership of the widely dispersed congregations all over the country with the assistance of Abero and Makebo. The acceptance of the proposal by the majority of Church leaders present (thirty-four leaders voted for, and only four against the proposal), signifies their acceptance of a schism as the only solution to a complex leadership problem.

The chief's reluctance to become fully involved in the conflict is clearly illustrated by his refusal to enforce another majority decision on the Church leaders, which was that one of the Land-Rovers should be turned over to Simon. Anrod opposed this proposal on the grounds that both cars belonged to Johane's own estate. Mudara, the senior Church councillor at the time, was then asked by the chief to resolve this issue. The consequence was predictable: no further action was taken to enforce the majority decision.

After the chief's meeting Simon and Anrod finally parted. Anrod was prepared to face a schism rather than allow Simon to assume power within the Church. Simon went away with the intention of having his name written in the District Commissioner's 'book' as the leader of a Church which, to him and his followers, was to represent the true Church of Johane Maranke. He erected a signpost at his homestead with the inscription:

African Apostolic Church
St. Simon
and
St. Johane

Johane's name is written beneath that of Simon to indicate the 'resting state' of the founder of the movement.

In 1964 Simon conducted his first independent *Paseka* near Mt. Nyengwe, which was attended by 477 people. To those senior leaders and relatives like Beremauro, Mudara, Moses and Bwizi (most of them *Rabaumah*-leaders), who sympathized with Simon and therefore attended this first *Paseka*, the lack of great numbers of participants must have come as an anticlimax in comparison with the thousands that used to come in the past. So they returned the following year to the more popular *Paseka* meeting of the parental body, which left Simon and Gwati as the main leaders of the newly formed schismatic Church.

Simon's following has since increased to more than a thousand members in the Maranke Reserve alone. He also conducts the local *Paseka* for several Apostle congregations at Sipolilo, Buhera, Jena (Victoria district) and Bikita. The general complaint of leaders who have thus far joined him, is the excessive demands of Abero and Makebo with regard to *Paseka* fees. They allege that £25 'petrol money' is now charged per *Paseka* centre, instead of the £5 which used to be given to Johane. Simon's Church has evidently become a place of refuge for malcontents in Abero's and Anrod's fold. It provides an outlet for those with frustrated leadership ambitions and with complaints about administrative malpractices. In 1966, when the major July festivities in Maranke took place, Obed, the senior of all the Bikita leaders, had an argument with Anrod. When an agreement could not be reached, Obed, followed by about fifty of the other Bikita Apostles together with their families, simply shifted their camp and were found the next day at Simon's *Paseka*, ten miles away.

3. THE APOSTOLIC SABBATH CHURCH OF GOD OF JOHANE MASOWE (OR GANDANZARA)

Another Spirit-type Independent Church which first came into being in the south-eastern regions of Rhodesia is Johane (formerly called Shoniwa) Masowe's *Apostolic Sabbath Church of God*. Sundkler gives us a brief description of Masowe's Messianic movement.[52] Like several other African Independent Church leaders, Masowe is believed to have 'died' and then to have been sent back to this world as the 'Messenger of God'. After he returned from the Marimba mountains in the Rusape district where he received his divine commission, he was no longer called Shoniwa, but Johane, because he had returned from the 'wilderness' like John the Baptist. His message was radical and apocalyptic: the imminence of the Day of Judgment, an assurance that his followers would not die; that Government, Churches and the sacraments were of the devil; that his followers should not erect Church buildings, etc. Having established himself as a 'Messiah' of the Shona and Ndebele in the early 1930's, Masowe first moved to Johannesburg, then lived for some years in Bechuanaland. Afterwards, he and his followers, called the vaHossana, settled in the Korsten slum, near Port Elizabeth, in 1947. Here the Masowe group, of whom many were vaShona, become known as the Korsten basketweavers. Characteristic of Masowe's leadership is his claim to a divinely changed identity after a 'resurrection'. He was no longer Shoniwa '. . . for Shoniwa was dead; but he was John Masowe, the Son of God, sent out by God in order to prepare the judgment. Jesus had come in the person of John Masowe, descendant of the original people of God, speaking the original language of mankind, Shona.'[53]

Masowe's Church does not feature prominently in the Gutu, Bikita and Victoria districts any longer. A considerable following still seems to exist in the eastern districts, between his home district Rusape, and Umtali. Infor-

52. Sundkler, *op. cit.*, pp. 323-325.
53. *Ibid.*, p. 324.

mants from Chingombe assert that Masowe's Apostles are also found in the vicinity of Gwelo, Que Que and Bulawayo. I did not particularly study this movement, but it is worth mentioning because it forms the background to the formation of the Church of the *Shinga Postora* (Courageous Apostles) which came into being in the Gutu district during my stay in Chingombe. The prime movers of the *Shinga Postora*, Prophet Elison Mutingwende of Chingombe, and Rev. (*mufundisi*) Daniel Dziro of Nyamande, both belonged to Masowe's group before they started their own 'Church'. Their activities[54] give an idea of what can happen to the 'floating membership' of a Church when its leader has lost contact with his followers.

Irregular contact with their leader and the secretive nature of Masowe's operations have left the Gutu Hossanas with brief and somewhat vague recollections about the origin of their Church. They know about the 'death' of Masowe, but Elison Mutingwende gives a different account of this event from that found in Sundkler's book. He holds that Shoniwa was imprisoned at Salisbury where he 'died' after having received treatment in hospital. According to Elison:

'Shoniwa was buried near the Harare mountain before he arose from the dead on the third day. While dead, he saw a staff which was singing, "Hossana, Hossana!" This staff and some garments were given to him when he returned to the world. When the police saw that he had risen from the dead they were greatly surprised. The Government gave him a Bible and told him to bring the Gospel to the people. On his preaching tours he met Johane Maranke who was troubled by Spirit-possession. He laid hands on Johane and for some time the two of them worked together. Johane first broke away to form his own Church and then Barnabas of Buhera district broke away. Barnabas quarrelled with Masowe about the consumption of sweet beer [*mangisi*]. He said that the prophet Isaiah allowed such beer to be drunk . . . We know Masowe by the names of Shoniwa Masowe or as Gandanzara. He is still alive. I saw him last in Bechuanaland in 1952, when he was living in Port Elizabeth. We believe that he has not yet died, but we do not know when he will return. We do not know of his doctrine about not dying . . . all the Hossanas die as other people do!'

Samuel Dziro recalls that he had last seen Gandanzara in 1924, when the latter passed through the Gutu district on a preaching tour. 'We do not know where he is now, but he did send a letter occasionally when Church funds were needed, and some of the other leaders came out here in former years for joint meetings. Some people say that he went north on a preaching cam-

54. To be described in a chapter dealing with 'Prophetism and Wizardry', in Volume 2.

paign and that he nearly reached the ocean beyond Tanganyika. We did not use the sacraments because Johane said, "The sacraments are only to be used in heaven". He did not allow us, as lesser leaders, to baptize in Jordan. Only he baptized. Now we have decided to baptize people ourselves because we are afraid people may die and be rejected by God because they are not baptized.'

Sundkler's reference to Masowe as the 'secret Messiah' certainly rings true according to these two accounts, because the movements of their leader were an enigma to Elison and Dziro. If Dziro's date of meeting Masowe is correct, this Apostolic leader must have been active before Johane Maranke made his appearance. Although the Maranke Apostles do not acknowledge any former link with the Masowe Apostles, it is possible that Johane was influenced by Masowe himself, or by Masowe's followers, during his stay in Umtali. Sundkler again indicates that Masowe himself had originally been influenced by Watch Tower doctrines.

Whether Masowe 'died' in Rusape or in Salisbury does not affect his claim that he had received supernatural sanction for his work, which, according to Sundkler, 'is the first necessity for the one who would be recognized as a Messiah.'[55] Elison's reference to Masowe's resurrection, and the so-called 'Government's approval' of his calling, are probably later efforts to strengthen the mythical history of Masowe. The first serves to emphasize the similarity between his task and that of Christ, and the second to provide an element of credibility to his supposed resurrection. Actually Barnabas of Buhera was Masowe's main contact with the scattered Gandanzara disciples in Gutu, until he (Barnabas) died in the early 1950's. Although Barnabas had broken with Masowe on the beer issue, and although he was recognized by the Gutu factions as the principal regional leader, men like Elison and Dziro still regarded themselves as Masowe followers. Their isolation from the main body of Hossanas became more or less complete after the death of Barnabas. The lengthy absence of their 'Messiah' raised doubts in their midst. The exclusive claims of an absent Messiah became untenable, not least because of the increasing emphasis of other Spirit-type Churches on the absolute necessity of baptism in Jordan as a prerequisite for salvation. Who was going to baptize their children or new followers if their own 'Messiah' failed to return? And why did all the other Churches set such store by the use of the sacraments? As time went by and their principal leader did not appear to solve their problems, the Gandanzara believers began to join other Independent Church groups, or merely fell back upon their traditional practices. Elison

55. Sundkler, *op. cit.*, p. 325.

MAP 3 DISTRICTS WHERE FIELD-

Distribution of land; Locati
Surveyed Independent Chu

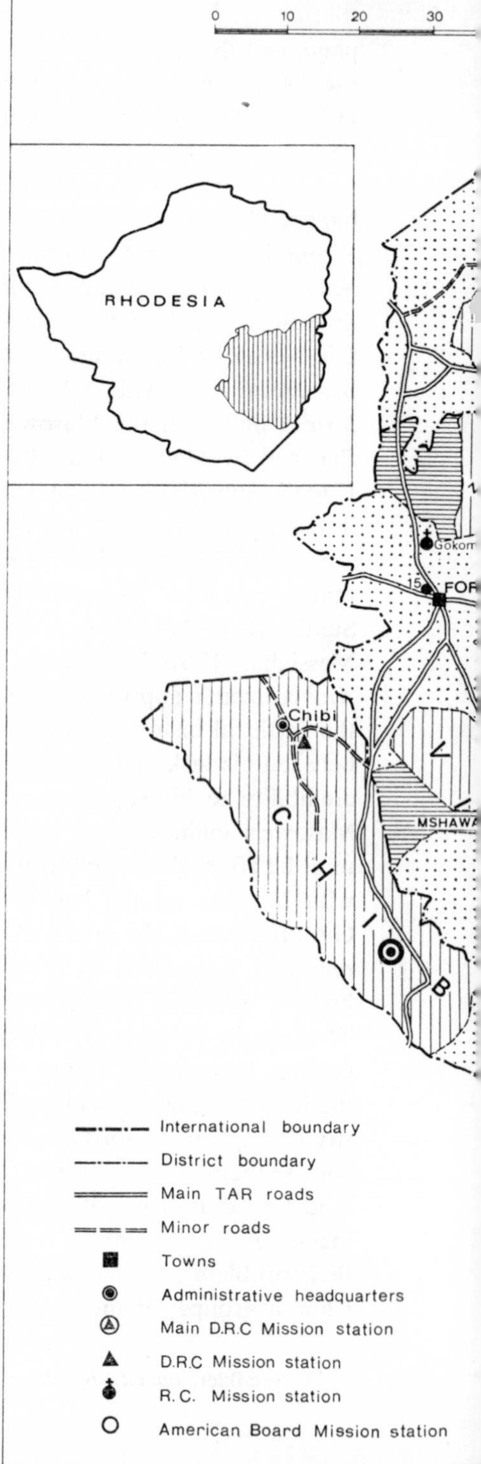

0 10 20 30

RHODESIA

Gokom

15 FOR

Chibi

CHIBI

MSHAWA

- ⦿ *Main Independent Church headquarters*

1. ZION APOSTOLIC FAITH MISSION (Bishop Andreas Shoko)
2. ZION APOSTOLIC CHURCH OF SOUTH AFRICA (Bishop David Masuka)
3. ZION CHRISTIAN CHURCH (Rev. Samuel Mutendi)
4. ZION APOSTOLIC CHURCH (Bishop Makamba)
5. AFRICAN APOSTOLIC CHURCH OF JOHANE MARANKE (Priest Abero)
6. FIRST ETHIOPIAN CHURCH (Bishop Nheya Gavure)
7. AFRICAN CONGREGATIONAL CHURCH – CHIBARIRWE – (Rev. Zvekare Sengwayo)
8. AFRICAN REFORMED CHURCH at *Shonganiso* Mission (Rev. Jonas Zvobgo)

- • *Minor Independent Church headquarters of schismatic leaders*

9. Rev. Joram Gwai – seceded from Mutendi's ZCC
10. Bishop Nehemia Chengerai – seceded from Makamba's ZAC
11. Bishop Nehemia Gotore (ZION SABBATA) – advanced schism from ZAC of SA
12. Bishop Kudzerema (ZAC OF JESUS CHRIST) – seceded from Masuka's ZAC of SA
13. Bishop Matthew Zungura (ZCC) – successor of Makuti, who seceded from the ZCC
14. Bishop Zacheo (ZION PROTESTANT CHURCH) – advanced schism from ZAC of SA
15. Evangelist David Mabika – seceded from the ZCC
16. Rev. Moses Ruwana – influential *Chibarirwe* leader
17. Rev. Kumani Sibambo – seceded from the ACC to from the ARC (see No. 8 above)

International boundary
District boundary
Main TAR roads
Minor roads
Towns
Administrative headquarters
Main D.R.C Mission station
D.R.C Mission station
R.C. Mission station
American Board Mission station

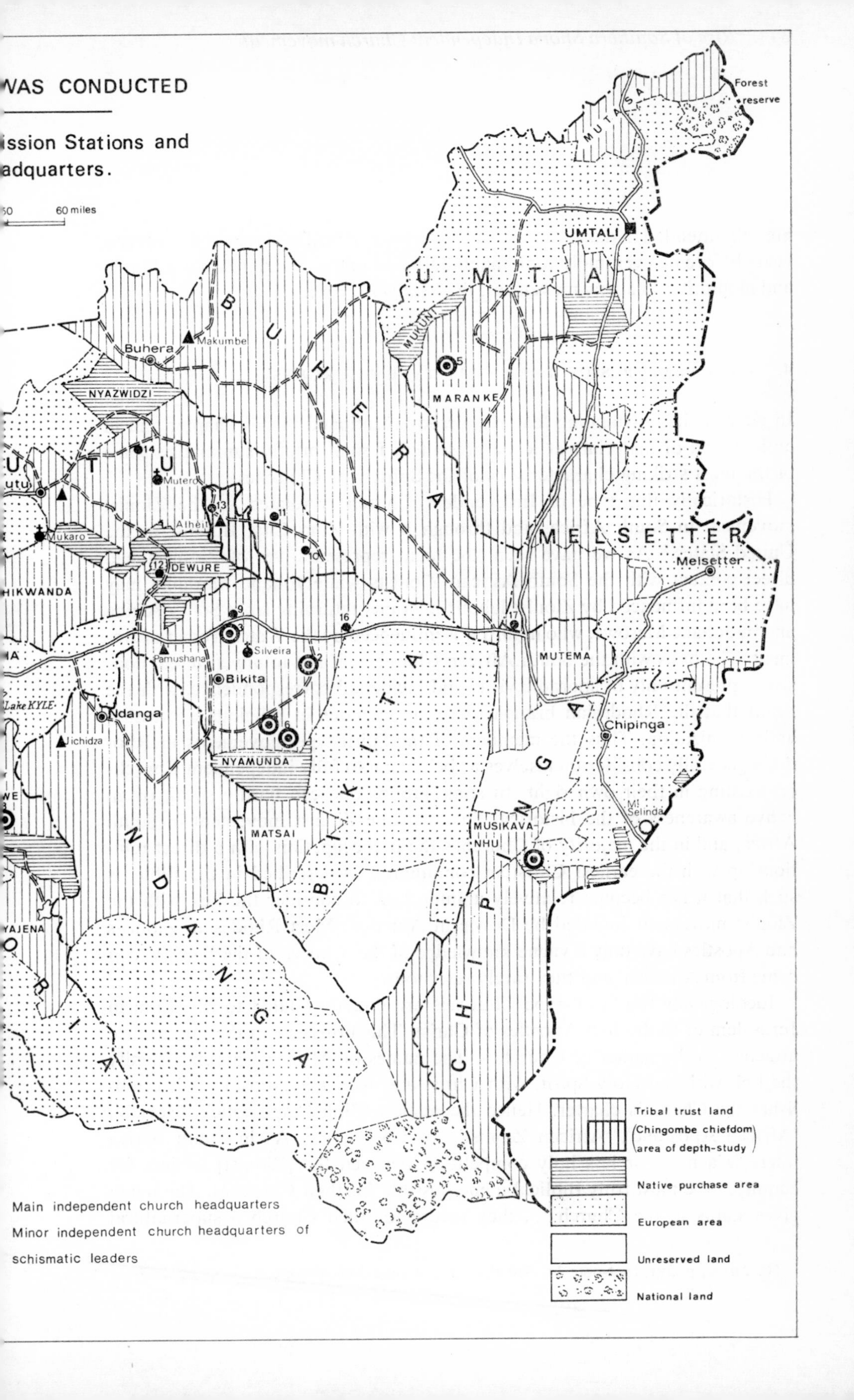

WAS CONDUCTED
ission Stations and
adquarters.
60 miles
Forest reserve
MUTASA
UMTALI
U M T A L I
B U H E R A
Makumbe
Buhera
NYAZWIDZI
MUKUNI
MARANKE
Mutero
Alheit
Mukaro
DEWURE
HIKWANDA
MELSETTER
Melsetter
Pamushana
Silveira
Bikita
MUTEMA
Lake KYLE
Ndanga
Jichidza
NYAMUNDA
Chipinga
MATSAI
Mt Selinda
MUSIKAVANHU
B I K I T A
N D A N G A
C H I P I N G A
YAJENA
Tribal trust land
(Chingombe chiefdom area of depth-study)
Native purchase area
European area
Unreserved land
National land
Main independent church headquarters
Minor independent church headquarters of schismatic leaders

himself attended Ndaza Zionist and Maranke Apostle services for several years before he eventually took the initiative to revive Gandanzara's 'Church' and mould it into a new movement, the *Shinga Postora*.

4. MAIN FEATURES OF THE SPIRIT-TYPE CHURCHES

In view of the outstanding features already mentioned in this chapter and in anticipation of material yet to be presented, I shall briefly summarize some of the most striking characteristics of the Spirit-type Churches.

Historically this type of Independent Church is related to the Zionist movement in South Africa, and through it with Zion City, Illinois, in the United States.[56] As we have seen, the main representatives of Zionism had direct contact with the South African Zionists while Johane Maranke may have been influenced by Zionist labour migrants returning from South Africa and by Johane Masowe, who in turn was influenced by the Watch Tower movement. The links with the South African Churches, if not totally severed, consist at present only of sporadic visits and incidental correspondence, with the result that the Rhodesian branches are autonomous in religious expression and organization. Thus the members of the Spirit-type movements in Rhodesia generally consider themselves as belonging to fully independent Churches, existing in their own right. In some groups one can hardly speak of an active awareness of the historical link with the Zionist movement in South Africa, and in the majority of Churches the preoccupation with a direct relationship with the earliest Christian community, as described in the Bible, is such that it has become relatively unimportant to consider the link with the Zionist movement founded by Dowie in America. Most Rhodesian Zionists and Apostles have only a vague knowledge of the 'Church of the Spirit which came from America' and they rarely refer to it.

Ideologically the Spirit-type Churches are directly related to Mt. Zion in Jerusalem or to the first Apostles of Christ. This brings us to the importance attached to the names of Churches. The names of African Churches signify the link with the Holy Spirit, with Christ and with His Apostles – it establishes the Church's charter. Hence the names: 'Zion', 'Apostolic', 'Moriah', 'African Apostolic', 'African Zionist', 'of Christ', etc. As in South Africa 'there is a more or less holy competition between the [Zionist] leaders for acquiring the most truly Biblical name possible for their Churches. The name gives status to the Church . . . they secure for their Church a supernatural

56. *Supra*, p. 291, foot-note 15. See also Zionist genealogical table.

bond with these holy guarantees and they signify a charter showing the spiritual strength of the Church.'[57]

Mention has been made of the fact that the then young labour migrants, Mutendi and Andreas Shoko, were deeply impressed by the Sotho Zionists' adherence to a proper Biblical name for their Church. In addition there was the significant discovery that the name 'Dutch Reformed Church' was not to be found in the Bible.

A good example of the desire to establish a direct link with the first Christian community is to be found in Mutendi's diagrammatic representation of Christianity since the time of Christ. According to this diagram, which is kept in the Church office of Zion City, the first group of Christians up to about 400-500 A.D. belonged to the 'Zion Church'. Then the Apostles founded the Catholic Church as an extension of the 'Zion Church', the latter somehow failing to perpetuate itself properly. From the Catholic Church branched the Montanists, Celtic Church, Waldenses, Lollards and others, which groups dwindled away, while the two other branches – the Ethiopian Church founded by the eunuch of Ethiopia and the Greek 'Catholic' Church – continued to exist as *important* (according to the diagram's lines) movements in Christianity up to the year 1900, with the branches of the Anglo-Saxon and Calvinist (including the DRC and the *Chibarirwe*) Churches clearly indicated. Then, in 1923, still in the main diagrammatic line of Christianity, appears the Zion Christian Church of the Rev. Samuel Mutendi as the true continuation of the early 'Zion Church'. The other Zionist groups in Rhodesia are presented as the branches of the main Zion Christian Church. The exact relationship of the ZCC with the preceding Churches is not as important as the fact that this Church now appears, diagrammatically at least, on the same level as the formerly discontinued Zion Church, on the 'main line' of Christianity and as a true representation of the ancient and authentic Christian community (see diagram – Appendix V).

Although more attention is paid in religious life to the work of the Holy Spirit than that of Christ, the names or constitutions of these movements usually bear a close association with Jesus Christ. Thus the secessionist Zionist leader, Kudzerema, calls his Church the *Zion Apostolic Church of Jesus Christ* and Bishop Komboni Vambire his, the *African Zion Church of Jesus.* In his constitution Mutendi lays down as the basis of his Zion Christian Church that it shall be called 'Zion, City of the living God, Heavenly Jerusalem, innumerable company of angels; general assembly and Church of all (Hebr. 12 : 12-23) and built upon the foundations of the Apostles and

57. Sundkler, *op. cit.*, p. 59.

prophets, *Jesus Christ Himself being the chief cornerstone* (Eph. 2 : 20)' – my italics.[58] The Apostles claim, however, that the Zionists, through their emphasis on 'Zion', are less authentic than they themselves and that one can only be a true follower of Christ as an Apostle. The very name of their Church gives them a monopoly on Christian discipleship. They are the ones who have responded to the call of Christ, they, the divinely elected descendants of the neglected house of Ham, are now given the responsibility of spreading God's word among Africans.

The Church's name and its interpretation also signifies the main program of each group. In the Zionist camp one aims at realizing in the African setting something of the community of believers as it is believed to have functioned in ancient Jerusalem and as one believes the coming Kingdom of God should be realized in this existence. To be a Zionist, and therefore a citizen of the heavenly Holy City, finds expression in a wide range of activities varying from the mere assertion of belonging to Zion during sermons in the smaller Ndaza Zionist groups, to the all-embracing and group-consolidating activities of actually building 'Jerusalem' at Mutendi's headquarters. Additional distinctions such as 'Zion Sabbata' or 'Zionist Protestant' point at doctrinal differences between different Zionist groupings, such as keeping the Sabbath instead of the Sunday, or a stricter application of the Zionist code in reaction to compromising laxity of some leaders within the movement. The Apostles, in turn, interpret their movement's designation literally in the sense that they have been commissioned to live like Christ's first Apostles. They, too, seek to establish a cohesive body of believers, but their discipleship does not include the building of a central 'city' as a kind of religious refuge for the believers. Small-scale communities are only allowed to develop at the recognized healing centres. For the rest, the task of a true Apostle is to move about and spread God's word and not to get involved in such time-consuming projects as building Churches and schools.

Only a few of the Spirit-type Churches have constitutions. These are sometimes drawn up when a Church applies for official recognition.[59] If compared, the constitutions of Mutendi's ZCC and Komboni's *African Zion Church of Jesus* reflect significant differences. The former, drawn up with the aid of a European lawyer, describes the basis and organizational structure of the Church; the functions of committees, duties of office-bearers, use of funds, succession to leadership and marriage procedure (see Appendix VII, No. 1). The latter starts off with the ten commandments in modified form,

58. Constitution of the Zion Christian Church, Appendix VII.
59. *Infra*, pp. 427-431.

and then proceeds to define the major activities of the Church. Therefore it is a combination of elementary Church law, Church confession and constitution, all in one. One of the most outstanding features of Komboni's constitution is that it excludes the first four commandments and commences with the fifth: 'Honour thy Father and thy Mother that thy days may be long upon the land (Ex. 20 : 12).' This is no mere coincidence nor the subjective preference of an individual Church leader, for it shows the African's concern with the horizontal relation in society, man's religiously defined obligations to his fellowman, starting with his nearest kith and kin. The vertical relationship between man and God is not really excluded or of secondary importance. It is a presupposed reality, a basis for the horizontal relations between man and man. As such, it encompasses all Church laws which, in the African setting, starts off with the interrelations of the most vital social unit, the elementary family. A special appreciation of the fifth commandment by African Christians probably derives from the similarity which they perceive between this law and the traditional emphasis on sound relations between parents and children, relations which used to be perpetuated and strengthened through ancestor worship. Neither has this similarity escaped the notice of traditionalists. Nowadays it is not uncommon to hear some of them refer to the fifth commandment as a justification for ancestor worship. It is argued that God's commandment not only applies to this existence, but that parents should also be honoured after their death and that *kupira midzimu* is the obvious way of doing so.

Komboni's constitution reflects a trait common to most Independent Churches, of the Spirit as well as the Ethiopian type, namely the effort of leaders to create a cohesive community of believers in which close fellowship is regulated in the first place by a well-defined code of interpersonal relations. In order to be of real meaning and to create a spiritual home for adherents such a code – couched as it is in Biblical terms – is adapted to customary patterns of behaviour and receives similar emphases in its application.

Ritually and doctrinally there are numerous variations between the different Spirit-Churches. But in spite of the emphasis on superficial differences by secessionist leaders in their endeavours to establish a particular identity distinct from other groups, or to justify a split from some parental group, a remarkable uniformity emerges on closer examination. As 'Churches of the Spirit (*makereke dzoMweya*)' all these groups pay special attention to the work of the Holy Spirit. This is evident not only in sermons but in most ritual activities. The Spirit always manifests His presence through speaking in tongues and through prophetic revelations. The Spirit cleanses the water of 'Jordan' for baptism – virtually all these groups practise baptism through immersion in 'Jordan' –, the Spirit reveals the hidden sins of novices about to be baptized and He possesses and inspires the novice during or after baptism. In the name of the Holy Spirit, Church laws are upheld and through His revelations the inner sanctity of Church members determined before their participation in the all-important Communion service during *Paseka* festivities. Thus the whole control system within these movements hinges on the professed work of the Holy Spirit.

Most Spirit-type movements practise faith-healing. Here, again, it is the Spirit who reveals, through the prophetic healer, the causes and nature of illness and who prescribes therapeutical treatment; through His superior power evil spirits are exorcised. Faith-healing has become one of the major attractions of the entire prophetic movement. It meets the need of Africans to combat the spiritual forces which pose a threat to their well-being. It is at this point, however, that syncretistic tendencies are most apparent, for although *nganga* practices are explicitly rejected, and with it all forms of ancestor worship, the prophetic healer's activities include remarkable parallels with those of the *nganga*. In the prophet's effort to secure for his followers a prosperous existence, safeguarded against the onslaughts of evil forces, he uses holy water and in some instances a wide variety of sanctified objects, symbolic of God's protective powers, the use of which is not entirely free from the traditional conception of the function of magical objects.

The attitude of the Spirit-type Churches towards the African community at large varies considerably. On the one hand one finds the somewhat exclusionist Apostles and some Ndaza Zionist groups, who emphasize the sanctity of the in-group in relation to outsiders to such an extent that their Church programs exclude a broad approach to general social improvement. On the other hand the Zion Christian Church and some of the larger Ndaza Zionist groups seem less tied down by doctrinal strictures and are more comprehensively involved in their society. Mutendi's direct involvement in tribal politics, his aim to establish schools for the advancement of Africans – Zionists and non-Zionists alike – and the encouragement of his followers to acquaint themselves with modern agricultural techniques through participation in Government-sponsored schemes, reflect a more comprehensive conception of the task of the Church. This comprehensive approach in turn leads to an ambivalent attitude towards the European Administration. For, in spite of a reaction to European domination and some signs of protest, co-operation in the educational and agricultural fields has led to the acceptance of Western-orientated values and in some cases to explicit appreciation for what the Government has done on behalf of Africans.

The more closed Spirit-type organizations tend to foster stronger and more obvious anti-European sentiments than the others. Sundkler's description of the South African Separatist movements conveys the impression that the strongest reactionary sentiments in relation to white rule is generated in the Ethiopian-type Churches. Their program is said to include the slogan 'Africa for the Africans'.[60] In Rhodesia the general picture is different. Here, all the Independent Churches, as essentially all-African movements, are concerned to a greater or lesser extent with the African's cause, but it is in some of the Spirit-type Churches – especially the *vaPostori* – rather than in the 'Ethiopian' movement that the strongest note of protest against the European political and religious dominance can be observed. One of the most important reasons for this difference is the geographically more restricted and predominantly rural adherence of the *Chibarirwe*, *Topia* and African Reformed Churches, compared to the substantial numbers of Zionist and Apostolic members in the urban centres where contact with the main streams of African nationalist aspirations and politics is more direct. In addition, the contact of Maranke Apostolic leaders with affiliated Church members and with socio-political developments in independent African states to the north of Rhodesia probably contributes towards more overt forms of antagonism against Europeanism than is the case in other prophetic groups.

60. Sundkler, *op. cit.*, p. 54.

5

The Ethiopian-type Churches

The Independent Churches which in this study are referred to as 'Ethiopian' are in the first place non-prophetic Church groups that lay no claim to special manifestations of the Holy Spirit. Distinct from the Spirit-type Churches, described in the previous chapter, the most 'Ethiopians' do not practise baptism by immersion in 'Jordan'. Their services tend to be less emotional, they do not as a rule exorcise spirits or indicate witches, they have less strictures or 'taboos' with regard to the use of beer, medicine, pork, etc., and their Church services follow the pattern of the Protestant Mission Churches more closely than do the prophetic movements. Sundkler's main distinction for Bantu Churches of the Ethiopian type in South Africa is that they have 'seceded from the White Mission Churches chiefly on racial grounds.'[1] As mentioned in the previous chapter, the racial factor is significant, to a greater or lesser degree, in *all* the Shona Independent Churches and it is not a main feature distinguishing 'Ethiopians' from Zionists, Apostles or other Independent Church groups. There are in fact indications that the First Ethiopian Church (FEC) belongs to the least racially-minded, i.e. the least militantly anti-European category, of all the Independent Churches dealt with in this study. The most common categorical factors that distinguish the Spirit-type from the Ethiopian-type Churches are religious and organizational rather than socio-political.

Classical Ethiopianism, as it was known in South Africa at the turn of the century, had distinctly racial overtones, and for that reason the Anglican bishop in Rhodesia warned the Chief Native Commissioner as early as 1903 that this society represented 'political and social aspirations' among the Africans that could lead to considerable racial trouble.[2] As a result the foreign leaders of the American Negro Mission representing the African Methodist Episcopal Church (AMEC), were deliberately kept out of the Colony, despite early efforts to obtain permission of entry. Ethiopianism nevertheless pene-

1. Sundkler, 1961, p. 53.
2. Ranger in *Religion in Africa*, 1964, p. 57.

trated the Colony at an early stage, when the Fingo labourers and farmers were brought into the country to settle amongst the Ndebele in the vicinity of Bulawayo. Rev. Magatho, a Sotho minister who had joined the AMEC, was the main leader in those early years. He founded a Church and school near the Bulawayo location in 1906. It was in this region, but on a more limited scale, and also among the Sotho settlers in the Fort Victoria district that Magatho exerted some influence. We cannot here give a detailed description of this initial rise of Ethiopianism in Rhodesia. Ranger provides us with a brief but sound account of its development and of Rev. Magatho's close involvement in the political development between 1906 and 1920, especially his participation in the efforts of the Ndebele to acquire land for a 'National Home'.[3]

It is of importance for this study to take note of the extension of early Ethiopianism to the Fort Victoria area. Magatho's influence was mainly confined to the Sotho settlers. Yet in 1909 it was alleged by ruralists that the efforts of a Karanga syndicate to buy a Company farm was inspired by Magatho. The question arises therefore whether the AMEC had in fact taken root amongst the Southern Shona at this early date, and whether it had influenced the rise of other Ethiopian-type Churches at a later date. Ethiopianism at this stage, it would seem, was mainly supported by the Ndebele, and although the Shona in the Victoria and surrounding districts were familiar with its political sentiments, one cannot speak of a significant Shona membership on a widely organized basis before the 1930's. Chidembo, the first Shona bishop of the First Ethiopian Church (FEC) in the Bikita district, was in touch with the Ndebele 'Ethiopians' for a short while, after he had actually introduced a type of Ethiopianism in the Colony that had already been divorced from American Negro supervision in South Africa. There are no indications that Chidembo had been influenced by the AMEC movement in the Colony before he left for South Africa as a labour migrant. Similarly, Sengwayo's African Congregational Church (*Chibarirwe*) was inspired by direct contact with South African Church leaders and not in the first place by influences coming from the early Ethiopian movement in the Colony. It seems therefore that the AMEC – which is not strictly speaking an African Independent, but a Negro-directed Mission Church – had a restricted sphere of influence in the Victoria area. At present the main Shona adherence to this Church is in the towns where most of its activities take place, while the 'proper' Shona Independent Churches, especially the Ethiopian-type ACC

3. *Ibid.*, pp. 57-62.

(*Chibarirwe*) and the FEC, are mainly rural Churches. To the rise of these latter two movements we must now turn our attention.

1. THE AFRICAN CONGREGATIONAL CHURCH (CHIBARIRWE)

a) *Dissent of American Board Church leaders*

The African Congregational Church was founded in the Union of South Africa in 1917, when Gardiner Mvuyana, a Zulu Church leader, broke away from the American Board Mission. Mvuyana, as one of the most 'powerful leaders and best preachers that Zulu Congregationalism has known'[4] had considerable influence among Africans on the Rand, where he worked from time to time, as well as in Natal and in Zululand. The new Church was recognized by the S.A. Government in 1937. After Mvuyana died, influential leaders such as Samuel Dube and L. M. Makhoba succeeded to his position. It is with these leaders that some of the Rhodesian labour migrants came into contact between 1920 and 1930.

The main figure in Rhodesia who started with the ACC and was later to become its President, is Mheke Zvekare Sengwayo, a muRozvi[5] from the Chipinga district. At present he lives on a small farm of 160 acres, in Chief Musikavanhu's territory near the African township of Chibunji. Sengwayo completed Std. 2 at Mt. Selinda, the main Mission centre of the American Board. Together with Makoni and Dzukuso, two other Africans of the Chipinga district, he was trained as an evangelist. These fellow students were allowed to continue their studies for the ministry, while Sengwayo was required to work as an evangelist once he had finished his preliminary training. Sengwayo's school qualifications were well below the minimum requirements for an advanced course of theological study. While training as an evangelist he was far from young and the father of five children, factors which further complicated his chances of realizing his ideal of becoming a real *mufundisi* (Church minister). In the late 1920's he was sent out to Chief Mutema's chiefdom as an evangelist. He relates:

'In Mutema's chiefdom I had to co-operate with Teacher Chabva, but we did not work well together because he wanted to be an evangelist as well as a teacher. He reported me to the missionaries, who decided that he should preach in the Church building while I had to preach in the villages only. I

4. Sundkler, *op. cit.*, p. 45.
5. *Mutupo:* Moyo; *chidao:* Chirandu.

then told the missionaries that I would not complete the course at the Bible school, that I would go to my own village and preach there to my own people. They tried to persuade me to complete my studies and preach in the Church, but I refused, saying that I would rather go home. When the matter was brought before the Church council, they did me a great disfavour. They were jealous of me and told me to stop my evangelical activities. So I left their service and trained as a builder in Chipinga. The missionaries advised the European for whom I was working to send me away. They said I was a bad man. When I worked for another man, the same thing happened. This time the missionaries even arranged for another builder to replace me. I was bitterly disappointed and left for my home in the tribal area. From that day I was convinced that the missionaries did not like me at all.'

Sengwayo's account conveys the bitterness that resulted from thwarted leadership ambitions. It is possible that he never fully realized, or never wanted to realize, why the missionaries required other students for the ministry. To him his exclusion meant a personal humiliation. His appearance before the Church council, where some of those whom he had come to regard as his opponents were sitting in judgment on him, only served to deepen his resentment. To what extent the missionaries did in fact oppose him after his departure for Chipinga is not clear, but it is likely that after such a disappointment he was bound to blame the Mission Church for his setback as a builder.

Soon after returning to his homestead, Sengwayo was employed at the Native Commissioner's office as a messenger. During his next four years of employment at Chipinga he regularly participated in the Holy Communion services conducted by the American Board missionaries, which shows that he had not yet severed all his ties with the Mission Church. In this period he came into contact with representatives of several Independent Churches. The FEC leaders working under Bishop Chidembo tried to win him over, but 'his heart refused'. He must also have obtained much firsthand knowledge about the Ndaza Zionist activities and doctrines, because part of his task was to report to the Native Commissioner on Zionist activities. According to the Native Commissioner at Chipinga, 'Zvekare, the ex-native messenger, who has been temporarily appointed detective to watch activities of above-mentioned [Zion Apostolic City] sect, has now visited most of the kraals in which Zionist emissaries are said to have taught their peculiar dogmas of late.'[6] The administrative authorities were concerned at the time about the reports of children being lured away from their schools by Zionist preachers. Sengwayo, how-

6. Native Commissioner, Chipinga, to Chief Native Commissioner, Salisbury, 10th February, 1933. National Archives, File S 138/140.

ever, soon became too well known in the district to be of further use as a 'detective'. He therefore settled on the piece of land which he had purchased, and for some time turned his mind to farming.

The crops of the first year yielded approximately £150, which in those years was no mean achievement. As a result Sengwayo was seriously tempted to turn to business on a large scale. He considered building a store on his farm, but, as he himself stated, the Voice of God kept troubling him: 'In 1938, while I was sowing out in the fields, a voice came to me and reminded me of the talents that should not be hidden. I replied that I badly wanted to preach the Gospel but was refused by the missionaries because I had not yet "passed". So I was confused and did not know what to do. The voice replied, "Go and see the Government" [*hurumende*: which to Sengwayo meant the local NC].'

From this account it appears that Sengwayo's training as an evangelist had been negligible, but that he had retained a strong sense of vocation. A 'voice' regularly urged him to continue his preaching activities. To the Native Commissioner he was a trusted man of standing, but to the missionaries he was a troublemaker, a 'bad' man. The latter's attitude towards him caused inner conflict and resentment. Small wonder that the voice directed him towards a person and institution where he had formerly experienced recognition and appreciation for his personal capabilities.

In spite of a growing apprehension about the increase of 'Separatist' Church activities in his district, the local NC was sympathetically disposed towards Sengwayo, when the latter arrived at the office with a preacher's certificate to 'apply for his own Church'. Yet the NC delayed the matter after deliberations with Rev. Orner, the representative leader of the American Board, who pointed out that serious repercussions could be expected if Sengwayo was officially permitted to campaign for a Church of his own. Eventually, in 1938, Sengwayo was sent to Salisbury to see the Chief Native Commissioner (CNC). By that time he had a list of 12 male followers – all of whom had left the American Board after they were charged with polygamy – who wanted to join him if recognition for an African Church could be obtained. When the Chief Native Commissioner asked Sengwayo in what kind of Church he was interested, he promptly replied, 'An African Congregational Church!'

Sengwayo's own narrative of his discussion with the CNC conveys the impression that the name African Congregational Church simply came from his lips by chance. He prefers not to mention that he had meanwhile been in contact with a certain K. Sibambo, a muNdau, then living near the Birchenough Bridge, who had told him about the African Congregational Church of Mvuyana in South Africa. Sibambo himself was a member of the American Board, but he was closely acquainted with several ACC leaders when he worked in South Africa as a labour migrant in the late 1920's. He had actually advised Sengwayo to travel to South Africa, where he would stand a chance of being ordained as a minister, once he had joined Mvuyana's movement. Sengwayo's reluctance to mention the role Sibambo played at this stage probably stands in connection with the latter's secession from the Rhodesian ACC at a later date. According to Sengwayo the CNC told him of a real African Congregational Church in Johannesburg and of the advisability of contacting the leaders of this Church. He offered to assist Sengwayo in making arrangements for a visit to South Africa.

Sengwayo experienced considerable trouble with the customs authorities at the Rhodesian border and was detained for a short while at Messina, before he was allowed to proceed on his journey in South Africa. Of his visit to the Transvaal he gives the following account:

'I got off at Doornfontein where I met Samuel Dube, the main leader of the African Congregational Church. I reached him by asking the people about his whereabouts as I moved around. I also met Ndwendwe, who had seceded from Mvuyana. Both he and Mvuyana had succeeded in organizing "*Chibarirwe*"[7] Churches. They had all broken away from the American Board. The following Sunday I was asked to preach in Johannesburg. People who attended the service were very pleased and gave me 10/– as a token of appreciation for my sermon on the children of Jacob who were sent to Egypt in search of food. They understood that I had come, like the children of Jacob, in search of the Word of God, of which we as Africans were deprived in Rhodesia. The same day they appointed me as a leader [*mufundisi*] in their Church.'

Sengwayo's ideal of becoming a Church minister had at last been fulfilled He returned to Rhodesia with newly attained credentials. The NC at Chipinga accepted these, but warned Sengwayo not to go and preach to the members of the American Board. The NC was afraid that serious trouble might arise 'amongst his children', says Sengwayo. In 1940 Sengwayo was invited by the Rev. Dube to attend a big Church conference at Durban. There he met most

7. *Chibarirwe:* derived from *kubara* or *kubereka* ('to give birth') literally means 'that which was born for us'. Broadly speaking the name means 'heritage of our fathers, that which has not been derived from others, our very own'. It was to become the popular name of the ACC in Rhodesia and is descriptive of this group's reaction to the Mission Churches and its reversion to the customs of the forefathers. Sengwayo's reference to this name in connection with the two South African Churches, indicates that he regarded them as based on the customs of their fathers.

of the senior leaders of the ACC – Dube, Makhoba and Ndwendwe – who promised him financial aid for the erection of a big Church in Rhodesia. On the last Sunday of the proceedings, Sengwayo's official consecration as minister took place through the laying-on of hands.

After his return to Rhodesia, Sengwayo achieved full Government recognition for his Church in 1942. He kept up a regular correspondence with Dube for several years, but could obtain no further permission for regular visits to South Africa. In his opinion the Administration's refusal to give him a travelling pass was due only to the radical opposition from the American Board missionaries. A certain Rev. Marsh visited him on occasion, trying to dissuade him from continuing his campaigning activities. 'When I refused', Sengwayo recalls, 'this man was greatly angered. He saw that I would not listen to him and he therefore complained to the Government.'

The apprehension of the American Board missionaries was not unfounded. On account of Sengwayo's activities between 1942 and 1945 they had lost many Church members among whom several prominent Church leaders. Sengwayo's initial endeavour to win new converts was confined to the Ndau chiefdoms in the Chipinga district, where he told the people that he had 'brought' a truly African Church of their own tribe (*rudzi*). All those who found it difficult to remain in the European Churches because of their difference in customs (*tsika*) were welcome to join the ACC. A permissive attitude towards beer drinking and polygamy was the main attraction of the new movement. For many Africans this lenient approach came as a liberation from the rigidly applied and Western-orientated Church laws by European missionaries, which a great number of them regarded as an intrusion into the highly prized field of their own customs, and not as a mode of operation belonging to the essence of Christianity.

Sengwayo had by this time taken a second wife. Rev. Dzukuso and Rev. Pahla, who had received their theological training at Mt. Selinda, left the American Board in those years and joined the *Chibarirwe*. They, too, had taken second wives. The reasons why these ministers left their Mission Church were more complex, however, than merely their reaction to the Mission Church's prohibition of the customary practice of polygamy. Apart from taking second wives, both these leaders had purchased farms, Pahla in the Zamchia Native Purchase Area (Chipinga district) and Dzukuso in the Nyahunda NPA (Bikita district). Thus they had vested agricultural interests when they left the Mission Church. Pahla held that, by mistake, another Church official had been appointed minister in his place after he, Pahla, had been chosen by the missionaries to go to South Africa for further training. 'After my journey had been cancelled', he says, 'the local congregation could not afford the salaries of two ministers, so I retired from active Church service and settled down on my farm.' It was only when he had left the American Board that he added his father's second wife, after the old man's death, to his own household. In view of Pahla's case I would therefore suggest that at least some of the American Board leaders left the Mission Church as prospective rather than as recognized polygamists, and that at the time of their secession, additional aggravating factors such as limited salaries, were at stake. Furthermore it would seem that for many 'master farmers' the ownership of a farm was synonymous to having a polygamous household. Several of them have stated during interviews that, 'to have many wives and children is the only way for us Africans of securing a reliable labour force for the farm', and that 'it is a necessity!' It is not unlikely that men like Sengwayo, Pahla and Dzukuso, indeed considered this factor when they purchased their farms.

Sibambo, who had originally informed Sengwayo of the ACC, joined him in 1942. He became the first evangelist of the new Church and for a time was the Church president's most trusted associate. As advisor on Church organization he was of great help, because he was the only person besides Sengwayo who had actually 'seen' the customs of the Church in South Africa. Of the future ACC leaders he was the only one who had not become a polygamist. As to his reasons for joining the ACC, he emphasizes that he had never experienced trouble with the American Board missionaries. 'I merely saw that the Africans had come of age [*vatema vatanga kukura*] with regard to the things that the missionaries had taught us. I joined the new Church to see if we could succeed in managing our own Church affairs, independently of others.'

Up to 1945 most of the important Church meetings were held in Ndau territory. The ACC was a tribal Church in so far as the nuclear body of Church leaders (Dzukuso, Pahla and Sibambo), and the majority of followers of those years were vaNdau. The picture was soon to change, however, once DRC leaders joined the movement.

b) *DRC factions join the ACC*

Moses Ruwana, a muDuma from Bikita, was for many years the most popular evangelist of the Dutch Reformed Church. He had joined the Mission Church at Pamushana in 1916, completed Std. 4 and went to Morgenster, the main Mission station, for evangelist training. For twelve years he served as an evangelist in Chief Ziki's chiefdom (Bikita district) where he became known as a zealous Church worker and a powerful preacher. Rev. Botha, who was stationed at Pamushana Mission at the time, was impressed with Ruwana's work and recommended him for further theological training. Ruwana and four other promising evangelists were chosen in 1937 to follow a course for the ministry at Morgenster.

At this time Ruwana experienced serious domestic trouble. His wife had stopped 'bringing forth blood' (*kubudisa ropa*) after she had given birth to one daughter. She had therefore failed to present her husband with the all-important male name-bearer, a situation which according to customary law justified substitutory arrangements. Their marriage, pre-arranged by their parents, and in earlier years avoided by Ruwana as long as possible, had never been a success. Once she was past child-bearing age, Moses's wife spent long periods away from home. In this connection he says, 'By the time I went to Morgenster, I had gone through great suffering [*matambudziko*] because I had not known a woman for six years.' To him it must have come as a bitter disappointment when his domestic misfortunes inhibited his progress to the highest ranks of leadership in the Church; an achievement which seemed to be within his reach. In 1938 he was bypassed for re-election to continue with the theological studies. Instead he was sent back to the Ziki chiefdom to continue his work as an evangelist.

In 1944 he eloped with the daughter of Maruta, who was then the acting Rozvi chief in Bikita. When the matter became known to the DRC missionaries at Pamushana in 1945, she had already conceived. *Roora* arrangements had been settled. Rev. Louw Jr. visited Ruwana and entreated him to continue with his evangelistic work until the end of the year, when his case would be brought before the Church council. Ruwana was deeply moved by the plea of this missionary, whom he respected for his integrity. 'I told Rev. Louw', he says, 'that I would change the *roora* payment into payment of damages[8] [which would have implied the cancellation of the marriage arrangements]. The woman could then go and stay with her relatives at Bovora, where she could rear my child. I told her that she was free to marry somebody else, because I had to return to the Mission. I said to her, "I cannot bear exclusion from the Holy communion" [*Handigino kugara kunze kweChirayiro*].'

Sincere though his intentions may have been, they were never carried out. Before the end of that year Bishop Mutendi visited Ruwana three times to win the influential evangelist for the Zion Christian Church. Ruwana refused on the grounds that true prophecies had ended in Old Testament times, that the Zionists incorrectly emphasized Old Testament 'Church laws' and that

8. See Holleman (1952, p. 244) in connection with *Maputiro:* payment of damages.

they had diverged from the true way of Jesus Christ. The ACC to him was a different proposition altogether. Sengwayo, advised by Dzukuso, invited him to a Church meeting at Tanganda. Moses professed to have been greatly impressed by this African Church. Its forms of religious expression corresponded to those he had been used to; it enjoyed Government recognition, and the office of Church minister (*mufundisi*) included similar duties, such as the administration of the sacraments, as its counterpart in the Mission Church.

For some time Moses was in doubt whether to join the ACC, but then a letter from Sengwayo clinched the matter for him. Sengwayo wrote: 'I have heard of your intention to part with your second wife. Why? Such action would be wrong, because there is nothing wrong with a second wife. It is only a matter of different customs [*itsika dzinosiyana koga*]. Amongst the Europeans there is no heathen with two wives. Even if you are a European heathen you have only got one wife . . .' The implication was obvious: a second wife for an African is a matter of custom and not necessarily a return to heathenism. The Europeans had wrongly identified one of their customs with the essence of Christianity. Moses was convinced, and in 1946 he and his second wife were accepted in the new fold.

During the first few years, while he held a junior position in the ACC, Moses tended to confine his activities to the eastern sector of Bikita and he would join the vaNdau at their weekend meetings in the Chipinga district. Such loyalty as he undoubtedly still had for his parental Church, kept him from venturing into 'their territory' at this stage. Once he was ordained as a minister in 1950, however, he immediately started operating on a wide scale amongst DRC backsliders and reactionaries in the Gutu, Buhera, Victoria and Chibi districts. His consecration as a minister marks the beginning of a major thrust, of what had been a predominantly Ndau Church with mainly post-American Board Church members, into new territory where the DRC influence had been most strongly felt. The ceremony itself represented the first major ACC conference west of the Sabi river. Paul Sengwayo, the president's eldest son, arrived at Ruwana's village with a truck packed with Chipinga Church members. All five *vafundisi* (Sengwayo, Dzukuso, Pahla, Sibambo and Makoni – the latter also a former American Board minister) laid hands on Ruwana, each with a special message of inspiration for the new leader. The impression this ceremony made on Ruwana is best described in his own words: 'I felt greatly honoured because this was the first big Church meeting outside Chipinga territory. As I knelt down to receive their benediction my chest grew so heavy in me, that I thought I would die.'

The difference in the attitudes of individual missionaries to Independent Church activities is illustrated in the visits of two European DRC missionaries shortly after Moses's ordination. Rev. X came to Ruwana with the sole purpose of persuading him to leave the new Church, in view of its seemingly negative effect on other DRC members. Rev. Y, on the other hand, came to inquire about Moses's new status and to congratulate him on his ordination. After they had shaken hands, Moses understood him to have said, 'Congratulations! You have found your own Church. I will ask our Church members to pray for you.' In principle neither of these missionaries fully accepted Ruwana's action, of which he was fully aware, but the personal involvement and understanding of Rev. Y made all the difference to him. It served to create the basis for future discussions on a personal basis.

Ruwana's campaigning activities were conducted according to a preconceived and carefully worked out plan. Personally or by correspondence he informed influential, former or discontented, DRC leaders in the abovementioned districts about the new Church. These leaders in turn would notify those who had left the Mission Church because of polygamy, discontented Mission Church members, backsliders and such traditionalists as showed interest in an all-African Church. In this way the news about the new Church soon spread over a wide area. Requests for Moses to come and 'receive' (*gamuchira*) or baptize new members came in from various tribal areas. As the movement gained impetus Ruwana was on the move continually.

In 1951 he was invited by Tinos Chirashanye of the vaMhari tribe (*mutupo*: Shumba; *chidao*: Siwanda), a former DRC evangelist, who lived south of Morgenster Mission in the Mushawasha Native Purchase Area (Victoria district), to come and finalize the preparatory work that had been done on behalf of the ACC in this district. On the 24th of April, Ruwana arrived at Gondoi store near Machitenda school, where a considerable number of people had gathered to meet the *mufundisi* of the new Church, of whom Tinos had told them. The next two days more than 80 adults were either baptized for the first time or officially 'received' into the ACC.[9] Ruwana kept a record of the names of the new members. He states that the majority of people who joined the ACC on this occasion were old women who had failed to pass the DRC catechism classes at Morgenster because of their inability to read or write. Their complaint was that the missionaries identified their inability to pass the catechism classes with a refusal on their part fully to accept God. As a free-lancer, Moses interpreted his own powers as including the right to appoint new Church officials. He wasted no time in appointing Tinos as evangelist. The latter had just left the Mission Church because he had taken a

9. Those who had been baptized in a Protestant Mission Church at an earlier date were not re-baptized, but 'received' through the laying-on of hands.

second wife. He resented the way in which an investigation had been conducted by Rev. X at his homestead during his absence. For the first two years Tinos was to accompany Ruwana on several tours before he was ordained as a minister in 1953, which enabled him to do Church work more independently.

Before Ruwana could return home, a messenger arrived from Majiri, a ward bordering on Mushawasha, with an invitation for him to visit Chief Chibwe. Preparatory work had been done in this area by Zvobgo – also a muMhari and kinsman of Tinos –, a former DRC teacher and Church deacon, who fell into disrepute after he had 'inherited' the two wives of his deceased elder brothers. In Majiri 38 people were admitted as members of the ACC. From there Ruwana travelled to Fort Victoria where word reached him that a group of former DRC members were awaiting his arrival in Zimuto's chiefdom. Tired though he was at this stage, he spent another week in Zimuto and added 29 more adult members to his Church, the majority of whom belonged to polygamous households.

Letters of invitation from Gutu and Buhera were awaiting Ruwana on his arrival back home. A certain Bota from Buhera had written to him: 'Why do you sit at home with such an important message? Must we die in darkness out here?' Moses accepted the challenge, knowing that the time had come for extensive journeys and long spells of absence from home. In this particular field he distinguished himself from all the other ACC leaders. Whereas the Ndau leaders primarily remained farmers, who only left their farms occasionally, Ruwana saw his task as a minister with a full-time occupation. He regarded the Church's entry-fees of 2/6, to be paid by each new adherent, as a partial source of his personal income. In Buhera he 'received' more than 100 people during his first visit. Bota was duly installed as evangelist to tend to the rapidly growing congregations, while Ruwana continued his journey.

Once he had entered Gutu territory, Ruwana had the advantage of the support of his sister's sons (*vazukuru*) who lived in the Munyaradze subchiefdom. From their homesteads he could operate in different directions, acting on their advice and making use of their influence. He started staying for periods of two weeks to several months in various sub-chiefdoms, such as Mazuru, Munyikwa and Chingombe, where he could 'receive', baptize and advise new Church members. In Chingombe, with its more than 100 villages and the DRC Mission station of Alheit at its centre, Ruwana enjoyed a major success. He found two DRC catechists, both of whom had left the Mission Church because of polygamy, and each of whom was directly related to the leading lineage members of the Rufura (mainly descendants of the Mudyanadzo house) and Hera (descendants of Mheresi) wards respectively.

These two men, Makomo and Mujeyi, were appointed as evangelists and in a matter of years managed through their own activities to establish eight congregations, to build three Church buildings (see map 4) and win the majority of Church-going kraalheads in the entire Chingombe area.[10]

In 1953 a Church conference was held in Gutu at the request of Ruwana. It was attended by the members of local congregations and all the senior leaders of the ACC. On this occasion Sengwayo was officially appointed president of the Church. Tinos Chirashanye of Mushawasha was ordained as minister for the Victoria congregations, and several evangelists 'received hands'. Amongst the newly appointed evangelists was Madyauta, who was to become the future minister of the Chibi congregations. The conference was important for various reasons:

In the first place it marked the beginning of an elaborate Church organization. The functions of each office-bearer were discussed and defined. Each Church circuit, with its boundaries in most cases demarcated according to the boundaries of the administrative districts, came under the jurisdiction of a *mufundisi* with a group of subordinate officials under his care.

Secondly, this conference all too clearly demonstrated the fact that in a few years' time the major influx of Church membership had shifted away from the Ndau area where Sengwayo had achieved his first success. The Chipinga faction of the Church now represented only a minority group, and Ruwana had in reality become the key-figure of the movement. Through his activities Church membership had spread over such a wide area, with so many of the new followers knowing Sengwayo only indirectly, that it had become impossible for the Church president to centralize powers with his own farm (map 3) as Church headquarters. He had to be satisfied with annual administrative conferences and Committee meetings being held in distant rural areas, in other words with a kind of 'floating Church headquarters' of unlocalized nature. Unlike most Spirit-type Churches and even the First Ethiopian Church, Sengwayo was therefore unable to conduct the major annual Communion service (*Chirayiro*) in the immediate vicinity of his homestead. This cost him the all-important personal link with the majority of his followers, a vital prerequisite for effective Independent Church leadership.

In the third place, Ruwana's own prestige among the ordinary Church members was generally enhanced by this conference, but at the same time he became suspect amongst his envious Ndau companions. They publicly queried

10. The first chapter in Volume 3 will deal with the composition of congregations in Chingombe.

his use of the above-mentioned entry-fees which they regarded as 'Church funds', in an effort to curb his growing popularity and influence.

After the 1953 conference the Church continued to expand rapidly in the Buhera, Gutu and Victoria districts. In Chipinga a stalemate was reached during the period preceding the first major schism in 1956 (see below), after which the membership in this district gradually decreased. A similar decline is noticeable at present in the Victoria district. Rev. Tinos Chirashanye had four well-organized congregations at Zimuto, Mushawasha, Majiri and Jena, constituting a total membership of well over a thousand adults, with one evangelist, two preachers and two overseers per congregation. Loss of membership in this case, as also happened to Sengwayo in the Chipinga district, coincided with a sharp decrease of the leader's individual activities because of old age and illness. Thus the personal influence of the local top-leader and the personal contact with his followers have a direct bearing on the vitality of the congregations under his care. Tinos and Sengwayo gave two additional reasons why many of their former followers lost interest: first, it was a matter of everybody aspiring to power (*ukuru*: leadership); if not duly satisfied, potential leaders turned to other groups. Secondly, an important reason for dissent was the conflict which continually arose between leaders and followers over the obligatory annual Church fees and the alleged misuse of Church funds by Church leaders. Finally, it should be mentioned that loss of Church membership was also due to the activities of the secessionist leaders, Sibambo and Zvobgo. Their initial success with a school in Majiri proved too strong an attraction for many ACC members.

In spite of the loss of Church membership in the Chipinga and Victoria districts, the ACC leaders in Gutu, Buhera and Chibi managed to establish stable congregations, with a constant increase of membership. The ACC at present comprises approximately 8,000 members with six ministers and a substantial body of sub-leaders. With the Gutu and Buhera district representing the strongest circuits of the Church, it can safely be stated that the majority of its members who had contact with Mission Churches prior to their ACC affiliation, have defected from the DRC – the strongest missionary agency operating in these districts. Apart from the American Board in Chipinga, the other Mission Church which lost some members to the ACC is the Swedish Lutheran Mission, which operates from Mnene, its main Mission station in the Belingwe district.

Ruwana mentions three important reasons why DRC members defect from the Mission Church:

1. People are 'chased away' (*kudzingwa*) from the Church when they take a second wife;

2. lack of African-administered schools, and
3. the loss of Shona customs in the Mission Church.

Both the first and the third reasons mentioned are concerned with Shona customs. To cater for the need of people who had broken away on these grounds, the ACC accepted such practices as polygamy, beer drinking and the use of Shona names during baptismal ceremonies. The monopoly of the Mission Church in the educational field (reason 2), it is felt, stands in direct relation to the threat of Shona customs becoming extinct. In the effort to counter this course of events, or at least do something to preserve such customs as they themselves regarded as relevant within the educational framework, the ACC planned to collect money for the erection of schools, a project which, as yet, has yielded meagre results.

Behind these specific causes of fission was the general urge for independence. The very existence of so many 'Dutch', 'American', 'Swedish' and other European 'tribal' Churches, was itself regarded as a justification for having a separate African Church. Tinos's comment during the last discussion he had with two prominent DRC missionaries before he finally left their Church illustrates this point:

'I accused the missionary leaders of misleading the Vakaranga people by not telling them the truth about all the different Churches belonging to the different "tribes", and therefore withholding from them the *right* of controlling their own Church. Isn't there a Dutch, a German and an English Church? They replied that I was being misled and that the name "Dutch Reformed" was to make way for "African Reformed Church", in the near future. I was angry at this stage and asked if the change of name would also entitle an African to take over the position of the DRC treasurer in order to handle the finances of this African Church.'

Independence for men like Tinos and Zvobgo did not, in the first place, imply freedom to practice polygamy and such Shona customs as they deemed suitable, but the elimination of what they considered to be the paternalistic implementation of DRC laws. What irked them was the radical application of Church laws by Europeans and those African Church leaders who assisted them, rather than the specific content of these laws. Tinos, for example, reacted strongly against an investigation conducted at his homestead during his absence. The investigation took place because it was rumoured that he had taken a second wife. He requested a full investigation to be conducted during his presence, but, he said, it was regarded unnecessary on the grounds of evidence already obtained.[11] What could possibly have been a fair and face-

11. It should be kept in mind, however, that the accounts of Independent Church

saving 'trial' for Tinos turned out to be a summary discussion in the Church council which resulted in a disqualifying conviction. Hence the secessionist use of the word '*kudzinga*' – to drive off – as descriptive of disciplinary measures taken by Church authorities. Zvobgo complains about the attitudes of the African overseers and the European missionaries at Jichidza Mission as regards his predicament after the second of his two elder brothers had died. This had left him at least partially responsible for two widows and eleven children. Whereas the overseers accused him of having fully inherited (*kugara nhaka*) the two women as wives, he insisted that he had merely accepted the responsibility of taking care of them and not for purposes of cohabiting with them. When the missionaries at Jichidza, acting on the advice of the local overseers (*vatariri*), refused to allow one of Zvobgo's inherited widows to live on the Mission premises, where her husband had been teaching before his death, Zvobgo left the Church. Rumour has it that he swore to take vengeance on the 'enemies' who were responsible for the death of his two brothers. For some time he established himself as a *nganga*, and it was hinted that he was feared for his knowledge of dangerous medicine.

c) *Schism*: *Formation of the African Reformed Church*

In 1947 Sengwayo became sub-chief in the Musikavanhu chiefdom. This position burdened him with so much additional responsibility that he decided to promote Sibambo to the position of *mufundisi* and to appoint him as temporary deputy of the new Church. So Sengwayo remained Church leader in name, but for all practical purposes Sibambo acted and was respected as the leader of the ACC between 1947 and 1951. It was not only the relation of mutual trust between him and Sengwayo, but also his earlier contacts with the South African Congregationalists, which made Sibambo the appropriate

leaders, on which this historical sketch is primarily based, do not always include a balanced consideration of all the factors involved at the time of secession from a Mission Church. As a result a somewhat one-sided picture, admittedly to the disadvantage of the Mission Church concerned, sometimes emerges. Tinos, for instance, emphasized what he considered to be the inconsiderate treatment of DRC missionaries in connection with his domestic affairs, but made no mention of the important fact that he was bypassed when a number of fellow DRC evangelists were chosen for advanced theological training. According to one of the leading missionaries who knew Tinos well, it was the latter's obvious frustration as a result of his exclusion from further theological training, rather than the reason mentioned above, which caused his dissent.

man for this position. He was the one who had 'seen' this Church in another country even before Sengwayo knew of its existence.

Representative leadership in the Independent Church has always been the seed-bed of future schism. In 1951 the growing strife among his Church leaders caused Sengwayo to return to fuller participation in Church affairs. He was actually requested to intervene when it became evident to the Church council that both Sibambo and Zvobgo were at loggerheads with the rest of the leaders.

Zvobgo was dissatisfied with the leadership of *Mufundisi* Tinos Chirashanye in the Victoria area. Tinos, according to him, was ill-equipped for the task. It was known, however, that Tinos's seniority in the Church was the main factor which delayed Zvobgo's own promotion as a Church leader. Sengwayo had made it clear that he did not wish to have two high-ranking Church leaders in the same area. But Zvobgo regarded himself as better qualified than Tinos. In the DRC circles he had been a teacher and catechist of high standing before he left the Mission Church in 1945, while Tinos had been a mere evangelist with lower educational qualifications. Through correspondence with his nephew, Mandondo, who was working as a labour migrant in South Africa, Zvobgo was informed of the existence of the ACC under Mvuyana, as well as a 'Reformed Church' among the Venda, led by a certain Dickson. Since 1945 he had therefore already begun propagating an African Independent Church in Majiri, that is, before coming into contact with Sengwayo. Now that his ideals and ambitions seemed to be thwarted by Tinos's leadership, he became increasingly critical of the lenient laws of Sengwayo's Church.

Sibambo, who was the only non-polygamist leader at the top of the ACC hierarchy, introduced a stricter code of Church laws soon after his appointment as Sengwayo's deputy. He publicly condemned polygamy and qualified it as a practice unworthy at least of the office-bearers of the Church. This uncompromising attitude was duly opposed by the rest of the ACC leaders, who accused Sibambo of wanting to turn the movement into a 'European Church'.

By the time Sengwayo returned to the Church as a full-time leader, he was confronted with a request from the Church council that the leadership of Sibambo be suspended. Sengwayo hesitantly succumbed to the pressure of the majority of leaders. It was clear to him though, that the wide influence of Sibambo could contribute towards a major crisis and the loss of many Church members, if the latter was summarily suspended by him. In a last desperate effort to get a grip on the situation Sengwayo led a delegation of Church officials to the District Commissioner's office at Fort Victoria. There he charged Sibambo with 'stealing his Church through the introduction of new

Church laws that were contrary to his own wish'. Sibambo, who had meanwhile opened discussions with Zvobgo about the possible formation of a new Church, was summoned to the office. There he argued:

'I decided to follow Sengwayo because he was proclaiming the truth. My main reason for joining this Church was to see if we could manage organizing our own independent Church, and not to separate completely from the Dutch Reformed, American Board and Methodist Churches, which were our first instructors. At that stage I did not know that Sengwayo and the others were going to organize "an African Church of many wives" [*kereke yavatema yokuwana vakadzi*]. When Sengwayo became chief, I was asked to lead the Church. In the course of time the other leaders demanded that all affiliated Church members be encouraged to become polygamists, with which I did not agree.'

During the ensuing discussions Sengwayo admitted that Sibambo had not been paid for his services as a Church leader, which satisfied the District Commissioner that this was not a case of 'a Church being stolen'. He even intimated, according to Sibambo, that a real Christian Church could not allow polygamy. His conclusion convinced Sengwayo that there was no basis for legal action against Sibambo, while Sibambo interpreted the outcome of these sessions as a green light for him to proceed, independently of the others, with his own religious activities.

Further discussions between Sibambo, Zvobgo and Mandondo led to the formation of the African Reformed Church in 1953.[12] The main laws in which the new Church differed from the ACC were that it did not allow polygamy or beer drinking and that marriages were only valid if they had been ritually sanctioned by the Church's marriage officer. Baptism in 'Jordan' was introduced, possibly to emphasize the difference between the ARC and the ACC. Sibambo obtained a confession from Zvobgo that he had trespassed in the past against the DRC laws on polygamy. In order to demonstrate his willingness to comply with the new laws, Zvobgo accordingly sent his 'inherited wives' back to their villages and publicly burnt his medicines. A period of three years' probation as an evangelist followed before he was ulti-

12. In her description of the rise of this Church, Sr. Mary Aquina (in *African Social Research*, 1966, No. 1, pp. 8-9) makes no mention of Zvobgo's contact with the *Chibarirwe* leaders and of the important role played by Sibambo. According to her 'Zvobgo set about founding his Church, which he called the 'Unreformed Church' because from the time of Jesus Christ until that day nobody had preached about it.' Although this name may have been used at first, I have heard no mention of it, and it does not seem to fit the explicit motivation of Sibambo and Zvobgo, which was to 'reform' certain *Chibarirwe* practices when they founded their *African Reformed Church.*

mately ordained as minister of the ARC in 1956. Mudikwane, leader of the AMEC in Fort Victoria, was specially invited as the representative of a 'true Ethiopian Church' to assist Sibambo with the ordination. At a later date Mandondo was also ordained, so that the ARC at present has three ordained ministers tending to their 800 to 1,000 members in the four adjacent Church circuits stretching from Sibambo's homestead at Birchenough Bridge in the east to Zvobgo's 'Mission station' at Majiri in the west.

It was during the initial break with the ACC leaders that the name *Chibarirwe* came to be regularly used.[13] Ruwana deliberately started using the term to emphasize his Church's acceptance of certain traditional customs. Sibambo rightly assumed that the term *Chibarirwe* was synonymous with polygamy, the consumption of beer, and traditional forms of divination (*kushopera*). 'Reformation' to him meant the expulsion of these three practices for which the *Chibarirwe* stood. But reformation (*kugadzirisa*: to set right) meant more to the ambitious new leader than the elimination of some old practices. It asked for a solid Church constitution – which was drafted in the late 1950's – a new hymnbook, own schools, and an effort to co-operate with other Protestant Churches. Zvobgo formulated the latter ideal as follows:

'We want to co-operate with the DRC. We do not despise this Mission Church because it is in this Church that we first found the good faith. The organization of our African Reformed Church is not directed at breaking down the work done by the DRC and other missionaries, but to further our own activities in the spirit of remembrance that our Church originated from the "vaDutchi", our spiritual fathers.'

Once permission had been obtained by Sibambo and Zvobgo to open a lower primary school in Majiri, the main drive and obsession of the ARC members in the following years became the erection of their own schools. Joint contributions by the four main congregations enabled Zvobgo and Mandondo to purchase the necessary building material and to construct the first three classrooms themselves. In 1956 the 'United Mission' (*Shonganiso Mission*), as the new school is fondly called, was officially opened with facilities for pupils from Sub. A to Std. 1. Ten years later the school was already promoted to higher primary level (Std. 6) with additional buildings, a staff of seven teachers and more than 340 pupils.

For the first few years the '*Shonganiso*' school was managed by 7th Day Adventist and Roman Catholic school managers, in accordance with ARC preference. Zvobgo, in spite of his ideals of co-operation with the DRC, had

13. *Supra*, p. 355. foot-note 7.

not forgotten his earlier experiences at Jichidza Mission. The *Shonganiso* venture had, moreover, been opposed by one of the DRC school superintendents. Zvobgo claims that he is now allowed to manage his schools all by himself. This makes him the proud holder of the three-fold position of school manager, schoolmaster and minister of religion. Efforts at co-operation had thus far been confined to preliminary, but somewhat stagnated, personal discussions between ARC and DRC leaders about the possibilities of ARC leaders receiving theological training at the Morgenster theological school.

2. THE FIRST ETHIOPIAN CHURCH (TOPIA)

a) *Spread of Ethiopianism to the Southern Shona*

Of the Independent Churches in the south-eastern districts the FEC is the oldest.[14] As far back as 1890, Mupambi Chidembo, a muNdau from Bikita, who worked as a cook at Olifantshoek in the Transvaal, came into contact with South African Ethiopian Church leaders. The young Chidembo was impressed by the claims of these leaders who propagated a segregated African Church. The charter of the new Church was found in Bible texts, such as Ps. 68 : 31 (*'Ethiopia shall soon stretch out her hand to God')* of which the 'correct interpretation' was supposed to give support to the argument that the Ethiopian Church was the oldest and therefore the most authentic in all Africa.[15]

It is improbable that Chidembo was motivated by reaction against Missions when he joined the Ethiopian movement. He had not received any form of education in a Mission school nor were there any missionaries working in the Bikita area who could have influenced him before he left for South Africa. It is an important fact, however, that he felt more at home with the members and leaders of the Ethiopian movement than with those of other denominations who were also operating in his new environment. Association with Ethiopian-type leaders led to his baptism, and Isaiah Charles (Chari) Chidembo, as he was then called, soon found himself in the fascinating ranks of

14. In this chapter the historical account of the ACC nevertheless appears before that of the FEC since President Sengwayo's activities as a Church leader date back further than that of Bishop Gavure, present leader of the FEC. Detailed particulars about the latter movement only concern the more recent phase of Church expansion under Gavure's leadership.

15. Sundkler, *op. cit.*, p. 39.

Church leadership. His twenty years' stay as a labour migrant in the Transvaal had enabled him to become fully acquainted with the laws and practices of the *First Ethiopian Church* before he returned to Rhodesia as a 'bishop' in 1910.

Preaching activities were at first confined to the Bikita district. Bishop Chidembo shifted his homestead several times in the Ziki, Masuka and Mazungunye chiefdoms, where he directed his evangelistic efforts at the Duma people living in the same locality. Consequently, several small Ethiopian-type congregations came into being, mostly within walking distance of the bishop's various homesteads. Several years after his return the 'Ethiopian' Church leader also moved into the Gutu, Ndanga and Chipinga districts. The growth of his Church in these territories was, however, limited until the enthusiasm and dedication of Gavure, the bishop's sister's son (*muzukuru*) and future leader of the movement, gave the campaigning activities the necessary impetus.

Bishop Chidembo never enjoyed the wide-spread influence of a Mutendi, Johane Maranke or a Moses Ruwana, nor was he of the same stature as these leaders. The journeys he undertook to Umtali and Bulawayo hint at the vision he may have had of a much wider Ethiopian Church expansion in Rhodesia, but which never reached fulfilment. Chidembo did manage to establish links with the leaders of the Ndebele Ethiopian Churches. Bishop Musweri assisted him in obtaining Government recognition for his Church, but this connection soon became as vague as the one with the Ethiopian Church in South Africa. At its peak, this Church under Chidembo's leadership may have counted two thousand members. By the time Gavure joined the Church in 1938, Chidembo had no more than a thousand followers in and around the Bikita district, of whom the majority knew little more about the origin of their Church than that Bishop Chidembo 'had brought the "*Topia*" with him from Johannesburg (*vaChidembo vabva Johni neTopia*).' Mutendi's rising popularity with the Bikita chiefs at the time, the increase of missionary activities in the educational field and Chidembo's failing health, were all factors that contributed towards a sharp decrease in the numbers of Church adherents. To many people Chidembo's claim that he had 'died' and returned after seven days with a 'book of instructions' for the Ethiopian Church, seemed but a feeble performance in comparison with the miracles performed by the influential Zionist leader at Moriah. Gavure laconically states that the only Church book left by Chidembo at his death was a Methodist hymnbook.

b) *Church expansion under a new leader*

When Gavure joined the FEC he lived at Norumedzo, a somewhat isolated area, tucked away between the mountains in Mazungunye's chiefdom. His maternal uncle (*sekuru*), Chidembo, had settled in their village and introduced the new Church. Gavure, who had never received any education and had never joined any Church, was struck by Chidembo's sincerity and enjoyed the bishop's preaching. His eagerness to learn more about the new message demanded a reading knowledge of the vernacular. This he obtained with the aid of his relatives. Chidembo lost no time in appointing the promising new member as one of his assistants. Gavure accompanied the old man on his preaching visits to the surrounding villages and within a few years became the trusted right-hand man of Chidembo.

Gavure spent two years (1941-2) as a labour migrant near Pretoria in the Transvaal, during which time he never made contact with other Ethiopian-type Church members. This in itself is a significant fact, because it shows that the relations between the South African and Rhodesian branches of the same Church were not maintained. This tendency was to some extent influenced by circumstantial factors, such as the development of inter-State relations and the difference in approach of the Rhodesian and South African Governments as regards the control of Independent Church movements, but also by the wish of some of the remote Church leaders to handle their own Church affairs independently of their 'superiors' in South Africa. As had happened to the Zionists, the distant Ethiopian congregations soon became autonomous. Gavure, while staying in South Africa, regarded himself as one of the future leaders of Ethiopianism in Rhodesia, and admits that he made no effort to attend Ethiopian Church services while in South Africa. His strong sense of vocation nevertheless became manifest in his request to the compound manager at Pretoria, where he stayed, to be allowed to preach. When this permission was granted, he continued his preaching activities and on one occasion converted fifteen co-workers, residing in the compound.

Back in Rhodesia, Gavure found that Chidembo had stopped his regular visits to his congregations due to old age and bad health. Many of the young Ethiopian leaders had backslid or joined other Churches. The Church's organization was in a deplorable state. In the same way as Ruwana was to take the initiative for the *Chibarirwe* later on, Gavure now travelled and preached on his own. In 1944 he succeeded in winning Simon Chapinga (Bikita) and Rainos Musasikwa (Zaka) for his Church. Both of these elderly men were his maternal uncles, and both were former DRC members. Their conversion to Ethiopianism marked the turning-point of the Church's history in Rhodesia. Having pledged full loyalty to their nephew Gavure, they assisted him in reviving what was left of the *Topia* movement in Bikita and Zaka districts. They also added many new members to their ranks.

In 1946 Gavure was appointed as a Church leader. He was singled out as special evangelist because of his important work as a preacher. Chidembo publicly approved of his work by draping one of his own garments around the shoulders of the young evangelist. He is reported to have said: 'See, there is my evangelist.' Two years later Gavure became *muongamiri*, which is the highest leading position below that of bishop. His quick promotion as a Church leader was partly due to the rapid growth of the Norumedzo and other congregations, which intensified the competition for leadership and inevitably hastened the promotion of those leaders who had been in the Church for some time. But more important was the devotion and the dignified persistence with which this man served the Church at a critical stage of its development and which earned him the respect of followers and opponents alike.

In 1952 Bishop Chari Chidembo died and a big Church conference, attended by senior representatives from each of the twenty to thirty congregations in the Bikita and Zaka districts (at that time the expansion in Gutu had hardly begun!), was held to appoint a successor. At first Sauro Muduma and David Mapfumvu were nominated on the grounds of their senior position as Church members. But the fifty Church leaders present were equally divided in their preferences. At this stage Gavure was nominated by some of the elder leaders who were aware of the fact that this young man's special relationship with the deceased bishop and his loyal service in the past had directly influenced the revival and life of the Church. With the exception of a few abstentions Gavure was unanimously chosen as Chidembo's successor. Sauro Muduma resented this and broke away from Gavure soon afterwards. Today he is a ward headman *(sadunhu)* with hardly any followers. David Mapfumvu was appointed as the Church's first *muongamiri*, a position which he held until he died.

The breach of the succession pattern (that of the senior son or agnatic relative replacing the deceased founding leader of the Church, which is normal practice in the Independent Churches) caused some hesitation amongst the Church members and provoked a few close relatives of Chidembo publicly to oppose Gavure. Everybody knew that Chidembo's only son, Macharutya, who was working in Johannesburg at the time, was likely to return sooner or later to claim the 'inheritance' (*nhaka*), i.e. Church leadership of his father, even though he had joined the Seventh Day Adventists and had done nothing in the past to promote the cause of his father's Church. Gavure, on the other hand, had given proof of outstanding leadership qualities and seemed a better spiritual leader than the deceased's son who had been living in the Transvaal for more than twenty years. Gavure therefore assumed his leadership with the knowledge of a possible challenge to his authority in the future.

In 1957 Bishop Gavure, who entertained good relations with Chief Mazungunye, went to see the latter in order to obtain permission for a Church building in his chiefdom. Mazungunye accompanied the *Topian* bishop to the district office at Bikita, where the authorities required a brief historical account of the Ethiopian Church. From Gavure's account it seems that the authorities knew very little about Chidembo's Church. This throws some light on the rather casual basis upon which these Churches were 'recognized' by the Government and the reason why some Church leaders were able to operate for many years and attain considerable followings without attracting much attention. The authorities were obviously more concerned with groups like the Mutendi Zionists, that had a more direct impact on the rural communities as a whole. Gavure presented the District Commissioner with a list of approximately 750 adult Church members in the Bikita, Zaka and Gutu districts, after which he was granted permission to build his Church on a surveyed site of seventy square yards. At a nominal rental of £1 a year, this piece of land became the cherished 'possession' of the *vaTopia*, and the symbol of their recognition by the State.

Gavure now called a major Church conference at which the matter was discussed at length. The Church was to be considerably larger than the majority of Independent Church buildings in the district – even that of Bishop Mutendi at Zion City. This must have meant a new incentive for the FEC, and a symbol of unity and prestige to which all the members could proudly contribute. As a sign of Government recognition it would place the Ethiopian Church on the same elevated level as the other larger Church movements that had 'their names written in the office books'. By placing his Church on this level of respectability Gavure consolidated his position as principal Church leader. He not only led the discussions on the building of the new Church but, more important, he supervised and did most of the building himself.

Gavure himself kept a meticulous record of the expenditure of Church funds. In 1967, when the building was nearing its completion, Gavure's books showed a total expenditure of £499.3.8 – a large amount by rural standards – with precise figures on funds still outstanding from each congregation. This financial aspect is of special importance in the African Independent Churches, because misappropriations of Church funds have often led to secessions. Fully aware of these dangers, Gavure scrupulously kept his financial records and invited Church members to check them whenever they wanted. In this respect Gavure has proved to be an exceptional Church leader. He is one of the few bishops who is completely trusted by the majority of subordinate Church officials as regards the handling of Church funds.

By means of regular Church meetings and building activities at his homestead (map 3) since 1956, Gavure managed to organize his widely scattered followers into a cohesive body with a centralized leadership. His Church became fully autonomous. Contacts with the Ndebele 'Ethiopians' were broken off before the death of Chidembo and the first bishop's contact with the South African leaders belongs to the remote past. There are as yet no signs of special efforts to link up with the South African Church leaders, nor with the African Methodist Episcopal Church, which was originally closely related to the all-African Ethiopian Church movement in South Africa, and which has a well organized centre at Fort Victoria.

The total FEC membership at present amounts to approximately 3,000 members. In Bikita the sixteen 'shadows of the Ethiopians' (*mapfute ava-Topia*)[16] fall under the regional leadership of *Muongamiri* (Church warden) Chapinga; the seventeen Zaka congregations fall under the control of *Muongamiri* Rinos Musasikwa. *Mufundisi* (Rev.) Bodias takes care of the ten Gutu congregations, the Rev. Maboko of the single congregation in Nyashanu (Buhera), and the Rev. Davidson Munanga of the Church's only urban congregation at Gatooma.

c) *Schism: Chidembo Jr.'s bid for leadership*

Macharutya, Chidembo's son, returned to Rhodesia in 1956 and attended his first FEC conference at Mudzingwa in Bikita. He stated at this meeting that he wanted to join the Church of his father since he felt no need to remain with the Seventh Day Adventists. Gavure made his wish known to the members of the Church and then told Macharutya that he had been accepted by the others as an Ethiopian Church member. Gavure also advised Macharutya to prepare a meeting at his house. This meeting would become an occasion of official welcome and recognition of the founder's son in his father's Church. Gavure attached only one condition, that Macharutya organize this meeting in co-operation with the regional leader of the Bikita district,

16. *Bvute* (pl. *mapfute)*: 'shadow'. This term calls to mind the shadows of the trees under which Church services are conducted. A *Topia* congregation is popularly referred to as a *bvute*.

Chapinga. At this meeting Macharutya was cordially welcomed and he was appointed as a deacon by Gavure. He was to work together with one of Gavure's evangelists near Chief Ziki's kraal.

Although Macharutya at first gave the impression that he was satisfied with his position in the Church, he had other intentions. He went to Chief Mazungunye and stated that he wanted the inheritance (*nhaka*) of his deceased father. Gavure was called. Mazungunye, who knew that Macharutya was a latecomer, told Macharutya that he had no claims, as Gavure was the one who had 'walked with his father' for many years, and whom Chidembo himself had preferred to be his successor. Gavure on this occasion stated that he was perfectly willing to share the leadership with Macharutya, but Macharutya was adamant. He wanted to become the one and only bishop, and told Gavure to step down. From his point of view it was a matter of all or nothing. Gavure naturally refused. Mazungunye stated publicly that Macharutya did not even know the ways and rules of the Church and that he favoured Gavure as leader of the *Topia* Church.

The strife continued and Macharutya repeatedly went back to Chief Mazungunye with complaints. After a while Mazungunye called Gavure once more and advised him to broach the issue in a meeting of the Church council (*dare rekereke*). Gavure summoned *Muongamiri* Chapinga and *Mufundisi* Mawere, two of his most trusted leaders, to attend the Church's *dare* session, while Macharutya was supported by Zuruzuru and Joshua Chabata (old followers of Chidembo, who resented Gavure's leadership). One of Chief Mazungunye's court councillors also attended the meeting, which took place at Chatindo in Bikita. On this occasion Gavure suggested that Macharutya Chidembo be appointed as bishop of the Ethiopian congregations in Chief Ziki's area (Bikita) and that the two of them co-operate as bishops. This was as fair a deal as Macharutya could expect. Gavure wanted to avoid a schism at all costs and said so. He thought that Chief Ziki and Chief Mazungunye could contribute towards Church unity, once two bishops had been appointed. Gavure also pointed out that Macharutya's promotion to the position of *mufundisi*, which had meanwhile taken place, was merely a sign of recognition of his relationship to the deceased bishop and not because of any work he had done in the Church. The matter remained unresolved at this meeting and yet another complaint was forwarded by Chidembo Jr. to Chief Mazungunye. Gavure repeated his offer and Chief Mazungunye once more accepted it as a feasible solution, but Chidembo's son would have none of it. He maintained his claim to full leadership of his father's Church, probably not only because of the prestige it would bring him, but possibly also for the financial advantage which he may have hoped to gain from it.

Yet at some stage Macharutya must have intimated acceptance of Chief Mazungunye's and Bishop Gavure's proposals, because Gavure arranged a meeting at which he proposed to confer the title of co-bishop on Macharutya. The meeting took place at the village of Macharutya. For Gavure it must have been a difficult time because he had to battle against the traditional succession pattern, which many Church members still regarded as the appropriate practice, applicable to Church leadership, in spite of their having chosen Gavure as Chidembo's successor. He also had to cope with the ambitions of his subordinate Church leaders, some of whom might be tempted to avail themselves of the circumstances to obtain a quick promotion.

Without making his intentions known to the followers of Gavure, Macharutya went to Mutendi and Dzukuso and asked them to come to the meeting in order to consecrate him as the Ethiopian Bishop and successor to his father. It is said that he told Mutendi and Dzukuso that he was the 'founder' of the Church, together with his father, and that both of them had played a role in establishing the Church in Rhodesia. He also won Chief Ziki (a follower of Mutendi, and possibly a relative of Chidembo) to his side. The arrival of all these dignitaries at the meeting came as a surprise to Gavure and his supporters. Mutendi, the most prominent Zionist leader in the district, Dzukuso, a *Chibarirwe* leader, and Chief Ziki, the local authority in tribal affairs, were the influential persons through whom Macharutya intended to sway the proceedings in his favour. His father had been well acquainted with these men, and he knew that they would favour him, Macharutya, as the 'legal' successor to his father's position, even if his claims about the origin of the Church proved to be shaky. Mutendi could be counted upon to support a leadership based on heredity, because this was the pattern he favoured for the succession in his own Church. He would also want to make use of the situation to gain more influence. There was no reason why he should back the young 'upstart' of the FEC, who had in fact outstripped the pride of Zion City with his large Church building and who, for some years at least, had been making more converts in the Bikita district, Mutendi's stronghold, than the miracle-maker of Moriah himself. Dzukuso favoured Chidembo Jr. because he was a friend of the old bishop, and regarded the succession of the deceased's son to his name and leadership as consistent with the 'ways of the fathers', which were so strongly emphasized in the *Chibarirwe* Church.

At the meeting which took place on the 6th of June, 1964, Dzukuso spoke first: 'I knew Chari Chidembo and I was present when he was buried. The relatives made it known that day that, if an ox could be found, we had to organize a feast in order to give the deceased's name to Macharutya.' It is important to note that Dzukuso did not actually say that it was Chidembo's wish that his son should also 'inherit' the Church leadership, but he might have implied this when he referred to the name-giving ceremony.

Mutendi played the main role during the proceedings. He addressed the meeting as follows: 'I have come here today because I have been called by Macharutya in connection with the "inheritance of his father" [*nhaka yababa*]. This *nhaka* cannot be taken by a foreigner [*mutorwa*], and therefore I have come today to give you, Macharutya, the name of your father, Chari Chidembo. This name belongs to you! I ask you to stand up.' Mutendi then asked Macharutya to name the leaders of the Church. Those who were pointed out were Tommy (Zaka district), Komichi (at Chief Ziki's), Philip and Sauro Muduma (who had already broken with Gavure before Macharutya's return from South Africa), both from Bikita. These members were the first converts of Chidembo and some of them had at that stage stopped participating in Church services. They were all called on to shake hands with the new Church leader. Mutendi laid hands on Macharutya, saying: '*You have come being you, Chari Chidembo. I am giving you the name and Church leadership* [*ubishopi*]. Do not be afraid of what the people might think or say. If anything arises in connection with your work that you do not fully understand, just come and ask our advice at Moriah.'

By naming Macharutya, Mutendi was acting contrary to customary usage. He assumed the role which should have been confined to one of Chidembo's relatives. Strictly speaking he had no authority for his action, but this was clearly an improvised *kugadzira* ritual, planned beforehand by Macharutya's supporters and aimed at conferring on him both name and leadership of his deceased father. While addressing Macharutya as the returned Chidembo, Mutendi even used the same words normally spoken during the name-giving part of the *kugadzira* ritual. Though the ancestors were not invoked during this semi-traditional ceremony, the legal implications were regarded as similar to those involved in a real *kugadzira*.

During the entire ceremony Gavure was ignored, except for a few derogatory remarks directed at him. Mutendi left, having urged the new 'Chidembo' to spread the Gospel. Before the meeting was closed, Chidembo's relatives threw gifts at the feet of their new leader as is the custom during name-giving ceremonies. They said: 'You have returned to us, Chari Chidembo, being you!'

Gavure asked Chief Ziki what he should do, as he had not expected this to happen. Ziki suggested that he also pay tribute to the new 'Chidembo'. By doing so, Gavure would actually have acknowledged Chidembo as the new leader of the Church. He therefore refused and went away. Only the close relatives of Chidembo Jr. accepted the new leader and honoured him with their presents. The other 'Ethiopians' left without participating in the ceremony. If Macharutya Chidembo had thought that he would succeed in rallying the majority of FEC members behind him, he was mistaken. Only the close relatives and a few disgruntled young leaders joined him. The majority of Church members remained loyal to Gavure. Scores of them felt that they owed him allegiance because he was the man who had taken the initiative and had urged many of them to join the Church at a time when Chidembo was only the frail old bishop and 'resting leader' of the Church.

From that day the schism between Gavure and Chidembo Jr. was definite and they never co-operated again. Chidembo became closely linked with Mutendi, and nowadays, whenever the Zionists hold a meeting at Chief Ziki's homestead, Chidembo with his few followers attend. Macharutya himself claims to have 200 members in Gutu (Chingombe), 400 in Ndanga and 130 in the Bikita district. He also claims to have jurisdiction over ten Church ministers, five evangelists, four deacons and a few overseers (*vatariri*). He makes no secret of his ambition to become the principal leader of 'the whole Ethiopian Church in Rhodesia'. The figures he mentions are based on wishful thinking. In Chingombe I did not come across a single FEC member who recognizes Macharutya as Church leader. The great majority of Church members whom he prefers to regard as his flock in reality pay allegiance to Bishop Gavure.

Gavure himself gave the following account of the whole matter:

'Up to the date of Chidembo's death there were no secessions worth mentioning. His followers were very few and it happened occasionally that some of them backslid and returned to the "ways of the world", but never did any of the Church leaders break away and take a large number of members with him. At the time when I became bishop there were few organized *mapfute* [congregations]. We did not total more than six congregations then, and in Gutu we had no followers at all.[17]

When I took over the leadership of the Church, the general conditions were favourable and the people flocked to the Church. While Chidembo was alive and while he was still active as a leader, the people were hesitant to follow him. They were afraid of being imprisoned because they saw the hardships of

17. That explains why only few FEC members in Gutu dispute the fact that Gavure succeeded Chidembo. I found that all the FEC members in the Chingombe chiefdom spoke with great respect of this man and that they never questioned his leadership. Most of them had never actually met Chidembo and from the time of their joining the Church they had direct contact with Bishop Gavure. To them, Chidembo was the founding leader whose name represented the link with the remote Ethiopian Churches in South Africa.

some of the other followers of African Churches. Besides, Chidembo was never really recognized by the Government! As soon as I was appointed as the Church's principal leader, I went to the DC's office and made known the fact that I had a Church and wanted to be officially recognized. Because of this move, the people who had wanted to join long ago saw that it was now safe and they joined us. I also went to Old Umtali Mission [American Methodists] and had the necessary preacher's certificates printed. The old man, Chidembo, had never really bothered much about the relationship with the authorities. He simply went around in the villages, preaching. He did this alone for a long time.

The main schism was that of Macharutya Chidembo. He now has only a few followers. Then there is Tommy of Zaka, whose breakaway is actually tied up with that of Chidembo Jr. and is therefore not of great significance. He disputed my leadership and said that he wanted to take charge of the Zaka congregations. He went to Chief Nhema, but the chief told him that he had no legal claim to leadership since he was my "child." The Zaka *vaongamiri* in any case refused to follow him. Ndinga, one of the kraalheads told me that he would rather run his own Church. Perhaps he had hopes of winning a large following, but the result of his actions was that he ended up with a few members living at his village. We are still good friends and see each other regularly. I have discussed the matter with him and we came to an agreement that he would hold his own services.

This Church will probably have a major split after my death. I am aware of the rumours that Chapinga and Rainos Musasikwa, my two maternal uncles [*vadzisekuru*], are already at loggerheads and that they refuse to co-operate with one another if I am absent. As the two most influential leaders they are already "campaigning" in their parishes, and it is known that, if I should fall away, the one would not accept the other as the bishop of the Church. If the Church council votes in favour of one or the other, the loser will try to start off on his own, taking as many members with him as he can. I know of this coming crisis but there is very little I can do about it. I have to carry on with the work at hand. I wish my eldest son, Ismael, to bear my name when I die. *Ismael must receive my name in my Church*!'[18]

It is interesting that Gavure's wish that his son should succeed him as leader of the Church reveals the same inclination as that of Macharutya when he made a bid for 'ecclesiastic' power on the grounds of genealogical descent. In spite of having seen what had happened to Chidembo, Gavure is honest enough to admit that he would like his name to be perpetuated in *his* Church.

18. Personal communication at the *Topia* Church headquarters in 1967.

In Shona philosophy this attitude is quite normal. Succession of his son to his own position is the only way in which Gavure can have his name perpetuated in the Church which he has built up himself. This wish is expressed in spite of the probability that Chapinga or Rainos will be elected as his successor, unless, of course, Gavure can retain the leadership long enough to offer his senior son a fair chance of establishing and proving himself as the future leader of the Church. But it is possible that Ismael, Gavure's senior son, may not be actively interested in the Church until his father's death, after which he may 'return' to his village to claim his '*nhaka*', in the same way as Chidembo Jr. did.

3. MAIN FEATURES OF THE ETHIOPIAN-TYPE CHURCHES

Historically the Southern Shona Ethiopian-type Churches have their roots in the 'Ethiopian' movement in South Africa. It is possible that Chidembo came into contact with members of the *Ethiopian Church* – one of the first movements of this type in South Africa – founded in 1892 by Mangena Mokone, a former Wesleyan minister. If this is so, Chidembo may also have been influenced by members of the *African Methodist Episcopal Church* because the *Ethiopian Church* of Mokone in its initial stages of development was closely associated with this Negro Mission Church, which was founded in 1816 by Richard Allen in Philadelphia.[19] All the other principal Shona leaders with whom we are concerned – Sengwayo, Sibambo and Zvobgo – had some form of contact with Mvuyana's *African Congregational Church* which had branched from the American Board Mission in 1917. Like the Rhodesian Zionist movement, all these Ethiopian-type Churches have, in practice, become fully autonomous and the links with their South African counterparts have barely more than ideological significance to the *Topia* members. The early termination of organizational contacts with the South African 'Ethiopians' has caused this connection to be a vague one, belonging to the remote past. In Rhodesia the rural Ethiopian-type Churches and the predominantly urban-centred African Methodist Episcopal Church recognize each other, but contact is maintained through mutual participation in outstanding events like the inauguration of a new leader or the opening of a Church building, rather than through regularized forms of co-operation.

19. Sundkler (*op. cit.*, p. 40) describes how Dwane, one of the outstanding leaders of the Ethiopian Church, visited the Uited States and incorporated the South African Church he represented into the AMEC.

Ideologically, a number of Ethiopian-type Churches claim to be linked to the first followers of Christ through the Church of Ethiopia, founded by the eunuch of that country, who was baptized by Philip, the Apostle of Jesus Christ. This ideological association with the earliest development of Christianity in Africa provides the Ethiopian-type Churches with a charter which is psychologically more satisfying than the indirect tie with the ancient Church traced through the complicated European Church history. Compared to the early development in Africa, the European Churches are regarded as latecomers, lacking the richness of 'true' Christianity. In this connection Aquina reports Zvobgo to have resigned at Morgenster Mission 'because he believed that Mvuyana [who is said to have visited Fort Victoria in 1947] had brought him news of the true Church, which traces its origin back to the Queen of Ethiopia who visited Solomon to learn from his wisdom, and who brought back soil with her from the Holy Land to found her Church . . .'[20] Although Aquina does not mention the personal factors involved in Zvobgo's dissent from the DRC, nor the key role played by Sibambo in the formation of the ARC, she correctly draws the attention to Zvobgo's concern with the origin of the 'truly African Church', and the influence of South African Separatist Church leaders on his religious life. The Italo-Abyssinian war of 1935, as Sundkler says, strongly encouraged the spread of an Ethiopian mythology in South Africa and stimulated the emergence of a 'mythical charter' of the Ethiopian-type Independent Churches. 'The Abyssinia ideology of the Ethiopians . . . is in essence an attempt to give to the independent Church an ancient Apostolic succession and a charter, linking their Church with the Bible.'[21] This attempt, as illustrated in the case of Zvobgo, undoubtedly affected the Rhodesian Independent Churches.

Yet the Abyssinia ideology, partly through lack of regular contact between the South African and Rhodesian Churches, had a less direct and less marked influence on the latter than on the former movements. Neither the name nor the correspondence or constitutions of the Shona Ethiopian-type Churches reflect a particular preoccupation with twentieth century events in Ethiopia or Abyssinia, as was the case with many of the South African 'Ethiopian' Churches founded in the 1930's and 40's.[22] Only the name *First Ethiopian Church* is reminiscent of the link with Christianity in the North African state. And even so this name, to the followers of Bishop Gavure, is less loaded with political overtones than in the south, since it conveys to them primarily the

20. Aquina, 1966, p. 8.
21. Sundkler, *op. cit.*, pp. 57-58.
22. *Ibid.*, p. 57.

idea of the *first* Church in Africa, i.e. the early Church in Ethiopia, and the *first* independent African Church (presumably the one founded by Mokone) in South Africa. *Chibarirwe*, the popular designation of Sengwayo's African Congregational Church, reflects the emphasis on adaptation to tribal customs, and 'African Reformed' refers primarily to the reformation of what Sibambo and Zvobgo regarded as the distortion of the Christian marriage in the ACC.

In the official 'Church books' of these two Churches no specific mention is made of the Church or the Christian kingship in the state, Ethiopia. The explanation of the African Church's origin in the African Reformed Church's hymnbook,[23] relates the founding of this movement to the experiences of some of the Israelite tribes, as described in the Old Testament, and from this angle seeks to establish the legitimacy of its existence. It is stated that the Roman Catholic Church was the first Christian Church, from which all other Churches branched off according to the diverse convictions of their founding leaders. Then, one day, an African had a dream in which his attention was drawn to Joshua 22 : 1-34. When he awoke and read this portion in the Bible, he was greatly struck by the narrative of the three tribes of Israel – Reuben, Gad and Manassah – who, because they were living on the far side of the river Jordan, built an altar and installed a priest on behalf of their children. To the dreamer this message was an indication of the African Church's right of existence. In the same way as the Israelites were apprehensive of the religious developments on the other side of Jordan, so the established Mission Churches questioned the formation of an African Church. But the Israelite army, sent out against these tribes, was satisfied with the explanation that the new altar was erected on behalf of the children who were growing up without proper instruction. So the three tribes were left in peace. Likewise the established Mission Churches also accept (the inference is that they are expected to accept!) the formation of the African Church. 'Don't be astounded', it says in the hymnbook, 'for each race has its own Church, and it is good to found a Church in accordance with the laws of the Government . . . The African Church was not founded with the intention of breaking with other Churches or opposing the Government, but to honour God, so that He may bless us and may lead us in truth.'[24]

It is possible that the founding leader, whose name is not mentioned in the ARC hymnbook, was in fact the Zulu, Mvuyana, with whom Sibambo and Zvobgo (through his nephew, Mandondo) were in contact. The explanation

23. *Nziyo dzeKereke yaVatema:* Hymns of the African Church, *Shonganiso* Mission, African Newspapers Ltd., Salisbury.

24. *Ibid.*, pp. 3-4.

30. Zvekare Sengwayo, president of the ACC (*Chibarirwe*), closing an out-door meeting with prayer.

31. *Mufundisi* Moses Ruwana, key-figure of the *Chibarirwe* movement, and his second wife, both in official attire.

32. Rev. Zvobgo and Mandondo, two prominent leaders of the African Reformed Church, in discussion at *Shonganiso* Mission.

33. Bishop Nheya Gavure of the First Ethiopian Church, reading the Bible in preparation of a Church service.

of the Church's origin, apart from signifying the importance of dreams as valid revelations from God,[25] reflects the attempt to link the Church directly to the Bible. Reference to the state, Ethiopia, may have been left out on purpose, for purely diplomatic reasons. On the other hand this omission should caution us not to over-emphasize the importance of the Ethiopia-Abyssinia ideology for all the Churches classified as 'Ethiopian'. What *is* important to men like Sibambo and Zvobgo is to find convincing Biblical justification for their movement, irrespective of whether or not the link with the ancient people of God is traced through Ethiopia. The particular preference for the three tribes of Israel on the far side of Jordan might well derive from more than a mere revelatory dream. For, incidentally, both Sibambo and Zvobgo have their following on the other side of large rivers, away from the main centres of the Mission Churches to which they formerly belonged: Sibambo's main sphere of influence stretching across the Sabi river beyond the American Board's 'domain' at Mt. Selinda, and Zvobgo having built the *Shonganiso* Mission within a few hundred yards of the Mtilikwe river, on the side opposite the comparatively powerful Morgenster Mission some twenty miles away.

As far as attitudes towards the African community are concerned, the Ethiopian-type Churches are generally comprehensively involved or at least aim at such involvement in society. Although only the ARC has thus far succeeded in building and managing its own school, all these Churches are interested in the educational advancement of Africans. In the *Chibarirwe* 'constitution' it is laid down that Church funds should be used for 'the work of the African Congregation everywhere in this country of Rhodesia . . . e.g. for the building of Churches and schools.'[26] The ARC is even more explicit in its constitution – which is a description of the Church's aims rather than of its structure and organization – about its desire to be fully involved in the education of Africans.[27] This Church has a well-defined working program, covering a wide field of social and religious tasks. The poor and the needy should be helped; the consumption of beer is sharply attacked on the grounds of the negative effect of alcohol on a person's physique and appearance; the young should be instructed about sexual behaviour and marriage; the exclusionist attitudes of tribalism should be overcome . . . 'All Africans must live in unity and honour each other without taking blood relationship into consideration', and laziness

25. Dreams play a less significant role in the Ethiopian-type than in the Spirit-type Churches, but there is no doubt of their being regarded as a reliable channel through which divine messages are communicated to the living. Dream accounts, still to be presented in Volume 2, bear out this point.

26. See Appendix VII.

27. Appendix VII, ARC constitution – c.

with all its detrimental results should be overcome through diligent work.[28] In many respects *Topia* practices correspond to those of the ARC, while the *Chibarirwe*, true to its name, has a more lenient view of beer drinking and also of traditional rituals. Being less interested in ritual purity and food taboos than the Spirit-type groups, the 'Ethiopian' movement generally has a more open attitude towards society at large and provokes fewer reactions from traditionalists.

In their relations with the European Government and Mission, the Ethiopian-type Churches among the Southern Shona are characterized by a similar ambivalence as those in South Africa.[29] On the one hand there is reaction and protest; mostly in camouflaged form and less overt in public statements than in the sermons of some of the Spirit-type Churches, as mentioned in the previous chapter. The slogan 'Africa for the Africans' is not expressly included in their working program, as in South Africa. On the other hand, one finds appreciation for and a modelling of Church practices on those of the Protestant Mission Churches. ARC involvement in the educational field probably contributed towards Sibambo and Zvobgo drawing up a constitution which is surprisingly positive in relation to Missions and Government. In the first two articles it is stated that the African Church only wants to increase the light already lit by the Mission Churches and that it honours the 'ministers of the white skin' who had initially brought the Africans out of darkness.[30] The land development schemes of the Government are praised; God, Government and the Church ministers are all envisaged as working in unison. Thus the Government is regarded as a 'restorer of peace' and a 'bestower of prosperity' if its laws are obeyed. Lack of prosperity is ascribed to the incapability of honouring and fearing the European Government and African chiefs. 'This [incapability] shows that we did not assimilate properly all the words we are taught by our "ministers of the white skin" who showed us their love while teaching us everything.'[31] Africans are explicitly encouraged to honour the Government and African chiefs.

Ritually, we have already characterized the Ethiopian-type Churches as conforming to Mission Church patterns. Their sermons are less emotional, frequently less fragmentary in Bible interpretation, and focusing more on single themes, as taught in Mission evangelist schools, than is the case in the Spirit-type Churches. In the *Chibarirwe* and ARC hardly any dancing takes

28 Appendix VII, ARC constitution – d, g, h, i, k.
29. Sundkler, *op.cit.*, p. 54.
30 Appendix VII, ARC constitution – a and c.
31. Appendix VII, ARC constitution.

place during services. Nevertheless, the 'Ethiopian' camp comprises great differences, varying from the left-wing group which incorporates some Spirit-type practices, to the right wing which follows the Protestant Mission (predominantly DRC and Methodist) Churches more closely. The *Topia* Church falls under the former category. Here, singing and dancing takes a central place. The use of holy water, of the bishop's holy staff, faith-healing and exorcism have all been introduced as valid practices, though less prominent than in the Zionist and Apostolic Churches. The ARC stands at the opposite end, for, in spite of the recognition of baptism through immersion which differs from that of the DRC, such important parallels to the Mission policy as monogamy, marriage in Church, catechetical instruction and strict prohibition of beer drinking have been reintroduced to counter the far-reaching accommodation of the *Chibarirwe*.

6

Conflict and recognition

In this chapter we shall deal with the attitudes of the Administration, tribal authorities and Missions towards the Independent Churches and the reaction of the African Church leaders to the repressive measures imposed on their religious activities. The main focus is on the Government's policy, and in this respect the material in the National Archives in Salisbury provided the main source of information. But this presented some serious limitations. In the first place, the interest of the former Native Commissioners in the Independent Churches was generally a political one, with the result that their official reports and correspondence throw little light – from the administrative angle – on the sociological and religious aspects of the emergent 'sects'. Secondly, there was a tendency to report exclusively on those Independent Churches that interfered with African education or that were suspected of spreading seditious ideas. Consequently many of the smaller groups have gone unrecorded (as far as I traced the files to the early 1930's). No mention is made, for instance, of the early rise of Chidembo's First Ethiopian Church. Thirdly, I was prevented by statute law from having access to the material of the past thirty years. Consequently there is a gap in our knowledge relating to a period which is of vital importance for an understanding of the development of relations between the Administration and the Independent Church leaders. Much therefore remains to be done in this field in the future.

As far as the four major Southern Shona Church movements are concerned, the files available in 1967 contained elaborate information on the Zionist movement, but even then the records of the important period in the late 1930's and the 1940's, when official recognition was granted to some of the Zionist groups, remained inaccessible. No reference to the Apostolic movement of Johane Maranke could be found in the main files on 'Separatist Churches', although it can be taken for granted that Johane's activities and those of his followers did not go unnoticed, even in the early 1930's. The surveyed Ethiopian-type Churches, having achieved official recognition at a much later date, were obviously not included in the files available. Fortunately we have in Mutendi's ZCC Rungano a fairly accurate 'canonized' historic account of his relations with the Administration and missionaries up to the period when his Church was officially 'recognized', or rather tolerated, by the administrative authorities. His account reflects the mood of Africans in response to the Government's effort to control and curb their 'sectarian' activities – and for this reason it will be treated at some length in this chapter.

Strictly speaking the period before the advent of Zionism amongst the Southern Shona falls outside the scope of this study, but a brief review of the measures taken by the Chartered Company officials against some of the early Pentecostal, Ethiopian and other movements will serve as a background for a fuller appreciation of Government policy in the years subsequent to Responsible Government in 1923. In the period from 1923 to 1930 an effort was made to introduce legislation to control the activities of indigenous Church leaders more effectively. This effort was one of the indications of the stiffening opposition of the Government towards Pentecostalism. But the conflict between indigenous Church leaders and Administration reached its peak only after 1930, when it became apparent that local congregations of the Spirit-type Churches were mushrooming all over the country, especially in the central, southern and eastern Shona areas. To the three distinct periods – before 1923, 1923 to 1930, and after 1930 – we will now turn our attention.

1. GOVERNMENT POLICY AND AFRICAN REACTION

a) *The Chartered Company's control of religious activities* (*up to 1923*)

There were two good reasons why, in the opinion of the early Rhodesian administrators, they should pay attention to the political implications of the work done by the leaders of the African Independent Churches. In the first place there were significant indications of political ambition and ideals in the Independent religious movements of the surrounding territories, such as Northern Rhodesia, Nyasaland and South Africa. In the South African Ethiopian movement the slogan 'Africa for the Africans' could be heard, and to the north the far-reaching effect of the Chilembwe rising was evident. In the second place the Administration realized that in African society there was no clear-cut distinction between religious and political institutions in the past and that the traditional world-view, for some time to come, would have a considerable influence on the behaviour of the indigenous population. This attitude of the Southern Rhodesian Administration is aptly reflected at a later date in the annual report of the Native Commissioner, Charles Bullock:

'It is to be emphasized that the tribes affected [by Independent Church movements], have reached only the second stage of evolution. There are therefore fundamental differences between their social structure and our own; e.g. they are in a state in which political and religious institutions have not yet been differentiated ... That which is concerned with religion qua religion with us, is necessarily also political with them.'[1] In Rhodesia the role played by officers of the High-God cult during the Rebellions of 1896-7 went on record as a warning of the far-reaching influence of religious authorities. As Ranger points out, 'they [the administrative authorities] remembered only too well the key-role played by the traditional religious authorities in the rebellions of 1896 and 1897, and in their anxious supervision of the independent churches they were merely [I would say "to some extent"] transferring their suspicions from the spirit mediums and priests of Mwari to separatist and independent preachers and teachers.'[2]

In view of this background it is understandable that the authorities were reluctant to grant permission to the representative Negro Church leaders of the African Methodist Episcopal Church to enter the country. When Bishop Coppin, for instance, requested permission to visit the country in 1903 the Chief Native Commissioner sought the advice of the Anglican bishop of Mashonaland, and having been 'appropriately informed' by the reverend bishop, turned down the request. Amongst other things the Anglican bishop stated that 'This society [the AMEC] ... advocates "higher" education, makes comparisons between the political and social position of the American negro

1. NC, Sinoia, Report for year ending 31st Dec. 1928, National Archives, File S 84/A/293.
This chapter contains numerous comments of Government officials, most of them representatives of the old Native Affairs Department. To avoid confusion as regards the various administrative levels at which these officials were operating, it should be kept in mind that the Chief Native Commissioner (CNC), stationed at Salisbury, headed the Native Department and simultaneously acted as Secretary of Native Affairs. Senior representatives of the Native Department in Mashonaland and Matabeleland for many years were the two Superintendents of Natives, stationed at Fort Victoria and Bulawayo respectively; with subordinate Native Commissioners operating at local district levels. With the reorganization of African Administration in 1962, the old Native Affairs Department became the Ministry of Internal Affairs, the office of Provincial Commissioner was introduced and the term Native Commissioner (NC) was replaced by that of District Commissioner (DC). This explains the alternate use of the abbreviations NC and DC in the text. For a more comprehensive account of the hierarchic order within the whole system of African Administration, and the changes introduced in the course of time, see Holleman, 1969, pp. 15-19, 258f.

2. Ranger, in *Religion in Africa,* 1964, p. 53.

and the African native, talks of a great Native Church to arise in Africa, insists on the autonomy of the black race, need for unity, and so forth.' He went on to say that he was not likely to depreciate any legitimate aspirations, 'but there is a distinct danger, to my mind, that aspirations may be manufactured for political, social or even religious reasons, and a *manufactured* political cry on the part of the NATIVES of this country is bound to become a *RACIAL CRY* to an even much more dangerous extent than the manufactured political cry of the Dutch . . . [this refers to the "Afrikaner Bond" in South Africa].'[3]

That the Administration was unable to prevent the spread of Ethiopianism to Rhodesia is illustrated by the role played at a fairly early date by Rev. Magatho of the AMEC, among the Fingos around Bulawayo and the Sotho settlers near Fort Victoria. The Chief Native Commissioner did not hold Magatho's efforts to erect independent African schools in high esteem. In 1908 he reported that 'a few pseudo native schools are conducted by representatives of the AMEC, otherwise known as the Ethiopian movement. This particular sect endeavours to discourage the attendance of natives at schools conducted by Europeans. This body is known as confusing political propaganda with religious teaching.'[4] At first the erection of independent African schools took place on a loose basis because there were no legal strictures on the founding of schools not subsidized by the Government. Due to the low standards of some of these Ethiopian-type schools and also to the revolutionary sentiments propagated, the Chartered Company in 1912 prohibited the erection of African schools without the permission of the Director of Education. Schools that proved, upon inspection, to be of a very low standard could be closed down altogether.[5]

The early AMEC leaders in Matabeleland not only operated in the field of education, they also participated in political manoeuvres concerning the purchase of land, which resulted in their close association with the Ndebele drive for a 'National Home'. Rev. Magatho himself had managed to purchase a farm near Bulawayo in 1906. His influence was also felt further afield, when two Sotho syndicates bought land in the Fort Victoria district and, as Ranger says, Magatho was 'alleged to be behind the attempt of a Karanga group in the same area to obtain a Company farm.' The local DRC missionary

3. Anglican bishop of Mashonaland to CNC, 25th Feb. 1903, National Archives, File A/11/2/18/3.
4. Ranger, 1964, p. 58.
5. Gann, 1965, p. 205.

predicted that 'such a farm will become a harbour for those who are dissatisfied with church government and discipline.'[6]

Alarmed at the spreading influence of these Ethiopian Church leaders, the Company authorities decided to turn down applications for land by Ethiopian or Ethiopian-inspired African purchasers. They were aware that the Ethiopian-type Church leaders represented the link between the Ndebele leaders – such as Nyamanda – who were pressing for a 'National Home', and the African political movements in South Africa.

Matthew Zwimba's 'Original Church of the White Bird' (*Shiri Chena*), founded in 1915, presented the administrative authorities with a problem totally different from that posed by the AMEC leaders who were for the greater part Fingo or Sotho foreigners from South Africa and who, for that reason, did not appeal specifically to the Shona or Ndebele past. Zwimba belonged to the chiefly clan of his district and was determined to elevate some of the deceased African rebels of 1896-7 to sainthood. As Ranger indicates, 'the very name of the Church contained a double reference to Christian and traditional sources of authority; the white bird stood both for the dove of the Holy Spirit and for the traditional messenger of the High-God, Mwari, to mankind.'[7] The sentiments of Zwimba's Church were obviously not favourably looked upon by the authorities, and when he applied for the recognition of his Church in 1915 – pleading that the Administrator should be as lenient to him as to the missionaries coming from overseas – his request was turned down. At first Zwimba was only warned to stop his religious activities, unless they were conducted under European supervision, but when he disregarded this warning, drastic action was taken. Having discovered the new Church's list of rebel martyrs, the authorities imprisoned its founding leader on the grounds of spreading seditious ideas. Zwimba escaped, but was later detained several times for offences such as refusing to pay taxes, sending the Administration an 'official declaration of war' and other acts of defiance. Zwimba's following, which had always remained limited, gradually dwindled away.

Another religious group which the Administration kept under close surveillance in those years was the Watch Tower movement. Before 1923 this movement had hardly begun to win members among the indigenous population, but the apprehensive authorities had a close watch kept on some of the Nyasa leaders, working in the Colony as labour migrants. When, in 1917, the Nyasaland Government expressed its opinion that the Watch Tower

6. Ranger, 1964, p. 59; and Gono's application for land, 1904, in Archives, File L 2/1/175.

7. *Ibid.*, p. 54.

movement was a menace to all forms of Government and proved to be hostile towards European Missions, the Rhodesian authorities deported a great number of Nyasa members of this movement. Ranger comments on this purge as follows: 'The Watch Tower in Southern Rhodesia seemed to have been destroyed and the administration must have felt a certain satisfaction when seven Watch Tower deportees from Southern Rhodesia were responsible for the very considerable disorders in Northern Rhodesia a year later in 1918.'[8]

The Zionist teaching, introduced in Matabeleland by Mabhena and Ndebele – of the *Christian Apostolic Church of Zion* – in 1918, caused one of the missionaries to complain about the negative influence of this movement on missionary work. The local Native Commissioner agreed that 'this is not the Ethiopian Church, but seems a bit worse if anything.' He also thought it possible that 'under a cloak of religion they may spread propaganda which would tend to unsettle the natives.'[9] The reports made by the Criminal Investigation Department between 1918 and 1921 nevertheless indicated that Zionist preaching was not always as politically negative as was at first assumed. During sermons there were often exhortations to pay taxes and to obey the law. Greater cause for alarm were the activities of the two Pentecostalist leaders, Luttig, a European from South Africa, and Dingiswayo, a Nyasa preacher, the early representatives of the *Apostolic Faith Church.* That this Church fell into disrepute with the authorities soon after it commenced work in the Catooma district is reflected in the Chief Native Commissioner's comment in 1919: 'Faith-healing and emotionalism are prominent features of this sect. The psychic and moral effect of such teaching, to my mind, must tend to foster delusions among the native community . . . Emissaries of such sects are a menace to the Administration by stirring up discontent among the natives.'[10] As stated before, action was soon taken against both these Church leaders. Dingiswayo was deported in 1923, after he had broken with Luttig and had started operating on behalf of the CCAC in Zion; and Luttig was prohibited from entering the Shiota reserve.

The system of control during the period of Company rule was common to most colonies under British rule. It implied that all foreign Missions had to be licenced by the British Foreign Office, which involved a guarantee of loyalty to the British Government. After the first World War the system was changed at the request of the South African Government, to give greater powers of control to the local Governments. Both the South African and

8. See correspondence in Archives, File RC 2/9/5/8.
9. NC, Insiza, to Superintendent of Natives, Bulawayo, 1918, Archives, File N 3/5/3.
10. CNC to Secretary of Administrator, 1919, Archives, File S 84/A/275.

Rhodesian Governments were anxious to stop the entry of some of the American Pentecostal Missions who were regarded as the bearers of sentiments and forms of worship that stimulated separatism and which, by implication, fostered the spread of Ethiopianism. In 1921 the British Government tried to modify this system by delegating the powers of controlling the entry of missionaries to the Conference of Missionary Societies in Britain, the Foreign Missions Conference of North America or the Archbishop of America – a system which the Government of India had adopted. The Rhodesian authorities strongly disapproved of the move. Such modifications would have left them virtually without control over the entry of missionaries whom they wished to debar from the Colony. Especially during the first World War the Administration emphasized the necessity of a strict entry control. In this connection the Commandant-General commented that 'once a missionary arrives in the country, no matter what he does or what he preaches, it is impossible to deal with him, as his practices come under the head of bona fide religious tenets! This being so, when it is known beforehand that an applicant is an extremist, it is well to refuse permission for him to enter the territory.'[11]

This system proved ineffective when it came to the control of entry of South African and Rhodesian citizens. South African-born men like Luttig, who had joined the AFC in South Africa, had free access to Rhodesia, with the result that the influence of such Pentecostal groups as the AFC, Assemblies of God, Full Gospel and CCAC in Zion inevitably found their way into Rhodesia, although their foreign missionaries were kept out. Other methods therefore had to be devised. These will be dealt with in the following subsection. What was soon to become a more pressing problem, however, was the control of indigenous Church leaders who started roaming the country on preaching campaigns. Towards the end of its reign the Chartered Company had not yet introduced legislative measures for such a control. A reason for this was, of course, that only after Responsible Government had been granted to Southern Rhodesia did the activities of newly returned Zionist labour migrants – which marked the beginning of the movement's growth among the central, southern and eastern Shona – become an acute problem.

11. Minute of Commandant-General, 6th Nov. 1918, Archives, File 3/6/5.

b) *Government opposition to Anglo-American Pentecostalism and all-African Zionism (1923-1930)*

i) *First efforts to initiate legislative measures*

In 1923, when Rhodesia was granted Responsible Government, the experience of the authorities of the Native Department with sectarian movements had been limited to the few we mentioned in the previous section. The effort to pass legislation controlling unrecognized religious bodies was stimulated in the first place by the experiences of the Government with the Watch Tower since 1917, and also by the anticipation of an increase of indigenous sects in the Colony. Soon after the new Government came to power the Chief Native Commissioner wrote to the Premier's Secretary: 'This Colony has been assailed by Separatist bodies from the South and the North. Those from the South have not thrived hitherto and it is the Watch Tower movement which, albeit its propaganda has been largely limited to Northern natives, accentuates our need for protective measures. Our indigenous population will more than probably become increasingly receptive to such subversive ideas, to encounter which the proposed legislation will undoubtedly assist us.'[12] In a letter to the Native Department during the same period the CNC agrees with the view of the Superintendent of Natives on the 'desirability of legislation for the better control of Native Separatist bodies.' It was clear to him 'that hostility of European control of Missions and the denouncing of their doctrine is preached by the leaders of the [Watch Tower] movement. At present,' he continued, 'the energies of this particular sect are confined to native foreigners but there are other Separatist bodies with headquarters at Johannesburg [AMEC and CCAC in z] the representatives of which are endeavouring to establish themselves among the indigenous natives and whose doctrines are not in reality varying from that of the Watch Tower movement.'[13]

The view of the CNC in 1924 about Separatist bodies 'with their headquarters in Johannesburg' was actually based on what had happened in Matabeleland rather than in Mashonaland. This can be deduced from the reactions to a questionnaire on the Separatist Churches sent to Native Commissioners and Superintendents of Natives in 1923. This questionnaire contained questions on the reasons for secession, educational standards of leaders, doctrines and practices, causes of spread of Separatist Churches, etc. It formed part of an enquiry conducted by a Government Commission in

12. CNC to Secretary of Premier, 10th April 1924, Archives, File S 138/106, titled: 'Control of Unrecognized Religious Denominations 1923-1929'.

13. CNC to Native Affairs Department, 20th April 1924, Archives, File S 138/106.

South Africa under the leadership of Dr. C. T. Loram – after the tragic incident with Mgijima's Israelite movement at Bullhoek in 1921.[14] Nearly all the Commissioners in Shona-speaking areas informed the CNC that they were unable to fill in the questionnaire because there were no Separatist movements in their districts or provinces. Of the northern Shona territories the NC of Marandellas (Posselt) stated, 'I am not in a position to answer the questionnaire as I have no knowledge of native Separatist Churches . . . this Church [the AFC of Luttig] has not come into active existence in my district and I understand that the Government has refused to recognize the denomination.' The NC of Sinoia reported that as far as he knew there were no movements towards separation in his district. Similar reactions came from Goromonzi and Hartley. From the south-east the NC of Umtali bluntly stated: 'There are no Separatist movements in this area' and from the south the Superintendent of Natives for the Victoria Province (which includes the Gutu, Bikita, Ndanga, Victoria and Chibi districts) reported that, 'as there are no Separatist Churches in the Victoria circle and I have no detailed knowledge of the movement elsewhere, I am not in a position to supply any of the information asked for, nor have any of the NC's of the circle been able to supply any. The leading local missionary bodies to whom I addressed enquiries have not replied and it can therefore be assumed that they know nothing of the matter.'[15]

The Superintendent of Natives at Bulawayo (Jackson) was the only authority capable of furnishing the CNC with detailed information, due to the presence of 'Separatist' movements in his (Ndebele) province. He mentioned the presence of the Watch Tower, African Methodist Episcopal Church, Zion Apostolic and Christian Catholic Apostolic Church in Zion movements. Concerning their aims he comments that these are 'religious and social with no more, at present, than a suggestion of political aims.' 'The Watch Tower sect' he observed, 'is going ahead more than other bodies probably on account of latitude of doctrines but here again it is observed that the proselytes, by which I mean converts, are mostly northern natives of Nyasaland . . . Those Separationists which come from the South cannot be said to be flourishing or increasing and their spread is not marked. By officials they are regarded as a *danger in embryo* because of the political spread of ideas in the Union. They are *not an existent active danger at present* (my italics).'

This passage reflects the general attitude of the Administration at the time. With the exception of the repressive measures against Zwimba's activities, restrictions up to that stage had been motivated by the anticipation of trouble

14. Sundkler, 1961, p. 73.
15. Archives, File N 3/5/6, titled: 'Native Churches - SEPARATIST MOVEMENT'.

as a result of what was happening in the surrounding territories and not because the Churches in Rhodesia were regarded as a direct political threat. The authorities actually regarded the effort of these 'Independents' in the educational field as ineffective. 'In the matter of secular education', wrote Jackson, 'they are so defective as to offer little inducement to the natives at large and for that reason they are not at present making much headway. At any rate the efficient organization of the organized non-Separationist bodies is at present more attractive to the natives. The Separationists are too hampered by lack of funds.'[16]

The opinions expressed in 1923 by Herbert Taylor, the CNC, in answer to the South African Commission's enquiries, are of great interest because it can be regarded as the most representative judgment of a Government authority at the time, based on information concerning the whole Colony. Taylor estimated that the Watch Tower and the CCAC in Zion counted a thousand adherents each, the African Episcopal Church fifty members, and that Zwimba's *Shiri Chena* Church had become totally defunct. He was basically in agreement with the Superintendent of Natives at Bulawayo that the doctrines of the Separatist Churches contained 'no more than just a suggestion of political aims at present; that the poor secular educational qualifications of the teachers offer but little inducement to the natives of the Colony generally and principally' and that Separationist bodies were inefficiently organized through lack of funds. Like Jackson, he also regarded these Churches as an embryonic and not as an immediate active danger. 'The attitude of non-seceding natives', he stated, 'appears to be uninterested. The heathens are not interested to any appreciable extent and it should be emphasized that these bodies are more particularly proselytizing organizations, endeavouring to obtain adherence from old established organizations.' Taylor's judgment on the attitudes of heathens and 'non-seceding natives' was quite accurate, since all the principal leaders of the Zionist Churches admit the active opposition of traditionalists and tribal authorities during the initial stages of their religious activities. His enumeration of several causes – in order of importance – for the spread of Separatism also gives evidence of a sound insight in the driving powers behind this movement:

1. 'The spread of Education which has led to the desire for a control in their own religious matters;
2. A feeling in the native mind that the non-Separatist Churches have broken away from the simplicity and Biblical teaching which has in the older organizations been overlaid with [Western!] ceremony and doctrine;

16. Superintendent of Natives, Bulawayo, Archives, File N 3/5/6.

3. The desire of many who think that they possess the gift of teaching to instruct and lead their people without intervention of the European clergy;
4. The fact that the teachers are of the same class as the taught; and
5. An intense fervour which finds its natural outlet in a somewhat hysterical outpouring.'

The CNC furthermore pointed out that none of these Churches could be classified as definitely anti-European, apart from individual teachers who showed a tendency in this direction; that their relationship to political organizations was indirect, partly because the 'native political organizations have as yet taken no distinct line'. None of the sects operating in the country showed a tendency towards 'Christian polygamy'; only the Watch Tower movement allegedly condoned a certain looseness in matters pertaining to sexual ethics. No instance of the misappropriation of Church funds had been brought to his notice.[17]

On the whole these observations of the CNC reveal a balanced, well-informed and moderate attitude. The religious activities of the Separatist Churches did not seem a cause for undue anxiety.

But the mood of the Administrators changed rapidly as the increased activities of European-organized Pentecostal movements called for stricter control. In 1924, only a year after he had reported on the absence of Separatist movements in his district, the NC of Marandellas notified the CNC that he did not consider Mr. Luttig's presence to be in the interest of the natives of Shiota reserve. 'In the natives' interests I am averse to increasing further the number of denominations granted Mission facilities in the reserves as tending only to confuse the native mind and leading to a vaccillating faith.'[18] The NC of Gwanda also voiced his alarm at the increase of religious societies and commented, 'I cannot but think that the immense number of societies such as this must be confusing to the native mind. There appears to be no control over native schools established for teaching in Religion only and the present application [of the Free Gospel Church] again raises the question whether legislation is not desirable with a view of giving some power of control in these matters.'[19] Significantly, both these Native Commissioners were worried about the confusion caused amongst Africans by the activities of too many religious bodies in their districts. Towards the end of the previous year the CNC had already drawn the attention of the Minister of Internal Affairs

17. CNC to Dr. C. T. Loram, Pietermaritzburg, 1923, Archives, File N 3/5/6.
18. NC, Marandellas, to CNC, Nov. 1924, Archives, File S 138/176.
19. NC, Gwanda, to Superintendent of Natives of Matabeleland, 1st Sept. 1924, Archives, File S 138/176.

to 'the confusion caused in the native mind by the very teachings of numerous sects and churches at present at work in the country . . .'[20]

In the effort to achieve greater control through legislation, the Rhodesian authorities could learn from the legislative measures which the South African Commission of Inquiry intended proprosing to its Government, as well as the new system of control set out in the Northern Rhodesia Proclamation, No. 28 of 1921. In South Africa, legislation on the conditions of recognition of Separatist Churches was not passed until 1925,[21] with the result that the Rhodesian Department of Native Affairs in 1923 had only an outline of the measures proposed by the Commission of Inquiry. The essence of this policy was that Government should tolerate such movements as long as they were free of subversion of public order, that 'no christian marriage, no renting of land, no registration for exemption, no railway or other concessions should be allowed until the Church and ministers have become registered' and that the 'sole condition of recognition for registration should be that the Church is a *stable organization* and its ministers are responsible persons fit to emphasize the civil duties of ministers of religion.'[22]

The Northern Rhodesia Proclamation which was originally devised for taking drastic legal action against the Watch Tower movement, nevertheless received preference. Commenting on the South African proposals the Superintendent of Natives for Matabeleland stated: 'I am in general agreement concerning the [S.A.] Government's attitude as suggested and hope that a similar move will be adopted in Southern Rhodesia . . . I think the suggestions of the N.R. Proclamation are preferable as they are more thorough.'[23] A few months later the CNC advised the Premier that the 'model for our guidance exists in the Northern Rhodesia Proclamation.' He warned that 'interference with religious freedom is something which requires delicate handling', but then continued to state that 'where freedom is misused and

20. CNC to Secretary of Native Affairs, 13th Dec. 1923, Archives, File S 138/148.

21. Sundkler, 1961, p. 74.

22. Included in Questionnaire forwarded to Rhodesian Commissioners, 1923, Archives, File N 3/5/6. The actual conditions for a Church's recognition as a 'stable organization' were the following:
a) 6 congregations of at least 50 full members, each of them not nearer than 25 miles from each other, b) a continued existence of at least 5 years, c) a separate Church building for each congregation, d) a standard discipline agreeing with the ideals of Christian teaching and ethics, e) ministers especially trained for the work, and f) the minister to be certified by the magistrate as a suitable person for the exercise of the several functions of this office.

23. Superintendent of Natives, Matabeleland, in reply to 1923 Questionnaire, Archives, File N 3/5/6.

allowed to degenerate into licence, the sort of thing which we have had of late . . . it becomes necessary to place it under some control.' 'The Northern Rhodesia Proclamation', he stated, 'shows no undue scruples on the point and in the interests of all sections of the population may be followed. There should be a definition of the term "recognized religious denomination" as in the N.R. Proclamation and I can see no reason why, to allay possible fears, a full list should not be scheduled of all "recognized religious bodies".'[24] The CNC furthermore recommended that section 10 of the N.R. Proclamation be recast to suit the Rhodesian situation. It would then read: 'All natives engaged in religious teaching or preaching should hold certificates of authorization, if they belong to recognized religious denominations from the missionary in charge of the mission to which they belong, or if they do not belong to any recognized religious denomination, from the Chief Native Commissioner. No such certificate will remain valid for a period of more than one year from the date on which the same was granted . . . The aforegoing might necessitate a definition of the term "missionary in charge". If so, it may be defined as a European missionary in charge of missionary work in a district or districts who is duly accredited by this Government.'[25] This suggestion actually implied that all powers of authorization of purely indigenous Church groups or of European controlled Pentecostal Missions, not recognized by the Government, be vested in the Chief Native Commissioner.

Preference for the N.R. Proclamation did not mean that discussions in Southern Rhodesia were restricted mainly to evidence from the Northern territories. Advice was actually sought from the Native Affairs Department of the Union of South Africa. On one occasion, when the CNC informed the Minister of Native Affairs of the confusion caused by the activities of numerous sects, he referred to an article in a South African newspaper to illustrate 'that the natives themselves are opposed to these newer churches and such things . . .' In this particular article on 'Religious Freedom' one Ezekiel Mahabane of Amanzimtote, Natal, launched an all-out attack on Separatist movements:

'It [religious freedom] has today resulted in the establishment of innumerable sects, the majority of which read the Bible without understanding it and this misconception of the Bible has led to its misinterpretation which affects circulation of misinterpreted ideas to the bulk of the natives in the pagan world . . . They are a demoralizing and deleterious element in the entire Bantu population . . . I urge that prominent leaders of all the recognized

24. CNC to Secretary of Premier, 10th April 1924, Archives, File S 138/106.
25. *Ibid.*, File S 138/106.

churches take immediate steps against this contagious disease. I am of the opinion that some of the natives took this privilege of freedom of religion to a destructive instead of a constructive limit. One cannot conceive the possibility of the propagation and dispersal of the Gospel to the natives of the pagan world when there are derogatory elements working against.'[26]

From this and other critical views expressed by members of the African community in South Africa and Rhodesia the Administration must have drawn some comfort and justification for its proposed legislation. The general consensus amongst the Native Commissioners may have been similar to that of the Chief Native Commissioner in that they regarded the non-seceding sector of the African community as sceptical of the 'Separatist movement'. There are, however, indications of a divergence of opinion amongst the NCs concerning the nature of control of these movements. Unfortunately the files do not reveal much in this respect, but the comment of the Native Commissioner at Mazoe, for instance, reflects a trend of thought different from that of the fellow Commissioners who advocated strict control. Having stated that the Watch Tower movement in his district was not anti-European, he said, 'I am of the opinion that the *suppression of the inevitable movement of the natives towards Separatist Churches is undesirable because it is doomed to failure*. It is however desirable to *keep a very watchful eye* on possible political propaganda, it being obvious that the soil of the Separatist Organization must prove a fruitful one for the production of anti-European ideas (my italics).'[27] He obviously preferred a tolerant approach, with intervention only in cases of subversive political propaganda.

A bill 'regulating the teaching and preaching by natives' was drafted in 1923.[28] As the nature of the proposed measure was 'discriminatory' and therefore, in terms of the Constitution, required the approval of the Imperial Government, the Chief Native Commissioner thought it wise to have the draft submitted to the Missionary Conference first. 'The Conference', he wrote, 'may safely be relied upon to advise the Government as to rights of which it is in a sense the acknowledged guardian.'[29] But if the CNC had bargained on the support of the missionary bodies owing to their opposition to the activities of what they regarded as sectarian movements, his confidence must have been shaken. A left-wing missionary faction, acting under the inspiration of men like Cripps and White, managed to sway the Conference against the proposed

26. E. Mahabane, *Religious Freedom*, in Abanthu Batho, 13th Dec. 1923; CNC to Secretary of Native Affairs, 1923, Archives, File S 138/148.

27. NC, Mazoe, in reply to questionnaire, Archives, File S 138/148.

28. *Supra*, p. 237.

29. CNC to Secretary of Premier, 10th April, 1924, File S 138/106.

legislation on the grounds that it was an infringement of religious liberty. John White afterwards recollected that Cripps 'stood up in the Missionary Conference pleading with the passion and pathos of one of the old Hebrew prophets that there should be no restriction imposed upon any African whom God had called to preach the Gospel.' According to the recorded proceedings of the Conference, 'he [Cripps] asked, if a man was convinced of truth, should he not say "Lord! send me", but "Lord! I have no certificate from the Native Department." How would Christ have suffered at the hands of a State organization such as this Ordinance proposes to set up?'[30] The nature of White's opposition to the introduction of stricter measures of control by the Administration comes out clearly in a letter to Frank Mussell. 'I note', he wrote, 'that four American fundamentalists have not been allowed to enter Rhodesia because the Government considered that their teaching was distracting to Africans. On this question I have repeatedly fought the Government and have contended that it is not their function to say who shall or shall not preach the Gospel. To talk about "disturbing the natives" is bunkum. That does not concern ministers when it pleases them to pass an Ordinance. If it is as I saw it reported, then this new encroachment on our religious freedom ought to be strenuously resisted. With the credentials he had our Lord would never have got past Plumtree.'[31]

The apparent ease with which men like John White questioned the sincerity of the ministers' concern for the interests of Africans raises the question whether these 'left-wing' missionaries fully appreciated the complexity of the problems confronting the Administration. It should be borne in mind that White's and Cripps's opposition to the Administration derived from their wish to avoid too close an association with the Government in the eyes of the Africans. This attitude led to exaggerated statements which did not always do justice to Government officials who tried to act in the interest of the African people. On the other hand it should also be considered that the proposed legislation was, to a great extent, based on the anticipation of the future effects of the Separatist movement on the African population. A great number of missionaries, especially from the Shona territories, had not yet encountered such movements in their districts, with the result that the proposed system of control may have seemed unduly severe or premature to them. 'Practical necessity' did not, therefore, play a prominent role in the considerations of quite a number of missionaries. Cripps and White could

30. T. O. Ranger, *State and Church* (unpublished article), p. 10; with reference to the Proceedings of the Southern Rhodesia Missionary Conference, 1924.
31. *Ibid.*, p. 11.

fight the Administration's proposals on the grounds that it militated against the *sacrosanct* principle of religious freedom. Viewed primarily from this angle, the proposals stood little chance of acceptance. It nevertheless remains doubtful if the Conference would have summarily rejected the draft bill if it had been forwarded to them a few years later, *after* the missionaries had actually felt the pressure of the mushrooming Independent movements in their districts. It is possible that they would then have welcomed a system of control, at least in a modified form.

Without the support of the Missionary Conference it would have been futile to forward the proposed legislation to the British Government, which, as had become evident in the past, took a lenient view of religious activities in the British colonies. Having dropped the bill, the Native Department, as Ranger says, 'had to continue to deal with Separatist preachers by the same "informal" measures of coercion combined with prosecution under various statutes and proclamations not connected with religious teaching at all, which had served it in the past.'[32]

ii) *The control of Anglo-American Pentecostalism*

In the 1920's the Administration was particularly concerned about the spread of such Anglo-American originating Pentecostalist bodies as the Apostolic Faith Church, Full Gospel, Assemblies of God and the Christian Catholic Apostolic Church in Zion, which they regarded as the carriers of Separatism. It did not have a high esteem for the working methods of the representatives of these bodies. In 1927, for instance, the NC at Marandellas urged that no facilities be granted to a certain Mr. Bowden 'to open a Mission in any of the Native reserves. He is, if I am not mistaken, of a denomination calling itself the Assemblies of God, readily baptizing all and sundry without any preliminary instruction.'[33] Soon afterwards the Director of Education raised the same note of criticism with reference to the Full Gospel Church. 'Certainly it would, in my opinion, be a mistake', he wrote to the Assistant CNC, 'to afford recognition to a mission body which has a practice of "readily baptizing all and sundry without any preliminary instruction" which I note is the opinion of the NC of Marandellas. In the circumstances I would be glad if you would be so good as to suggest a means of enquiry.'[34] At an earlier date, when the activities of the Full Gospel Church had been brought to the notice of the

32. *Ibid.*, p. 16.

33. NC, Marandellas, to Director of Education, 27th Jan. 1927, Archives, File S 138/176.

34. Director of Education to Assistant CNC, 2nd Feb. 1927, Archives, File S 138/176.

Minister of Native Affairs, he had remarked: 'I cannot say I am particularly impressed by the name of this sect or whatever it is. I presume that the word "full" is not intended to indicate the amount of attendance so much as the quality of the creed dispensed and it seems to contain by implication the somewhat unpleasant suggestion as to the quality of the article provided by rival denominations.'[35]

These and other comments made by the authorities reveal the lack of an objective criterion by which these movements could be weighed and evaluated. With the withdrawal of the African Preacher's bill in 1924 the legal position – of which the Attorney General had already said in 1923, 'under our general law no provision exists for a formal recognition of missionary societies, as such' – was simply perpetuated. Unlike in South Africa and Northern Rhodesia, where the conditions for recognition had a clearly specified legal basis, the authorities in Rhodesia had no such legalized guide-line, with the result that the recognition of religious bodies was subjected to an arbitrary system, dependent on the subjective judgment of members of the Native Department. Consequently the opinion of local Commissioners about missionaries of the Anglo-American Pentecostal groups in their districts played a role in determining the Administration's attitude. Thus, the favourable impression made by the Rev. Hooper of the Full Gospel Church seems to have contributed towards a gradually more lenient approach by the authorities towards this particular denomination. The Director of Education mentions in 1927 that he had 'learnt from him [Rev. Hooper] that the Full Gospel Mission is a Protestant body of normal character . . . which has no particular views or practices which differ from any other Protestant mission body.' The CNC agreed, 'I have met Mr. Hooper. He is certainly feasible and of good address . . .'[36] On the other hand, there were men like 'Brother' Luttig, whose unstable career caused the authorities to view his activities with some apprehension and disapproval. During his stay at Gatooma, Luttig was first connected with the AFC, then successively with the Pentecostal Mission, the Assemblies of God and the Full Gospel Church. The unpredictability of this missionary – to whom an Anglican church leader referred as a 'well-meaning but foolish old man' – irked the authorities and contributed towards their reluctance to give scope to such Pentecostal groups as he represented. In Shiota, for instance, Luttig and Dingiswayo, the Nyasa preacher, started off by making converts for the Apostolic Faith Church. Dingiswayo then took a

35. Secretary of Premier to CNC, Salisbury, 20th Aug. 1925, Archives, File S 138/176.

36. Director of Education to CNC, 2nd February 1927; CNC to Director of Education, 28th Jan. 1927, Archives, File S 138/176.

large number of followers with him into the fold of the CCAC in Zion, and after his deportation from the Colony Luttig tried to win these former members of his Church over, not to the AFC however, but to the Full Gospel Church. Native Commissioners therefore had sound grounds to complain about the confusion of the 'native mind' by sectarian movements, and it is not surprising that the NC at Marandellas considered Luttig's presence in the Shiota reserve as undesirable.

Although the conditions of recognition were arbitrary, the practical effect on the work of those Missions who were refused recognition was considerable. The Government could severely curtail their activities by refusing them facilities normally granted to the established Mission bodies, such as the entry of European missionaries into the tribal areas (reserves), the granting of land-leases for Mission sites or the permission to build schools. In this way the 'unrecognized' Mission bodies were kept in a state of perpetual uncertainty as to the advisability of expanding their work in the Colony. Even though a number of these bodies were not induced by such measures to turn their energies elsewhere, their efforts were frustrated and retarded. 'We have been at a loss', Rev. Hooper of the then still 'unrecognized' FGC wrote to the CNC, 'to know just how far we could proceed with our work in Southern Rhodesia ... I can assure you that we are sincere in our desire to properly supervise our native work but we feel that this continued uncertainty makes it most difficult to do so.'[37]

Because official recognition was of such cardinal importance to the Pentecostal Churches, petitions were continually sent to the CNC. Some of these contained promises of loyalty, verging on the absurd, to the Government, or pathetic pleas to be granted educational and other rights. As 'overseer' of the Pentecostal Mission, Luttig, for instance, pleaded for recognition in the following words: '... to assist us grant us our petition. We have promises and we want to abide by our promises to play the game and to co-operate in conjunction with other societies at present operating in this territory. Your consent is needed and we shall be recognized as member of the SRM [Southern Rhodesia Mission] societies. If I did not have the native's interests at heart (I must say I love the native) I would not have troubled you in the least. I believe you know the native lies deep in my soul. I willingly would leave civilization behind and go and live with these despised people and help them and lift them up for God. Sir Herbert, give us our opportunity, I endeavour you. We will show our sincerity. We will also pay our rent for the site. The people in Chiota reserve beg for a school. Grant it them please. I have tried

37. Rev. Hooper to CNC, Salisbury, 22nd Nov. 1928, Archives, File S 84/A/275.

so long and have always received a negative reply . . . Sir Herbert, with you lies the issue – God grant you grace in this our application . . .'[38] This application for recognition, like the preceding ones, was of no avail.

Mr. Buren von Schumaker, head of the CCAC in Zion in South Africa, again, was at pains to defend the 'good name' of his organization after the Nyasa preacher, Dingiswayo, who had operated on behalf of this Church, was deported from Rhodesia. He wrote to the CNC at Salisbury explaining Dingiswayo's position. This preacher, according to Von Schumaker, had faked his ministerial credentials, for when he left the Missionary Conference held in South Africa 'he was not an ordained minister but the local conductor of an unordained class.' Therefore 'anyone he [Dingiswayo] had ordained to the ministry was void of official authority.' Having reorganized the CCAC in Zion in South Africa, Von Schumaker told the CNC in Rhodesia that his Church was not a 'careless and fanatical organization' and that they wanted to 'obtain a place of usefulness in the service of the people'. 'Zion's work', he stated, 'is in no way associated with the fanatical movements such as the trans-evangelistic movements which work the natives into a frenzy, by so-called visions, tongues, trances and false claims to prophecy. . . . WE WAIT THE TIME WHEN WE SHALL BE GRANTED THE OPPORTUNITY TO PROVE TO YOUR GOVERNMENT THE AIM AND OBJECT OF OUR ZEAL FOR THE NATIVES OF SOUTH AFRICA . . . . WE DESIRE ONLY TO DEFEND THE GOOD NAME OF OUR ORGANIZATION AND AID THE OFFICIALS OF ANGLO-SAXON GOVERNMENTS TO CONTROL WITH AUTHORITY THE NATIVE AND BID HIM ATTAIN TO A PLACE OF USEFULNESS AS A SERVANT PEOPLE.' (Von Schumaker's capitals.)[39]

On more than one occasion the Rhodesian authorities sought the advice of the Native Affairs Department of the South African Government. In 1923 the Secretary of Native Affairs, for example, informed the Rhodesian CNC that the *Apostolic Faith Church* is a 'stable body under European control in the Union of South Africa where it is accorded the usual privileges enjoyed by other Christian bodies. Its doctrines and general teachings are in accordance with Christian principles.' Information concerning the *Zion Apostolic City* was also supplied.[40]

The Rhodesian authorities soon decided that they could not follow the South African example of what they regarded as an indiscriminate approval of practically all religious societies. In 1927 the CNC wrote to the Director of

38. Luttig to CNC, 1924, Archives, File S 138/176.

39. Buren von Schumaker to CNC, 16th Febr. 1929, Archives, File S 138/140.

40. Secretary of Native Affairs (South Africa) to CNC, Salisbury, 24th Dec. 1923, Archives, File S 138/148.

Education that 'the practice of seeking advice from the Union Native Affairs Department in matters affecting Religious Sects has been discontinued of late for the reason that all sects are apparently approved without discrimination and it is not desirable to reproduce in this Colony a universal tolerance of Native matters – religious and educational – that exists in the Union.'[41] This interpretation of what was happening in South Africa is somewhat misleading, for although the basic interpretation of 'religious freedom' of the South African Government at the time was more liberal than that of the Rhodesian Government, it should be kept in mind that this latitude did not involve indiscriminate official recognition of sectarian movements, as the Rhodesian CNC thought. In spite of the legal machinery it had created in 1925, the South African Government had, in fact, by 1948 only recognized eight of the eight-hundred 'Separatist' Churches (i.e. 1%)[42] – whereas the arbitrary basis of recognition in Rhodesia actually enabled the Native Department to afford 'recognition' to a greater percentage of 'sectarian' movements than was the case in South Africa. On the one hand this left sufficient scope for strict repressive measures when the Commissioners considered these necessary, but it also enabled them (especially after 1935 when a gradual change of attitude towards the 'Separatists' began to take place) to apply more flexible and liberal criteria than were current in South Africa.

The control of the 'unrecognized' Pentecostal Churches presented the Administration with a complex problem. Between 1923 and 1930 there seems to have existed a divergence of opinion between the CNC and the CID (Criminal Investigation Department) regarding the exact line of action to be taken. After the deportation of Dingiswayo, resolute action, if not a thorough purge of the principal leaders, was recommended by the Superintendent of the CID. The CNC was hesitant to adopt such drastic measures. In a letter to the Prime Minister he stated, 'I am in agreement with the opinion of the Commissioner of Police that the deportation of the leaders of these sects [CCAC in Zion and Full Gospel] is not to be recommended. I am of the opinion that if the recommendations suggested by the Superintendent of the CID were adopted, it would convey the impression to the members of these sects that the Government was really concerned and feared these activities.' He thought that a stern warning addressed to these sectarian leaders might have a deterring effect on their activities. Having rejected the idea of outright deportation, he nevertheless proposed that officials be instructed to 'warn these leaders and their followers that, should they act in any matter prejudicial to good government, they would be de-

41. CNC to Director of Education, 28th Feb. 1927, Archives, File S 138/176.
42. Sundkler, 1961, p. 77.

ported from the Colony.'[43] In practice it was far from clear to some Government officials what the exact nature of repressing or controlling action should be. There was no prohibition of purely evangelistic activities, and permission to African preachers to enter the tribal areas could hardly be withheld. But, as soon as permission to preach was granted to preachers of 'unrecognized' Churches, there was a danger of their interpreting such concessions as an official encouragement to expansion, or as a promise of future official recognition. Confronted with this kind of problem the CNC had to advise the officials as best he could. In 1926 the Assistant Superintendent of the CID, for example, sent him the credentials of two evangelists, Unkulungi and Muzhuru of the Full Gospel Church. 'As this church is not recognized by the Government, will you please inform me', read the request, 'whether these or any other natives have permission to reside and preach in the reserves, and if not, should the attached credentials be confiscated. I understand that these two natives have built a church in the Seki reserve . . .'[44] Acting on this enquiry the CNC informed the NC at Goromonzi: 'They are reported to have built a Church in the Seki reserve and are preaching there. I have instructed them to report to you with this letter and to obtain your permission if they want to preach in your district. I would point out that *this denomination is not recognized by the Government* and that no encouragement should be given to the members thereof. I would, however, further point out that *there is no law to prevent an indigenous native from carrying on purely evangelistic work in the reserves* (my italics)'.[45] Unfortunately no further details about this case were included in the official files, but it seems that the credentials of these two leaders were not confiscated. Having cautioned the NC not to encourage this 'unrecognized' Church, the CNC actually left the issue to the former's discretion. The NC had to determine himself whether the leaders of this sect were 'carrying on purely evangelistic work' or not.

Another example of the lack of clarity is found in the correspondence between the CNC and the Director of Education concerning the application of the Full Gospel leaders for official recognition. 'The question arises', wrote the Director of Education, 'of how the claim of the Full Gospel Church to be a desirable addition to the societies already engaged in missionary work in Rhodesia, can be investigated . . . In the circumstances I would be glad if you would be so good as to suggest a means of enquiry . . .' In his reply the CNC mentioned that he had seen Rev. Hooper and 'For my part and before

43. CNC to Premier, 3rd Sept. 1924, Archives, File S 138/140.
44. Assistant Superintendent, CID to CNC, 25th March 1926, Archives, File S 138/176.
45. CNC Bowker, to NC at Goromonzi, 1926, Archives, File S 138/176.

advising that the Government should accord recognition to this new sect, which may be a veritable mushroom for all I know, and before allowing its [European] ministers access to the Native Reserves, I feel that there should be *more solid assurance as to its religious tenance* and its Educational work as has yet been forthcoming . . . (my italics).'[46] He furthermore pointed out that the Missionary Conference had refused to 'include this new sect'. The fact remains, however, that he had circumvented the Director of Education's request concerning a 'means of enquiry' and that there was neither a clear indication of what precisely he meant with 'more solid assurance' nor an indication of how he intended to obtain it.

This kind of manoeuvring leaves one with the impression of indecision and vagueness about measures that might be adopted – apart from withholding the coveted document of recognition – to discourage the sectarian leaders.

Whereas the control of indigenous *African* Church leaders of 'unrecognized' bodies proved to be a source of misunderstanding, the policy concerning the *European* ministers of these sects was more precise. Those of Anglo-American descent who requested entry into the Colony were either refused entry, as was the case with Von Schumaker, or otherwise they were allowed to visit the colony only temporarily in order to supervise the members of their Church. But even then the Government emphasized that such concessions did not constitute official recognition of the Church concerned. Thus, in 1927, the CNC informed Rev. F. Burke of the Njelele Mission at Louis Trichardt (Transvaal) that permission was granted to Rev. Daniel to visit the Gwanda reserve temporarily for purely evangelistic activities. 'You will understand', he concluded, 'that such permission is given only at the pleasure of the Government and does not constitute official recognition by the Government of your Mission.'[47]

Such then were the precautionary measures taken by the Government in the 1920's. There were objections to the negative influence of the pentecostal emotionalism and the confusion caused by the influx of unstable sectarian groups. But the deepest motivation for repressive action remained the desire to prevent – as the Acting Administrator had already stated in 1919 – 'any sort of accession of strength to these [American] professors and teachers of unusual creeds . . . [who] hold and teach views in regard to native questions which are not altogether acceptable out here.'[48]

46. Director of Education to CNC, 25th Feb. 1927, Archives, File S 138/176.

47. CNC to Rev. Burke, Njelele Mission, 25th Jan. 1927, Archives, File S 138/176.

48. Correspondence concerning the Seventh Day Adventists 1919-1921, Archives, File A 3/6/8, in Ranger, *State and Church*, p. 5.

iii) *The control of all-African Zionism*

Soon after the Superintendent of Natives for the Victoria Province had reported in 1923 that 'no Separatist Churches' were operating in the Southern Shona districts, the situation changed. Mtisi and Masuka at first did not attract much attention, but soon after Mutendi's arrival in 1923 the Zionist movement grew rapidly, to the alarm of the local authorities. As a result of his former experience as a policeman Mutendi had a fair idea of how far he could go without provoking the local authorities to take strong repressive action. He steered clear of seditious preaching. His message obviously contained scriptural applications to the specifically African situation that could be interpreted by the authorities as having political implications, but he was careful to avoid an overt attack on the European Government.

Mutendi's increasing popularity in the Bikita and surrounding districts, however, soon confronted the NCs with the problem of control. In reply to their enquiries the Assistant CNC in 1925 informed the Superintendent of Natives at Fort Victoria that 'the Government has refused recognition of this [ZAFM] society. There is no law', he continued, 'prohibiting purely religious teaching. It will be in your knowledge that a bill to regulate such preaching and teaching was printed but not proceeded with last year. Secular teaching on the other hand is controlled by Ordinance 7 of 1912, but if Mutendi's ministrations are purely evangelistic that cannot be prevented. It may be that interference with children against the wish of their parents and baptizing them under the conditions described amount to a sort of assault. I regret that I can offer no helpful suggestion.'[49] Since Mutendi had committed no serious offence the authorities at Bikita decided to follow up the hint of the Asst. CNC by detaining Mutendi on the grounds that he had interfered with children against the will of their parents. Mutendi himself narrates in the *Rungano* (the Church's canonized history) how the chief and elders reported him to the Native Commissioner for 'spoiling the country'. They alleged that he 'plunged their children into the rivers' and that he and his followers destroyed their cattle at night through 'spirit-possessed lions' (*zvitebwe*). Mutendi was now repeatedly detained and forbidden to preach in the name of the Zion Apostolic Faith Mission, to which he was affiliated at first. The *Rungano* has it that he 'stayed at the mouth of jail' in those days, but it added that these measures did not deter him from preaching. It is actually suggested that the local NC developed some respect for this 'man of God', especially after he had successfully prayed for the removal of a swarm of locusts. While Mutendi

49. Assistant CNC to Superintendent of Natives, Fort Victoria, 21st April, 1925, Archives, File S 138/148.

was under arrest the NC is said to have summoned him to give him a chance of 'proving' that he was worshipping the true God. He had to pray for the removal of a great swarm of locusts which was then ravishing the crops. When Mutendi had performed the miracle the surprised NC is said to have stated: 'You are now free. Go and worship your God at your own village, but do not travel and preach from one village to another.'[50]

Towards 1926 the Native Commissioners of the Southern Shona districts expressed grave concern at the spread of Zionism under indigenous leadership in their districts. The minutes of the Conference of Native Commissioners held at Fort Victoria in June 1926 illustrate their concern. Point 6 of the agenda dealt exclusively with the 'control of native preachers who are not under European supervision'. The discussions mainly concerned the activities of Mutendi and his subordinate leaders in the Bikita district. According to the minutes the NC of Bikita introduced the whole problem by reading the official correspondence with regard to the ZAFM. 'He stressed the fact that the natives in his district themselves had raised objections to the activities of these teachers and their methods. They had approached him on the matter and had asked him to stop these men preaching as they had such a bad effect on the young people. He drew attention to the fact that the teachers were not working under European control. He pointed out that very far-reaching consequences might be expected and that teaching of any type can be introduced under the guise of religious teaching.' The Native Commissioner said further that the problem of control was a complex one because the leaders were indigenous inhabitants of the Colony who could not be debarred from entering the tribal areas. He suggested that African preachers should be prevented from continuing their activities unless they were associated directly with a European leader residing in the country. 'Without such power [of control]', he continued, 'he found himself in a very invidious position . . . He found himself unable to take any action which was in any way adequate to the situation. He was powerless in the matter. He felt that such a situation undermined his authority over and above other evils which were accruing . . .' In the discussions that followed it was generally agreed that greater control was needed. The 'Bullhoek incident' in South Africa was mentioned to emphasize the necessity of control, but not a single concrete proposal for adequate control was made. It was eventually decided to refer the whole issue to the Secretary of Native Affairs and to invite his attention to 'the present *dangerous state of affairs* due to lack of control (my italics).'[51]

50. Appendix IV, *Rungano,* Chapter 21:1-6.
51. Minutes of the Conference of Native Commissioners, Fort Victoria, No. 10-11,

We have noted that the Bikita NC's assertion that complaints were raised by members of the indigenous population was not unfounded. Neither was the NC's reference to the undermining of his authority exaggerated. His frustration, resulting from insufficient control of the situation, is even portrayed in Mutendi's handbook, which states that the Commissioner scolded the chiefs (as 'bloody fools'), and sent them away for having changed their minds about Mutendi after they had first come to him to request this man's deportation from the country.[52] This incident reveals to what extent the NC had become dependent on the complaints of the indigenous population in the effort to curb the Zionist leaders' activities effectively.

Mutendi repeatedly tried to obtain official recognition for his Church. His first trip to Salisbury to see the CNC took place after he had received and distributed preaching certificates from Johannesburg. He probably entertained the hope of persuading the authorities to recognize the ZCC which he had helped to found in 1925, and which was 'registered' in the Government Buildings in Pretoria. According to the *Rungano* he was not given a decisive reply in Salisbury but was sent back with the promise that his 'papers' would be forwarded to the local NC at Bikita. Back in Bikita he found that the former NC had been transferred to Fort Victoria. The new NC who 'was not yet familiar with the issues of the new district', allowed Mutendi to carry on with religious work at his village.[53]

After his visit to Lekhanyane in 1925-6 Mutendi was again faced with charges from the indigenous population. This time it was the parents of the young women who had accompanied him on his journey who complained at the NC's office that their children had been 'stolen' by this 'impostor'. They are reported to have told the authorities on Mutendi's arrival, 'There he is, he has returned; put him in jail because we do not want to see him any longer!' The night before his arrest Mutendi had a warning dream, but 'the voice' assured him that he would not be imprisoned. At the district headquarters the charges against Mutendi indeed proved to be insufficiently serious for a conviction and he was soon released.[54]

The Zionist leaders were keenly aware of the limitations of the Government authorities to control religious matters. The inconsistence of successive local Native Commissioners in their efforts to deal with the expanding new

June, 1926. Present on this occasion were the Native Commissioners of Fort Victoria, Bikita, Chibi, Gutu and Chilimanzi.

52. Appendix IV, *Rungano,* Chapter 22:1-2.
53. Appendix IV, *Rungano,* Chapter 23:1-5.
54. Appendix IV, *Rungano,* Chapter 26:6-7.

movement, spoke for itself. It was obvious that the European Administration desired to check its influence, but is was equally obvious that the local representatives of Government at district level had no legal means of eliminating the key figures – apart from brief detentions – as long as these men confined their efforts to purely evangelistic activities. The *Rungano* even states that the Government was puzzled by the expansion of Mutendi's Church. 'The Government did not know how the Church could develop in such a way that its members were, for instance, to be found in Gutu.'[55] Thus the historical facts are here presented in a way which suggests that this 'man of God' was actually outwitting the Government authorities, a factor of great psychological value to the ZCC members. In Gutu, as in the surrounding areas, the expansion of the ZCC had become an established fact towards the close of this period. A pole-and-mud Church was built for Sunday services, but whenever trouble arose secret services were conducted in the mountains.

c) *Continuation of the strife and the breakthrough after 1930*

The European-directed Pentecostal Churches persisted in their efforts to achieve official recognition in Rhodesia after 1930, but the Government was equally persistent in refusing to grant them the required privileges. Instead of becoming more permissive the Native Department, in collaboration with the CID, stepped up restrictive measures, especially in the case of the CCAC in Zion. When a certain Titus Nyafunga from Pietersburg in the Transvaal sent an application to the Native Department for the establishment of a branch of the CCAC in Zion in Rhodesia with headquarters in Salisbury, the CID was requested to investigate the activities of this Church's leaders. They found that a Church building had been erected on a location plot at Salisbury, belonging to one S. Kufmann.[56] The CNC then informed the Minister of Native Affairs . . . 'that two non-indigenous natives desired to open a church at Kufmann's plot in the location. There is no European representative of their Church in the Colony. Therefore, in accordance with the previous ruling of the Honourable the Minister of Native Affairs, recognition cannot be granted to this denomination. Unfortunately this does not mean that they can be prevented from opening a church and preaching as we have no control over that aspect of the matter. All that can be done is to ask the CID to

55. Appendix IV, *Rungano,* Chapter 27:4.

56. Report of Sergeant of CID to CNC, Archives, File S 138/140, titled: 'Zionist Activities: Means to suppress the spread of the cult.'

assist us in keeping a watch over the movement with a view to interference if anything seditious transpires . . .'[57]

Here then we find the guiding principle according to which control over the activities of the Pentecostal and 'Separatist' Churches was to be exerted. The absence of a European representative of the Church concerned was sufficient ground for the refusal of recognition and hence also for withholding the right to participate in the educational field. Religious leaders of unrecognized Churches were to be watched and could be prosecuted if they preached sedition or 'taught anything else than religion' i.e. interfered in the field of secular education. Suspect leaders could be kept under close surveillance by the CID.

When it became evident that the Zionists were much less occupied with subversive political propaganda than was anticipated, and that insufficient evidence of subversion existed, the authorities increasingly directed their attention to the so-called interference of the sectarian Church leaders in the field of education. In Matabeleland there was the case of Mabhena who, on behalf of (Mabilitsa's) *Christian Apostolic Church in Zion*,[58] applied for a school in the Insiza district. In this case the CNC informed the Acting Superintendent of Natives at Bulawayo that 'Mabhena should be informed that, as his denomination is not under European supervision, his application to open kraal schools cannot be granted.'[59] When Mabhena declined to close his 'schools' the CNC advised that he should be prosecuted under act 7 of 1912 for unlawfully opening schools. The Director of Native Development informed the CNC that he 'had no clearly worded report from the Circuit Inspector attached to this department as to the effect that he inspected the school personally and has found that this is doing academic work of a nature which is not '*teaching in religion only*'. If you prefer it, I propose to ask the inspector that he make this the subject of an ad hoc visit in order to determine whether prosecution could be proceeded with.'[60] To this proposal the CNC agreed. He thought that 'the case could be greatly strengthened if your Circuit Inspector could definitely state that teaching other than religion definitely takes place.'[61]

The problem with some of these so-called 'schools' was that they were religious centres in the first place, engaged in instruction of a semi-academic

57. CNC to Secretary of Premier of Native Affairs, 30th March 1932, Archives, File S 138/140.

58. *Supra*, p. 391.

59. CNC to Acting Superintendent of Natives, Bulawayo, Archives, File S 138/140.

60. Director of Native Development, 1932, Archives, File S 138/140.

61. Director of Native Development, 1932, Archives, File S 138/140.

nature. Ironically, both the authorities and the African Church leaders involved preferred to regard such centres as 'schools' – but for widely diverging reasons. The former, because it provided them with a sound reason for prosecution and therefore of control, and the latter, because they were anxious to have African controlled educational centres, after the example of the larger Missions.

In the Southern and Eastern Shona districts, where the Ndaza and Mutendi Zionists were operating, the conflict with the local authorities in the early 1930's also centred around the educational issue. Here it was not only a matter of Zionist leaders opening so-called 'schools' but of some of them deliberately encouraging children to leave the Mission schools. In order to reconstruct the nature of the conflict between the Zionists and the local authorities we shall first of all concern ourselves with the Ndaza Zionists and then with Mutendi's Zion Christian Church.

i) *The Ndaza Zionists*

The *Zion Apostolic City* (or Zion City) movement, initially introduced by Mtisi in the south-eastern districts, was carefully watched when leaders began to interfere with the established village schools. In Chipinga district, which had become the stronghold of Mtisi's followers, special detectives were sent out into the tribal areas to watch Zionist activities. Zvekare Sengwayo, later to become the President of the *Chibarirwe* Church, was one of these detectives. In 1933, the NC of Chipinga reported that Zvekare 'has now visited most of the kraals in which Zionist emissaries are said to have taught their peculiar dogmas of late.' On this particular occasion Sengwayo, to whom the NC referred as a 'very useful detective', did not find much that was new, but information was passed to the NC all the same that two or three Zionists were 'attempting to lure the children from the established kraal schools in the Mutambara native reserve to the North.' The NC concluded that he intended going out to the village schools concerned in order personally to speak to the parents of the children.[62]

The interference of these Zionists with school attendance caused the CNC to make enquiries from the Native Department at Pretoria. Afterwards he told the NC at Chipinga that the South African Native Affairs Department had informed him that 'little is known of the *Zion Apostolic City* beyond the fact that it is one of the most recently established of the numerous native mushroom sects which has sprung into existence as a result of schismatic tendencies. The Church', he went on to say, 'is not recognized for Government

62. NC, Chipinga, to CNC, Salisbury, 10th Feb. 1933, Archives, File S 138/140.

privileges in the Union. The NC at Potgietersrust has been asked to get in touch with Johnson [leader of the ZAC at Potgietersrust who was consecrating African labour migrants returning to Rhodesia] with a view to discontinuing the issue of credentials.'[63]

A certain amount of confusion as to the different divisions of the Ndaza Zionists characterizes the official correspondence. David Masuka's *Zion Apostolic Church of South Africa* was represented in the same eastern districts as Mtisi's movement and the authorities were inclined to classify the robed Zionists in these areas with the numerically strongest *Zion Apostolic City Church*. When, for instance, the NC of Rusape sent the CNC a ministerial credential of a certain Willie Charewa, who belonged to David's ZAC of SA, bearing David's signature,[64] the CNC replied: 'The credentials you received from Charewa are obviously an ignorant imitation and it is probable that the name of the Church was misquoted. It may be the Zion Apostolic City of the new location – Potgietersrust, Transvaal. One J. C. Johnson is sending out emissaries from there or giving credentials to Southern Rhodesia natives returning from work.'[65] In this case the CNC, who was probably not aware of Masuka's leadership of the local branch of Mhlangu's ZAC of SA, was mistaken in his assumption. Charewa had not misquoted the Church's name, but had received his credentials from Masuka, who at that stage had started acting independently of his South African superior, Mhlangu, and for that very reason was distributing handwritten imitations of the original ZAC of SA certificates.

Whatever their views about the classification of Ndaza Zionists, the authorities were gravely concerned about the rise of this movement. The above-mentioned Willie Charewa was described by the local NC as 'a far from suitable person to be preacher [who] has been convicted of stock theft and theft of native tax besides other minor offences.' The NC admitted that no complaints had been received from any of the village headmen living in the same locality, but stated that he had nevertheless forbidden Charewa to continue building his Church.[66] More serious still was the accusation made by the American Board missionaries at Mt. Selinda (Chipinga district) that the Zionists were responsible for the deterioration of school attendance at, and the ultimate closing of the Musane school in the Mutema tribal area. It is not clear from the files which of the Ndaza Zionist groups were involved. The report

63. CNC to NC, Chipinga, 1933, Archives, File S 138/140.
64. See the so-called 'imitated' credentials of Willie Charewa, Appendix VI.
65. CNC to NC, Rusape, 30th May 1933, Archives, File S 138/140.
66. NC, Rusape, to CNC, 25th May 1933.

on Zionist activities in the Mutema area, submitted by the Rev. H. J. Orner of Mt. Selinda to the Director of Native Development, reveals the following:

'At Mutema, the first of the activities of these people was towards the end of last year [1931] when two young men originally from that section of the country returned *from Johannesburg*, and began to work in the reserves as evangelists. They frequently attended the services at our schools and once or twice caused some disturbance during a service at the Mutema school. The NC had a talk with them shortly after that time and they immediately quietened down. About two months ago another native with the name of Jeremiah came from Johannesburg and declared himself a Zionist priest. The activity flared up again. Jeremiah began holding meetings almost nightly 3 to 400 yards from our Musane school and these were also held nearly every night at the kraal only a few hundred yards from our Mutema school. On Sunday Zionist meetings were held both at Tanganda and Musane rivers and frequently "converts" were baptized in these rivers. *The chief message with these people is that education is not a good thing and nobody ought to go to school* though lately they have been promising the people to open their own schools after ours have been done away with and to teach only the ChiNdau language. They also preach that *those who have joined the Church of the white missionaries have the mark of the beast on their foreheads*, as mentioned in Revelations, as the white man is the beast since he came out of the sea . . . We white missionaries and our followers are not christians, because we do use medicine when we are ill and also because we teach that Church members ought to support the Church by their gifts. This it seems is wrong because salvation is free. At the time of the recent visit of the High Commissioner and the Governor the meeting was held at Mutema. The natives belonging to this movement did not attend as the Governor and the High Commissioner themselves are the beast as said in Revelation. *As a result of this movement we had to close the Musane school* and as you already know the attendance at Mutema has dropped to that of about 25. According to the latest reports we hear that some of the heathen natives and the chiefs are becoming tired of these people because of their treatment of the girls and because of other reasons, so we hope it will soon meet with a natural death (my italics).'[67]

This report once more highlighted the fact that Zionism was brought into the country by labour migrants returning from the Transvaal. Rev. Orner was convinced that the Zionists were fully responsible for the deterioration of the

67. Report of Rev. Orner (6th Oct. 1932) to Director of Native Development.

situation at some of the Mission schools and he accused them of strong anti-European sentiments – an aspect which at this early stage could hardly have been a predominant feature of the Zionist movement. In all probability the American missionaries, because of their own subjective involvement in the religious field, and possibly because of personal prejudices, were inclined to over-emphasize the negative aspects of this movement and to blame the 'sectarian upstarts' for failures that in fact resulted from a multiplicity of factors (not least from the effects of the economic slump in the 1930's) and were not caused only by the Zionist 'attacks' on missionary work.

By way of contrast the local NC demonstrated a much more balanced attitude towards the Zionists. In his reply to the CNC's enquiry, he stated, 'It is so that up to the present time I have not found any evidence of subversive or seditious preaching by the men who have taken on themselves to spread the new sect . . . These men have been interrogated by me in my office and they all have denied all the allegations made against them by the teachers of the American Board Mission and so far it has not been possible to find any independent witness to substantiate those allegations which at most seem to me do not go beyond the fulmigations to be expected always and everywhere from the first converts of a new religion. I do not think that the connection between the activities of these people and waning school attendance complained of is as close as Mr. Orner seems to think . . .' According to the NC's judgment the situation was not serious enough to call for prosecution. 'I propose to continue my present policy', he told the CNC, 'of watching these people as closely as I can without as far as possible letting them know that I am doing so, lest by appearing to be concerned about their preaching we should cause the movement to assume an importance in the eyes of the natives which it might not otherwise acquire.'[68] This NC acted on the assumption that outright suppression would only stimulate the growth of this movement and consequently he favoured a cautious and more tactful approach. The severity of measures taken against the Zionists therefore greatly depended on the personal judgment of local NCs.

In some of the other districts where the Ndaza Zionists were operative a similar cautious approach was adopted. In Buhera, for example, it became evident towards the end of 1932 that the work of a certain Panganai had an effect on the school nearest to his village. Towards the end of that year the Assitant NC reported that 'as a result of Zionist teachings the DRC Mission school established at Nemadziwa's has lost a great number of its adherents, the attendance having dropped from about 40 to 10 pupils . . .'[69] and in March

68. NC, Chipinga, to CNC, Salisbury, 13th Oct. 1932, Archives, File S 138/140.

of the following year it was reported of the same school that the teacher had complained about another twelve or more of his pupils having fallen away.[70] Although it was obvious in this case that Zionist activities had a direct effect on school attendance the local NC could report that there was *no evidence of any subversive propaganda.* As in Chipinga, it was decided not to take strong action but to have a close watch kept on sectarian activities. In the words of the local NC: 'I am watching the situation. The next patrol will bring the alleged Zionist preacher for interrogation.'[71] Judging from the archival material of the early 1930's on the two above-mentioned districts, it would seem that the propagation of subversion was rather an exception than a rule with the Ndaza Zionists. Indirect interference with school attendance mainly served to alert the authorities. In such cases they interrogated and warned Zionist leaders, but generally prosecution took place only if there was sufficient indication that a leader had unlawfully endeavoured to open a 'school' for academic instruction.

By way of comparison the ZAFM under the leadership of Andreas Shoko had a more peaceful entry in the Chibi district (at least as far as its relations with the Administration were concerned) than Mtisi's and Masuka's Churches in the East. Jeremiah, one of Andreas's subordinate leaders who seceded from him in 1948, was mistaken by the authorities for the principal leader of the movement. In 1931 the CNC notified the Superintendent of Natives at Fort Victoria that he preferred 'not to accord official recognition to this movement, but as Jeremiah's actions seem to be harmless there is no need to interfere with him as long as he confines his activities to his own kraal.' He furthermore regarded it unnecessary to provide Jeremiah with a pass 'which he would undoubtedly regard as official recognition'[72] (as was the case with other all-African Zionist Churches). Official recognition was simply withheld on the grounds that the Church did not have a European supervisor in the country. Provided the Church leaders' activities proved harmless, the attitude was one of tolerance. Another condition for tolerance, as illustrated in the case of Mutendi, was that the leader had to confine his activities to his own village.

69. Assistant NC, Buhera, to NC, The Range, Enkeldoorn, 26th Oct. 1932.
70. NC, Buhera, to NC, The Range, Enkeldoorn, 11th March 1933. Archives, File S 138/140.
71. *Ibid.*, File S 138/140.
72. CNC to Superintendent of Natives, 10th Dec. 1931. Archives, File S 138/140.

ii) *The Zion Christian Church*

As the most influential Zionist leader in the Southern Shona districts, Mutendi's evangelistic activities had a far-reaching impact, directly and indirectly, on the work of missionaries in the educational field. It was alleged that he had opened two 'schools' – one in the Gutu and one in the Bikita district – where he was teaching without permission.[73] He was convicted on both charges. The nightly services and the frequent spells of Spirit-possession had an effect on the behaviour of school children in the Bikita, Zaka, Ndanga and Gutu districts. Rev. Roux, the DRC school superintendent at Jichidza Mission in the Zaka district, complained to the authorities about the behaviour of Abisai, one of his teachers, who seemed to be following Mutendi's example in some respects. One of the Zaka district officers investigated the matter and sent Rev. Roux the following report:

'I have occasion to reprimand your native Abisai over the following matter. It appears that on Saturday, 30th May, he held a meeting on his own at Mutingwe school . . . There was a large gathering of children and young people who stayed for two nights – leaving on the Monday morning. During the time that they were there it is reported that there was much singing both day and night and that some of the young boys and girls became hysterical, throwing themselves on the ground in convulsions and making weird noises. I know you are aware of this unbalanced behaviour which is gradually becoming a feature among the young people. It is similar to the hysteria practised in "*kubatwa neshavi*", but now referred to as "*kubatwa noMweya*". The matter was reported to me by a number of elders in the vicinity of Mutingwe school. They seemed to be much concerned about the carrying on at this meeting and the behaviour of the young people. I submit every endeavour should be made to prevent this growing habit of young people throwing themselves into hysterics under the cloak of religion. I particularly ask you to warn all your native teachers in this district to use their influence to stop it. And furthermore that all-night meetings of young people will not be tolerated.'[74]

To the minds of local NCs there was little doubt about the connection between this type of hysterical manifestations of children at village schools and Mutendi's work. Both the Commissioners at Zaka and Bikita for this reason favoured severe repressive measures against Mutendi. 'It appears to me', remarked the NC of Zaka, 'that Abisai – a teacher of the Dutch Reformed

73. The NC of Bikita informed the Superintendent of Natives at Fort Victoria on the 28th of August 1931, that 'Mutendi was convicted of opening a school and teaching at the school without permission. He was charged on two counts, one of his schools being in this district and the other in Gutu.' Archives, File S 138/140.

74. J. L. Oliver to Rev. J. Roux, 5th June 1931, Archives, File S 138/140.

Church – is adopting the same methods as Mutendi at Bikita district and I feel that if *strong action could be taken against Mutendi* it would have a good effect as he appears to be the leader (my italics).'[75] The NC of Bikita pointed out that the connection between teacher Abisai and Mutendi lay in the similarity of their night meetings. He included the following brief summary of what he regarded to be the procedure adopted during such a meeting: 'He [Mutendi] sends one of his elders to a certain place and tells him to let the people know he will be there on a particular night. At or about that time he goes to this place and beats a drum. This is a sign to all the young people in the neighbourhood to proceed to where he is. On their arrival he holds a short service in which he works himself up into a hysterical paroxysm of religious mania, throws himself about and makes noises like a baboon barking. After this he leads all the people up a hill. By this time they are all imitating Mutendi. All this is done by night. I have heard that these gatherings on occasion can last for three nights. It can be seen from the aforegoing that it appears that there is a connection between Mutendi and Abisai.' Having indicated the person whom he regarded as the source of 'religious mania' and having obviously based his description of Mutendi's activities on the biased reports of African informants, the NC continued, 'What I would like would be *some means whereby Mutendi could be stopped.* The elder men strongly disapprove of these meetings. I do not see what legal action can be taken to prevent him holding them (my italics).' But the NC was meanwhile inventing his own crude methods to stop Mutendi. He reports that a certain headman Nebarwe had come to see him about a possible means of stopping Mutendi, who had visited his kraal. 'All I could do', he concluded laconically, 'was to tell Nebarwe if he [Mutendi] came again was to *give him a hiding*.'[76]

In their distant offices the superiors of the Native Commissioners thought differently and were more reluctant about the application of strict measures. The Superintendent of Natives at Fort Victoria reminded the CNC of a similar outbreak of 'hysterical cum-religious mania' in the past, that had died away of its own accord. He suggested that school inspectors be advised to speak to the school teachers of village schools when they are on their rounds of inspection.[77] In the same connection the CNC pointedly stated, 'It is difficult

75. In the same letter to the Superintendent of Natives at Fort Victoria, dated 5/8/'31, the NC of Zaka states that the NC at Gutu had informed him a few days before that Mutendi had entered his district to hold a large meeting amongst the natives there. Archives, File S 138/140.

76. NC, Bikita, to Superintendent of Natives, Fort Victoria, 25th August, 1931, Archives, File S 138/140.

77. Superintendent of Natives, Fort Victoria, to CNC, Salisbury, 8th July, 1931, Archives, File S 138/140.

under any circumstances to take action in these cases. In the present instance the information is much too vague to permit anything being done . . . Mutendi was once convicted for not obeying a lawful order. What specific charge can now be brought against him which would permit strong action being taken?'[78]
Due to the lack of appropriate evidence and legislation there was little else these Government officials could do than warn the indigenous Church leaders in the hope of dissuading them from continuing their campaigning activities. Towards the end of that turbulent year the CNC himself was forced to hand down such a warning when Chief Ndanga brought two local ZCC leaders, operating in his chiefdom, to the CNC's office with the request that they be permitted to continue their religious teaching. 'I refused and warned them that if they disobeyed, steps would be taken at once', he later informed the Superintendent at Fort Victoria.[79] He did not then indicate what measures he intended to take against such 'trespassing' Church leaders.

The disturbances ascribed to Mutendi and his followers in 1931 were brought to the notice of the Minister of Native Affairs. He instructed the CNC to issue a circular to all the NCs to the effect that no Churches were to be built in the tribal areas without the permission of the CNC. These instructions were forwarded to the Superintendent of Natives at Fort Victoria in June 1932 under a covering minute headed 'Rhodesia Mission'. In accordance with these instructions the NCs at Bikita and Zaka stepped up repressive measures against the Zionists, such as demolishing some of the huts that had been erected as Church buildings. Towards the end of that year the NC at Bikita informed the Superintendent of Natives at Fort Victoria that he had eliminated a certain Jack Tichiwanga's Church. He thought this Zionist leader to be one of the ZCC secessionists.[80] The NC at Zaka reported that he had ordered a hut, used for Zionist teaching at Zvimene's kraal, to be pulled down. He justified this step firstly with reference to the protests vented by local chiefs and headmen against Zionist 'schools' during a meeting held earlier that year, and secondly, with reference to the CNC's minute 'Rhodesia Mission'.[81] In both areas the movement of Mutendi and his subordinate leaders were kept under close watch. Mutendi himself was called in by the NC of Bikita, to report on his distribution of teaching certificates, while his son-in-law, Finias Gumbo, who was the senior representative of the ZCC in the Zaka

78. CNC to Superintendent of Natives, Fort Victoria, 14th August, 1931, Archives, File S 138/140.

79. CNC to Superintendent of Natives, Fort Victoria, Dec. 1931, Archives, File S 138/140.

80. NC, Bikita, to Superintendent of Natives, Fort Victoria, 23rd Nov. 1932.

81. NC, Zaka, to Superintendent of Natives, Fort Victoria, 18th Oct. 1932.

district – and who, today, features prominently in the movement as a minister – was closely watched after he had been ordered to discontinue teaching the Zionist faith. In Zaka an office messenger was especially appointed to patrol the area and report on Zionist activities.[82] Apart from pulling down unauthorized buildings and prohibiting the establishment of so-called Zionist 'schools', the Commissioner at Zaka stated in his report that he had also 'adopted the policy of insisting on the Zionist followers in particular and the residents at the infected kraals in general to carry out all laws and regulations in existence, such as prompt payment of tax and dog-tax, and the registration of marriage, etc. I have also told the parents that they have proper schools established under the DRC and that the Government will not countenance the opening of schools which are not under the direct supervision of some European denomination.' According to him the proof of the effectiveness of this policy was that the number of children in attendance at the school near Zvimene had risen from 49 in August to 120 in October. The teacher who had been responsible for the last inspection reported back to him that the Zionist movement had died out quickly in that area.[83] It is clear from the later development of Zionism in this district that the so-called 'dying-out' of this Church was but a temporary decrease of activities and not by any means a total rejection of the Zionist faith.

Mutendi's rising popularity over a wide area and the impact of Zionist activities on the rural environment thus caused the Native Department to impose more drastic measures. The CNC who had cautioned the local Commissioners to moderate action in 1931, condoned the destruction of improvised Church buildings of unrecognized sects towards the end of 1932. His minute to the Native Commissioners actually gave them greater powers of control. In a letter to the Secretary of the Minister of Native Affairs he argued that a natural corollary of this minute (which stipulated that no Churches were to be built without the CNC's permission) 'would seem to be that an unauthorized building may be removed.' By pulling down a Zionist building the NC of Bikita therefore 'appears to have acted on that assumption.' In conclusion, the CNC recommended that the action of the NC at Bikita be approved, because, as he saw it, 'the activities of such unauthorized bodies as the Zion Apostolic Mission [he was here actually referring to Mutendi's ZCC] are bound to lead to serious trouble if they are not checked.'[84]

82. See letters of Zaka and Bikita Native Commissioners to the Superintendent of Natives, Fort Victoria; Oct.-Dec. 1932, Archives, File S 138/140.

83. NC, Zaka, to Superintendent of Natives, Fort Victoria, 18th Oct. 1932.

84. CNC to Secretary of Premier of Native Affairs, 28th Sept. 1932, Archives, File S 138/140.

We must now turn to Mutendi's *Rungano* and briefly follow the sequence of events from the Zionist point of view up to the time when 'official recognition' was finally granted to this Church. Unfortunately the information in the official records comes to an end when the breakthrough in the official attitude towards the Independent Churches was about to take place. Consequently we have to rely on the Zionists' presentation of this important phase of development. It should be noted in this connection that, apart from an understandably subjective interpretation of events – especially those pertaining to Mutendi's performance of miracles –, the historical survey in the *Rungano* is remarkably accurate. The narrative of those events that could be checked by comparison with other sources all proved to be a fair description of what had happened, and there is no reason to question the veracity of the records dealing with the relations between Church and State.

Mutendi's clashes with the authorities in the early 1930's over the erection of so-called 'schools' in Gutu and Bikita, which led to his conviction, are treated in some detail. Inspector Mather is said to have come across the Zionist 'place of worship' in Gutu. He referred to it both as a school and as a Church. 'I will call your leader and have him arrested', he said, 'because you are not allowed to build churches without permission from Salisbury.' The elders of the district rejoiced when they heard what Mather had said because they were greatly opposed to their children attending the night meetings of Mutendi in the mountains.[85] After Mather had seen Mutendi and had notified the provincial authorities at Fort Victoria, the Zionist leader was summoned to appear in court. When it became apparent that Mutendi was in serious trouble, those subordinate leaders who were present during the court session denied that they knew him. It seems, however, that Mutendi was temporarily released or acquitted, partly as a result of the evidence of a European who had seen him operating in the Gutu district.[86] It is possible that this court case did in fact add to Mutendi's prestige. The next day a great number of people came to see him. 'They came running to see the man who had performed such great things.' A big service was held and several people were converted after they had seen 'the big deeds of God being done through the hands of Rev. Samuel Mutendi.' Some Europeans also attended the service. One of them told Mutendi that he believed him to be the minister of truth and offered to order proper garments for him to wear from overseas – presumably in the hope of persuading Mutendi to join his own Church – which offer Mutendi refused.[87] Soon after these events Mutendi had to appear in

85. Appendix IV *Rungano,* Chapter 27:5-8.
86. Appendix IV, *Rungano,* Chapter 29:1-7.
87. *Ibid.,* Chapter 30:1-3.

court again. This time he was charged with luring children into the mountains and with erecting a Church ('school', according to the Administration) without authorization from the Government. He was sentenced to seven weeks imprisonment.[88]

Mutendi was determined to obtain the coveted permission from the CNC to continue with his religious activities. Once out of jail, he again set out for Salisbury, this time on foot. In the *Rungano* the hardships of the ZCC leader are emphasized. He travelled at night 'when the leopards roar' and he travelled without resting or eating properly. In Salisbury he was warned by 'a sergeant' that he would be imprisoned for three years if he continued his Zionist activities. The CNC sternly warned him, 'We will not allow you to preach even once!' whereupon the 'man of God' left the office with 'great sorrow in his eyes'.[89] These threats did not deter Mutendi from continuing his work. On his return journey he was inspired by God to persevere in doing His work. Back at his village, when the people came to inquire whether he had been successful at Salisbury, he preferred not to state outright that he had been refused permission. Knowing that his followers feared arrest, he decided to give them the impression that the Church had actually been recognized but that they still had to worship in secret for a while. In this way he tried to stop his followers from defecting. He encouraged them by reading to them such verses as Isaiah 62 : 1: 'Because of Zion I will not remain silent, because of Jerusalem I will not rest . . .' This must have been an extremely difficult period for Mutendi, who was keenly aware that his Church was being branded as the scapegoat for all sorts of misfortunes that befell people living in the tribal areas. It seemed that both European officials and African tribal authorities were inclined to 'hate his Church'. 'Those who could barely think or speak used to say: "We are troubled by the Zionists" ', runs the account of the *Rungano*.[90] Secessionist leaders saw their chance and several of them (Manhiwa, Shiri, Mageza, Bariravafumi and others – see Chapter 4) formed their own little Church groups after they had publicly disclaimed any association with the 'troublemaker', Mutendi. Individual Church members defected to other Churches or simply stopped worshipping.

Chapter 35 of the *Rungano* provides us with a vivid description of the hardships of Mutendi's followers in the early 1930's. Due to the regular patrol by policemen in the district, the Zionists had to walk 'facing backwards' when they went to their secret places of worship. The women were cautioned to

88. *Ibid.*, Chapter 32:7-9.
89. *Ibid.*, Chapter 33:1-6.
90. *Ibid.*, Chapter 34:1-7.

wear dark clothes on such occasions to avoid detection. 'They suffered greatly, holding their services in caves, in the bush and in the fields when the maize had grown tall. They carried their hoes when they went to pray to give the impression that they were going to the fields.' ZCC members were sometimes detained, but they were always released soon afterwards. The African police is said to have regarded this strange course of events as resulting from some hidden power of Mutendi, whereby he confused the authorities and prevented them from reaching a final solution. Once all the Zionist leaders were ordered by the police to throw down their 'holy staves' in the office yard. The African police thought that in this way they had overpowered Mutendi, but the *Rungano* has it that Mutendi's staff became invisible to the police and they failed to collect it with the others.[91] Thus the conflict with the African police and local European representatives of Government, the detentions and warnings without prosecutions and convictions, served to strengthen the Zionists in their determination to continue worshipping God in their own way. Simultaneously their leader gained a prominence which he would otherwise not have reached.

Some exaggerations are to be found in the *Rungano*, such as in Chapter 35 : 3, where it is stated that the Zionists 'hardly spent a day without being arrested', but it is probably true that regular dealings with the police did serve to make them more defiant and courageous. Verse 3 concludes with the assertion that the Zionists no longer feared the police and that they joked about 'going to the fields' when they were summoned to the district office.

The change in Government policy came in 1937. After an attempt by Mutendi to call in the aid of Lekhanyane from South Africa, it must have become evident to the officials that Mutendi was willing to go to any lengths to achieve some sort of recognition for his Church. His attempt to arrange a visit for Lekhanyane who, according to his reasoning, had achieved official recognition for the ZCC in South Africa and therefore could possibly help him persuade the Rhodesian Government to do likewise in Rhodesia, once more demonstrated his persistence. It is possible that the Administration had come to realize the futility of repressive measures and that their experiences with the Zionists had convinced them that the leaders of this Church did not really propagate subversion, or at least did not pose a serious threat to law and order. They may also have felt that permission to hold public Zionist meetings would give them a better chance of controlling the movement than when it was forced to operate secretly. Whatever the motivation for greater leniency, Mutendi was advised to consult a lawyer. The *Rungano* mentions

91. *Ibid.*, Chapter 35:1-8, 11.

a certain Bouchet at Fort Victoria, who presumably assisted Mutendi in drawing up a constitution for his Church. Permission was granted in 1937 to conduct services in public. This 'recognition' did not imply a complete breakthrough, because the Zionist leaders were still bound to a number of conditions, such as a prohibition of their operating beyond the borders of their own tribal wards and districts. But even these strictures were overcome in the course of time, because the ZCC members persistently extended their activities – 'little by little until they were allowed to preach wherever they preferred.'[92]

That the Zionist movement remained subject to surveillance and control is illustrated in a few sentences in the *Rungano* concerning the opening of Mutendi's Church in 1951. The opening ceremony was delayed 'because the NC, Gandazhara ["Dry skin"] had left, and was succeeded by someone who did not know the Church. The Church's opening was therefore stopped by the Europeans. They refused.'[93] Later that year another NC, referred to by the Zionists as Daramu, permitted them to open their Church. The true state of affairs remains somewhat obscured, but I have the impression that the differences of approach of the successive Native Commissioners and Mutendi's ability to co-operate with or irritate them personally had a far-reaching effect on the development of his Church. The unpredictability of what would happen next must have had a confusing and frustrating effect on the Zionists. The lack of an objective criterion, according to which their Church could be evaluated once and for all, and the considerable powers of the local NCs to affect their activities, made the Zionists dependent on their relations with each

92. *Rungano,* Chapter 36:1-6. In the archival files a single indication of a change of policy was to be found. In a letter to the Supt. of Natives, dated 23/11/'37, the NC of Chibi stated that he had issued Jeremiah, the local leader of the ZAFM, with a pass. This pass, of course, did not at the time constitute full recognition in the same sense as the larger established denominations were recognized, but it signifies the change of attitude of local authorities. Concerning this same leader the CNC had written in 1931: 'It is unnecessary to provide him [Jeremiah] with a pass, which he would undoubtedly see as official recognition.' (File S 138/140.) In 1937 the authorities were at least willing to risk such misinterpretation, through the issue of a pass. The local NC at Chibi included the following description of Jeremiah's activities: 'It appears that Jeremiah has several adherents – all males, all relatives, all members of the same kraal, who had been baptized by Jeremiah. They meet at the kraal under a tree, under which tree a breastwork of stones had been built. They pray and read from the N.T. together. Jeremiah does not teach or preach [?] He has no superior in the organization to whom he is responsible here in Rhodesia. He conceived it his duty to do some religious work as there is no church operating in that area . . . Rev. Edward S. [obviously Eduard of Basutoland] who is the General Overseer of the world is a native.' NC, Chibi to Superintendent of Natives, 23/11/'37; File S 138/140.

93. Appendix IV, *Rungano,* Chapter 42:8.

successive NC. One threatened to have their leader whipped, another allowed him to preach and baptize at his village; yet another allowed him to proceed with the building of his Church and a fourth prevented the same Church from being opened. Small wonder that the eventual opening of Mutendi's Church building in 1951 came as a kind of catharsis of pent-up emotion. 'On that day the people greatly rejoiced', runs the moving account of the *Rungano*. 'They said: "Today we enter our Church in public [*pachena*: in the open, i.e. legally]". But those who had started with the Church and who had encountered all the trouble already mentioned, wept at the remembrance of their suffering when they were worshipping in the mountains.' The Rozvi chief, who officially opened the Church, and other speakers expressed their appreciation for Mutendi's perseverance in the face of many years of affliction.[94]

Fourteen years after he was first allowed to conduct public services and twenty-eight years after he had returned from the Transvaal as a Gospel messenger of Zion for the first time, Mutendi stood before a large gathering of people who had come from far and wide to attend the opening of his Church. In his address he proudly told the people that, through his own hardships, he had paved the way for the Vakaranga to preach God's word without fear. He claimed that this was the first Church in the country with an all-African leadership, tactfully adding that this did not mean that his followers were the only true Christians, as he regarded those Africans in Mission Churches as Christians too. His Church was a sign of God's grace among Africans, which enabled them to do the work of God on their own (*pachedu poga*). The contempt of others for his Church, he said, was no matter of surprise, because only the 'chosen ones' could be expected to give praise to it. In conclusion he thanked God who had given him the strength to establish His Church amongst the Africans.[95]

This address and other passages in the *Rungano* leave no doubt about Mutendi's own views and those of his followers. The Christian character of Mission Churches was not disputed, but the Zion Christian Church was *the* all-African Church in Rhodesia. There was 'no other way' in which Zionism came to Rhodesia. The true foundation of Zionism in the country was to be found in Mutendi's Church, and the basis for this assertion was that 'we don't hear of anybody else who had suffered continually on behalf of this African Zionist Church.' The *Rungano* emphasized, and correctly so, the fact that Mutendi bore the brunt of suppressive measures while the Ndaza leaders were lying low. 'Even David Masuka in that period of hardship did not have

94. *Ibid.*, Chapter 42:8; 43:1-13.
95. *Ibid.*, Chapter 44:3-8.

his own Church but pretended to be one with Mutendi until all the trouble had passed.' Mutendi and Masuka are likened to Moses and Aaron, with the inference that Masuka was actually playing an assisting role next to the main figure during the periods of tribulation.[96] These claims are not altogether true. Actually numerous Ndaza leaders were, from an early date, operating independently of Mutendi, and his was not 'the only way' in which Zionism came to the country. It remains a fact, however, that he had become the most outstanding and legendary Zionist leader in the country, admired by a great number of Africans for his courageous and indomitable perseverance in the face of persistent opposition.

d) *The basis and privileges of official recognition*

After the administrative officials had started issuing passes to them in the late 1930's all the leaders of major Church groupings and a large number of leaders of small schismatic bodies obtained the much coveted 'official recognition'. The criterion of recognition, however, has remained somewhat arbitrary. Legislation was never passed in Rhodesia (as was the case in South Africa) laying down the conditions by which recognition of the Independent Churches could be regulated. In the words of the Provincial Commissioner of the Victoria Province, 'recognition of these Churches is *not governed by any statute* but at times it is necessary for government departments to afford recognition to these Churches, for example, when they grant leases for Churches in the Tribal Trust Lands. Provided they do not do anything which is contrary to the laws of this country', he added, 'these churches have freedom of expression in the same way as any other Church.'[97]

In practice there are two types of 'official recognition'. In the first place a Church leader obtains a slip of paper from the local Native Commissioner on which it is stated that he is the acknowledged religious leader of a specific group of people.[98] The issue of such a 'pass' often takes place in an offhand and informal way, as the casual handwritten piece of paper which constituted the 'recognition' of Gavure's Ethiopian Church in 1954 illustrates (see Appendix VI). A former and a present District Commissioner of Gutu – Mr. De Bruyn and Mr. Menzies – both stated that such 'passes' are given on

96. *Ibid.*, Chapter 47:6-8.

97. Provincial Commissioner, Fort Victoria, to author, 10th Nov. 1967.

98. See Nheya Gavure's 'pass' issued at the Bikita District Office in 1954. It simply reads: 'I am satisfied that Nheya 12983A Bikita, is looked upon as the head of the Ethiopian Church in the Bikita district.' Signed by the local NC – Appendix VI.

a rather loose basis, similar to the official recognition granted to traditional herbalists or diviners. 'If these Church leaders want to be recognized', Menzies stated, 'they come to the office and I must then establish that they are a bona fide religious group. Sometimes a list of names of their followers is required and it must then be established, mainly from the reports of Native Messengers, that they are of good repute and then the leader receives a piece of paper, stating that he is acknowledged at the office and that his group is a true bona fide religious group.' The DC also stated that he disliked this particular responsibility because he saw no reason for interference with worship. 'They themselves have the wish to be recognized in that sense', he said, 'so we give them the recognition.'[99]

It is interesting to note that, since there is no specific criterion for the size of the Church group, this kind of recognition is determined by the personal judgment of the DC concerned. *He* has to decide whether the applicant's following is large enough to justify 'recognition'. In the majority of cases the DC is in the position to obtain a fairly accurate account of the Church leader's activities and the size of his following from the departmental messengers who come from the same area. The value of this type of recognition is primarily that it constitutes a kind of 'legal basis' upon which permission to conduct large Church meetings in the tribal areas can be obtained. Such permission must be obtained from the local tribal authorities[100] and from the district police, and these seldom refuse permission for such meetings if the Church leader can produce a pass with the DC's signature on it. Church leaders generally attach great value to these 'passes' because they regard it as a kind of safeguard against interference by the police, especially during periods of political upheaval. Against the background of repressive measures in the past, it is of great importance to any Church leader to be able to assure new converts that his or her Church is accepted by the authorities and that its name is 'written in the books of the Government'.

The second type of recognition is an advanced stage of the former type. It concerns the grant of leases for Church buildings and, in exceptional cases, for schools. More particulars are required when Churches and schools are to be built. As in the past, these applications are considered at a higher administrative level. Particulars concerning the number of followers, names of

99. Personal communication, 1967.

100. See, by way of example, the permission for a Church meeting that was afforded by Chief Nhema to Bishop Gavure of the FEC in 1954 (Appendix VI). Such scraps of paper with the permission of tribal authorities scribbled on it, are often kept together with the Church leader's ministerial card and 'letter of permission' from the DC as a manifestation of the Church's prestige and importance.

office-bearers, organizational aspects, credentials[101] and sometimes also the constitutions of Churches are filled in at the district office and the forms forwarded to the CNC for his consideration. Evidence must be produced that the headman in whose ward the particular site is situated has consented to the erection of a Church or school. In order to erect schools, European supervision is required, an aspect which will be dealt with when we discuss the schools of Mutendi and of Sibambo's African Reformed Church at *Shonganiso* Mission.

It seems that a Church constitution is not required as an absolute prerequisite, even for the second type of recognition. The Provincial Commissioner at Fort Victoria informed me that there are no Separatist Church constitutions filed in his office[102] and at the Gutu district office none were to be found either. As for the more than twenty principal leaders of Independent Churches interviewed, only Bishop Mutendi of the ZCC, Bishop Komboni Vambire of the African Zion Church of Jesus and Rev. Sibambo of the ARC (*Shonganiso*) were in possession of complete drafts of Church constitutions.[103] The others either did not have a constitution or, in one or two cases, could not find all their 'Church papers'. A number of factors, such as the rate of development of a Church, the ambitions or sophistication of individual leaders, their standing with the different DCs, made some leaders draw up constitutions for their Churches while others did not. A leader like Mutendi, who was determined to achieve full recognition for his movement and who had ideals of erecting schools, had his Church constitution drafted by a lawyer, more or less provoked by the repressive measures against his unrecognized Church. Nheya Gavure, who obtained recognition on behalf of a much smaller following and at a much later date than Mutendi, when circumstances generally had changed, was not required to produce a constitution. Other leaders again were satisfied merely with the 'pass' obtained from their local DC.

From the administrative point of view there are thus three main categories of Independent Churches: firstly the 'unrecognized' small groups that are tolerated by the officials and have freedom of religious expression as long as the leaders refrain from subversive propaganda; secondly, the locally recognized Churches that have acquired an official standing with the authorities; and thirdly, the Churches that have acquired recognition from departmental headquarters at Salisbury. This latter category includes both Churches with-

101. See Appendix VI for an example of ministerial credentials.
102. Provincial Commissioner, Fort Victoria, to author, 10th Nov. 1967.
103. See Appendix VII.

out constitutions, such as the *Chibarirwe* and the *Topia* Churches that are allowed to build Churches, as well as those Churches with constitutions, such as the ZCC and ARC which have acquired the all-important permission to open schools and the additional privileges of having one or more of their Church leaders appointed as marriage officers. This classification[104] indicates that 'official recognition' does not automatically constitute the whole range of possible privileges. Comparatively few Independent Churches have in fact acquired the right to build Churches and schools, or to appoint marriage officers.[105]

'Freedom of religious expression' therefore has its specific connotations in the Rhodesian setting. Strictly speaking any indigenous law-abiding religious leader can obtain permission to conduct services for his followers and carry on purely evangelistic work, as long as he proves to have a bona fide following. It must also be stated that during my research period there was a remarkable leniency of approach by local DCs and a cordiality of relationship between some DCs and local Independent Church leaders. But the desire to control these movements nevertheless has remained and this accounts to some extent for the withholding of full privileges in a few exceptional cases. Generally they are still suspect of subversive activities, in spite of observations of Commissioners like Menzies, who stated that he had no experience, at Gutu and at Buhera, of the interference of Separatist Churches with State security, and of De Bruyn (former DC of Gutu) who commented that none of the Separatist Churches operating in the Chingombe chiefdom officially participated as such in the political disturbances caused by ZANU during the early 1960's.[106] As in the past, these groups are regarded as an 'embryonic danger' and their activities are closely watched. One District Commissioner pointed out that 'the potential danger lies in X's effective organization, not as it functions at present, but in the way it could be manoeuvred into political channels in the future . . . It is very difficult', he added, 'to predict what these groups would do if we have a change of circumstances.' The Independent

104. This classification is simply used for the sake of clarity. The Government authorities do not officially distinguish between the categories of Churches as mentioned above.

105. The granting to Church leaders of concession rates on railway fares is not included in the list of privileges attainable by recognized Churches, as is the case in South Africa. See Sundkler, 1961, pp. 77-79.

106. Mr. De Bruyn says that the *Chibarirwe* Church did not operate as a politically militant body. He actually relied on the Zionist and Apostolic groups to curb the extremist political activities and accepted the assertion of some of the prophetic leaders that they were preventing their followers from joining the extremist political parties.

Churches causing concern at the moment are obviously the larger movements with an effective country-wide organization. Although repressive measures are not now as evident as they were in the past, there are indications that the movements of some of the outstanding Church leaders have been confined to within the borders of the Colony. The common knowledge that they are being watched and that members of the CID from time to time attend their services, has cautioned the majority of leaders to be careful when expressing themselves on political issues.

2. THE ATTITUDES OF TRIBAL AUTHORITIES

The historical survey of the rise of the Independent Church movement has already revealed that its leaders came into conflict with the tribal authorities as well as with the European Administration. Several letters of NCs and CNCs contained comments on the opposition of kraalheads and chiefs to Zionist practices. This point was sometimes over-emphasized by administrators who relied on the pleas coming from the African community to control the movement of 'Separatist' leaders and who used it as an argument to urge the introduction of greater powers of control. In 1932 the CNC, for example, based his argument in favour of stricter control over the building of Churches on the fact that 'all the chiefs and kraalheads in the Bikita district are opposed to its [the ZCC of Mutendi's] practices',[107] and the NC at Bikita himself stressed the local elders' disapproval of Mutendi's activities, when he pressed for 'some means whereby Mutendi could be stopped.'[108] There is undoubtedly some truth in these allegations because the Church leaders themselves refer to the initial struggle with the tribal authorities. But it is also true that right from the start a number of kraalheads and ward heads sympathized with, and were actually baptized into the budding new Churches.

We now briefly trace the nature of the conflict between the opposing tribal authorities and Church leaders, as well as the notable change of attitude that followed the first period of antagonism. There are mainly two reasons why the Spirit-type Church leaders encountered a much stiffer and sometimes fiercer resistance from the chiefs, ward and village headmen, than did the Ethiopian-type leaders. In the first place they started operating amongst the Southern Shona rural inhabitants at an earlier date than the 'Ethiopians' did, at a time when the conservative tribal communities still offered effective

107. CNC to Secretary of Premier, Archives, File S 138/140.
108. NC, Bikita, to CNC, Salisbury, 25th Aug. 1931, Archives, File S 138/140.

resistance to the large Mission Churches. The tribal authorities represented an inward-looking community, not favourably disposed towards social or religious change, and maintaining a united front – even though it was sometimes only by way of passive resistance – to foreign influence. When the first Zionist labour migrants began to return to the Southern Shona territories in the early 1920's, the chiefs and headmen still held influential religious leadership positions which were closely related to their tribal political activities. The Zionists introduced something new which, the tribal authorities intuitively felt, appealed to their tribal folk (even if the attraction was at first mainly confined to the young people) and which therefore posed a threat to their own religio-political positions. To the chiefs, and especially the staunch supporters of traditional religion, the new movement came as a shock, and their reaction against this intrusion proved to be bitter and sharp. Secondly, the creeds and practices of the Spirit-type Churches contrasted sharply with those of the Ethiopian-type Churches. The very nature of the former militated more directly against the traditional thought-patterns and rituals than did the latter movement, and provoked indignation and protest. There was the strong apocalyptic message of prophetic leaders, who propagated the imminence of the coming judgment, the direct attacks on all forms of ancestor worship, *shavi-possessions,* the use of medicine and all kinds of magical objects procured from *nganga,* as well as the prohibition of beer drinking. Although the prophetic Church leaders seldom deliberately undermined the authority of local headmen, their activities were felt to be disruptive of traditional society. The prophets were supplanting the *nganga,* they lured the children into the mountains with their entertaining and vivid forms of worship, they attracted many women with their promises and rumoured successes in granting fertility, and they appealed to a spiritual authority beyond the traditional realm, an authority which claimed to have the power of chasing away any spirit, including the powerful *ngozi* – above all, they represented a Power which refused compromise with the mediating ancestral spirits. The Ethiopian Churches, on the other hand, were not generally as spectacularly organized. They represented smaller numbers, had a less radical message concerning ancestor worship and traditional practices, condoned the use of beer, medicine and visits to traditional diviners, in short, they were regarded as 'the Churches of our forefathers'.

From the tribal political point of view the latter Churches were easier to control, the actions of their leaders proved to be more predictable, and their compromising attitude concerning the attitudes of kraalheads and ward heads in the traditional *mukwerere* rituals was interpreted as a sign of tribal loyalty. As far as the FEC is concerned no indications were found of any conflict between Chidembo and the local chiefs or ward heads. Gavure, his successor, was on a good footing with the Bikita chiefs ever since he became the principal leader of this Church. His relationship with Chief Mazungunye in particular was of a friendly and confidential nature. Sengwayo, the president of the *Chibarirwe* Church, acted as chief himself for a few years. Having worked as a detective during the period when Zionist activities provoked tribal authorities into opposition, he was well acquainted with the attitudes of chiefs towards African Independent Churches in the Chipinga district. He could therefore avoid the mistakes other Church leaders had made by the time he started to organize his own Church. Eventually it was not from the side of the chiefs and practising traditionalists, but from the missionaries of the American Board that he experienced the strongest opposition to his work.

Considering the Spirit-type Churches, it is noteworthy that the Maranke Apostles somehow seem to have provoked less hostility and opposition from the local chiefs and headmen in the Maranke reserve than did the Zionist in other Shona districts. For their message was at least as radical as, if not more uncompromising than, that of the Zionists, and their doctrine was very similar. The reasons for the greater leniency shown by the chiefs towards the Apostles should be sought elsewhere. A factor to be considered is that Johane launched out on his first campaign well after the first wave of indignant protest against the activities of the leaders of the Ndaza Zionist leaders had already subsided. Of greater importance during the first few years of the Church's development was Johane's kinship link with the acting Chief Maranke. The chief was favourably disposed towards Johane, who was his daughter's son (*muzukuru*), and made no attempt to stop the development of the new movement. This attitude was adopted by most of the chiefs of the surrounding chiefdoms. Johane's growing prestige and power in the religious field posed no threat to the local contestants for the tribal positions of authority. Was he not the son of a foreigner (*mutorwa*) who had no claim to tribal leadership? Johane was therefore in a position essentially different from that of a man like Mutendi, who was a kinsman of the royal Rozvi lineage, himself a kraalhead with definite stakes in the Rozvi chieftainship, being a senior representative of one of the senior Rozvi houses. Mutendi's rising popularity and considerable influence in Rozvi territory was bound to provoke the envy and suspicion of his fellow contestants. Joram's schism bears proof of this.[109] Then there was the ceaseless boundary conflict between the more numerous Duma factions and the Rozvi tribe in the Bikita district. Against this background Mutendi's success was no reason for rejoicing among the Duma

109. See p. 313. for a description of the strife between Mutendi and Joram.

chiefs. They certainly did not welcome the idea of a prominent Rozvi operating on a massive scale in their chiefdoms. A comparison between Johane's Apostolic and Mutendi's Zionist movement shows that circumstantial factors, apart from the actual impact of the Churches on the environment, played a role in conditioning the attitudes of fellow Africans holding positions of tribal authority.

But even the favourable disposition of the chiefs towards Johane's Church did not imply that he and his followers met with no opposition. Some of the kraalheads and village leaders did in fact protest against the Apostolic activities in their villages. In the 'New Revelation' (*Umboo utsva*), Chapter 16 : 1, Johane tells how the Holy Spirit led him to conduct services at Wendumba's. 'I reached a village at Majeese and asked permission to conduct a service. *The elders of the village* [*vakuru vemusha*] *refused and chased us all away*. A voice told us to make a fire in the bush nearby and to start singing . . . Many people followed us to that place.' In spite of such manifestations of disapproval one cannot speak of a general wave of tribal opposition against the Apostolic movement, followed by a large-scale change of attitude, as was the case with the Zionists. The tribal odds did not weigh as heavily against Johane and his fellow leaders during the first phase of Church expansion as they did against Mutendi, Masuka, Andreas Shoko and other Southern Shona Zionist leaders.

What then were the specific objections raised by the chiefs and traditionalists against the Zionists? Andreas Shoko says that four charges were made against him by the Chibi elders in 1933, when all the chiefs of the district and the local NC came to his village for an '*indaba*'. They accused him and his followers of: 1) eating the bones of deceased people in the mountains, 2) polluting the public water during baptism ceremonies, 3) abducting the women of others by force, and 4) causing droughts. The first charge reveals a disapproval of the Zionists' activities in the mountains at night. The highly emotional and prolonged spells of spirit-possession, followed by preaching and singing in the mountains, was not to their liking. Feasting at night was not uncommon to the traditionalists, but then it was done at the village under the guardianship of the protecting *midzimu*. To those who did not participate in the Zionist meetings the mountain sessions at night contained a secretive element. Was this not the time when witches operate? Are the witches not fond of opening up graves and removing the flesh or ribs of deceased people? Thus the allegation of the Zionists' eating the bones of the dead implied a somewhat generalized and veiled accusation of witchcraft. There was no proof to substantiate this charge, but in Shona terms it was the strongest possible protest against what they regarded as the disruption of traditional society. The accusation of 'eating bones' was the essence of the traditionalists' verdict and involved all other accusations. In other words, the Zionists leaders were 'witches' and 'sorcerers' because they polluted water, stopped the rain from falling and disrupted family life. They were regarded as a threat to social harmony.

There was some truth about the pollution of water. A baptismal ceremony in a shallow pool, as I have witnessed, does turn the water into a muddy state for several hours, and if such a pool happens to be used for domestic or other purposes, complaints are bound to be made, especially in times of drought when water is scarce.

The Zionists were not 'abducting the women by force', but the attraction of this movement for females and the fact that some of the faith-healers were able to acquire many wives through their activities, naturally stimulated resentment and prejudice in other quarters.

The accusation that the Zionists caused droughts was provoked by the claims of some prophets that they could bring rain through prayer. This placed them in direct opposition to the traditional messengers (*vanyai*) of Matonjeni and the many who still believed that rain and fertility depended on the goodwill of the oracular deity at the rain shrines in the Matopos. The Zionists had aroused the anger of Mwari, the God of *Mabweadziva* (the rocks of the pool), so that He kept the rain from falling.

None of these charges led to legal prosecution. Convincing evidence that Bishop Andreas Shoko had disrupted the rural community was not tendered. As he himself says, 'The NC and the chiefs simply went away after the *indaba* and left me in peace.' Similar charges were also made against other Ndaza leaders. Bishop Makamba relates how, while he was still working under David Masuka, they were frequently accused by the tribal elders of 'disturbing the country'. 'They accused us of eating their goats like leopards, taking away their women and eating the bones of deceased people in the mountains.' At times the kraalheads tried to take action themselves by charging Zionists for minor offences at village courts. Bishop Makamba mentions one such incident when he conducted a service at one of the Bikita villages. The kraalhead called a village *dare* and charged him (Makamba) with disrespectful action, because he had killed an ox for the Zionist participants and sent the beast's neck to the kraalhead, instead of the customary front leg (*bandauko*). This was interpreted as a deliberate insult to the kraalhead's authority. Bishop Masuka was called in to reprimand his junior official before the *dare* dismissed the case.

In the eyes of the traditional authorities Mutendi was the main culprit. His spells of Spirit-possession were said to arouse the *zvitebwe* spirits which sowed destruction among the stock of his opponents (*Rungano* 17 : 1; 21 : 1); he 'stole' the people's children by taking them along on long journeys (*Rungano* 26 : 6); he misled their children by luring them into the mountains (21 : 1) and he committed the 'crime' of 'plunging' people into the pool of water (21 : 1). One of the reasons why Mutendi was at the same time the most popular and the most despised Zionist leader lies in his rare combination of personal qualities. He had the courage and self-confidence of an independent spirit refusing to be intimidated by the threats of his opponents. But these traits were blended by his magnetic personality, a sense of justice and a strange humility which won him the respect and devotion of his followers. Some of the tribal elders regarded him as an arrogant fool. When he had the audacity to stop the preparations for the funeral of Chief Rukuni's daughter, some of the elders threatened him with guns if he did not succeed in 'raising her from the dead' (*Rungano,* Chapter 18). The tribal elders in the Gutu district rejoiced when they heard of Inspector Mather's threat to have Mutendi imprisoned (27 : 7), and the chiefs in the Bikita district at one stage requested his removal, because he 'broke down the country (*kuputsa nyika*)' – *Rungano* 22 : 1.

The change of attitude among the chiefs came in the 1940's after the ZCC had been 'recognized' by the Government. Mutendi's prophets prophesied that his former enemies would become 'members of his house'. As public opinion changed, several chiefs began to turn to Mutendi for help in times of drought. 'One day during a dry year', runs the account of the *Rungano*, 'Chief Marozva requested rain. Rev. Mutendi told him to return to his home where he would find the rain falling. Disbelieving, Marozva returned, but soon after his departure it started raining, so that he had to travel in the rain, praising God.' Mutendi also visited Chief Chingombe at a time when his people were suffering as a result of drought. The chief showed Mutendi the scorched fields and asked him for rain, to which the bishop promptly replied, 'Let us pray together for the rain to fall here'. According to the *Rungano* it started raining soon after they had prayed together in the fields, and as a result 'all the people praised Mwari with one heart.'[110]

Mutendi's adaptation of his Church's liturgy to meet the constant need of the subsistence farmer for good rainy seasons played an important role in attracting chiefs to his Church. His reputation as a 'rainmaker' spread far and wide. Several chiefs were baptized into his Church after they became convinced of his power to invoke rain. In 1951 the Rozvi chief at Bikita publicly praised Mutendi during the opening ceremony of his Church, which

110. Appendix IV, *Rungano,* Chapter 38:2, 3, 7.

reveals the change in attitude of chiefs in Mutendi's home district where he had, at first, experienced the strongest opposition. Three influential Duma chiefs, Ziki, Mazungunye and Ndanga of the Bikita and Zaka districts later joined the Church and in 1965 Mutendi's following included no less than 15 affiliated chiefs and sub-chiefs, a larger adherence of notables than any of the other Independent Churches in the country could claim. Mutendi's royal Rozvi descent undoubtedly played a role in attracting chiefs to his movement. His erection of a 'Zion City' as the centre of a wide-spread sphere of influence must have appealed to the sentiments of tribal leaders (as much as it aroused the envy of others), who had not forgotten the glories of the once powerful Rozvi dynasty. In this all-African Church, with its remarkable headquarters, the chiefs probably sensed an organized kind of extra-tribal unity which reminded them of the unifying leadership of the Rozvi Mambos. Was the religious factor not one of the main pivots of intertribal unity during the period of Rozvi rule with Zimbabwe as its headquarters? In the present-day political situation Mutendi does not publicly invoke the Rozvi past, but it does seem significant that Shona chiefs pay tribute to him during the large *Paseka* meetings, in similar fashion as one would honour a king. The most outstanding example of a demonstration of loyalty by a chief was witnessed during the July *Paseka* festival in 1966 when 'paramount' Chief Nyashanu rounded off his sermon by rolling over and over in the dust at Mutendi's feet to demonstrate to the large meeting of Zionists how much he respected the 'man of God'. When I asked an informant why Mutendi had such success with the Shona chiefs, he briefly answered: 'Mutendi is a real muRozvi!'

Thus we see how conflict made way for recognition. Chiefs, ward headmen and scores of kraalheads not only recognized the Independent Church movement but they joined these Churches and were themselves promoted to positions of honorary or active leadership within the various clerical hierarchies. One of the surest signs of the recognition of the Independent Churches by tribal authorities is the willingness of affiliated tribal dignitaries to have judgment passed on their domestic behaviour by their Church superiors. In the Gutu district I observed how a chief, who was a junior evangelist of the AACJM, subjected himself to the long, formal enquiry held by his senior Apostolic 'judges' (*vatongi*) after he had broken off the relationship with his future bride in a manner unacceptable to the moral code of the Apostles. Within the Church he accepted the verdict of leaders who, in everyday life, were commoners under his own secular authority. On the other hand, Church leaders may appeal to their local chief's tribunal when they are themselves in trouble. We have seen this happen during the schismatic conflicts, in the 'Ethiopian' case of Gavure against Chidembo Jr., and between

Simon and Anrod of the Apostles. Such cases foster a sense of mutuality and understanding between tribal chiefs and Independent Church leaders.

Recognition or toleration by the majority of chiefs did not, of course, result in a universal appreciation of these Churches by the rest of the community. The traditionalists such as the Matonjeni messengers and *nganga* especially resented the partial usurpation of their own influential positions by these prophetic leaders. They continued to oppose the Spirit-type Churches and whenever droughts occurred, they branded the leaders of these groups as the source of trouble. As recently as 1965 Andreas Shoko and his Ndaza subordinates were singled out by the Chibi traditionalists as scapegoats when the rain was late in coming. The Matonjeni messenger at Bikita (then) revealed that Mwari waMatonjeni, the oracular deity, had announced a continuous drought in the country as a punishment for Mutendi, the false rainmaker. The Zionists simply returned the compliment by ascribing the drought to the unwillingness of the heathens (*vahedeni*) to turn to the Christian Mwari.

3. THE ATTITUDES OF MISSION CHURCH LEADERS

A more appropriate characterization of the contact between Mission and Independent Church leaders than the heading of this chapter – conflict and recognition – would be 'conflict and negation'. Whereas the European Administration and tribal authorities more or less recognized the Independent Churches after the early period of conflict, the Mission authorities opposed, and are continuing to oppose, the Independent Churches and have virtually lost all contact with their leaders. The official policy of the larger European-directed denominations is clearly set against any form of recognition of, or co-operation with, the 'Separatists'. The basic concept of the Catholic Church more or less excludes the possibility of viewing the 'Separatist movements' as Churches. Persons who have belonged to any of these Church groups are rebaptized when they join the Catholic Church. The DRC makes a distinction beween the Negro-directed AMEC and the other 'Separatist' Churches. Members of the former Church can be accepted into the DRC fold, as is also the case with Roman Catholic, Seventh Day Adventist, Church of Christ, Free Methodist and a few other Churches, after an enquiry has been made by the DRC council. But the Zionist, Apostolic Faith (including the Maranke Apostles), Watch Tower, Full Gospel and *Chibarirwe* Churches are classified as 'stray Churches' (*makereke dzakatsauka*) and of these it is stated in the DRC's Law Book: 'We cannot co-operate with these Churches at all . . . Members of these Churches must attend catechism classes for two years if they want to join our Church.' They are also to be re-baptized.[111]

The intensity of opposition by the European missionaries during the initial phases of Separatism depended to a great extent upon the nature of the schisms and the direct or indirect effects upon the different missionary enterprises. In the Chipinga district, where the American Board experienced the rise of the Zionist movement as a direct blow to their educational endeavours, the European missionaries reacted strongly. The above-mentioned report of Rev. Orner on Zionist activities indicates the serious view taken by the American Board leaders and their inclination to present the Ndaza Zionist to the Administration in such a bad light as to invite repressive measures. An even greater blow to this Mission was the loss of Evangelist Sengwayo and, shortly afterwards, of several other prominent Church leaders. I have not been able to check Sengwayo's allegations, but he was convinced that on at least two occasions the American Board missionaries actually interfered with his work as a builder in the Chipinga township after he had left the evangelist school. Rev. Orner tried to persuade the Native Commissioner not to permit Sengwayo to organize his own Church, and Rev. Marsh personally tried to dissuade Sengwayo from continuing his independent evangelical work. These direct efforts to obstruct their religious activities only led to bitterness and the determination, on the part of the African leaders, to expand their own Churches. One can compare the attitude of these missionary leaders to men like Stewart of Lovedale and François Coillard, to whom Sundkler refers as the 'missionary patriarchs' of the past who had personally baptized and confirmed their flocks, who regarded Ethiopianism as destructive to missionary work, and who consequently tried to win back the members of their flock who had strayed.[112]

The opposition of DRC missionaries to the Zionist Church movement was less intense and overt than that of the American Board leaders. One of the reasons for their more complacent attitude was that the majority of principal leaders were either not affiliated to the DRC before joining Zionism or, like Mutendi and Andreas Shoko, had lost contact with the missionaries during their stay in South Africa. Moreover, the first impact of Zionist activities was only indirectly felt at Morgenster, the DRC headquarters. There was no massive loss of Church membership and the chief Zionist leaders were, moreover, further removed from the main centre of the DRC than was the case with the American Board centre at Mt. Selinda.

111. See *BUKU YEMIRAIRO,* No, 122, 123, 124, pp. 31-32.
112. Sundkler, 1961, p. 61.

It was again Mutendi who proved to be a thorn in the flesh. His rising popularity and the influence of his meetings on schoolchildren aroused such concern that the DRC missionaries decided to investigate his work with a view to curtailing, if possible, his influence. Mutendi's *Rungano* contains two chapters on this enquiry. It refers to a meeting at Pamushana Mission to 'determine whether he [Mutendi] had received permission to preach, and to enquire into his healing activities.' At first it was decided to send the Rev. Orlandini because he was a 'stern man', who could possibly intimidate Mutendi. But strange things are believed by the Zionists to have happened that day. First the car, and then the bicycle on which Orlandini set out for Mutendi's village, broke down. Reading between the lines of the *Rungano* one finds a suggestion here of mystical intervention to the detriment of the missionaries. After Orlandini's failure the missionaries decided to send the Rev. Louw Jr., the son of '*Sekuru*' Louw who could speak to Mutendi in a gentle manner. Having seen what had happened to Rev. Orlandini, the new delegate decided to travel to 'Zion City' on foot.[113]

The discussion between Rev. Louw and Bishop Mutendi, described from the Zionist point of view, portrays Zionist reaction to missionary intervention. When Louw questioned Mutendi about his ministerial credentials and registration certificate (*chiputa*), the bishop countered by asking the minister since when was he doing the job of a policeman. When the European minister, surprised at such arrogance, in turn asked if Mutendi had a bad spirit, the 'man of God' simply stated that such questions did not hurt him. Were not the believers of olden times also accused of having bad spirits? Rev. Louw would, among other things, have asked if Mutendi compared himself to Jesus Christ, a question which suggests that the missionaries were at this early stage already anticipating Messianic tendencies. In the *Rungano* Mutendi preferred to leave this question unanswered, but in the concluding section of Chapter 20 he likens his discussion with Rev. Louw to the experiences of Jesus, as described in Mark 11 : 27f. This refers to the question of the priests and scribes about the authority behind His actions, to which Jesus reacted by asking them if the baptism of John was from heaven or from men. 'To this event', says the *Rungano*, 'we liken Mutendi's experiences when they ask him where his authority comes from and when they ask to see his preaching certificates.' The most important point in this chapter, however, is the suggestion that Rev. Louw ultimately 'recognized' Mutendi's Church. After Mutendi had shown him his ministerial credentials, Louw is alleged to have said, as if to himself: 'This man has a task. Let us leave him undisturbed. Let us leave

113. Appendix IV, *Rungano*, Chapter 19:2-5.

him at it!'[114] What may very well have been resignation on the part of the missionary was interpreted by the Zionist leader as a gesture of recognition. The lack of contact and active opposition from the side of the DRC missionaries following this encounter was obviously due to their acceptance of the inevitable, and not to their belief that the Zionists were performing an essentially Christian task.

Similar trends are also noticeable in the contacts of European missionaries with *Chibarirwe* leaders. As long as there was a chance of persuading men like Moses Ruwana or Tinos Chirashanye to remain in the DRC, regular contact between missionaries and potential schismatic leaders was maintained and encouraged by the missionaries. Of this trend we have an example in Rev. Louw Jr.'s efforts to persuade Ruwana to continue working in the DRC (efforts which were to some extent appreciated by Ruwana), and the discussion of Tinos with two missionary leaders before his secession. But once such leaders had joined one of the Shona Independent Churches, and sometimes only *after* one or two last attempts to win back such a leader, contact between them and the missionaries usually broke down completely. Ruwana mentions the visits of two DRC missionaries after he had become affiliated to the ACC (*Chibarirwe*). The one was actively opposed to Ruwana's pretentions as a leader of a 'Separatist Church' – a stray Church! – while the other was sympathetically disposed. Such examples illustrate the impossibility of making generalizations about the attitudes of missionaries. On a personal level some of the missionaries were indeed inclined towards sympathetic understanding.

At present there is still a tendency amongst both European and African leaders of the DRC to ignore or deliberately evade contact with the Independent Church leaders, especially on the local congregational level. There are several reasons for this:

Firstly, the Mission Church leaders have become used to regarding these movements as 'stray Churches', as the official policy defines them; Churches that are responsible for spreading false doctrines, and whose leaders do not 'listen to reason'. Rev. Brand, European minister at Pamushana Mission, states: 'We see the Zionists as non-Christians. They are the object of missionary work as any other heathen group; they are only more difficult to convince . . . I do not see the use of visiting the Zionists. *You simply cannot convince them of a different viewpoint* (my italics).' Rev. Shiri, African minister at Alheit Mission, comments in a similar vein: 'These stray Churches are rival groups that twist the truth . . . *I do not know the Separatist leaders here in Chingombe*. The leaders act like madmen and spread untruth. They

114. *Ibid.*, Chapter 20:1-4.

know they are following the wrong tracks, but they will not come to reason. They base their teachings solely on the Old Testament and not on what Jesus said.'[115]

Secondly, there is the not altogether unfounded assumption that, if Mission Church leaders take the initiative in establishing contact with the Independent Church leaders, the latter would interpret this as a sign of recognition. Such action, it is feared, would have a confusing effect on the members of the Mission Church itself. Rev. Brand, whose living quarters at Pamushana are within half-an-hour's drive from Bishop Mutendi's 'Zion City', refrains from visiting the Zionist bishop. 'The people will interpret any visit I pay the Zionists as an indication of recognizing their practices', he says. 'In this way we shall weaken the position of our own Church and strengthen that of the Zionists.' For similar reasons Rev. Shiri at Alheit avoids contacting Separatist Church leaders living in his vicinity. It should be stated, however, that the educational leaders on the Mission stations, such as Mr. Gopoza and Mr. Chindanya at Alheit, are in regular contact with the 'stray Church' leaders. Schoolmaster Chindanya, who regards the Spirit-type Churches as being definitely non-Christian and as Churches of the uneducated that will die away as the general standard of education rises, has less qualms about possible misinterpretation of his contact with 'Separatist' leaders. For instance, Madyaruto, a kraalhead and influential FEC leader near Alheit Mission, visited him regularly in 1967 to discuss educational matters.[116]

Thirdly, the lack of contact can be ascribed to the practical problem that both African and European ministers are overburdened with work. European missionaries, often involved in a wide field of activities, in addition to their congregational work or teaching assignments, have little time for anything else. The shortage of African ministers and the wide dispersal of congregations make it impossible for some ministers to meet the Synod's requirements of paying regular pastoral visits to all the members of their own flock. Much time is spent in travelling to outposts in order to accomplish the essential duties of a tight program. Separatist Church leaders are therefore only met by chance, usually in passing, and long personal discussions can seldom take place.

115. Personal communication, 1967.

116. Mission Church leaders in the educational field usually come into regular contact with the Independent Church leaders. The chances of the rural population interpreting such contact as a form of recognition is less than is the case if ministers of religion take up contact, since it is accepted that school managers and schoolmasters have the task of dealing with the parents of schoolchildren irrespective of their Church affiliation.

In the fourth place, it seems that missionaries are still inclined to underestimate the importance of the Independent Churches. The nature of the growth of these movements, and the seemingly unimportant small congregations scattered all over the rural areas, may have contributed towards this view. In 1967 a prominent DRC theologian, with many years of experience as a missionary in Rhodesia, wrote that the Separatist movement generally has not succeeded in attracting large numbers from the DRC Mission Churches.[117] It is true that amongst the Southern Shona the DRC never experienced a dramatic schism with a large number of members breaking away *en masse* in a relatively short span of time, but it is also true that large numbers of individual DRC members or potential Church members have in the course of years defected to the so-called 'Separatist' Churches. To the missionary who stays at a Mission station for a few years, the loss of a small number of Church members may seem relatively unimportant, and the manifestation of 'small' and seemingly unstable Separatist congregations may lead him to believe that this is but a passing phenomenon and not a serious challenge to the Mission Church. The occasional reports of Mission Church members having been baptized by prophets during a witch-hunt, or under stress of illness, are often treated by the Mission Church leaders as a side-issue of passing importance. The prophetic 'twisters of truth' are often ignored, their methods of operation only superficially considered and those Mission Church members who have had the misfortune of being forced into a mass baptism[118] by their kraalhead receive a light sentence of three or six months of Church discipline.

The lack of contact with 'Separatist' leaders is also evident from the comments of other Mission Church leaders. Father Urayai, the African RCC priest at Mutero, for instance, was hesitant to call the Independent Churches Christian or non-Christian because, he admitted, 'I do not know the *vaPostora*, and I do not know what the differences are between the Zionists and Apostles. I have only heard of the *Chibarirwe* and *Topia* Churches, but I have not had the time or means to meet them . . . I have not yet seen a prophet being possessed by the Spirit, but I think that they possibly resort to the traditional practices. Occasionally I have met individual members of these Churches, but I have not yet met one who could give me the proper facts about his Church.'

In recent years some Mission Church leaders have begun to take a greater interest in this phenomenon. Practical necessity made the DRC council con-

117. Van der Merwe, 1967, p. 18.

118. In Volume 2 we will pay attention to several mass baptisms which were conducted by Zionist and Apostle prophets in order to detect witches or resolve village feuds.

sider the treatment of defecting Church members[119] and the possibility of conducting joint meetings with the Separatists.[120] Individual missionaries like Rev. Esterhuizen, theological lecturer at Morgenster Mission, are paying attention to the 'Separatist' movements and one or two seminars for missionaries were devoted to this subject. Rev. Esterhuizen has made special efforts to establish personal ties with Rev. Zvobgo of the ARC (*Shonganiso* Mission) at Majiri in the Victoria tribal area, and the possibilities of allowing Zvobgo's followers to attend the theological school have been discussed. In a seminar held at Morgenster, in 1964, Esterhuizen indicated that Sibambo and Zvobgo's ARC differed a great deal from the original *Chibarirwe*, in that it disallowed polygamy, opposed 'heathen practices' and had strong Christological emphases. He argued that this Church could not be classified as a 'sectarian movement' and recommended that 'points of contact' be established, that ARC (*Shonganiso*) students be allowed entry to the teacher's training schools and that candidates with the appropriate qualifications also be allowed entry into the theological school.[121] Several European missionaries of the DRC feel that the chance of co-operating with Zvobgo and his followers should not be missed. One of them emphasized that the admission of *Shonganiso* theological students would give the Mission a chance of positively influencing the ministry of such leaders, but others again were somewhat apprehensive about the influence of such 'non-affiliated' elements on the Mission community. In this case only one particular group was concerned, which seems to 'have returned to the ways of the Mother Church' and which

119. In 1954 the Church council determined that the names of Mission Church members who defected to 'Separatist Churches' should not be cancelled immediately. After such members had belonged to Separatist Churches for a year they should be asked if they want to re-join the Mission Church. Only then, and after they had been properly warned, are their names to be scrapped from the Church books. Those 'Separatists' who wanted to return to the Mission Church, it was decided, should attend the catechism classes for 6 months and publicly confess their acceptance of the Mission Church doctrines before the congregation, before they are accepted in the fold once more. Those who returned after a warning were exempted from catechism, but had to make the public confession. See also law No. 159 in Church lawbook.

120. In 1966 the matter of joint meetings was discussed by the Church council in view of renewed efforts at interChurch co-operation, especially in some of the urban areas. A warning note was sounded: 'Our congregations should be careful about holding Church meetings with the Separatist Churches. The congregation must consult the Church council before giving a reply [to requests for such meetings]. It should be carefully considered whether such meetings are beneficial to the Kingdom of God.'

121. Title of Seminar: 'Ondersoek na die Ontstaan, Verspreiding, Aard en Invloed van die Separatistiese Kerk bekend as die 'Crying Church' en nou as African Congregational en ook African Reformed Church.'

was therefore regarded as non-sectarian. But officially contact has not yet been sought with the 'real sects' – the Zionists, the Apostles and the *Chibarirwe* groups.

Of great significance is the more lenient attitude of the younger second and third generation Mission-trained African Church leaders. Discussions with the DRC theological students at Morgenster Mission in 1967 revealed that only one or two of the older men were prepared to regard the 'Separatists' as being definitely non-Christian or heathen. The others either stated that the rich variety of these Churches made it impossible to categorize them, or regarded them as 'sub-Christian' or as 'deteriorated forms of Christianity'. Prophetic activities were sharply criticized as *nganga* practices with a Christian veil, and one or two students maintained that beer and polygamy were the sole attractions of the *Chibarirwe* Church. Significant, however, were the qualifications made by some of them:

'The members of these stray Churches are believers, but they lack the true interpretation in preaching . . .'

'The people who go to the prophets to be helped in times of illness or crisis are true believers who want to follow God. But the only thing that spoils these Churches are the doctrines coming from the leaders . . .'

'Their teachings are not sound . . . but if you want to repent you can repent in any of these Churches.'

The students were doubtful about the possibility of associating officially with the Spirit-type Churches, but of the Ethiopian-type Churches (*Chibarirwe*, ARC and *Topia*) it was stated that '*we must have a strong fellowship* with the members of these Churches and we must emphasize the positive aspects we find in them. In order to make contact with them it would be good if men from the ARC of Zvobgo are enrolled in this school – if we can agree on the essential points.' Although little has been done so far by the present DRC leaders about establishing official ties that could lead to such 'strong fellowship', the attitude of the African Church leaders of tomorrow indicate possible changes in future policy.

In Roman Catholic circles a number of Church leaders have also become increasingly aware in recent years of the importance of getting acquainted with the practices of the Independent Churches. On the academic level the publications of Sr. Mary Aquina OP has drawn the attention to this phenomenon.[122] I myself was invited to address the priests of Southern Mashonaland on Rhodesian Zionism and was struck by the interest shown by most of the par-

122. Aquina in *African Social Research,* June 1966; in *Africa,* April 1967 and in *Africa,* April 1969.

ticipants. As in DRC circles, there is of course a certain amount of scepticism regarding the value of associating with the leaders of the Independent Churches, but some priests are at least trying to reach 'Separatist' leaders and discuss matters with them. One of them, Fr. Alois Erni, gives a description of a Zionist service he attended and of several discussions he had with a Zionist 'bishop' and preacher. Of special interest is Erni's mention of five arguments used by the Ndaza Zionists against the Roman Catholic Church.

1. 'Are you people better than we? They – the Catholics – offer to the *vadzimu*, drink beer like anything and break the marriage.
2. Why are we not allowed to honour God in our own way? We don't do wrong in having our own meetings.
3. Show us what is written in the Bible about Mass. We also have Holy Communion.
4. You don't baptize properly because the people are not immersed into the water as is written in the Bible.
5. Why is the Pope so rich while Christ was so poor?'

Erni admits that Aquina had nearly convinced him that 'he would never convert them'. 'But I soon found out', he tells us, 'that the way of love opens many doors for them. Mutual understanding grew remarkably after the *vadzimai* [RCC women] of Mapiravana had gone to help the blind woman of the [Zionist] preacher to harvest her *zviyo* [groundnuts] for the children. A lift or a friendly joke broke down big parts of the wall between us. The other day I read in the *Southern Cross* that our Pope said: "Let us pray for our separated brethren. It may be that union is nearer than we believe".'[123]

Deliberate efforts to establish ties with the 'separated brethren' have been made by only a few as yet, and the motivation behind such action seems basically to be the winning of such 'Separatists' for the Catholic faith and not of recognizing these movements in their own rights. This trend is consistent with the theological objections still raised in Catholic – as well as Protestant – Church circles, to entering into official theological discussions with the 'Separatists' as ecumenical partners. Nevertheless, the efforts of individuals to establish contact should be positively evaluated in so far as they aim at dialogue and at eliminating the isolation and prejudices of the past.

123. Erni in *Guti*, February, 1966.

Summary and preliminary conclusions

This first volume represents only a broad introduction to a more detailed analysis of the organizational and religious activities of the Southern Shona Independent Churches. I therefore limit myself to a brief recapitulation of background factors and to some preliminary conclusions concerning the origin and nature of development of the major movements.

1. SOCIO-ECONOMIC FACTORS

In describing the socio-economic setting of the Southern Shona our attention has been mainly directed at the tribal areas, for two reasons: firstly, the vast majority of Africans still live in the rural areas (as has been indicated in Chapter 1); and secondly, the rural environment proved to be an ideal setting fort he recruitment of Independent Church membership (an aspect to be discussed fully in the next volume). Here one finds the largest concentrations of IC adherents and the heartbeat of large-scale religious activities.

Rural society has been sketched in its territorial divisions: those of village, ward and chiefdom, each with its distinctive yet interrelated patterns of activities and systems of authority. Apart from these are the separate but overlapping kin-groups, such as the *rudzi* (clan), a territorially widely scattered and as such a non-political unit; the *chizvarwa* (lineage segment) which functions as a corporate unit; the politically significant *imba* ('house'); and the *mhuri* ('kindred') which is the basic kin-grouping at village level whose members share the important experiences of life. Within these groups the mutual behaviour of individuals is conditioned by the all-important seniority principle, varying from the rigid super and subordination between close agnates to the relative equality between *sekuru* (maternal uncle) and *muzukuru* (sister's son). Despite the impact of Western culture on Shona society, the reciprocal obligations within the kinship system have remained largely intact. Its important bearing on the growth of Independent Churches and on their leadership structures has become evident in the preceding chapters and will be referred to below.

In order to avoid confusion the term 'tribe' is used in a twofold sense: 1) with a territorial connotation, to indicate both a politically integrated community within defined boundaries and the name of the ruling patrilineage around which tribal unity is built, here in particular with reference to the Rufura of Gutu; and 2) to differentiate between the lineages, clans and, by implication, the diverse tribal origins of the members of a single community, e.g. those of the Rufura, Hera, Duma, Rozvi, and other elements of the Chingombe chiefdom. This distinction enables one to formulate with some precision the 'tribalistic' or 'non-tribalistic' composition of various Church groups.

In the urban environment a different set of social values and forces is emerging. A multi-tribal and constantly changing urban population, without a politically dominant kin-group to maintain social cohesion and stability, furthers a breakdown of traditional sanctions. The seniority and heredity principles are replaced by other determinants of leadership, e.g. individual capability, efficiency, educational standard and financial standing. The religious and social significance of the *chizvarwa* and the tribal political role of the *imba* are lost in this milieu, in which the elementary family unit, if only temporarily, is relatively isolated from the familiar network of interlineage and clan ties – circumstances which accelerate the process of individualization. Situations of close contact with Europeans in everyday life and in economic enterprise co-exist with a system of rigid social segregation, a feature which is emphasized in the geographic separation of the African township from the European residential areas. The urban setting stresses the discrepancy between African and European income and creates a more acute awareness of racial insulation than is the case in remote rural districts where many tribesmen have but sporadic contact with Europeans. The frustrations and tensions generated among Africans as a result of these conditions may find some outlet in the religious activities of the Independent Churches, whose answer to racial segregation is a Church 'apart'. Nevertheless, the urban environment has not (yet), for the Southern Shona at least, become the seedbed of religious separatism as one might have expected.

In connection with land allocation mention was made of an important difference between the Shona and Ndebele territories, in that the former, since the arrival of the Europeans, has been in a more advantageous position. I have suggested that the Southern Shona Independent Churches should not, in the first place, be characterized as a land protest movement, a point of view which will receive more attention in Volume 2. Nevertheless, the two highly controversial land acts, mentioned in Chapter 1, did provoke African reaction and contributed towards a psychological state conducive also to religious dissent. The land pressure in Chingombe, where a considerable percentage of farmers have to sustain themselves and their families on patches of land smaller than the standard allocation, is a constant source of discontent and resentment. In this way the land question forms part of the complexity of factors stimulating the growth of the Independent Churches.

The economic situation in the rural areas is based upon regular subsistence farming supplemented by additional sources of income, of which periodic participation of males in the wage labour market in the urban centres is the most important. Labour migration causes an uneven sex ratio in the rural areas so that females predominate in the rural Independent Church congregations. This trend is less evident in remote tribal areas, e.g. Chingombe, than in those bordering on large industrial centres. The continual movement of wage labourers to and from the towns and the retarded development of a stable core of townsmen facilitate the process of rural-urban interaction, thus perpetuating a strong undercurrent of traditional beliefs and practices in the urban environment, despite the above-mentioned change of values. Economically there is still a wide gulf between the average standards maintained by Africans and Europeans respectively. In rural and urban African society, however, a certain economic stratification, with the emergence of a relatively prosperous upper class, is discernible. The question of whether the Independent Churches can be identified with a particular economic stratum will be dealt with in the following volume.

2. TRADITIONAL RELIGION

The Shona High-God has been sketched as an ambivalent deity with both masculine and feminine, immanent and transcendent attributes. Mwari is primarily a God of fertility, but He is also interested in politics, tribal and national, and He imposes moral sanctions on His people. He stands in close relation to the ancestral spirits who act as mediators between Him and living men. Especially the tribal spirits (*mhondoro*) are considered to be close to Mwari. Wielding power to protect and afflict or kill, the ancestral spirits (*midzimu*) have a direct and far-reaching influence on the lives of their living descendants. Divinatory and healing powers are attributed to the alien *shavi* spirits. They can also impart a wide variety of socially constructive or destructive skills tot heir hosts. Some are believed to dwell close to Mwari at Matonjeni while others 'come from afar'. They operate independently or in unison with the ancestral spirits. The dreaded *ngozi* is the vengeful spirit of an untimely deceased person, with considerable powers of causing misery in the family of the culprit responsible for his death. The belief in magical powers complement the belief in a hierarchically structured yet diffuse spirit world. Generally speaking, the *nganga* (diviner-herbalist) is the specialist who harnesses these powers to the benefit of society while the wizard (*muroyi*), and especially the witch, turns them towards destructive ends.

Traditional beliefs and practices among the Southern Shona have a remarkable resilience, whether in overt of camouflaged form. In a rural area where Christianity has exerted its influence for at least 70 years through medical and educational institutions, and where the majority of people claim affiliation to a Mission or Independent Church, the old beliefs still continue to exist. Many Church supporters still regard the God of Matonjeni as the rain-giving God, the *midzimu* are still believed to threaten their well-being if neglected, the *shavi* spirits are still the inspiring agents of contemporary *nganga* practices, and the *varoyi* are still believed to cause the ailments or deaths of their victims. Even the old network of interrelated rituals, despite changes and minor breakdowns, continues to exist with surprising tenacity. The Mwari cult has remained intact and in some districts a resurgence of the cult's influence has taken place in recent years. *Vanyai*, the cult messengers, continue to visit Matonjeni as representatives of the central, southern and eastern tribal areas of Rhodesia.

Then there is the key ritual, the *kugadzira,* which is still performed in the tribal areas on behalf of many deceased adults, whether stripped of some of its traditional connotations or still interpreted as a proper induction of the deceased's spirit into the ancestral realm. *Mukwerere* rain rituals are conducted on a wide scale and Christians frequently participate directly by attending, or indirectly by contributing the required finger millet for sacrifical beer. Family rituals have been partly driven underground. They are less numerous than before and a *gono guru* ('big bull' dedicated to a senior home-ancestor) will no longer be found in the cattle kraal of every homestead. Yet there is still a general tendency to revert to traditional religious practices during periods of family crises, or when all other aids in a situation of stress seem to have failed. As the result of modern medical aid and the activities of Zionist and Apostolic prophets the *nganga* have lost their former influential positions in some areas. But, as I have pointed out in connection with northern Chingombe, they seem to be as numerous as ever, and they remain the 'king-pins' of traditional religion, fostering the kind of philosophy and beliefs to which Independent Church prophets adapt their activities with obvious success. I shall return to this point in the following volume.

European missionaries, on the whole, seem to be insufficiently aware of the prevalence of traditional rituals in their environment. Restricted by their

Western-type ecclesiastic institutions and programs, largely conditioned by their own cultural and theological presuppositions, they have often failed to establish real contact with the thought-world of the African. A negation or rejection of traditional religion on Biblical grounds hampered their understanding of the fusion of old and new in African Christianity, which had emerged even in the Mission Churches. Ill-equipped or disinclined to gauge the degree of participation of Church adherents in traditional religion, or to assess the penetration of Christianity into the deeper layers of the African mind, some Missions derived a questionable satisfaction from the numerical rather than the 'qualitative' progress of their flocks.

The frequent failure of Missions to cope with the real issues in the lives of traditionalists or of their African converts left a vacuum which the Independent Church leaders were well equipped to fill. In this respect the latter have a distinct advantage over the former. Familiarity with existing practices and beliefs facilitates their task of presenting the tenets of Christianity to the African mind, if not at a deeper level, then at least in a more appropriate idiom. As will be illustrated in a subsequent study, much of the success of the Independent Churches derives from an intuitive assessment and recognition of the strength of traditional religion and the subsequent dialogue – involving both partial adaptation and rejection – with the High-God, ancestral and alien spirit cults.

3. MISSIONS, TRIBAL AND ADMINISTRATIVE AUTHORITIES

In the effort to determine the reasons why more people with a Protestant than a Roman Catholic background join the Independent Churches, the policies and strategies of the DRC and the RCC have been considered on a comparative basis. With reference to Sundkler's thesis, that in South Africa the emphasis on the 'Self' in the Protestant policy of promoting self-supporting, self-propagating and self-governing Churches, and the application of a segregation policy in the Church, are the two main reasons for secession from the Mission Churches, I have discussed the similarities and differences between the DRC and RCC policies and practices.

In connection with the 'planting' of a Mission Church I have argued that the Shona Protestant Church was not envisaged as a separate Church by the founding leader, Rev. A. A. Louw, nor was the emphasis exclusively on the Self. It was the retarded process of evolution to *self*-determination and the persisting paternalistic control of missionaries, rather than a premature move towards establishing an independent Mission Church, which encouraged an atmosphere favourable to secession. I have also pointed out that, despite the theoretical differences between the DRC and the RCC, the latter emphasizing *implantatio ecclesiae* – through which the local Church develops as an integral component of the institutionally unified, universal Roman Church –, the *practical* approach of missionaries in both camps with regard to Church growth in the field has much in common. Both Mission Churches, for instance, moved cautiously with the training of African Church leaders and with the delegation of administrative powers to these officials. Thus Sundkler's first value premise does not furnish a satisfactory explanation for secession from Mission Churches and the growth of Independent Churches in Southern Shona territory. Nor does Niederberger's postulation, that the DRC's separation of individual conversion and the founding of a Church (resulting in a '*kirchliches Vakuum*' between Mother and Mission Church), fully explain why the DRC loses more of its members to Independent Churches than the RCC does.

As regards race relations, the RCC's official policy, leaning towards racial integration, and that of the DRC which argues that 'practical necessity' dictates its application of racial segregation, stand directly opposed to each other. It is only in the past two decades, however, with the upsurge of African nationalism and through the publication of critical Catholic pastorals, that this difference has become more evident to the African public. During the initial phases of Independent Church formation, between 1920 and 1945, this difference was much less prominent. It is conceivable that, with the Catholic authorities becoming increasingly critical of the Government's racial policy and more outspoken on behalf of African aspirations and rights, in contrast to a more neutral ('political non-involvement') stand of the DRC, this factor may grow in importance as a reason for secession from the latter Church.

I have argued that both Mission Churches were burdened with the stigma of being 'Government agents', partly because of their ownership of vast stretches of land in the form of Mission farms, and partly because of their close co-operation with the Government in the educational field. The missionaries of both camps were, moreover, identified in the eyes of the Africans with the privileged white class. Even the patterns of social life on Mission stations had much more in common than their theoretically different viewpoints reveal. On the one hand, the DRC missionaries were more flexible and liberal in their dealings with the Africans than the Church policies formulated by the Synod in the far south would suggest. On the other hand, the Catholic missionaries to some extent preserved an element of 'social distance' between black and white on their Mission stations like that of most other European-directed Churches, in spite of their views on racial equality. It would therefore be misleading, because of the present polarization between Catholic Church and State on the racial issue, to single out this factor as a major reason for the higher incidence of individual secession from the Protestant than from the Catholic fold.

Both Mission Churches established their influence through a wide network of schools, and from the start the educational system contained the 'seeds of Separatism'. The paternalistic control of missionaries was bound to provoke reaction, as did the subjective criteria initially applied to the selection of African teachers. There was also the insufficiently clear distinction between Church and school, which contributed towards the superficial attitude of some Africans to Church membership. I discussed the effective use by the Roman Catholics of lower primary schools as a recruitment area for Church membership, and how the DRC, because of its shortage of higher primary and secondary school facilities, suffers a greater loss of Church membership than the RCC. In the rural areas the closing down of a number of DRC schools, on account of the economic slump in the 1930's, and the disappointment of Africans who were beginning to respond to the challenge of education, coincided with the first wave of Independent Church growth. A trend which may emerge more prominently in the future is the progressive loss of African support generally, and a falling off of membership in both Mission Churches, as a result of inter-denominational rivalry.

A major reason for the higher incidence of individual secession from the DRC than from the RCC is the more rigid approach of the former to traditional customs and religious practices. I have indicated that a strict system of Church discipline which tends to become formalistic in its application and which sometimes gives insufficient spiritual support to disciplined members, has adversely affected DRC membership.

In contrast with this Church's outright repudiation of customary practices, such as beer drinking, visits to *nganga,* and traditional forms of marriage – all of which are punishable by the Church council according to set rules – the Catholics not only allow several of these, but also deal with defaulting Church members in private. The latter practice reduces the feeling of public humiliation and the resulting tendency for a trespasser to secede.

The difference between the two Mission Churches emerges most sharply in their approach to the ancestral cults. Whereas the one looks upon all forms of ancestor 'worship' and divination as trespasses against the first commandment, the other accommodates its own ritual practices to the point of including addresses to the *midzimu.* Despite a host of theological problems and possible objections to the latter approach, it does have the psychological advantage of assimilating something typically African, thus evading the creation of a gulf between old and new which may drive people to search elsewhere for compensatory forms of religious expression. The DRC approach, however, consistent with Calvinist theology, has the disadvantage that – if formalized – it appears to some Africans as yet another manifestation of European intolerance and his disparagement of an essential element in the African personality and identity. In view of the centrality of the ancestors in African religion and philosophy, theological reflection on this subject is needed. My next volume will provide examples of how the various Independent Churches cope with the still dominant beliefs in the traditional spirit world. Theologians of the Mission Churches, concerned with a 'theology of the ancestors', will do well to study the attitudes and methods of their IC counterparts.

Another factor, not mentioned in Chapter 3, is the translation and dissemination of the Scriptures in the vernacular. Barrett demonstrates statistically 'that the availability of the Bible in the language of a tribe greatly increases the prospects of independency arising.'[1] Neill, in his foreword to Barrett's study, considers the difference between Protestant and Catholic approach to the translation and distribution of the Scriptures as an important reason why the latter have been less troubled by breakaway movements. He states that he can affirm from personal observation in Africa 'that the new attitude to the Scriptures in the Roman Catholic Church and the encouragement to read them which is now almost universal are producing exactly the same spirit of questioning and enquiry. It seems likely that in future the Roman Catholic Church will be faced in many areas with problems similar to those with which the Protestant missions have been wrestling for almost a century.'[2] It is not unlikely that the initial reluctance of the Roman Catholics, also in Mashonaland, to spread the Scriptures among the Shona laity (they have only recently produced their first version of the entire NT in Shona) has contributed towards their success in maintaining ecclesiastic solidarity, and that they, too, with the fostering of a more critical and independent approach through individual Bible study, may find themselves increasingly confronted with the problem of small-scale yet frequent secession.

The attitude of the authorities of the Mission Churches to the Independent Churches is characterized as one of 'conflict and negation', rather than 'conflict and recognition'. With the exception of individual missionaries who have taken a special interest in the so-called 'Separatists' and who make an effort

1. Barrett, 1968, p. 105.
2. *Ibid.*, pp. XV-XVI.

to meet their representatives, there is little official contact and no organized form of co-operation between the leaders of these Churches. The main reasons for this lack of contact at the official level have been mentioned in Chapter 6, namely:

1. the dogmatic view of the Mission Churches that the 'Separatists' are stray Churches, sects, or even non-Christian;
2. the conviction of some missionaries that any initiative to establish contact with prominent IC personalities might be wrongly interpreted as a formal recognition of these movements;
3. the practical problem of a full program which leaves Mission Church authorities little time to engage in other than regular ecclesiastic activities; and
4. a tendency to underestimate the importance of the Independent Churches.

These four aspects have caused a regrettable ignorance in Mission circles about the life, faith and organization of the Independent Churches. The older generation of Mission Church officials – European and African – tend to view the Separatists as their opponents, 'sheep-stealers' who rob members of their flock, and as 'twisters of the truth'. The Separatist acceptance of polygamy causes some to look upon these 'Churches of many wives' as an inferior expression of Christianity, or as decidedly non-Christian.

Aware of the attitudes of Mission Churches, the IC officials react by accusing missionaries of disregarding some of the essentials of Christianity. Nevertheless, theirs is an ambivalent attitude, because they regret their own relative isolation and secretly or openly aspire to be recognized by, and co-operate with, the major Mission Churches. It is this tendency which should be positively regarded as a starting-point for the establishment of meaningful ties between Mission Church and Independent Church, should the former prove willing to take the latter seriously.

As regards the tribal authorities, these at first protested violently against the budding Independent Churches, especially those of the Spirit type. They regarded the new prophetic movements as a direct threat to their religio-political position and, as a result, co-operated with the Government in an effort to curb their activities. The prophets were supplanting *nganga* practices more effectively than European doctors were able to do. They attracted young people and women in large numbers, and they challenged the traditional spirit world in the name of a 'foreign' Spirit, whom they declared to be more powerful than all other spirits. Small wonder that the prophetic leaders came to be regarded by some chiefs and headmen as wizards (*varoyi*) – disrupters of society. After the first wave of protest a gradual change took place as the tribal authorities came to appreciate the indigenous character of the all-African movements, and discovered that they could benefit from them. Despite the continuing distrust and antagonism, especially on the part of staunch traditionalists, many tribal authorities now became supporters of the new movements, which provided them with an outlet for the frustrations caused by their complicated position of being expected by their own folk to represent African interests while having to co-operate with European authorities. Here they could indirectly vent their feelings and participate in relatively free organizations without prejudicing their Government-sponsored positions. In Mutendi's Church, with its numerous adherent chiefs, the faded glory of the Rozvi dynasty seems to come to life during the major annual festivals.

Since the inception of the Shona Independent Churches, the Administration has tended to regard these as a political 'danger in embryo', as well as educationally ineffective because of their lack of funds. Alarmed by the activities of European-inspired Pentecostal movements in the surrounding countries, restrictive measures were imposed on the entry and movement of foreign missionaries. Early efforts by the Administration to pass legislation for the control of African preachers were abandoned after a draft bill had been discussed and rejected by the Missionary Conference on the grounds that it was an infringement of religious liberty. As a result, administrative authorities had to deal with the new religious movements without a specifically designed criterion of evaluation. This placed a special onus on the judgment of individual District Commissioners. Although the Rhodesian authorities at one stage intended to deal with the 'Separationists' more drastically than the South African Government, whom they regarded as liberal and over-tolerant on this point, they eventually operated on an arbitrary basis without any statute law regulating the recognition of religious bodies. A certain indecision and vagueness concerning the criteria and the methods of control to be applied therefore marks the correspondence between departmental headquarters and local district authorities.

After 1930, coercive methods in the field of education were introduced to check the activities of influential leaders like Rev. Mutendi. Unauthorized 'school buildings' were pulled down and the trespassing Church officials prosecuted. Possibly the authorities regarded this as a more effective measure of control than merely keeping the main leaders under surveillance in case they indulged in seditious preaching. In the late 1930's official recognition was granted to Mutendi's movement on the condition that its evangelistic activities be geographically restricted. We have traced the account in the ZCC *Rungano* ('History') of Mutendi's first fruitless applications for such recognition, the subsequent change in the Government's attitude, followed by a greater leniency of administrative officials at the local level, and the consolidation of Mutendi's influence over a wide area.

The present-day grounds for official recognition of the Independent Churches are still arbitrary, depending to a great extent on the personal judgment of local District Commissioners or, in exceptional cases, on the overriding views of departmental headquarters at Salisbury. Even unrecognized religious movements are tolerated as long as their creeds and practices do not present a threat to law and order. Nevertheless, a close surveillance is still being kept on the activities of the Independent Churches, and they are still regarded as a potential danger. Yet some District Commissioners hold the movements with which they are acquainted in high esteem, and claim that they have thus far encountered no organized political resistance from them.

4. OLD AND NEW IN THE GROWTH OF THE INDEPENDENT CHURCHES

The major attraction of the IC movement lies in its remarkable ability to combine vital aspects of the old order – the basic structure of African society, beliefs, sentiments and philosophy – with the new religion, Christianity. On the one hand one can speak of adaptation, in so far as traditional customs are incorportated into Church life. The Gospel is presented, for instance, in a typically African guise. On the other hand, and by means of the new message coming to grips with the old religion at a truly existential level, a rejection or at least deliberate transformation of some of its facets takes place. One has to unravel the strains of old and new in the Independent Church context to arrive at an evaluation of this movement, to determine its strength and weaknesses. I intend to pursue this aim in the following volumes. In our description of the rise of the movement at least some idea has been obtained of the process of adaptation and rejection, and this calls for some concluding comments.

a) *Family and tribal Churches?*

The subjects of recruitment appear to be the kin-groups familiar to Shona society. A new Church leader nearly always confines his initial activities to his own kindred. In the case of Mutendi the first converts belonged to his own *chizvarwa*, i.e. his brothers, sons and daughters; or to the 'houses' (*dzimba*) of familiar Rozvi kinsmen, as the first mass baptism at Mupamawonde indicates. Mutendi's campaigning team, during the first phase of Church development, consisted of his *mhuri*, i.e. his wives, children, maternal and affinal kin all of them belonging to the same neighbourhood. Likewise Johane Maranke at first concentrated on, and made use of, the aid of members of his own *chizvarwa* and *mhuri*. It was his father, paternal uncle and his two brothers – all members of the same *chizvarwa* – who were first confronted with the new message. Soon afterwards some of the in-laws, such as Ruka Mataruka, and maternal kin, e.g. cousins Simon and Gwati, were informed and they duly acknowledged Johane's divine assignment. Thus the *imba* ('house') of Momberume (Johane's father) was closely associated with the Apostolic movement and members of Johane's *mhuri* became the bearers of the new faith. It follows that, in the case of influential Independent Church personalities, the religious significance of the entire family group changes. Instead of the *chizvarwa* manifesting its unity during a propitiatory ceremony in honour of a common ancestral spirit, it does so in the entirely different context of Church meetings conducted by one or more of its members.

In addition, the important leadership positions of the budding Church are usually allocated to relatives of the principal leader. The latter tends to appoint such agnates in the leadership hierarchy as are naturally subordinate to him, e.g. his younger brothers and sons, while he reserves some important positions for maternal kin, i.e. for a *sekuru* (mother's brother), *muzukuru* (sister's son) or maternal cousin, who, through relationships of particular intimacy and relative equality, are likely to become reliable allies willing to respect his authority. We have seen how Johane appointed his maternal cousin, Simon, as his right-hand man and first prophet of the movement, with Anrod, Johane's elder blood brother and therefore his senior, in a position of junior prophet, subordinated to Simon. We have also noted that Bishop Gavure of the FEC called in the aid of two of his *vadzisekuru* (maternal uncles), Chapinga and Musasikwa, when he started with his revivalistic work in Bikita and Zaka. These two men became the senior regional officials of the *Topia* movement in these districts. Senior agnates, who are in a position of superordination to the Church leader, are mostly placed low down in the leadership hierarchy, or else they are given honorary positions – as was the case with Johane's father – with restricted executive powers.

In some respects one could therefore speak of 'family Churches', in that the Independent Church groups originate as family efforts, extend themselves by exploiting kinship ties and consolidate their top leadership within the ranks of one or several overlapping kin-groups. Due also to the initial development of such movements within the boundaries of a single *nyika*, that is within a geographically distinct tribal community, and because of their frequent close association with the politically dominant lineage which constitutes tribal unity, the Independent Churches appear to have distinctly tribalistic leanings. Mutendi, for instance, launched his movement in Rhodesia by first of all directing his campaigning activities at his Rozvi kinsmen in the Bikita district.

In view of these features one may ask whether kinship ties and tribal loyalties do not obscure or supersede the actual basis on which a community of Christian believers should be founded, that is, faith in and loyalty to Jesus Christ. Does individual conversion feature prominently enough as a condition for Independent Church membership or are these movements merely religious 'clubs' consisting of relatives and tribal members drawn together by natural loyalties under pressure of socio-political circumstances? Although it cannot be denied that in some cases ulterior motives play a role in Church membership and that the psychological pressure of relatives turning to a particular Church overrides the religious motives of some of its members, it should be emphasized that Biblical criteria are seldom completely superseded by the old order. In reality the qualifications 'family' and 'tribal' can only be applied to the Independent Churches with some important reservations. For in most cases it is only during the initial phase of development that the focus is on the Church leader's own *chizvarwa* and *mhuri*, or on the tribal group to which he belongs. Soon a number of other people join the movement, and also *vatorwa* (foreigners) are appointed, next to the leader's relatives, in the leadership hierarchy on the grounds of their ability. And so the group acquires a multi-tribal character as it develops beyond the boundaries of the leader's tribe. Moreover, there is usually a definite accent on individual conversion, public confession of sin, demonstration of a contrite spirit and on controlled initiation into the new community of believers through baptism, in order to prevent superficial recruitment. Family baptisms admittedly still take place at an advanced stage of Church development, as will be described in the following volume, but then with sufficient emphasis on the Christian transformation of each of its members, so as to exclude those who feel they cannot meet the prescribed conditions, and to subject the young baptized members to constant religious instruction. Ultimately the Christian ideal of a 'community of believers in Christ' prevails. With the exception of a few of the smaller schismatic groups, all the Independent Churches included in this study consist of communities of believers transcending the loyalties of family and tribal configurations. The fact that kinship ties do not lose their significance in these movements, but are utilized in recruitment and determine Church leadership up to a point, may be seen as the way God inspires men in the African setting.

b) *Church leadership*

That a fusion of old and new can lead to questionable forms of Church life and to a misunderstanding of certain functions within the community of believers, despite the group's predominantly Christian character, is best illustrated in the combination of diverging leadership patterns. A clear distinction is not always made between customary principles of seniority and heredity in contrast with the Biblical criteria of moral standard and spiritual maturity, with the result that persons often become Church officials on the grounds of the former rather than the latter qualifications. As the Church grows, and frequently after the Church leader has consolidated his own position by appointing relatives in key positions of the nuclear Church community, a shift of emphasis may take place. Instead of, or in combination with, kinship ties and seniority of membership, religious zeal, conformity to group norms, charismatic potential, social standing and Bible knowledge become the norms for appointment and promotion in the leadership hierarchy. Nevertheless, there remains a vast difference between the Mission-type clergy with its extensive theological training as a precondition for promotion to the highest ranks, and the Independent Church leadership which offers access to prominent positions in the group, irrespective of such Western-type of training.

This difference enhances the attraction which the Independent Churches hold for persons who have leadership ambitions, but are not qualified to make headway in the Mission Church context. A compensatory outlet for the frustrated ambitions of former Mission Church members, as well as for persons deprived of political power, is provided by the hierarchic structure of the Independent Church. Here almost any adult male, willing to serve the Church group, can attain to a position of some prestige. To many ruralists an uneventful and often colourless existence acquires new perspective and meaning through appointment in some IC office. With a clear division of responsibilities throughout the entire congregation, the Church, in its ritual context, corresponds with, and forms an effective substitute for the *chizvarwa* or other traditional ritual unit with its comprehensive distribution of religious functions among the nuclear body of interrelated participants. In IC congregations, which are normally small, more persons are actively engaged in a variety of roles during Church ceremonies than in the Mission Churches, where most members of comparatively larger congregations remain essentially passive during services or public events.

But the indigenized patterns of Church leadership also carry the 'seeds of separatism'. This becomes evident during leadership succession crises arising after the death of the founding leader. In the Spirit-type Churches, for instance, the prophetic healer, through close ties with his followers, manages to maintain a firm yet precariously balanced Church unity during his lifetime. But as soon as he dies, the effort to perpetuate his cohesive influence through his heir meets with serious trouble. Invariably the succession of the senior son to his deceased father's ecclesiastic position (for which Biblical justification is sought in the kingship succession patterns of ancient Israel) is opposed by regional Church officials who, though willing to co-operate with the founding leader, are now reluctant to accept the authority of someone whom they regard as their junior.

The roots of the secessions that follow are to be found in the traditional segmentation patterns. In much the same way as the second and third generation descendants of a common ancestor segment into ritually independent houses with the passing away of the agnatic family heads, or in the same way as village segments hive off from an overpopulated main village, secessionist leaders 'hive off' from the parental Church group after the death of its founding leader. Though Mutendi did not, strictly speaking, secede from the South African part of the ZCC, the autonomy of his own group of followers in Rhodesia became an established fact after the death of Enginasi Lekhanyane, the founding leader. In David Masuka's Zionist movement it was only after the main leader's death that the major schisms took place, which left his senior son with only a handful of loyal supporters. Likewise, the most serious secession in Johane Maranke's group took place when Abero and his younger brothers inherited the Church leadership from their father. Even in the *Topia* movement, where the Church conference is supposed to elect a successor to the main leader on other grounds than blood relationship, the claims of the deceased Bishop Chidembo's son caused a major upheaval and the dissent of several members from an otherwise stable Church community. It should be stated, however, that, in spite of the disrupting effect of this type of schism on the solidarity of the original group, it also carries the impulses of renewed Church expansion, because the ambitious secessionist leader, having established the independency of his own fold, seeks to extend his influence through intensified recruitment activities.

In the performance of a more or less Christianized version of the *kugadzira* ritual, when the senior son inherits both his father's name and the Church leadership, the integration of old and new emerges most strikingly. Stripped of its traditional religious connotations, the transformed ceremony nevertheless retains its jural significance in the family context, with the added implication that the succeeding son also becomes life-long head of the 'Church family'. That this ceremony creates serious problems through the attempt to combine elements of two basically incompatible systems was shown by

Simon's objection to the identification of Johane's personal belongings and Church property as inheritable property, when Abero inherited the deceased Johane's estate (*nhaka*). Although Simon did not oppose a hereditary succession to Church leadership, he disputed the implication of vesting all central authority, administrative powers and rights to Church property in the inner circle of Johane's relatives. Until clearer distinctions between old and new principles are evolved, and as long as customary concepts of inheritance predominate ceremonial procedure during such crises, the danger of disruptive schisms will continue to exist as a corollary to IC leadership succession.

c) *Attitudes to traditional religion and customs*

In the rejection of certain traditional religious practices and the incorporation of some of the old customs lies the strength of the Independent Churches. From the outset the leaders of the prophetic movements launched an attack on all forms of ancestor 'worship'. Mutendi and Johane publicly renounced *pira midzimu* ceremonies, they burned the personal charms and medicines which converts had obtained from *nganga*, and they introduced the prophetic office which could detect and deal with wizardry in order to safeguard members of the movement from such destructive practices. In the case of Johane Maranke the destruction of the family's *gono guru* (the bull dedicated to the family spirits) as a symbolic rejection of the ancestral cult, and the efforts to convince his mother of the necessity to reject her function as spirit medium, signified how drastically this Apostolic leader applied his Church's creed.

Why could the Spirit-type Church leaders successfully attack traditional practices and sustain this seemingly damning attitude to the 'ways of the fathers' in their recruitment techniques, while a similar policy seems to have the opposite effect on membership in the Mission Churches? Broadly speaking there are two important reasons for this. In the first place, there is a great difference between the rejection of something so intimately woven into the fabric of African society as ancestor 'worship' by *outsiders*, who do so on doctrinal grounds and sometimes deprecatingly, and the criticism which comes from within that society – not halfheartedly, because the missionary suggested it, but from an inner conviction based on personal experience. Psychologically the Independent Church leader's attack has the advantage of being more convincing because he himself sets the example of rejecting in the name of a stronger Power, the beneficial powers attributed to the ancestors, while it is sensed by Africans that the missionary is not confronted with a similar existential choice. On the other hand, there are staunch traditionalists who do not seek Church membership and who react even more sharply to the prophetic movements than to the Mission Churches, because in their eyes the prophets, by their effective substitution of *nganga* practices, pose a greater threat to traditional religion than the Mission Churches do.

In the second place, the Spirit-type Church leaders substituted the old rituals with adapted Church practices more effectively than did the Mission Churches. Mention has been made of Mutendi's and Johane's dreams and visions, their possession by the Holy Spirit – through whose powers they could exorcise evil spirits –, their use of faith-healing as a recruitment technique, and of the centrality of Jordan baptisms right from the start. Practically all these practices have parallels in the old religion. Dreams, acknowledged channels of communication between the traditional spirit world and the living, were regarded as valid manifestations of divine guidance by the new movements. Instead of an ancestral or *shavi* spirit summoning a relative or host through dreams to perform a particular task, an angel or messenger of God now calls someone to join the community of believers. The conveyance of knowledge or certain skills to spirit mediums through spirit-possession was replaced by the all-important possession of the elect by the Holy Spirit. Under the guidance of this new agent faith-healing and rainmaking miracles are being performed, which take the place of a *shavi*-inspired *nganga's* medical aid and the procurement of rain through the High-God cult and *mukwerere* rituals. Jordan baptisms, in which the symbolic use of water plays a central role, corresponds with the former ritual purification and fortifies the believer against the attacks of malignant powers as the traditionalist *mbanda* treatment against *ngozi* attacks is supposed to do. Thus the Christian message and all that goes with it is introduced into African society in a truly African guise.

Faith-healing, one of the most potent attractions of the Spirit-type Churches, highlights more than any other practice the confluence of old and new. Based on a rejection of divination as practised by the *nganga*, it nevertheless concerns itself with the very forces which the *nganga* regards as the cause of ailment. The Holy Spirit, too, indicates that ancestral spirits, witchcraft or other personal forces are the main source of affliction. In other words, the prophet recognizes and deals with the psychological causes of the patient's trouble in terms which are familiar to the latter. Therapeutical treatment, however, reveals to what extent the prophet dissociates himself from the type of solution prescribed by the traditional doctor. Instead of advising ancestral propitiation to regain the protection of the guardian spirits, liberation from the afflicting agent through the healing power of God is emphasized. Magical medicaments and charms are supplanted by objects symbolizing the curative powers of the Christian God.

Most Ethiopian-type Churches share with the prophetic movements a permissiveness towards traditional forms of marriage, e.g. elopement (*kutizisa*) and polygamy. This feature contrasts sharply with Mission Church policy (Chapter 3) and enhances the popularity of these indigenized movements, as can be seen in the account of the rise of the *Chibarirwe*. But this tolerance goes further in the Ethiopian-type than in the prophetic Churches. The *Chibarirwe,* for example, allows beer drinking and introduced the use of typically African instead of Biblical names at baptisms. In this Church, too, the confrontation with the ancestral world is less direct. Visits to *nganga* are allowed and affiliated members are seldom disciplined for participation in propitiatory rites. Consequently, tribal dignitaries, for example kraalheads, who want to belong to a Christian community without totally having to reject their inherited ancestral ritual obligations, show a special preference for Churches of the Ethiopian type. Unlike the substitution of ancestral cults with prophetic activities, Ethiopian-type leaders either evade outright repudiation of the old practices; or, as the *Chibarirwe* President Sengwayo did, they seek to justify the sustained contact of Church members with the forefathers' spirits as a God-given institution.

These differences, which will be discussed in much greater detail in the next volume, are important for a differentiated evaluation of the various IC movements. When, for example, it comes to a critical Biblical appraisal of traditional rituals and beliefs within the inner circle, the Ethiopian-type Churches, which some observers may be inclined to regard favourably on account of their organizational and liturgical similarities with the Protestant Mission Churches, may in fact prove to be less advanced than the prophetic movements.

Appendices

Witchcraft Suppression Act chapter 50

To suppress the practice of pretended witchcraft
[18th August, 1899.]

Ord. 14, 1899

Short title.

1. This Act may be cited as the Witchcraft Suppression Act (*Chapter* 50).

Interpretation of term.

2. In this Act 'witchcraft' includes the 'throwing of bones', the use of charms and any other means or devices adopted in the practice of sorcery.

Punishment for imputation of witchcraft.

3. Whoever imputes to any other person the use of non-natural means in causing any disease in any person or animal or in causing any injury to any person or property, that is to say, whoever names or indicates any other person as being a wizard or witch shall be guilty of an offence and liable to a fine not exceeding one hundred pounds or to imprisonment for a period not exceeding three years, or to corporal punishment not exceeding twenty lashes or to any two or more of such punishments.

Punishment for imputation of witchcraft by habitual or reputed witch doctor or witch finder.

4. Whoever, having so named and indicated any person as a wizard or witch, is proved at his trial under section three to be by habit and repute a witch doctor or witch finder shall be liable, on conviction, in lieu of the punishment provided by section three to a fine not exceeding two hundred and fifty pounds or to imprisonment for a period not exceeding seven years or to corporal punishment not exceeding thirty-six lashes or to any two or more of such punishments.

Punishment for employing witch doctor or witch finder.

5. Whoever employs or solicits any other person–
   a) to name or indicate any other person as a wizard or witch; or
   b) to name or indicate by means of witchcraft or by the

application of any of the tests mentioned in paragraph b) of section *eight* or by the use of any non-natural means any person as the perpetrator of any alleged crime or other act complained of; or

c) to advise him or any other person how by means of witchcraft or by any non-natural means whatsoever the perpetrator of any alleged crime or other act complained of may be discovered;

shall be guilty of an offence and liable to a fine not exceeding twenty-five pounds, or in default of payment to imprisonment for a period not exceeding six months.

Punishment for witch doctor or witch finder practising witchcraft or supplying witchcraft materials.

6. Whoever, professing a knowledge of so-called witchcraft or of the use of charms, either as a witch doctor or witch finder, advises or undertakes to advise any person applying to him how to bewitch or injure any other person or any property, including animals, and any person who supplies any other person with the pretended means of witchcraft, shall be guilty of an offence and liable to the punishments provided by section *four*.

Punishment for applying means or processes of witchcraft for the injury of persons or property.

7. Whoever, on the advice of a witch doctor or witch finder or any person pretending to the knowledge of witchcraft or the use of charms, or in the exercise of any pretended knowledge of witchcraft or of the use of charms, uses or causes to be put into operation such means or processes as he may have been advised or may believe to be calculated to injure any other person or any property, including animals, shall be guilty of an offence and liable to the punishments provided by section *four*.

Punishment for the naming or indicating of thieves, etc., by witchcraft, charms, etc.

8. Whoever–

a) by the exercise of any witchcraft, conjuration, use of charms or of any other unnatural means pretends to discover where or in what manner any property supposed or alleged to have been stolen or lost may be found or to name or indicate any person as a thief or perpetrator of any crime or any other act complained of; or

b) in the pretence of discovering whether or not any other person has committed any crime or any other act complained of, applies or advises the application or causes to be applied to such person the 'boiling water test' (that is to say the dipping by such other person of any of his limbs or portion of his body into boiling water), whether such dipping is voluntary or compelled, or administers or advises or causes the administration of, to such other person, with or without his consent, any emetic or purgative;

shall be guilty of an offence and liable to the punishments provided by section *four*.

Money, etc., received as payment or received for practice of witchcraft, etc., shall be deemed to have been received by fraud, and punishment for such fraud.

9. Any money, animal or other thing received by any person by way of payment or reward for, or in respect of an exercise or pretended exercise of so-called witchcraft or of the use of charms, or for or in respect of advising a person as to any mode or method of bewitching or injuring, by non-natural means, any other person or property, including animals, or for or in respect of indicating any person who by non-natural means is supposed to have bewitched or injured any other person or any property, including animals, or for or in respect of the performance of any of the acts mentioned in section *eight*, shall be deemed to have been obtained by fraud, and the person so receiving such money, animal or other thing shall be liable to be prosecuted for fraud and to suffer such punishment as is by law provided for such offence.

Treatment of 'shamhu' (disciplinary) cases by the Pamushana Church council *

The quarterly session is called *Rangano yeChiunga* (Council meeting of the Congregation). Rev. A. B. – European missionary and head of the Mission station (grandson of Rev. A. A. Louw) – and Rev. M., the African minister in charge of the local Church circuit, alternately act as chairman of these and other Church council sessions. This particular meeting was attended by overseers (*vatariri*), elders and deacons of the DRC congregations surrounding Pamushana, and chaired by Rev. B.

CASE 1. POLYGAMY
Accused absent.

Mutariri C: briefly reports on a Church member who has taken a second wife. Accused was notified that the matter would be reported to the Church council. *Rangano* unanimously decides (after hardly any discussion) on *shambu isingatarwi* (unconditional discipline) i.e. expulsion from use of sacraments until member agrees to meet the Church regulations and requests reinstatement. C. will notify accused accordingly.

CASE 2. HEALING TREATMENT BY INDEPENDENT CHURCH (APOSTOLIC) PROPHET
Accused absent.

Mutariri C: '*Mai* X was baptized in "Jordan" by one of the *vaPostora* [African Apostolic Church of Maranke] prophets. Her intention was not to join the prophet's Church permanently, but she was ill and baptism was the only way in which she could obtain the prophet's [diagnostic] prophecy. I notified *Mai* X that I will report this matter to the *dare* [Church "court"], to which she agreed. She said that she is not now attending the services of the *vaPostora*.'

Rev. B: 'This is not allowed by the Church, so what do we do?'

Mutariri Mb: 'This woman was being tempted under difficult circumstances, so she went in search of aid elsewhere. *We must search for the reason of her action amongst ourselves*! We were late in going to this woman in her distress. We should have assisted *Mai* X as a group of Church elders [my italics].'

* Held in March 1967 and translated from Chikaranga.

Rev. B: '*Mutariri* C, have you been to the sick woman?'

Mutariri C: 'What could I do? I heard of *Mai* X's illness only after she had been to the prophet. I have not been notified beforehand.'

Rev. B: 'This is *mhaka huru* [a serious case]. You, *vatariri*, must report illness to me as soon as possible because I do not always know of such cases.'

Mutariri Z: 'If a person is ill he is influenced more easily than usual. We must therefore in the first place think how to bring such a person back to the Church. We should punish her but *not cast her out completely* [*kuvarasha chose chose*]. If I have cattle in the garden I chase them away. Let us leave this woman alone [i.e. treat this case with great consideration].'

Rev. M: 'There is no excuse for this woman, because anyone can come and say that they have been forced through circumstances to trespass Church laws. If we punish this woman it does not show that we do not have sympathy with her, but it is the same as giving a person a jail sentence, for his own and others' good. What she has done causes other members to stumble . . .

You *vatariri* must regularly visit the sick and pray for them: I suggest *shamhu* [Church discipline] of 6 months.'

Mutariri K: 'Is there not any permanent law in our Church dealing with people that temporarily join other Churches and then come back?'

Rev. M: 'No, we do not treat this woman along those lines, but as someone who has visited a *nganga*. It is the attendance of a kind of healing ceremony which is not permitted by our Church. [Note: For disciplinary purposes, visitations to *nganga* and prophets are treated in the same way.] It is the same as kushopera [divination through *hakata* or divining bones].'

Rev. B: 'It should not be less than 6 months.'

The two ministers search in the law book for the appropriate regulation. When they do not find it, 'sentence' is postponed to a later date.

CASE 3. ADULTERY *(Upombwe)*
Olivia absent.

Mutariri J: 'Olivia has conceived, and when I investigated the matter, I found that the boy is not sure about marrying this girl. He refuses to *roora* her.'

Rev. B: 'This is then a case of straightforward adultery. Should we give one year, plus the ruling: "until she has married", or just one year and then see what happens?'

Mutariri C: 'We must sentence her one year for adultery and ask *Mutariri* J to check on the matter and report back to the *dare*.'

Mutariri K: 'Yes, we must do it in this way and if the woman is finally refused by the boy, but wants to return to the Church after a year, we must accept her.'

Rangano decides: 1 year *shamhu*; with *Mutariri* J checking to see if proper marriage arrangements are made.

CASE 4. ELOPEMENT MARRIAGE *(Kutizisa)*
Shumirai absent.

Mutariri: 'Shumirai has eloped with her boy friend. Shall we consider this as a case of *upombwe* [adultery]?'

Rev. B: 'What *shamhu* do we give her?'

Rangano: (general consensus without discussion) It is adultery. Sentence: 1 year *shamhu*. Shumirai may return to Church afterwards if she is properly married.

CASE 5. INHERITANCE MARRIAGE *(Kugara nhaka)*
Rosa Gani absent.

Mutariri L: 'Rosa had been "inherited" by one of the relatives of her deceased husband, but she has now left the man and said that she no longer wants to accept such conditions. The man has also said: "I don't want her any longer!" The woman still lives at his farm in the Purchase Area but she is economically independent of him because she has her own field.'

Other vatariri: 'Are you sure that they are separated? Why does she still stay at the farm?'

Mutariri L: 'This matter had been discussed before and I was sent to investigate the matter. I have asked the man's real wife to find out what the actual situation is, and she assures me that it is all finished now. They have refused to live together completely.'

Mutariri Mb: 'As far as I know, these people have returned to the Church. The woman, Rosa, is old [i.e. beyond child-bearing] and she can stay with her children. She was probably forced into *nhaka* by the man, but is now taken care of by her children.'

Rev. B: 'The case is now clear. The woman was given *shamhu* earlier on and she asks to return.'

Rangano: The *shamhu* is lifted. Rosa can return to the Church (i.e. participate in the Holy Communion).

CASE 6. ADULTERY
Chengeto absent.

Mutariri: 'Chengeto was taken as wife by Joëre Sibanda without a proper Church marriage.'

Rangano: (No discussion) *Upombwe*! 1 year *shamhu* + condition of marriage.

CASE 7. JOINING INDEPENDENT CHURCH *(Chibarirwe)*
Regina Moyo absent.

Mutariri L: 'Regina joined the *Chibarirwe* two years ago. She says that she joined against her will, because her husband forced her.'

Rev. M: 'This woman must be given "*shamhu isingatarwi*" [unconditional discipline], because we do not know what will happen in future and when it will happen. She could have remained in our Church if she really wanted to. The door remains open if she wants to return.'

Rev. B: 'Unconditional *shamhu* seems a bit too drastic, so let us change it to "*shamhu kusvika vadzoka*" [discipline until she returns]. She really has no interest in the *Chibarirwe* but followed her husband, which factor we must consider.'

Mutariri L: 'We must know when we *tonga* [judge] what it all amounts to. There is a difference between being forced to join another Church and just going there out of one's own free will. What do we do if Regina returns tomorrow? Do we just accept her and say that there is no *shamhu*, or what?'

Rev. B: 'She must get a specific *shamhu* to illustrate that the Church disagrees. She must be an example otherwise others take it lightly and think that they can go to other Churches and just be received back if they prefer to do so. We do this so that people should not *shovora* [make light of] the sacraments.'

Rangano decides: *Shamhu* until she returns. If she returns within a few days her *shamhu* is lifted at the next meeting of the Church council.

CASE 8. VISIT TO 'NGANGA' IN CONNECTION WITH WITCHCRAFT
Regina absent.

Mutariri M: 'A traditionalist [girl with no Church affiliation] fell ill and accused Regina [DRC member] of having bewitched her. In order to prove her innocence, Regina and two others went to a *nganga* to have him throw the *hakata*.'

Rev. B: 'The case is as follows: somebody fell ill and accused Regina of witchcraft. They quarrelled and Regina went to a *nganga*. Afterwards they went to Regina's father and a dispute ensued. The parents of the sick girl then refused to attend Church services although they are communicant members. They did not want to attend together with Regina, the witch.'

Mutariri M: 'We must find a proper way of judging this case because the village *dare* has failed to sort it out.'

Mutariri Mb: 'The sick girl became *penga* [mad] and made the accusation during her father's absence, which procedure is never allowed. I suggest that the matter be investigated.'

Mutariri J: 'Regina is guilty because she went to *shopera* [lit. divine]. In our Karanga custom there is always an accusation in cases of serious illness or death. The accused should not have paid attention to the accusation. The Church is also at fault. We do not tend to the sick regularly, and *we do not tell the people often enough that God allows illness – so they just go to the nganga.*'

Author questions: 'Who accompanied Regina? What did the *nganga* say? Was Regina's grandmother regarded as a witch?'

Mutariri answers: 'Regina went to the *nganga* with her uncle and the kraalheads of both villages. The *nganga* said: "It is untrue! You, Regina, are not a witch!" After this favourable verdict Regina returned to the village *dare* to proclaim her innocence. The sick girl was then accused of falsely charging Regina. The village members are not satisfied to leave the matter at that. I don't know if Regina's grandmother was a witch and it is impossible for me even to try to obtain such information.

The father of Regina refused to even attend the village *dare*, but Regina wanted to be fully cleared, so she took the initiative. It was then that the two families *pesana'd* [separated] and the sick girl's parents refused to attend Church services because they had failed to accept the *nganga's* verdict.'

Rev. B: 'Regina is guilty because she went to the *nganga* and her father is not guilty because he refused to take an active part in the whole affair.'

Rangano: 'We appoint a commission of three to investigate the matter and report at the next Church *dare*.'

CASE 9. ADULTERY
Sophia Shiri absent.

Mutariri K: 'Sophia became pregnant and then went to her boy's home, but he refused to marry her. She then came to me and asked me to report to her father that she had been refused. The father and I called a village *dare* and sent for the boy. He admitted that it was his child, but that he no longer wanted to marry the girl. He had to pay "damages". This therefore is a clear case of adultery.'

Rangano: 1 year *shamhu* for Sophia.

CASE 10. ADULTERY (*nhaka:* inherited wife)
Josias Chisi absent.

Mutariri Mb: 'Josias lived with the wife of his deceased younger brother. He is under Church discipline for this offence. The woman has now left him and he is busy negotiating to marry another woman. Josias has served his term; he will soon have one proper wife. The *shamhu* must be lifted.'

Rangano: 'Josia's *shamhu* is now officially lifted.'

CASE 11. ELOPEMENT MARRIAGE
Bettina Shoko absent.

Mutariri: 'Bettina went to stay with her boyfriend while the *roora* negotiations were still under way. She had gone out of her own free will. She had forced the pace [*kumanikidza*] of the arrangements. She is not pregnant yet.'

Rangano: 'This is *upombwe hwokuwanisa* [adultery with intent of marriage].' Bettina is served with 1 year *shamhu* + condition of proper marriage.

Meeting closed with prayer.

Supplement to the (RCC) burial rite *

1. THE SPRINKLING OF THE HOUSE AFTER THE BURIAL OF THE DECEASED

The priest stands at the door of the house, saying: The Lord be praised!

All: Forever.

Priest: Let us pray: Almighty God, please guard this house in which Your child, N, who was redeemed by Christ on the cross, lived. Shield it so that nothing may touch it. Let Your angels guard it so that no enemy may come within reach of it. Christ, our Lord, You delivered him, do now also present this our request to God the Father.

All: Amen.

Priest: Let us pray: Almighty God, who empowered water to bring forth a person anew, chase away every evil thing in this house with this holy water.

In the name of the Father . . . (sprinkling the house three times).

All: Amen.

Priest: comes out of the house, stands at the door incensing the house (burning incense), saying: We incense this house with holy incense so that every single destroyer wanting to enter it may be burnt in the eye and choke in the strong incense (smoke) of Christ, our Redeemer, in the name of the Father, the Son and the Holy Ghost.

All: Amen.

Then the priest enters the house and incenses it completely.

Leave-taking before departure

Priest stands at the door, faces the people, saying: Almighty God, Father, Son and Holy Ghost, descend on all these Your children, bless them and be with them forever!

* Translated from Chikaranga.

MAGADZIRO echiKRISTE (CHRISTIAN CEREMONIES FOR ACCOMODATING THE SPIRIT OF THE DECEASED)

2. PRESENTATION OF THE GRAIN

On the day the grain is presented [to the deceased] the priest prays the prayer [written] below. If the priest cannot attend, the prayer is offered by a relative of the deceased, one who is a believer. Now, when the grain has been prayed for in this manner, it must still be sanctified by the priest. If possible the priest must be at the house of the deceased the day the grain is produced. All the people in the house kneel, facing the pot-shelf [*rukuva*].

Priest: The Lord be praised.

All: Forever.

Priest: Give him eternal rest, Lord.

All: May holy light shine on him forever.

Priest: Let him rest in peace, in the grace of God.

All: Amen.

The relative of the deceased who offers this prayer kneels while pouring out the holy water and says: *Nhingi* [name of the deceased here inserted], if you have not yet reached Mwari, where your relatives and all the saints are; or if you are still in Purgatory, see this grain which we have produced, so that we may gather [call together] the people who intercede on your behalf before Christ, who has delivered you in order to call you to Himself in heaven, where all your relatives, the saints and the everlasting joy of heaven are.

N and N and N (mentioning the dead relatives): This is the grain with which we have gathered the people so that they may cause your child to reach Mwari, where you are. If he is not there yet, ask Christ, his Redeemer, to take him out of Purgatory and to place him in heaven.

Priest: God, our Father, Father of N, here is the grain which we have brought and with which we have gathered the people so that they may cause Your child to reach You. If You have not yet taken him, do receive him, please, abiding with him in eternal joy in heaven. Christ, our Lord, please present this our request to God the Father.

All: Amen.

Priest: I sprinkle this grain with appeasing water so that it may demonstrate the appeasement which we ask to be applied to you [addressing deceased] by the blood of Christ, Who died for you on the cross; in the name of the Father, the Son and the Holy Ghost (while pouring out the holy water).

All: Amen.

All the women ululate, saying: Let Christ be praised.

All the men clap hands, saying: Let Christ be praised.

Priest: Let his spirit and the spirits of the dead believers rest in peace.

All: Amen.

In the absence of a priest the relative offers all these prayers. If the grain has already been sanctified by the priest, he has only to pray the written prayer called: 'The prayer of the priest'.

3. BLESSING OF THE NGOMBE (COW OR OX)

The priest goes with the relatives to the cattle kraal. On seeing the cattle he says: May the Lord be praised.

All: Forever.

The relatives say [to deceased]: N, this is the beast we are killing on the day of interceding for you.

Priest: May they who eat it thank God for all His gifts to you. May they pray for you that eternal joy be your portion.

All: Amen.

Priest: I sprinkle this beast with the water of appeasement as a sign of the appeasement we ask to be bestowed on you by the blood of Christ; in the name of the Father, the Son and the Holy Ghost.

All: Amen.

The women ululate, the men clap, saying: Let Christ be praised.

In the absence of a priest, a relative of the deceased must officiate.

4. BLESSING OF THE BEER

The priest goes with the relative to where the beer is kept, to the *musumo* pot behind the door.

Priest: God be praised.

All: Forever.

Priest: Brother N, if you have not yet arrived at the place where God is, where your relatives are or the saints, this is the beer, with which we have gathered the people who will cause you to reach God, your relatives and the saints. Christ, our Lord, You died for Him, please open heaven to him.

All: Amen.

Priest: God, accept Your child, N, and live with him forever.

All: Amen.

Priest: Christ, You who died for him, please open heaven to receive him.

All: Amen.

Priest: I sprinkle this beer with the water of appeasement to show the renewing we beg you to be given by the blood of Christ Who redeemed you on the cross, i.e. if you are in Purgatory; in the name of the Father, the Son and the Holy Ghost.

All: Amen.

The women ululate, the men clap hands and all say: Let Christ be honoured. If the priest cannot attend, all the prayers must be said by a relative.

5. BLESSING OF THE GOAT (GRIEF FOR THE DEATH OF A PERSON)

A goat is made to stand at the doorstep of the house of deceased. The priest and relatives of the deceased stand behind the goat with the holy water and coals or ashes of the palm tree, which was sanctified on Palm Sunday.

Priest: God be praised.

All: Forever.

Priest: Let us pray: Our Lord Jesus Christ, it is You who saved N with Your blood which flowed on the cross. Take him now to live with You, that is, if he has not yet arrived. Let the blood of this goat be a sign of Your exoneration and deliverance of him from all his sins of fighting, of cruelty, of angry hatred and illwill towards his relatives or friends; in the name of the Father, the Son and the Holy Ghost (while he sprinkles the goat and coals with holy water).

All: Amen.

Relative (nobody else) rubs the coals on the throat of the goat, saying: Jesus our Saviour, please forgive N all his sins, especially his sins of anger. N, go now to your Lord, with a pure heart; in the name of the Father, the Son and the Holy Ghost. Amen.

6. GOING TO THE GRAVE

Very early in the morning (the priest having consecrated the beast and the beer the previous evening) the people gather at the house of the deceased.

Priest: Look, my relatives [brothers], we are gathered here to cause N to reach God and all the others belonging to him – that is, if he has not yet arrived in heaven. We do this in the way he chose while still alive.

Relative: It is you yourself and nobody else who said you wanted to follow Christ. Look, some of your fellow believers have come to pray for you, to help you to reach God and the others so that you also may rejoice with them if you have not yet arrived there. It is you who desired all this. Here are they who came.

Priest: Please give him eternal rest, Lord.

All: Let holy light enlighten him forever.

Priest: Let him rest in peace.

All: Amen.

Priest: Let us pray: Our Lord Jesus Christ, Saviour of all people, Saviour of N, look, we have gathered here to bring Your N to You Who saved him on the cross with Your precious blood. Here he is, take him now with You into eternal joy. Forgive him all his sins against You, that he may find eternal peace. You always judge in partnership with the Father and the Holy Ghost, forever. Amen.

7. THE ACCOMMODATING PRAYER USED DURING THE BURIAL RITE IS NOW SAID

8. THE PRIEST SPRINKLES THE GRAVE WITH HOLY WATER

He says: I sprinkle you with the water of appeasement so that you may be 'cooled off' by the blood of Christ in the name of the Father, the Son and the Holy Ghost.

All: Amen.

Then *the priest* burns incense on the grave, saying: I incense you with heavenly incense (smoke). May its smell drive away your enemies and the evil spirits; in the name of the Father, the Son and the Holy Ghost.

9. HOLY MASS

There on the grave the priest performs the Mass and preaches. After the Mass everybody goes home singing holy hymns. Arriving at the house of the deceased, the priest says: May his spirit and the spirits of all the dead believers rest in the peace and the grace of God.

10. INHERITANCE

a) The day before the inheritance [is discussed] *the sister's son* [*muzukuru*] sprinkles the heir, i.e. the one who inherits the name of the deceased, with holy water, saying: You are N [mentioning the hereditary name]. May God guard you always. You, N, guard this one who has been given your name, that he may have a family well pleasing to God, a family that will not disappear but go on and on – in the name of the Father, the Son and the Holy Ghost.

b) At a little brook: The *muzukuru* washes the inheritor of the name, saying: May this water with which I am washing you be a sign of the baptismal water washing away your sin.

c) He gives him sticks (*tsvimbo*), saying: May these sticks be symbolical of the stick of the Cross with which you fight Satan.

d) The *inheritor* of the name sits on a sleeping-mat while the *muzukuru* says: Today, see, you are N, you are his avenger, may God guard you! And you, N, keep this child of ours, he has taken your name, be his intercessor before God; in the name of the Father . . . (sprinkling water over the name-bearer). Rejoicing, etc.

The inheritance

The woman and the man who seem likely to accept each other as part of the inheritance (i.e. the man who inherits the wife of deceased) must tell the priest privately how it should be arranged for them so that he can find them the solution to the law forbidding a man to take the wife of his brother.

Crossing the bow

The woman crosses the bow, having first said: In the name of God I jump over this bow to prove that I have not 'burnt my husband's grave' [committed adultery].

Then she jumps and says: In the name of the Father (jump), the Son (jump) and the Holy Spirit (jump).

The women ululate and the men clap hands.

Now follows the rite of the inheritance:

Priest: We rely on the Lord.

All: Who created heaven and earth.

Priest: Let us pray: Our Lord Jesus Christ, our Saviour, we ask that everything we do here may be in accordance with Your laws and pleasing to You, honouring You. Do not let anyone be compelled to act against his will or contrary to Your wishes. You are the eternal judge, together with the Father and in co-operation with the Holy Ghost, Amen.

Paternal aunt of the woman: This water shows what things you regard as helpful, to keep you alive, to relieve you and to enable you to please God.

Woman: I believe God.

The women shout and rejoice while the men clap their hands.

Woman: God, my Lord, please help me, so that this step I am taking here may also be pleasing to You.

Sendeka uta ('to place the bow against something' – acceptance of the inheritance):

Priest: May the Lord be honoured.

All: Forever.

Heir: With this beer I prove to You, my God, and to you, N, that I have become the guardian of your wife and of everything relating to your family. Keep on being our intercessor before God that He may shield us from all spiritual and physical danger. Christ our Lord, do teach us to carry our cross always so that we too may have eternal life.

Priest: I sprinkle this beer with the water of appeasement that we may illustrate the appeasement which we ask for you through the blood of Christ, Who redeemed you on the cross; in the name of the Father, the Son and the Holy Ghost.

The women ululate, the men clap their hands, saying: Christ be praised.

In conclusion (to the 'day of the grave' or the 'day of inheritance'):

Relative of deceased: Beloved relatives, see we have reached the end of our task. We thank God that everything went well. Let us now pray the final prayer: ... In the name of the Father ... God, our Lord, thank You for keeping us everywhere You worked today. Now, do accompany us right up to our homes. Mercifully guard the household of N, which he left here, and shield it from all trouble. spiritually and physically. Christ our Lord, please present this our request to God, the Father. Let the spirit of N and the spirits of all deceased believers rest in peace and in the mercy of God.

Thanksgiving hymn follows.

Excerpts from Mutendi's ZCC-'Rungano' on the growth of his Church in relation to Government (conflict and recognition), tribal authorities and DRC missionaries *

Chapter 17
1. A spirit of fear came over the elders [*vakuru*] of the country and they said, 'His [Mutendi's] preaching and prophecies arouse the *zvitebwe* [from *chitebwe*: maneless lion into which an avenging spirit has entered] at night, which then eats our cattle.'

2. But these matters only served to give him [Mutendi] more power.

Chapter 19 (Sub-title: *Enquiries about the source of Mutendi's powers*)
2. In those days of the signs [reference is here made to the performance of healing miracles and the raising of the dead girl at Rukuni, as described in the preceding chapters of the *Rungano*] the DRC ministers were still wondering what was happening there [at Mutendi's village]. So they called a meeting at Pamushana Mission. They congregated to determine whether he [M] had received permission to preach and to enquire into his healing activities.

3. The meeting decided to send a representative to find out where this power [or authority] which enabled him to do all these things came from. Then Rev. Orlandini was sent because he was a stern man and they reasoned that he would make enquiries in a harsh way which would intimidate him [M].

4. When that minister drove off in his car a strange thing happened because the car 'died' on the road and it had to be taken back. He then took a bicycle but once more it was of no avail because the bicycle broke down before he could reach [Mutendi's village], with the result that he had to turn back.

5. The missionaries then decided to send Rev. Louw, the son of 'the owner of the Church' [the founder of the DRC mission in Mashonaland] whom we call grandfather [*sekuru*]. They said, 'He will go and speak in a gentle manner.' Rev. Louw was afraid that if he travelled by car or bicycle it would break down again, so he travelled on foot, taking a muKaranga, Johannes Muchengeti, with him.

Chapter 20
1. He found Samuel working in the fields. The minister [*muneri*] enquired, 'Is it true that you have your own Church and that you baptize people in a river?' Samuel replied, 'Yes, I am doing as you have heard.' *Muneri* asked, 'Where do you get

* Translated from Chikaranga.

the power [*simba*] to do these things? Have you got a "registration certificate" [*chitupa*]?' Samuel retorted, 'How is it that *muneri* has today changed from being a minister to being a policeman? Have you become a policeman, *muneri*?' *Muneri* said, 'Has a bad spirit entered you? Why do you question me in such manner?' Samuel replied, 'Will I fear today when I hear that I have a bad spirit as if I am the first person to have a bad spirit? Did not the believers of old also hear that they had bad spirits? For that reason it [your question] does not hurt me at all.'

2. *Muneri* said, 'Do you want to compare yourself with the believers of old? Did they pretend to be like Jesus? Or is it that you yourself are Jesus? If both of us see that the child resembles the father, will he [the child] pretend to be the father? Cannot a child resemble his father and yet remain a child?'

3. They left the fields and went to his house to see the preaching certificates he had brought with him from Johannesburg. After he [Rev. Louw] had seen them he said to himself, 'This man has a task, let us leave him undisturbed; let us leave him at it.'

4. This is the same kind of event as is described in Mark 11 : 27 where it says: 'And they came again to Jerusalem. And when Jesus was walking about in the temple the chief priests and the scribes and the elders came to Him, and said to Him, 'By what authority are You doing these things?' Jesus told them, 'I will ask you a question. Answer Me and then I will tell you by what sort of authority I do these things. Was the baptism of John from heaven or from men?'

To this event we liken Mutendi's experiences when they ask him where his authority comes from and when they ask for his preaching certificates [*zvitupa zvokuparidza*].

Chapter 21 (Sub-title: *Troubles*)

1. In those days of the missionaries [1924], troubles arose, because the elders and chiefs of the country reported Samuel Mutendi at the [NC's] office, saying that this man had spoilt [*kunyangadza*] the country. He takes our children and 'plunges them into the rivers' and all his followers eat our cattle at night in the form of *zvitebwe* [spirit-possessed lions].

2. On account of these matters the authorities arrested him and forbade him to preach in the name of that Church, the Zion Apostolic Faith Mission. But it was a surprising matter because whenever he came out of detention he resumed his preaching.

3. This man was repeatedly arrested because of his wish to preach. He continually stayed at the 'mouth of the jail' but he never remained there very long nor did he stop preaching.

4. (Sub-title: *The miracle of the locusts in jail*)

One day he was arrested, he and Masuka together. They were kept in jail for a long time.

5. While they were in jail a swarm of locusts came and ravished [the crops]. The commissioner said, 'Let Mutendi, who professes to worship Mwari, together with his followers, come out, and let them pray for the removal of these locusts,

which will reveal to us whether they worship the true God.' Samuel emerged, took his staff and prayed, pointing the staff at heaven. All the locusts were driven back by a strong wind which arose.

6. All those present were greatly surprised at the sight of God's power. As a result the Commissioner, who was equally surprised, said, 'You are now free; go and worship your God at your village; but do not travel and preach from one village to another!' So they were freed with great joy, praising God and saying, 'God performs His work in His own Church only.'

Chapter 22 (Sub-title: *The Chiefs totally refuse to recognize Mutendi*)
1. After he [M] had been released for a few days only, the chiefs again went to the office and complained that the Commissioner had 'reinstated' the man who had spoilt the country, while it was their wish that he should remain in jail until he had renounced [his Church work]. Many chiefs refused to acknowledge him and some went to the office to state that they did not want this man in their *nyika.* They said, 'Let him return to the place where he came across this Church.' Those who wanted him removed were Goto, Madzivanyika and Gumunyu. They said, 'This man causes much trouble. Our chiefdoms are spoilt by him, so that it will be better if he leaves us. Let him return to Johannesburg where he found his Church!'

2. The Commissioner also consented and picked up his pen to cross out Mutendi's name so that he could return from where he had come with his Church. Then Goto stood up and said, 'Sir, we cannot drive this "child of ours" away, because we have fetched him from Chipinda where he was living. It is our child whom we have fetched to stay with us. How can we now drive him away?' The Commissioner asked, 'Is this your child?' All replied, 'Yes, *Mambo*!' The Commissioner said, '*Buratifuru demiyo*!' [bloody fools, damn you!] go away!' So all of them returned to their villages, taking their child with them.

Chapter 23 (Sub-title: *Visit to Salisbury*)
1. Soon after he had returned to his village, he was summoned to the office to receive the preaching certificates which had been sent from Johannesburg by his fellow minister, Enginasi Lekhanyane.

2. After receiving the certificates he decided to go to Harare [Salisbury] to ask permission for his Church from the Government. He was accompanied by Jacobo. But when he saw that the money was not enough for both of them, he left Jacobo at Chatsworth and proceeded alone.

3. Having arrived at Harare he went alone to the office. When the official saw him in the office he asked, 'Are you the one who was nearly chased from this country?' He replied, 'Yes, sir.' His lordship [the Chief Native Commissioner] said, 'If a person had gone to work at Selukwe will he not, on his return, tell his relatives what he had seen?' He said, 'You may go, I will send your *tsamba* [possibly letter of recognition] to the Commissioner of your district.'

4. Mutendi returned by way of Fort Victoria, where he met the Commissioner of Bikita who had meanwhile been transferred. It was prophesied before he left his home that Commissioner Mangwaya would be transferred.

5. The Commissioner told him to proceed to Bikita, where he waited till *Ishe* Maponese [new NC of Bikita] arrived. Since he was not yet familiar with the circumstances of the new district he told Mutendi to go and preach at his village and baptize only those who were willing. So he returned to preach and baptize.

Chapter 26 (Sub-section: *The arrest of Samuel*)

6. When he arrived home [after his visit to the Transvaal in 1925-6 when he and Lekhanyane founded the ZCC] he found trouble awaiting him. The people accused him of having taken the children of others to South Africa. The parents of those who had accompanied him reported him at the office, saying, 'Our children were "stolen" by that man whom we have requested to be driven off; he had taken our children with him to Johannesburg.'

7. They simply said on his arrival, 'There he is, he has returned, put him in jail because we don't want to see him any longer!' The night before he went to the office he dreamt that the sun was approaching him, until he cried out in a loud voice, 'Yowee, I am burning!' A voice replied, 'This is the sign that you will be arrested tomorrow, without anything being proved against you.' He arose, greatly alarmed. In the morning he was arrested and taken to the office but they could not find him guilty of any offence. Thus the court dismissed the matter and permitted him to return. He then returned to his village.

Chapter 27

4. Thus the expansion of the Church became an established fact, but the Government did not know how the Church could develop in such a way, that, for instance, its members were found in Gutu. There, at Gutu, very many believers were to be found and a Church for Sunday services had been built. They continued in this way for a long time, but when trouble arose they used to worship in the mountains.

5. (*The arrest of Rev. Samuel Mutendi*)
In those days the inspector of schools passed through Gutu. When he reached the place where they [the Zionists] worshipped, he said to them, 'Where have you obtained permission to build schools?' They replied, 'Our leader at Bikita has sent us to do all this.'

6. This inspector's name was Mather. So he said, 'I will call your leader and have him arrested because you are not allowed to build Churches without permission from Salisbury.'

7. When the elders of that district heard what had happened they said, '*Toko waro*! [i.e. he deserved it] because our children were led astray by this man who led them into the mountains.' So you [M] can now stop bothering the children who were living in the mountains.

8. Mather went to Rev. Samuel Mutendi and asked him, 'Why do your followers take the children to the mountains? Who allowed you to build Churches in other districts?' So he was summoned to come to the court at Fort Victoria where he could tell them who had allowed him to do such things.

Chapter 29

1. He took some of the elders with him to Fort Victoria. When they arrived they entered the court to be judged. When those who were with [Mutendi] saw that it was indeed a 'heavy' and serious matter, they feared greatly. They all deserted him and said, 'We do not know this man.' Johannes Shoko [as the highest ranking sub-leader of the ZCC] who was present said, 'I come from Bedi mine where I have a job; I do not know this man. We have just met.'

7. But the European, Chari, who knew him [M] and who had seen him at Vunjere [in the Gutu district] witnessed in his favour and said, 'Don't do this! I know the work of this man.' Because of this witness, he [M] 'survived'. Within the ranks of both the Europeans and the Africans there were those who greatly feared because of what they had seen that day.

Chapter 30

1. The next day a great number of people gathered. They came running to see the man who had performed such [great] things.

2. On that day many people heard a sermon on the greatness of God. Many people were also converted on that day when they saw the big deeds of God being done through the hands of Rev. Samuel Mutendi.

3. The Europeans were astounded, so that one of them said, 'You are a minister of truth. Don't you want us to find you some garments for the ministry? We will order you some very nice things from England, which you can wear and which will become you.' But he refused, saying, 'I cannot accept other garments from you because these are the ones we wear. They are similar to those worn by one of my ministers in Johannesburg.' So he refused and they left him alone.

Chapter 32

7. He was called once more to the court where he was accused of taking the children of other people into the mountains for prayer and of building a 'Church' [school] without the permission of the Government.

8. He was sentenced to one month and three weeks imprisonment. He stayed in jail a long time, until some of the members of the Church decided to help him.

9. They called a meeting and said, 'Let us help our minister who is in jail, by freeing him with money.' The believers then contributed with 'one heart'; they collected money and went to free him, and he was free.

Chapter 33. Journey to Salisbury.

1. When he came out of prison he decided to go to Salisbury to ask permission to conduct services in public.

2. He [accompanied by some of his followers] went to Salisbury on foot, travelling at night when the leopards roar. They kept walking without rest.

3. They met with great hardships because they did not want to rest a single day.

5. ... When they arrived they began by seeing the sergeant. The sergeant said, 'If you want Zionism again you will have to spend three years in prison!'

6. Because God wanted the case to be brought out into the open He encouraged Mutendi to speak to the 'chief' [the Chief Native Commissioner]. The Commissioner said, 'We won't even allow you to preach once!' When he heard this he left the office with great sorrow in his eyes.

Chapter 34. Return from Salisbury

1. He returned without joy, but his heart simply said, 'We will not stop doing the work of God.' It was God who inspired him like that because nobody was so brave under such circumstances.

2. They walked and came across the same hardships in the bush, as before ...

3. When he reached home, a great number of followers gathered, saying, 'We are going to hear what has passed at Salisbury, and whether we are allowed to worship in public like others.'

4. But others, who were sceptical of the truth, said, 'Let us say that we have been permitted, because if we say that we have been refused the people will be too frightened to worship with us.'

5. He [M] said, 'We won't remain silent until the name of Zion is officially recognized.' They were strengthened, reading from Isaiah 62 : 1: 'Because of Zion I will not remain silent, because of Jerusalem I will not rest until His justice appears in a glow and His redemption like a burning torch.'

6. So in those days he said that they had been officially recognized, but they had to worship secretly. In this way he encouraged the people not to backslide because at that time the people greatly feared to be arrested. They worshipped secretly because they were afraid of the policemen who were sent out to report on Zionist activities, so that they could be arrested.

7. The Church was hated by all the Europeans and Africans and everybody else; those who could hardly think or speak used to say, 'We are troubled by the Zionists.'

Chapter 35. The misfortunes of the Zionists

1. The prejudice against the Zionists became very strong. Therefore they used to say, 'When we go to worship we walk facing backwards in order to evade those who try to find us'. The women were not allowed to wear white headdresses, or other white garments, to avoid detection.

2. They suffered greatly, holding their services in caves, in the bush and in the maize fields when the maize had grown tall. They carried their hoes when they went to pray so as to give the impression that they were going to the fields [to work].

3. Otherwise they went separately and met at a specified place. But hardly a

day passed without someone being arrested, until they no longer feared the policemen, because, as they said, 'We are going to the fields,' meaning: the Office.

4. One day Johannes Shoko asked a policeman, 'Why do you keep troubling us by arresting us day after day and each time releasing us again? Today you will be put to shame again by observing us return.'

5. The policeman replied, 'We know that Mutendi wears his beret when he goes to the office. When he is cross-examined he just touches it a few times, which renders the police incapable of arriving at a solution in connection with this man. That is why the people proudly say, 'We will not be detained long.'

6. Once, when he was arrested, he left his beret and went with his staff only. So they [the police] decided to take away the Zionists' staves – also that of Rev. Samuel Mutendi.

7. Rev. Mutendi threw down his staff in the office yard together with those of the others. The police gathered all the staves of the others but Mutendi's remained lying there. None of the people present could see it except the Zionists.

8. They said, 'Today we have overpowered him by taking away this staff', but he picked up his staff and went away.

11. ... One year, when they went to Johannesburg, they arrived at Messina and found the road blocked by policemen. Rev. Mutendi pointed his staff at the police, after which they were allowed to pass without interference. They continued their journey, praising Mwari.

Chapter 36. The journey to the Transvaal

1. In 1937 they went with buses to the Transvaal to call in Lekhanyane's assistance with the organization of their Church here in Rhodesia which had caused so much trouble. These two men [Mutendi and Lekhanyane] were doing the work of God together, with love and in truth.

2. When he [Lekhanyane] was requested to come with his followers to Rhodesia, an enemy penetrated the inner circle with the result that Lekhanyane was not permitted by that Government [of South Africa] to come here.

3. The people advised him [Mutendi] to consult a lawyer on these matters. In the flesh he was alone but in spirit they [M and L] were one.

4. A lawyer by the name of Bouchet, who practised in Fort Victoria, was consulted and did his best to help this man to gain official recognition for the Zion Christian Church.

5. Thus they eventually [1937] received official permission to worship in public. The condition was that they should not preach everywhere, but confine their activities to their own wards [*matunhu*]. But they refused and continued [expanding their activities] little by little until they were allowed to preach wherever they wished.

6. The word of God then progressed without too much trouble.

Chapter 38. Expansion of the work [the chiefs change their mind]
2. The prophets now declared: 'Your enemies will become members of your family'. The chiefs who had opposed him became his 'relatives' because, whenever there were droughts, the chiefs requested rain from Mutendi.

3. One day, during a dry year, Chief Marozva requested rain. Mutendi told him to return home where he would find the rain falling. Disbelieving, Marozva returned, but soon after his departure it started raining so that he had to travel in the rain, praising Mwari.

7. . . . The minister [M] said he wanted to go to Chief Chingombe where he wanted to preach God's word. When he arrived in Chingombe he noticed that the chief was expecting him. The chief took him to his fields to show him how his crops had been parched by the sun. Chief Chingombe said to Rev. Samuel Mutendi, 'Do you see that all my grain is burnt by the sun? What will I and my people eat?' So he asked for rain. The minister said, 'Let us pray together for the rain to fall here!' Both of them prayed on the spot and the rain started falling. All the people praised Mwari with one heart.

Chapter 42. The opening of the newly built Church in Jerusalem
8. . . . When the Church was completed arrangements were made for an opening ceremony, but it was a troublesome matter because the NC, Gandazhara, ['Dry skin'] had left and was succeeded by someone who did not know this Church. The Church's opening was therefore stopped by the Europeans. They refused permission.

Chapter 43
1. In 1951 Mwari performed a great work which led to the opening of the Church. Daramu was the NC at that time.

2. The Church meeting was held in July of that year. Many people gathered for the occasion. Our Rozvi chief, Gopo, was also present and he opened the Church.

7. On that day the people greatly rejoiced, saying, 'Today we enter our Church in public [*pachena* – in the open].' But those who had started the Church and had encountered all the trouble mentioned, wept at the remembrance of their suffering while they were worshipping in the mountains.

8. When the people had entered the Church building and many were left outside because there was not sufficient space inside, Chief Gopo opened the ceremony with a sermon.

9. He preached forcefully, praising the *mufundisi* [M] who had persevered in the face of all the affliction up to that day . . .

10. He said to the Zionists, 'Today you may enter your Church with joy and worship your God publicly.'

13. A DRC teacher who had strongly opposed Mutendi's work and who had accompanied Rev. Louw Jr. when the latter visited Mutendi, also preached: 'I

did not know that this man would persevere courageously up to this day because at first I laughed at him. Today I am greatly surprised at this man at whom I laughed . . .'

Chapter 44

3. After the others had spoken, the 'owner of the job' – Rev. Samuel Mutendi, the Bishop – stood up. He described all the hardships he had to endure in order to achieve recognition for this Church.

4. He also stated that he had prepared the way for all the Vakaranga to preach the word without fear; because this was the first Church of the Africans in the country. He said, 'This is the first African Church with all-African leadership, which is based on the word of God.'

5. He said that this did not mean that his followers were the first truly African Christians, for the Africans were already Christians when they attended the European Churches,

6. – those [Mission Churches] to whom we are grateful up to this day, for although we are Africans, they supported us. But now the grace of God was found amongst us Africans so that we can do the work of God on our own [*pachedu poga*] –

7. Rev. S. Mutendi said, 'I believe the work I am doing does not please those who did not send me, but He who has sent me is greatly pleased.' As for the contempt of others, this Church is merely *Jikinya ra Marumbi* – [the laughing-stock of the Europeans]. It is easy to blame somebody – everybody can do so. Only the chosen ones give praise [to this Church].'

8. He said, 'I thank God who gave me the strength for this work of founding His Church among the Africans.'

Chapter 47

6. If we refer to the African Church we mean the Zionist Church, because that is the only one you will find here in Rhodesia with the new foundation of Zion. There is no other way [than this, the ZCC] in which the Zionist Church came to this country. We don't hear of anybody else who had suffered and suffered continually on behalf of this African Zionist Church. Even David Masuka in that period of hardship did not have his own Church but pretended to be one with Mutendi until all the troubles had passed. Afterwards he started working on his own.

7. In the difficult days they [Mutendi and David] co-operated as Aaron and Moses did when they were sent to Egypt. In the old days David likewise assisted Samuel.

When the Church was recognized it seemed as if they were divided, but it was a partition of sorts – not a complete separation.

Mutendi's diagrammatic representation of Christianity

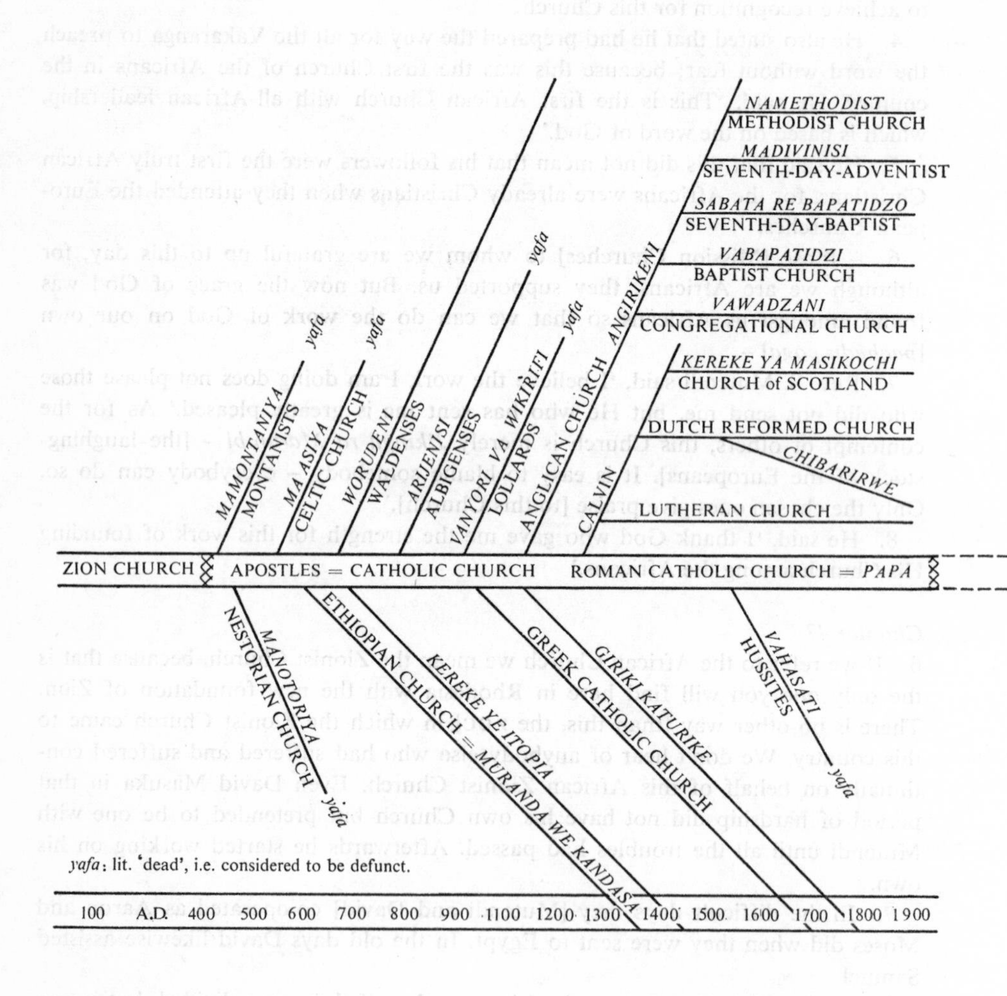

yafa: lit. 'dead', i.e. considered to be defunct.

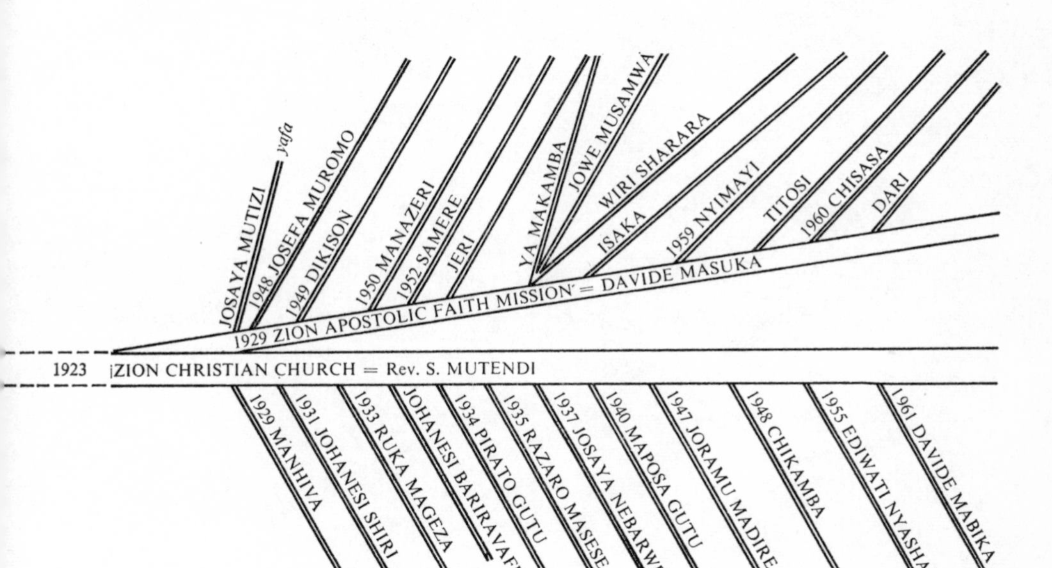
1923 ZION CHRISTIAN CHURCH = Rev. S. MUTENDI
1929 ZION APOSTOLIC FAITH MISSION = DAVIDE MASUKA
JOSAYA MUTIZI
yafa
1948 JOSEFA MUROMO
1949 DIKISON
1950 MANAZERI
1952 SAMERE
JERI
YA MAKAMBA
JOWE MUSAMWA
WIRI SHARARA
ISAKA
1959 NYIMAYI
TITOSI
1960 CHISASA
DARI
1929 MANHIVA
yafa
1931 JOHANESI SHIRI
yafa
1933 RUKA MAGEZA
JOHANESI BARIRAVAFUMI pamuti usinazita
1934 PIRATO GUTU
yafa
1935 RAZARO MASESE
yafa
1937 JOSAYA NEBARWE
yafa
1940 MAPOSA GUTU
yafa
1947 JORAMU MADIRE
1948 CHIKAMBA
1955 EDIWATI NYASHANU
yafa
1961 DAVIDE MABIKA

Examples of the 'papers' and credentials of Independent Church leaders

On opposite page from left to right and top to bottom

34. Bishop Gavure's 'Church papers'.

a) Permission to conduct Church meeting, by Chief Nhema.
b) Letter or 'pass' constituting official recognition by local Native Commissioner.
c) Native Commissioner's permission for a local Church meeting.
d) Bishop Gavure's ministerial credentials.

a, b

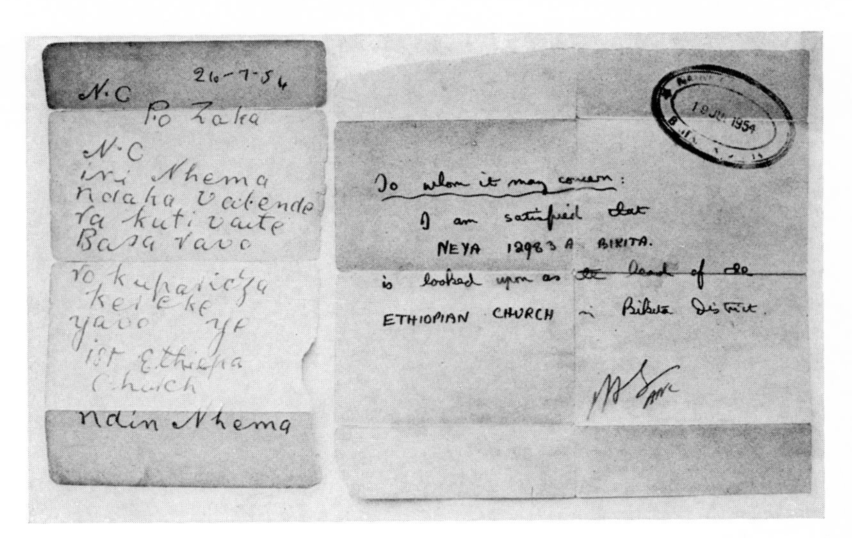

N.C 26-7-54
P.O Zaka
N.C
iri Nhema
ndaka vakende
va kutivate
Basa vavo
vo kuparidza
kereke
yavo ye
1st Ethiopia
Church
Ndin Nhema

1 JUL 1954

To whom it may concern:
I am satisfied that
NEYA 12983 A BIKITA.
is looked upon as the head of the
ETHIOPIAN CHURCH in Bikita District.

c

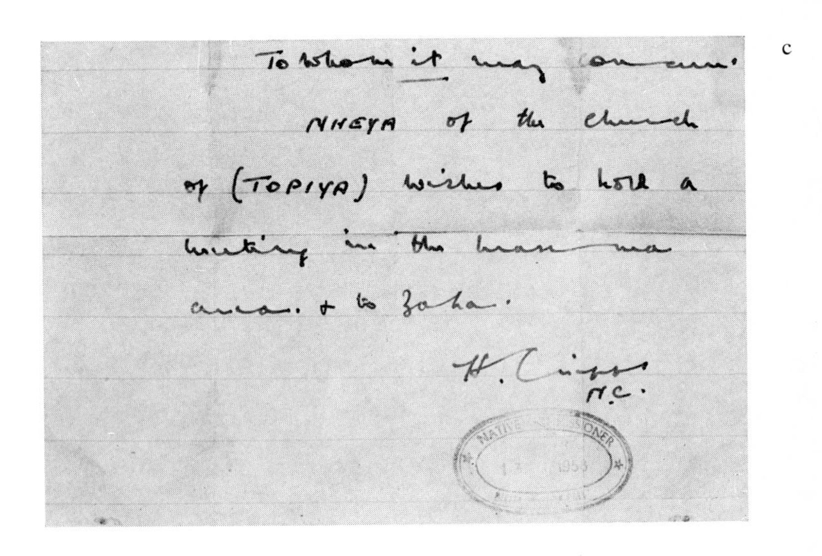

To whom it may concern.
NHEYA of the church
of (TOPIYA) wishes to hold a
meeting in the [illegible]
area. + to Zaka.

H. Cripps
N.C.

NATIVE COMMISSIONER
1953

d

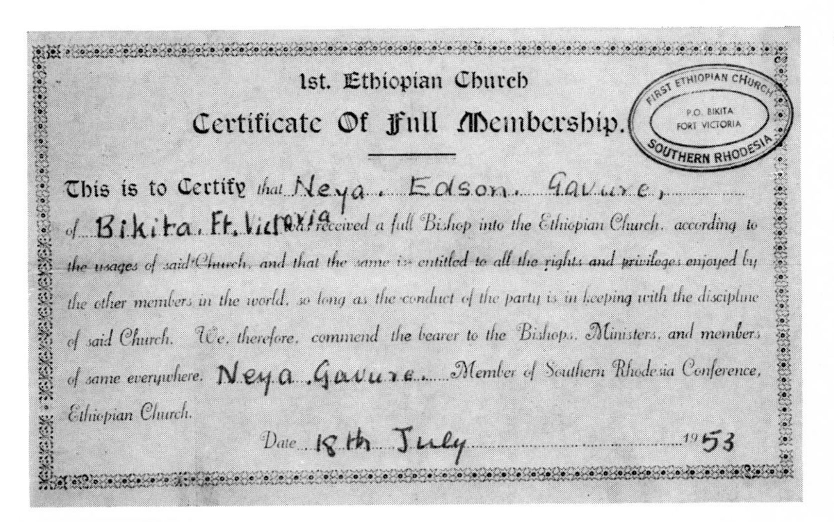

1st. Ethiopian Church

Certificate Of Full Membership.

FIRST ETHIOPIAN CHURCH
P.O. BIKITA
FORT VICTORIA
SOUTHERN RHODESIA

This is to Certify that Neya Edson Gavure, of Bikita, Ft. Victoria was received a full Bishop into the Ethiopian Church, according to the usages of said Church, and that the same is entitled to all the rights and privileges enjoyed by the other members in the world, so long as the conduct of the party is in keeping with the discipline of said Church. We, therefore, commend the bearer to the Bishops, Ministers, and members of same everywhere. Neya Gavure Member of Southern Rhodesia Conference, Ethiopian Church.

Date 18th July 1953

SIO APOStolic church of South Africa

Built upon the
oundation of the
postles and
rophets, Christ
imself being
e chief cornerstone
phesian 2: 19-22

SIONAPOSTORICHARICH OF SOATHAFRCA

Heb 13-8

Jesus christ the same yester
and to day and for ever
Hebrew, 13 - 8

Ministerial Credentian

his is to certify that the Bearer Willie Charehwa
Chiduku Reserve Dist Rusapi has been ordained
as to the Office of Minister Apointee.

He has Aithority

To preach the Gospel of Jesus christ. Mark 16-15
To pray for the sick with laying on hands. Mark 16-18
o bury the dead. 1 Corinthian 15
Headquatters Address P.O. Box 4870.
Johannesburg

To Consecrate Children, Mark 10-1
To Baptize believers, Matthew 28-1
To Administe The Lord Super
1 cor 11- 23-30 John 2-1-2

3-4-1933

Minister in Charge
Rev. DAVIDA
Mutto Gezewa wolo

35. The 'imitated' credentials of Willi Charewa.

Independent Church constitutions

1. CONSTITUTION OF THE ZION CHRISTIAN CHURCH*

Be it hereby known that whereas the Zion Church (hereafter referred to as the Church) was founded in Rhodesia in the year 1924;

Whereas, owing to the increase in membership and the growth of activities and ministrations, it has been found necessary to draw up a constitution of the Church; and whereas it is desirable to consolidate all laws, rules and regulations governing and appertaining to the Church;

Now, therefore, the undersigned, representing all the ecclesiastical officers and members of the congregations set opposite our names, do hereby resolve and agree that the following shall be the constitution of the Church: –

NAME AND HEADQUARTERS

The name of the Church shall be the Zion Christian Church.
Its headquarters shall be at Bikita.

EXECUTIVE

Life Senior Elder Founder:
Samuel Mutendi, Director Superintendent.

THE SONS OF THE FOUNDER

Upon the death or retirement of the Founder, one of his sons will be elected to Senior Eldership. The Church will choose one with exemplary character to be the Bishop in place of his father. The sons are 23 in number.

MINISTERS

Johannes Shoko, Aroni Makusha, Samson Gutu, Isaka Moyo, Jositos Makore, Razorosi Chilimanzi, Josaya Buhera, Jakopo Muroyi, Pirosi Mapanzure, Elias Chibi, Pauls Makombe, Anania Nyamhonda.

EVANGELISTS

Pitros Shava, Finias Moyo, Peter Moyo, Ezekia Betta, Shadrick Mazinhu, Moro-

* Changes were made in the original English text to correct language mistakes only.

dikai Shoko, David Sithole, Pauls Shoko, Simon Mepo, Pianos Shoko, Ezekia Masarire.

ANNUAL CONFERENCE

Conference shall be held annually upon a fixed date.

CONSTITUTION

The Conference shall consist of:

a) All Ordained Ministers;

b) All Lay Preachers;

c) Two delegates to be elected from the Officers of the Church by each congregation of not less than 25 persons.

LAY STANDING COMMITTEE

The Lay Standing Committee shall consist of the General Secretary and not less than four (4) Class Leaders. It shall deal with all matters of the Church which do not fall within the province of the Ecclesiastical Committee or Finance Committee.

BUSINESS COMMITTEE

Each of the aforesaid Committees shall appoint a Secretary, to whom all communications regarding the respective Committees shall be addressed. The Committees shall keep proper records of all matters submitted to them and of their findings therein, and shall in due course report all such matters at the Annual Conference.

CONTROL OF COMMITTEES

Each of the said Committees shall have full control of matters submitted to them respectively and their decisions shall be binding upon all parties; but so that any person or persons feeling aggrieved by the finding of any Committee may appeal to the Conference for its reconsideration of such decisions, and the action of the Conference herein shall be final and binding upon any member and adherent of the Church.

CLASS LEADERS

Any Ordained Minister shall have the right to appoint one or more members of the Church to be leader of Church classes in the congregation under his charge.

It shall not be necessary for Conference to confirm the appointment of such Class Leaders unless the majority of members of such congregation shall object to such appointment.

FUNDS

The funds of the Church shall be raised by its members, and otherwise as may be determined by Conference, and all moneys received shall be paid over to the

General Secretary at the Church. He shall be bound and obliged to pay the same into an account in Barclays Bank D.C.O. in Salisbury or such other bank as Conference may approve of, in the name of the 'Zion Christian Church.' All payments to be made on behalf of the Church shall be made by means of cheques drawn on this account.

The Chairman of the Finance Committee and the General Secretary of the Church are authorized to operate this account.

TRUSTEES

The Annual Conference shall elect not less than three (3) nor more than five (5) of its members to be the Trustees of the Church, and all the Church property shall be held by these Trustees, and, in the case of immovable property, shall be registered in the names of such Trustees.

The Trustees shall hold the said property for the said Church upon condition that only Ordained Ministers or Lay Preachers appointed by Conference shall hold service therein.

They shall further deal with such property in such manner as they may be directed by the members of the quarterly meeting of the congregation within whose area the property is situated; and so that the property shall remain in all cases in the hands of the Church, and not of any particular congregation.

ACTIONS

All actions instituted either on behalf of the Church or against it shall be brought in the name of or against the General Secretary in his capacity as such, and the General Secretary shall be authorized by a joint resolution of the Lay and Finance Committees to institute or defend any such action.

DENOMINATION

Our aim is to organize a denomination for the spread of the word of God and the Gospel of our Lord Jesus Christ in the world, since the above pillars have seen and still see with deepest Christian anxiety, the deplorable spiritual and mental condition of our people who inhabit the colonies of the world, which the word of God declares shall be lighted up with the glorious rays of the sun of righteousness. We further remember with deep emotion the last command of our ascending Lord: 'Go ye into the world and preach the Gospel to all nations', and desiring to show our love by our obedience, we resolve to constitute ourselves into a distinct denomination with various colonies to have and enjoy the free use and benefit of all premises acquired on behalf of the said congregation for rendering effectual the tasks created by purchase of ground, gifts, donations, legacies, bequests or trusts made to or in favour of the said people who are members of the said denomination or those who have come under the jurisdiction of this denomination without distinction of race and colour.

BASIS

The Church shall be designated Zion, City of the living God, Heavenly Jerusalem, innumerable company of angels; general assembly and Church of all (Heb. 12: 12-23) and is built upon the foundations of the apostles and prophets, Jesus Christ Himself being the chief cornerstone (Ephesians 2: 10).

ORDER OF PRAYER

We adopt the Common Prayers as the Apostles used when the Holy Ghost within constraineth, or healing order to lay hands on the sick and pray: 'Ye are the children of the Lord Your God, ye shall not cut yourselves nor make any baldness between your eye for the dead.' (Deut. 14 : 1).

Is any person sick among you? Let him call for the elders of the Church and let them pray over him, anointing him with oil in the name of the Lord (James 5 : 14).

DUTIES OF JUNIOR AND SENIOR ELDER

The President shall preside over all conventions which are summoned and have power in the Church over all Ministers. Subject to an appeal to the annual Conference, he will sign all documents and labour assiduously for the promotion of the Church. He will guard the spirit of the Church constitution to be observed. He will, in conjunction with presiding Ministers and full Ministers, ordain candidates selected and presented to him for ordination while the annual Conference is in session. He will have the power to remove, suspend or change Ministers after investigation by a committee composed of not less than three members of Ministers and Missionaries. In the absence of the Bishop, the Senior Elder, the annual Conference may select a Chairman among the presiding sons of the Founder. Should a vacancy occur during the interval of the Conference, the Executive Church Council will fill it until the annual Conference is held.

DUTIES OF MINISTERS

Ministers are ordained and have authority to preach the Gospel of Jesus Christ (Matt. 28: 19-20) to lay hands on and pray for the sick (Mark 16: 17-18; James 5: 13-15), to consecrate children (Mark 10: 17-18), to baptize believers, and to bury the dead (1 Cor. 15; Rev. 14-15).

DUTIES OF DEACONS

They have authority to preach the Gospel of Jesus Christ (Matt. 28: 19-20), to lay hands on and pray for the sick (Mark 16: 17-18; James 5: 13-15), to bury the dead (1 Cor. 15; Rev. 14:13). Jesus Christ said: 'Ye shall receive power, after that the Holy Ghost is come upon you, ye shall be my witness unto the uttermost parts of the earth' (Acts 1 : 8).

SENIOR ELDER

The founder shall be the Senior Elder and shall remain so for the whole of his life, and upon his death or retirement one of the founder's sons shall be elected to Senior Eldership. The Senior Elder who has remained in service for a period of not less than 10 years shall receive a sum of £15 (fifteen pounds) every quarter, i.e. £60 (sixty pounds) annually. This will be spent as he wishes.

The first, second and third widows of the Senior Elder shall receive a yearly amount of £24, £18, £12 respectively upon the death of their husband. Any additional widow shall be cared for by the Church.

MARRIAGE

Members of the Church are strictly prohibited to marry outside the Church, and all marriages should be reported to the Church Conference beforehand. No marriage ceremonies are to be held outside the Church. The Church Conference has full control over the second or following marriage. Only the Bishop can conduct a marriage ceremony in the Church.

The Church members are not bound strictly to marry only one wife, nor did God blame those who married more than one wife. The first man in the history of the Bible who was the husband of two wives, was Ramek, but we do not read that God accused him of that. We read of him in the Book of Genesis 4 : 19.

Abraham was called the friend of God, and yet he married two wives. Jakobo, who first earned the name Israel, was the husband of four wives. God often pointed out the sins of the people, but why not in this case?

David, the King, married more than one wife, as we read in the Second Book of Samuel, Chapter 15 : 16. But we do not read that he was lost for that reason. Solomon, too, married many wives, and it is obvious that his heart was turned away after other gods. Solomon did not turn away from the true God because he had married many wives but because he married many strange women, amongst others the daughter of Pharaoh, who drew him to idolatry. We are irrational if we think that monogamy is a way of preventing sin from entering the family according to Christian experience. God married Adam, the first man, to one wife, through whom sin penetrated into the family. This we write to some who think that marrying many wives is the gateway of sin in the family.

We read in the first book of Kings, 16 : 31, that Ahab was married, outside the Church, to a Zidonian princess who did not know Jehovah, but Baal; so the King served Baal and worshipped him. Verse 33 of the same book says: 'And Ahab made a grove; and Ahab did more to provoke the Lord God of Israel to anger than all the Kings of Israel that were before him.' This was a marriage to one wife, and yet it led to this situation. You can marry one wife who practises heathenism, and expect to turn away from God at any time. But you can marry a hundred Christian wives, and remain in Christianity for the rest of your life. For further proofs, we may read the following books: (II Samuel 5 : 12); (Chronicles 14 : 3); (I Samuel 1 : 2); (Judges 8 : 30); (Isaiah 4 : 1); (Judges 12 : 8). If we read these books, we shall have wisdom to know what God wants and what he does not want; because all wisdom is found in the Bible, and we shall know the commandments of God and the commandments of man. But Jesus said: 'In vain they shall worship me, teaching for doctrine the commandments of man.' Let us consider carefully if we are not teaching for doctrine the commandments of man.

This is the amended Constitution of the Zion Christian Church. It was constituted in the ZION CITY MORIAH,

NYIKA HALT,
P.B. 9072,
FORT VICTORIA.

2. CONSTITUTION OF THE AFRICAN ZION CHURCH OF JESUS

(Copy of Bishop Komboni Vambire's application for recognition of his Church, in which he included his 'Constitution')

Psalm 87 Verses 2-5.
Peter 2 Verses 2-5.

The African Zion Church of Jesus,
Bishop J. Komboni Vambire,
Mucheke African Township,
P.O. Box 215,
FORT VICTORIA.
26th April, 1963.

My name is J. Komboni Mukiva Vambire, R.C. 14782 Gutu. I became a Christian of the Zion Church on the 3rd May, 1945. I am a Citizen of Fort Victoria, and have been ever since 1940 (23 years).

I was promoted to be a Church Bishop on the 9th October, 1961. My Church Laws are accepted by everybody, and my Constitution is as follows:

1. Exodus 20 verse 12: Honour thy Father and Mother that thy days may be long upon the land.
2. Thou shalt not sin.
3. Thou shalt not commit adultery.
4. Thou shalt not steal.
5. Thou shalt not bear false witness against thy neighbour.
6. Thou shalt not covet thy neighbour's house.
7. Thou shalt not covet thy neighbour's wife.
8. A man shall not take his father's wife (Deut. 22 verse 30).
9. Thou shalt love thy neighbour as thyself (Math. 22 verse 30).
10. Neither shalt thou desire thy neighbour's wife (Deut. 5 verse 21).
11. The children of this world marry, and are given in marriage (Luke 20 verse 34).

12. And if a man entice a person that is not betrothed and lie with her, he shall marry her as his wife (Exodus 22 verse 16).

13 We have permission to drink medicine or to go to the Hospital: For Isaiah told the people to take a lump of figs, and use it for a plaster upon the boil, and he would recover (Isaiah 38 verse 21), (Luke 10 verses 33, 34), (2 Kings 20 verse 17).

14. Whatever tree is medicine, we eat of it (Gen. 1 verse 29). We preach everywhere (Math. 28 verse 15). So they took the money and did as they were told. And this saying is commonly used among the Jews to this day.

15. We baptize them in the name of Jesus. (Math. 28 verse 19 says: Go ye therefore and teach all nations, baptizing them in the name of the Father and of the Son, and of the Holy Ghost.)

16. To solemnize the Lord's Supper (Luke 22 : 7, 19). Then came the day of unleavened bread, when the passover must be killed. Verse 19: And he took bread and gave thanks and broke it and gave unto them, saying, 'This is my body which is given unto you, this do in remembrance of me.'

17. To consecrate children (Mark 10 verse 13). And they brought young children to him so that he should touch them, and his Disciples rebuked those who brought them.

18. When you go to Church, take off your shoes. Joshua 5 verse 15: And the Captain of the Lord's Host said unto Joshua, take thy shoes from thy feet, for the place thou standeth on is holy and Joshua did so.

19. We praise God with trumpets (Psalm 150 verses 1-5). Verse 3: praise Him with the sound of the trumpet; praise Him with psaltery and harp.

20. To bury the dead (1 Cor. 15; Rev. 12 : 13). To lay hands on the sick and pray for them (Mark 16 : 17, 18).

21. Psalm 8, verse 2-5.
Peter 2 verse 2-8.

ADMITTANCE OF PEOPLE INTO MEMBERSHIP OF THE AFRICAN ZION CHURCH OF JESUS

1. Every member of the Church, if married, must have one wife married according to Christian rites. Our leaders will be selected only from people of good standing who conform to the idea of one wife, who do not drink beer, who lead a clean life and can influence others to lead a decent and clean life as taught by Christ Himself. Any member who marries a second wife will cut himself off from Church membership, but can attend Church only to hear the word of God. This will apply to those who drink beer and lead an unexemplary life.

2. The Church, by preaching the word of God to all people without selecting, will admit into membership anybody who repents and accepts Christ's way of life. Nobody who has repented will be refused membership because of his past history, which may have been un-Christian.

3. Members will in future be asked to give contributions under the following headings: Class gifts, Baptism fee, Harvest collections, Annual contributions for Gospel extension. All these funds will be used to pay the workers of the Church and also to pay for Church materials which are indispensable to the work, e.g. books, etc.

3. AFRICAN CONGREGATIONAL CHURCH (CHIBARIRWE)
(translated from Chikaranga)

Committee of the circuit
Every circuit has its own committee chosen by the people of that particular area. In the case of a large circuit, eight people, six men and two women, are chosen, and for a smaller area four men and two women are chosen (in addition to the elders). In the case of a small circuit one or two men and one woman are chosen.

This committee treats (judges) the small, unimportant matters in conjunction with an overseer. At the end of the year a new committee is elected. A popular person (having acted according to the wishes of the people) may be re-elected.

Executive committee
This is the chief committee, since every circuit has representatives on this committee, chosen at the big meeting of the year. After three years the Superintendent and the General Secretary are elected again. This is how they do it: if they find that a person is chosen again he holds office for another three years.

This committee pays the ministers' salaries and they regulate the allocation of money. In consultation with the ministers they decide about the ordination of a new minister. They have power to draw money from the Bank.

They arrange the transfer of ministers in a joint meeting with the ministers, after having heard the reports of the circuits concerning the work of the various ministers.

Their General Secretary keeps the minutes. It is he who records the decisions made in the meetings of the circuits (when the various circuits come together).

The meeting of the ministers also has its secretary, a minister who records the decisions taken.

The money collected by the circuits is deposited in the Bank in the presence of two ministers and a third man chosen from among the people. This money must be for the work of the African Congregation everywhere in this country of Rhodesia where it is needed – e.g. for the building of Churches and schools. Nobody will be allowed to use this money for anything but the work of the Church.

These decisions were supported by the chief worker of the African Congregation so that they may be 'powerful' laws for all the circuits. Therefore he who does not follow or obey them breaks the all-important law made by the circuits and their leader, Rev. Z. M. Sengwayo, President of the African Congregation.

4. CONSTITUTION OF THE AFRICAN REFORMED CHURCH

The order and aims of the African Church – (translated from Chikaranga)

a) The African Church will try, wherever possible, to increase the light started by the Churches of our leaders who taught us to know God in the right way.

b) This Church honours the ministers 'of the white skin' who brought us out of darkness. It honours our Government who did so much for the black people living in the dwelling-places in the mountains, and for restoring peace in the country.

c) This Church desires to help in building its schools under the guidance of the Government. All believers must be taught how to live decently so that this faith may have roots and renown like the other Churches.

d) The African Church tries very hard to comfort, help and console the poor and the needy; to honour also the chiefs of the country.

e) It teaches the people to hate sin and uncleanness – of their bodies – teaching them to live decently so that all the unconverted will desire to believe in Jesus Christ. This is the reason why the Government tried in many ways to uplift the people by appointing Land Development Officers and Agricultural Demonstrators all over the country, because the homes and gardens were so filthy. This is clearly seen by everybody today, viz., that God, the Government and the Ministers are all working in unison.

f) If a man disobeys the law of the Government and all the chiefs, he cannot obey the rules of the Church. The man who obeys the laws of the Government will prosper. Likewise the man who obeys the laws of the Church will eventually go to heaven when he dies and live happily there.

g) No Church can have peace when its members are intoxicated with beer, and so the African Church does not allow beer drinking, because there are many corpses of people, destroyed by beer. All uncleanness, untidiness, all unmentionable filth are the result of beer. There is no knowledge or faith if a person does not hate beer. Before the Government appointed Agricultural Demonstrators in the villages, the home of a drunkard resembled a pigsty, smelling only of the dregs of beer and of vomit. A man who goes to a beer party, after washing himself and dressing properly, will be filthy all over when he returns in the evening.

h) The Church teaches *Ruwadzano*, that is, a peaceful relationship between husband and wife and with their whole family. And so the Spirit of God will dwell in that home. It also teaches that our children, boys and girls, must live together in harmony. It teaches that girls should be instructed about their marriage by the mothers when they are alone. If two or three women are unable to solve the problems, then the matter must be referred to the Mothers' meeting at the end of the month.

Here, good and sound teaching must be given by the women who a) have the knowledge, and b) have not brought dishonour on their homes, whose lives are above reproach: 1 Tim. 3 : 1. The leader must be a person whose life is free from fault or blame.

Our girls often behave wrongly and improperly simply because they are not taught properly about right relationships, especially with boys.

In many ways they misbehave because of lack of knowledge:

i) having been given in marriage while still a little child;
ii) failure to get on with boys;
iii) disrespect towards others in the village;
iv) laziness, and
v) carelessness about cleanliness, in other matters and about boys.

We desire that our children should behave in such a way that after marriage their lives shall be happy. The African Church wants to co-operate with the Churches which taught us, so that our race may progress without disgracing their forebears. These things prove to us that our race is unable to teach our boys and girls.

i) This Church teaches that the Black Skin [Africans] must unite and help one another in times of trouble and receive one another with open arms without enquiring about his origins, whether he is a Malawian, muZezuru, muKaranga, muNedebele, muShangaan or a muSotho. But we only look at his skin. All Africans must live together in unity and honour each other without taking blood relationship into consideration [lit. without saying: 'he is not my father or grandfather']. Let us honour everybody, provided his skin is black. Then the Government and God will also honour us.

i) We are incapable of honouring and fearing the Government, therefore we do not prosper.
ii) We are incapable of honouring our employers for whom we work.
iii) We cannot do the work we are supposed to do although we receive payment at the end of the month.
iv) We are incapable of honouring our country's chiefs. This shows that we did not assimilate properly all the words we were taught by our ministers 'of the white skin', who showed us their love while teaching us everything.

j) The African Church teaches:

i) that we must honour and fear our leaders;
ii) we must honour our chiefs;
iii) we must honour our Government and humble ourselves even when we are judged and punished, because our Lord Jesus said so; when He found the people paying their taxes he did the same. Jesus said: 'If we do not honour our employers we shall not be able to honour God whom we have not seen.'
iv) He, in conclusion, spoke the most important word, above all other things: 'Love everyone, and love your neighbours as you love yourself!' This is the great law.

k) The African Church teaches that we must not be lazy but work diligently, so that we can have enough. Laziness results in:

i) theft,
ii) hooliganism,
iii) disobedience towards parents and Government,

iv) *ubinya* – one who rapes, steals and murders, ana
v) bad temper.

All these things have as their source: laziness.

So, if a person wants to follow Jesus, he must not be lazy, because laziness is the pillow of Satan.

Glossary of Shona terms and phrases

baba	father; *babamukuru,* father's elder brother; *babamunini (mudiki),* father's younger brother.
badza	hoe.
bakuro	(syn. for *ngombe youmai*: 'motherhood' cow or heifer) gift of husband to wife's mother (apart from official *roora* payment).
bandauko	front leg of animal, often given to superior person in recognition of such a person's authority.
bani	plain; open level land.
basa	work; *basa rouvangeri,* evangelistic work.
benzi	fool, idiot.
bere	hyena, frequently associated with witchcraft (as a witch's familiar.)
bira	ritual service for the propitiation of ancestral spirits (see *kupira*).
bona	see *kugadzira.*
buku	book; *buku yemirairo,* lawbook.
bvene	baboon (also *gudo*).
bvute	(syn. *mvuri):* shade; *bvute reTopia,* congregation of the First Ethiopian Church.
Changani	Shangaan.
chapungu	battaleur eagle.
chembere	woman past child-bearing age.
Chibarirwe	derived from *kubara* or *kubereka,* 'to give birth': that which was born for us; in the Independent Church context it means 'heritage of our fathers, that which has not been derived from others, our very own', and as such is the popular designation of the African Congregational Church.
chibereko	'fruit', child or child-bearing power (from *kubereka,* to bear offspring).
chidao	sub-clan name; laudatory form of address.
chidoma	witch's familiar; animal of psychic nature, conceived of as smaller than a polecat.
chidziva	little pool (dim. of *dziva*).
chikonye	small worm.
chikoro	school, sometimes used as syn. for Church.
chikwerete	debt.
chimutsamapfiwa	see *kumutsa mapfiwa.*
chipanda	lit. 'forked stick'; the sister to whom a man is linked for the provision of his marriage cattle.

chiparadza — last sharing out of beer in conclusion of ritual procedure or of ordinary beer drink; *kuparadza,* disperse.

chipo (pl. *zvipo*) — gift.

chipondamabwe — lit. 'pounding of the rocks'; thunderstorm or hail.

chiposo — an act of sorcery in which the malignant substance or particles are believed to the 'thrown at' the victim; *kuposa,* derived from *kuposha* or *kupotsa,* literally means 'to throw'.

chipuna — *shavi* spirit of the healing type.

chirayiro — lit. 'evening meal'; in the Mission Church context this term refers to the Holy Communion; *kudya chirayiro,* to participate in ('eat') the Lord's Supper.

chiremba — doctor; designation frequently used for a female diviner-herbalist.

chirungu — European ways; European influence generally.

chisi — day on which work (in the lands) is forbidden by the tribal tutelary spirit.

chitema — lit. 'black thing'; sin; *handina chitema nemi,* 'I have nothing against you'.

chitsinga — physical disorder caused by an act of sorcery; see *kutsinga.*

chitupa — registration certificate.

chiuchiro — token gift of respect; *kuuchira,* to show respect through the clapping of hands.

chizvarwa — segment of patrilineage; the descendants of one man over several generations.

chuma — beads, love token.

dambudzo (pl. *matambudzo*) — tribulation, suffering.

danga — cattle kraal; *danga ramai,* lit. 'kraal of the mother'; matri-estate.

dangwe — firstborn child; (from *kutanga,* to begin).

dare — meeting-place; tribal court; *dare rekereke,* Church 'court' or council.

demoni — demon, evil spirit.

denga — sky, heaven; *denga rakwewa kure,* 'the heaven has drawn far away', i. e. it withholds its rain; see *kugadzira matenga.*

divisi — magical charm to damage crops of others or to cause abundance in one's own fields.

dondo — bush; *mweya uri mudondo,* 'the spirit [of deceased person] is in the bush', i.e. the deceased has not yet attained full ancestorhood, his or her spirit is still 'outside' since the induction rite has not yet been performed.

doro — beer; *doro rokubvuma,* acceptance beer, which is brewed as a sign of a new spirit medium's willingness to act as mouthpiece of a family or tribal spirit; *doro rokugadzira,* sacrificial beer used during the induction rite; *vasengi vedoro,* bearers of the beer.

dudziro — explanation.

dumbu — stomach, womb; *kubva mudumbu rimwe,* to come (persons born) from one womb, or persons with a common spiritual heritage.

dunhu	tribal ward.
dura	granary (little hut, usually built on the face of granite rock) for threshed grain.
dzidzo	lesson.
dziva	pool; *Dzivaguru,* Great Pool, praise-name of the Shona High-God, Mwari.
dzvene	holy; see *Mweya mutsvene.*
dzviti	invader; *muDziviti,* a Ndebele person (when negatively appraised by a muShona).
gomo	mountain (pl. *makomo*).
gona	horn; *gona rouroyi,* horn of wizardry; container of malignant medicine.
gono	bull; *gono guru* (big bull), *gono romusha* (bull of the homestead), *gono rababa* (father's bull): the animal dedicated to the family's senior ancestral (or more distant guardian) spirit for ritual purposes; the term 'father's bull' indicates that this animal is usually selected from the *roora* herd a father receives from his daughter's suitor.
gota (or *mukurukota)*	councillor of headman or chief.
guta	city; *guta renjuzu,* city of the *njuzu* (*shavi* healing) spirits, believed by some to exist below a pool of water.
guvi	hole in a rock (in which water collects), used to soak finger millet before it is used for brewing sacrificial beer.
hakata	wooden divining slabs; this term is sometimes used as a general indication of all kinds of objects used for divination.
hanzvadzi	reciprocal kinship term between brother and sister.
hosana	male children of God – especially dedicated to the traditional High-God and with special functions in the ancient, oracular cult; or followers of the Apostolic leader, Johane Masowe.
hosho	rattle.
hosi	first (i.e. senior) wife.
hospitara	hospital.
huru (guru)	big, great, see *simba guru.*
hurumende	government.
hwamanda	kudu horn used as a musical instrument.
imba	hut, 'house'; group of descendants of one person, male or female.
imbwazukuru	she-goat given by a man to his mother-in-law, who offers it to her grandmothers in recognition of their services in rearing her daughter.
impi	Ndebele term for regiment.
indaba	Ndebele term for a meeting of tribal dignitaries.
induna	Ndebele term for tribal dignitary.
ishe	chief.
jinda	member of the ruling lineage, and especially one occupying a position of authority.
jira	blanket.
jukwa	*shavi* spirit, closely associated with the traditional High-God and with His rainmaking powers.

katekisma	catechism.
kereke	Church; *kereke yakatsauku,* a stray Church; *kereke yoMweya,* Church of the (Holy) Spirit; popular designation of Zionist and Apostolic Independent Churches.
kubata	hold; *kubata pamimba,* 'to grip the womb' (this action is ascribed to a spirit which wants to prevent childbirth), *kubata zita,* 'to hold the name', i.e. succession to a deceased's name during the *kugadzira* ritual.
kubatwa nomweya	to be possessed by the spirit *(noMweya:* by the [Holy] Spirit).
kubuda	'to come out'; *mweya wabuda,* 'the spirit has come out' (implication: the spirit possesses its host); *shavi igere kubuda zvakanaka,* the *shavi* spirit has not yet 'come out' properly.
kubudisa ropa	to bring forth (menstrual) blood.
kuchengeta	to keep; *kuchengeta mhuri,* to keep or protect the family – a function ascribed to the ancestral spirits.
kudarika uta	'to cross (a deceased person's) bow', a method of finding out during the *kugadzira* procedure if a widow has remained chaste after her husband's death.
kudya	to eat; *kudyisa,* to bewitch by adding harmful medicine to the victim's food; *kudyiwa nomuroyi,* 'to be eaten by a witch' (the witch is supposed to remove parts of the liver, intestines, etc.) as a result of which the victim wastes away.
kudzidza	to learn.
kudzikira bango	'to drive in a peg' as a sign of confirmation of the establishment of a new village.
kudzinga	to chase away.
kudzivisa	to rule out, prevent.
kuenzanisa nyanya	to settle a dispute informally.
kufa	to die.
kufamba	to walk; *mufi unofamba pose-pose,* the (spirit of the) deceased 'walks' about everywhere.
kugadzira	to settle the spirit of a deceased person; this term indicates the induction rite through which the spirit of a deceased relative is 'brought back home' and simultaneously elevated to the status of ancestorhood; also referred to as *bona,* 'to give or sustain life' and as *kurova guwa,* lit. 'to hit the grave'.
kugadzira matenga	'to fix the heavens', i.e. to procure rain from the spirit world through the performance of rain rituals.
kugadzira musha	to take the necessary magical measures in order to safeguard one's homestead against misfortune; see *kupinga musha.*
kugamuchira	to receive; welcome.
kugara	to be seated.
kugara nhaka	to inherit, or to succeed to, a deceased person's estate or position; *kugarwa nhaka,* to become an inherited wife of one of the deceased husband's agnatic kinsmens; *kugova nhaka,* to distribute a deceased's estate (see also *kuparadza nhumbi); mugari wenhaka,* heir.
kuheduka	to backslide spiritually.

kuita mhere-mhere	to cry out (or mourn) loudly.
kukomborera	to bless.
kukudza	to honour.
kukumbira	to ask, to propose for marriage; *kukumbira mvura,* to ask for rain; see *kukwira makomo.*
kukusha	to sprinkle.
kukwira makomo	lit. 'to climb the mountains'; this term is descriptive of the *mukwerere* ritual since the request for rain is usually made to the tribal ancestors on a hill or mountain where their graves are to be found.
kumanikidza	to enforce.
kumema	to make first payment of *roora* (bridewealth) in a regular proposal marriage.
kumira pamukova	to stand at the door; descriptive of the protective function of the home ancestors; by 'standing at the door' the *midzimu* prevent evil forces from entering the dwelling places of their living descendants.
kumutsa mapfiwa	'to raise the cooking stones'; to provide the substitute for a prematurely deceased wife; *chimutsamapfiwa,* wife substituted for deceased relative.
kumutsa murimo	'to raise or revive the medicine', i.e. to continue the magical practices of the deceased forebears; *muroyi wokumutsa murimo,* hereditary witch who continues the practices of one of her matrilineal forebears.
kunamata	to employ praise greeting in order to obtain favour; to worship; *kunamatira,* to intercede on behalf of.
kunetsa	to be troublesome.
kunyengetera	to persuade or pray; *munyengetero,* humble persuasion, prayer meeting.
kuparadza nhumbi	'to scatter the belongings', to distribute the belonings of a deceased person, usually during the *kugadzira* ritual procedure.
kupembera	to dance joyfully.
kuperekedza	to escort; *kuperekedza mukadzi,* 'to accompany a woman' usually when she proceeds to her groom's village after the *roora* requirements have been met, or when she returns to her home-village with some form of compensation in the case of marriage negotiations being discontinued.
kupfungaidza	to incensate.
kupfuka	to haunt, turn against; *mudzimu wapfuka,* the ancestral spirit has turned against me.
kupinga musha	'to buttress or peg the homestead', i.e. to treat one's house with protective medicine, e.g. to drive magical pegs into the ground at the corners of the back and front yard to ward off the attacks of evil forces.
kupira	to offer for, propitiate (from *kupa:* to give).
kuposa	to bewitch; see *chiposo.*
kupururudza	to ululate in rejoicing, applauding.
kuputsa	to smash; *kuputsa nyika,* 'to break up the country' in the sense

of disturbing the existing order; *kuputsika mudziva,* to fall into the pool (part of the baptismal procedure adopted in some of the Spirit-type Churches).

kuramba — to refuse.

kurangarira — to remember.

kurasha — to throw away; *kurasha munhu,* to cast out a person from a particular community, e.g. religious grouping; *kurasha tsika dzamadzibada,* to cast away (in the sense of rejecting or neglecting) the customs of the forefathers.

kurinda — to guard or protect; *kurinda mhuri, t*o protect the family; one of the most important services rendered by the 'home ancestors' (*midzimu yapamusha*).

kuruma — 'to bite'; descriptive of the traditional doctor's treatment of a bewitched patient, when he literally 'bites out' the malignant substance from the afflicted person's body.

kurwadza — to hurt; common term which indicates the negative action undertaken by a neglected ancestor against his or her forgetful descendants.

kusendeka uta — to accept an inherited wife during the formal *sendeka uta* ceremony – which is part of the *kugadzira* procedure.

kusenga — to carry.

kuseredza manhindi — to cause the consumed meat to settle down (usually through drinking some beer).

kusevenza — to work.

kushandura jeko — lit. 'to change the menstrual pain'; i.e. change the sex of a coming child if a woman has previously born children of one sex only.

kushata — to become bad; *zvakashata,* evil; *kushatirwa,* to be angered or offended.

kushopera — to divine by throwing divinatory bones or slabs; *akashoperwa,* the divining bones have been thrown on his account.

kusika — to create; *musiki,* creator.

kusimbisa — to authorize.

kusiyana — to differ, disagree; *siyano,* difference.

kusunungura — to unfasten; *kusunungura zivi,* to release from sin, to pardon.

kutamba — to play; *kutamba mashavi,* to dance in honour of the *shavi* spirits; *kutamba majukwa,* to dance in honour of the *jukwa* spirits when a request for rain is made to the ancestral spirits.

kutasva — to mount, or ride; *mukadzi uyu unotasva bere,* 'this woman rides a hyena', i.e. she practises witchcraft at night and makes use of a hyena (the most common witch familiar); *ndataswa nomuroyi,* 'I was ridden by a witch'; after a bad night's rest a person may complain that he was unwittingly being used by a witch, as a result of which he had to carry her wherever she preferred to practise her nocturnal activities.

kutemera — to make incisions on a person's body through which medicine is applied; *muroyi wokutemerwa,* a witch who willingly accepts her profession by having witchcraft medicine rubbed into her body through incisions made by other witches.

kutenda	to believe; *ndinotenda Mwari,* I believe in God.
kutenga	to buy.
kuteya	to trap, to ensorcel; *ndateyiwa gumbo,* 'my leg was trapped', i.e. I was ensorcelled by treading on the medicine of a sorcerer or witch; see *kutsinga.*
kutizisa	to cause to run away; to elope with a lover.
kutonga mhosva	to judge a judicial case.
kutonhodza	to cool off, to assuage the anger of a troublesome spirit; *donhodzo,* any cooling or appeasing drink (e.g. libation on grave).
kutsamwisa	to provoke the anger of, to displease.
kutsinga	to ensorcel with malignant medicine which is placed as a leg trap in the victim's path; after contact, the medicine is believed to pass through the leg to various parts of the body where it causes the intended harm; see also *chiposo* and *kuteya.*
kuuraya	to kill.
kuumba ukama	'to strengthen the relationship'; many people regard the strengthening of the relationship between two families as the essential function of *roora* payment.
kuviga	to conceal; *kuviga mufi,* to bury a dead person.
kuwana	to obtain; *kuwana mukadzi,* to 'find' (and by implication marry) a woman.
kuzarura mukova	to open the door; if an ancestral spirit is said to 'open the door' it means that he has withdrawn his protection from his relatives, which leaves them vulnerable to the onslaughts of their enemies (an act of retaliation caused by the livings' neglect of their ancestral spirits); see *kumira pamukova.*
kuzvarirwa	to contract a credit marriage by pledging one's daughter to another family without her prior knowledge.
mabvazuva	lit. 'where the sun comes from'; the east.
mabweadziva	'the rocks of the pool'; popular designation of the rain shrines in the Matopo hills where the voice of Mwari is to be heard.
madzivanyika	the great ones (spirits) of the land.
mai	mother.
mambo	king, chief; in the past this term was used for the Rozvi rulers.
mangisi	sweet, unmalted beer.
manyahana	healing spirit, well known among the Manyika tribes.
marudzi	tribal spirits, cf. *mhondoro.*
masungiro	gift by husband to his wife's parents after consummation of marriage in recognition or anticipation of first conception.
Matangakugara	You, who sat first - one of the names of the Shona High-God.
mate	spittle; *mate emvura,* spittle of rain, which is requested from the tribal spirits during *mukwerere* ritual procedure.
Matonjeni	the Matopo hills; *Mwari waMatonjeni,* 'God of the Matopo hills'; popular name of the raingiving God.
Mawanikwa	You, who were found to exist - one of the names of the Shona High-God.
mbanda	powdered medicine.
mbonga	woman dedicated (usually as a young girl) to the service of the

	Shona High-God, Mwari; sometimes referred to as 'the wife of Mwari'; *mbonga-svikiro,* the *mbonga* female who acts as spirit medium in the cult cave during oracular sessions at Matonjeni.
mbudzi	goat; see *imbwazukuru.*
mbuya	grandmother.
mhandara	girl of marriageable age.
mhezi	scabies.
mhofu	eland.
mhondoro	tribal spirit; *mhondoro yamatenga,* great spirit of the skies, whose involvement in human affairs is of multi-tribal significance.
mhosva huru	an important issue.
mhuka	wild animal, buck; *mhuka huru,* great antelope; this is the *chidao* of some Hera clans.
mhunga	bulrush millet.
mhuri	family, multi-lineal group of kinsmen living in the same locality.
mimba	womb; see *kubata pamimba.*
Mlimo	Ndebele syn. for the Shona word, Mwari (God).
muchakata	cork tree; this tree through its shade and fruit symbolizes the protective and sustaining function of the ancestral spirits; it is the tree most frequently selected by the Southern Shona for ritual purposes; a *rushanga* (pole enclosure, symbolizing the dwelling place of the ancestral spirits) is usually built around the trunk of a *muchakata.*
muchengeti	keeper; guardian.
muchinda	see *jinda.*
muduku	young one, junior.
mudzimu	ancestral spirit; *midzimu yapamusha,* 'home ancestors'; patri and matrilineal ancestors directly concerned with the welfare of a family group; *midzimu mikuru isina mitupo,* great (and remote) ancestors with no identifiable clan-names; see *mhondoro yamatenga.*
mufumi	a wealthy person.
mufundisi	minister of religion.
mugari wenhaka	see *kugara nhaka.*
muhedeni	heathen.
mukadzi wamapoto	'woman or wife of the cooking pots'; a woman who stays with an adult male (usually a labour migrant) in an urban area on a basis of temporary and unofficial 'matrimony'; one of the main tasks of such a woman is to 'see to the pots', i.e. to do the cooking.
mukoma	a man's elder brother or a woman's elder sister.
mukombe	calabash, ladle.
mukuru	elder, dignitary.
mukute	water tree (*Syzygium*).
mukutu	quiver.
mukuwasha	son-in-law.
mukwerere	rain ritual during which the senior tribal spirits are propitiated

	at their graves and/or at a *rushanga;* these rituals are conducted at the commencement of each rainy season or if rains have failed; it is also called *mutoro.*
mumiriri	mediator.
munhu	a person.
mununguna	a man's younger brother or a woman's younger sister.
munyai	messenger, a representative; a *munyai* in the High-God cult organization is the person who maintains contact between the local district he represents and the priest colony at the cult centre; he annually visits the cult centre at Matonjeni to request rain for his district and to discuss local matters of general significance.
munyori	secretary.
muongamiri	Independent Church official of senior rank whose task it is 'to call others together', i.e. to lead the members of his congregation(s); from *kuunganidza,* 'to gather or call together'.
muphuwira	love-potion used by females to attract a prospective lover or to regain the love of a husband.
mupinzi webasa	'the controller of the job' (from *kupinza,* to admit); in the High-God cult the *mupinzi webasa* is the high priest who is in control of the ritual activities at the cult cave.
muPostora	an Apostle; follower of Johane Maranke or Johane Masowe.
muramu	potential husband or wife.
murapi	healer; doctor.
murevo	pot of beer especially offered to senior ancestral spirit as notification that sacrificial beer has been prepared; as such it is the 'pot of address' (*murevo* is derived from *kureva,* to tell); during ritual procedure it symbolizes the presence of the *midzimu;* it is also called the *musumo.*
murombo	poor person.
muromo	mouth.
muroora	daughter-in-law.
muroyi	wizard (sorcerer or witch); *muroyi wedzinza* or *muroyi wokumutsa murimo,* hereditary witch who operates at night under the direction of an ancestral and/or *shavi* spirit; *muroyi wemasikati,* 'sorcerer of the afternoon', i.e. he whose medicines also work in daytime; *muroyi vokutemerwa,* 'a witch who has been incised'.
murume	male, husband.
murungu	European; see *chirungu.*
masese	beer sediment.
musha	village, home.
mushonga	medicine (all-inclusive term indicating both Western-type and African medicines, e.g. magical preparations); syn. *muti* or *murimo.*
mushozowa	wild tree with exceptionally hard wood; sometimes associated with *ngozi* exorcism.
musiki	creator; *Musikavanhu,* Creator of mankind (praise-name of the High-God, Mwari); *musikarudzi,* progenitor of the tribe.

musumo	'pot of address' or 'pot of introduction'; used during propitiatory rites; from *kusuma,* to make preliminary remarks before distributing beer to guests; see *murevo.*
muswe	tail.
mutariri	overseer.
mutema	a black; an African; *vatema vatanga kukura,* lit. 'the blacks have begun to become big', i.e. the Africans have come of age.
mutongi	judge, councillor, e.g. chief or headman in the tribal court.
muTopia	member of the First Ethiopian Church.
mutorwa	foreigner; a person who does not belong to one's own lineage.
mutumbu	lit. 'the whole physical body'; compensation in the form of cattle and/or a *mhandara* (marriageable girl) payed to the relatives of an avenging *ngozi* spirit, by the afflicted party.
mutupo	clan name.
Muumbapasi	'Founder of the land (name of the Shona High-God, Mwari).
muvengi	enemy (*kuvenga,* to hate).
muvimi	hunter.
muviri	physical stature; body.
muZioni	a Zionist.
muzukuru	'grandchild'; nephew, niece.
mvura	water, rain.
mvuri	shade.
mwana	child.
Mwari	God (most common name of the Shona High-God).
mweya	spirit; *Mweya mutsvene,* Holy Spirit (the Manyika and especially the followers of Johane Maranke use the word *Mudzimuneira* instead of *Mweya mutsvene*); *mweya wakaipa,* evil spirit.
ndara	file snake *(Mehelya capensis).*
nengure	sparrow-like black bird.
nganga	diviner-herbalist.
ngombe youmai	see *bakuro.*
ngombe yovutete	'cow or heifer of the aunt'; payable by a deceased male's name-bearer or other descendants to the deceased's sister, who acts as ritual officiant during the 'home-bringing' (*kugadzira)* ceremony conducted on behalf of the deceased.
ngomwa	a barren female or a sterile male.
ngozi	avenging spirit; harmful or dangerous influence of any kind.
nhaka	see *kugara nhaka.*
nhimbe	collective beer party for work (mainly in the fields).
nhopi	mash made from pumpkin.
nhumbi	thing, possession.
njuzu	*shavi* spirit, associated with water and with healing activities.
nkonkoni	gnu; wildebeest.
Nyadenga	'Possessor of the sky'; praise-name of the Shona High-God.
nyama	meat; *nyama yokudzor*a, meat that pacifies.
nyika	land, tribal territory, country.
nziyo	hymn.
nzungu	ground or monkeynut (*Arachia hypogaea*); to be distinguished from nyemba, groundnut or cow pea (*Vigina unguculata*).

nzvimbo — place; space to be occupied.
panze — outside.
Paseka — Paschal ('Passover') celebrations; popular name of annual festivals conducted at the Church headquarters (or in outlying congregations) of the Spirit-type Churches.
pedo — near; *midzimu iri pedo nesu,* the ancestors are near to us; *ukama uri pedo,* a close relation; mostly of persons in the same lineage.
Pendi — 'Pentecost'; popular name for the major July gathering of the *vaPostori* at their Church headquarters in the Maranke reserve.
pose-pose — everywhere, all over.
Postora — see *muPostora* (also pronounced as *muPostori).*
rabaumah — derived from *liebumah* – the spelling generally adopted by the *vaPostori* – indicates the topmost ranks in each of the major offices of baptist, prophet, evangelist and healer.
rangano — conference; *Rangano Huru,* Church conference (of the DRC).
risipambvi — gentle rain.
roora — bridewealth; marriage compensation.
ropa — blood.
rudzi — 'kind' or 'species'; tribe, clan, patrilineage.
rukuva — pot-shelf.
rukweza — finger millet (*Eleusine corocana*).
rungano — tale, history.
runyaradzo — consolation ceremony conducted on behalf of the relatives of the recently deceased.
rupasa — reed mat.
ruponeso — salvation *(kuponesa,* to give or sustain life).
rushanga — temporary pole enclosure frequently built around the trunk of a *muchakata* for ritual purposes; see *muchakata.*
rutsambo — bracelet; original marriage proposal token; now common term for the cash element of the marriage compensation.
ruvunzo — token of introduction to negotiations in a regular proposal marriage.
sabuku — 'keeper of the book', village headman; cf. *samusha.*
sadunhu — headman of tribal ward.
sadza — thick porridge; *sadza risingaperi,* 'eternal porridge', spiritual 'food' (message) of eternal life.
samukadzi — 'keeper of the wife'; paternal aunt; a man's sister (usually his *chipanda*) who holds authority over his wife and acts as executrix of his estate after his death.
samusha — 'keeper of the village', original term for village headman.
sango — multi-purpose charm carried around the upper arm.
sekuru — grandfather or mother's brother.
shamhu — thin stick with which to beat a person; cane; syn. for Dutch Reformed Church discipline; *shamhu isingatarwi,* unconditional Church discipline; *shamhu youpombwe,* Church discipline for persons who have committed adultery.
shavi — alien spirit which does not belong to the lineage of the host whom it possesses; the various types of *shavi* spirits impart a

variety of skills, e.g. healing, hunting, dancing, blacksmithing, etc. to their hosts; *shavi yokurapa,* a healing *shavi* spirit; *shavi youroyi,* a *shavi* spirit which inspires wizardry; *kutsika shavi,* 'to tread on the *shavi*', i.e. to tread on an object identified with such a spirit and in this way attract it; *kubatwa neshavi,* 'to be caught hold of by a *shavi* spirit', to fall possessed.

Shinga Postora	'Courageous Apostles' (schismatic group with its roots in Johane Masowe's Apostolic movement); *kushinga,* to be diligent or brave.
shiri	bird.
shoko	monkey, clan name of the Mbire priests at Matonjeni.
shumba	lion.
shurire	bad omen.
simba	strength; power; *simba guru,* great power; see *kusimbisa.*
siyano	see *kusiyana.*
sungano	bond, association.
svikiro	spirit medium.
tateguru	paternal grandfather or great-grandfather.
tezvara (or *mukarabwe)*	father-in-law; *vatezvara,* general term of reference to a man's family-in-law.
Topia	'Ethiopianism', see *muTopia.*
tsika	custom, convention; *tsika yenyika,* custom of the chiefdom (or more generally of the country).
tsime	well; source of water supply.
tsvimbo	walking or hunting stick.
tswanda	basket.
ubishopi	leadership position of a bishop.
ukama	kinship; *ukama hwokutamba,* 'playful relationship' of the type which is least dominated by the general principle of super and subordination in the Shona kinship structure, e.g. that between an uncle (*sekuru*) and his sister's son (*muzukuru*).
ukuru	leadership; *ukuru hwekereke,* Church leadership.
umboo utsva	new revelation.
upfu	meal, flower.
upombwe	illicit sexual intercourse; adultery.
ura utete	thin intestines.
uredzi (or *chiredzwa)*	fee or compensation for rearing of a child; some people describe the *roora* payment as *uredzi hwavabereki,* compensation for the bride's parents for rearing her.
uroyi	wizardry; see *kuroya.*
vamwene	husband's sister who is the 'owner' of his wife.
vana wamabuku	'children of the books', schoolchildren.
vatete	paternal aunt; see *samukadzi.*
Wedenga	the One in heaven; name of the Shona High-God, Mwari.
Wokumusoro	the One above; i.e. Mwari.
zenda	*shavi* spirit conveying hunting skills; *zenda rabuda! 'zenda* has come out!' triumphant exclamation when a hunter brings down quarry with well aimed shot.

zhezha	edible tuber.
Zimbabwe	from *dzimba dzamabwe,* 'houses of stone'.
zvingweme	*shavi* spirits (origin unknown to author).
zvipo	see *chipo.*
zvipusha	epilepsy.
zvitebwe	(pl. for *chitebge*): *shavi* spirits, which cause destruction to the cattle of their enemies by entering maneless lions and then proceeding to kill.
zviyo	any cultivated grain crop (sometimes restricted to finger millet).

Abbreviations

AACJM	African Apostolic Church of Johane Maranke
ACC	African Congregational Church
AFC	Apostolic Faith Church
AMEC	African Methodist Episcopal Church
ARC	African Reformed Church
ASCGJM	Apostolic Sabbath Church of God of Johane Masowe
AZCJ	African Zion Church of Jesus
BSAC	British South African Company
BSAP	British South African Police
CCAC in Z	Christian Catholic Apostolic Church in Zion
C OF C	Church of Christ
CID	Criminal Investigation Department
CNC	Chief Native Commissioner
CSR	Casual Sample, Reserve
CST	Casual Sample, Town
DC	District Commissioner
DRC	Dutch Reformed Church
FEC	First Ethiopian Church
FG	Full Gospel (Church)
IC	Independent Church
IRM	International Review of Missions
LMS	London Missionary Society
MC	Mission Church
Meth.	Methodist (Church)
NADA	Native Affairs Department Annual
NC	Native Commissioner
NGB	Nederlandse Geloofsbelydenis (Dutch Confession of Faith)
NPA	Native Purchase Area
RCC	Roman Catholic Church
RSS	Random Sample Survey (conducted in the Chingombe chiefdom)
SRBCC	Southern Rhodesian Bantu Christian Conference
SZC	Sabbath Zion Church
TTL	Tribal Trust Land
UDI	Unilateral Declaration of Independence
YMCA	Young Men's Christian Association
YWCA	Young Women's Christian Association
ZACJC	Zionist Apostolic Church of Jesus Christ

ZAC OF SA	Zion Apostolic Church of South Africa
ZAFM	Zion Apostolic Faith Mission
ZCC	Zion Christian Church
ZPC	Zion Protestant Church

Bibliography

A. BOOKS AND PERIODICAL ARTICLES CITED

ABRAHAM, D. P. 'The Roles of Chaminuka and the Mhondoro Cults in Shona Political History', in *The Zambesian Past*, edited by E. Stokes and R. Brown, Manchester, 1966.

ANDERSSON, E. *Messianic Popular Movements in the Lower Congo*, Studia Ethnographica Upsaliensis, XIV, London, 1958.

AQUINA, M. 'Christianity in a Rhodesian Tribal Trust Land', *African Social Research*, No. 1, June 1966.

—, 'The People of the Spirit: An Independent Church in Rhodesia', *Africa*, Vol. XXXVII, No. 2, April 1967.

—, 'Zionists in Rhodesia', *Africa*, Vol. XXXIX, No. 2, April 1969.

BALANDIER, G. *Sociologie actuelle de l'Afrique noire*, Paris, 1955.

BARRETT, D. B. *Schism and Renewal in Africa – An Analysis of Six Thousand Contemporary Religious Movements*, Oxford University Press, London, 1968.

BAVINCK, J. H. *Inleiding in de zendingswetenschap*, Kampen, 1954.

—, *The Impact of Christianity on the Non-Christian World*, Grand Rapids, 1949.

BEATTIE, J. *Other Cultures – Aims, Methods and Achievements in Social Anthropology*, London, 1964.

BERKOUWER, G. C. *De algemene openbaring – Dogmatische studiën*, Kampen, 1951.

—, *De mens het beeld Gods – Dogmatische studiën*, Kampen, 1957.

BLAKE THOMPSON, J. and SUMMERS, R. 'Mlimo and Mwari: Notes on a Native Religion in Southern Rhodesia', in *NADA*, Salisbury, 1956.

BLAUW, J. *De ontmoeting der godsdiensten*, Horstcahier 35, Uitgave Kerk en Wereld, Driebergen, 1968.

BOEHI, B. 'From my Diary', *Guti*, Sept./Oct., 1963.

BÜHLMANN, P. W. *Die christliche Terminologie als missionsmethodisches Problem*, Schöneck-Beckenried, Switzerland, 1950.

BULLOCK, C. *The Mashona*, Juta, Cape Town, 1927.

BURKE, T. J. M. *Catholic Missions – Four great Encyclicals*, New York, 1957.

CRAWFORD, J. R. *Witchcraft and Sorcery in Rhodesia*, International African Institute, London, 1967.

DANEEL, M. L. *The God of the Matopo Hills – An Essay on the Mwari Cult in Rhodesia*, Africa Study Centre Communications, Leiden, 1970.

DU PLESSIS, J. P. *The Evangelization of Pagan Africa – A History of Christian Missions to the Pagan Tribes of Central Africa*, Juta, Cape Town, 1929.

DURAND, J. J. F. *Una Sancta Catholica in Sendingsperspektief*, Amsterdam, 1961.

ERNI, A. 'You will never convert them', *Guti*, Febr. 1966.

Evans-Pritchard, E. E. *Witchcraft, Oracles and Magic among the Azande*, Oxford, 1937.
Fortes, M. 'Some Reflections on Ancestor Worship in Africa', in *African Systems of Thought*, edited by M. Fortes and G. Dieterlen, London, 1965.
Fortune, G. *Bantu Languages of the Federation*, Rhodes Livingstone Papers, No. 14, London, 1959.
Freitag, A. 'Die Fortschritte des einheimischen Hierarchie in den Missionsländern in den letzten dreissig Jahren (1920–1950)', in J. Beckmann, *Der einheimische Klerus in Geschichte und Gegenwart*, Schöneck-Beckenried, 1950.
Frey, E. J. '70 Years St. Peter and Paul's Mission', *Guti*, Sept./Oct. 1963.
Frey, F. 'The Discrepancy', *Guti*, July 1964.
Gann, L. H. *History of Southern Rhodesia – Early Days to 1934*, London, 1965.
Garbett, G. K. 'The Land Husbandry Act of Southern Rhodesia', in *African Agrarian Systems*, edited by D. Biebuyck, Oxford, 1963.
—, *The Political System of a Central African Tribe with particular reference to the Role of Spirit Mediums* (Ph.D. thesis), Manchester, 1964.
Gelfand, M. *Shona Ritual*, Juta, Cape Town, 1959.
—, *Shona Religion*, Juta, Cape Town, 1962.
—, *Medicine and Custom in Africa*, Edinburgh and London, 1964 (I).
—, *Witch Doctor – Traditional Medicine Man in Rhodesia*, London, 1964 (II).
—, *An African's Religion – The Spirit of NyaJena*, Juta, Cape Town, 1966.
—, *The African Witch*, Edinburgh and London, 1967.
Gensichen, H. W. *Missionsgeschichte der neueren Zeit*, Göttingen, 1961.
Gerdener, G. B. A. *Reguit Koers Gehou*, Kaapstad, 1951.
Gray, R. *The two Nations – Aspects of the Development of Race Relations in the Rhodesias and Nyasaland*, Oxford University Press, London, 1960.
Holleman, J. F. 'Some Shona Tribes in Southern Rhodesia', in *Seven Tribes of British Central Africa*, edited by E. Colson and M. Gluckman, London, 1951.
—, *Shona Customary Law*, Oxford University Press, London, 1952 (2nd Edition, London, 1969).
—, *Accommodating the Spirit amongst some North-Eastern Shona Tribes*, Rhodes Livingstone Paper, No. 22, London, 1953.
—, *African Interlude*, Cape Town, 1958.
—, *Chief, Council and Commissioner – Some Problems of Government in Rhodesia*, Van Gorcum, Assen, 1968.
Howman, R. 'Chiefs and Headmen in Southern Rhodesia', in *From Tribal Rule to Modern Government*, edited by Apthorp, Rhodes Livingstone Institute, Lusaka, 1959.
Hughes, A. J. B. *Report on an Experimental Sample Socio-Economic Survey, Conducted in Gutu Tribal Trust Land*, July 1963, – Department of Conservation and Extension, Salisbury, 1965.
Inauen, B. 'Gregorian Chant in Africa', *Guti*, Aug. 1962.
Johnson, R. W. M. *African Agricultural Development in Southern Rhodesia:* 1945–1960, A Publication of the food research institute, Stanford University, 1964.
Kilchmann, J. 'Opportunism', *Guti*, June 1964.
Knoob, W. *Afrikanisch-christliche Bewegungen unter den Bantu*, (Ph.D. thesis), Cologne, 1961.
Kuper, H. 'The Shona' in *The Shona and Ndebele of Southern Rhodesia*, by H. Kuper, A. J. B. Hughes and J. van Velsen, International African Institute, London, 1955.
Latourette, K. S. *The Twentieth Century outside Europe*, Vol. V. of series: *Christianity in a Revolutionary Age*, London, 1963.
Louw, A. A. *Andrew Louw van Morgenster*, Kaapstad, 1965.

MBITI, J. S. *African Religions and Philosophy*, Heineman, London, 1969.
MICHLIG, J. 'Zum silbernen Jubiläum unserer Mission', *Guti*, Sept./Oct. 1963.
MULDERS, A. *Missiegeschiedenis*, Bussum, 1957.
MURPHREE, M. W. *Christianity and the Shona*, London School of Economics – Monographic Series on Social Anthropology, No. 36, London, 1969.
NIEDERBERGER, O. *Kirche – Rasse – Mission, Die Missionsauffassung der Niederländisch-Reformierten Kirchen von Süd Afrika*, Schöneck-Beckenried, Switzerland, 1959.
PALLEY, C. *The Constitutional History and Law of Southern Rhodesia, 1888–1965*, Oxford, 1966.
PAUW, B. A. *Religion in a Tswana Chiefdom*, London, 1960.
RANGER, T. O. 'The early History of Independency in Rhodesia', in *Religion in Africa*, Papers presented at the International African Seminar, Edinburgh, 1964.
—, 'The Role of Ndebele and Shona Religious Authorities in the Rebellions of 1896 and 1897', in *The Zambesian Past*, edited by E. Stokes and R. Brown, Manchester, 1966.
—, *Revolt in Southern Rhodesia, 1896–7*, Heineman, London, 1967.
—, 'State and Church in Southern Rhodesia (1919 to 1939)', Unpublished article.
REA, F. B. 'The Future of Mission Education in Southern Rhodesia', *IRM*, 1960.
ROGERS, C. A. and FRANTZ, C. *Racial Themes in Southern Rhodesia – The Attitudes and Behaviour of the White Population*, Yale, 1962.
RUBIO, J. 'Three important Letters', *Guti*, June 1965.
RUTISHAUER, J. 'The Great Temptation', *Guti*, June 1966.
SHEPPERSON, G. 'Church and Sect in Central Africa', *Rhodes Livingstone Journal*, No. 33, Oct. 1963.
SMITH, E. W. *The Way of the White Fields in Rhodesia – A Survey of Christian Enterprise in Northern and Southern Rhodesia*, London, 1928.
—, *African Ideas of God*, London, 1950.
SUMMERS, R. 'Carl Mauch on Zimbabwe Ruins', *NADA*, Salisbury, 1952.
SUNDKLER, B. G. M. *Bantu Prophets of South Africa*, London, 1948 (2nd revised edition, London, 1961).
TANNER, R. E. S. *Transition in African Beliefs*, Maryknoll, New York, 1968.
TAYLOR, J. V. *The Primal Vision – Christian Presence amid African Religion*, SCM Press, London, 1963.
TAYLOR, J.V. and LEHMANN, D.A., *Christians of the Copperbelt - The Growth of the Church in Northern Rhodesia*, London, 1961.
TRACEY, H. 'What are Mashavi Spirits?' *NADA*, 1934.
TYLOR, E. B. *Primitive Culture*, London, 1871.
VAN DER MERWE, W. J. *The Development of Missionary Attitudes in the Dutch Reformed Church in South Africa*, Cape Town, 1934.
—, 'Some History of the Vakaranga in the Gutu Reserve', *NADA*, Salisbury, 1936.
—, *Shona Idea of God*, Morgenster Mission Press, 1952.
—, *The Day Star arises in Mashonaland*, Morgenster Mission Press, 1953.
—, *Gesante om Christus wil*, Kaapstad, 1967.
VON SICARD, H. *Mwari der Hochgott der Karanga*, in Wiener Beiträge zur Kulturgeschichte und Linguistik, Jahrgang 6, 1944.
WARNECK, G. *Evangelische Missionslehre* III, Gotha, 1897.
WINTERHALDER, W. 'Life in the Early Days', *Guti*, Sept./Oct. 1963.
—, 'The Discrepancy', *Guti*, Aug. Sept. 1964.
YOUNG, T. C. 'The Idea of God in Northern Nyasaland', in *African Ideas of God*, edited by E. W. Smith, London, 1950.

YUDELMAN, M. *Africans on the Land*, Harvard University Press, Cambridge, Massachusetts, 1964.

B. OFFICIAL PUBLICATIONS

Report of the Land Commission – 1925, Government Printer, Salisbury, 1926.
Survey of the Native Educational Development (by B. Grimston), Government Printer, Salisbury, 1937.
Report of the Secretary for Native Affairs and Chief Native Commissioner for the Year 1947, Government Printer, Salisbury, 1948.
What the Land Husbandry Act means to the Rural African and to Southern Rhodesia, Government Printer, Salisbury, 1955.
Report of the Secretary for Native Affairs, Salisbury, 1960.
Report of the Mangwende Reserve Commission, Government Printer, Salisbury, 1961.
Report of the Robinson Commission of Inquiry, Government Printer, Salisbury, 1961.
Report of the Southern Rhodesia Education Commission (by A. V. Judges and Commission), Government Printer, Salisbury, 1962.
Final Report of the April/May Census of Africans in Southern Rhodesia, Government Printer, Salisbury, 1964.
The Economics of African Education, Government Printer, Salisbury, 1967.
Notes and Queries on Anthropology, Sixth Edition, Revised by a Committee of the Royal Anthropological Institute, London, 1964.

C. CHURCH BOOKS, PERIODICALS AND PAMPHLETS

1. *Mission Churches*

General:

International Review of Missions, Commission of the World Mission and Evangelism of the World Council of Churches, Geneva.
Acts: Reformed Ecumenical Synod, 1963 and 1968.

Dutch Reformed:

Die Kerkbode, Die Verenigde Kerkblad van die Ned-Geref. Kerke in Suid-Afrika, (Kaapstad).
NG-Statistiese Opgawe, 1925–1955.
Statements on Race Relations, Report of the Ad Hoc Committee for Race Relations, appointed by the Federal Council of Dutch Reformed Churches, Johannesburg, 1960.
KATEKISMA – *(Catechism) – neDudziro yeDzidzo dzeDutch Reformed Church*, Morgenster Misson Press, 1966.
BUKU YEMIRAIRO – *Rules and Regulations of the African Reformed Church*, Morgenster Mission Press, 1967.

Roman Catholic:

Guti, Missionary Periodical of the Gwelo Diocese, Catholic Mission Press, Gwelo.
Peace through Justice, Pastoral Instruction of the Catholic Bishops of Southern Rhodesia, Catholic Mission Press, Gwelo, 1961.

Problems of our People, Pastoral Instruction of the Catholic Bishops of Southern Rhodesia, Catholic Mission Press, Gwelo, 1963.
A Plea for Peace, Pastoral Instruction of the Catholic Bishops of Southern Rhodesia, Catholic Mission Press, Gwelo, 1965.
Memorandum of the Missionary School Policy in the Diocese of Gwelo, in *Guti*, May 1966.
Statistics of the Gwelo Diocese, in *Guti*, June 1966.
Kuvigwa kwomunhu – (Burial Rite), Mambo Press, Gwelo, 1967.

2. *Independent Churches*

Constitution of the Zion Christian Church, Mimeographed, no date.
Zion Christian Church Rungano, (i.e. ZCC 'History'), Mimeographed, Salisbury, no date.
Nziyo yeKereke yaVatema – Hymns of the African Church, *Shonganiso* Mission, African Newspapers, Ltd., Salisbury, no date.
Nziyo dze African Congregation Church, African Newspapers, Ltd., Salisbury, no date.

Index of authors

Index of key words, names and subjects

Mutendi's 'Jerusalem', 313, 346, 490
Jesuit(s), 79, 190-2, 247
Jichidza, DRC Mission station, 189, 365, 369, 418
jinda, *see*: *muchinda*
jira, 99, 119, 181